THE BEST TEST PREPARATION FOR THE
ADVANCED PLACEMENT EXAMINATION

EUROPEAN HISTORY

Miles W. Campbell, Ph.D.
Professor and Chair, Department of History
New Mexico State University
University Park, New Mexico

Niles R. Holt, Ph.D.
Professor of History
Illinois State University
Normal, Illinois

William T. Walker, Ph.D.
Associate Professor and Chair, Department of Humanities
Philadelphia College of Pharmacy and Science
Philadelphia, Pennsylvania

Research & Education Association
61 Ethel Road West • Piscataway, New Jersey 08854

The Best Test Preparation for the
ADVANCED PLACEMENT EXAMINATION
IN EUROPEAN HISTORY

Printed in the United States of America

Library of Congress Control Number 00-132018

International Standard Book Number 0-87891-863-9

Research & Education Association
61 Ethel Road West
Piscataway, New Jersey 08854

REA supports the effort to conserve and
protect environmental resources by
printing on recycled papers.

CONTENTS

AP EUROPEAN HISTORY COURSE REVIEW 1

SIX PRACTICE EXAMS

ABOUT RESEARCH & EDUCATION ASSOCIATION

Research & Education Association (REA) is an organization of educators, scientists, and engineers specializing in various academic fields. Founded in 1959 with the purpose of disseminating the most recently developed scientific information to groups in industry, government, high schools, and universities, REA has since become a successful and highly respected publisher of study aids, test preps, handbooks, and reference works.

REA's Test Preparation series includes study guides for all academic levels in almost all disciplines. Research & Education Association publishes test preps for students who have not yet completed high school, as well as high school students preparing to enter college. Students from countries around the world seeking to attend college in the United States will find the assistance they need in REA's publications. For college students seeking advanced degrees, REA publishes test preps for many major graduate school admission examinations in a wide variety of disciplines, including engineering, law, and medicine. Students at every level, in every field, with every ambition can find what they are looking for among REA's publications.

While most test preparation books present practice tests that bear little resemblance to the actual exams, REA's series presents tests that accurately depict the official exams in both degree of difficulty and types of questions. REA's practice tests are always based upon the most recently administered exams, and include every type of question that can be expected on the actual exams.

REA's publications and educational materials are highly regarded and continually receive an unprecedented amount of praise from professionals, instructors, librarians, parents, and students. Our authors are as diverse as the subject matter represented in the books we publish. They are well-known in their respective disciplines and serve on the faculties of prestigious high schools, colleges, and universities throughout the United States and Canada.

ACKNOWLEDGMENTS

In addition to our authors, we would like to thank Dr. Max Fogiel, President, for his overall guidance, which brought this book to completion; Larry B. Kling, Quality Control Manager of Books in Print, for his supervision of revisions; Omar J. Musni, Editorial Assistant, for coordinating revisions; and Marty Perzan for typesetting the manuscript.

ABOUT THIS BOOK

This book provides an accurate and complete representation of the Advanced Placement Examination in European History. The six practice tests and the review section are based on the most recently administered AP European History Exams. Each test includes every type of question that you can expect to appear on the actual exam. Following each practice exam is an answer key complete with detailed explanations. The explanations discuss both the correct and incorrect responses and are designed to clarify the material for the student.

By studying the review section, completing all six tests, and studying the answer explanations, students can discover their strengths and weaknesses and prepare themselves for the actual AP European History Examination.

Teachers of Advanced Placement European History and Social Studies courses will also find this book of great use. The book can be used as supplemental text in planning courses and practicing for the exam. It will provide teachers with specific information concerning the level, scope, and type of material found on the actual exam.

ABOUT THE TEST

The Advanced Placement program is designed to allow high school students to pursue college-level studies while attending high school. The three-hour exam is usually administered to high school students who have completed a year's study in a college-level European history course. The results are then used for determining course credit and/or placement level in college.

The Advanced Placement European History course is designed to represent college-level history studies. Students are expected to leave the course with college-level writing skills, knowledge of historical events and concepts, and an ability to interpret historical documents. The course is intended for students who possess strong backgrounds in history and writing.

The exam is divided into two sections:

1. **Multiple-choice**: This section consists of 80 multiple-choice questions designed to measure the student's ability to understand and analyze European history from the Renaissance to the recent past. This section tests factual knowledge, scope of preparation, and knowledge-based analytical skills. The student has 55 minutes to complete this section of the exam, which counts for 50 percent of the final grade.

2. **Free-response**: This section is composed of three essay questions designed to measure the student's ability to write coherent, intelligent, well-organized essays on historical topics. The essays require the student to demonstrate mastery of historical interpretation and the ability to express views and knowledge in writing. They may relate documents to different areas, analyze common themes of different time periods, or compare individual and group experiences which reflect socioeco-

nomic, racial, gender, and ethnic differences. Part A consists of a mandatory 15-minute reading period, followed by 45 minutes in which the student must answer a document-based question (DBQ). In Part B the student must answer two essay topics out of the six that are given. The student has 30 minutes to write each of the essays. In determining the score for the free-response section, the DBQ is weighted 45 percent while the two thematic essays are weighted 55 percent. The entire free-response section counts for one-half of the final grade.

These topics are broken down as follows:

Political and Diplomatic History	35-45%
Social and Economic History	30-40%
Intellectual and Cultural History	20-30%

The basic chronology of the exam runs from the high Renaissance to the present. The time periods are covered as follows: 50% from 1450 to 1789, 50% from 1789-1996. Major late medieval events bearing upon post-1450 events may also be included.

ABOUT THE REVIEW SECTION

This book begins with a comprehensive review of European history designed to give the student an idea of what type of information can be found on the exam. The review discusses the following historical time periods and events in depth:

1450 to 1648: The Renaissance, Reformation, and the Wars of Religion
Martin Luther; the European Wars of Religion; the Thirty Years' War; the Age of Exploration; the Scientific Revolution; the Peace of Westphalia

1648 to 1789: Bourbon, Baroque, and the Enlightenment
The Peace of Westphalia; Mercantilism; Beginnings of Modern Science and the Enlightenment; Bourbon France; the Hapsburgs; the Hohenzollerns; the English Civil War; the Restoration; Peter the Great and Russia; the Papacy; the Ottoman Turkish Empire in Europe; Baroque and Rococo

1789 to 1848: Revolution and the New European Order
The French Revolution; the Era of Napoleon; the Congress of Vienna; the Industrial Revolution; the Impact of Thought Systems on the European World; the Concert of Europe; the Revolutions of 1848

1848 to 1914: Realism and Materialism
The Failure of the Revolutions; Realpolitik and Nationalism; the Crimean War; Capitalism and the New Left; Karl Marx; the Second French Republic and the Second Empire; Imperial Russia; the Balkan States and the End of the Ottoman Empire; the New Imperialism; the Age of Bismarck; Darwin, Wagner, and Freud; the Coming of the Great War

1914 to 1935: World War I and Europe in Crisis

The Russian Revolutions of 1917; the Paris Peace Conference 1919 – 1920; Weimar Politics; Benito Mussolini and Italian Fascism; Soviet Russia; the Death of Lenin and the Rise of Josef Stalin; the Rise of Adolf Hitler and Nazism; the League of Nations

1935 to 1996: World War II to the Demise of Communism

Including: The Great Democracies; the Cold War; Loss of European Overseas Empires; Spreading Communism; Russian-American Relations; Nuclear Weapons and the Arms Race; Changes Under Yeltsin; the Balkan Crisis; the Persian Gulf War; the Arab-Israeli Peace Movement; the European Community; NATO's Changing Role; Cultural and Social Developments Since World War II

In addition to studying the review presented in this book, test-takers should acquaint themselves with current issues, thereby gaining the necessary perspective on modern European events.

SCORING THE EXAM

The multiple-choice section of the exam is scored by crediting each correct answer with one point and deducting one-fourth of a point for each incorrect answer. Unanswered questions receive neither a credit nor a deduction. The free-response essays are graded by over 200 instructors and professors who gather together each June for a week of non-stop AP essay grading. Each essay booklet is read and scored by several graders. Each grader provides a score for the individual essays. The score for the DBQ is a number on a scale from 0 to 15, 0 being the lowest and 15 the highest. Each topic-based essay receives a score from 0 to 9. These scores are covered up so that the next grader does not see them. When the essays have been graded completely, the scores are averaged, one score for each essay, so that the free-response section is comprised of three scores.

The total weight of the free-response section is 50 percent of the total score. The multiple-choice section also comprises 50 percent of the total score. Each year the overall grades fluctuate because the grading scale depends upon the performance of students in past AP administrations. The following method of scoring and the corresponding chart will give you an **approximation** of your score. It does not indicate the exact score you would get on the actual AP European History exam, but rather the score you achieved on any of the sample tests in this book.

SCORING THE MULTIPLE-CHOICE SECTION

For the multiple-choice section, use this formula to calculate your raw score:

_____ – (_____ x 1/4) = _____ (round to the nearest whole number)
 number   number   raw
  right   wrong   score

SCORING THE FREE-RESPONSE SECTION

For the free-response section, use this formula to calculate your raw score:

_____ + _____ + _____ = _____ (round to the nearest whole number)
 DBQ   essay   essay   raw
 essay   #1   #2   score

You may want to give your essays three different grades, such as a 13, a 10, and an 8, and then calculate your score three ways: as if you did well, average, and poorly. This will give you a safe estimate of how you will do on the actual exam. Try to be objective about grading your own essays. If possible, have a friend, teacher, or parent grade them for you. Make sure your essays follow all of the AP requirements before you assess the score.

THE COMPOSITE SCORE

To obtain your composite score, use the following method:

1.13 x _____ = _____ (weighted multiple-choice score—**do not round**)
          multiple choice
          raw score

2.73 x _____ = _____ (weighted free-response score—**do not round**)
         free-response
         raw score

Now, add the two weighted sections together and round to the nearest whole number. The result is your total composite score. Compare your score with this table to approximate your grade:

AP Grade	Composite Score Range
5	114–180
4	91–113
3	74–90
2	49–73
1	0–48

These overall scores are interpreted as follows: 5-extremely well qualified; 4-well qualified; 3-qualified, 2-possibly qualified; and 1-no recommendation. Most colleges will grant students who earn a 3 or above either college credit or advanced placement. Check with your school guidance office about specific school requirements.

STUDY SCHEDULE

The following is a suggested six-week study schedule for the AP European History Exam. You may condense or expand this schedule depending on how soon you will be taking the actual exam. Set aside time each week, and work straight through the activity without rushing. In this way, you will be sure to complete an adequate amount of studying, and be confident and prepared on the day of the actual exam.

Week	Activity
1	Acquaint yourself with the AP European History Exam by reading the Preface and About the Test. Take AP European History Practice Test 1. Read through **all** of the detailed explanations carefully (not just for those that you answered incorrectly). Make a note of any sections that are difficult for you, or any questions that are still unclear after reading the explanations. Review the specific field of difficulty in the AP European History Course Review included with this book, or by using the appropriate textbooks and notes.
2 and 3	Study the review material included in this book. Do not study too much at any one time. Pace yourself, so that you can better comprehend what you are reading. Remember that cramming is not an effective means of study.
4	Take AP European History Practice Tests 2 and 3. Read through all of the detailed explanations. Make a note of anything that you find difficult or unclear after reading the explanations. Use our AP European History Course Review and your textbooks, notes, or course materials to review those areas that need clarification.
5	Take AP European History Practice Tests 4 and 5. Read through all of the detailed explanations. Make a note of anything that is causing you difficulty. Use our AP European History Course Review and your textbooks, notes, or course materials to review those areas that need clarification
6	Take AP European Practice Test 6. Read through all of the detailed explanations. Continue reviewing any material that you are finding difficult. Compare your progress between each of the practice tests. Note any sections where you are able to improve your score, and sections where your score remained the same or declined. Use any time remaining for extra study in areas that require added attention.

AP
EUROPEAN
HISTORY

◆

COURSE REVIEW

1 THE RENAISSANCE, REFORMATION AND THE WARS OF RELIGION (1450-1648)

THE LATE MIDDLE AGES

The Middle Ages ("medieval" is the French word) were chronologically between the classical world of Greece and Rome and the modern world. The papacy and monarchs, after exercising much power and influence in the high Middle Ages, were in eclipse after 1300. During the late Middle Ages (1300 – 1500) all of Europe suffered from the Black Death. While England and France engaged in destructive warfare in Northern Europe, in Italy the Renaissance had begun.

THE CHURCH AND CRITICISMS

The church was a hierarchical or pyramidal organization, with the believers at the base. These believers were ministered to by priests, who in turn were supervised by bishops . All were under the leadership of the pope. Monks, nuns, and friars existed outside the pyramid but were usually governed by the pope as well.

In the late Middle Ages, numerous criticisms were directed against individuals and church practices, but not the idea of the church itself or Christian beliefs.

Corruption was widespread, with numerous decisions within the church's bureaucracy being influenced by money, friendship, or politics. Simony – the purchase of church positions, such as a bishopric, rather than appointment to the positions based upon merit – was commonplace.

Pluralism also existed. A man could hold more than one office in the church even though he would not be able to do both jobs at once. He might hire an assistant to do one of the jobs for him or it might be left undone. As he could not be both places, he was also open to the criticism of absenteeism.

These criticisms, and others, such as those concerning extravagance, excessive wealth, political involvement, and sexual improprieties, were part of the hostility to the clergy called anticlericalism. Those who criticized were often attacked by the church as heretics

John Wycliff (1320 – 1384), an English friar, criticized the vices of the clergy, taxes collected by the pope, transubstantiation, and the authority of the pope. As he believed the church should follow only the Scriptures, he began translating the Bible from Latin into English. Wycliff's ideas were used by the peasants in the revolt of 1381, and his followers, Lollards, survived well into the fifteenth century.

John Huss (1369 – 1415), a Czech priest with criticisms similar to Wycliff's, produced a national following in Bohemia which rejected the authority of the pope. Huss was burned at the stake at the Council of Constance.

Lay Piety

In the Rhine Valley of Germany, mystics , such as Meister Eckhart (1260 – 1327) and Thomas à Kempis (1379 – 1471), sought direct knowledge of God through the realm of inner feelings, not observance of church rituals.

Gerard Groote (1340 – 1384) began a semi-monastic life for laymen in the Low Countries. The Brethren of the Common Life ran schools and led lives guided by the Christian principles of humility, tolerance, and love, all unconcerned with the roles of the institutional church.

POPES

The papacy, recognized as the leader of the western church since at least the thirteenth century, encountered a series of problems in the late Middle Ages which reduced the prestige of popes and interfered with their ability to deal with the problems underlying the criticisms.

Babylonian Captivity

In 1305, after a confrontation with the king of France, a new pope, Clement V was elected. He was a Frenchman and never went to Rome, settling instead in Avignon, near the French kingdom. While not held captive by the French kings, the popes in Avignon were seen as subservient to them. Also, the atmosphere was one of luxury, and the popes concentrated on money and bureaucratic matters, not spiritual leadership. Popes resided in Avignon from 1309 to 1377.

Great Schism

In 1377 Pope Gregory XI returned to Rome, ending the Babylonian Captivity, but dying soon afterward. Disputes over the election of his successor led to the election of two popes, one of whom stayed in Rome (Urban VI). The other, (Clement VII), returned to Avignon. The monarchs chose different sides (England and Germany for Rome; France, Scotland, Aragon, Castile, Portugal, and Italian city-states for Avignon), while neither pope prosecuted any reforms of the church. The existence of two popes lasted until 1417.

Conciliar Movement

An effort was initiated to have the church ruled, not by the pope, but by everyone in the church, such as bishops, cardinals, theologians, and abbots, as well as laymen. The idea gained impetus from the existence of two popes and the abuses they were not correcting. Marsiglio of Padua (1270–1342), author of *The Defender of the Peace*, argued that the church was subordinate to the state and that the church should be governed by a general council.

Efforts after 1409 by councils at Pisa (1409) and Constance (1414–8) united the church under one pope (Martin V) but failed to effect any reform of abuses, as all such efforts ended in struggles between the pope and councils over power in the church. Martin and his successors rejected the conciliar movement.

Renaissance Popes

After 1447, a series of popes encouraged and supported much artistic work in Rome. While their personal lives were often criticized for sexual laxness, these popes took more interest in political, military, and artistic activities than in church reform. Sixtus IV (1471–84) started the painting of the Sistine Chapel which his nephew, Julius II (1503–13), whom Sixtus had promoted within the church, finished with the employment of Michelangelo to paint the ceiling. Julius also successfully asserted his control over the Papal States in central Italy. These popes did not cause the Reformation, but they failed to do anything which might have averted it.

THE HUNDRED YEARS' WAR

The governments of Europe partially broke down in the late Middle Ages, as violence within and war without dominated the scene. Towards the end of the period monarchs began to reassert their power and control. The major struggle, between England and France, was the Hundred Years' War (1337 – 1453).

The English king was the vassal of the French king for the duchy of Aquitaine, and the French king wanted control of the duchy; this was the event that started the fighting. The English king, Edward III, had a claim to the French throne through his mother, a princess of France.

Additionally, French nobles sought opportunities to gain power at the expense of the French king. England also exported its wool to Flanders, which was coming under control of the king of France. Finally, kings and nobles shared the values of chivalry which portrayed war as a glorious and uplifting adventure.

The war was fought in France, though the Scots (with French encouragement) invaded northern England. A few major battles occurred — Crecy (1346), Poitiers (1356), Agincourt (1415) — which the English won due to the chivalrous excesses of the French. The fighting consisted largely of sieges and raids. Eventually, the war became one of attrition; the French slowly wore down the English. The technological changes during the war included the use of English longbows and the increasingly expensive plate armor of knights.

Joan of Arc (1412 – 1431), an illiterate peasant girl who said she heard voices of saints, rallied the French army for several victories. Due to Joan's victories, Charles VII was crowned king at Rheims, the traditional location for enthronement. Joan was later captured by the Burgundians, allies of England, and sold to the English who tried her for heresy (witchcraft). She was burned at the stake at Rouen.

Results of the Hundred Years' War

England lost all of its Continental possessions, except Calais. French farmland was devastated, with England and France both expending great sums of money. Population, especially in France, declined.

Both countries suffered internal disruption as soldiers plundered and local officials left to fight the war. Trade everywhere was disrupted and England's wool trade to the Low Countries slumped badly. To cover these financial burdens, heavy taxation was inflicted on the peasants.

In England, the need for money led kings to summon parliaments more often, which gave nobility and merchants more power. No taxes could be levied without parliamentary approval. Parliamentary procedures and institutions changed, giving nobles more control over government (impeachments). Representative government gained a tradition which enabled it to survive under later challenges.

A series of factional struggles led to the deposition of Richard II in 1399. After the Hundred Years' War ended the nobility continued fighting each other in the War of the Roses (1450 – 1485), choosing sides as Lancastrians and Yorkists.

In France, noble factions contended for power with the king, who refused to deal with noble assemblies. The king faced various problems, while holding certain advantages. First of all, the Duchy of Burgundy was virtually independent. Secondly, there was no national assembly to confront, but only a series of provincial bodies. Thirdly, the monarch had the right to levy a tax on salt, the gabelle, and a national tax, the taille, which exempted nobles and clergy. Lastly, a royal standing army existed so that reliance on nobles became unnecessary.

In both countries the war led to the growth of nationalism, the feeling of unity among the subjects of a country. Kings in both countries used propaganda to rally popular support. Hatred of the enemy united people, and military accomplishments fed national pride.

Literature also came to express nationalism, as it was written in the language of the people, instead of in Latin. Geoffrey Chaucer (1340 – 1400) portrayed a wide spectrum of English life in the Cantebury Tales, while Francois Villon (1431 – 1463), in his Grand Testament, emphasized the ordinary life of the French with humor and emotion.

THE HOLY ROMAN EMPIRE

After prolonged struggles with the papacy in the 13th century, the Holy Roman Emperor had little power in either Germany or Italy. After 1272, the empire was usually ruled by a member of the Hapsburg family, which had turned its interest to creating possessions in Austria and Hungary. The Ottoman Turks, following the conquest of Constantinople in 1453, continually pressed on the borders of the Empire.

In 1356 the Golden Bull was issued. This constitution of the empire gave the right of naming the emperor to seven German electors, but gave the pope no role.

The Swiss cantons gradually obtained independence, helped by stories such as that of William Tell.

In Italy, city-states, or communes, dominated by wealthy merchants, continued their efforts to obtain independence from the emperor.

In many cities, the governments became stronger and were dominated by despots (Milan had the Visconti and later the Sforza; Florence came under the control of the Medici) or oligarchies (Venice was ruled by the Council of Ten). Other smaller city-states disappeared as continual wars led to larger territories dominated by one large city.

THE NEW MONARCHS

After 1450, monarchs turned to strengthening their power internally, a process producing the "New Monarchy." However, several difficulties hindered their efforts.

The general economic stagnation of the late Middle Ages combined with the increasing expense of mercenary armies to force monarchs to seek new taxes, something traditionally requiring the consent of the nobles.

Additionally, nobles, long the chief problem for kings, faced declining incomes and rising desires to control the government of their king. If not fighting external foes, they engaged in civil war at home with their fellow nobles.

Unfortunately for the monarchs, many weak, incompetent or insane kings hindered their efforts.

Opposition to Monarchian Power

Nobles claimed various levels of independence under feudal rules or traditions. Forming an assembly provided some sort of a meeting forum for nobles. Furthermore, the core of royal armies consisted of nobles; monarchs were solaced only by the appearance of mercenary armies of pike which reduced royal reliance on noble knights. Many of the higher clergy of the church were noble born.

Additionally, some towns had obtained independence during times of trouble. Church and clergy saw the pope as their leader.

Help for France's Monarchy

The defeat of the English in the Hundred Years' war removed the external threat. The defeat of the duchy of Burgundy in 1477 removed a major military power holding part of eastern France. Trade was expanded, fostered by the merchant Jacques Coeur (1395 – 1456). Louis XI (1461 – 1483) demonstrated ruthlessness in dealing with his nobility as individuals and collectively in the Estates General.

Help for England's Monarchy

Many nobles died in the War of the Roses. Nobles were controlled by a royal court, the Star Chamber. Standard governmental procedures of law and taxation were developed.

Help for Spain's Monarchy

The marriage of Isabella of Castile (1474 – 1504) and Ferdinand of Aragon (1478 –1516) created a united Spain. Navarre was conquered in 1512. Moslems were defeated at Granada in 1492.

Additionally, sheep farming was encouraged through a government organization, the Mesta. An alliance with a group of cities and towns, the Hermandad, was formed in opposition of the nobility. Finally, reform and control of the church was enacted through the Inquisition.

THE BLACK DEATH AND SOCIAL PROBLEMS

The bubonic plague ("Black Death") is a disease affecting the lymph glands, which causes death quickly. Existing conditions in Europe encouraged the quick spread of disease. There was no urban sanitation, and streets were filled with refuse, excrement and dead animals. Houses were made of wood, clay and mud with straw roofs. Living conditions were overcrowded, with families often sleeping in one room or one bed. Poor nutrition was rampant, due to population pressures on food supplies. There was also a general lack of personal cleanliness.

Carried by fleas on black rats, the plague was brought from Asia by merchants and arrived in Europe in 1347. The plague affected all of Europe by 1350 and killed perhaps 25 to 40 percent of the population, with cities suffering more than the countryside.

Consequences

Some of the best clergy died because they attempted to help the sick; the church was left to the less competent or sincere. With fewer people, the economy declined. Additionally, Jews were killed due to a belief that they poisoned wells of Christians.

A general pessimism pervaded the survivors. Flagellants whipped and scourged themselves in penance for sins which they believed caused the plague. Literature and art reflected this attitude, including such examples as the Dance of Death, which depicted dancing skeletons among the living.

Population

By 1300, Europe's population had reached the limit of available food resources and famines became common. A series of consequences manifested after the decline of population after 1350.

Wages became higher as the remaining workers could obtain better wages or move; governments often responded with laws trying to set wage levels, such as England's Statute of Laborers (1351). Serfdom ended in many places. Guilds were established which limited membership, and cities limited citizenship in efforts to obtain or protect monopolies. The Hanseatic League of German cities controlled the Baltic trade in the 14th and early 15th centuries. Finally, sheep farming increased and, as sheep needed fewer workers, the necessary enclosures of open fields in England eliminated peasants and their villages.

Peasant Revolts

Records do not reveal major peasant revolts prior to the 13th century. New conditions following the Plague led to increased revolutionary activity.

Taxation was increased due to the Hundred Years' War. Higher wages were desired after the Black Death. Rising expectations were frustrated after a period of relative prosperity. Hostility to aristocrats increased, as expressed in the words of a priest, John Ball, one of the leaders of the English Peasants' Revolt: "When Adam delved and Eve span / Who was then the gentleman?"

A number of subsequent revolts ensued. In England, the largest of these, the Peasants' Revolt of 1381, involved perhaps 100,000 people. France experienced the *Jacquerie* in 1358. Poor workers revolted in Florence in 1378.

The Low Countries, Germany, Sicily, Spain, and at other times in England and France all experienced similar occurences.

THE RENAISSANCE

The Renaissance occurred mainly in Italy between the years 1300 and 1600. New learning and changes in styles of art were two of the most pronounced characteristics of the Renaissance. The Renaissance contrasts with the Middle Ages in that the Renaissance was secular, not religious. Also, the individual, not the group, was emphasized during the Renaissance. The Renaissance occurred in urban, not rural, areas.

Italian city-states, such as Venice, Milan, Padua, Pisa, and especially Florence were the home to most Renaissance developments, which were limited to the rich elite.

Jacob Burckhardt, in *The Civilization of the Renaissance in Italy* (1860), popularized the study of the period and argued that it was a strong contrast with the Middle Ages. Subsequent historians have often found more continuity with the Middle Ages in terms of the society and its traditions. Whether the term applies to a cultural event or merely a time period is still debated.

Definitions

Renaissance – French for 'rebirth'; the word describes the reawakening, rebirth, of interest in the heritage of the classical past.

Classical past – Greece and Rome in the years between 500 B.C. and 400 A.D. Humanist scholars were most interested in Rome from 200 B.C. to 180 A.D.

Humanism – The reading and understanding of writings and ideals of the classical past. Rhetoric was the initial area of study, which soon widened to include poetry, history, politics, and philosophy. Civic humanism was the use of humanism in the political life of Italian city-states. Christian humanism focused on early Church writings instead of secular authors.

Individualism – Behavior or theory which emphasizes each person and is contrasted with corporate or community behavior; or, theory in which the group is emphasized at the expense of the individual. Renaissance individualism sought great accomplishments and looked for heroes of history.

Virtu – The essence of being a person through the showing of human abilities. This ability could be displayed in speech, art, politics, warfare, or elsewhere by seizing the opportunities available. For many, the pursuit of virtu was amoral.

Florentine or Platonic Academy – located in a country house and supported by the Medici, the leading Florentine political family, a group of scholars who initially studied the works of Plato, the ancient Greek. The leading members were Marsilio Ficino (1433 – 1499) and Pico della Mirandola (1463 – 1494).

Causes

While no cause can be clearly identified as the source of the Renaissance, several categories have been suggested by historians.

The first explanation is for economic reasons. Northern Italy was very wealthy as a result of serving as intermediary between the silk- and spice-producing East and the consuming West of England, France and Germany. Also, Italian merchants had built great wealth in the cloth industry and had often turned to international banking. This wealth gave people leisure to pursue new ideas, and money to support the artists and scholars who produced the new works.

Political interactions may have also contributed to the sweeping changes. Struggles between the papacy, the Holy Roman Empire, and merchants during the Middle Ages had resulted in the independence of many small city-states in northern Italy. This fragmentation meant no single authority had the power to stop or redirect new developments. The governments of the city-states, often in the hands of one man, competed by supporting artists and scholars.

Historical influences were also at hand. Northern Italian cities were often built on the ruins of ancient Roman ones, and the citizens knew of their heritage.

Finally, an influx of new ideas occurred. The appearance of men fleeing the falling Byzantine Empire brought new ideas, including the study of Greek, to Italy. Also, during the numerous wars between the Italian city-states, contestants sought justifications for their claims in the actions of the past, even back to the classical past. Finally, the study of Roman law during disputes between the popes and the Holy Roman Emperors led to study of other Roman writers.

LITERATURE, ART, AND SCHOLARSHIP

Literature

Humanists, as both orators and poets, were inspired by and imitated works of the classical past. The literature was more secular and covered more subjects than that of the Middle Ages.

Dante (1265 – 1321) was a Florentine writer who spent much of his life in exile after being on the losing side in political struggles in Florence. His *Divine Comedy*, describing a journey through hell, purgatory, and heaven, shows that reason can only take people so far and then God's grace and revelation must be used. Dealing with many other issues and with much symbolism, this work is the pinnacle of medieval poetry.

Petrarch (1304 – 1374), who wrote in both Latin and Italian, encouraged the study of ancient Rome, collected and preserved much work of ancient writers, and produced much work in the classical literary style. He is best known for his sonnets, including many expressing his love for a married woman named Laura, and is considered the father of humanism.

Boccaccio (1313 – 1375) wrote *The Decameron*, a collection of short stories in Italian, which meant to amuse, not edify, the reader.

Castiglione (1478 – 1529) authored *The Book of the Courtier* which specified the qualities necessary for a gentleman – including the development of both intellectual and physical qualities – and leading an active, non-contemplative life. Abilities in conversation, sports, arms, dance, music, Latin and Greek, he advised, should be combined with an agreeable personal demeanor. The book was translated into many languages and greatly influenced Western ideas about correct education and behavior.

Art

Artists also broke with the medieval past, in both technique and content.

Medieval painting, which usually depicted religious topics and was used for religious purposes, was idealized. Its main purpose was to portray the essence or idea of the topic. Renaissance art sometimes used religious topics, but often dealt with secular themes or portraits of individuals. Oil paints, chiaroscuro, and linear perspectives all combined to produce works of energy in three dimensions.

Medieval sculpture was dominated by works of religious significance. The idealized forms of individuals, such as saints, were often used in the education of the faithful who could not easily deal with concepts. By copying classical models and using free standing pieces, Renaissance sculptors produced works celebrating the individualistic and non-religious spirit of the day.

Medieval architecture included the use of pointed arches, flying buttresses, and fan vaulting to obtain great heights, while permitting light to flood the interior of the building, usually a church or cathedral. The result gave a 'feeling' for God rather than the approach through reach. The busy details, filling every niche, and the absence of symmetry also typify medieval work.

Renaissance architects openly copied classical, especially Roman, forms, such as the rounded arch and squared angles, when constructing town and country houses for the rich and urban buildings for cities.

Several artists became associated with the new style or art.

Giotto (1266 – 1336) painted religious scenes using light and shadow, a technique called chiaroscuro, to create an illusion of depth and greater realism. He is considered the father of Renaissance painting.

Donatello (1386 – 1466), the father of Renaissance sculpture, produced, in his *David*, the first statue cast in bronze since classical times.

Masaccio (1401 – 1428) emphasized naturalism in *Expulsion of Adam and Eve* by showing real human figures, in the nude, with three-dimensions, expressing emotion.

Leonardo da Vinci (1452 – 1519) produced numerous works, including *The Last Supper* and *Mona Lisa*, as well as many mechanical designs, though few were ever constructed.

Raphael (1483 – 1520), a master of Renaissance grace and style, theory and technique, represented these skills in The School of Athens.

Michelangelo (1475 – 1564), a universal man, produced masterpieces in architecture, sculpture (*David*), and painting (the Sistine Chapel ceiling). His work was a bridge to new, non-Renaissance style called Mannerism.

Scholars

Scholars sought to know what is good and to practice it, as did men in the Middle Ages. However, Renaissance people sought more practical results and did not judge things by religious standards. Manuscript collections enabled scholars to study the primary sources they used and to reject all traditions which had been built up since classical times. Also, scholars participated in the lives of their cities as active politicians.

Leonardo Bruni (1370 – 1444), civic humanist, served as chancellor of Florence, where he used his rhetorical skills to rouse the citizens against external enemies. He also wrote a history of his city and was the first to use the term humanism.

Lorenzo Valla (1407 – 1457), authored *Elegances of the Latin Language*, the standard text in Latin philology, and also exposed as a forgery, the Donation of Constantine, which had purported to give the papacy control of vast lands in Italy, as a forgery.

Machiavelli (1469 – 1527), wrote *The Prince*, which analyzed politics from the standpoint of reason, rather than faith or tradition. His work, amoral in tone, describes how a political leader could obtain and hold power by acting only in his own self interest.

THE RENAISSANCE OUTSIDE ITALY

The Renaissance in the rest of western Europe was less classical in its emphasis, as well as more influenced by religion, particularly that of Christian humanism.

In the Low Countries, artists still produced works on religious themes but the attention to detail in the paintings of Jan van Eyck (1385 – 1440) typifies Renaissance ideas. Later artists include the nearly surreal Pieter Brueghel (1520 – 1569) and Rembrandt van Rijn (1606 – 1669).

In Mainz, Germany, around 1450, the invention of printing with movable type, traditionally attributed to Johann Gutenberg, enabled new ideas to be spread throughout Europe more easily. Albrecht Durer (1471 – 1528) gave realism and individuality to the art of the woodcut.

Many Italian artists and scholars were hired in France. The Loire Valley chateaux of the 16th century and Rabelais' (1494 – 1553) Gargantua and Pantagruel reflect Renaissance tastes.

Interests in the past and new developments did not appear in England until the 16th century. Drama, culminating in the age of Shakespeare, is the most pronounced accomplishment of the Renaissance spirit in England.

In Spain, money from the American conquests supported much building, such as the Escorial, a palace and monastery, and art, such as that by El Greco (1541 – 1614), who is often considered to work in the style of Mannerism.

CHRISTIAN HUMANISM

Theme

Much of the Renaissance outside of Italy focused on religious matters through the study of writings of the early Christian church, rather than through those of the secular authors of Rome and Greece.

Elements

Although they used the techniques of the Italian humanists in the analysis of ancient writings, language and style, Christian humanists were more interested in providing guidance on personal behavior.

The work on Christian sources, done between 1450 and 1530, emphasized education and the power of the human intellect to bring about institutional change and moral improvement. The many tracts and guides of Christian humanists were directed at reforming the church, but led many into criticisms of the church, which resulted in the Reformation. Additionally, the discovery that traditional Christian texts had different versions proved unsettling to many believers.

Though many Christian humanists were not clergymen, most early reformers of the church during the Reformation had been trained as Christian humanists.

Christian Humanism, with its emphasis on toleration and education, disappeared due to the increasing passions of the Reformation after 1530.

Biographies

Desiderius Erasmus (1466 – 1536), a Dutchman and the most notable figure of the Christian humanist movement, made new translations of the Greek and Latin versions of the New Testament in order to have 'purer' editions. His book *In Praise of Folly* satirizes the ambitions of the world, most especially those of the clergy. A man known throughout the intellectual circles of Europe, he emphasized the virtues of tolerance, restraint, and education at the time the church was fragmenting during the Reformation. Erasmus led a life of simple piety, practicing the Christian virtues, which led to complaints that he had no role for the institutional church. His criticisms of the church and clergy, though meant to lead to reforms, gave ammunition to those wishing to attack the church and, therefore, it is said "Erasmus laid the egg that Luther hatched."

Thomas More (1478 – 1536), an English laywer, politician, and humanist, wrote *Utopia* (a Greek word for 'nowhere'). Mixing civic humanism with religious ideals, the book describes a perfect society, located on an imaginary island, in which war, poverty, religious intolerance, and other problems of the early 16th century do not exist. *Utopia* sought to show how people might live if they followed the social and political ideals of Christianity. Also, in a break with medieval thought, More portrayed government as very active in the economic life of the society, education, and public health. Though a critic of the church and clergy of his day, More was executed by Henry VIII, king of England, for refusing to countenance Henry's break with the pope in religious matters.

Jacques Lefevre d'Etables (1454 – 1536), the leading French humanist, produced five versions of the Psalms, his *Quincuplex Psalterism*, which challenged the belief in the tradition of a single, authoritative Bible. Also, his work on St. Paul anticipated that of Luther.

Francesco Ximenes de Cisneros (1436 – 1517), leader of the Spanish church as Grand Inquisitor, founded a university and produced the *Complutensian Polyglot Bible*, which had Hebrew, Greek, and Latin versions of the Bible in parallel columns. He also reformed the Spanish clergy and church so that most criticisms of the later reformers during the Reformation did not apply to Spain.

THE REFORMATION

The Reformation destroyed Western Europe's religious unity, andinvolved new ideas about the relationships among God, the individual, and society. Its course was greatly influenced by politics, and led, in most areas, to the subjection of the church to the political rulers.

Earlier threats to the unity of the church had been made by the works of John Wycliff and John Huss. The abuses of church practices and positions upset many people. Likewise, Christian humanists had been criticizing the abuses.

Personal piety and mysticism, which were alternative approaches to Christianity and did not require the apparatus of the institutional church and the clergy, had been appearing in the late Middle Ages.

MARTIN LUTHER (1483 – 1546) AND THE BEGINNINGS

Martin Luther was a miner's son from Saxony in central Germany. At the urgings of his father, he studied for a career in law. He underwent a religious experience while traveling, which led him to become an Augustinian friar. Later, he became a professor at the university in Wittenberg, Saxony.

Religious Problems

Luther, to his personal distress, could not reconcile the problem of the sinfulness of the individual and the justice of God. How could a sinful person attain the righteousness necessary to obtain salvation? During his studies of the Bible, especially of Romans 1:17, Luther came to believe that personal efforts – good works such as a Christian life and attention to the sacraments of the church – could not 'earn' the sinner salvation but that belief and faith were the only way to obtain grace. "Justification by faith alone" was the road to salvation, Luther believed by 1515.

Indulgences

Indulgences, which had originated in connection with the Crusades, involved the cancellation of the penalty given by the church to a confessed sinner. Indulgences had long been a means of raising money for church activities. In 1517, the pope was building the new cathedral of St. Peter in Rome. Also, Albrecht, Archbishop of Mainz, had purchased three church positions (simony and pluralism) by borrowing money from the banking family, the Fuggers. A Dominican friar, John Tetzel, was authorized to preach and sell indulgences, with the proceeds going to build the cathedral and repay the loan. The popular belief was that "As soon as a coin in the coffer rings, the soul from purgatory springs," and Tetzel had much business. On October 31, 1517, Luther, with his belief that no such control or influence could be had over salvation, nailed 95 theses, or statements, about indulgences to the door of the Wittenberg church and challenged the practice of selling indulgences. At this time he was seeking to reform the church, not divide it.

Luther's Relations with the Pope and Governments

In 1519 Luther debated various criticisms of the church and was driven to say that only the Bible, not religious traditions or papal statements, could determine correct religious practices and beliefs. In 1521 Pope Leo X excommunicated Luther for his beliefs.

In 1521 Luther appeared in the city of Worms before a meeting (Diet) of the important figures of the Holy Roman Empire, including the Emperor, Charles V. He was again condemned. At the Diet of Worms Luther made his famous statement about his writings and the basis for them: "Here I stand. I can do no other." After this, Luther could not go back; the break with the pope was permanent.

Frederick III of Saxony, the ruler of the territory in which Luther resided, protected Luther in Wartburg Castle for a year. Frederick never accepted Luther's beliefs but protected him because Luther was his subject. The weak political control of the Holy Roman Emperor contributed to Luther's success in avoiding the penalties of the pope and the Emperor.

Luther's Writings

An *Address to the Christian Nobility of the German Nation* (1520) argued that nobles, as well as clergy, were the leaders of the church and should undertake to reform it.

The *Babylonian Captivity* (1520) attacked the traditional seven sacraments, replacing them with only two.

The *Freedom of the Christian Man* (1520) explains Luther's views on faith, good works, the nature of God, and the supremacy of political authority over believers.

Against the Murderous, Thieving Hordes of the Peasants (1524), written in response to the Peasants' Revolt, stated Luther's belief that political leaders, not all people, should control both church and society.

By 1534 Luther translated the Bible into German, making it accessible to many more people as well as greatly influencing the development of the German language. Also, his composition, "A Mighty Fortress is Our God," was the most popular hymn of the 16th century. The printing press enabled Luther's works to be distributed quickly throughout Germany.

Subsequent Developments of Lutheranism

Economic burdens being increased on the peasants by their lords, combined with Luther's words that a Christian is subject to no one, led the peasants of Germany to revolt in 1524. The ensuing noble repression, supported by Luther, resulted in the deaths of 70,000 to 100,000 peasants.

At a meeting of the Holy Roman Empire's leading figures in 1529, a group of rulers, influenced by Luther's teachings "protested" the decision of the majority – hence the term "Protestant." Protestant originally meant Lutheran but eventually was applied to all Western Christians who did not maintain allegiance to the pope.

After a failure of Protestant and Catholic representatives to find a mutually acceptable statement of faith, the Augsburg Confession of 1530 was written as a comprehensive statement of Lutheran beliefs.

Led by Philip Melanchthon (1497 – 1560), the "Educator of Germany," Lutherans undertook much educational reform, including schools for girls.

Denmark became Lutheran in 1523 and Sweden in 1527.

Lutheran rulers, to protect themselves against the efforts of Charles V, the Holy Roman Emperor, to re-establish Catholicism in Germany, formed a defensive alliance at Schmalkald, the Schmalkaldic League, in 1531.

Wherever Lutheranism was adopted, church lands were often seized by the ruler. This made a return to Catholicism more difficult, as the lands would need to be restored to the church.

After warfare in the 1540's, which Charles V won but was unable to follow up because his treatment of defeated political rulers in Germany offended the nobility of the Empire, the Peace of Augsburg (1555) established the permanent religious division of Germany into Lutheran and Catholic churches. The statement "cuius regio, eius religio" ("whose region, his religion") meant that the religion of any area would be that of the ruling political authority.

OTHER REFORMERS

Martin Luther was not so much the father as the elder brother of the Reformation, because many other reformers were criticizing the church by the early 1520's.

Ulrich Zwingli (1484 – 1531) introduced reforming ideas in Zurich in Switzerland. He rejected clerical celibacy, the worship of saints, fasting, transubstantiation, and purgatory. Rejecting ritual and ceremony, Zwingli stripped churchs of decorations, such as statues. In 1523 the governing council of the city accepted his beliefs. Zurich became a center for Protestantism and its spread throughout Switzerland.

Zwingli, believing in the union of church and state, established in Zurich a system which required church attendance by all citizens and regulated many aspects of personal behavior – all enforced by courts and a group of informers.

Efforts to reconcile the views of Zwingli and Luther, chiefly over the issue of the Eucharist, failed during a meeting in Marburg Castle in 1529.

Switzerland, divided into many cantons, also divided into Protestant and Catholic camps. A series of civil wars, during which Zwingli was captured and executed, led to a treaty in which each canton was permitted to determine its own religion.

Anabaptists

Anabaptist (derived from a Greek word meaning to baptize again) is a name applied to people who rejected the validity of child baptism and believed that such children had to be rebaptized when they became adults.

As the Bible became available, through translation into the languages of the people, many people adopted interpretations contrary to those of Luther, Zwingli, and the Catholics.

Anabaptists sought to return to the practices of the early Christian church, which was a voluntary association of believers with no connection to the state. Perhaps the first Anabaptists appeared in Zurich in 1525 under the leadership of Conrad Grebel (1498 – 1526), and were called Swiss Brethren.

In 1534, a group of Anabaptists, called Melchiorites, led by Jan Matthys, gained political control of the city of Munster in Germany and forced other Protestants and Catholics to convert or leave. Most of the Anabaptists were workers and peasants, who followed Old Testament practices, including polygamy, and abolished private property. Combined armies of Protestants and Catholics captured the city and executed the leaders in 1535. Thereafter, Anabaptism and Munster became stock words of other Protestants and Catholics about the dangers of letting reforming ideas influence workers and peasants.

Subsequently, Anabaptists adopted pacifism and avoided involvement with the state whenever possible. Today, the Mennonites, founded by Menno Simons (1496 – 1561), and the Amish are the descendents of the Anabaptists.

John Calvin

John Calvin (1509 – 1564), a Frenchman, arrived in Geneva, a Swiss city-state which had adopted an anti-Catholic position, in 1536 but failed in his first efforts to further the reforms. Upon his return in 1540, Geneva became the center of the Reformation. Calvin's Institutes of the Christian Religion (1536), a strictly logical analysis of Christianity, had a universal, not local or national, appeal.

Calvin brought knowledge of organizing a city from his stay in Strasbourg, which was being led by the reformer Martin Bucer (1491 – 1551). Calvin differed from Luther, as Calvin emphasized the doctrine of predestination (God knew who would obtain salvation before those people were born) and believed that church and state should be united.

As in Zurich, church and city combined to enforce Christian behavior, and Calvinism came to be seen as having a stern morality. Like Zwingli, Calvin rejected most aspects of the medieval church's practices and sought a simple, unadorned church. Followers of Calvinism became the most militant and uncompromising of all Protestants.

Geneva became the home to Protestant exiles from England, Scotland, and France, who later returned to their countries with Calvinist ideas.

Calvinism ultimately triumphed as the majority religion in Scotland, under the leadership of John Knox (1505 – 1572), and the United Provinces of the Netherlands. Puritans in England and New England also accepted Calvinism.

REFORM IN ENGLAND

England underwent reforms in a pattern differing from the rest of Europe. Personal and political decisions by the rulers determined much of the course of the Reformation there.

The Break with the Pope

Henry VIII (1509 – 1547) married Katherine of Aragon, the widow of his older brother. By 1526 Henry became convinced that his inability to produce a legitimate son to inherit his throne was because he had violated God's commandments (Leviticus 18:16, 20:21) by marrying his brother's widow.

Soon, Henry fell in love with Anne Boleyn and decided to annul his marriage to Katherine in order to marry Anne. The pope, Clement VII, the authority necessary to issue such an annulment was, after 1527, under the political control of Charles V, Katherine's nephew. Efforts to secure the annulment, directed by Cardinal Wolsey (1474 – 1530) ended in failure and Wolsey's disgrace. Thomas Cranmer (1489 – 1556), named archbishop in 1533, dissolved Henry's marriage, which permitted him to marry Anne Boleyn in January 1533.

Henry used Parliament to threaten the pope and eventually to legislate the break with Rome by law. The Act of Annates (1532) prevented payments of money to the pope. The Act of Restraint of Appeals (1533) forbade appeals to be taken to Rome, which stopped Katherine from appealing her divorce to the pope. The Act of Supremacy (1534) declared Henry, not the pope, as the head of the English church. Subsequent acts enabled Henry to dissolve the monasteries and to seize their land, which represented perhaps 25% of the land of England.

In 1536, Thomas More was executed for rejecting Henry's leadership of the English church.

Protestant beliefs and practices made little headway during Henry's reign as he accepted transubstantiation, enforced celibacy among the clergy and otherwise made the English church conform to most medieval practices.

Protestantism

Under Henry VIII's son, Edward VI (1547 – 1553), a child of ten at his accession, the English church adopted Calvinism. Clergy were allowed to marry, communion by the laity expanded, and images were removed from churches. Doctrine included justification by faith, the denial of transubstantiation, and only two sacraments.

Catholicism

Under Mary (1553 – 1558), Henry VIII's daughter and half-sister of Edward VI, Catholicism was restored and England reunited with the pope. Over 300 people were executed, including bishops and Archbishop Cranmer, for refusing to abandon their Protestant beliefs. Numerous Protestants fled to the Continent where they learned of more advanced Protestant beliefs, including Calvinism at Geneva.

Anglicanism

Under Elizabeth (1558 – 1603), who was Henry VIII's daughter and half-sister to Edward and Mary, the church in England adopted Protestant beliefs again. The Elizabethan Settlement required outward conformity to the official church, but rarely inquired about inward beliefs.

Some practices of the church, including ritual, resembled the Catholic practices. Catholicism remained, especially among the gentry, but could not be practiced openly.

Some reformers wanted to purify (hence "Puritans") the church of its remaining Catholic aspects. The resulting church, Protestant in doctrine and practice but retaining most of the physical possessions, such as buildings, and many powers, such as church courts, of the medieval church, was called Anglican.

REFORM ELSEWHERE IN EUROPE

The Parliament in Ireland established a Protestant church much like the one in England. The landlords and people near Dublin were the only ones who followed their monarchs into Protestantism, as the mass of the Irish people were left untouched by the Reformation. The Catholic church and its priests became the religious, and eventually, the national, leaders of the Irish people.

John Knox (1505 – 72), upon his return from the Continent, led the Reformation in Scotland. Parliament, dominated by nobles, established Protestantism in 1560. The resulting church was Calvinist in doctrine.

France, near Geneva and Germany, experienced efforts at establishing Protestantism, but the kings of France had control of the church there and gave no encouragement to reformers. Calvinists, known in France as Huguenots, were especially common among the nobility and, after 1562, a series of civil wars involving religious differences resulted.

The church in Spain, controlled by the monarchy, allowed no Protestantism to take root. Similarly Italian political authorities rejected Protestantism.

THE COUNTER REFORMATION

The Counter Reformation brought changes to the portion of the Western church which retained its allegiance to the pope. Some historians see this as a reform of the Catholic church, similar to what Protestants were doing, while other see it as a result of the criticisms of Protestants.

Efforts to reform the church were given new impetus by Luther's activities. These included new religious orders such as Capuchins (1528), Theatines (1534) and Ursulines (1535), as well as mystics such as Teresa of Vaila (1515 – 1582).

Ignatius of Loyola (1491 – 1556), a former soldier, founded the Society of Jesus in 1540 to lead the attack on Protestantism. Jesuits, trained pursuant to ideas found in Ignatius' *Spiritual Exercises*, had dedication and determination and became the leaders in the Counter Reformation. In addition to serving in Europe, by the 1540's Jesuits, including Francies Xavier (1506 – 1552), traveled to Japan as missionaries.

Popes resisted reforming efforts because of fears as to what a council of church leaders might do to papal powers. The Sack of Rome in 1527, when soldiers of the Holy Roman Emperor captured and looted Rome, was seen by many as a judgment of God against the lives of the Renaissance popes. In 1534, Paul III became pope and attacked abuses while reasserting papal leadership.

Convened by Paul III and firmly under papal control, the Council of Trent met in three sessions from 1545 to 1563. It settled many aspects of doctrine including transubstantiation, the seven sacraments, the efficacy of good works for salvation, and the role of saints and priests. It also approved the "Index of Forbidden Books."

Other reforms came into effect. The sale of church offices was curtailed. New seminaries for more and better trained clergy were created. The revitalized Catholic church, the papacy, and the Jesuits set out to reunite Western Christianity.

Individuals who adopted other views but who had less impact on large groups of people included Thomas Muntzer (d. 1525), Caspar Schwenckfeld (d. 1561), Michael Servetus (d. 1553), and Lelio Sozzini (d. 1562).

DOCTRINES

The Reformation produced much thought and writing about the beliefs of Christianity. Most of the major divisions of the Western church took differing positions on these matters of doctrine. Some thinkers, such as Martin Bucer, a reformer in Strasbourg, believed many things, such as the ring in the marriage ceremony, were "things indifferent" – Christians could differ in their beliefs on such issues – but with the increasing rigidity of various churches, such views did not dominate.

The role of the Bible was emphasized by Protestants, while Catholics included the traditions developed by the church during the Middle Ages, as well as papal pronouncements.

Catholics retained the medieval view about the special nature and role of clergy while Protestants emphasized the 'priesthood of all believers,' which meant all individuals were equal before God. Protestants sought a clergy that preached.

Church governance varied widely. Catholics retained the medieval hierarchy of believers, priests, bishops, and pope. Anglicans rejected the authority of the pope and substituted the monarch as the Supreme Governor of the church. Lutherans rejected the authority of the pope but kept bishops. Most Calvinists governed their church by ministers and a group of elders, a system called Presbyterianism. Anabaptists rejected most forms of church governance in favor of congregational democracy.

Most Protestants denied the efficacy of some or all of the sacraments of the medieval church. The issue which most divided the various churches came to be the one called by various names: the Eucharist, the mass, the Lord's supper, the communion.

According to the belief of Transubstantiation, the bread and wine retain their outward appearances but the substances are transformed into the body and blood of Christ; this was a Catholic doctrine.

According to the belief in Consubstantiation, nothing of the bread and wine is changed but the believer realizes the presence of Christ in the bread and wine ("a piece of iron thrust into the fire does not change its composition but still has a differing quality"); this was a Lutheran doctrine.

Other views included ones that the event was a symbolic one, utilizing the community of believers. It served as a memorial to the actions of Christ, or was a thanksgiving for God's grant of salvation.

The means of obtaining salvation differed. Catholics believed in living the life according to Christian beliefs and participating in the practices of the church – good words. Lutherans accepted the notion of Justification by faith – salvation cannot be earned and a good life is the fruit of faith. Calvinists believed in Predestination – that salvation is known only to God but a good life can be some proof of predestined salvation; this was a Calvinist doctrine.

Relation of the church to the state also differed. Catholics and Calvinists believed the church should control and absorb the state; when God is seen as ruling the society, this is a theocracy. Lutheran and Anglican belief held that the state controls the church. Anabaptists held that the church ignores the state.

RESULTS

By 1560, attitudes were hardening and political rulers understood the benefits and disadvantages of religion, be it Catholic or Protestant. The map of Europe and its religions did not change much after 1560.

Political rulers, be they monarchs or city councils, gained power over and at the expense of the church. The state thereafter could operate as an autonomous unit.

Religious enthusiasm was rekindled. While most of the reforms came from the political and religious leadership of the societies involved, the general populus eventually gained enthusiasm – an enthusiasm lacking in religious belief since far back into the Middle Ages.

All aspects of Western Christianity undertook to remedy the abuses which had contributed to the Reformation. Simony, pluralism, immoral or badly educated clergy were all attacked and, by the 17th century, considerably remedied.

Protestantism, by emphasizing the individual believer's direct contact with God, rather than through the intermediary of the church, contributed to the growth of individualism.

Thinkers have attempted to connect religious change with economic developments, especially the appearance of capitalism. Karl Marx, a nineteenth-century philosopher and social theorist, believed that capitalism, which emphasized hard work, thrift, and the use of reason rather than tradition, led to the development of Protestantism, a type of Christianity he thought especially attractive to the middle class who were also the capitalists.

Max Weber, a later 19th-century sociologist, reversed the argument and believed that Protestantism, especially Calvinism, with its emphasis on predestination, led to great attention being paid to the successes and failures of this world as possible signs of future salvation. Such attention, and the attendant hard work, furthered the capitalist spirit.

Most writers today accept neither view but believe Protestantism and capitalism are related; however too many other factors are involved to make the connection clear or easy.

THE WARS OF RELIGION

The period from approximately 1560 to 1648 witnessed continuing warfare, primarily between Protestants and Catholics. Though religion was not the only reason for the wars – occasionally Catholics and Protestants were allies – religion was the dominant cause of the bloodshed. In the latter half of the 16th century, the fighting was along the Atlantic seaboard between Calvinists and Catholics; after 1600, the warfare spread to Germany where Calvinists, Lutherans, and Catholics fought.

Warfare and the Effects of Gunpowder

Cannons became effective; therefore, elaborate and expensive fortifications of cities were required. Long sieges became necessary to capture a city.

The infantry, organized in squares of three thousand men and armed with pikes and muskets, made the cavalry charge obsolete.

Greater discipline and control of armies were required to sustain a siege or train the infantry. An army once trained would not be disbanded, due to the expense of retraining. The order of command and modern ranks appeared, as did uniforms.

The better discipline permitted commanders to attempt more actions on the battlefield, so more soldiers were necessary. Armies grew from the 40,000 of the Spanish army of 1600, to 400,000 in the French army at the end of the 17th century.

War and Destruction

Devastation of the enemy's lands became the rule. Armies, mostly made up of mercenaries, lived by pillage when not paid and often were not effectively under the control of the ruler employing them. Peasants, after such devastation and torture to reveal their valuables, left farming and turned to banditry.

THE CATHOLIC CRUSADE

The territories of Charles V, the Holy Roman Emperor, were divided in 1556 between Ferdinand, Charles' brother, and Philip II (1556-98), Charles' son. Ferdinand received Austria, Hungary, Bohemia and the title of Holy Roman Emperor. Philip received Spain, Milan, Naples, the Netherlands, and the New World. Both parts of the Hapsburg family cooperated in international matters.

Philip was a man of severe personal habits, deeply religious, and a hard worker. Solemn (it is said he only laughed once in his life, when the report of the St. Bartholomew's Day massacre reached him) and reclusive (he built the Escorial outside Madrid as a palace, monastery and eventual tomb), he devoted his life and the wealth of Spain to making Europe Catholic. It was Philip, not the pope, who led the Catholic attack on Protestants. The pope and the Jesuits, however, did participate in Philip's efforts.

Sources of the Power of Philip II

The gold and silver of the New World flowed into Spain, especially following the opening of the silver mines at Potesi in Peru.

Spain dominated the Mediterranean following a series of wars led by Philip's half-brother, Don John, against Moslem (largely Turkish) forces. Don John secured the Mediterranean for Christian merchants with a naval victory over the Turks at Lepanto off the coast of Greece in 1571.

Portugal was annexed by Spain in 1580 following the death of the king without a clear successor. This gave Philip the only other large navy of the day as well as Portuguese territories around the globe.

Nature of the Struggle

Calvinism was spreading in England, France, the Netherlands, and Germany. Calvinists supported each other, often disregarding their countries' borders.

England was ruled by two queens, Mary (1553 – 58), who married Philip II, and then Elizabeth (1558 – 1603), while three successive kings of France from 1559 to 1589 were influenced by their mother, Catherine de' Medici. Women rulers were a novelty in European politics.

Monarchs attempted to strengthen their control and the unity of their countries, a process which nobles often resisted.

CIVIL WAR IN FRANCE

Francis I (1515 – 47) obtained control of the French church when he signed the Concordat of Bologna with the pope, and therefore had no incentive to encourage Protestantism.

With the signing of the Treaty of Cateau-Cambresis in 1559, the struggles of the Hapsburgs and Valois ended, leaving the French with no fear of outside invasion for a while.

John Calvin was a Frenchman and Geneva was near France, so Calvinist ideas spread in France, especially among the nobility. French Calvinists were sometimes called Huguenots.

Three noble families, – Bourbon, Chatillon, and Guise – sought more power and attempted to dominate the monarchs after 1559. Partly due to politics, the Bourbons and Chatillons became Calvinists.

When Henry II (1547 – 59) died as a result of injuries sustained in a tournament, he was succeeded, in succession, by his three sons (Francis II, 1559–60, Charles IX 1560 – 74, Henry III 1571–89), each influenced by their mother, Catherine de' Medici (1519 – 89), and often controlled by one of the noble families. Though the monarch was always Catholic until 1589, each king was willing to work with Calvinists or Catholics if it would give him more power and independence.

The Wars

A total of nine civil wars occurred from 1562 to 1589. The wars became more brutal as killing of civilians supplanted military action.

The St. Bartholomew's Day Massacre on August 24, 1572, was planned by Catherine de' Medici and resulted in the deaths of 20,000 Huguenots. The pope had a medal struck commemorating the event and the king of Spain, Philip II, laughed when told of the massacre.

As a result of St. Bartholomew's Day and other killings, Protestants throughout Europe feared for their future.

Several important figures were assassinated by their religious opponents, including two kings (Henry III and Henry IV). The two leading members of the Guise family were killed at the instigation of the king, Henry III, in 1588.

Spain intervened with troops to support the Catholics in 1590.

Henry of Navarre (1589 – 1610)

A Calvinist and member of the Bourbon family, Henry of Navarre became king in 1589 when Henry III was assassinated. Personally popular, Henry began to unite France but was unable to conquer or control Paris, center of Catholic strength. In 1593 he converted to Catholicism saying "Paris is worth a mass." In this respect, he was a politique, more interested in political unity than religious uniformity.

In 1589 Henry issued the Edict of Nantes which permitted Huguenots to worship publicly, to have access to the universities and to public office, and to maintain fortified towns in France to protect themselves. The Edict was not a recognition of the advantages of religious tolerance so much as it was a truce in the religious wars.

THE REVOLT OF THE NETHERLANDS

The Netherlands was a group of seventeen provinces clustered around the mouth of the Rhine and ruled by the king of Spain. Each province had a tradition of some independence and each elected a stadholder, a man who provided military leadership when necessary. The stadholder often was an important noble and often became the most important politician in the province.

Since the Middle Ages the Netherlands had included many cities dominated by wealthy merchants. By 1560 the cities housed many Calvinists, including some who had fled from France.

Philip II, king of Spain, sought to impose on Netherland inhabitants a more centralized government, as well as a stronger Catholic church closely following the decrees of the Council of Trent. Philip's efforts provoked resistance by some nobles, led by William of Orange (1533 – 84), called "the Silent" because he discussed his political plans with very few people. An agreement and pledge to resist, called the Compromise of 1564 and signed by people throughout the provinces, led to rebellion.

Philip sent the Duke of Alva (1508 – 1583) with 20,000 soldiers to suppress the rebellion. Alva established the Council of Troubles (called the Council of Blood by its opponents) which executed several thousand Calvinists as heretics. Alva also imposed new taxes, including a sales tax of 10%. Most significantly, the Inquisition was established.

The resistance to Alva included groups of sailors, called Sea Beggars, and the opening of the dykes to frustrate the marches of the Spanish armies. In 1576 the unpaid Spanish sacked Antwerp, an event called the Spanish Fury, which destroyed Antwerp's commercial supremacy in the Netherlands.

The Calvinist northern provinces and the Catholic southern provinces united in 1576 in the Pacification of Ghent, but were unable to cooperate. They broke apart into two religious groups: the Calvinist Union of Utrecht (approximately modern day Netherlands) and the Catholic Union of Arras (approximately modern day Belgium).

International attention was attracted when a son of Catherine de' Medici attempted to become the leader of the revolt and when the English sent troops and money to support the rebels after 1585.

The Spanish were driven out of the northern Netherlands in the 1590's, and the war ended in 1609, though official independence was not recognized by Spain until 1648. Thereafter, the independent northern provinces, dominated by the province of Holland, were called the United Provinces and the southern provinces, ruled by the king of Spain, the Spanish Netherlands.

ENGLAND AND SPAIN

Mary (1553 – 58)

The daughter of Henry VIII and Katherine of Aragon, Mary sought to make England Catholic. She executed many Protestants, earning her the name "Bloody Mary" from her opponents.

To escape persecution, many of the English went into exile on the Continent where, settling in Frankfurt, Geneva, and elsewhere, they learned more radical Protestant ideas.

Cardinal Pole (1500 – 58) was one of Mary's advisers and symbolized the subordination of England to the pope.

Mary married Philip II, king of Spain, and organized her foreign policy around Spanish interests. They had no children.

Elizabeth (1558 – 1603)

A Protestant, though one of unknown beliefs, Elizabeth achieved a religious settlement between 1559 and 1563 which left England with a church governed by bishops and practicing Catholic rituals, but maintaining a Calvinist doctrine. This was seen as a via media – a middle way between extremes – by its supporters, or an impossible compromise of Protestantism and Catholicism by its opponents.

Puritans sought to purify the English church of the remnants of its medieval heritage and, though suppressed by Elizabeth's government, were not condemned to death.

Catholics, who sought to return the English church to an allegiance to the pope, participated in several rebellions and plots.

Mary, Queen of Scots, had fled to England from Scotland, in 1568, after alienating the nobles there. It was she, in Catholic eyes, who was the legitimate queen of England. Several plots and rebellions to put Mary on the throne led to her execution in 1587.

Elizabeth was formally excommunicated by the pope in 1570. A politique interested in the advancing English nation, Elizabeth did not "make windows into men's souls".

In 1588, as part of his crusade and to stop England from supporting the rebels in the Netherlands, Philip II sent the Armada, a fleet of over 125 ships, to convey troops from the Netherlands to England as part of a plan to make England Catholic. The Armada was defeated by a combination of superior English naval tactics and a wind which made it impossible for the Spanish to accomplish their goal.

Peace between Spain and England was signed in 1604. England remained Protestant and an opponent of Spain as long as Spain remained a world power.

THE THIRTY YEARS' WAR

Calvinism was spreading throughout Germany. The Peace of Augsburg, which settled the disputes between Lutherans and Catholics in 1555, had no provision for Calvinists. Lutherans gained more territories through conversions and often took control of previous church states – a violation of the Peace Augsburg. A Protestant alliance under the leadership of the Calvinist ruler of the Palatinate opposed a Catholic League led by the ruler of Bavaria.

The Bohemian Period (1618 – 25)

The Bohemians rejected a Hapsburg as their king in favor of the Calvinist ruler of Palatinate, Frederick. They threw two Hapsburg officials out a window – the "defenestration of Prague."

Frederick's army was defeated at White Mountain in 1620, Bohemia was made Catholic, and the Spanish occupied Frederick's Palatinate.

The Danish Period (1625 – 29)

The army of Ferdinand, the Holy Roman Emperor, invaded northern Germany, raising fear amongst Protestants for their religion and local rulers for their political rights. Christian IV (1588 – 1648), king of Denmark, led an army into Germany in defense of Protestants but was easily defeated. After defeating Christian, the Holy Roman Emperor sought to recover all church lands secularized since 1552 and establish a strong Hapsburg presence in northern Germany.

The Swedish Period (1629 – 35)

Gustavus Adolphus (1611–32), king of Sweden, who was monetarily supported by France and the United Provinces, that wanted the Hapsburgs defeated, invaded

Germany in defense of Protestantism. Sweden stopped the Hapsburg cause in the battle of Breitenfeld in 1630, but Gustavus Adolphus was killed at the battle of Lutzen in 1632.

The Swedish-French Period (1635 – 48)

France, guided by Cardinal Richelieu (1585 – 1642), supplied troops in Germany, as the war became part of a bigger war between France and Spain.

Treaty of Westphalia (1648)

The presence of ambassadors from all of the belligerents, as well as many other countries made settlement of nearly all disputes possible. Only the French-Spanish war continued, ending in 1659.

The principles of the Peace of Augsburg were reasserted, but with Calvinists included. The pope's rejection of the treaty was ignored.

The independence of the United Provinces from the king of Spain, and the Swiss Confederacy from the Holy Roman Empire, was recognized. Individual German states, numbering over three hundred, obtained nearly complete independence from the Holy Roman Empire.

Miscellaneous

Not all issues were ones of Protestants versus Catholics. The Lutheran ruler of Saxony joined the Catholics in the attack on Frederick, at White Mountain, and the leading general for the Holy Roman Emperor, Ferdinand, was Albrecht of Wallenstein, a Protestant.

The war brought great destruction to Germany, leading to a decline in population of perhaps one-third, or more, in some areas. Germany remained divided and without a strong government until the 19th century.

Results

After 1648, warfare, though often containing religious elements, would not be executed primarily for religious goals.

The Catholic crusade to reunite Europe failed, largely due to the efforts of the Calvinists. The religious distribution of Europe has not changed significantly since 1648.

Nobles, resisting the increasing power of the state, usually dominated the struggle. France, then Germany, fell apart due to the wars. France was reunited in the seventeenth century; Germany was not.

In most political entities, politiques, such as Elizabeth I of England and Henry IV of France, who sought more to keep the state united than to insure that a single religion dominated, came to control politics.

The branches of the Hapsburg family, the Austrian and the Spanish, continued to to cooperate in international affairs. Spain, though a formidable military power until 1648, began a decline which ended its role as a great power of Europe.

THE GROWTH OF THE STATE AND THE AGE OF EXPLORATION

In the 17th century the political systems of the countries of Europe began dividing into two types, absolutist and constitutionalist. While no country typified either type and all countries had part of both, the countries can be divided in their focus. England, the United Provinces, and Sweden moved towards constitutionalism, while France was adopting absolutist ideas.

Overseas exploration, begun in the 15th century, expanded, as the wealth of the New World flowing to Spain became apparent to the rest of Europe. Governments supported such activity in order to gain wealth, as well as to preempt other countries.

Definitions

Constitutionalism meant rules, often unwritten, defining and limiting government. Seeking to enhance the liberty of the individual as well to advance the individual as a person were goals; in this manner constitutionalism shaded over into Liberalism. Constitutional regimes usually had some means of group decision making, such as a parliament, but a constitutional government need not be a democracy and usually was not. Consent of the governed provided the basis for the legitimacy of the regime, its acceptance by its subject.

Absolutism emphasized the role of the state and its fulfillment of some specific purpose, such as nationalism, religion, or the glory of the monarch. The usual form of government of an absolutist regime was, in the seventeenth century, kingship, which gained its legitimacy from the notion of divine right or the traditional assumption of power.

Nobles and bourgeoisie, depending on the country, provided the chief opposition to the increasing power of the state. In constitutionalist states, they often obtained control of the state, while in absolutist states they became servants of the state.

POLITICAL THOUGHT

The collapse of governments during the wars of religion, and the subjection of one religious group to the government of another, stimulated thought about the nature of politics and political allegiances. The increasing power of the monarchs raised questions about the nature and extent of that power.

Both Protestants and Catholics developed theories of resistance to a government. Luther and Calvin had disapproved of revolt or rebellion against government. John Knox's *Blast of the Trumpet Against the Terrible Regiment of Women* (1558) approved rebellion against a heretical ruler. His text was directed against Mary, Queen of Scotland.

In France, Huguenot writers, stimulated by the St. Bartholomew Day's Massacre, developed the idea of a covenant (contract) between people and God and between subjects and monarch. If the monarch ceased to observe the covenant, the purpose of which was to honor God, the representatives of the people (usually the nobles or others in an assembly of some sort) could resist the monarch.

Catholic writers, such as Robert Bellarmine, saw the monarch as being given authority, especially religious authority, by God. With the pope as God's deputy on earth, the pope could dispose of a monarch who put people's souls in jeopardy by wrong beliefs.

Jean Bodin (1530 – 96), in response to the chaos of France during the civil wars, developed the theory of sovereignty. He believed that in each country one power or institution must be strong enough to make everyone else obey; otherwise chaos results from the conflicts of institutions or groups of equal power. Bodin provided the theoretical basis for absolutist states.

Resistance to the power of monarchs was based upon claims to protect local customs, "traditional liberties" and "the ancient constitution." Nobles and towns appealed to the medieval past, when sovereignty had been shared by kings, nobles, and other institutions.

The struggles in the seventeenth century produced varying results. At the extremes, an absolutist country was ruled by a monarch from whom all power followed, while a constitutional country would limit government power and have a means of determining the will of the people, or at least some of them.

The French king dispensed with all representative institutions, dominated the nobility, and ruled directly. The nobles controlled the English government through the representative institution of Parliament. In Germany, various components of the Holy Roman Empire defeated the Emperor and governed themselves independently of him.

ENGLAND

Problems Facing English Monarchs

The English church was a compromise of Catholic practices and Protestant beliefs and was criticized by both groups. The monarchs, after 1620, gave leadership of the church to men with Arminian beliefs.

Arminius (1560 – 1609), a Dutch theologian, had changed Calvinist beliefs so as to modify, slightly, the emphasis on predestination. English Arminians also sought to emphasize the role of ritual in church services and to enjoy the "beauty of holiness," which their opponents took to be too Catholic. William Laud (1573 – 1645), Archbishop of Canterbury, accelerated the growth of Arminianism.

Opponents to this shift in belief were called Puritans, a term that covered a wide range of beliefs and people. To escape the church in England, many Puritans began moving to the New World, especially Massachusetts. Both James I and Charles I made decisions which, to Puritans, favored Catholics too much.

In financial matters, inflation and Elizabeth's wars left the government short of money. Contemporaries blamed the shortage on the extravagance of the courts of James I and Charles I. James I sold titles of nobility in an effort to raise money but this annoyed the nobles with older titles, as well as debased the entire idea underlying nobility.

The monarchs lacked any substantial source of income and had to obtain the consent of a Parliament to levy a tax. The monarchs would face numerous concerns in dealing with a parliamentary body.

First of all, a Parliament only met when the monarch summoned it. Though Parliaments had existed since the Middle Ages, there were long periods of time between Parliamentary meetings. Parliaments consisted of nobles and gentry with a few merchants and lawyers. The men in a Parliament usually wanted the government to remedy grievances as part of the agreement to a tax. In 1621, for the first time since the Middle Ages, the power to impeach governmental servants was used by a Parliament to eliminate men who had offended its members.

The Counties

The forty English counties had a tradition of much local independence. The major landowners – the nobles and the gentry – controlled the counties and resented central government interference.

James I (1603 – 25)

James ended the war with Spain and avoided any other entanglements, despite the problem that the Thirty Years' War in Germany involved his son-in-law, who was the ruler of the Palatinate and a Protestant hero. The Earl of Somerset and then the Duke of Buckingham served as favorites for the king, doing much of the work of government and dealing with suitors for royal actions.

Charles I (1625 - 49)

Henrietta Maria, a sister of the king of France and a Catholic, became his queen. Charles stumbled into wars with both Spain and France during the late 1620's.

A series of efforts to raise money for the wars led to confrontations with his opponents in Parliaments. A "forced loan" was collected from taxpayers with the promise it would be repaid when a tax was voted by a Parliament. Soldiers were billeted in subjects' houses during the wars. People were imprisoned for resisting these royal actions.

In 1626, the Duke of Buckingham was nearly impeached because of his monopoly of royal offices and his exclusion of others from power. In 1628, Parliament passed the Petition of Right, which declared illegal the royal actions in connection with the loans and billeting.

Charles ruled without calling a Parliament during the 1630's. A policy of "thorough" – strict efficiency and much central government activity – was followed. Money was raised by discovering old forms of taxation. A medieval law which required all landowners with a certain amount of wealth to become knights was used to fine those who had not been knighted. All counties were forced to pay money to outfit ships – "ship money" – which had previously been the obligation only of coastal counties.

Breakdown

Charles, with the help of the Archbishop Laud, attempted to impose English rituals and the English prayer book on the Scottish church. The Scots revolted and invaded northern England with an army.

To pay for his own army Charles called the Short Parliament, but was not willing to remedy any grievances or to change his policies. In response, the Parliament did not vote any taxes. Charles called another Parliament, the Long Parliament, which attacked his ministers, challenged his religious policies, and refused to trust him with money.

Archbishop Laud and the Earl of Strafford, the two architects of "thorough," were driven from power. The courts of Star Chamber and High Commission, which had been used to prosecute Charles' opponents, were abolished. When the Irish revolted, Parliament would not let Charles raise an army to suppress them, as it was feared he would use the army against his English opponents. John Pym (1584 – 1643) emerged as a leader of the king's opponents in Parliament.

Civil War

In August, 1642, Charles abandoned all hope of negotiating with his opponents and, instead, declared war against them. Charles' supporters were called royalists or Cavaliers. His opponents were called Parliamentarians or Roundheads, due to the London apprentices amongst them who wore their hair cut short.

Historians differ on whether to call this struggle the Puritan Revolution, the English Civil Wars, or the Great Rebellion. The issues which precipitated the war were concerning religious differences and how much authority Charles should have in the government.

Charles was defeated. His opponents had allied with the Scots who still had an army in England. Additionally, the New Model Army, with its general Oliver Cromwell (1599 – 1658), was superior to Charles' army.

With the collapse of government, new religious and political groups, such as Levellers, Quakers, and Ranters, appeared.

Following the defeat of Charles, his opponents attempted to negotiate a settlement with him but, with that failing, he was executed on January 30, 1649, and England became a republic for the next eleven years.

The search for a settlement continued until 1689, when the nobles, gentry, and merchants, acting through Parliament, controlled the government and the monarchy.

FRANCE

Problems Facing the French Monarchs

The regions of France long had a large measure of independence, and local parliaments could refuse to enforce royal laws. The centralization of all government proceeded by replacing local authorities with intendants, civil servants who reported to the king.

The Huguenots, as a result of the Edict of Nantes, had separate rights and powers. They were, in effect, a state within the state. All efforts to unify France under one religion (Catholicism) faced both internal resistance from the Huguenots and the difficulty of dealing with Protestant powers abroad.

By 1650, France had been ruled by only one competent adult monarch since 1559. Louis XIII came to the throne at age 9 and Louis XIV at the age of 5. The mothers of both kings, Maria de' Medici and Anne of Austria, governed until the boys were of age. Both queens relied on chief ministers to help govern: Cardinal Richelieu (1585–1642) and Cardinal Mazarin (1602–61).

Henry IV (1589 – 1610)

Henry relied on the duke of Sully (1560 – 1641), the first of a series of strong ministers in the seventeenth century. Sully and Henry increased the involvement of the state in the economy, acting on a theory known as mercantilism.

Monopolies on the production of gunpowder and salt were developed. Only the government could operate mines. A canal was begun to connect the Mediterranean to the Atlantic.

Louis XIII (1610 – 43)

Cardinal Richelieu, first used by Louis' mother, became the real power in France. Foreign policy was difficult because of the problems of religion.

Due to the weakness of France after the wars of religion, Maria de' Medici concluded a treaty with Spain in 1611. In order to keep the Hapsburgs from gaining ascendancy in Germany, Richelieu supplied troops and money to Gustavus Adolphus, a Lutheran, after 1631.

The unique status of the Huguenots was reduced through warfare and the Peace of Alais (1629) when their separate armed cities were eliminated.

The nobility was reduced in power through constant attention to the laws and the mprisonment of offenders.

Breakdown

Cardinal Mazarin governed because Louis XIV (1643–1715) was a minor. During the Fronde, from 1649 to 1652, the nobility controlled Paris, drove Louis XIV and Mazarin from the city, and attempted to run the government. Noble ineffectiveness, the memories of the chaos of the wars of religion, and the overall anarchy convinced most people that a strong king was preferable to a warring nobility. The lack of impact of the movement was symbolized by the name of the Fronde, which meant a slingshot used by children to shoot rocks at carriages, but which caused no real damage.

Absolutism

By 1652, the French people were willing to accept, and the French monarchy had developed the tools, to implement a strong, centralized government. Louis XIV personally saw the need to increase royal power and his own glory, and dedicated his life to these goals. He steadily pursued a policy of "one king, one law, one faith."

OTHER CONSTITUTIONAL STATES

United Provinces

The seven provinces sent representatives to an Estates General, which was dominated by the richest provinces, Holland and Zealand, and which had few powers. Each province elected a stadholder, and a military leader. Usually, all of the provinces elected the same man, the head of the house of Orange.

Calvinism divided when Arminius proposed a theology that reduced the emphasis on predestination. Though the stricter Calvinism prevailed, Arminians had full political and economic rights after 1632, and Catholics and Jews were also tolerated, though with fewer rights.

The merchants dominating the Estates General supported the laxer Arminianism and wanted peace, while the house of Orange adopted the stricter Calvinism and sought a more aggressive foreign policy. In 1619, Jan van Oldenbarenveldt (1547 – 1619), representing the merchants, lost a struggle over the issue of renewing war with Spain to Maurice of Nassau, the head of the house of Orange. Until 1650, Maurice, and then William II, dominated, and the Dutch supported anti-Hapsburg forces in the Thirty Years' War. The merchants regained power, and Jan de Witt (1625 – 72) set about returning power to the provinces in 1653.

The 17th century witnessed tremendous growth in the wealth and economic power of the Dutch. The Bank of Amsterdam, founded in 1609, provided safe and stable control of money, which encouraged investments in many kinds of activities. Amsterdam became the financial center of Europe. The Dutch also developed the largest fleet in Europe devoted to trade, rather than warfare, and became the dominant trading country.

Sweden

Gustavus Adolphus (1611 – 32) reorganized the government, giving the nobles a dominant role in both the army and the bureaucracy. The central government was divided into five departments, each with a noble at its head. The very capable Axel Oxenstierna (1583 – 1654) dominated this government.

The Riksdag, an assembly of nobles, clergy, townsmen, and peasants, nominally had the highest legislative authority, The real power, however, lay with the nobles and the monarch.

From 1611 to 1650, noble power and wealth greatly increased. In 1650 Queen Christina, who wanted to abdicate and become a Catholic (which eventually she did in 1654), used the power of the Riksdag to coerce the nobles into accepting her designated successor.

As a result of Gustavus Adolphus' military actions, the Baltic became a Swedish lake and Sweden became a world power. Swedish economic power resulted fromdominating the copper mines, the only ones in Europe.

In both the United Provinces and Sweden, the government was dominated by rich and powerful groups who used representative institutions to limit the power of the state and produce non-absolutist regimes.

EXPLORATIONS AND CONQUESTS

Motives

Gold and silver were early and continuing reasons for explorations. Still further, the thrill of exploration explains the actions of many. Spices and other aspects of trade quickly became important, especially in Portuguese trade to the East Indies.

Religion proved to be a particularly strong motivation. To engage in missionary work, Jesuits, including Francis Xavier, appeared in India, Japan, and other areas by 1550. English unhappy with their church moved to North America in the 17th century.

Results

The wealth, especially the gold and silver of Mexico and Peru, enabled Spain to embark on its military activities. European inflation, which existed prior to the discoveries, was further fueled by the influx of gold and silver.

Disease killed perhaps 25 million, or eighty percent, of the Indians of the Americas. Syphilis appeared in Europe for the first time.

Many foods, such as potatoes and tomatoes, were introduced to Europe.

Europeans began transporting slaves from Africa to the Americas.

A large number of English settled in North America and a smaller number of Spaniards in Central and South America. Other areas were dotted by only a few Europeans.

Early Explorations

Portugal. Prince Henry the Navigator (1394 – 1460) supported exploration of the African coastline, largely in order to seek gold. Bartholomew Dias (1450 – 1500) rounded the southern tip of Africa in 1487. Vasco de Gama (1460–1524) reached India in 1498 and, after some fighting, soon established trading ports at Goa and Calicut. Albuquerque (1435 – 1515) helped establish an empire in the Spice Islands after 1510.

Spain. Christopher Columbus (1446 – 1506), seeking a new route to the (East) Indies, discovered the Americas in 1492. Ferdinand Magellan (1480 – 1521) started a voyage which first circumnavigated the globe in 1521 – 22. Conquests of the Aztecs by Hernando Cortes (1485 – 1547), and the Incas by Francisco Pizarro (1470 – 1541), enabled the Spanish to send much gold and silver back to Spain. Thus began the process of subjugating the American Indians.

In 1494, Spain and Portugal, with the treaty of Tordesillas, divided amongst themselves portions of the world they had newly discovered.

Other Countries. In the 1490's the Cabots, John (1450 – 98) and Sebastian (1474 – 1557), explored North America and, after 1570, various Englishmen, including Francis Drake (1545 – 96), fought the Spanish around the world. The English, discovering a route to Russia through the White Sea, commenced trading there. Jacques Cartier (1491 – 1557) explored parts of North America for France in 1534.

Early 17th-Century Explorations and Settlements

Governments took an increasing interest in settlements, seeking to control both them and trading ports from European capitals.

England's Virginia Company settled Jamestown in the Chesapeake Bay in 1607. Soon tobacco became a major export crop. Catholics were allowed to settle in Maryland after 1632. The Pilgrims arrived in Massachusetts in 1620. Other settlers of the Massachusetts Bay, chartered by the king in 1629, soon arrived. Between 1630 and 1650, over 20,000 people, unhappy with religious developments in England, emigrated to Massachusetts.

Various West Indies Islands were also settled.

Following Samuel de Champlain's (1567 – 1635) first efforts in 1603, the French explored the St. Lawrence River. Trade, especially for furs, was the goal. The Company of the Hundred Associates, founded in 1627, undertook the development of Canada. The West Indies attracted groups of investors, such as the Company of St. Christopher, which was organized in 1626.

The Dutch sent Henry Hudson (d. 1611) to explore North America in 1609, soon establishing settlements at New Amsterdam and in the Hudson River valley. The Dutch founded trading centers in the East Indies, the West Indies, and southern Africa. Swedes settled on the Delaware River in North America in 1638.

SCIENCE, LEARNING AND SOCIETY

The scientific revolution of the 16th and 17th centuries replaced religion as the explanation for the occurrences of the physical world. In contrast to religious articles of faith, the approach of science relied on experiment and mathematics. Learning, including the arts, moved away from Renaissance models to emphasize the emotions and individual variations.

While the family as an institution remained unchanged, much of society was transformed through population growth, inflation, and new patterns of landholding, trade, and industry.

THE SCIENTIFIC REVOLUTION

Astronomy, and to a lesser degree physics, first produced the new ways of thought called the scientific revolution.

The ideas of the ancient Greek, Aristotle (384 – 22 B.C.), provided the system of explanations. Aristotle believed that the motionless earth occupied the center of the universe, and that the sun, planets, and stars revolved around it in circular orbits determined by crystalline spheres. Aristotle's system was further refined by Ptolemy, a second-century astronomer, to make it correspond to the observed movements of the stars and planets.

Accepting both the Aristotelian idea that the circle is the closest to the perfect figure and, also, the Renaissance belief in simple explanations, Nicolaus Copernicus (1473-1543) suggested that the sun was at the center of the universe and that the earth and planets revolved around it in circular orbits. His *On the Revolutions of the Heavenly Spheres* was published in 1543, the year of his death. Copernicus' ideas that the universe was immense removed people from occupying the center of the universe, to inhabiting a small planet in a vast system. It also eliminated distinctions between the earth and the heavens.

Copernicus' views were not immediately accepted because they contradicted the words of the Bible. Although he posited circular orbits for the planets, his predictions of their locations were not accurate.

A Danish nobleman, Tycho Brahe (1546-1601) built the best observatory of his time, for which he collected extensive data on the location of the stars and planets. Brahe did not totally accept Copernicus' views, as he believed that the earth still occupied the center of the universe and that the other planets revolved around the sun, which, in turn, revolved around the earth.

Brahe's discovery of a new star in 1572, and the appearance of a comet in 1577, shattered beliefs in an unchanging sky and crystalline spheres.

Johannes Kepler's (1571 – 1630) reworking of Copernicus' theory and Brahe's observations produced the idea that the planets move around the sun in elliptical, not circular, orbits. The three new laws of Kepler accurately predicted the movements of the planets and were based on mathematical relationships.

Galileo (1564 – 1642) discovered four moons of Jupiter using a new invention of the time, the telescope. He also conducted other experiments in physics which related to the relationship of movement of objects and the mathematics necessary to describe the movement, such as that of the pendulum. A propagandist for science, Galileo defended his discoveries and mocked his opponents. The Catholic Church in Italy, where Galileo lived and worked, forced him to recant his views, which demonstrated the conflict of the older religious views and the new scientific approach.

Scientific Methodologies

The author of *Advancement of Learning* (1605) and an advocate of experimental approaches to knowledge, Francis Bacon (1561 – 1626) formalized empiricism, an approach using inductive reasoning. An Englishman, Bacon himself did few experiments but believed empiricism would produce useful, rather than purely theoretical, knowledge.

Beginning from basic principles, Rene Descartes (1596 – 1650) believed scientific laws could be found by deductive reasoning. Formulating analytic geometry, Descartes knew that geometry and algebra were related and that equations could describe figures. Later developments merged inductive experimentalism, with deductive mathematical rationalism, to produce today's epistemology method, used to obtain and verify knowledge.

Connections with the Rest of Society

During the Renaissance, many universities established the study of mathematics and physics. All of the great scientists involved in the changes in astronomy studied at universities.

The demands of explorers, especially those at sea, for more accurate measurements of the stars, increased attention on the details of the heavenly movements.

Warfare, particularly the developing use of artillery, required and permitted explanations involving precise measurements.

Initially, Protestant areas were more hostile than Catholic ones to the new learning. After Galileo, however, Catholic authorities led in trying to suppress the new ideas.

Consequences

The new approaches of the scientific method spread to inquiries far beyond astronomy and physics. Many sought new explanations as well as order and uniformity in all aspects of the physical world and society.

William Harvey (1578 – 1657) demonstrated the circulation of blood and the role of the human heart. Thomas Hobbes (1558 – 1679), an English writer on political theory, studied society. Using a few basic premises, he described politics in *Leviathan* (1651).

Blaise Pascal (1623 – 62), a French mathematician and scientist, developed several new ideas, including the basis for calculus. He worried, however, about the increasing reliance on science, which he believed could not explain the truly important things in life; those which can only be perceived by faith. Human beings, who had been at the center of the universe and the central link in the Great Chain of Being, became merely creatures in an unintelligibly vast universe.

Scientists slowly replaced the clergy as the people able to explain the happenings of the physical world. However, few of the discoveries – except for the aids to explorers – had any consequences on the lives of Europeans.

LITERATURE AND THE ARTS

Literature

Cervantes (1547 – 1616), a Spaniard, was a former soldier and slave concerned with the problems of religious idealism. *Don Quixote* (1605) satirized chivalric romances, describing a worldly-wise, skeptical peasant (Sancho Panzo), and a mentally unstable religious idealist (Don Quixote).

William Shakespeare (1564-1616) mixed country, court, and Renaissance ideas of the English in the 1600s, to produce tragedies, comedies, histories and sonnets. In addition to the timelessness of his themes, Shakespeare had a gift for skillfully portraying the psychological aspects of his characters. The unique manner in which he utilized the English language permanently altered its future use.

Influenced by the Renaissance while travelling in Italy, the Englishman, John Milton (1608 – 1674), had developed strong Puritan religious beliefs. *Paradise Lost* studied the motives of those who reject God. Milton took an active part in the troubles in England from 1640 to 1660, as secretary to a committee of Parliament.

Michel de Montaigne (1533 – 92), a Frenchman, became obsessed with death and the problems it raised. The inventor of the essay form, he adopted skepticism, embracing the doubt that true knowledge can be obtained, before turning to a belief in the value of individual self-study.

The Arts

Rejecting the balance and calm of Renaissance arts, Mannerists, who dominated painting and sculpture in the latter part of the sixteenth century, emphasized dramatic and emotional qualities. El Greco (1541 – 1614), a Greek who lived in Spain, took Mannerist qualities to the extreme.

17th century artists attempted to involve the viewer by emphasizing passion and mystery, as well as drama. Baroque, which emphasized grandeur, was connected with the Counter Reformation and monarchies, and was found primarily in Catholic countries.

The works of Bernini (1598 – 1680), such as his *David*, capture the appeal to emotion, the sense of tension in the object, and the subjects' human energy. Rubens (1577 – 1640), painting both religious and secular themes, conveyed the strength and majesty of his subjects.

In music, Monteverdi (1647 – 1643), using many new instruments, such as strings and woodwinds, wrote *Orfeo* (1607). He is known as the creator of the opera and the orchestra. Later in the 17th century, architecture, especially that of palaces, displayed the forces of power through the adoption of baroque forms.

SOCIETY

Hierarchy

A system whereby people, usually as members of groups, are ranked from highest to lowest in terms of power, wealth, or status, became the dominant view in the Europe of the 16th and 17th centuries.

Two major hierarchies existed: the countryside and the cities. Rural hierarchy consisted of landlords, peasants, and landless laborers. Urban hierarchy was comprised of merchants, artisans, and laborers. Clergy, lawyers, teachers, and civil servants fit somewhat awkwardly in both hierarchies.

New and expanding groups relied on education or wealth to open doors to older groups. People seeking to join the aristocracy often sought education as a means of acquiring noble status and behavior. Wealth permitted an artisan to become a merchant or, after a generation or two, a rich peasant to become a noble. The advantages of being in a higher group, besides the status, could include separate taxes and exemption from some taxes.

Social mobility – the changing from one group to another – was not accepted in the writings of the day, but did occur, though it was very hard to measure.

Demography

Exact numbers concerning population are not possible, as complete censuses do not exist. Following the Black Death and its repeated appearances in the fourteenth century, the population remained stagnant. Population began growing again in the sixteenth century and continued its upward climb until about 1650, when it levelled off for another century. The population of Europe nearly doubled between 1500 and 1650.

The population (very approximate) of some European countries in 1650 can be estimated at the following levels:

England	5.5 million
France	18.0 million
Holy Roman Empire	11.0 million
Italian peninsula	12.0 million
Spain	5.2 million
Sweden	1.5 million
United Provinces	1.5 million

Cities grew much faster than the population as a whole, as people migrated from the countryside. London grew from 50,000 in 1500 to 200,000 in 1650. Cities contained perhaps 10 to 20 percent of the total population of Europe.

The Family

The majority of households consisted of the nuclear family. A baby had a twenty-five percent chance of surviving to the age of one, a fifty percent chance of surviving to the age of twenty and a ten percent chance of reaching sixty. The average age of marriage was approximately 27 for men and 25 for women, though the nobility married younger. Few people married early enough or lived long enough to see their grandchildren.

The theory of family relationships, as expressed in sermons and writings, was one of patriarchy, with the father and husband responsible for, and in command of, the rest of the family. The reality of family relationships was more complex and, due to lack of sources, is not clear to historians.

Romantic love did exist, especially after marriage, but historians disagree as to whether it was the dominant element in forming marriages. Women, particularly in urban areas, shared in the work of their artisan and merchant husbands but rarely operated a business on their own.

The family was stable, as divorce was very rare.

Witchcraft

Witch-hunting, though found in the late Middle Ages, occurred primarily in the 16th and 17th centuries. Belief in witches was found among all parts of society - the educated, the religious, and the poor.

Historians and anthropologists provide many explanations as to why people believed in witches, and to why witch-hunting occurred when and where it did. Perhaps people needed a reason when things went badly. Another explanation is that the increased concern with religion, as a result of the Reformation, focused more attention on the role of the devil in life.

A charge of witchcraft could punish the aberrant, the nonconformist. Repression of sexuality could result in the projection of fears and hopes onto women, who then had to be punished. Though exact numbers are not possible, we know that thousands of witches were executed, with numbers varying from place to place.

Food and Diet

Bread was the staff of life - the chief item in the diet of the laboring classes. Vegetables included only peas and beans, as the vegetables from the Americas were not widely used by 1650. Meat and eggs were saved for special occasions except among the richer elements of society. Beverages included beer and wine, as milk was considered unhealthy except for the young.

Nobles and the bourgeoisie ate lots of rich meats, fish, cheeses and sweets, but consumed few vegetables or fruit. The English ate better than the rest of Europe, with the peoples of the Mediterranean areas being the worst-off. Local famines were still common, as governments lacked the ability to move food from one area of surplus to another of dearth.

The Economy

Inflation, sometimes called the price revolution, began around 1500 and continued until about the middle of the seventeenth century. Foodstuffs rose in price tenfold. The rise in population was the primary cause of the inflation, as there were more mouths to feed than food available. Another possible cause was the flow of silver from the Americas, which increased the amount of money available to buy things.

Farmers sought to increase output as the price of food rose. Land that had been idle since the Black Death of 1348 was brought under cultivation. In England, enclosures produced larger, more efficient farms, but resulted in fewer people living on the land. In Eastern Europe, landlords turned their lands into large wheat exporting operations and began the process of converting the peasants and laborers into serfs

Trade and industry grew, with the rest of the world as well as within Europe. Certain areas began to specialize: for example, the lands south and east of the Baltic produced wheat for northwestern Europe. The Dutch fleet dominated European trade.

The textile industry, the chief industry of Europe since the Middle Ages, underwent change. Regional specialization occurred on a larger scale. The putting-out system appeared, whereby the industry moved out of the cities into the countryside, and the process of production was divided into steps, with different workers doing each step.

Mercantilism

The conscious pursuit by governments of policies designed to increase national wealth, especially that of gold, became common in the seventeenth century. The chief aim was to obtain a favorable balance of international payments. Governments sought to create industries in order to avoid importing items.

2 BOURBON, BAROQUE, AND THE ENLIGHTENMENT (1648-1789)

HISTORICAL SETTING

The Thirty Years' War (1618–1648) had just ended, leaving a devastated Germany and Central Europe of some four hundred semi-autonomous states, referred to as "The Empire" (i.e., the Holy Roman Empire of the Middle Ages).

The Bourbon dynasty emerged stronger than the Hapsburgs, who had dominated Europe for a century and a half.

Peace of Westphalia (1648)

The principle that "the religion of the Prince is the religion of the realm" was extended to permit the Reformed faith (Calvinism) in Germany as well as Catholic and Lutheran Churches.

Dutch and Swiss republics were granted formal recognition as independent powers. Additionally, Sweden, Prussia, and France gained new territory.

Treaty of the Pyrenees (1659)

The war between France and Spain continued for eleven more years until Spain finally ceded to France part of the Spanish Netherlands and territory in northern Spain. A marriage was arranged between Louis XIV, Bourbon king of France, and Maria Theresa, daughter of the Hapsburg king of Spain, Philip IV.

War of Devolution (First Dutch War), 1667 – 68

After the death of his father-in-law, Philip IV, Louis XIV claimed the Spanish Netherlands (Belgium) in the name of his wife. The Law of Devolution granted inheritance to the heirs of a first marriage precedent to those of a second marriage. This law applied in private relationships to property rights, but Louis XIV applied it to political sovereignty.

France invaded the Spanish Netherlands with 50,000 troops in 1667 without a declaration of war. As a defensive measure, England, Holland, and Sweden formed the Triple Alliance.

Treaty of Aix-la-Chapelle (1668)

France received twelve fortified towns on the border of the Spanish Netherlands, but gave up Franche-Comté (Burgundy). Furthermore, the question of sovereignty over the Spanish Netherlands was deferred.

Second Dutch War (1672 – 78)

Louis XIV sought revenge for Dutch opposition to French annexation of the Spanish Netherlands. As a Catholic king, he also opposed Dutch Calvinism and republicanism.

France disputed the Triple Alliance by signing separate treaties with England (Charles II: Treaty of Dover, 1670) and with Sweden (1672).

In 1672, France invaded southern Holland with 100,000 troops. WILLIAM III of Orange became head of state. The Dutch opened the dikes to flood the land, saving Holland and the city of Amsterdam from the French.

At the war's end, the Peace of Nijmegan (1678 – 79) granted Holland all of its lost territory, while Spain and France exchanged more than a dozen territories.

Invasion of the Spanish Netherlands (1683)

France occupied Luxemburg and Trier and seized Lorraine while signing a twenty-year truce with The Empire.

The League of Augsburg was formed in 1686 to counteract the French and restore the balance of power. Members includedThe Empire, Holland, Spain, Sweden, the Palatinate, Saxony, Bavaria, and Savoy.

War of the League of Augsburg (1688 – 97)

The Glorious Revolution of 1688 brought William III of Orange and his wife, Mary, to the throne of England.

The War of the League of Augsburg opened the long period of Anglo-French rivalry which continued until the defeat of Napoleon in 1815. France fought against the two leading naval powers of the day, Holland and England, and in three theaters of war--the Rhine, in the Low Countries, and in Italy.

Known in North America as King William's War (1689 – 97), English and French colonials clashed along the New York and New England frontiers.

Treaty of Ryswick (1697)

France, England, and Holland agreed to restore captured territories. Fortresses in the Spanish Netherlands were to be garrisoned with Dutch troops as a buffer zone between France and Holland. Additionally, French sovereignty over Alsace and Strasbourg was acknowledged as permanent.

War of the Spanish Succession (1701 – 13)

Charles II, the last of the Hapsburg kings of Spain, died childless on November 1, 1700.

The king's will named Philip of Anjou, the grandson of Louis XIV and Maria Theresa, to be king of Spain. In 1698 King Charles had named Emperor Leopold's grandson, the seven-year-old Electoral Prince Joseph Ferdinand of Bavaria, as his sole heir. The boy died a few months later and in October 1700, and the king signed the new will in favor of Philip.

The Second Partition Treaty, however, signed by England, Holland, and France in May 1700, agreed that the son (later, Emperor Charles VI) of the Austrian Hapsburg Emperor Leopold would become king of Spain and Philip of Anjou would be compensated with Italian territories. (Both the mother and first wife of Leopold were daughters of Spanish kings.)

Issues involved in the War of the Spanish Succession concerned the future of the Spanish Empire. Additional primary causes concerned the possible separation of Austrian Hapsburg lands from Spain as well as the question of French/Bourbon strength in Spain.

In a sense, Charles II made war almost inevitable. Louis XIV had to fight for his grandson's claims against those of his enemy and Leopold had to do the same.

The Grand Alliance

William III, king of England, and Stadholder, of Holland, did not want to see the Spanish Netherlands fall into French control. England also faced Spanish and French competition in the New World. A merger of the Spanish and French thrones would result in a coalition of Spain and France against England and Holland in the Americas.

In response, England, Holland, The Empire, and Prussia formed the Grand Alliance in September 1701.

War

France and Spain were stronger on land. England and Holland controlled the sea.

The Battle of Blenheim, August 13, 1704, was a brilliant victory for England and the Duke of Marlborough, and one of the key battles of the war. It began a series of military reverses that prevented French domination of Europe.

At the great Battle of Ramillies, May 23, 1706, Marlborough shattered the French army in four hours and held onto the Netherlands.

In September 1709, the bloody Battle of Malplaquet had a contrasting result when the Allies lost 24,000 men and the French lost 12,000.

The allies invaded Spain and replaced Philip with Charles. The French and Spanish, however, rallied and drove the allies from both countries, restoring the Spanish throne to the Bourbons.

The war was known as Queen Anne's War (1702 – 13) in North America. England was faced for the first time with an alliance of its two great rival empires, Spain and France. Though the results there were inconclusive, English colonials were more reliable in fighting than Spanish and French.

Treaty of Utrecht (1713)

This was the most important European treaty since the Peace of Westphalia in 1648.

The Spanish Empire was partitioned and a Bourbon remained on the throne of Spain. Philip V (Philip of Anjou) retained Spain and the Spanish Empire in America. He explicitly renounced his claims to the French throne. The Hapsburg Empire in Central Europe acquired the Spanish Netherlands (Austrian Netherlands thereafter) and territories in Italy.

England took Gibraltar, Minorca, Newfoundland, Hudson's Bay, and Nova Scotia. France retained Alsace and the city of Strasbourg.

As a result, the Hapsburgs became a counterbalance to French power in western Europe, but no longer occupied the Spanish throne.

War of the Austrian Succession (1740 – 48)

Charles VI died in 1740 and his daughter ,23-year-old Maria Theresa (reigned 1740 – 80), inherited the Austrian Hapsburg Empire. Frederick the Great, age 28, (reigned 1740 – 86) had just inherited the Prussian throne from his father, Frederick William I. In 1840 Frederick suddenly invaded the Hapsburg territory of Silesia, and England joined Austria against Prussia, Bavaria, France, and Spain.

Frederick's brilliant military tactics won many victories. His long night marches, sudden flank attacks, and surprise actions contrasted with the usual siege warfare of the time.

The war was known in North America as King George's War (1744 – 48). Colonial militia from Massachusetts captured Louisburg, the fortified French naval base on Cape Breton Island commanding the entrance to the St. Lawrence River and Valley. Louisburg was returned to France after the war in exchange for Madras in India, which the French had captured.

The Treaty of Aix-la-Chapelle (1748), ended the war and Prussia emerged as one of the Great Powers. By retaining Silesia, Prussia doubled its population.

The Seven Years' War (1756 – 63)

Britain and France renewed hostilities as the French and Indian War (1754 – 63) began at the entrance to the Ohio Valley. At stake was control of the North American continent.

In Europe, Austria sought to regain Silesia with its important textile industry and rich deposits of coal and iron. Maria Theresa persuaded Louis XV to overlook their traditional Bourbon-Hapsburg enmity and aid Austria in a war with Prussia.

Russia, under Czarina Elizabeth (reigned 1741 – 62), joined the alliance. She disliked Frederick the Great intensely and feared Prussian competition in Poland. Great Britain provided Prussia with funds but few troops. Prussia was then faced with fighting almost alone against three major powers of Europe: Austria, France, and Russia. Their combined population was fifteen times that of Prussia.

The Seven Years' War was the hardest fought war in the eighteenth century. In six years Prussia won eight brilliant victories and lost eight others. Berlin was twice captured and partially burned by Russian troops. Still Prussia prevailed. In the process Prussia emerged as one of the Great Powers of Europe and established the reputation of having the best soldiers on the Continent.

William Pitt the Elder led the British to victory. The Royal Navy defeated both the French Atlantic and Mediterranean squadrons in 1759. Britain's trade prospered while French overseas trade dropped to one-sixth its pre-war level. The British captured French posts near Calcutta and Madras in India, and defeated the French in Quebec and Montreal.

In 1762 Elizabeth of Russia died and her successor, Czar Peter III, was a great admirer of Frederick the Great. Though he occupied the Russian throne only from January to July, he took Russia out of the war at a historically decisive moment.

By the Treaty of Hubertsburg (1763) Austria recognized Prussian retention of Silesia.

Treaty of Paris (1763)

France lost all possessions in North America to Britain. (In 1762 France had ceded to Spain all French claims west of the Mississippi River and New Orleans.) France retained fishing rights off the coast of Newfoundland and Martinique and Guadeloupe, sugar islands in the West Indies. Spain ceded the Floridas to Britain in exchange for the return of Cuba.

The American War for Independence as a European War, 1775 – 83

France entered the French-American Alliance of 1778 in an effort to regain lost prestige in Europe and to weaken her British adversary. In 1779 Spain joined France in the war, hoping to recover Gibraltar and the Floridas.

French troops strengthened Washington's forces. The leadership of French field officers such as Lafayette aided in strategic planning. Admiral DeGrasse's French fleet prevented the evacuation of Lord Cornwallis from Yorktown in the final decisive battle of the war in 1781. Rochambeau's and Lafayette's French troops aided Washington at Yorktown.

Treaty of Paris (1783)

Britain recognized the independence of the United States of America, and retroceded the Floridas to Spain.

Britain left France no territorial gains by signing a separate and territorially generous treaty with the United States.

ECONOMIC DEVELOPMENTS

Traditional Economic Conditions

Poverty was the norm during the Middle Ages. Infant mortality rate was 50% and sometimes half the surviving children died before reaching adulthood. As late as 1700, the overall life expectancy was 30 years of age.

Subsistence farming was the dominant occupation historically and famine was a regular part of life. One-third of the population of Finland, for example, died in the famine of 1696 – 97. France, one of the richer agricultural lands, experienced eleven general famines in the 17th century and sixteen in the 18th century.

Contagious diseases decimated towns and villages: smallpox, measles, diptheria, typhoid, scarlet fever, bubonic plague, and typhus.

Political and economic freedoms associated with the Protestant Reformation and biblical work ethic gradually began to change the economy of Europe as innovation, hard work, frugality, and entrepreneurship became the norm.

Social Institutions Necessary for Commerce and a Prosperous Economy

A prosperous economy needs a moral system as a base for reliance on a complex system of expectations and contracts. This was found both in traditional Catholic morality and in the Protestant Reformation of the 16th century. A modern economy could not function without confidence in people living up to their agreements with a sense of individual responsibility towards the following: 1) Credit; 2) Representations as to quality; 3) Promises to deliver products or to buy them when produced; 4) Agreements to share profits; 5) Honoring a bank check or bill of exchange; 6) Obligations of contracts – written or verbal.

The legal system in society reinforced individual morality with the recognition of legal enforcement of contracts and property claims--bills of exchange and banking (checks); insurance and payment of claims; recognition of property rights; and avoidance of confiscatory taxation.

Innovations in business arrangements abounded. Joint stock companies enabled enterprises to accumulate capital from many investors. Double entry bookkeeping provided a check on clerical accuracy, enabling managers to detect errors. Banknotes were used as a medium of exchange. The divided European political structure enabled merchants and businessmen to compete as they sought to locate themselves in places with a favorable business climate.

Mercantilism

There were several basic assumptions of mercantilism: 1) Wealth is measured in terms of commodities, especially gold and silver, rather than in terms of productivity and income-producing investments; 2) Economic activities should increase the power of the national government in the direction of state controls; 3) Since a favorable balance of trade was important, a nation should purchase as little as possible from nations regarded as enemies. The concept of the mutual advantage of trade was not widely accepted; and 4) Colonies existed for the benefit of the mother country, not for any mutual benefit that would be gained by economic development.

The philosophy of mercantilism had mixed results in the economy of Europe. On the one hand, the state encouraged economic growth and expansion. On the other, it tended to stifle entrepreneurship, competition, and innovation through monopolies, trade restrictions, and state regulation of commerce.

As a generalization, taxes were low enough not to discourage economic expansion since the expectations of the government from domestic society were small. There were relatively few administrative officials in a day when communication and transportation was slow. Compare France, one of the most bureaucratic states of Europe in the 18th century, with France in the 20th century. Then, 12,000 civil servants meant one bureaucrat for every 1,250 people. Today it is one for every 70 people.

The wars of the 17th and 18th centuries involved dynastic disputes, balance-of-power struggles, and mercantilistic competition for trade, raw materials, and colonies. Though economics was involved, it was not as important a factor as the more traditional power politics of international competition. It would have been less of a factor without some of the philosophical assumptions of mercantilism.

In the 19th century, more thought was directed toward encouraging economic initiative by average citizens to benefit temselves and by extention the entire country. Adam Smith's *The Wealth of Nations*, published in 1776, led the way to a more laissez-faire approach. Smith wrote at the beginning of the American War for Independence:

"To prohibit a great people ... from making all that they can of every part of their own produce, or from employing their stock and industry in the way that they judge most advantageous to themselves, is a manifest violation of the most sacred rights of mankind."

It was the Dutch and the English who led the way toward the concept of productivity as a measure of national wealth. As a result, Holland became one of the most productive countries in the world in the 17th century, and England in the 18th and 19th centuries. There was always a certain ambivalence, however, in the English attitude as laws like the Navigation Acts indicated. Such restrictive laws were passed in the early Industrial Revolution.

In France, Jean Baptiste Colbert (1619 – 1683), economic adviser to Louis XIV, used the government to encourage economic productivity and aided in the prosperity of France. But his dictatorial regulations were also counter-productive. For example, he forbade the emigration of skilled French workers and specified in detail methods of production. He also believed that foreign trade was a fixed quantity rather than one that grew with demand and lower prices. France, as most states, had high protective tariffs.

The lowering of interest rates also stimulated investment and productivity. Here England led the way: 1600: 10%; 1625: 8%; 1651: 6%; 1715: 5%; 1757: 3%.

Growth of Trade

Expansion of Europe's overseas trade resulted from the discovery of an all-water route to Asia around Africa as well as the discovery of the Western Hemisphere which provided an area of settlement and trade. The need for spices for food -preservation, and the desire for luxury goods from the Far East and the Near East, served as incentive.

Population growth expanded domestic markets far in excess of overseas trade. European population at the beginning of the seventeenth century was 70 million. By the end of the eighteenth century it had doubled. Productivity and economic growth increased even faster during the same period.

Innovative scientific and technological discoveries and inventions stimulated trade. Likewise, three-masted trading vessels lowered the costs of transportation and made possible trading over greater distances. Canal and road building also stimulated trade and productivity.

Capitalist systems of banking, insurance, and investment made possible the accumulation of capital essential for discovery and economic growth.

Urbanization was both a cause and a result of economic growth. Urbanization requires and creates a network of market relationships. Towns with prosperous tradeincreased in population while towns which did not prosper in trade quickly stagnated. Additionally, urbanization provided the opportunity and market for commercial services such as banking, insurance, warehousing, and commodity trading, as well as medicine, law, government, and churches.

Agricultural Changes

Feudal/manorial changes began in Europe, especially in England, and were replaced by absentee landlords and by commercial farms. Urbanization, increased population, and improvements in trade stimulated the demand for agricultural products.

The design of farm implements was improved. All-metal plows came into use in England as well as horse-drawn cultivators. Drainage and reclamation of swamp land was expanded. Experiments with crops, seeds, machines, breeds of animals, and fertilizers were systematically attempted.

Improvements in Transportation

The construction of canals and roads was of fundamental importance (Railroads were not developed until the 1830's).

The canal lock was invented in Italy in the 17th century soon after Holland began building canals.

The major rivers of France were linked by canals during the 17th century. England's coastal shipping made canals less pressing and so it was not until the 18th century that canals were built there.

All-weather roads were constructed after the mid-18th century when John Macadam (1756 – 1836) discovered that a gravelled and raised road-bed could carry vehicles year round.

Industrial Technology

Thomas Necomen in 1706 invented an inefficient steam engine as a pump. James Watt, between 1765 and 1769, improved the design so that the expansive power of hot steam could drive a piston. Later, Watt translated the motion of the piston into rotary motion.

The steam engine became one of the most significant inventions in human history. It was no longer necessary to locate factories on mountain streams where water wheels were used to supply power. Its portability meant that both steamboats and railroad engines could be built to transport goods across continents. Ocean-going vessels were no longer dependent on winds to power them.

At the same time, textile machines revolutionized that industry.

John Kay introduced the flying shuttle in 1733. James Hargreave invented the spinning jenny in 1770. Richard Arkwright perfected the spinning frame in 1769. Samuel Crompton introduced the spinning mule in 1779. Edward Cartwright invented the power loom in 1785.

Factors in Sustained Economic Growth

Innovation was a key elemet – by extension of trade and discovery of new resources; by lowering costs of production; by introducing new products and new ways of doing things; in organizing production and marketing methods; and in overcoming resistance to innovation.

The development of free enterprise stimulated new ideas. This was made possible where the state was not excessively involved in the economy. In England, the Puritan Revolution of the 1640's challenged the royal right to grant monopolies and trade privileges. The English common law afterwards adopted the principle of free enterprise open to all. With free enterprise came the responsibility of risk-taking with the possibilities of losses as well as profits.

Free movement of populations provided necessary labor resources. People "voted with their feet" and found their way to new jobs. Many moved to England from Europe. The population of England in 1700 was about 5.5 million and only 6 million by 1750. The economic growth during the last half of the century increased the population of England to 9 million by 1800, a fifty percent growth in a half century. Because of the Industrial Revolution of the 19th century, this figure doubled to 18 million by 1850.

BEGINNINGS OF MODERN SCIENCE AND THE AGE OF THE ENLIGHTENMENT

Scientific Revolution

Modern science had its origins in the 16th and 17th century "Scientific Revolution". "The Enlightenment" was an eighteenth century movement.

Nicholas Copernicus (1473 – 1543) discovered that the earth is but one of many planets revolving around the sun and turning on its own axis to make day and night. He demonstrated that the Greek mathematician, Ptolemy, was mistaken in his idea that the earth was a stationery planet in the center of the universe.

Tycho Brahe (1546 – 1601), a Danish nobleman, built an expensive observatory and systematically pursued Copernicus' theories.

Johann Kepler (1571 – 1630), the first great Protestant scientist and assistant to Brahe, discovered that the orbits of the planets are ellipses which complete their orbits in equal times. He explained the speed of the planets in their orbits and found that the planets do not move with the sun as focal point.

Galileo Galilei (1564 – 1642) was Professor of Physics and Military Engineering at the University of Padua. He was the first to use the telescope as a scientific instrument and built a powerful telescope himself. His discoveries and use of the telescope were a great aid in the voyages of discovery and had a direct effect on navigation. He provided artillery with a means of surveying distant targets for more accurate marksmanship. Galileo's discoveries in mechanics had far-reaching significance. He proved that all falling bodies descend with equal velocity, regardless of weight. He found that a long pendulum swing takes the same time as the short one, so that some force increases the speed of each swing by equal amounts in equal times.

Francis Bacon (1561 – 1626), Lord Chancellor of England, specified inductive method for scientific experimentation. Inductive observation, the development of hypotheses, experimentation, and organization were to be the keys to scientific inquiry.

Rene Descartes (1596 – 1650) wrote his *Discourse on Method* to build on the scientific method by using deductive analysis on scientific discoveries. He wrote that science must begin with clear and incontrovertible facts and then subdivide each problem into as many parts as necessary, following a step-by-step logical sequence in solving complex problems. Descartes was particularly a leader in mathematics and philosophy.

Scientific Societies

Scientific societies were organized in many European countries in the 17th century. Italy began the first scientific societies in Naples, Rome, and Florence. The Royal Observatory was established at Greenwich in 1675 and the Royal Society in 1662; private donations and entrance fees from members financed the society. The French

Academie des Sciences was founded in 1666. King Frederick I of Brandenburg-Prussia chartered the Berlin Academy of Sciences in 1700. Finally, Peter the Great founded the St. Petersburg Academy of Sciences in 1725.

Sir Isaac Newton (1642 – 1747) taught mathematics at Cambridge, was Master of the Royal Mint in London, and for twenty-five years was the President of the Royal Society. Most of his work was done in astronomy, the dominant science of the seventeenth century. He worked with magnification, prisms, and refraction. He used lenses with different curvature and different kinds of glass. Newton's greatest contribution, however, was in discovering his principle of universal gravitation, which he explained in *Philosophiae Naturalis Principia Mathematica*, published in 1687. He claimed to "subject the phenomena of nature to the laws of mathematics" and saw order and design throughout the entire cosmos.

Science and religion were not in conflict in the seventeenth and eighteenth centuries. Scientists universally believed they were studying and analyzing God's creation, not an autonomous phenomena known as "Nature." There was no attempt, as in the nineteenth and twentieth centuries, to secularize science. "Natural law," they believed, was created by God for man's use. A tension between the natural and the supernatural simply did not exist in their world view. The question of the extent of the Creator's involvement directly or indirectly in his Creation was an issue of the eighteenth century but there was universal agreement among scientists and philosophers as to the supernatural origin of the universe.

The Age of the Enlightenment

For the first time in human history, the 18th century saw the appearance of a secular world view to capture the imagination of many intellectuals. In the past some kind of a religious perspective had always been central to western civilization. This was true of the ancient Egyptians, Hebrews, Persians, Greeks, and Romans. It was also true of medieval Catholic Christendom and of the 16th century Protestant Reformation. By contrast, the 18th century philosophers, who declared themselves "enlightened," thought that "light" came from man's ability to reason. They rejected the idea that light must come from God, either through the Church (the Catholic position) or the Scriptures (the Protestant position). The Enlightenment opened the door to a secularized anthropocentric universe instead of the traditional theocentric view.

The philosophical starting point for the Enlightenment was the belief in the autonomy of man's intellect apart from God. The most basic assumption was faith in reason rather than faith in revelation. The "Enlightened" claimed for themselves, however, a rationality they were unwilling to concede to their opponents.

The Enlightenment believed in the existence of God as a rational explanation of the universe and its form, but that "god" was a deistic Creator who created the universe and then was no longer involved in its mechanistic operation. The mechanistic operation was governed by "natural law." Enlightenment philosophers are sometimes characterized as being either basically rationalists or basically empiricists.

Rationalists

Rationalists stressed deductive reasoning or mathematical logic as the basis for their epistemology (source of knowledge). They started with "self-evident truths" or postulates, from which they constructed a coherent and logical system of thought.

Rene Descartes (1596 – 1650) sought a basis for logic and thought he found it in man's ability to think. "I think; therefore, I am" was his most famous statement. That statement cannot be denied without thinking. Therefore, it must be an absolute truth that man can think. His proof depends upon logic alone.

Baruch Spinoza (1632 – 77) developed a rational pantheism in which he equated God and nature. He denied all free will and ended up with an impersonal, mechanical universe – a universe with no one there.

Gottfried Wilhelm Leibniz (1646 – 1716) worked on symbolic logic and calculus, and invented a calculating machine. He, too, had a mechanistic world-and-life view and thought of God as a hypothetical abstraction rather than persona.

Empiricists

Empiricists stressed inductive observation as the basis for their epistemology, in short, the scientific method. Their emphasis was on sensory experience.

John Locke (1632 – 1704) pioneered in the empiricist approach to knowledge and stressed the importance of environment in human development. He classified knowledge as 1) according to reason; 2) contrary to reason; and 3) above reason. Locke thought reason and revelation were both complementary and from God.

David Hume (1711 – 76) was a Scottish historian and philosopher who began by emphasizing the limitations of human reasoning and later became a dogmatic skeptic.

The people of the Enlightenment believed in absolutes; they were not relativists. They believed in absolute truth, absolute ethics, and absolute natural law. And they believed optimistically that these absolutes were discoverable by man's rationality. It wasn't long, of course, before one rationalist's "absolutes" clashed with another's.

The Enlightenment believed in a closed system of the universe in which the supernatural was not involved in human life. This was in sharp contrast to the traditional view of an open system in which God, angels, and devils were very much a part of human life on this earth.

The Philosophes

The Philosophes were popularizers of the Enlightenment, not professional philosophers. They were men and women "of letters," such as journalists and teachers. They frequented the salons, cafes, and discussion groups in France. They were cultured, refined, genteel intellectuals who had unbounded confidence in man's ability to improve society through sophistication and rational thought. They had a habit of criticizing everything in their path – including rationalism.

Francois-Marie Arouet (1694 – 1778) better known as Voltaire, was one of the most famous philosophes. He attended an upper-class Jesuit school in Paris and became well-known for his unusual wit and irreverence. His sharp tongue and "subversive" poetry led to an eleven-month imprisonment in the Bastille. Voltaire lived in England for several years and greatly admired the freedom in the relatively open English society. He accepted Deism and believed in a finite, limited God who he thought of as the Watchmaker of the universe. Characteristically, Voltaire relied on ridicule rather than reason to present his case.

Jean-Jacques Rousseau (1712 – 78) lived in Geneva until he was forced to flee to England because of what the government considered radical ideas. Rousseau thought of man in a simpler state of nature as "the noble savage" and sought to throw off the restraints of civilization. Rousseau saw autonomous freedom as the ultimate good. Later in life he decided that if a person did not want Rousseau's utopian ideas, he would be "forced to be free," an obvious contradiction in terms. Rousseau has been influential in western civilization for over two hundred years with his emphasis on freedom as a Bohemian ideal. His book on education, *Emile* (1762) is still popular, despite the fact that he left his five illegitimate children in an orphanage instead of putting his educational theories to work with his own children.

Chronology

The Enlightenment varied in emphasis from country to country; the French Enlightenment was not exactly the same as the English or German Enlightenment.

Distinctions can also be made chronologically in the development of Enlightenment thought. The end of the 17th and first half of the 18th century saw a reaction against "enthusiasm," or emotionalism and sought moderation and balance in a context of ordered freedom. From the mid-18th century the Enlightenment moved into a skeptical, almost iconoclastic phase where it was fashionable to deride and tear down. The last three decades of the 18th century were revolutionary, radical, and aggressively dogmatic in defense of various abstractions demanding a revolutionary commitment. "Love of mankind" made it one's duty to crush those who disagreed and thus impeded "progress." In short, the Enlightenment entered a utopian phase that became disastrous as it brought on the French Revolution.

The "Counter-Enlightenment"

The "Counter-Enlightenment" is a comprehensive term of diverse and even disparate groups who disagreed with the fundamental assumptions of the Enlightenment and pointed out its weaknesses. This was not a "movement," but merely a convenient category.

Theistic Opposition

German pietism, especially Count von Zinzendorf, (1700 – 60), leader of the Moravian Brethren, taught the need for a spiritual conversion and a religious experience. Methodism of the 18th century similarly taught the need for spiritual regeneration and a moral life that would demonstrate the reality of the conversion. Methodism was led by an Anglican minister, John Wesley, (1703 – 91). The Great Awakening in the English colonies in America in the 1730's and 1740's, led by Jonathan Edwards, had a similar result.

Roman Catholic Jansenism in France argued against the idea of an uninvolved or impersonal God. Hasidism in Eastern European Jewish communities, especially in the 1730's, stressed a joyous religious fervor in direct communion with God. Both of these were in sharp contrast to Deism, which at the same time gaining adherents in England.

Philosophic Reaction

Some philosophers questioned the fundamental assumptions of rationalist philosophy.

David Hume (1711–1776) for example, struck at faith in natural law as well as faith in religion. He insisted that "man can accept as true only those things for which he has the evidence of factual observation." (Then why accept Hume's statement as true?) Since the philosophes lacked indisputable evidence for their belief in the existence of natural law, Hume believed in living with a "total suspension of judgment." (But if one must be a dogmatic skeptic, then why not be skeptical about dogmatic skepticism?)

Immanuel Kant (1724 – 1794) separated science and morality into separate branches of knowledge. He said that science could describe the natural phenomena of the material world but could not provide a guide for morality. Kant's "categorical imperative" was an intuitive instinct, implanted by God in conscience. Both the ethical sense and aesthetic appreciation in human beings are beyond the knowledge of science. Reason is a function of the mind and has no content in and of itself.

BOURBON FRANCE

French Foreign Policy

France was the dominant European power from 1660 to 1713. Louis XIV, however, was unable to extend French boundaries to the Rhine River – one of his chief objectives.

From 1713 to 1789 no one European power dominated international politics. Instead, the concept of the Balance of Power prevailed. A readjustment of power was necessary in central and eastern Europe as a result of the decline of Sweden, Poland, and the Ottoman Empire. This period was characterized by a power struggle between France and England for colonial supremacy in India and in America.

France Under Louis XIV (1643 – 1715)

Louis XIV was vain, arrogant, and charming to the aristocratic ladies of his court. He was five feet five inches tall and wore shoes with high heels.

The king had great physical endurance for long hours of council meetings and endless ceremonies and entertainments. He seemed indifferent to heat and cold and survived a lifetime of abnormal eating.

Moreover, he aspired to be an absolute ruler with no one challenging his dictatorial powers.

The most significant challenge to royal absolutism in France in the 17th century was a series of three revolts (called *Frondes*, meaning "a child's slingshot") by some of the nobility and judges of the parlements or courts of Paris. Competition among the nobility, however, enabled the government to put down the revolts. All three of these occurred when Louis XIV was very young (ages 5 – 11) and made a lasting impression on him; he was determined that no revolt would be successful during his reign.

The king believed in absolute, unquestioned authority. Louis XIV deliberately got his chief ministers from the middle class in order to keep the aristocracy out of government. No members of the royal family or the high aristocracy were admitted to the daily council sessions at Versailles, where the king presided personally over deliberations of his ministers.

Council orders were transmitted to the provinces by intendants, who supervised all phases of local administration (especially courts, police, and the collection of taxes). Additionally, Louis XIV nullified the power of French institutions which might challenge his centralized bureaucracy.

Louis XIV never called the Estates-General. His intendants arrested the members of the three provincial estates who criticized royal policy; and the parlements were too intimidated by the lack of success of the *Frondes* to offer further resistance.

Control of the peasants, who numbered 95% of the French population, was accomplished by numerous means. Some peasants kept as little as 20% of their cash crops after paying the landlord, the government, and the Church. Peasants also were subject to the *corvee*, a month's forced labor on the roads. People not at work on the farm were conscripted into the French army or put into workhouses. Finally, rebels were hanged or forced to work as galley slaves.

Colbert, finance minister from 1661 to 1683, improved the economy and the condition of the royal treasury. He reduced the number of tax collectors; reduced local tolls in order to encourage domestic trade; improved France's transportation system with canals and a growing merchant marine; organized a group of French trading companies (the East India Company, the West India Company, the Levant Company, and the Company of the North); and paid bounties to ship builders to strengthen trade.

Palace of Versailles

Louis XIV moved his royal court from the Louvre in Paris to Versailles, twelve miles outside of Paris. The facade of his palace was a third of a mile long with vast gardens adorned with classical statuary, 1400 fountains, and 1200 orange trees.

In Paris, the court included six hundred people. At Versailles it grew to ten thousand noblemen, officials, and attendants. Sixty percent of the royal tax revenue was spent on Versailles and the upkeep of the court of Louis XIV.

The splendor of the court was in the beautiful gardens and Baroque architecture of the palace, in the luxurious furnishings of the apartments, and in the magnificent dress of men and women who went there. Often half of the income of nobles and their ladies was spent on clothing, furniture, and servants.

Extravagant amusements occupied the time of the aristocratic court: tournaments, hunts, tennis, billiards, boating parties, dinners, dances, ballets, operas, concerts, and theater. In order to celebrate the birth of his son in 1662, the king arranged a ball at the Palace of the Carrousel, which was attended by 15,000 people who danced under a thousand lights before massive mirrors.

Louis XIV's Policies Toward Christianity

The king considered himself the head of the French Catholic Church and claimed that the Pope had no temporal authority over the French Church. Louis XIV sided with the Jesuits against the Jansenists, or Catholics like Blaise Pascal who reaffirmed St. Augustine's doctrine of inherent depravity, i.e., that man is born by nature a sinner and salvation is only for the elect of God.

About a million French citizens were Protestant. Louis XIV attempted to eradicate Protestantism from France by demolishing Huguenot churches and schools, paying cash rewards to Protestants to convert to Catholicism, and by billeting soldiers in homes of those who refused to convert. In 1685 the king revoked the Edict of Nantes that had given many religious freedoms to Protestants at the time of Henry IV. The revocation took away civil rights from Protestants. Their children were required by law to be raised as Catholics. French Protestant clergymen were exiled or sent to the galleys. As many as 200,000 Huguenots fled from France – to England, Holland, and to English colonies in America. Protestantism did survive in France, but was greatly weakened.

France Under Louis XV (1715 – 74)

French people of all classes desired greater popular participation in government, rejecting royal absolutism. There was high resentment towards special privileges of the aristocracy. All nobles were exempt from certain taxes. Many were subsidized with regular pensions from the government. The highest offices of government were reserved for aristocrats. Promotions were based on political connections rather than merit. Life at Versailles was wasteful, extravagant, and frivolous.

There was no uniform code of laws, and a lack of justice in the French judicial system existed. The king had arbitrary powers of imprisonment. Government bureaucrats were often petty tyrants, many of them merely serving their own interests. The bureaucracy had become virtually a closed class within itself.

Vestiges of the feudal and manorial systems continued to upset the peasants, particularly when they were taxed excessively in comparison to other segments of society. The philosophes gave expression to these grievances and discontent grew.

Louis XV was only five years old when his great-grandfather died. Fifty-nine years later he too died, leaving many of the same problems he had inherited. Corruption and inequity in government were even more pronounced. Ominously, crowds lined the road to St. Denis, the burial place of French kings, and cursed the king's casket just as they had his predecessor.

France Under Louis XVI (1774–1792)

Louis XVI was the grandson of Louis XV. He married Marie Antoinette (1770), daughter of the Austrian Empress Maria Theresa.

Louis XVI was honest, conscientious, and sought genuine reforms, but he was indecisive and lacking in determination. He antagonized the aristocracy when he sought fiscal reforms.

One of his first acts was to restore to the French parlements their judicial powers. When he sought to impose new taxes on the under-taxed aristocracy, the parlements refused to register the royal decrees. In 1787 he granted toleration and civil rights to French Huguenots (Protestants).

In 1787 the king summoned the Assembly of the Notables, a group of 144 representatives of the nobility and higher clergy. At Versailles Louis XVI asked them to tax all lands, without regard to privilege of family; to establish provincial assemblies; to allow free trade in grain; and to abolish forced labor on the roads. The Notables refused to accept these reforms and demanded the replacement of certain of the king's ministers.

The climax of the crisis came in 1788 when the king was no longer able to achieve either fiscal reform or new loans. He could not even pay the salaries of government officials. By this time one-half of government revenues went to pay interest on the national debt (at 8%).

For the first time in 175 years the king called for a meeting of the Estates General (1789). When the Estates General formed itself into the National Assembly, the French Revolution was under way. Later in the radical phase of the revolution the National Convention voted 366 to 361 to execute the king, January 21, 1793.

SPAIN: HAPSBURG AND BOURBON

Spain in the Seventeenth Century

The Peace of Westphalia (1648) did not end the war between Spain and France; it continued for eleven more years. In the Treaty of the Pyrenees (1659), Spain ceded to France Artois in the Spanish Netherlands and territory in northern Spain. Marriage was arranged between Louis XIV, Bourbon king of France, and Maria Theresa, Hapsburg daughter of Philip IV, king of Spain. (Louis XIV's mother was the daughter of Philip III of Spain.)

The population of Spain in the 17th century declined as Spain continued expelling Moors from Spain, especially from Aragon and Valencia. In 1550 Spain had a population of 7.5 million; by 1660 it was about 5.5 million.

Formerly food-producing lands were deserted. In Castile sheep-raising took the place of food production. Food was imported from elsewhere in Europe. As production declined, inflation increased.

Work was looked upon as a necessary evil, to be avoided when possible. The upper classes preferred a life of cultured ease instead of developing and caring for their estates. Patents of nobility were purchased from the Crown, carrying with them many tax exemptions.

Capitalism was almost non-existent in Spain as savings and investment were viewed as beneath the dignity of the nobility. What industry there was in Spain – silk, woollens, and leatherwork – was declining instead of growing.

Catholic orthodoxy and aristocratic exclusiveness were high values in Spanish society. In 1660, the Spanish clergy numbered 200,000, an average of one for every thirty people.

The Spanish navy had ceased to exist by 1700; there were only eight ships left plus a few borrowed from the Genoese. Most of the soldiers in the Spanish army were foreigners.

Charles II (1665 - 1700)

Charles II, the last of the Spanish Hapsburg kings, was only four years old when his father, Philip IV, died. His mother, Marie Anne of Austria, controlled the throne as head of the council of regency. Afflicted with many diseases and of a weak constitution, the king was expected to die long before he did.

He intensely disliked the responsibilities of his office, and his timidity and lack of will power made him one of the worst rulers in Spanish history.

In 1680, he married Marie Louise of France and, on her death in 1689, he married Marie Anne of Bavaria. Since he had no child, Charles II's death in 1700 led to the War of the Spanish Succession.

Philip V (1700 - 1746)

The grandson of Louis XIV and the first Bourbon king of Spain was only seventeen years of age when he became king of Spain. The first dozen years of his reign were occupied with the War of the Spanish Succession which ended successfully for him. He modernized the Spanish army and brought it to a strength of 40,000 men.

Philip V centralized the Spanish government by using the intendant system of the French wherein the governors (or Intendants) of the provinces were under close supervision by the central government under the king. He abolished many pensions and government subsidies and restored fiscal health to the Spanish government.

Industry, agriculture, and ship-building were actively encouraged. The Spanish Navy was revived and the fleet was substantial by the end of his reign.

Philip V married the fourteen-year-old Marie Louise of Savoy, and when she died in 1714, he married Elizabeth Farnese of Parma. Philip V died during the War of the Austrian Succession and was succeeded by his son by Marie Louise, Ferdinand VI, who ruled for an uneventful thirteen years, 1746 – 1759.

Charles III (1759 – 1788)

Charles III had already had political experience as Duke of Parma and as King of the Two Sicilies. He was an able ruler and enacted many reforms during his long reign. Personally moral, pious, and hard-working, Charles III was one of the most popular of Spanish kings.

Charles helped to stimulate the economy by eliminating laws that restricted internal trade and by reducing tariffs. He encouraged new agricultural settlements and helped establish banks for farmers. He helped to create factories and gave them monopolies: woollens, tapestries, mirrors and glass, silks, and porcelain. Schools were established to teach the trades.

By the end of his reign the population of Spain had grown to 10.5 million.

Spain was a strongly Catholic country and Spanish intellectuals were not interested in the doctrines of the Enlightenment, repulsed by the irreligion of the philosophes. An ambassador wrote in 1789 that in Spain "one finds religion, love for the king, devotion to the law, moderation in the administration, scrupulous respect for the privileges of each province and the individual...."

AUSTRIAN HAPSBURGS AND CENTRAL EUROPE

History of the Hapsburgs

In 1273 Rudolph of Hapsburg was elected Holy Roman Emperor and gained permanent possession of Austria for the Hapsburg family. The Holy Roman Empire was still intact in the 18th century and consisted of 300 separate states, 51 free towns, and 1,500 free knights, each ruling a tiny state with an average of 300 subjects and an annual income of $500. The largest states of the Empire were the Hapsburg Monarchy, with a population of ten million inside the Empire and twelve million outside; Prussia, with a population of 5.5 million; Bavaria and Saxony, with a population of 2 million each; and Hanover, with a population of 900,000.

The Emperor also claimed authority over seventy-five small principalities.

The custom was to select the ruler of Austria as the Emperor because he alone had sufficient power to enforce Imperial decisions. (A brief exception was Charles VII of Bavaria.) After the War of the Spanish Succession (1701 – 13) and the Treaty of Utrecht (1713), the Spanish throne was occupied by a Bourbon, so Hapsburg power was concentrated in Austria. The Austrian Hapsburgs ruled the Empire: Naples, Sardinia, and Milan in Italy; the Austrian Netherlands (now Belgium); Hungary and Transylvania. Austria was not a national state; its lands included Germans, Hungarians, Czechs, Croats, Italians, Serbs, Rumanians, and others.

Government of the Austrian Empire

Since different parts of the Empire bore a different legal relationship to the Emperor, there was no single constitutional system or administration for all parts of the realm. The Emperor was duke of Austria, margrave of Styria, duke of Carinthia, Lord of Swabia, count of Tyrol, king of Bohemia, king of Hungary, Transylvania, Croatia, Slavonia and Dalmatia, besides his titles in Italy and the Austrian Netherlands.

The Hapsburg Empire had four chancelleries: the Austrian (with two chancellors); the Bohemian; the Hungarian; and the Translyvanian. There were also departments responsible for the affairs of Italy and the Austrian Netherlands.

In addition, the Central Government under the Emperor consisted of the Privy Council (Geheimer Rat) which discussed high policy; the Hofkammer, which made decisions regarding finance and trade; the Hofkriegsrat, which was the War Council; the Imperial Chancellery, which dealt with matters of Empire; and the Court Chancellery, which dealt with domestic matters.

Feudalism in the Hapsburg Empire

The lords of the manor had political as well as economic controls over the peasants. Peasants were under the judicial authority of the lord. They could not marry without the lord's consent. Their children could not work or serve an apprenticeship outside the estate. The peasant could not contract a loan or sell anything without the lord's consent. Peasants were obligated to the *corvée*, or compulsory labor, for as many as 100 days a year. Peasants were obliged to buy products supplied by the lord at the prices he set. There were tolls to pay, customs duties, duties on transactions, quit-rents and other taxes.

Music and Vienna

The most famous and popular of the arts in the Hapsburg Empire, and especially in Vienna, was music. Leopold I, a composer himself, was particularly significant as a patron of music. Royal concerts, ballets, and operas were part of the life of Vienna. Italians came to Austria, Bohemia, and Hungary to direct or improve their musical productions. The Slavs and Magyars excelled in singing and playing of instruments.

Adam Michna z Otradovic (1600 – 76) composed hymns based on Czech poetry and the famous St. Wenceslas Mass, honoring the national hero.

Emperor Leopold I (1658 – 1705)

Leopold I was the first cousin of King Louis XIV of France and also of King Charles II of Spain. He loved poetry, music, and was a patron of the arts. A devout Catholic, Leopold followed the advice of the Jesuits and sought to restrict severely his Protestant subjects. He employed German and Italian artists to build and decorate Baroque churches and palaces.

One of Leopold's most severe tests came with the Turkish invasion of Austria, and siege of Vienna itself, in 1683. The Turks were driven back by the Poles, Austrians, and Hungarians.

Emperor Leopold I was a key figure in the War of Spanish Succession.

Emperor Charles VI (1711 – 1740)

Following a brief reign by his older brother, Joseph I (1705 – 11), who died of smallpox at the age of thirty-three, Charles VI, son of Leopold I, came to the Austrian throne. Charles VI had a keen sense of duty and lived a conscientiously moral life. He was meticulous in his administration and personally involved in the details of governing.

Early in his reign he signed the Treaty of Szatmar with the Hungarians, recognizing their particular liberties and returning the Crown to St. Stephen. The Hungarian Chancellery was to be autonomous within the administration.

Maria Theresa (1740 – 1780)

Maria Theresa was not really the "Empress" although she was often referred to as such. First her husband and then her son was Emperor of the Holy Roman Empire. Technically she was "Queen of Bohemia and Hungary, Archduchess of Austria, ..." et. al.

Maria Theresa was a beautiful, courageous, high-minded, pious, and capable ruler. Her first reform was to increase the Austrian standing army from 30,000 to 108,000 by persuading the various estates to accept tax reforms and a tax increase. She gradually centralized the Empire and increased the power of the Austrian government.

Maria Theresa was a conservative Catholic, and considered the Church and the nobility to be the foundations of her state. She was concerned, however, with the freedom and well-being of her subjects and political realism was the hallmark of her reign. The two most important international events of her forty-year reign were the War of the Austrian Succession (1740 – 48) and the Seven Years' War (1756 – 63).

Joseph II (1765 – 1790)

Joseph II was co-regent with his mother for the last fifteen years of her reign. He sought to be an "enlightened despot" – with emphasis on despot. He wanted to govern decisively and forcefully, but rationally with the interests of his subjects in mind – at least as he envisioned them. He sought a full treasury, economy in government, and a strong military force. He sought to emulate the achievements and style of Frederick the Great of Prussia. His mother's adviser, Prince Anton von Kaunitz, provided a timely check on Joseph's ambitions. He wrote to the Emperor: "Despotic governments concern themselves with intimidation and punishment. But in monarchies [we must not forget] how much it is a joy worthy of a noble mind to govern free and thinking beings than to rule vile slaves."

Although the Emperor was a devout Catholic, he expanded the state schools of Austria and granted religious toleration to both Protestants and Jews. Joseph II died at the age of forty-nine, having suffered recent military defeats from the Turks and fearing both the growing power of Russia and revolts in the Austrian Netherlands.

PRUSSIA AND THE HOHENZOLLERNS

Brandenburg-Prussia in 1648

The Thirty Years' War had devastated Germany. Brandenburg had lost half its population through death, disease, and emigration.

Brandenburg was established by the Emperor Otto I in 950 A.D., and the ruler of Brandenburg was designated as an Elector of the Holy Roman Empire by Emperor Sigismund in 1417. By the time of the Thirty Years' War, despite its central location, Brandenburg was still an insignificant part of the Empire. By marriage, the House of Hohenzollern had also acquired widely-separated parts of the Empire. In the west, Hohenzollerns governed the duchy of Cleves and the counties of Mark and Ravensberg; in the east, they governed the duchy of East Prussia.

The Peace of Westphalia (1648) granted the Elector eastern Pomerania, three tiny bishoprics and the archbishopric of Magdeburg. Nothing in these possessions or any of the other disparate territories showed any promise of becoming a great power of Europe. Each province had its own estates, representing the towns and the nobility. They had little in common and no common administration. The terrain had no natural frontiers for defense and was not economically significant. Its population was sparse, its soil poor and sandy. It was cut off from the sea and was not on any of the trade routes of Europe.

Frederick William (1640 – 1688)

During his half-century reign the "Great Elector" established Prussia as a great power and laid the foundation for the future unification of Germany in the 19th century. He took the title "King of Prussia" since East Prussia lay outside the boundaries of the Holy Roman empire and thus was not in the jurisdiction of the Austrian Hapsburgs.

Frederick William was the nephew of King Gustavus Adolphus of Sweden and his wife was the granddaughter of William the Silent, hero of Dutch independence. He sought to emulate the government organization of the Swedes and the economic policies of the Dutch.

Frederick had been well-educated and spoke five languages. He was a strict Calvinist and settled 20,000 Huguenot refugees on his estates. He granted toleration, however, to both Catholics and Jews.

He encouraged industry and trade and brought in foreign craftsmen and Dutch farmers. In each province he established a local government, headed by a governor and chancellor, but with control from the central government in Berlin.

His most historically-significant innovation was the building of a strong standing army. He was able to do this only through heavy taxes, a rate of taxation twice as heavy as that of the French during the height of Louis XIV's power. But the Prussian nobility were not exempt from those heavy taxes, as were the French aristocracy.

The Elector sought to encourage industry and trade, but he was in danger of taxing it out of existence. New industries were started: woollens, cottons, linen, velvet, lace, silk, soap, paper, and iron products. One of his achievements was the Frederick William Canal through Berlin which linked the Elbe and Oder rivers and enabled canal traffic from Breslau and Hamburg to Berlin. He was the only Hohenzollern to be interested in overseas trade before Kaiser William II. But without ports and naval experience, the effort collapsed.

The central dynamic of Frederick William's life was his Calvinism, through which he became convinced of direct protection and guidance from God in all he did. He highly valued learning and founded the University of Pufendorf and the Berlin Library. He was greatly alarmed at the threat to Protestantism implied in Louis XIV's revocation of the Edict of Nantes in 1685 and joined the League of Augsburg in 1686.

Frederick I (1688 – 1713)

The Great Elector's son (i.e., Elector Frederick III and King Frederick I) was a weak and somewhat deformed man, but won the affection of his people as did no other Hohenzollern. He loved the splendor of the monarchy and elaborate ceremony. He built beautiful palaces and provided splendid uniforms of white satin edged with gold lace for his guards. Dinner was announced by twenty-four trumpeters. An orchestra played and the servants wore blue trimmed with gold lace.

Potsdam had been built by the Great Elector. Frederick I built a new palace in Berlin and Charlottenburg for his Queen, Sophie Charlotte, who joined her husband in the many philosophical and religious discussions common in the palace.

Frederick I founded the University of Halle in 1692, a center for two of the great concepts of the time, Pietism and Natural Law. The king welcomed as immigrants not only craftsmen, but also scholars such as Jacob Lenfant, historian of the Council of Trent, Isaac De Beausobre, translator of the New Testament, and Philip Speuer, a leading Pietist of his day. The Enlightenment philosopher Gottfried Wilhelm Leibnitz persuaded Frederick to found an academy of science.

Much of Frederick I's reign was spent at war. Prussia participated in the War of the League of Augsburg (1688 – 97) and the War of the Spanish Succession (1701 – 13). It did not gain territorially, but perpetuated the military tradition that was beginning. The costs of war were a heavy financial burden to the small state.

Frederick William I (1713 – 1740)

This king was quite different from his father. He cut the number of court officials drastically, not only for economy, but because he was impatient with ceremony.

He believed Prussia needed a strong standing army and a plentiful treasury and he proceeded to acquire both. Prussia's army grew from 45,000 to 80,000 during his reign, despite a population of only 2.5 million. Military expenditures consumed 80% of state revenues, compared with 60% in France and 50% in Austria. On the other hand, he only spent 2% of tax revenues to maintain his court, compared with 6% in Austria under Maria Theresa. Frederick built the fourth largest army in Europe, repaid all state debts, and left his successor a surplus of ten million thaler.

Prussia maintained a large standing army in order to avoid war, if possible. This policy was maintained during Frederick William's reign. The only time he went to war was when Charles XII of Sweden occupied Stalsund. Prussia immediately attacked and forced Sweden out of Stralsund. In 1720, Sweden agreed to the Prussian annexation of the port of Stettin and Pomeranian territory west of the river Oder.

Prussia continued close relations with Holland and with England. King George I of England was Frederick William's uncle and father-in-law. His mother was George I's sister and his wife was George's daughter.

Prussia developed the most efficient bureaucracy in Europe. In 1723 the king established a General Directory of four departments, each responsible for certain provinces. Taxes were high, but income from the royal estates (about one-third of the kingdom) largely paid for the army. The king made policy decisions and left it to the bureaucracy to work out the details.

Subordinate to the General Directory were the seventeen provincial chambers. Merit promotions rewarded efficiency and diligence. The civil bureaucracy as well as the military were based on the principle of absolute obedience and discipline.

For oversight, every provincial chamber included a special royal agent, or fiscal, to keep a close watch on how well the king's orders were carried out.. The king also required secret reports annually on all bureaucrats.

The whole Prussian bureaucracy consisted of only 14,000 poorly-paid civil servants (about 1/10th the proportionate number commonly found in 20th century European nations).

The king was a ceaseless worker and expected the same from those about him, including his son, the future Frederick the Great. The king entrusted his son's early education to his old governess, Mademoiselle de Rocoulles, a Huguenot refugee who taught Frederick to speak French better than German. The king regimented his son's education from 6:00 a.m. to 10:30 p.m. and the young boy learned all the fifty-four movements of the Prussian drill before he was five years old. The value that Frederick William placed on education is also demonstrated by the fact that he established a thousand schools for peasant children.

Frederick the Great (Frederick II: 1740 – 1786)

Frederick the Great inherited his throne at age 28. His father left him a prosperous economy, a full treasury, an income of seven million thalers, and an army of 80,000. Unlike his father, Frederick loved French literature, poetry, and music. He played the flute and wrote poetry all his life.

Frederick's philosophy of government soon became apparent. He wrote in 1740: "Machiavelli maintains that, in this wicked and degenerate world, it is certain ruin to be strictly honest. For my part, I affirm that, in order to be safe, it is necessary to be virtuous. Men are commonly neither wholly good nor wholly bad, but both good and bad ...." The king did not believe the state existed for the gratification of the ruler, but the ruler for the state: he must regard himself as "the first servant of the state". All his life, Frederick continued to ponder questions of religion, morality, and power. French literature dominated his reading.

In October 1740, the Emperor Charles VI died, and in December Frederick ordered a sudden attack on Silesia. Thus began twenty-three years of warfare where the Great Powers of Europe (France, Austria, and Russia) were aligned against Prussia. Their combined population was fifteen times that of Prussia. YetPrussia emerged a quarter century later with enlarged territories of rich land and nearly twice its former population, but at a cost of devastation. Prussia alone saw 180,000 killed and their entire society was seriously disrupted. Indeed, for a time, Frederick thought he would not survive "the ruin of the Fatherland." Instead, Prussia emerged as one of the Great Powers of Europe.

The remaining twenty-three years of the king's life were spent in re-building and reforming what he had very nearly destroyed. Frugality, discipline, and hard work, despite very high taxation, were the values stressed throughout the society. The king provided funds to rebuild towns and villages, used reserve grain for seed-planting, and requisitioned horses for farming. He suspended taxes in some areas for six months as an economic stimulant. He started many new industries. By 1773, 264 new factories had been built: sugar refineries, leather works, porcelain manufacturing, tobacco works, and so forth. The government drained marshes along the rivers and settled hundreds of families in colonizing former wastelands. He oversaw the reform of the judicial system in an attempt to produce a more equitable nation governed by law. His system was one of "constitutional absolutism."

In 1772, as part of the First Partition of Poland, Prussia acquired west Prussia thus linking most of its territories.

THE DUTCH REPUBLIC

Historical Background

The Netherlands (known today as Holland and Belgium) were governed by the Spanish Hapsburgs, but each of the seventeen provinces had its own special privileges and limited autonomy within the Spanish Empire.

During the Protestant Reformation of the 16th century, large numbers of Dutch were converted to Calvinism ("Reformed" Churches), especially in the North. Catholicism remained stronger in the South (now Belgium).

When Philip II, king of Spain, began demonstrating his determination to use the Spanish Inquisition to enforce laws against "heresy," the Netherlands began a revolt against Spain which continued intermittently for eighty years (1568 – 1648).

In 1578, the Duke of Parma restored many of the old privileges of self-government to the ten southern provinces and large numbers of Calvinists moved north. In 1581 the seven northern Dutch provinces, under the leadership of William the Silent, declared themselves independent of Spain. In 1588 the great Spanish Armada sent to attack both the English and the Dutch was partially destroyed by a storm and then defeated by the English seadogs.

In 1648 the Peace of Westphalia recognized the independence of the Republic of the United Provinces. This had already been conceded by Spain in the Treaty of Munster, January 20, 1648.

Government of the Netherlands

The Dutch republic consisted of the seven northern provinces of Zeeland, Utrecht, Holland, Gelderland, Overijssel, Groningen, and Friesland. Holland was the wealthiest and most powerful. Each province and each city was autonomous.

National problems were governed by the States General which consisted of delegates from the provinces which could act only on the instructions of the provincial assemblies. Each province had a Stadholder, or governor, who was under the authority and instructions of the assembly. In times of crisis the provinces would sometimes choose the same Stadholder, and he thereby became the national leader.

Dutch Economy

The 17th century was the Golden Age of the Dutch. Not only was it the Age of Rembrandt and other great Dutch painters, but the Netherlands was also the most prosperous part of Europe in the 17th century. It was also the freest. The Dutch did not have government controls and monopolies to impede their freedom of enterprise. As a result they became by far the greatest mercantile nation in Europe with the largest merchant marine in the world.

Medium-sized cities and ports such as Leyden, Haarlem, Gouda, Delft, and Utrecht (with populations from 20,000 to 40,000) were characteristic of the Netherlands. Amsterdam was the richest city in Europe with a population of 100,000. The quays and wharves of these Dutch cities were stocked with Baltic grain, English woollens, silks and spices from India, sugar from the Caribbean, salted herring, and coal.

The Dutch had almost no natural resources, but built their economy around the carrying of trade, mercantile businesses, and other service occupations. They were skilled in finishing raw materials. Coarse linens from Germany were bleached and finished into fine textiles. Furniture making, fine woollen goods, sugar refining, tobacco cutting, brewing, pottery, glass, printing, paper making, armament manufacturing, and shipbuilding were all crafts in which the Dutch excelled.

The Dutch taught accounting methods, provided banks and rational legal methods for settling disputes. Their low interest rate was a key to economic growth: 3%, half of the normal rate in England. The Dutch were discussed and written about all over Europe as champions of free enterprise and individual rights – in contrast to state absolutism, economic nationalism, mercantilism, and protective tariffs.

The Dutch East India Company and the Dutch West India Company were organized as cooperative ventures of private enterprise and the state. The various provinces contributed part of the capital for these ventures and the Companies were subject to the authority of the States General.

Dutch Art

The 17th century was the most significant in history for Dutch painting. Most of the Dutch painters came from the province of Holland. Rembrandt and Jan Steen were from Leyden; Cuyp came from Dordrecht; Van Goyen from the Hague; and Vermeer from Delft.

The artistic center of the Netherlands was Amsterdam where the Dutch school of painters was noted for their landscape and portrait painting, and especially for "genre painting" in which scenes of everyday life predominate. The Calvinist influence in Holland is reflected in their celebration, but not idealization, of God's Creation. The realistic portrait paintings show mankind as great and noble, but also flawed, or, as the Reformed Churches put it, "fallen creatures in a fallen world." Nevertheless, the flawed creation was still to be enjoyed and their pictures of Dutch life in the 17th century show it to be intensely joyful and satisfying in human relationships.

The Dutch painters were masters of light and shadow as were the later French Impressionists. They captured the subtlety and realism of an ordinary scene under the vast expanse of the sky; a storm at sea; or a rain shower "drifting across a distant landscape pursued by sunshine." It is an interesting comparison to contrast the equally-great Flemish contemporary school in the Spanish Netherlands strongly influenced by the counter-Reformation Baroque. Peter Paul Rubens from Antwerp is a good example.

Dutch Wars and Foreign Policy

The Peace of Westphalia (1648) ended eighty years of war between Spain and the Netherlands and resulted in independence for the Dutch Republic and continued Hapsburg rule of the Spanish Netherlands. After being freed from Spanish domination the Dutch were faced with a series of wars against England over trading rights and colonial competition. Then, Louis XIV's efforts to move into the Low Countries brought the Dutch into a drawn-out war with France.

The accession of William and Mary to the throne of England in 1688 brought an end to the warfare between the Dutch and English. In the War of the Spanish Succession, 1701 – 13, England and Holland fought against France and Spain.

ENGLAND, SCOTLAND AND IRELAND

The English Civil War (1642 – 1649)

One of the underlying issues in this conflict was the constitutional issue of the relationship between king and Parliament. (Could the king govern without the consent of Parliament or go against the wishes of Parliament?). In short, the question was whether England was to have a limited, constitutional monarchy or an absolute monarchy as in France and Prussia.

The theological issue focused on the form of church government England was to have – whether it would follow the established Church of England's hierarchical, episcopal form of church government, or acquire a presbyterian form?

The episcopal form meant that the king, the Archbishop of Canterbury, and the bishops of the church would determine policy, theology, and the form of worship and service. The presbyterian form of polity allowed for more freedom of conscience and dissent among church members. Each congregation would have a voice in the life of the church and a regional group of ministers, or, "presbytery," would attempt to insure "doctrinal purity."

The political implications for representative democracy were present in both issues. That is why most Presbyterians, Puritans, and Congregationalists sided with Parliament and most Anglicans and Catholics sided with the king.

Charles I (1625 – 1649)

Charles I inherited both the English and Scottish thrones at the death of his father, James I. He claimed a "divine right" theory of absolute authority for himself as king and sought to rule without Parliament. That rule also meant control of the Church of England.

The king demanded more money from Parliament. Parliament refused and began impeachment proceedings against the king's chief minister, the duke of Buckingham, who was later assassinated in 1628. Charles then levied a forced "loan" on many of the wealthier citizens of England and imprisoned seventy-six English gentlemen who refused to contribute. Sir Randolph Crew, Chief Justice of the King's Bench, was dismissed from office for refusing to declare those "loans" legal. Five of the imprisoned men applied for writs of *habeas corpus*, asking whether the refusal to lend money to the king was a legal cause for imprisonment. The court returned them to jail without comment.

By 1628 both houses of Parliament – Lords and Commons alike – united in opposition to the king.

The Petition of Right (1628)

The Parliament in effect bribed the king by granting him a tax grant in exchange for his agreement to the Petition of Right. It stipulated that no one should pay any tax, gift, loan, or contribution except as provided by Act of Parliament; no one should be imprisoned or detained without due process of law; all were to have the right to the writ of *habeas corpus*; there should be no forced billeting of soldiers in the homes of private citizens; and that martial law was not to be declared in England.

The Parliament of 1629

In the midst of a stormy debate over theology, taxes, and civil liberties, the king sought to force the adjournment of Parliament. But when he sent a message to the Speaker ordering him to adjourn, some of the more athletic members held him in his chair while the door of the House of Commons was locked to prevent the entry of other messengers from the king. (That famous date was March 2, 1629.) A number of resolutions passed. Innovations towards Catholicism or Arminianism were to be regarded as treason. Whoever advised any collection of taxes without consent of

Parliament would be guilty of treason. Whoever should pay a tax levied without the consent of Parliament would be considered a betrayer of liberty and guilty of treason.

A royal messenger was allowed to enter the Commons and declared the Commons adjourned and a week later Charles I dissolved Parliament – for eleven years, 1629 – 40. Puritan leaders and leaders of the opposition in the House of Commons were imprisoned by the king, some for several years.

Religious Persecution

The established Church of England was the only legal church under Charles I, a Catholic. Within the Church of England (i.e., Anglican Church), specific ministers might be more Catholic, Arminian Protestant, or Puritan (with both Calvinist and Lutheran emphases).

Conventicles were harshly suppressed. (Conventicles were secret meetings for worship in which the authorized Prayer Book was not used, but the Bible and the Psalter were.)

William Laud, Archbishop of Canterbury, sought to enforce the king's policies vigorously. Arminian clergymen were to be tolerated, but Puritan clergymen silenced. Criticism was brutally suppressed. No book or pamphlet could legally be printed or sold without a license. Puritans who wrote secret pamphlets were punished harshly: In 1630 Alexander Leighton was whipped, pilloried, and mutilated for printing An *Appeal to Parliament* in which he challenged episcopacy. Three others had their ears cut off; one was branded on the cheek with the letters, SL (Seditious Libeler). Several were executed.

National Covenant of Scotland (1638)

Dissatisfaction with royal absolutism reached a crisis in Scotland when representatives of the Scottish people met at Greyfriars Kirk in Edinburgh in 1638 to sign a national protest against the policies of King Charles, who was king of Scotland as well as king of England. The nobility and barons met and signed the National Covenanton one day and the burgesses and ministers, the next. The covenant affirmed the loyalty of the people to the Crown but declared that the king could not re-establish the authority of the episcopate over the church. (The Church of Scotland had a presbyterian form of church government since the Reformation of the sixteenth century under John Knox.)

King Charles foolishly declared everyone who signed the National Covenant a rebel and prepared to move an army into Scotland.

War in Scotland

King Charles called out the militia of the northern counties of England and ordered the English nobility to serve as officers at their own expense. A troop of the king's horses entered Scotland only to find their way blocked by a large Scots army. They returned south of the border without fighting.

Charles signed the Pacification of Berwick with the Scots in June, 1639, by which each side would disband its forces and a new General Assembly of the Church of Scotland and a Scottish Parliament would determine the future constitution of the government. The Church General Assembly confirmed the actions of its predecessor; the Scottish Parliament repealed laws in favor of episcopacy and increased its own powers; and the Scottish army remained in existence.

The Short Parliament

For the first time in eleven years the king convened the English Parliament to vote new taxes for the war with Scotland. Instead the Commons presented to the king a long list of grievances since 1629. These included violations of the rights of Parliament; of civil rights; of changes in church order and government; and of rights of property ownership. In anger the king again dissolved Parliament, which had met only from April 13 to May 5, 1640.

The Scots Invade

The Scots invaded the two northern counties of Northumberland and Durham unopposed. Charles called a Great Council of Lords such as had not met in England for over two hundred years. They arranged a treaty with the Scots to leave things as they were.

The Long Parliament

The king was cornered: he had no money, no army, and no popular support. He summoned the Parliament to meet in November 1640. The Commons immediately moved to impeach one of the king's principal ministers, Thomas Wentworth, Earl of Strafford.

Strafford's trial began in March 1641, and lasted three weeks without a verdict. He was accused of treason for subverting the fundamental laws of the realm with an arbitrary and tyrannical government. Treason was traditionally defined as an offense against the king, so the indictment read instead that he was guilty of "treason against the nation."

With mobs in the street and rumors of an army enroute to London to dissolve Parliament, a bare majority of an under-attended House of Lords passed a bill of attainder to execute the Earl. Agonizingly distraught, but fearing mob violence as well as Parliament itself, the king signed the bill and Strafford was executed. Archbishop William Laud was also arrested, and eventually tried and executed in 1645.

The House of Commons passed a series of laws to strengthen its position and to better protect civil and religious rights. The Triennial Act provided that no more than three years should pass between Parliaments. Another act provided that the current Parliament should not be dissolved without its own consent. Various hated laws, taxes, and institutions were abolished: the Star Chamber, the High Commission, power of the Privy Council to deal with property rights. Ship money, a form of tax, was abolished and tonnage duties were permitted only for a short time. The courts of common law were to remain supreme over the king's courts.

The Commons was ready to revoke the king's powerg over the Church of England, but there was disagreement over what form the state church would take: episcopal, presbyterian, or congregational. Puritans were in the majority.

Rebellion in Ireland and the Grand Remonstrance

Irish Catholics murdered thousands of their Protestant neighbors. The Commons immediately voted funds for a large army, but questions remained whether it was to be a parliamentary army or a royal army under the control of the king.

The Grand Remonstrance listed 204 clauses of grievances against the king and demanded that all officers and ministers of the state be approved by Parliament.

The English Civil War Begins

With mobs in the streets and gentlemen carrying swords to protect themselves, men began identifying themselves as Cavaliers, in favor of the king, or Roundheads, if they supported Parliament.

In one of his most foolish actions as king, Charles then ordered his Attorney General to prepare impeachment proceedings against five of the leading Puritans in the House of Commons. When the House refused to surrender their members to the custody of the king, Charles went in person to Parliament with four hundred soldiers to arrest the five members. While the five slipped away from Westminster to London, mobs turned out into the streets, including four thousand from Buckinghamshire who sought to defend their hero, Sir John Hotham.

The king withdrew to Hampton Court and sent the Queen to France for safety. In March 1642, Charles II went to York and the English Civil War began.

The Division of the Country

To some extent every locality was divided between supporters of the king and supporters of Parliament. Geographically, though, the north and west of England sided with the king, and the south and east, with Parliament. The Midlands was competitive between them.

Eighty great nobles sided with the king, thirty against him. The majority of the gentry supported the king, a large minority were for Parliament. The yeomen tended to side with the gentry of their areas; the peasants wanted to avoid the fighting.

A few London merchants were Royalists, but most businessmen in various towns sided with Parliament. London, which was strongly Presbyterian, supplied Parliament with many men and much money.

Parliament had two great advantages. The navy and merchant marine supported Parliament. They brought in munitions and revenue from customs as foreign trade continued. They hindered the coastal towns behind the king's lines. Parliament also had control of the wealthier and more strategic areas, including London, and were able to secure the three principal arsenals: London, Hull, and Portsmouth.

The King Attacks London

Charles put together a sizeable force with a strong cavalry and moved on London, winning several skirmishes. He entered Oxford but was beaten back from London. Oxford then became his headquarters for the rest of the war.

Oliver Cromwell

Oliver Cromwell, a gentleman farmer from Huntingdon, led the parliamentary troops to victory, first with his cavalry, which eventually numbered eleven hundred, and then as lieutenant general in command of the well-discliplined and well-trained New Model Army.

Early Stages of the War

The early part of the war went in favor of the king. Lincolnshire, Cornwall, and Devon were occupied by two of the king's armies in 1643. The Queen returned from France with reinforcements and supplies. The king planned a three-pronged assault on London, but was beaten back by the Earl of Essex. Charles sought allies among Irish Catholics and Parliament sought aid from Presbyterian Scotland.

In January 1644, a well-equipped Scottish army of 21,000 crossed into England, thereby greatly upsetting the military balance. The Duke of Newcastle, the king's general was forced into York and there besieged. Prince Rupert came to his rescue from the west, but precipitated the battle of Marston Moor in July 1644. Cromwell decisively defeated the king's cavalry in a royalist disaster. The north was now in Parliamentary hands.

The king was not beaten yet, however. James Graham, the Marquis of Montrose, raised troops for the king in the Scottish Highlands, much to the consternation of the Lowlands Scots.

Parliament reconstructed and improved its army, giving Oliver Cromwell the top command. In June 1645, Charles marched into enemy territory and was crushed by Cromwell's "Ironsides" at Naseby. The king was then a fugitive and surrendered himself to the Scots in May 1646.

Controversy Between Parliament and the Army

The majority of Parliament were Presbyterians, wanting to extend the Scottish National Covenant idea to England. Many soldiers, however, were Independents who believed in democracy in politics and congregational control of the church.

During the Civil War, under the authority of Parliament the Westminster Assembly convened to write a statement of faith for the Church of England that was Reformed or Presbyterian in content. Ministers and laymen from both England and Scotland participated for six years and wrote the *Westminster Confession of Faith*, still a vital part of Presbyterian theology.

When the war ended, Parliament ordered the army to disband without receiving the pay due them. The army refused to disband and in 1647 Parliament sought to disperse them by force. The plan was to bring the Scottish army into England and use it against the men who had won the war.

The army refused to obey Parliament and arrested the king when he was brought across the border. In August the army occupied London and some of their leaders wrote an "Agreement of the People" to be presented to the House of Commons. It called for a democratic republic with a written constitution and elections every two years, equal electoral districts and universal manhood suffrage, freedom of conscience, freedom from impressment, equality before the law, and no office of king or House of Lords.

The Death of the King

On the night of November 11, 1647, the king escaped from Hampton Court and went to the Isle of Wight. He had made a secret agreement with the Scots that he would establish Presbyterianism throughout England and Scotland if they would restore him to his throne.

The Second Civil War followed in 1648 but it consisted only of scattered local uprisings and the desertion of part of the English fleet.

The Scots invaded England but were defeated by Cromwell at Preston, Wigan, and Warrington in the northwest of England. After these victories the English army took control. London was again occupied. The army arrested 45 Presbyterian members of Parliament, excluded the rest and admitted only about 60 Independents, who acted as the "Rump Parliament."

The army then tried Charles Stuart, formerly king of England, and sentenced him to death for treason. They charged him with illegal deaths and with governing in a tyrannical way instead of by the constitutional system of limited power that he had inherited. The execution of the king particularly shocked the Scots because the English had specifically promised not to take the king's life when the Scots delivered him into English hands.

The Commonwealth (1649 - 1653)

After the execution of the king, Parliament abolished the office of king and the House of Lords. The new form of government was to be a Commonwealth, or Free State, governed by the representatives of the people in Parliament.

The entirety of the people, however, were not represented in Parliament. Many large areas of the country had no representatives in Parliament. The ninety Independents that controlled Parliament did not want elections.

The Commonwealth was in effect a continuation of the Long Parliament under a different name. Parliament was more powerful than ever because there was neither king nor House of Lords to act as a check.

The Commons appointed a Council of State and entrusted it with administrative power. Thirty-one of its forty-one members were also members of Parliament.

Opposition to the Commonwealth

Royalists and Presbyterians both opposed Parliament for its lack of broad representation and for regicide. The army was greatly dissatisfied that elections were not held, as one of the promises of the Civil War was popular representation.

The death of the king provoked a violent reaction abroad. In Russia the czar imprisoned English merchants. In Holland Royalist privateers were allowed to refit. An English ambassador at the Hague and another in Madrid were murdered by Royalists. France was openly hostile.

Surrounded by enemies, the Commonwealth became a military state with a standing army of 44,000. The army, with career soldiers, was probably the best in Europe, and the best paid. Forty warships were built in three years. The North American and West Indian colonies were forced to accept the government of the Commonwealth.

Ireland

In the summer of 1649 Cromwell landed in Dublin with a well-equipped army of 12,000. Despite a coalition of Protestant Royalists and Irish Catholics, the Irish did not put together an army to oppose him. Instead they relied on fortresses for safety.

Drogheda was the scene of the first massacre when Cromwell ordered the slaughter of the entire garrison of 2800. Another massacre took place at Wexford.

This campaign of terror induced many towns to surrender; by the end of 1649 the southern and eastern coast was in English hands. In 1650, Cromwell captured Kilkenny and left the rest of the conquest to others.

The lands of all Roman Catholics who had taken part in the war were confiscated and given in payment to Protestant soldiers and others. Two-thirds of the land in Ireland changed hands, controlled mostly by Protestant landlords.

Scotland

Scottish Presbyterians, offended by the Independents' control of the English Parliament and by the execution of the king, proclaimed Charles II as their king. Charles accepted the National Covenant and agreed to govern a Presbyterian realm.

On September 3, 1650, Cromwell defeated the Scots at Dunbar, near Edinburgh, and killed 3,000, taking 10,000 prisoner. The next year King Charles II led a Scots army into England, which was annihilated almost to the last man at Worcester. Charles was a fugitive for six weeks before escaping to France.

The Protectorate (1653 –1659)

When it became clear that Parliament intended to stay in office permanently without new elections, Cromwell took troops to Parliament and forced all members to leave, thus dissolving the Parliament.

Cromwell had no desire to rule either as king or military dictator. He called for new elections – but not under the old system, most office holders in the new system were chosen by Independent or Puritan churches.

Cromwell then agreed to serve as Lord Protector with a Council of State and a Parliament. The new government permitted religious liberty, except for Catholics and Anglicans.

England was not strongly opposed to military rule, particularly after Cromwell divided the country into twelve districts with a major general in charge of each.

Oliver Cromwell died on September 3, 1658. After Cromwell's death a new Parliament was elected under the old historic franchise.

The Restoration (1660 – 1688)

The new Parliament restored the monarchy, but the Puritan Revolution clearly showed that the English constitutional system required a limited monarchy, with the king as chief executive – but not as absolute ruler. Parliament in 1660 was in a far stronger position in its relationship to the king than it ever had been before.

Charles II (1660 – 1685)

Thirty years of age at the Restoration, the new king was dissolute, lazy, affable, intelligent, a liar, and a cunning deceiver. He loved the sea and the navy and was interested in science and trade. Because he had so little interest in religion, he was willing to be tolerant.

While still on the Continent, Charles II issued the Declaration of Breda in which he agreed to abide by Parliament's decisions on the postwar settlement.

The Convention Parliament (1660)

Parliament pardoned all those who fought in the Civil War except for fifty people listed by name. Of these, twelve were executed for "regicide."

Royalists whose lands had been confiscated by the Puritans were allowed to recover their lands through the courts, but those who had sold them should receive no compensation. That meant that both Roundheads and Cavaliers would be the landowners of England.

To raise money for the government, Parliament granted the king income from customs duties and an excise on beer, ale, tea, and coffee. Feudalism was largely abolished.

The Clarendon Code

Of England's 9,000 parish churches, 2,000 were pastored by Presbyterian ministers 400 by Independents, and the rest by Anglicans. The Cavalier Parliament, elected early in 1661, sought to drive out all Puritans and exclude them from public and ecclesiastical life.

The Corporation Act of 1661 excluded from local government any one who refused to swear to the unlawfullness of resistance to the king and those who did not receive communion according to the pattern of the Church of England. The Act of Uniformity in 1662 issued a new Prayer Book and ordered ministers either to accept it or resign their positions and livelihood. 1,200 pastors refused and vacated their churches.

The Conventicle Act of 1664 and 1670 imposed harsh penalties on those who attended religious services which did not follow the forms of the Anglican Church. The

Five-Mile Act, 1665, prohibited ministers from coming within five miles of a parish from which they had been removed as pastor. A licensing act permitted the Archbishop of Canterbury and the bishop of London to control the press and the publishing of books.

The effect of all this was to divide England into two great groups – the Anglican Church and nonconformists. The church was purged of Puritans and regained its property. It levied tithes and controlled education at all levels. Nonconformists were excluded from the universities, from government, from many professions, and from membership in the House of Commons. Some, of course, became Anglicans outwardly but did not believe what they professed. Nonconformists became shopkeepers, artisans, small farmers, merchants, bankers, and manufacturers. Their diligence, thrift, and self-discipline brought prosperity. They were strengthened by the rise of Methodism in the 18th century.

Disasters for England

War with the Dutch cost enormously in ships and money. The bubonic plague hit London in 1665, killing 68,000. The Great Fire of London in 1666 destroyed 13,000 homes, 84 churches, and many public buildings, none covered by insurance.

Scotland's Independence

Scotland regained her independence at the restoration of Charles II in 1660. The Earl of Middleton was made the King's Commissioner in the Scottish Parliament and commander of the army in Scotland. Some of the Scottish Presbyterian ministers reminded the king of the National Covenant of 1638 and of his own covenant-oath in 1651, pledging that Scotland be governed according to Presbyterian polity and principles.

The king arrested the Marquis of Argyle, leader of the Covananters and a Presbyterian He was charged with treason for his "compliance with Cromwell's government." Argyle and James Guthrie were both executed.

Charles II declared himself head of the Church of Scotland and decreed that the episcopal form of hierarchical church government would be used in Scotland.

In 1661 the Scottish Parliament declared that the National Covenant was no longer binding and prohibited anyone to renew any covenant or oath without royal permission.

Samuel Rutherford, influential author of *Lex Rex* and Principal of St. Mary's College, St. Andrews, was cited by the Privy Council for treason in 1661, but died before a trial could be held.

A dictatorship was established in Scotland to enforce episcopacy and rule by approved bishops. The government demanded absolute obedience and used illegal detention. Drastic fines were levied on hundreds of people suspected of being sympathetic to the Covenanters. Presbyterianism was outlawed and hundreds of ministers lost their positions.

By 1666 the covenanters finally took to arms against oppression and captured the commanding general at Dumfries.

Perhaps as many as 18,000 ordinary people died for the cause of religious liberty in the persecution that followed. Dragoons were sent to prevent people from meeting in the files and in "unlicensed" homes for the purpose of worshipping God and studying the Bible. Others were fined for not attending the parish church.

Archbishop James Sharp was assassinated by a group of over-zealous Covenanters on May 3, 1679. Covenanting leaders immediately repudiated the action, but it led to pitched battles between the king's troops and covenanters.

The last two years of Charles II reign in Scotland were known as The Killing Times because of the wholesale slaughter of hundreds who were shot down without trial if they refused to take the oath of objuration of the Covenant.

Charles II died on February 5, 1685, in his 56th year and received Roman Catholic absolution on his deathbed.

James II (1685 – 1688)

The new king, fifty-one years of age, was the brother of Charles II. He had served as Lord Admiral and commanded an English fleet against the Dutch.

James II began his reign in a strong position. The Whigs were weak and the Tories were in overwhelming strength in Parliament. They immediately voted the king an income from customs for life.

James II, a strong Roman Catholic, was determined to return England to Catholicism. He proceeded to appoint Catholics to many of the high positions in his government. In 1685, he created a court of Ecclesiastical Commission with power over the clergy and suspended the bishop of London from office. Three colleges at the University of Oxford were put under Roman Catholic Rule. (Oxford was an Anglican and Tory stronghold and so the king was jeopardizing his own supporters.)

In April 1687, King James issued a Declaration of Indulgence which declared both Catholics and nonconformists free to worship in public and to hold office. This was a bold move, but the nonconformists knew that the king's intent was to enable Catholics to eventually control the government. Instead of supporting the king, the nonconformists secured a promise from the Anglicans that they would eventually be given toleration.

The Glorious Revolution of 1688

The leaders of Parliament were not at all willing to sacrifice the constitutional gains of the English Civil War and return to an absolute monarchy. Two events in 1688 goaded them to action.

In May, James reissued the Declaration of Indulgence with the command that it be read on two successive Sundays in every parish church. Archbishop Bancroft and six bishops petitioned the king to withdraw his command. They printed and distributed their petition to the king. This was a technical violation of the law and the king ordered them prosecuted for publishing a seditious libel against his government. When a London jury reached a verdict of "not guilty," it was clear that the king did not have popular support.

On June 10, 1688, a son was born to the king and his queen, Mary of Modena. They had been married for fifteen years and their other children had died. As long as James was childless by his second wife, the throne would go to one of his Protestant daughters, Mary or Anne. The birth of a son, who would be raised Roman Catholic, changed the picture completely.

A group of Whig and Tory leaders, speaking for both houses of Parliament, invited William and Mary to assume the throne of England. William III was Stadtholder of Holland and son of Mary, the daughter of Charles I. Mary II was the daughter of James II by his first wife, Anne Hyde. They were both in the Stuart dynasty.

William was willing to assume the English throne only if he had popular support and only if accompanied by his own Dutch troops, despite the irritation their presence would cause in England.

The Dutch feared that King Louis XIV would attack Holland while their army was in England, but the French attacked the Palatinate instead and eliminated that fear. Louis XIV offered to James II the French fleet but James declined what would have been very little help. King Louis thought that William's invasion would result in a civil war which would neutralize both England and Holland, but he was mistaken. On November 5, 1688, William and his army landed at Torbay in Devon. King James offered many concessions, but it was too late. He advanced with his army to Salisbury, then returned to London, and finally fled to France.

William assumed temporary control of the government and summoned a free Parliament, which met in February 1689. Whigs and Tories met in a conciliatory spirit though party differences soon became evident. The Whigs wanted a declaration that the throne was vacant in order to break the royal succession and give the king a parliamentary title. The Tories declared that the king had abdicated so as to avoid admitting that they had deposed him. William and Mary were declared joint sovereigns, with the administration given to William.

The English Bill of Rights (1689) declared the following: 1) The king could not be a Roman Catholic; 2) A standing army in time of peace was illegal without Parliamentary approval; 3) Taxation was illegal without Parliamentary consent; 4) Excessive bail and cruel and unusual punishments were prohibited; 5) Right to trial by jury was guaranteed; and 6) Free elections to Parliament would be held.

The Toleration Act (1689) granted the right of public worship to Protestant nonconformists but did not permit them to hold office. The Act did not extend liberty to Catholics or Unitarians, but normally they were left alone.

The Trials for Treason Act (1696) stated that a person accused of treason should be shown the accusations against him and should have the advice of counsel. They should also not be convicted except upon the testimony of two independent witnesses.

Freedom of the press was permitted, but with very strict libel laws.

Control of finances was to be in the hands of Commons, including military appropriations. There would no longer be uncontrolled grants to the King.

The Act of Settlement in 1701 provided that should William or Anne die without children (Queen Mary had died in 1694) the throne should descend, not to the exiled Stuarts, but to Sophia, Electress Dowager of Hanover, a granddaughter of King James I, or to her Protestant heirs.

Judges were made independent of the Crown. Thus, England declared itself a limited monarchy and a Protestant nation.

Queen Anne (1702 – 1714)

Much of Queen Anne's reign was occupied with the War of the Spanish Succession (1702 – 13). The reign of Queen Anne is also called the Augustan Age of English elegance and wealth. Anne was a devout Anglican, a semi-invalid who ate too much and was too slow-witted to be an effective ruler. She had sixteen children, none of whom survived her.

The most important achievement of Queen Anne's reign was the Act of Union (1707), which united Scotland and England into one kingdom. The Scots gave up their Parliament and sent forty-five members to the English House of Commons and sixteen to the House of Lords. Presbyterianism was retained as the national church.

Eighteenth Century England

Following the Act of Settlement in 1701 and Queen Anne's death in 1714, the House of Hanover inherited the English throne in order to insure that a Protestant would rule the realm.

The Hanover dynasty was as follows: George I (1714–1727); George II (1727–60); George III (1760–1820); George IV (1820–30); William IV (1830–37); and Queen Victoria (1837–1901).

Because of the English Civil War, the Commonwealth, and the Glorious Revolution of 1688, the Hanovers were willing to rule as King-in-Parliament, which meant that to rule England, the king and his ministers had to have the support of a majority in Parliament. Sir Robert Walpole, who served forty-two years in the English government, created the office of Prime Minister, a vital link between king and Parliament. Other famous 18th century prime ministers were the Duke of Newcastle, George Grenville, William Pitt, the Elder (Earl of Chatham), Lord North, and William Pitt the Younger.

The loss of England's North American colonies in the American War for Independence (1775–83) was a major blow to the British Empire. Also during this period Ireland received very harsh treatment under British rule.

In March 1689, James II arrived in Dublin with 7,000 French troops and was joined by Irish Catholics seeking independence from England. Protestants fled to Londonderry which withstood a siege of 105 days. In June 1690, William landed in Ireland with an army of 36,000 and at the Battle of Boyne completely defeated James, who fled to France.

Repercussions in Ireland were harsh: no Catholic could hold office, sit in the Irish Parliament, or vote for its members. He could enter no learned profession except medicine. He was subject to discriminatory taxation. He could not purchase land or hold long leases.

The American War for Independence gave hope to the Irish that they might obtain autonomy or independence. British troops were withdrawn from Ireland to be sent to America and an Irish militia was formed.

The British did grant concessions to the Irish between 1778 and 1783. Roman Catholics could inherit property and hold long-term leases. The Irish Parliament was given its independence but continued to be controlled by Protestants. Executive officials continued to be appointed by the English Crown.

In 1800, the Irish Parliament was persuaded to vote itself out of existence in exchange for one hundred seats in the British House of Commons and thirty-two places in the House of Lords.

Scotland, at this time, was the scene of Jacobin efforts to restore the Stuarts to the throne.

In 1688 the Scots declared that James had "forfeited" the Scottish throne which they offered to William and Mary, with the understanding that Scotland would be Presbyterian. Some of the Highland clans, however, turned out in defense of James. They were defeated at the Battle of Killiecrankie in July 1689.

The settlement with William and Mary was marred by the brutal Glencoe Massacre of 1692, in which the Campbell clan slaughtered a large group of Macdonalds after giving them shelter and hospitality. In 1715, James II's son, then twenty-seven years old, raised an army of 10,000 Highlanders in a revolt. James Francis Edward Stuart, the "Old Pretender," was soundly defeated and fled to France. In 1745, James Francis Stuart's son, Charles Edward, the "Young Pretender," then in his mid-twenties, obtained two ships from the French and sought to incite an uprising in Scotland, winning lasting fame as "Bonnie Prince Charlie."

His spirit and ambition won him the backing of several Highland chiefs. He was a natural leader and his men respected him for enduring the hardships of the common soldier.

Charles was able to capture the city of Edinburgh, but not the fortified castle. Soon he was forced to retreat north to Inverness. At Culloden, in April 1746, he was completely defeated. The rebellion was followed with harsh English reprisals. There were many executions and parts of the Highlands were devastated. The Highlanders were disarmed and even the Highland kilt and tartan were forbidden.

SCANDINAVIA

Sweden in the Thirty Years' War

King Gustavus Adolphus drove the Imperial forces from Pomerania in 1630. Swedish troops occupied all of Bohemia, organized a new Protestant Union, and invaded Bavaria. Gustavus Adolphus was killed in 1632 in the Battle of Lutzen.

In the fall of 1634, Imperial forces decisively defeated the Swedish army at Nordlingen. The Treaty of Prague (1635) restored Catholic and Protestant lands to their status as of 1627.

Catholic France allied with Protestant Sweden against the Hapsburg Empire during the last phase of the war from 1635 – 1648. Sweden acquired western Pomerania as part of the Peace of Westphalia (1648), ending the Thirty Years' War.

Swedish Empire

The high point of Swedish power in the Baltics was in the 1650's. Population of the Swedish Empire including the German provinces was only three million, half of whom were Swedish.

Sweden was not a large or productive country. Maintaining a strong standing army proved to be too much of a strain on the economy. Sweden sought to control the trade of the Baltic Sea with its important naval stores, but even at the height of Swedish power only 10% of the ships in the Baltic trade were Swedish; 65% were Dutch.

Swedish provinces in the Baltic and in Germany were impossible to defend against strong continental powers such as Russia, Prussia, or Austria.

Political Situation

After the death of Gustavus Adolphus in 1632, the government was effectively controlled by an oligarchy of the nobility ruling in the name of the Vasa dynasty.

Christina, the daughter of Gustavus Adolphus, became queen at six years of age and ruled from 1632 to 1654. At age twenty-eight, she abdicated the throne to her cousin and devoted the rest of her life to the Catholic faith and to art.

Charles X Gustavus reigned from 1654 to 1660 during the First Northern War against Poland, Russia, and Denmark.

Poland ceded Livonia to Sweden by the Treaty of Olivia (1660). Denmark surrendered to Sweden the southern part of the Scandinavian Peninsula by the Treaty of Copenhagen (1660).

Charles XI (1660 – 1697) became king at age eleven. When he came of age, he spent the rest of his life attempting to regain powers lost to the Council. For this, he secured the aid of the Lower Estates of the Riksdag who in 1693 declared that Charles XI was "absolute sovereign King, responsible to no one on earth, but with power and might as his command to rule and govern the realm as a Christian monarch." This was in dramatic contrast to the centuries' long struggles in Holland and England to constitutionally limit their kings.

King Charles XII (1697 – 1718) came to the throne at age 15 and reigned for twenty-one years. He spent most of his life at war and was an outstanding military leader in the Great Northern War (1700 – 1721).

Denmark, Saxony, Poland, and Russia formed an alliance to destroy the Swedish Empire. In February 1700, Poland attacked Swedish Livonia and Denmark invaded Holstein. The Swedish navy defeated the Danes and attacked Copenhagen, forcing Denmark to make peace.

Charles then shifted his attention to Estonia and routed a Russian invasion in the Battle of Narva, inflicting heavy losses. Charles was then eighteen years of age.

The next several years were spent fighting in Poland, defeating both the Poles and the Russians. But in 1709, the Russians, outnumbering the Swedish forces two-to-one, defeated them. Peter the Great then took the Baltic provinces of Livonia and Estonia from Sweden.

Years of warfare, poor government, and high taxes finally led to Charles XII's alienation from his people. In 1718 he was killed by a stray bullet.

Eighteenth Century Sweden

The loss of the Empire meant a move to a more democratic, limited monarchy and the new freedom led to a sharp increase in peasant enterprises and independence. The Swedish economy prospered.

By 1756, parliament considered itself the sovereign Estates of the realm and many civil liberties were established. Principal decisions of government were made by the Riskdag (Parliament).

Under Gustavus III there was a temporary return to royal absolutism until he was assassinated in 1792.

Scandinavian Relations

Finland was part of the Swedish Empire in the seventeenth century and Norway was part of Denmark. In the early nineteenth century Sweden gave up Finland but acquired Norway as an autonomous part of a union of the two nations.

Denmark

Frederick III (1648 – 1670), established himself as absolute ruler.

Frederick IV (1699 – 1730) fought in the Northern War and achieved a rough parity in the Baltic with Sweden, but accepted Swedish control in the south of the Scandinavian Peninsula.

Christian VII experimented with both enlightened despotism and reforms that allowed more civil liberties and economic freedoms to the Danish people.

RUSSIA OF THE ROMANOVS

Ivan III (1442 – 1505)

Ivan III, "Ivan the Great," put an end in 1480 to Mongol domination over Russia. He married Sophie Paleologus (1472), the niece of the last emperor of Constantinople. (The Byzantine Empire was conquered by the Ottoman Turks in 1453). Ivan took the title of Caesar (i.e., Czar) as heir of the Eastern Roman Empire (i.e., Byzantine Empire). He encouraged the Eastern Orthodox Church and called Moscow the "Third Rome," many Greek scholars, craftsmen, architects, and artists were brought to Russia.

Ivan IV (1533 – 1584)

Ivan IV, "Ivan the Terrible," grandson of Ivan III, began westernizing Russia.

A contemporary of Queen Elizabeth, he welcomed both the English and the Dutch and opened new trade routes to Moscow and the Caspian Sea. English merchant adventurers opened Archangel on the White Sea and provided a link with the outer world free from Polish domination.

The "Time of Troubles" followed the death of Ivan IV in 1584 when the ruling Muscovite family died out. The Time of Troubles was a period of turmoil, famine, power struggles, and invasions from Poland.

The Romanov Dynasty

The Romanov dynasty ruled Russia from 1613 to 1917. Stability returned to Russia in 1613 when the Semski Sobor (estates general representing the Russian Orthodox Church, landed gentry, townspeople, and a few peasants) elected Michael Romanov as czar from 1613 to 1645.

Russia, with a standing army of 70,000, was involved in a series of unsuccessful wars with Poland, Sweden, and Turkey. In 1654, Russia annexed the Ukraine with its rich farmlands. The Ukranians were supposed to be granted full autonomy, but in the end were not.

It was under Michael Romanov that Russia continued its expansion into contiguous territory and created an enormous empire across Asia to the Pacific. Westernization, begun under Ivan IV, continued under Michael Romanov.

The Russian army was trained by westerners, mostly Scotsmen. Weapons were purchased from Sweden and Holland. Four Lutheran and Reformed Churches and a German school were established in Moscow. Western skills and technology, western clothes and customs became accepted in Russia. By the end of the 17th century, 20,000 Europeans lived in Russia, developing trade and manufacturing, practicing medicine, and smoking tobacco while Russians began trimming their beards and wearing western clothing.

Western books were translated into Russian. In 1649, three monks were appointed to translate the Bible for the first time into Russian. The Raskolniki (Old Believers) refused to accept any Western innovations or liturgy in the Russian Orthodox Church and were severely persecuted as a result. In twenty years, 20,000 of them were burned at the stake, but millions still called themselves Old Believers as late as 1917.

Peter the Great (1682 – 1725)

Peter was one of the most extraordinary people in Russian history. He was nearly seven feet tall with physical strength so great that he could bend a horse shoe with this bare hands. His restless energy kept him active doing things incessantly, perpetually at work building boats, extracting teeth, dissecting corpses, shoemaking, cooking, etching, writing dispatches and instructions sometimes for fourteen hours a day. He did not understand moderation and could be cruel and vicious. He often whipped his servants, killed people who angered him, and even tortured his son to death. When he received good news, he would sometimes dance around and sing at the top of his voice.

Peter was born in 1672, the son of Czar Alexis' second wife, Natalia. When Peter was only four years old, his father died and the oldest son Theodore ruled until 1682, when he also died without an heir. For seven years Peter and his older half-brother ruled with the older half-sister Sophia as regent. Discovering a plot by Sophia to kill him, Peter, in 1689, banished her to a monastery and began ruling in his own right with his mother Natalia as regent. When she died in 1694, Peter, at age 22, took over the administration of the Russian government.

The driving ambition of Peter the Great's life was to modernize Russia and he needed the West to accomplish that. At the same time he wanted to compete with the great powers of Europe on equal terms.

Peter visited western Europe in disguise in order to study the techniques and culture of the West. He worked as a carpenter in shipyards; attended gunnery school; and visited hospitals and factories. He sent back to Russia large numbers of European technicians and craftsmen to train Russians and to build factories, some of which were larger than any in the West. By the end of Peter's reign Russia produced more iron than England (though not more than Sweden or Germany).

Wars of Peter the Great

Peter built up the army through conscription and a 25-year term of enlistment. He gave flintlocks and bayonets to his troops instead of the old muskets and pikes. Artillery was improved and discipline enforced. By the end of his reign Russia had a standing army of 210,000 despite a population of only 13 million. Peter also developed the Russian Navy.

In 1696, Peter sailed his fleet of boats down the Don River and took Azov on the Black Sea from the Turks.

The Great Northern War (1700 – 1721)

In 1699 Peter allied with Poland and Denmark against Sweden.

Charles XII, the 18-year-old Swedish king, defeated the Russian army of 35,000, capturing its artillery and most of its senior officers.

The main Swedish effort, though, was against Poland but the Swedish war lasted for twenty years. In 1706, Sweden again defeated Russia at Grodno, but in 1709 Peter won at Poltava.

The Treaty of Nystad (1721) ended the war. Russia returned Finland. Livonia (Latvia) and Estonia became part of the Russian Empire. Russia now had possessions on the Baltic Sea and a "window on the West."

St. Petersburg

The building of this great city (now Leningrad) out of a wilderness and making it the capital as well as one of the two principal cities of Russia, was one of Peter's crowning achievements. Construction began in 1703, done by conscripted labor and supervised by the czar himself.

Peter sought to make St. Petersburg look like Amsterdam. It became a cosmopolitan, lively city with French theater and Italian opera. His palace imitated Versailles with its terraces, fountains, cascade, art gallery, and park. St. Petersburg was built mostly of stone and brick rather than from traditional Russian wood.

The czar ordered a specific number of noble families to move to St. Petersburg and build their houses according to Peter's plans. At Peter's death in 1725, St. Petersburg had a population of 75,000, the largest city in northern Europe.

Reforms Under Peter the Great

The czar ruled by decree (ukase). Government officials and nobles acted under government authority, but there was no representative body.

All land-owners owed life-time service to the state, either in the army, the civil service, or at court. In return for government service they received land and serfs to work their fields.

Conscription required each village to send recruits for the Russian army. By 1709, Russia manufactured most of its own weapons and had an effective artillery.

The Russian navy, mostly on the Baltic, grew to a fleet of 850 ships, but declined sharply after Peter's death.

Taxes were heavy on trade, sales, and rent. The government also levied a head tax on every male.

State-regulated monopolies brought income to the government, but stultified trade and economic growth and in the long-run were counter-productive economically. Half of the two hundred enterprises begun during Peter's reign were state-owned; the rest were heavily taxed.

Peter sought unsuccessfully to link the main rivers by canals. Thousands died in the effort but only one of his six great canals was completed: St. Petersburg was linked to the Volga by canal in 1732.

The budget of the Russian government at the end of Peter's reign was three times its size at the beginning, 75% of which was spent on the military. Peter also established naval, military, and artillery academies.

The Russian secret police ferreted out opposition and punished it as subversion.

The Swedish model was followed in organizing the central government. Russia was divided into twelve provinces with a governor in charge. This decentralized many of the functions previously performed by the national government.

Industrial serfdom mean that workers were brought and sold amongst the factories and invariably created inferior products.

Russia had a "conditional land tenure" system with the Czar as the theoretical owner of all land in a Russian-style feudal system where both nobility and serfs served the state.

When the Patriarch of the Russian Orthodox Church died in 1700, Peter abolished his authority and began treating the Church as a government department. He eventually gave governing authority to a Holy Synod.

18th Century Russian Czars After Peter the Great

Catharine I, who ruled from 1725 to 1727, was the second wife of Peter the Great.

Peter II (1727 – 30) the son of Alexis and grandson of Peter the Great, died at age 15.

Anna (1730 – 40) was dominated by German advisers. Under her rule the War of the Polish Succession (1733 – 35) gave Russia firmer control over Polish affairs. War against the Turks (1736–39) gave Azov to Russia once again. Russia agreed not to build a fleet on the Black Sea.

Ivan VI (1740 – 41) was overthrown by a military coup.

Elizabeth (1741 – 62) was the youngest daughter of Peter the Great. This was the Golden Age of the aristocracy as they freed themselves from some of the obligations imposed on them by earlier czars. Russia entered the Seven Years' War (1756 – 63) during Elizabeth's reign.

Peter III (1762) was deposed and killed in a military revolt.

Catharine II ("the Great"; 1762 – 96) continued the westernization process begun by Peter the Great. The three partitions of Poland, in 1772, 1793, and 1795 respectively, occurred under Catharine II's rule. Russia also annexed the Crimea and warred with Turkey during her reign.

ITALY AND THE PAPACY

The Papacy

For the first time in its long history the papacy was of secondary importance in European diplomacy. There were a number of factors contributing to the decline of the papacy:

1) The Protestant Reformation of the 16th century and the emergence of many Protestant kingdoms throughout Europe.

2) The emphasis on limited constitutional government adopted in the Protestant Reformation and accepted by many non-Protestants as well.

3) The relatively few sanctions available to the pope in an international atmosphere of realpolitik.

4) The beginnings of secularization of Europe through the growing influence of the Enlightenment.

5) The anti-clericalism associated with the Enlightenment spread a desire to reduce the power and economic holdings of the church in traditionally Catholic countries. Anti-clericalism reached a climax in the French Revolution.

6) The lack of papal leadership in countering the above. Most of the 17th and 18th century popes were more concerned about administering their own territories than with the wider political milieu.

Pope Innocent X (1644 – 55) protested against the Peace of Westphalia (1648) because it acknowledged the rights of Lutherans and Calvinists in Germany, but the diplomats at Westphalia paid him little attention.

Quiet obscurity characterized the next three popes, Alexander VIII (1655 – 67), Clement IX (1667 – 69), and Clement X (1670 – 76), though they did clash with King Louis XIV over the prerogatives of the Church versus the prerogatives of the Crown, particularly in the appointment of bishops.

Innocent XI (1676 – 89) was scrupulous in financial matters and worked actively against the Turkish invasion of Europe. He subsidized Poland's relief of Vienna in the great campaign against the Turks in 1683.

Clement XI (1700 – 21) sided with France in the War of the Spanish Succession and in the course of the war, the Papal States were invaded by Austria. Clement renewed the condemnation of Jansenism, which had made extraordinary progress in France. (Jansenism was an Augustinian Catholic reform movement akin to Protestant Calvinism in its theology.)

Benedict XIV (1740 – 58), much influenced by the Enlightenment, sought to salvage some of the Church's lost influence in absolute European states by compromising the state's influence in nationally-established Catholic churches.

Clement XIV (1769 – 74) ordered the Jesuit Society dissolved (July 21, 1773).

Pius VI (1775 – 99) felt the full force of French radical anti-clericalism, which finally led to the French invasion of the Papal States in 1796.

17th and 18th Century Italy

Italy in the 17th and 18th centuries remained merely a geographic expression divided into small kingdoms, most of which were under foreign domination. Unification of Italy into a national-state did not occur until the mid-nineteenth century.

In the 17th century Spain controlled most of the Italian peninsula. Spain owned Lombardy in the north and Naples, Sicily, and Sardinia, in the south. Lombardy (or

Milan) was the most valuable to Spain in the 17th century because of its strategic importance, linking Spain with Austria and with Flanders (through Franche Comt). It served as a barrier to French invasion of Italy. Naples and Sicily were not scenes of foreign invasion as was the north of Italy.

Independent Italian States

The Duchy of Tuscany had lost its earlier eminence in art and literature. The prosperous Republic of Genoa did not influence European affairs. The Republic of Venetia no longer challenged Turkey in the eastern Mediterranean.

Savoy

Savoy was the only state with a native Italian dynasty. In the early 16th century, Savoy was a battleground between the French and the Spanish.

Emmanuel Philibert, Duke of Savoy (1553 – 80), was rewarded by the Holy Roman Emperor with the restoration of the independence of Savoy. He built Savoy as a modern state.

Charles Emmanuel I (1580 – 1630), maintained his independence by playing off France diplomatically against Spain and vice versa. Neither country could permit the other to gain a foothold in strategic Savoy, so Savoy remained independent.

Victor Amadeus (1630 – 37), married Marie Christine, Louis XIII's sister, thus increasing French influence in Savoy. Charles Emmanuel II (1637 – 75) was similarly dominated by France.

Victor Amadeus II (1675 – 1731), championed the Protestant Vaudois against Louis XIV. He joined William of Orange and the League of Augsburg against France. France defeated Savoy and forced Savoy to change sides. Nevertheless, the Peace of Ryswick confirmed Savoy's independence and left Savoy the leading Italian state and an important entity in the balance of power.

In 1713 Victor Amadeus was awarded Sicily and in 1720 exchanged Sicily to Austria for the island of Sardinia. henceforth he was known as the King of Sardinia.

Charles Emmanuel III (1731 – 1773) joined France and Spain in the War of the Polish Succession in an unsuccessful attempt to drive Austria out of Italy. Savoy sided with Austria in the War of the Austrian Succession and received part of Milan as a reward.

The French Revolution and Napoleon's invasion of Austria completely changed the situation for Italy and in the 19th century Italian unification was achieved under a Sardinian king, Victor Emmanuel II.

THE OTTOMAN TURKISH EMPIRE IN EUROPE

Christian Europe versus Islamic Mediterranean

During the Middle Ages the Islamic Empire included Spain, North Africa, and the Middle East. Expansion of Islam into Europe was blocked by France in the West (and, after 1492, by Spain) and by the Byzantine Empire in the East. When Constantinople fell to the Ottoman Turks in 1453, Eastern Europe was open for Islamic expansion by force of arms.

Hungary and the Hapsburg Empire became the defenders of Europe. Under Suleiman the Magnificent (d. 1566) the Turks captured Belgrade and took over nearly half of Eastern Europe. Ottoman power extended from the Euphrates River to the Danube.

Turkish Decline in the 17th AND 18th Centuries

The Sultan headed an autocratic and absolutist political system, often controlled by intrigue, murder, and arbitrary capital punishment. Most Sultans were more preoccupied with their harem than with affairs of state.

Government finance was based more on spoils of war, tribute, and sale of offices than on a sound economy. The Turkish military and bureaucracy were dependent on the training and loyalty of Christian slaves, the famous Janissaries and officials of the Sultan's Household.

Mohammed IV (1648 – 1687)

His reign was characterized by the efficient rule of an Albanian dynasty of grand viziers, the Kiuprilis. Thirty thousand people were executed as the Sultan and grand vizier purged all opposition to their will.

In 1683, the Turks besieged Vienna with 200,000 men for six weeks, intending to take Vienna as they had Constantinople two centuries earlier. John Sobieski, the king of Poland, with 50,000 Polish troops, went to the relief of the city and of the Hapsburg Empire. The Turks massacred 30,000 Christian prisoners and were defeated in a terrible slaughter.

Mustapha II (1695 – 1703)

Austrian and Polish armies defeated the Turks again, killing 26,000 in battle and drowning 10,000. The Treaty of Karlowitz (1699) recognized Austrian conquests of Hungary and Transylvania. The Ottoman Empire never recovered its former power or aggressiveness.

Ahmed III (1703 – 1730)

In 1711, the Turks attacked the Russians and forced Peter the Great to surrender and restore the Black Sea part of Azov.

In 1716, Austria destroyed 20,000 men in forcing the Turks away from Belgrade, and overran Serbia. The Treaty of Passarowitz (1718) ceded the rest of Hungary and the great fortress of Belgrade to Austria. The Sultan abdicated in the face of a rebellion of the Janissaries.

Mahmud I (1730 – 1754)

Power was wielded by the chief eunuch in Mahmud's harem, Bashir, an Abyssinian slave who elevated and deposed sixteen grand viziers.

Austria and Russia coalesced to dismember the Turkish Empire. Russia regained Azov in 1737, but Austria was defeated and gave up Belgrade in 1739.

The Janissaries disintegrated as an effective military force when the Sultan began selling the rank of Janissary to anyone willing to pay for it.

Provincial governors also became more independent of the Sultan.

Abdul Hamid I (1774 – 1789)

In the Treaty of Kutchuk-Kainardji (1774) Catherine the Great forced the Turks to surrender the Crimea and to recognize Russia's right to protect Eastern Orthodox Christians in the Balkans.

Russia and Austria declared war on Turkey in 1788 and Austria re-captured Belgrade in 1789.

The Ottoman Empire was no longer an important power in Europe. Competition to take over parts of Eastern Europe, especially the Balkans, was called the "Eastern

Question" in European history and was a causal factor in starting World War I.

CULTURE OF THE BAROQUE AND ROCOCO
Age of the Baroque (1600 – 1750)

The baroque emphasized grandeur, spaciousness, unity, and the emotional impact of a work of art. The splendor of Versailles typifies the baroque in architecture: gigantic frescoes unified around the emotional impact of a single theme is baroque art; the glory of Bach's *Christmas Oratorio* expresses the baroque in music. Art reflects the world-and life-view (*Weltanschauung* – way of looking at the world) that is dominant in a given age. To better understand the 17th and 18th centuries, one needs to see the values, philosophy, and attitude of the age reflected in baroque art, architecture, and music. Although the baroque began in Catholic counter-reformation countries to teach in a concrete, emotional way, it soon spread to Protestant nations as well and some of the greatest baroque artists and composers were Protestant (e.g., Johann Sebastian Bach and George Frideric Handel).

Baroque Architecture

Michelangelo's work provided much of the initial inspiration for baroque architecture. A dynamic and unified treatment of all the elements of architecture combined in the baroque. Oval or elliptical plans were often used in baroque church design. Gianlorenzo Bernini (1598 – 1650) was perhaps the leading early baroque sculptor as well as an architect, and great painter. Bernini's most famous architectural achievement was the colonnade for the piazza in front of St. Peter's Basilica in Rome. Louis XIV brought Bernini to Paris to plan a design for the completion of the palace of the Louvre, but the final design selected was that of Claude Perrault (1613 – 1688).

Louis XIV's magnificent palace at Versailles was particularly the work of Louis LeVau (1612 – 70), and Jules Mansart. The geometric design of the palace included the gardens which excel in symmetry and balance. The many fountains are also typical of the baroque.

Baroque Art

Baroque art concentrated more on broad areas of light and shadow rather than on linear arrangements as in the High Renaissance. Color was an important element because it appealed to the senses and was more true to nature. The baroque was not as concerned with clarity of detail as with the overall dynamic effect. It was designed to give a spontaneous personal experience.

Leaders in baroque painting were Annibale Carracci (1560 – 1609) from Bologna and (Michelangelo Merisi) Caravaggio (1573 – 1610) from near Milan. They are known for the concrete realism of their subjects. Their work is forceful and dramatic with sharp contrasts of light and darkness (*chiaroscuro*).

The Flemish painter Peter Paul Rubens (1577 – 1640) is one of the most famous of baroque artists. He emphasized color and sensuality.

There existed, of course, other types of painting along with the baroque. An example was the school of Italian genre painters known as bamboccianti who painted street scenes of Roman peasant life on a small scale.

Rembrandt Van Rijn (1606 – 1669) the great Dutch painter, was so unique that he could not be considered typically baroque. Nicolas Poussin (1595 – 1665) also followed a different line of reasoning. His paintings were rationally organized to give with precision a total effect of harmony and balance; even his landscapes are orderly.

Baroque Music

A major underlying presupposition of baroque music was that the text should dominate the music rather than the music dominating the text, as was done formerly. The idea that music can depict the situation in the text and express the emotion and drama intended was a major innovation of the baroque period. Instead of writing lyrics appropriate to a musical composition, the lyrics or libretto came first and was determinative in the texture and structure of the composition. Dissonance was used freely to make the music conform to the emotion in the text. Devices of melody, rhythm, harmony, and texture all contribute to emotional effects.

The baroque was a conscious effort to express a wide range of ideas and feelings vividly in music. These were intensified by sharp contrasts in the music and a variety of moods experienced: anger, excitement, exaltation, grandeur, heroism, wonder, a contemplative mood, mystic exaltation.

Bach's "St. Matthew Passion" illustrates this with a frenzied effect of cruelty and chaos obtained by a double chorus of four voices singing, "Crucify him! Crucify Him!" The jubilant Easter Oratorio reflects the triumph of the Resurrection. Violins and violas maintain a steady progression of pizzicato chords to depict the gentle knocking of Christ in the cantata, "Behold I stand at the door and knock...."

The splendor and grandeur of baroque art and architecture was similarly expressed in baroque music. Giovannia Bargieli (1555 – 1612) pioneered this effect when he placed four groups of instruments and choirs, each complete in itself, in the galleries and balconies of St. Mark's Cathedral in Venice. The baroque followed his lead and Bargieli laid the foundation for the modern orchestra.

The concerto, involving interaction between a solo instrument and a full orchestra, was also an innovation of the baroque. Antonio Vivaldi (1678 – 1741) pioneered the concerto and standardized a cycle of three movements. The major-minor key system of tonality was also developed during the baroque period.

The baroque developed a new counterpoint, different from that of the Renaissance. There was still a blending of different melodic lines, but those melodies were subordinated to the harmonic scheme. Bach was particularly successful in balancing harmony and counterpoint and melody with polyphony. George Frideric Handel (1685 – 1759) was a master of baroque grandeur, especially in his dramatic oratorios. He brought to life in his music a poetic depth and his use of the chorus profoundly affected his audiences. Handel was like a painter who was at his best with gigantic frescoes that involved his audience in the whole uplifting experience.

Rococo

Rococo comes from a French word meaning shell or decorative scroll. It describes a tendency towards elegance, pleasantness, and even frivolity. It is in contrast to the impressive grandeur of the baroque. It has a similar decorativeness without the emotional grandeur of the baroque. It is simpler, but not plain. The effect was more sentimental than emotional.

The leader in the Rococo movement was France, and Francois Boucher (1703 – 1770) was one of the most famous French rococo painters. His paintings are elegant, delicate, innocent, and sensual all at the same time, as his paintings of Madame de Pompadour and Diana well illustrate.

Characteristics of the rococo can be found in the compositions of both Franz Josef Haydn (1732 – 1809) and Wolfgang Amadeus Mozart (1759 – 1791).

3 REVOLUTION AND THE NEW EUROPEAN ORDER (1789-1848)

THE FRENCH REVOLUTION I, 1789 – 1799

The shape of the modern world first became visible during ten years of upheaval in France, between the years 1789 and 1799. Radical ideas about society and government were developed during the 18th century in response to the success of the "scientific" and "intellectual" revolutions of the preceding two centuries. Armed with new scientific knowledge of the physical universe, as well as a new view of the human capacity to detect "truth," social critics assailed the existing modes of thought governing political, social, religious and economic life.

Thus, the modern world that came of age in the 18th century was characterized by rapid, revolutionary changes which paved the way for economic modernization and political centralization throughout Europe. The ideas and institutions created by the revolutionaries would be perpetuated and extended by Napoleon Bonaparte, who conquered and converted Europe.

IMPACT OF THE SCIENTIFIC REVOLUTION (C. 1500 – 1700)

The Scientific Revolution revolutionized human thinking about both the physical universe and themselves. This new body of independent, scientific knowledge, based on measuring devices and new methods of observation and interpretation, suggested that humans would understand the operation of the physical world through use of their reason - aided by the modern scientific method of inquiry.

The "scientific method" involved identifying a problem or question, forming an hypothesis (unproven theory), making observations, conducting experiments, interpreting results with mathematics, and drawing conclusions.

Pioneers

Nicolaus Copernicus (1473 – 1543) rejected the geocentric (earth-centered) view of the universe and suggested a heliocentric (sun-centered) view. Thus began the tradition of modern scientific thinking.

Galileo Galilei (1564 – 1642) developed a powerful telescope and confirmed Copernicus' theories.

Tycho Brahe (1546 – 1642) is considered the greatest astronomer of the late 16th century. Having built one of the earliest modern observatories, he kept meticulous celestial observations.

Johannes Kepler (1571 – 1630) used Brahe's observations to prove that a mathematical order existed in the planetary system; he proved mathematically that the planets revolve around the sun.

Isaac Newton (1642 – 1727) discovered the laws of motion, gravity and inertia. By building on earlier discoveries he developed a systematic interpretation of the operation of the universe (Newtonian View of the Universe), wherein natural scientific laws all worked together to provide a clear and comprehensive explanation of the physical universe. After Newton, the scientific method was not solely a matter of theory or observation, but of both. Little wonder then that the poet Alexander Pope could write: "Nature and nature's laws lay hid in the night; God said, Let Newton be! and all was light."

Philosophical Trends

Empiricism (inductive method of reasoning) was advanced by Sir Francis Bacon (1561 – 1626), who believed knowledge was gained through systematic observation of the world and tested by experiment.

Rationalism (deductive method of reasoning) was advanced by René Descartes (1596 – 1650), who rejected the senses as a basis for knowledge and argued that reality could be known only by reasoning from self-evident axiomatic principles: "*Cogito ergo sum*" ("I think, therefore I am").

Consequences

The Scientific Revolution gave birth to the modern scientific community, whose goal was the expansion of knowledge based on modern scientific methods that rejected traditional knowledge.

It likewise convinced many persons that all the complexities of the universe, (including human relations), could be reduced to relatively simple mechanical laws such as those found in the physical universe.

INFLUENCE OF THE ENLIGHTENMENT (C. 1700 – 1800)

The Scientific Revolution gravely undermined the foundation on which the traditional social order of the 18th century rested, by producing a revolution in the world of ideas which seriously challenged the status quo. The enlightenment was a response to economic and political changes at work in European society. It heralded the coming of a new secular society.

The Philosophes: Agents of Change

The new learning was promoted by a relatively small number of thinkers called philosophes — not philosophers in a traditional sense, but rather, social activists for whom knowledge was something to be converted into reform. They were not always original thinkers, but moreso, popularizers of leading reformist thought. The philosophes believed their task was to do for human society what the scientists had done for the physical universe: apply reason to society for the purpose of human improvement, and in the process, discover the natural laws governing God, humans, and society.

While they came from virtually every country in Europe, most of the famous social activists were French. This was probably due to the fact that France was the center of this intellectual revolution.

Voltaire (1694 – 1778), considered the most brilliant and influential of the philosophes, argued for tolerance, reason, limited government and free speech.

Denis Diderot (1713 – 1784) served as editor of the *Encyclopedia*, the bible of the enlightenment period. This twenty-eight volume work was a compendium of all new learning; no self-respecting reformer would be found without a set.

Baron de Montesquieu (1689 – 1756) authored *The Spirit of the Laws* (1748), in which the separation of powers theory was found. Montesquieu believed such a separation would keep any individual, (including the king), or group, (including the nobles), from gaining total control of the government.

Jean Jacques Rousseau (1712 – 1778) wrote *The Social Contract* (1762) in an attempt to discover the origin of society and to propose that the composition of the ideal society was based on a new kind of social contract.

The dissemination of enlightenment thought was largely accomplished through philosophes touring Europe or writing and printing books and essays, the publication of the *Encyclopedia* (1751), and the discussions in the salons of the upper classes. The salons became the social setting for the exchange of ideas, and were usually presided over by prominent women.

Major Assumptions of the Enlightenment

Human progress was possible through change of one's environment; i.e., better people, better societies, better standard of living.

Humans were free to use reason to reform the evils of society.

Material improvement would lead to moral improvement.

Natural science and human reason would discover the meaning of life.

Laws governing human society would be discovered through application of the scientific method of inquiry.

Inhuman practices and institutions would be removed from society in a spirit of humanitarianism.

Human liberty would ensue, as individuals became free to choose what reason dictated, or required, as good.

Enlightenment Effect on Society

Changes or reform must be instituted when institutions cannot demonstrate a rational base of operation.

Religion. Deism or "natural religion" was inaugurated, which rejected traditional Christianity by promoting an impersonal God who does not interfere in the daily lives of the people. The continued discussion of the role of God led to a general skepticism associated with Pierre Bayle (1647 – 1706), a type of religious skepticism pronounced by David Hume (1711 – 1776), and a theory of atheism or materialism advocated by Baron Holbach (1723 – 1789).

Political Theory. John Locke (1632 – 1704) and Jean Jacques Rousseau (1712 – 1778) believed that people were capable of governing themselves, either through a political (Locke), or social (Rousseau), contract forming the basis of society. However, most philosophes opposed democracy, preferring a limited monarchy that shared power with the nobility.

Economic Theory. The assault on mercantilist economic theory was begun by the physiocrats in France, who proposed a "laissez-faire" (non-governmental interference) attitude toward land usage, which culminated in the theory of economic capitalism associated with Adam Smith (1723 – 1790) and his slogans of free trade, free enterprise and the law of supply and demand.

Attempting to break away from the strict control of education by the church and state, Jean Jacques Rousseau advanced the idea of progressive education, where children learn by doing and where self-expression is encouraged. This idea was carried forward by Johann Pestalozzi, Johann Basedow and Friedrich Frobel, and influenced a new view of childhood.

Psychological Theory. In the *Essay Concerning Human Understanding* (1690), John Locke offered the theory that all human knowledge was the result of sensory experience, without any preconceived notions. He believed that the mind at birth was a blank slate (tabula rasa) that registered the experience of the senses passively. According to Locke, since education was critical in determining human development, human progress was in the hands of society.

Gender Theory. The assertion of feminist rights evolved through the emergence of determined women who had been denied access to formal education, yet used their position in society to advance the cause of female emancipation. The enlightenment salons of Madame de Geoffren and Louise de Warens are an example of self-educated women taking their place alongside their male counterparts. One woman fortunate enough to receive education in science was Emilie du Chatelet, an aristocrat trained as a mathematician and physicist. Her scholarship resulted in the translation of Newton's work from Latin into French. The writing of Lady Mary Montagu and Mary Wollstonecraft promoted equal political and educational rights for women. Madame Marie Roland was an heroic figure throughout the early but critical periods of the French Revolution, as she attacked the evils of the Ancient Regime.

Era of "Enlightened Despotism"

Most philosophes believed that human progress and liberty would ensue as absolute rulers became "enlightened." The rulers would still be absolute, but use their power benevolently, as reason dictated. Their reforms were usually directed at increasing their power rather than the welfare of their subjects. Their creed was "Everything for the people, nothing by the people."

Most of the philosophes opposed democracy. According to Voltaire, the best form of government was a monarchy in which the rulers shared the ideas of the philosophes and respected the people's rights. Such an "enlightened" monarch would rule justly and introduce reforms. Voltaire's influence, as well as that of other philosophes, on Europe's monarchs produced the "enlightened despots" who nonetheless failed to bring about lasting political change. Some famous "despots" included Frederick "the Great" of Russia (1740 – 1786), Catherine "the Great" of Russia (1762 – 1796), and Joseph II of Austria (1765 – 1790).

Influence of the American Revolution

The American Revolution acted as a "shining beacon" to Europeans anxious for change, and helped prove that people could govern themselves without the help of monarchs and privileged classes.

France, the center of Enlightenment thought, was particularly vulnerable. Eighteenth-century ideas about the "Rights of Man" and the "Consent of the Governed" were discussed widely in French salons, as well as in the rest of Europe. French reformers believed that their nation was a perfect example of everything wrong with society. Philosophes and their admirers were galvanized into action.

Finally, the concept of revolution was validated as a legitimate means to procure social and political change, when it could not be effected through existing avenues. the The American Revolution, however, was not a radical revolution but a conservative movement: it preserved the existing social order and property rights, and led to a carefully thought-out constitutional system built on stability and continuity.

CAUSES OF THE FRENCH REVOLUTION

Cumulative Discontent with the Ancient Regime

The rising expectations of "enlightened" society were demonstrated in the increased criticism directed toward government inefficiency and corruption, and toward the privileged classes. The social stratification model failed to correspond to the realities of wealth and ability in French society. The clergy (First Estate) and nobility (Second Estate), representing only two percent of the total population of twenty-four million, were the privileged classes and were essentially tax exempt. The remainder of the population (Third Estate) consisted of the middle class, urban workers and the mass of peasants, who all bore the entire burden of taxation and the imposition of feudal obligations. As economic conditions worsened in the 18th century, the French state became poorer, and totally dependent on the poorest and most depressed sections of the economy for support, at the very time this tax base had become saturated.

The mode of absolute government practiced by the Bourbon dynasty was wed to the "Divine Right of Kings" philosophy. This in turn produced a government that was irresponsible and inefficient, with a tax system that was unjust and inequitable, and without any means of redress because of the absence of any meaningful representative assembly. The legal system was chaotic, with no uniform or codified laws.

The economic environment of the 18th century produced a major challenge to the state-controlled French economy (mercantilism), as businessmen and bankers assailed the restrictive features of this economic philosophy. With the growth of new industrial centers and the philosophic development of modern capitalist thought, the middle classes began to assert themselves, demanding that their economic power be made commensurate with political and social power – both of which were denied them. Within France, the estate system allowed the few to monopolize all economic benefits, while the many were "invisible." Thus, an inequitable and inefficient tax system haunted those least able to pay, while the mass of peasants had an additional burden – that of performing feudal obligations for the privileged classes, as well as the payment of outdated feudal taxes and fees.

The intellectual currents of the 18th century were responsible for creating a climate of opposition based on the political theories of John Locke, Jean Rousseau, Baron Montesquieu and other philosophes; the economic ideas of the French physiocrats and Adam Smith (the "Father of Modern Capitalism"); and the general reform-minded direction of the century.

Immediate Cause: Financial Mismanagement

The coming of revolution seemed a paradox in a nation that was one of the largest and richest nations in the world, with a population around twenty-four million and a capital city (Paris) which was considered the crossroads of Enlightenment civilization. Dissatisfaction with the way France was administered reached a critical stage during the reign of King Louis XVI (1774 – 1792).

The deepening public debt was of grave concern, and resulted from (1) the colonial wars with England, 1778 – 1783; (2) French participation in the American War of Independence; (3) maintaining large military and naval establishments; and (4) the extravagant costs of maintaining the Royal Court at Versailles. Unable to secure loans from leading banking houses in Europe (due to poor credit rating), France edged closer to bankruptcy.

Between 1730 and the 1780s, there was an inflationary spiral which increased prices dramatically, while wages failed to adjust accordingly. Government expenses continued to outstrip tax revenues. The "solution" to the debt problem was to either increase the rates of taxation or decree new taxes. The French tax system could not produce the amount of taxes needed to save the government from bankruptcy because of the corruption and inefficiency of the system. The legal system of "*Parlements*" (Courts), controlled by the nobility, blocked tax increases as well as new taxes in order to force the king to share power with the Second Estate.

As France slid into bankruptcy, Louis XVI summoned an Assembly of Notables (1787) in the mistaken hope they would either approve the king's new tax program, or consent to the removal of their exemption from the payment of taxes. They refused to agree to either proposal.

Estates General Summoned

Designed to represent the three estates of France, this ancient feudal body had only met twice, once at its creation in 1302 and again in 1614. When the French parlements insisted that any new taxes must be approved by this body, King Louis XVI reluctantly ordered it to assemble at Versailles by May, 1789. Each estate was expected to elect their own representatives. As a gesture to the size of the Third Estate, the king doubled the number of their representatives. However, the Parlement of Paris decreed that voting in the Estates General would follow "custom and tradition," i.e., by estate unit voting. Therefore the First and Second estates, with similar interests to protect, would control the historic meeting despite the increased size of the Third Estate.

Election fever swept over France for the very first time. The 1788 – 89 election campaign is sometimes considered the precursor of modern politics. Each estate was expected to compile a list of suggestions and complaints called "cahiers" and present them to the king. These lists of grievances emphasized the need for reform of government and civil equality. Campaigning focused on debate and the written word (pamphlets). The most influential writer was the Abbé Siéyès and his pamphlet, "What is the Third Estate?"; the answer was "everything."

The election campaign took place in the midst of the worst subsistence crisis in 18th century France, with widespread grain shortages, poor harvests, and inflated bread prices.

Finally, on May 5, 1789 the Estates General met and was immediately outraged over the voting method, i.e., voting by unit and not per capita. Each estate was ordered to meet and vote separately. The third estate refused and insisted on the entire assembly remaining together.

PHASES OF REVOLUTION

The National Assembly, 1789 – 1791

After a six-week deadlock over voting methods, the Third Estate declared itself the true National Assembly of France (June 17). They were immediately locked out of their meeting place by order of Louis XVI. Instead they assembled in an indoor tennis court, where they swore an oath never to disband until they had given France a constitution (Tennis Court Oath). The third estate had assumed sovereign power on behalf of the nation. Defections from the First and Second Estates then caused the king to recognize the National Assembly (June 27), after dissolving the Estates General. At the same time, Louis XVI ordered troops to surround Versailles.

The "Parisian" revolution began at this point. Angry because of food shortages, unemployment, high prices, and the fear of military repression, the workers and tradesmen began to arm themselves. On July 14 they stormed the ancient fortress of the Bastille in search of weapons. The fall of this hated symbol of royal power gave the revolution its baptism of blood. The king recalled his troops from Versailles. The spirit of rebellion spread to the French countryside, triggered by a wave of rumor and hysteria. A feeling of fear and desperation called "The Great Fear" took hold of the people. They attacked the manor houses, symbols of the upper class wealth, in an effort to destroy the legal records of their feudal obligations. The middle class responded to this lower class violence by forming the National Guard Militia to protect property rights. Hoping to put an end to further violence, the National Assembly voted to abolish feudalism in France and declare the equality of all classes (August 4). A virtual social revolution had taken place peacefully. The assembly then issued a constitutional blueprint, the "Declaration of the Rights of Man and Citizens" (August 26), a guarantee of due process of law and the sovereignty of the people. The National Assembly now proceeded to its twin functions of governing France on a day-to-day basis and writing a constitution.

Among the achievements of the National Assembly were the following:

1) *Secularization of Religion* — Church property was confiscated to pay off the national debt. The Civil Constitution of the Clergy (1790) created a national church with 83 bishops and a like number of dioceses. All clergy were to be democratically elected by the people and have their salaries paid by the state. The practical result was to polarize the nation over the question of religion.

2) *Governmental Reform* — To make the country easier to administer, the Assembly divided the country into 83 departments (replacing the old provincial boundary lines) governed by elected officials. With a new system of law courts, France now had a uniform administrative structure - 83 dioceses, departments and judicial districts.

3) *Constitutional Changes* — Despite a failed attempt by Louis XVI and his family to escape from France (June 20, 1791), to avoid having to approve the Constitution of 1791, the National Assembly completed what may have been its greatest task. They transformed France into a constitutional monarchy with a unicameral Legislative Assembly. Middle class control of the government was assured through an indirect method of voting and property qualifications.

The Legislative Assembly, 1791 – 1792

While the National Assembly had been rather homogeneous in its composition, the new government began to reflect the emergence of political factions in the revolution that were competing for power. The most important political clubs were republican groups, such as the Jacobins (radical urban) and Girondins (moderate rural), while the Sans-culottes (working-class extreme radical) were a separate faction with an economic agenda.

The focus of political activity during the ten-month life of the Legislative Assembly was the question of "war." Influenced by French nobles who had fled France beginning in 1789 (*Émigrés*), the two largest continental powers, Prussia and Austria, issued the Declaration of Pillnitz (August, 1791), declaring the restoration of French monarchy as their goal. With a sharply polarized nation, mounting political and economic chaos, and an unpopular monarch, republican sentiment gained strength, as war against all monarchs was promoted to solve domestic problems. Ideological fervor and anti-Austrian sentiment drove the Legislative Assembly to declare war on Austria (April, 1792). Unprepared, the French revolutionary forces proved no match for the Austrian military. The Jacobins blamed their defeat on Louis XVI, believing him to be part of a conspiracy with Prussia and Austria. Mobs reacted to the threat, made by the invading armies, to destroy Paris (Brunswick Manifesto) if any harm came to the royal family, by seizing power in Paris and imprisoning the king. The Legislative Assembly came under attack and obliged the radicals by suspending the 1791 Constitution, ordering new elections based on universal male suffrage, for the purpose of summoning a national convention to give France a republican form of government.

The National Convention, 1792 – 1795

Meeting for the first time in September, 1792, the Convention abolished monarchy and installed republicanism. Louis XVI was charged with treason, found guilty and executed on January 21, 1793. Later the same year, the queen, Marie Antoinette would meet the same fate.

By the spring of 1793 the new republic was in a state of crisis. England and Spain had joined Austria and Prussia in opposing the revolution. Food shortages and counter-revolution in western France threatened the radicals' grip on the revolution. A power struggle ensued between Girondins and Jacobins, until the Jacobins ousted their political enemy and installed an emergency government to deal with the external and internal challenges to the revolution. A Committee of Public Safety, directed by Maximilien Robespierre, responded to the food shortages and related economic problems by decreeing a planned economy (Law of the Maximum), which would also enable France to urge total war against its external enemies. Lazare Carnot, known as "The Organizer of Victory," was placed in charge of reorganizing the French army. The entire nation was conscripted into service (*Levée en masse*), as war was defined as a national mission.

The most notorious event of the French Revolution was the famous "Reign of Terror" (1793 – 1794), the government's campaign against its internal enemies and counterrevolutionaries. Revolutionary Tribunals were created to hear the cases of accused enemies brought to "justice" under a new Law of Suspects. Approximately 25,000 people throughout France lost their lives. Execution by guillotine became a spectator sport. A new political culture began to emerge, called the "Republic of Virtue." This was Robespierre's grand scheme to de-Christianize France and inculcate revolutionary virtue. The terror spiraled out of control, consuming leading Jacobin leaders (Danton, DesMoulins, and Hébert), until no one could feel secure in the shadow of Robespierre's dictatorship. On July 27, 1794 Robespierre was denounced in the Convention, arrested, and executed the next day, along with his close associate St. Just.

The fall of Robespierre was followed by a dramatic swing to the right called the Thermidorian Reaction (1794). Tired of terror and virtue alike, the moderate bourgeoisie politicians regained control of the National Convention. The Girondins were readmitted. A retreat from the excesses of revolution was begun. A new constitution was written in 1795, which set up a republican form of government. A new Legislative Assembly would choose a five-member executive, the Directory, from which the new regime was to take its name. Before its rule came to an end, the Convention removed all economic controls, which dealt a death blow to the Sans-culottes. Finally, the Convention decreed that, at least for the first two years of operation, the new government reserve two-thirds of the seats in the Legislative Assembly for themselves.

The Directory, 1795 – 1799

The Constitution of 1795 set the tone and style of government in France: voting and holding office was reserved to property owners. The middle class was in control. They wanted peace in order to gain more wealth, and to establish a society in which money and property would become the only requirements for prestige and power. These goals confronted opposition groups such as the aristocracy, who in October, 1795, attempted a royalist uprising. It might have succeeded were it not for the young Napoleon Bonaparte, who happened to be in Paris at the time and loyally helped the government put down the rebellion. The Sans-culottes repeatedly attacked the government and its economic philosophy but, leaderless and powerless, they were doomed to failure. Despite growing inflation and mass public dissatisfaction, the Directory government ignored a growing shift in public opinion. When elections in April, 1797 produced a triumph for the royalist right, the results were annulled and the Directory shed its last pretense of legitimacy.

Military success overshadowed the weak and corrupt Directory government.

French armies annexed the Austrian Netherlands, the left bank of the Rhine, Nice and Savoy. The Dutch republic was made a satellite state of France. The greatest military victories were won by Napoleon Bonaparte, who drove the Austrians out of northern Italy and forced them to sign the Treaty of Campo Formio (October, 1797) in return for which the Directory government agreed to Bonaparte's scheme to conquer Egypt and threaten English interests in the East.

The Directory government managed to hang on for two more years, thanks to the military successes. But a steady loss of support continued in the face of a government that was bankrupt, filled with corruption and unwilling to halt an inflationary spiral that was aggravating the already impoverished masses of French peasants. The spirit of revolution was being crushed in the land, and this fear gave rise to a conspiracy to save the Revolution and forestall a royalist return to power. Led by the famous revolutionary, the Abbé Siéyès, Napoleon Bonaparte was invited to join the conspirators, which he did upon returning from Egypt. On November 9, 1799, they ousted the Directory. The conspirators quickly promulgated a new constitution which established the Consulate Era.

European Reaction to the Events of 1789 – 1799

Liberals and radicals hailed the birth of liberty and freedom. Among those who explicitly defended the French Revolution were the German philosophers Immanuel Kant and Johann Fichte, the English scientist Joseph Priestly, and the American pamphleteer Tom Paine. Not all reaction was favorable. Conservatives predicted that societal anarchy would ensue everywhere if the French revolutionaries succeeded. Friedrich Von Gentz' and Edmund Burke's, 1790 "Reflections on the Revolution in France" remains to this day the classic statement of the conservative view of history. It was the romantic poet William Wordsworth who captured the sense of liberation and limitless hope inspired by the French Revolution:

"Bliss it was in that dawn to be alive
   But to be young was very heaven."

Results

The first ten years of revolution in France destroyed the old social system replaced it with a new one based on equality, ability and the law; guaranteed the triumph of capitalist society; gave birth to the notion of secular democracy; laid the foundations for the establishment of the modern nation-state; and gave the great mass of the human race what it had never had before except from religion: hope.

THE FRENCH REVOLUTION II: THE ERA OF NAPOLEON, 1799–1815

After the first ten years of revolution, the 1799 shift to a new group in power did not prepare anyone in France for the most dramatic changes that would distinguish this era from the changes of government of the past ten years. France was about to be mastered by a legendary "giant" and Europe overwhelmed by a mythical titan.

Background of Napoleon's Life

Napoleon was born of Italian descent on the island of Corsica, August 15, 1769 to a prominent Corsican family one year after France annexed the island. He pursued a military career while advocating Corsican independence. He associated with Jacobins and advanced rapidly in the army when vacancies were caused by the emigration of aristocratic officers. His first marriage was to Josephine de Beauharnais, who was divorced by Napoleon after a childless marriage. In 1810 Napoleon arranged a marriage of state with Marie Louise, daughter of the Austrian emperor. Their son was known as Napoleon II, "King of Rome."

Napoleon was a military genius whose specialty was artillery. He was also a charismatic leader with the nationalist's clarity of mind and the romantic's urge for action. Napoleon galvanized a dispirited, divided country into a unified and purposeful nation at the price of individual liberty.

Role in Directory Government, 1795 – 1799

In 1793 Napoleon was responsible for breaking the British siege of Toulon. Because of his loyalty to the revolution, he was made Commander of the Army of the Interior, after saving the new Directory government from being overthrown by a Parisian mob in 1795. He was selected to lead an army into Italy in the Campaign of 1796, against the First Coalition (1792 – 97), where he defeated the Austrians and Sardinians and imposed the Treaty of Campo Formio (1797) on Austria, effectively ending the First Coalition. England was thereby isolated.

The election results of 1797 forced the Directory government to abandon the wishes of the country and establish a dictatorship of those favorable to the revolution ("Post-Fructidorian Terror"). After defending the government, Napoleon launched his invasion of Egypt (1798), only to have his navy destroyed by England's Lord Nelson at the Battle of the Nile. Napoleon and the French army were isolated in North Africa.

Popular indignation against the Directory government, along with financial disorder and military losses, produced a crisis atmosphere in France. Fearing a return to monarchy, a group of conspirators headed by the Abbé Siéyès decided to save the revolution by overthrowing the Directory. Napoleon was invited to furnish the armed power, and his name, to the takeover (Coup d'État Brumaire, November 9, 1799).

Consulate Period, 1799 – 1804 (Enlightened Reform)

The new government was installed on December 25, 1799 with a constitution which concentrated supreme power in the hands of Napoleon.

Executive power was vested in three consuls, but the First Consul (Napoleon) behaved more as an enlightened despot than revolutionary statesman. His aim was to govern France by demanding obedience, rewarding ability and organizing everything in orderly hierarchical fashion.

Napoleon's domestic reforms and policies affected every aspect of society and had an enduring impact on French history. Among the features were the following:

1) strong central government and administrative unity;

2) religious unity (Concordat of 1801 with the Roman Catholic Church);

3) financial unity (Bank of France), emphasizing balanced budget and rigid economy in government;

4) economic reform to stimulate the economy, provide food at low prices, increase employment and allow peasants to keep the land they had secured during the revolution; and

5) educational reforms based on a system of public education under state control (University of France).

The Legal Unity provided the first clear and complete codification of French law (Code Napoleon), which made permanent many of the achievements of the French Revolution. It stipulated equality before the law, freedom of conscience, property rights, abolition of serfdom, and the secular character of the state. Its major regressive provisions denied women equal status with men, and denied true political liberty.

Thus, in the tradition of enlightened despotism, Napoleon repressed liberty, subverted republicanism and restored absolutism to France.

Empire Period, 1804 – 1814 (War and Defeat)

After being made Consul for Life (1801), Napoleon felt that only through an Empire could France retain its position and relate to other European states. On December 2, 1804, Napoleon crowned himself Emperor of France in Notre-Dame Cathedral.

Militarism and Empire Building

Beginning in 1805 Napoleon engaged in constant warfare that placed French troops in enemy capitals from Lisbon and Madrid to Berlin and Moscow, and temporarily gave Napoleon the largest empire since Roman times. Napoleon's Grand Empire consisted of an enlarged France and satellite kingdoms, as well as coerced allies.

The military campaigns of the Napoleonic Years included the War of the Second Coalition (1798–1801), the War of the Third Coalition (1805 – 1807), the Peninsular War (1808 – 1814), the "War of Liberation" (1809), the Russian Campaign (1812), the War of the Fourth Coalition (1813 – 1814), and the Hundred Days (March 20 – June 22, 1815)

French-ruled subject peoples viewed Napoleon as a tyrant who repressed and exploited them for France's glory and advantage. Enlightened reformers believed Napoleon had betrayed the ideals of the Revolution.

The downfall of Napoleon resulted from his inability to conquer England; economic distress caused by the Continental System (boycott of British goods); the Peninsular War with Spain; the German War of Liberation; and the Invasion of Russia.

The actual defeat of Napoleon was the result of the Fourth Coalition and the Battle of Leipzig ("Battle of Nations"). Napoleon was exiled to the island of Elba as a sovereign with an income from France.

After learning of allied disharmony at the Vienna peace talks, Napoleon left Elba and began the "Hundred Days" by seizing power from the restored French king, Louis XVIII.

Napoleon's gamble ended at Waterloo in June 1815. He was now exiled as a prisoner of war to the South Atlantic island of St. Helena, where he died in 1821.

Evaluation

The significance of the Napoleonic era lies in the fact that it produced the first egalitarian dictatorship of modern times. Although Napoleon ruled France for only fifteen years, his impact had lasting consequences on French and world history. He consolidated revolutionary institutions. He thoroughly centralized the French government. He made a lasting settlement with the Church. He also spread the positive achievements of the French Revolution to the rest of the world.

Napoleon also repressed liberty, subverted republicanism, oppressed conquered peoples, and caused terrible suffering.

The Napoleonic Legend, based on the personal memoirs of Napoleon, suggest an attempt by Napoleon to rewrite history by interpreting past events in a positive light.

THE POST-WAR SETTLEMENT:
THE CONGRESS OF VIENNA, 1814 – 1815

The Congress of Vienna met in 1814 and 1815 to redraw the map of Europe after the Napoleonic era, and to provide some way of preserving the future peace of Europe. While Europe was spared a general war throughout the remainder of the 19th century, the failure of the statesmen who shaped the future in 1814–1815 to recognize the forces unleashed by the French Revolution, such as nationalism and liberalism only postponed the ultimate confrontation between two views of the world: change and accommodation, or maintaining the status quo.

The "Big Four"

The Vienna settlement was the work of the representatives of the four nations that had done the most to defeat Napoleon: England, Austria, Russia and Prussia.

Prince Klemens Von Metternich, who represented Austria, epitomized conservative reactionism. He resisted change, and was generally unfavorable to ideas of liberals and reformers because of the impact such forces would have on the multinational Hapsburg Empire.

Lord Castlereagh was England's representative. His principal objective was to achieve a balance of power on the continent by surrounding France with larger and stronger states.

Karl Von Hardenberg, as chancellor, represented Prussia. His goal was to recover Prussian territory lost to Napoleon in 1807 and gain additional territory in northern Germany (Saxony).

Czar Alexander I represented Russia. He was a mercurial figure who vacillated between liberal and reactionary views. The one specific "non-negotiable" goal he advanced was a "free" and "independent" Poland, with himself as its king.

While Perigord Talleyrand, the French Foreign Minister, was not initially included in the early deliberations, he became a mediator where the interests of Prussia and Russia clashed with those of England and Austria. He thereby brought France into the ranks of the principal powers.

The "Dancing Congress"

This European gathering was held amid much pageantry. Parties, balls, and banquets reminded the delegates what life had been like before 1789. This was intended to generate favorable "public opinion" and occupy the delegates, since they had little to do of any serious nature.

Principles of Settlement: Legitimacy, Compensation, Balance of Power

"Legitimacy" meant returning to power the ruling families deposed by more than two decades of revolutionary warfare. Bourbon rulers were restored in France, Spain and Naples. Dynasties were restored in Holland, Sardinia, Tuscany and Modena. Papal States were returned to the Pope.

"Compensation" meant territorially rewarding those states which had made considerable sacrifices to defeat Napoleon. England received far-flung naval bases (Malta, Ceylon, Cape of Good Hope). Austria recovered the Italian province of Lombardy and was awarded adjacent Venetia as well as Galicia (from Poland), and the Illyrian Provinces along the Adriatic. Russia was given most of Poland, with the Czar as King, as well as Finland and Bessarabia. Prussia was awarded the Rhineland, three-fifths of Saxony and part of Poland. Sweden was given Norway.

"Balance of Power" meant arranging the map of Europe so that never again could one state (like France) upset the international order and cause a general war.

Encirclement of France was achieved through the following: a strengthened Netherlands, by uniting Belgium (Austrian Netherlands) to Holland to form the Kingdom of the United Netherlands, a much larger state north of France; Prussia receiving Rhenish lands bordering on the eastern French frontier; Switzerland receiving a guarantee of perpetual neutrality; enhancing Austrian influence over the Germanies by creating the German Confederation (Bund) of thirty-nine states, with Austria designated as President of the Diet (Assembly) of the Confederation; and Sardinia having its former territory restored, with the addition of Genoa.

Enforcement Provisions (Concert of Europe)

Arrangements to guarantee the enforcement of the status quo as defined by the Vienna settlement now included two provisions. The "Holy Alliance" of Czar Alexander I of Russia, which was an idealistic and unpractical plan, existed only on paper. No one except Alexander took it seriously. The "Quadruple Alliance" of Russia, Prussia, Austria and England provided for concerted action to arrest any threat to the peace or balance of power.

England defined concerted action as the great powers meeting in "Congress" to solve each problem as it arose, so that no state would act unilaterally and independently of the other great powers. France was always believed to be the possible violator of the Vienna settlement.

Austria believed concerted action meant the great powers defending the status quo as established at Vienna against any change or threat to the system. Thus, liberal or nationalist agitation was unhealthy for the body politic.

Congress System

From 1815 to 1822, European international relations were controlled by the series of meetings held by the great powers to monitor and defend the status quo: the Congress of Aix-la-Chapelle (1818); the Congress of Troppau (1820); the Congress of Laibach (1821); and the Congress of Verona (1822).

The principle of collective security required unanimity among members of the Quadruple Alliance. The history of the Congress System points to the ultimate failure of this key provision in light of the serious challenges to the status quo after 1815

Evaluation

The Congress of Vienna has been criticized for ignoring the liberal and nationalist aspirations of so many peoples. Hindsight suggests the statesmen at Vienna may have been more successful in stabilizing the international system than we have been able to do in the 20th century. Not until the unification of Germany in 1870 – 71 was the balance of power upset; not until World War I in 1914 did Europe have another general war. But hindsight also instructs us that the leading statesmen at Vienna underestimated the new nationalism generated by the French Revolution, that they did not understand the change that citizen armies and national wars had effected among people in their attitude toward political problems. The men at Vienna in 1815 underestimated the growing liberalism of the age and failed to see that an industrial revolution was beginning to create a new alignment of social classes and to create new needs and issues.

THE INDUSTRIAL REVOLUTION

In the late 19th century the English historian Arnold Toynbee began to refer to the period since 1750 as "The Industrial Revolution." The term was intended to describe a time of transition when machines began to significantly displace human and animal power in methods of producing and distributing goods.

These changes began slowly, almost imperceptibly, gaining momentum with each decade, so that by the midpoint of the 19th century, industrialism had swept across Europe west to east, from England to eastern Europe. Few countries purposely avoided industrialization because of its promise of material improvement and national wealth.

The economic changes that constitute the "Industrial Revolution" have done more than any other movement in Western civilization to revolutionize Western life, by imparting to our cultures a uniqueness which never before, or perhaps since, has been matched or duplicated.

England Begins the Revolution in Energy and Industry

Essentially, the "Industrial Revolution" describes a process of economic change from an agricultural and commercial society into a modern industrial society. This was a gradual process, where economic, social and political changes nonetheless produced a veritable revolution, which Arnold Toynbee was the first to identify. He placed the origins of this remarkable transition in England.

Roots of the Industrial Revolution could be found in the following: 1) the Commercial Revolution (1500 – 1700), which spurred the great economic growth of Europe brought about by the Age of Discovery and Exploration, which in turn helped to solidify the economic doctrines of mercantilism; 2) the effect of the Scientific Revolution, which produced the first wave of mechanical inventions and technological advances; 3) the increase in population in Europe from 140 million people in 1750 to 266 million people by the mid-part of the 19th century (more producers, more consumers); and 4) the political and social revolutions of the 19th century, which began the rise to power of the "middle class", and provided leadership for the economic revolution.

England began the economic transformation by employing her unique assets:

1) a supply of cheap labor, as the result of the enclosure movement which created unemployment among the farmers (yeomen); those former agricultural laborers were now available for hire in the new industrial towns;

2) a good supply of coal and iron, both indispensable for the technological and energy development of the "revolution";

3) the availability of large supplies of capital from profitable commercial activity in the preceding centuries, ready to be invested in new enterprises;

4) a class of inventive people who possessed technological skill and whose independence and non-conformity allowed them to take risks;

5) as a colonial and maritime power, England had access to the raw materials needed for the development of many industries;

6) England had a government which was sympathetic to industrial development and well-established financial institutions ready to make loans available; and

7) after a long series of successful wars, England was undevastated and free to develop its new industries, which prospered because of the economic dislocations caused by the Napoleonic Wars.

Early Progress

The revolution occurred first in the cotton and metallurgical industries, because those industries lent themselves to mechanization.

A series of mechanical inventions beginning in 1733 and, lasting until 1793, would enable the cotton industry to mass- produce quality goods.

The need to replace wood as an energy source led to the use of coal, which increased coal mining and resulted ultimately in the invention of the steam engine and the locomotive as inventions which sought to solve practical problems.

The development of steam power allowed the cotton industry to expand and transformed the iron industry. The factory system, which had been created in response to the new energy sources and machinery, was perfected to increase the amount of manufactured goods.

A transportation revolution ensued, in order to distribute the productivity of machinery as well as deliver raw materials to the eager factories. This led to the growth of canal systems, the construction of hard-surfaced "macadam" roads, the commercial use of the steamboat demonstrated by Robert Fulton, and the railway locomotive made commercially successful by George Stephenson.

Subsequent revolution in agriculture made it possible for fewer people to feed humankind, thus freeing people to work in factories or in the many new fields of communications, distribution of goods, or services like teaching, medicine and entertainment.

Spread of Industrialization to Europe and the World

During the first fifty years of the 19th century, industrialism swept across Europe west to east, from England to eastern Europe. In its wake, all modes of life would be challenged and transformed.

The Challenges to the Spread of Industrialism

Continental economic growth had been retarded by the wars of the Napoleonic period.

Because England was so technically advanced, European countries found it difficult to compete. However, catching up to England was made easy by avoiding the costly mistakes of early British experiments and by using the power of strong central governments and banking systems to promote native industry. But on the continent there was no large labor supply in cities; iron and coal deposits were not as concentrated as in England.

Route of Industrialization

England was the undisputed economic and industrial leader until the mid-19th century. The industrialization of the continent occurred mostly in the latter half of the 19th century, and, in the southern and eastern regions, in the 20th century.

By 1830 industrialism had begun to spread from England to Belgium, France and other scattered areas of Europe. These successful industrial operations were due to the exportation from England of machines, management and capital. Germany was slower in following English methods until a tariff policy was established in 1834 (the *Zollverein*), which induced capital investment in German manufacturers.

Growth of Industrial Society

The undermining and eventual elimination of Western society's traditional social stratification model (i.e., clergy, nobility and the masses) would be the result of the Industrial Revolution.

The Bourgeoisie: The New Aristocracy

The middle class were the major contributors as well as the principal beneficiaries of early industrialism. They measured success in monetary terms and most tended to be indifferent to the human suffering of the new wage-earning class. The industrial bourgeoisie had two levels: 1) upper bourgeoisie, i.e., great bankers, merchants and industrialists who demanded free enterprise and high tariffs; and, 2) lower bourgeoisie, i.e., small industrialists, merchants and professional men who demanded stability and security from government.

The Factory Worker: The New Wage-Earning Class

The Industrial Revolution created a unique new category of people who were dependent on their job alone for income, a job from which they might be dismissed without cause. The factory worker had no land, no home, no source of income but his job. During the first century of the Industrial Revolution the factory worker was completely at the mercy of the law of supply and demand for labor.

Working in the factory meant more self-discipline and less personal freedom for workers. The system tended to depersonalize society and reduced workers to an impersonal status. The statistics with regard to wages, diet, and clothing suggest overall improvement for the workers, with some qualifications, since some industries were notoriously guilty of social injustices. Contemporary social critics complained that industrialism brought misery to the workers, while others claimed life was improving. Until 1850 workers as a whole did not share in the general wealth produced by the Industrial Revolution. Conditions would improve as the century wore on, as union action combined with general prosperity and a developing social conscience, to improve the working conditions, wages, and hours first of skilled labor, and later of unskilled labor.

Social Effects of Industrialization

The most important sociological result of industrialism was the urbanization of the world. The new factories acted as a magnet, pulling people away from their rural roots and beginning the most massive population transfer in history. Thus the birth of factory towns and cities that grew into large industrial centers.

The role of the city changed in the 19th century from governmental and cultural centers, to industrial centers with all the problems of urbanization.

Workers in cities became aware of their numbers and their common problems, so cities made the working class a powerful force by raising their consciousness and enabling them to unite for political action, to remedy their economic dissatisfaction.

It is in this urban setting that the century's great social and political dilemmas were framed: working class injustices, gender exploitation and standard-of-living issues.

Family structure and gender roles within the family were altered by the growth of industrialism. Families as an economic unit were no longer the chief unit of both production and consumption, but rather, consumption alone.

New wage economy meant that families were less closely bound together than in the past; the economic link was broken. Productive work was taken out of the home (cottage) and placed elsewhere. As factory wages for skilled adult males rose, women and children were separated from the workplace. A new pattern of family life emerged.

Gender-determined roles in the home and domestic life emerged slowly. Married women came to be associated with domestic duties ,while the male tended to be the sole wage earner.

Single women and widows had much work available, but that work commanded low wages and low skills and provided no way to protect themselves from exploitation.

Marriage as an institution in the wage economy began to change. Women were now expected to create a nurturing environment to which the family members returned after work. Married women worked outside the home only when family needs, illness or death of a spouse required them to do so.

Evaluation

The Industrial Revolution conquered and harnessed the forces of nature: water power, coal, oil, and electricity all provided power to replace human effort. The amount of wealth available for human consumption increased. Vast amounts of food, clothing and energy were produced and distributed to the workers of the world. Luxuries were made commonplace, life expectancy increased and leisure time was made more enjoyable.

But the workers would not begin to share in this dramatic increase in the standard of living until the second half of the 19th century, when all the evils associated with the factory system (low wages, poor working conditions, etc.) and early industrialism in general were corrected. In the first century of industrialism the wealth created went almost exclusively to the entrepreneur and the owner of capital—the middle class.

IMPACT OF THOUGHT SYSTEMS (ISMS) ON THE EUROPEAN WORLD

The mind set of Western civilization was being challenged in the first half of the 19th century by the appearance of numerous new thought systems. Not since the 18th century Enlightenment had humans sought to catalog, classify and categorize their thoughts and beliefs. Several of these systems of thought acted as change agents throughout the 19th century, while others would flow into the 20th century and continue to define the modern world.

Romanticism

Romanticism was a reaction against the rigid classicism, rationalism and deism of the 18th century. Strongest in application between 1800 and 1850, the romantic movement differed from country to country and from romanticist to romanticist. Because it emphasized change it was considered revolutionary in all aspects of life. It was an atmosphere in which events occurred and came to affect not only the way humans thought and expressed themselves, but also the way they lived socially and politically.

Characteristics

Romanticism appealed to emotion rather than to reason (i.e., truth and virtue can be found just as surely by the heart as by the head), and rejected classical emphasis on order and the observance of rules (i.e., let the imagination create new cultural forms and techniques).

It also rejected the enlightenment view of nature as a precise harmonious whole (i.e., viewed nature as alive, vital, changing and filled with the divine spirit), as well as the cold impersonal religion of Deism (i.e., viewed God as inspiring human nobility;

deplored decline of Christianity).

Romanticism further rejected the Enlightenment point of view of the past, which was counter-progressive to human history (i.e., viewed the world as an organism that was growing and changing with each nation's history unique), and expressed vital optimism about life and the future.

Romantics enriched European cultural life by encouraging personal freedom and flexibility. By emphasizing feeling, humanitarian movements were created to fight slavery, poverty and industrial evils.

Romantic Literature, Art, Music, and Philosophy

English romantics like Wordsworth and Coleridge epitomized the romantic movement, along with Burns, Byron, Shelley, Keats, Tennyson, Browning and Scott. The greatest German figures were Goethe, Schiller, Heine and Herder. French romantics were Hugo, Balzac, Dumas and Stendahl. The outstanding Russian exponents were Pushkin, Dostoevski and Turgenev. Among the greatest American figures were Longfellow, Cooper, Irving, Emerson, Poe, Whitman and Thoreau.

The leading romantic painters in popular taste were the Frenchmen Millet and David, the Englishmen Turner and Constable, and the Spaniard Goya. Gothic Revival Style marked the Romantic era in architecture.

Music did not change as dramatically as did literature. Classical forms were still observed, but new ideas and innovations were increasing. Beethoven was a crossover, while straight romantics would include Brahms, Schumann, Schubert, Berlioz, Chopin and Von Weber.

Romantic philosophy stimulated an interest in Idealism, the belief that reality consists of ideas, as opposed to materialism. This school of thought (Philosophical Idealism), founded by Plato, was developed through the writings of 1) Immanuel Kant whose work, *Critique of Pure Reason*, advances the theory that reality was two-fold — physical and spiritual. Reason can discover what is true in the physical, but not in the spiritual, world; 2) Johann Gottlieb Fichte, a disciple of Kant, and Friedrich Schelling, collaborator of Fichte; and, 3) Georg Wilhelm Hegel, the greatest exponent of this school of thought. Hegel believed that an impersonal God rules the universe and guides humans along a progressive evolutionary course by means of process called dialecticism; this is an historical process by which one thing is constantly reacting with its opposite (the thesis and antithesis), producing a result (synthesis), that automatically meets another opposite and continues the series of reactions. Hegel's philosophy exerted a great influence over Karl Marx who turned the Hegelian dialectic upside down to demonstrate that the ultimate meaning of reality was a material end, not a higher or spiritual end, as Hegel suggested.

Impact

Romanticism destroyed the clear simplicity and unity of thought which characterized the 18th century. There was no longer one philosophy which expressed all the aims and ideals of Western civilization. Romanticism provided a more complex, but truer, view of the real world.

Conservatism

Conservatism arose in reaction to liberalism and became a popular alternative for those who were frightened by the violence, terror and social disorder unleashed by the French Revolution. Early conservatism was allied to the restored monarchical governments of Austria, Russia, France and England. Support for conservatism came from the traditional ruling classes, as well as the peasants who still formed the majority of the population. Intellectual ammunition came from the pens of the Englishman Edmund Burke; the Frenchmen, Joseph de Maistre and Louis de Bonald; the Austrian Friedrich Gentz; and many of the early romantics. In essence, conservatives believed in order, society and the state; faith and tradition.

Characteristics

Conservatives viewed history as a continuum which no single generation can revoke.

Conservatives believed the basis of society was organic, not contractual. Society was not a machine with replaceable parts. Stability and longevity, not progress and change, mark a good society.

The only legitimate sources of political authority were God and history. The social contract theory was rejected because a contract cannot make authority legitimate.

Investing society with the theory of individualism ignored humans as social beings and undermined the concept of community, which was essential to life. Conservatives said self-interest does not lead to social harmony, but to social conflict.

Conservatives argued that measuring happiness and progress in material terms ignored humans as spiritual beings.

Conservatives rejected the philosophy of natural rights and believed that rights did not pertain to people everywhere, but were determined and allocated by a particular state.

With its exaggerated emphasis on reason and intellect, the conservatives denounced the philosophes and reformers for ignoring each human as an emotional being and for underestimating the complexity of human nature.

To conservatives, society was hierarchical, i.e., some humans were better able to rule and lead than those who were denied intelligence, education, wealth and birth.

Impact

Conservatism was basically "anti-" in its propositions. It never had a feasible program of its own. The object of their hatred was a liberal society which they claimed was antisocial and morally degrading. While their criticisms contained much justification, conservatives ignored the positive and promising features of liberal society. Conservative criticism did poke holes in liberal ideology, and pointed toward a new social tyranny, the aggressive middle class.

Liberalism

The theory of liberalism was the first major theory in the history of Western thought to teach that the individual is a self-sufficient being, whose freedom and well-being are the sole reasons for the existence of society. Liberalism was more closely connected to the spirit and outlook of the enlightenment than to any of the other "isms" of the early 19th century. While the general principles and attitudes associated with liberalism varied considerably from country to country, liberals tended to come from the middle class or bourgeoisie, and favored increased liberty for their class and indirectly, for the masses of people, as long as the latter did not in their turn ask for so much freedom that they endangered the security of the middle class. Liberalism was reformist and political rather than revolutionary in character.

Characteristics

Individuals are entitled to seek their freedom in the face of arbitrary or tyrannical restrictions imposed upon them.

Humans have certain natural rights and governments should protect them. These rights include the right to own property, freedom of speech, freedom from excessive punishment, freedom of worship, and freedom of assembly.

These rights are best guaranteed by a written constitution, with careful definition of the limits to which governmental actions may go. Examples include the American Declaration of Independence (1776) and the French Declaration of Rights of man (1789).

Another view of liberalism was presented by individuals who came to be known as the utilitarians. Their founder, Jeremy Bentham, held the pleasure-pain principle as the key idea – that humans are ordained to avoid pain and to seek pleasure.

Bentham equated pleasure with good and pain with evil. The goodness or badness of any act, individual or public, was found by balancing the pleasure against the pain it caused. Thus one came to test the utility of any proposed law or institution, i.e., "the greatest happiness of the greatest number."

Liberals advocated economic individualism (i.e., laissez-faire capitalism), heralded by Adam Smith in his 1776 economic masterpiece, *Wealth of Nations*. They regarded free enterprise as the most productive economy, and the one that allowed for the greatest measure of individual choice.

Economic inequality will exist and is acceptable, liberals held, because it does not detract from the individual's moral dignity, nor does it conflict with equality of opportunity and equality before the law.

Economic liberalism claimed to be based on the realities of a new industrial era. The "classical economists" (Thomas Malthus and David Ricardo) taught that there were inescapable forces at work – competition, the pressure of population growth, the iron law of wages, and the law of supply and demand – in accordance with which economic life must function. It was the duty of government to remove any obstacle to the smooth operation of these natural forces.

Internationally, liberals believed in the balance-of-power system and free trade because each track allowed individual nations the opportunity to determine its own course of action.

Liberals believed in the pluralistic society as long as it did not block progress. War and revolutionary change disrupt progress and enlarge the power of government.

Education was an indispensable prerequisite to individual responsibility and self-government.

Early 19th Century Advocates of Liberalism

In England, advocates included the political economists, the utilitarians and individuals like Thomas Robington Macaulay and John Stuart Mill; in France, Benjamin Constant, Victor Cousin, Jean Baptiste Say and Alexis de Tocqueville; in Germany, Wilhelm von Humboldt, Friedrich List, Karl von Rotteck and Karl Theodor Welcker.

Impact

Liberalism was involved in the various revolutionary movements of the early 19th century. It found concrete expression in over ten constitutions secured between 1815 and 1848 in states of the German Confederation. Its power was demonstrated in the reform measures that successive British governments adopted during these same decades. It affected German student organizations and permeated Prussian life.

Alexis de Toqueville spoke for many liberals when he warned against the masses' passion for equality, and their willingness to sacrifice political liberty in order to improve their material well-being. These fears were not without foundation. In the 20th century, the masses have sometimes shown themselves willing to trade freedom for authority, order, economic security and national power.

Nationalism

The regenerative force of liberal thought in early 19th century Europe was dramatically revealed in the explosive force of the power of nationalism. Raising the level of consciousness of people having a common language, a common soil, common traditions, a common history, a common culture and a shared human experience, to seek political unity around an identity of what or who constitutes the nation, was aroused and made militant during the turbulent French Revolutionary era.

Characteristics

Early nationalist sentiment was romantic, exuberant and cosmopolitan, as compared to the more intense, hate-filled nationalism of the latter half of the 19th century.

The breakdown of society's traditional loyalties to church, dynastic state and region began during the course of the 18th century. Impelled by the French Revolutionary dogma, new loyalties were fashioned — that people possessed the supreme power (sovereignty) of the nation and were, therefore, the true nation united by common language, culture, history, etc. Only then would people develop the sense of pride, tradition and common purpose which would come to characterize modern nationalism.

Nationalism, as loyalty to one's nation, did not originate in the early 19th century. Men and women have been fighting for, and living and dying for, their respective countries for hundreds of years. It wasn't until the early 19th century that this feeling and motivation changed into something far more intense and far more demanding than it had been. The focus of the loyalty changed from dynastic self-interest, to individual self-interest as part of a greater collective consciousness.

Impact

Nationalistic thinkers and writers examined the language, literature and folkways of their people, thereby stimulating nationalist feelings. Emphasizing the history and culture of the various European peoples tended to reinforce and glorify national sentiment.

Most early 19th century nationalist leaders adopted the ideas of the German philosopher-historian Johann Gottfried Herder (1744 – 1803), who is regarded as the father of modern nationalism.

Herder taught that every people is unique and possesses a distinct national character, or *Volksgeist*, which has evolved over many centuries. No one culture or people is superior to any other. All national groups are parts of that greater whole which is humanity.

Herder's doctrine of the indestructible *Volksgeist* led to a belief that every nation has the right to become a sovereign state encompassing all members of the same nationality. Since most Western states contained people of many different nationalities, and few states contained all the members of any one nationality, nationalism came to imply the overthrow of almost every existing government.

Evaluation

Because of its inherently revolutionary implications, nationalism was suppressed by the established authorities. Yet it flourished in Germany, where conservative and reactionary nationalists competed with a somewhat more liberal form of nationalism associated with intellectuals like Fichte, Hegel, Humboldt and Von Ranke. In Eastern Europe, conservative nationalists stressed the value of their own unique customs, culture and folkways, while Western European nationalists demanded liberal political reforms. The influence of the Italian Nationalist Mazzini and the Frenchman Michelet in stimulating nationalist feeling in the West was a key ingredient.

It should be noted that there was always a fundamental conflict between liberalism and nationalism. Liberals were rationalists who demanded objectivity in studying society and history, while nationalists relied on emotion and would do anything to exalt the nation, even subvert individual rights. By the late 19th century nationalism was promoting competition and warfare between peoples and threatening to douse liberal ideas of reason and freedom.

Socialism

With the chief beneficiaries of industrialism being the new middle class, the increasing misery of the working classes disturbed the conscience of concerned liberal thinkers (Bentham and Mill), who proposed a modification of the concept of laissez-faire economics. Other socially concerned thinkers, observing the injustices and inefficiencies of capitalistic society, began to define the social question in terms of human equality and the means to be followed in order to secure this goal. As cures for the social evils of industrialism were laid out in elaborate detail, the emerging dogma came to be called socialism.

Characteristics

Since biblical times humans have been concerned with the problem of social justice, but it was not until the 19th century that it possessed a broader intellectual base and a greater popular support than it had ever enjoyed in the past. The difficulty with the existing system, according to social critics of the day, was that it permitted wealth to be concentrated in the hands of a small group of persons and deprived the working classes of a just share in what was rightfully theirs. A social mechanism had to be developed so a just distribution of society's wealth could be attained. The result was a variety of approaches.

The Utopian Socialists (from *Utopia*, Saint Thomas More's book on a fictional ideal society) were the earliest writers to propose an equitable solution to improve the distribution of society's wealth. While they endorsed the productive capacity of industrialism, they denounced its mismanagement. Human society was to be organized as a community rather than a mixture of competing, selfish individuals. All the goods a person needed could be produced in one community.

Generally, the utopians advocated some kind of harmonious society, some form of model communities, social workshops or the like, where the ruthless qualities of an individualistic capitalism would disappear.

Utopian ideas were generally regarded as idealistic and visionary, with no practical application. With little popular support from either the political establishment or the working classes, the movement failed to produce any substantial solution to the social question. Leading Utopian thinkers included Henri de Saint-Simon (1760 – 1825), Charles Fourier (1772 – 1837), Robert Owen (1771 – 1858), and Louis Blanc (1811 – 1882).

The Anarchists rejected industrialism and the dominance of government. Auguste Blanqui (1805 – 1881) advocated terrorism as a means to end capitalism and the state.

Pierre Joseph Proudhon (1809 – 1865) attacked the principle of private property because it denied justice to the common people.

Christian Socialism began in England circa 1848. Believing that the evils of industrialism would be ended by following Christian principles, the advocates of this doctrine tried to bridge the gap between the anti-religious drift of socialism and the need for Christian social justice for workers. The best-known Christian Socialist was the novelist Charles Kingsley (1814 – 1875), whose writings exposed the social evils of industrialism.

"Scientific" Socialism, or Marxism, was the creation of Karl Marx (1818 – 1883), a German scholar who, with the help of Friedrich Engels (1820 – 1895), intended to replace utopian hopes and dreams with a brutal, militant blueprint for socialist working class success. The principal works of this revolutionary school of socialism were *The Communist Manifesto* and *Das Kapital (Capital)*.

The theory of Dialectical Materialism enabled Marx to explain the history of the world. By borrowing Hegel's dialectic, substituting materialism and realism in place of Hegel's idealism, and inverting the methodological process, Marx was able to justify his theoretical conclusions.

Marxism consisted of a number of key propositions: 1) The economic interpretation of history, i.e., all human history has been determined by economic factors (mainly who controls the means of production and distribution); 2) The class struggle, i.e., since the beginning of time there has been a class struggle between the rich and the poor or the exploiters and the exploited; 3) Theory of Surplus Value, i.e., the true value of a product was labor and, since the worker received a small portion of his just labor price, the difference was surplus value, "stolen" from him by the capitalist; 4) Socialism was inevitable, i.e., capitalism contained the seeds of its own destruction (overproduction, unemployment, etc.); the rich will grow richer and the poor will grow poorer until the gap between each class (proletariat and bourgeoisie) is so great that the working classes will rise up in revolution and overthrow the elite bourgeoisie to install a "dictatorship of the proletariat". As modern capitalism is dismantled, the creation of a classless society guided by the principle "From each according to his abilities, to each according to his needs," will take place.

Evaluation

Ideologies (isms) are interpretations of the world from a particular viewpoint. They are, or imply, programs of action, and thrive where belief in general standards and norms has broken down. The proliferation of so many thought systems, and movements based on them, after 1815, suggest that the basic division of society was between those who accepted the implications of the intellectual, economic, and political revolutions of the 18th and early 19th centuries, and those who did not. The polarization in ideology was the result.

EUROPE IN CRISIS, 1815 – 1833: REPRESSION, REFORM AND REVOLUTION

The Vienna peace settlement signaled the triumph of the political and social conservative order in Europe. The dangerous ideas (Liberalism and Nationalism) associated with the French Revolution and Napoleonic period had been "contained" by the territorial provisions of the 1815 agreement. The status quo had been once again defined. "Order" and "stability" was expected in the European state system.

Underestimating the power of ideas, the Conservative leadership after 1815 was, instead, faced with a dramatic confrontation between those who had been converted to the "new" ideas (which required political changes), and the traditional ruling classes, who were reluctant to make any accommodation with the believers in the "new" ideas. The result of such confrontation in most states was government-sponsored repression followed by revolution. Few states chose to respond to the call for liberal reform. Only nationalist impulses in Greece and Belgium were successful, for reasons which could hardly comfort liberals. The intellectual climate of Romanticism provided a volatile atmosphere in which these events unfolded.

Post-War Repression, 1815 – 1820

Initially, the great powers followed the lead of the Austrian statesman Prince Metternich (1773 – 1859) in suppressing any direct or indirect expression of liberal faith. Most leaders attempted to reinstitute conservative means of governmental control, in order to prevent reforms in the direction of greater participation by more people in government. The literate middle class, supported by urban workers, demanded reform and were willing to use violence to obtain it.

England

The Tory (Conservative) government that defeated Napoleon was in control of England. Facing serious economic problems that had produced large numbers of industrial unemployed, the conservatives tried to follow a reactionary policy.

The Corn Law of 1815 effectively halted the importation of cheaper foreign grains, aiding the Tory land-holding aristocracy, but increasing the cost of bread, and driving the poor and unemployed to protest and demand parliamentary reform.

The Coercion Acts of 1817 suspended "habeas corpus" for the first time in English history; provided for arbitrary arrest and punishment; and drastically curtailed freedom of the press and public mass meetings.

The "Peterloo Massacre" of 1819 occurred when several members of a large crowd, who were listening to reformers demand repeal of the Corn Laws and other liberal changes, were killed, with hundreds of others injured when police authorities broke up the meeting.

The Six Acts of Parliament in 1819, in response to the "Peterloo" episode, were a series of repressive measures which attempted to remove the instruments of agitation from the hands of radical leaders and to provide the authorities with new powers.

The Cato Street Conspiracy of 1820 took place when a group of extreme radicals plotted to blow up the entire British cabinet. It provided new support for repression by the Tories, as well as discrediting the movement for parliamentary reform.

By 1820 England was on the road to becoming a reactionary authoritative state, when numerous protests among younger Tories argued that such repressive legislation was not in the English tradition, and that the party itself might need to change its direction.

France

France emerged from the chaos of the long revolutionary period (1789 – 1815) as the most liberal large state on the continent. The period from 1815 – 1830 is always referred to as the Restoration era, signifying the return of the legitimate royal dynasty of France — the infamous Bourbon line.

Louis XVIII (reign 1814 – 1824) governed France as a Constitutional Monarch, by agreeing to observe the "Charter" or Constitution of the Restoration Period. This moderate document managed to limit royal power, grant legislative powers, protect civil rights, and uphold the Code Napoleon and other pre-restoration reforms.

Louis XVIII wished to unify the French populace, which was divided into those who accepted the Revolution and those who did not. The leader of those who did not was the Count of Artois (1757–1836), brother of the king and leader of the Ultra Royalists.

The 1815 "White Terror" saw royalist mobs murder thousands of former revolutionaries.

New elections in 1816 for the Chamber of Deputies resulted in the Ultras being rejected, in favor of a moderate royalist majority dependent on middle class support. The war indemnity was paid off, France was admitted to the Quadruple Alliance (1818), and liberal sentiment began to grow.

In February, 1820, the Duke of Berri, son of Artois and heir to the throne after his father, was murdered. Royalists charged that the left (Liberals) were responsible and that the king's policy of moderation had encouraged the left.

Louis XVIII began to move the government more and more to the right, as changes in the electoral laws narrowed the eligible voters to the most wealthy, and censorship was imposed. Liberals were being driven out of legal political life and into near-illegal activity. The triumph of reactionism came in 1823, when French troops were authorized by the Concert of Europe to crush the Spanish Revolution and restore another Bourbon ruler, Ferdinand VII.

Austria and the Germanys

Throughout the first half of the 19th century the Austrian Empire and the German Confederation were dominated by Prince Metternich, who epitomized conservative reactionism. To no other country or empire were the programs of liberalism and nationalism potentially more dangerous. Given the multi-ethnic composition of the Hapsburg empire, any recognition of the political rights and aspirations of any of the national groups would mean the probable dissolution of the empire.

It was Napoleon who reduced over 300 German states to 39, and the Congress of Vienna which preserved this arrangement under Austrian domination. The purpose of the German confederation (Bund) was to guarantee the independence of the member states, and by joint action, to preserve all German states from domestic disorder or revolution. Its organization of government was a Diet (assembly), presided over by Austria, as President.

The two largest states in the confederation were Austria and Prussia. Austria was ruled by the Hapsburg dynasty and, through Metternich's anti-liberal and nationalist pathology, held the line against any change in the status quo.

Prussia was ruled by the Hohenzollern dynasty, a very aggressive royal family when it came to expanding the borders of this northern German state, sometimes at the expense of other German rulers. For a short time after 1815 German liberals looked to Prussia as a leader of German liberalism, because of liberal reforms in government enacted after a humiliating defeat at the hands of Napoleon. These reforms were intended to improve the efficiency of government and were not the portent of a general trend. The Prussian government and its traditional ruling classes (Junkers) intended to follow the lead of Metternich in repressing all liberal-nationalist agitation.

Liberal-nationalist agitation was highly vocal and visible in and among German universities in the first half of the 19th century. Student organizations, such as the Burschenschaften, were openly promoting political arrangements that seemed radical and revolutionary at the time.

At the Wartbug Festival (1817), students burned various symbols of authority. Russian agent Kotzebue was assassinated in 1819 by Karl Sand, a student member of the

Burschenschaften.

The Carlsbad Diet (1819) was summoned by Metternich to end the seditious activity of German liberals and nationalists. The passage of a series of decrees effectively ended the activities of these change-agents. In fact, the movement was driven underground.

Russia

From 1801 to 1825 Czar Alexander I governed this traditional authoritarian state. A man of many moods, this Russian emperor thought he was called upon to lead Europe into a new age of benevolence and good will. After the Congress of Vienna, he became increasingly reactionary and a follower of Metternich.

Alexander I was torn between an intellectual attraction to the ideas of the Enlightenment and reform, and a very pragmatic adherence to traditional Russian autocracy (absolutism).

With the help of liberal adviser, Michael Speransky, plans were made for a reconstruction of the Russian government, due to the czar's admiration for Napoleon's administrative genius. This and other liberal policies alienated the nobility, and Speransky was dismissed.

Alexander I came to regard the Enlightenment, the French Revolution and Napoleon in biblical terms, seeing all three as anti-Christian. Turning to a new reactionary advisor, General Arakcheiev, repression became the order of the day. There could be no toleration of political opposition or criticism of the regime. The early years of possible liberal reform had given way to conservative repression.

REVOLUTIONS I (1820 – 1829)

Nationalism, liberalism and industrialism were all key factors in the outbreak of revolution during the first half of the 19th century. All three "isms" were opposed by the conservative groups of the population (royalists, clergy, landed aristocracy), who were rooted in the way of life before the French Revolution. Promoting the new forces of change was a younger generation, the heirs of the Enlightenment who believed in progress. Romanticism was the atmosphere against which these events were played out.

The International System: The Concert of Europe

At the 1815 Congress of Vienna, the enforcement provisions of the settlement were designed to guarantee stability and peace in the international arena. The Quadruple Alliance (Austria, Russia, Prussia, England) that had defeated Napoleon was to continue through a new spirit of cooperation and consultation that would be referred to as the "Concert of Europe." At the suggestion of Lord Castlereagh, England's Foreign Minister, foreign policy issues affecting the international order would be worked out in a series of meetings or Congresses, so that no one nation could act without the consent of the others. But under the leadership of Metternich, the Congress system became the means to preserve the political status quo of autocracy in Europe against all revolutionary ideas. The Congress system was short-lived because the continental powers could not always agree on cooperative action, and the English refused to support interference in the domestic affairs of nation-states. In the end, each nation became guided by its own best interests.

The Congress System of Conferences.

The Congress of Aix-la-Chapelle (1818) arranged for the withdrawal of the allied army of occupation from France, and the admission of France into the concert of Europe (Quintuple Alliance).

The Congress of Troppau (1820) was summoned by Metternich because of the outbreak of revolution in Spain. A policy statement (Protocol of Troppau),which would authorize armed intervention into any state that undergoes revolutionary change, was opposed by England.

The Congress of Laibach (1821) authorized Austrian troops to end the revolution-ary changes in the Kingdom of the Two Sicilys, where revolutions had spread from Spain. No decision was made concerning Spain.

The Congress of Verona (1822) was called because of the continuing Spanish Revolution and the outbreak (1821) of revolution in Greece. When Russia, Prussia and Austria agreed to support French intervention in Spain, the new English Foreign Minister, George Canning (1770 – 1827), (Viscount Castlereagh had committed suicide), withdrew England from the Concert of Europe. Verona marked the effective end of the Congress system.

The Monroe Doctrine and the Concert of Europe

British fears that Metternich would attempt the restoration of Spain's colonies, then revolting in Latin America, prompted George Canning to suggest, and then support, the foreign policy statement of the United States of America known as the Monroe Doctrine (1823) ,which prohibited any further colonization and intervention by European powers in the Western Hemisphere.

England hoped to replace Spain in establishing her own trading monopoly with these former Spanish colonies. Throughout the 19th century British commercial interests dominated Latin America.

Latin America in Revolution

Inspired by the French Revolution and the Napoleonic period, the rise of Latin American nationalism between 1804 and 1824 would witness the end of three centuries of Spanish colonial rule and the emergence of new heroes such as Toussaint L'Ouver-ture, Jose San Martin, Bernardo O'Higgins, Simon Bolivar and Miguel Hidalgo.

The Revolutions of the 1820s

Spain (1820 – 1823). Beginning in January 1820, a mutiny of army troops under Colonel Rafael Riego began, in opposition to the persecution of liberals by the restored monarch, King Ferdinand VII. The Congress of Verona (1822) authorized a French army to invade Spain and crush the revolutionaries.

Italy (1820 – 1821). Incited to revolution by the activities of secret liberal-nationalist organizations ("carbonari"), liberals revolted in Naples in July 1820, protest-ing the absolute rule of Ferdinand I of the Kingdom of the Two Sicilys. The Congress of Laibach (1821) authorized Austria to invade and suppress the rebels. An attempted uprising (1821) in Piedmont was crushed by Austrian forces.

The Greek Revolt (1821 – 1830). The revolution which broke out in Greece in 1821, while primarily a nationalist uprising rather than a liberal revolution, was part of a larger problem known as "The Eastern Question." Greece was part of the Ottoman Empire, whose vast territories were gradually being recessed throughout the 18th and early 19th centuries. The weakness of the Ottoman Empire and the political and economic ramifications of this instability for the balance of power in Europe kept the major powers in a nervous state of tension.

Because of conflicting interests, the major powers were unable to respond in any harmonious fashion for several years. The revolt was a leading political question in Europe throughout the 1820s. Occurring in the Romantic era, the revolt touched the sensitivities of romantics in the West. A Greek appeal to Christian Europe did not move Prussia or Austria, but did fuse England, France and Russia into a united force that defeated a combined Turco-Egyptian naval force at Navarino Bay (1827). Greek independence was recognized through the Treaty of Adrianople (1829).

Russian intervention on the side of Greek revolutionaries was based on Russian national interest (i.e., any dimunition of Ottoman power increased Russian chances of further expansion into the Turkish empire).

Greek nationalism triumphed over the conservative Vienna settlement, and three of the five great powers had aided a movement that violated their agreement of 1815. The self-interests of the great powers demonstrated the growing power of nationalism in the international system.

The Decembrist Uprising in Russia (1825). The death of Alexander I on December 1, 1825 resulted in a crisis over the actual succession to the throne and, in turn ,produced the first significant uprising in Russian history. The expected succession of Constantine, older brother of Alexander I, who was believed somewhat more liberal than the late czar, did not materialize. Instead, the younger brother Nicholas, no liberal by any measure, prepared to assume the throne that Constantine had actually renounced.

Hoping to block Nicholas' succession, a group of moderately liberal junior military officers staged a demonstration in late December, 1825, in St. Petersburg, only to see it quickly dissipated by artillery attacks ordered by Czar Nicholas I.

The Decembrists were the first upper-class opponents of the autocratic Russian system of government, who called attention to the popular grievances among Russian society. The insurrection developed in Nicholas I a pathological dislike for liberal reformers.

A program called "Official Nationality,"with the slogan, "Autocracy, Orthodoxy and National Unity," was designed to lead Russia back to its historic roots. Through it, Nicholas I became Europe's most reactionary monarch.

Domestically, Russia became a police state with censorship and state-sponsored terrorism. There would be no representative assemblies, and education was not only limited, but university curricula were carefully monitored. A profound alienation of Russian intellectual life ensued.

In foreign affairs the same extreme conservatism was demonstrated. The Polish Revolution of 1830 – 31 was crushed, and Russian troops played a key role in stamping out Hungarian nationalism in the Hapsburg Empire, during the revolutionary uprisings of 1848 – 49. Russia's traditional desire for expansion in the direction of the Ottoman Empire, produced a confrontation between France and Russia over who was entitled to protect Christians and the Holy Places in the Near East. When the Sultan of Turkey awarded France the honor, Nicholas I was prepared to go to war against Turkey to uphold Russia's right to speak for Slavic Christians. The result was the Crimean War (1854 – 56), which Russia would lose. Nicholas I died (1855) during the course of fighting this war.

England Chooses Reform Over Revolution

The climax of repression in England was the Six Acts of Parliament (1819). Yet even as these laws were enacted, younger conservative politicians were questioning the wisdom of their party elders (Wellington, Castlereagh), and calling for moderation. During the 1820s, a new group of younger Tories would moderate their party's unbending conservatism.

Reform was promoted by George Canning and Robert Peel, in opposition to the reactionary policies of earlier Tory leaders. With the help of liberal Whig politicians, enough votes were found to put England on the road to liberal reform.

Canning inaugurated a liberal policy in foreign affairs, including abandonment of the Congress System. Robert Peel reformed prisons and the outdated criminal code, as well as established an efficient metropolitan police force ("Bobbies").

Mercantile and navigation acts were liberalized, enabling British colonies to trade with nations other than England.

The 1673 Test Act, which was a religious test used for barring non-Anglicans from participation in the government, was repealed. The Catholic Emancipation Act (1829) granted full civil rights to Roman Catholics. It was in defiance of the Test Act, which was prompted by the election of the Irish leader Daniel J. O'Connell to the British Parliament.

The momentum for liberal reform would continue into the 1830s, as Britain realized that accommodation with the new merchant and financial classes was in the spirit of English history. The acid test of liberal reform, however, would come to focus on the willingness of Parliament to repeal the Corn Laws and reform itself.

REVOLUTIONS II, 1830 – 1833

The Conservative grip on Europe following the turbulence of the 1820s was very quickly challenged, when revolution broke out in France in 1830. By then, the forces of liberalism and nationalism had become so strong that they constituted major threats to the security of many governments. In eastern Europe, nationalism was the greater danger, while in the West the demands of middle class liberals for various political reforms grew louder.

France: The July Revolution

The death of King Louis XVIII in 1824 brought his brother Charles, Count of Artois and leader of the Ultra Royalists, to the throne as Charles X, and set the stage for a return to the Old Regime or revolution.

Attempting to roll back the revolutionary gains, Charles X alienated the moderate forces on the right as well as the entire left. Continued violations of the Charter enabled French voters to register their displeasure in the elections of 1827 by giving the liberals a substantial gain in the Chamber of Deputies.

In 1829, when Charles X appointed a ministry led by the Prince of Polignac, who was the personification of reactionism in France, liberals considered this a declaration of war. Elections in 1830 produced a stunning victory for the liberals. Charles X responded by decreeing the Four Ordinances, which would have amounted to a royal *Coup d'État* if not stopped. The spark of revolt was set off by the radicals of Paris, with the workers and students raising barricades in the streets with the intention of establishing a republic. Charles X abdicated and fled France.

The Liberals in the Chamber of Deputies, under the leadership of Adolphe Thiers, preferred a constitutional monarchy without a Bourbon ruler. With the cooperation of Talleyrand and Lafayette, they agreed on Prince Louis Philippe, head of the Orleans family and cousin to Charles X.

France was now controlled by the bourgeoisie of upper-middle class bankers and businessmen. King Louis Philippe was "the Bourgeoisie King" who would tilt the government towards these interests. While the July Monarchy of Louis Philippe was politically more liberal than the restoration government, socially it proved to be quite conservative.

The news of the successful July Revolution in France served as a spark ("When France sneezes, the rest of Europe catches cold") to revolutionary uprisings throughout Europe.

The Belgian Independence Movement (1830 – 1831)

Since being merged with Holland in 1815, the upper classes of Belgium had never reconciled themselves to rule by a country with a different language, religion and economic life. Inspired by the news of the July Revolution in France, a revolt against Dutch rule broke out in Brussels, led by students and industrial workers. The Dutch army was defeated and forced to withdraw from Belgium by the threat of a Franco-British fleet. A national Congress wrote a liberal Belgian Constitution. In 1831, Leopold of Saxe-Coburg (1831 – 1865) became king of the Belgians. In 1839, the Great Powers declared the neutrality of Belgium.

Poland (1830 – 1831)

The new czar of Russia, Nicholas I (reign 1825 – 1855), had the first opportunity to demonstrate his extreme conservatism in foreign policy when a military insurrection broke out late in 1830, in Warsaw. This nationalist uprising challenged the historic Russian domination of Poland. The Russian garrison was driven out of Poland; the czar was deposed as king of Poland; and the independence of Poland was proclaimed by a revolutionary government.

Nicholas I ordered the Russian army to invade Poland; it ruthlessly proceeded to crush the nationalist rebellion. Poland became "a land of graves and crosses." The Organic Statute of 1832 declared Poland to be an integral part of the Russian empire.

Italy (1831 – 1832)

Outbreaks of liberal discontent occurred in northern Italy, centering on Modena, Parma, and the Papal States. The inspiration for Italian nationalists who spoke of a unification process was (1) Guiseppe Mazzini and his secret revolutionary society called Young Italy; and (2) the Carbonari, the secret nationalist societies, which advocated the use of force to achieve national unification. Still too disorganized, the Italian revolutionaries were easily crushed by Austrian troops under Metternich's enforcement of the Concert of Europe's philosophy. Still, the Italian Risorgimento (resurgence of the Italian spirit) was well under way.

Germany (1830 – 1833)

The Carlsbad Decrees of 1819 had effectively restricted freedom throughout Germany. At the news of France's July Revolution, German university students and professors led street demonstrations that forced temporary granting of constitutions in several minor states. These expressions of liberal sentiment and nationalistic desires for German unification were easily crushed by Metternich's domination of the German Confederation (Bund), and his influence over Prussia.

Great Britain: Reform Continues

The death of King George IV and the accession of King William IX in 1830 resulted in a general parliamentary election in which the oppositional political party, the Whigs, scored major gains with their platform calling for parliamentary reform. With the Tory party divided, the king asked the leader of the Whig party, Earl Grey (1764 – 1845) to form a government.

Immediately, a major reform bill was introduced, designed to increase the number of voters by fifty percent and to eliminate underpopulated electoral districts ("Rotten Boroughs") and replace them with representatives for the previously unrepresented manufacturing districts and cities.

After a national debate, new elections, and a threat from King William IV to alter the composition of the House of Lords, the Great Reform Bill of 1832 was enacted into law. While the Reform Bill did not resolve all political inequities in British political life, it marked a new beginning. Several more notable reforms would begin to redraw the sociological landscape of British life.

Evaluation

Neither the forces of revolution nor those of reaction, were able to maintain the upper hand between 1789 and 1848. Liberalism and nationalism, socialism and democracy were on the march, but the forces of conservatism and reaction were still strong enough to contain them. The polarization of Europe was becoming ever so clear: the liberal middle class West, which advocated constitutionalism and industrial progress; and the authoritarian East, which was committed to preserving the status quo. The confrontation would continue until one or the other side would win out decisively.

The Revolutions of 1848

The year 1848 is considered the watershed of the 19th century. The revolutionary disturbances of the first half of the 19th century reached a climax, in a new wave of revolutions that extended from Scandinavia to southern Italy, and from France to Central Europe. Only England and Russia avoided violent upheaval.

The issues were substantially the same as they had been in 1789. What was new in 1848 was that these demands were far more widespread and irrepressible than ever before. Whole classes and nations demanded to be fully included in society. The French Revolution of 1789 came at the end of a period ("Ancien Regime"), while the revolutions of 1848 signaled the beginning of a new age. Aggravated by a rapid growth in population and social disruption caused by industrialism and urbanization, a massive tide of discontent swept across the western world.

Generally speaking, the 1848 upheavals shared in common the strong influences of romanticism, nationalism, and liberalism, as well as a new factor of economic dislocation and instability throughout most of Europe. Some authorities believe that it was the absence of liberty that was most responsible for the uprisings.

Specifically, a number of similar conditions existed in several countries: 1) severe food shortages caused by poor harvests of grain and potatoes (e.g., Irish Potato Famine); 2) financial crises caused by a downturn in the commercial and industrial economy; 3) business failures; 4) widespread unemployment ; 5) a sense of frustration and discontent of urban artisan and working classes as wages diminished; 6) a system of poor relief which became overburdened; 7) living conditions which deteriorated in the cities, and; 7) the power of nationalism in the Germanys and Italys, as well as Eastern Europe, to inspire the overthrow of existing governments. Middle class predominance with the unregulated economy continued to drive these liberals to push for more reform of government and for civil liberty. They pursued this by enlisting the help of the working classes in putting more pressure on the government to change.

Republicanism: Victory in France and Defeat in Italy

In France, working class discontent and liberals' unhappiness with the corrupt regime of King Louis Philippe (reign 1830 – 1848) – especially his minister Guizot –

erupted in street riots in Paris on February 22 – 23, 1848. With the workers in control of Paris, King Louis Philippe abdicated on February 24, and a provisional government proclaimed the Second French Republic.

Heading the provisional government was the liberal Alphonse Lamartine (1790 – 1869), who favored a moderate republic and political democracy. Lamartine's bourgeoisie allies had little sympathy for the working poor, and did not intend to pursue a social revolution, as well.

The working class groups were united by their leader Louis Blanc (1811 – 1882), a socialist thinker who expected the provisional government to deal with the unemployed, and anticipated the power of the state being used to improve life and the conditions of labor. Pressed by the demands of Blanc and his followers, the provisional government established national workshops to provide work and relief for thousands of unemployed workers.

The "June Days" revolution was provoked when the government closed the national workshop. A general election in April resulted in a National Assembly, dominated by the moderate republicans and conservatives under Lamartine who regarded socialist ideas as threats to private property. The Parisian workers, feeling that their revolution had been nullified, took to the streets in revolution.

This new revolution (June 23 – 26) was unlike previous uprisings in France. It marked the inauguration of genuine class warfare; it was a revolt against poverty and a cry for the redistribution of property. It foreshadowed the great social revolutions of the 20th century. The revolt was extinguished after General Cavaignac was given dictatorial powers by the government. The June Days confirmed the political predominance of conservative property holders in French life.

The new Constitution of the Second French Republic provided for a unicameral legislative (with the National Assembly designating themselves as the first members), and executive power vested in a popularly-elected president of the Republic. When the election returns were counted the candidate of the government, General Cavaignac, was soundly defeated by a "dark horse" candidate, Prince Louis Napoleon Bonaparte (1808 – 1873), a nephew of the great emperor. On December 20, 1848, Louis Napoleon was installed as President of the republic.

It was clear the voters turned to the name of Bonaparte as a source of stability and greatness. They expected him to prevent any further working class disorder. However, the election of Louis Napoleon doomed the Second Republic. He was a Bonaparte, dedicated to his own fame and vanity, and not republican institutions. In December, 1852, Louis Napoleon became Emperor Napoleon III, and France retreated from republicanism again.

Italian nationalists and liberals wanted to end Hapsburg (Austrian), Bourbon (Naples and Sicily), and papal domination and unite these disparate areas into a unified liberal nation. A revolt by liberals in Sicily in January, 1848, was followed by the granting of liberal constitutions in Naples, Tuscany, Piedmont, and the Papal States. Milan and Venice expelled their Austrian rulers. In March, 1848, upon hearing the news of the revolution in Vienna, a fresh outburst of revolution from Austrian rule occurred in Lombardy and Venetia, with Sardinia-Piedmont declaring war on Austria. Simultaneously, Italian patriots attacked the Papal States, forcing the Pope, Pius IX, to flee to Naples for refuge.

The temporary nature of these initial successes was illustrated by the speed with which the conservative forces regained control. In the north, Austrian Field Marshal Radetsky swept aside all opposition, regaining Lombardy and Venetia and crushing Sardinia-Piedmont. In the Papal States, the establishment of the Roman Republic

(February 1849), under the leadership of Giuseppe Mazzini and the protection of Giuseppe Garibaldi, would fail when French troops took Rome in July, 1849, after a heroic defense by Garibaldi. Pope Pius IX returned to Rome cured of his liberal leanings. In the south and in Sicily the revolts were suppressed by the former rulers.

Within eighteen months the revolutions of 1848 had failed throughout Italy. Among the explanations for these failures were the failure of conservative, rural people to support the revolution; the divisions in aim and technique among the revolutionaries; the fear the radicals aroused among moderate groups of Italians, who would be needed to guarantee the success of any revolution; and the general lack of experience and administrative ability on the part of the revolutionists.

Nationalism Resisted in Austrian Empire

The Hapsburg Empire was vulnerable to revolutionary challenge. With its collection of subject nationalities (more non-Germans than Germans), the empire was stirred by an acute spirit of nationalism; its government was reactionary (liberal institutions were non-existent); and its social reliance on serfdom doomed the masses of people to a life without hope. As soon as news of the "February Days" in France reached the borders of the Austrian Empire, rebellions began. The long-suppressed opponents of the government believed the time had come to introduce liberal institutions into the empire.

Vienna

In March 1848, Hungarian criticism of Hapsburg imperial rule was initiated by Magyar nationalist leader, Louis Kossuth (1802 – 1894), who demanded Hungarian independence. Students and workers in Vienna rushed to the streets to demonstrate on behalf of a more liberal government. The army failed to restore order and Prince Metternich, the symbol of reaction, resigned and fled the country. Emperor Ferdinand I (reign 1835 – 1848) granted a moderately liberal constitution, but its short-comings dissatisfied more radical elements, and continual disorder prompted the emperor to flee from Vienna to Innsbruck, where he relied on his army commanders to restore order in the Empire. The Austrian imperial troops remained loyal to the Hapsburg crown. Prince Schwarzenberg was put in charge of restoring Hapsburg control.

A people's committee ruled Vienna, where a liberal assembly gathered to write a constitution. In Hungary and Bohemia, revolutionary outbreaks indicated ultimate success.

The inability of the revolutionary groups in Vienna to govern effectively made it easier for the Hapsburgs to lay siege to Vienna, in October 1848. The rebels surrendered, and Emperor Ferdinand abdicated in favor of his eighteen-year-old nephew, Francis Joseph (reign 1848 – 1916), who promptly restored royal absolutism.

The imperial government had been saved at Vienna through the loyalty of the army, and the lack of ruling capacity on the part of the revolutionaries. The only thing the revolutionaries could agree on was their hatred of the Hapsburg dynasty.

Bohemia

Nationalist feeling among the Czechs or Bohemians had been smoldering for centuries. They demanded a constitution and autonomy within the Hapsburg Empire.

A Pan-Slav Congress attempted to unite all Slavic peoples, but accomplished little, because divisions were more decisive among them than was unified opposition to Hapsburg control.

In June, 1848, Prague submitted to a military occupation, followed by a military dictatorship in July, after all revolutionary groups were crushed.

Hungary

The Kingdom of Hungary was a state of about twelve million under Hapsburg authority. Magyars or Hungarians, who represented about five million subjects of the emperor, enjoyed a privileged position in the empire. The remaining seven million Slavic and Rumanian natives were powerless.

In March, 1848, Nationalist leader Louis Kossuth took over direction of the movement, and tamed a more radical Hungarian rebellion; Hungarian autonomy was declared in April, but failed to win popular support for the revolution because of the tyrannical treatment of the Slavic minorities. Because the government in Vienna was distracted by revolutions everywhere in the empire in the summer and fall of 1848, Louis Kossuth had time to organize an army to fight for Hungarian independence.

War between Austria and Hungary was declared on October 3, 1848, and Hungarian armies drove to within sight of Vienna. But desperate resistance from Slavic minorities forced the Hungarians to withdraw. Hungary was invaded by an Austrian army from the West, in June, 1849, and a Russian army (Tsar Nicholas I of Russia offered assistance to new emperor Francis Joseph) from the north. Along with Serbian resistance in the south and Rumanian resistance in the east, the combined opposition proved too much for Louis Kossuth's Hungarian Republic (proclaimed in April 1849), which was defeated. Kossuth fled into exile, while thirteen of his guards were executed. Not until Austria was defeated by Prussia, in 1866, would Hungary be in a position again to demand governmental equality with the Austrians.

Italy

Charles Albert, King of Sardinia, having granted his people a constitution, and hoping to add the Hapsburgs' Italian holdings to his kingdom, declared war on Austria. Unfortunately, the Sardinian army was twice defeated in battle (Custozza and Novara) by the Austrian General, Radetsky.

King Charles Albert abdicated in favor of his son, Victor Emmanuel, who was destined to complete the unification of Italy in the second half of the 19th century.

The Revolutions of 1848 failed in Austria for several reasons. The subject nationalities sometimes hated each other more than they despised Austria. The Hapsburgs used the divisions between the ethnic groups as an effective weapon against each. The imperial army had remained loyal to its aristocratic commanders, who favored absolutism. There were too few industrial workers and an equally small number of middle class. The industrial workers could not exert any political power, and the middle class feared working-class radicalism and rallied to the government as defender of the status quo.

Liberalism Halted in the Germanies

The immediate effect of the 1848 Revolution in France was a series of liberal and nationalistic demonstrations in the German states (March, 1848), with the rulers promising liberal concessions. The liberals' demand for constitutional government was coupled with another demand: some kind of union or federation of the German states. While popular demonstrations by students, workers, and the middle class produced the promise of a liberal future, the permanent success or failure of these "promises" rested on Prussian reaction.

Prussia, The Frankfurt Parliament and German Unification

Under King Frederick William IV (reign 1848 – 1861), Prussia moved from revolution to reaction. After agreeing to liberalize the Prussian government following street rioting in Berlin, the king rejected the constitution written by a specially-called assembly. The liberal ministry resigned and was replaced by a conservative one. By the fall the king felt powerful enough to substitute his own constitution, which guaranteed royal control of the government, with a complicated three-class system of indirect voting that excluded all but landlords and wealthy bourgeoisie from office. This system prevailed in Prussia until 1918. Finally, the government ministry was responsible to the king and the military services swore loyalty to the king alone.

Self appointed liberal, romantic, and nationalist leaders called for elections to a constituent assembly, from all states belonging to the German Bund, for the purpose of unifying the German states. Meeting in May, 1848, the Frankfurt Parliament was composed of mostly intellectuals, professionals, lawyers, businessmen and middle class. After a year of deliberation over questions of (1) monarchy or republic; (2) federal union or centralized state; and (3) boundaries (i.e., only German-populated or mixed nationalities), the assembly produced a constitution.

The principal problem facing the Frankfurt Assembly was to obtain Prussian support. The smaller German states generally favored the Frankfurt Constitution, as did liberals throughout the large and middle-sized states. Austria made it clear that it was opposed to the work of the Assembly and would remain in favor of the present system.

The Assembly leaders made the decision to stake their demands for a united Germany on King Frederick William IV, of Prussia. They selected him as emperor in April, 1849, only to have him reject the offer because he was a divine-right monarch, not subject to popularly-elected assemblies. Without Prussia there could be no success, so the Frankfurt Parliament dissolved without achieving a single accomplishment.

The Prussian King Frederick William IV had his own plans for uniting Germany. Right after refusing a "crown from the gutter," he offered his own plan to the German princes, wherein Prussia would play a prominent role, along with Austria. When Austria demanded allegiance to the Bund, the Prussian king realized pushing his plan would involve him in a war with Austria and her allies (including Russia). In November, 1850, Prussia agreed to forego the idea of uniting the German states, at a meeting with Austria called the "Humiliation of Olmutz." Austrian domination of the German Bund was confirmed.

Great Britain and the Victorian Compromise

The Victorian Age (1837 – 1901) is associated with the long reign of Queen Victoria, who succeeded her uncle, King William IV at the age of eighteen and married her cousin, Prince Albert. The early years of her reign coincided with the continuation of liberal reform of the British government accomplished through an arrangement known as the "Victorian Compromise." The Compromise was a political alliance of the middle class and aristocracy to exclude the working class from political power. The middle class gained control of the House of Commons, the aristocracy controlled the government, army, and Church of England. The process of accommodation was working successfully.

Highlights of the "Compromise Era"

Parliamentary reforms continued after passage of the 1832 Reform Bill. Laws were enacted abolishing slavery throughout the Empire (1833). The Factory Act (1831) forbade the employment of children under the age of nine. The New Poor Law (1834) now required the needy who were able and unemployed to live in workhouses. The Municipal Reform Law (1835) gave control of the cities to the middle class. The last remnants of the mercantilistic age fell with the abolition of the Corn Laws (1846) and repeal of the old navigation acts (1849).

Working class protest arose in the wake of their belief that passage of the "Great Reform Bill" of 1832 would bring them prosperity. When workers found themselves no better off, they turned to collective action of a political nature. They linked the solution of their economic plight to a program of political reform known as Chartism, or the Chartist movement, from the charter of six points which they petitioned Parliament to adopt - universal male suffrage, secret ballot for voting, no property qualifications for members of Parliament, salaries for members of Parliament, annual elections for Parliament, and equal electoral districts.

During the age of Victorian Compromise these ideas were considered dangerously radical. Both the middle class and aristocracy vigorously opposed the working class political agenda. Chartism as a national movement failed. Its ranks were split between those who favored violence and those who advocated peaceful tactics. The return of prosperity, with steady wages and lower food prices, robbed the movement of momentum. Yet the chartist movement came to constitute the first large-scale, working class political movement that workers everywhere would eventually adopt if they were to improve their situation.

After 1846 England was more and more dominated by the middle class; this was one of the factors that enabled England to escape the revolutions which shook Europe in 1848. The ability of the English to make meaningful industrial reforms gave the working class hope that its goals could be achieved without violent social upheaval.

Evaluation

The revolutions of 1848 began with much promise, but they all ended in defeat for a number of reasons. They were spontaneous movements which lost their popular support as the people lost their enthusiasm. Initial successes by the revolutionaries were due less to their strength than to the hesitancy of governments to use their superior force. Once this hesitancy was overcome, the revolutions were smashed. They were essentially urban movements, and the conservative landowners and peasants tended, in time, to nullify the spontaneous actions of the urban classes. The middle class, who led the revolutions, came to fear the radicalism of their working class allies. While in favor of political reformation, the middle class drew the line at social engineering, much to the dismay of the laboring poor. Divisions among national groups, and the willingness of one nationality to deny rights to other nationalities, helped to destroy the revolutionary movements in central Europe.

However, the results of 1848 – 1849 were not entirely negative. Universal male suffrage was introduced in France; serfdom remained abolished in Austria and the German states; parliaments were established in Prussia and other German states, though dominated, to be sure, by princes and aristocrats; and Prussia and Sardinia-Piedmont emerged with new determination to succeed in their respective unification schemes.

The Revolutions of 1848 – 1849 brought to a close the era of liberal revolutions that had begun in France in 1789. Reformers and revolutionists alike learned a lesson from the failures of 1848. They learned that planning and organization is necessary; that rational argument and revolution would not always assure success. With 1848 the Age of Revolution sputtered out. The Age of Romanticism was about to give way to an Age of Realism.

EPILOGUE: THE VIEW FROM
MID-19TH CENTURY EUROPE

A new age was about to follow the Revolutions of 1848-1849, as Otto von Bismarck, one of the dominant political figures of the second half of the 19th century, was quick to realize. If the mistake of these years was to believe that great decisions could be brought about by speeches and parliamentary majorities, the sequel would soon show that in an industrial era new techniques involving ruthless force were all too readily available. The period of *Realpolitik* — of realistic, iron-fisted politics and diplomacy — was about to happen.

By 1850 all humankind was positioned to become part of a single, worldwide, interacting whole. Based on military technology and industrial productivity, no part of the world could prevent Europeans from imposing their will.

The half century after 1850 would witness the political consolidation and economic expansion that paved the way for the brief global domination of Europe. The conservative monarchies of Sardinia-Piedmont and Prussia united Italy and Germany by military force, and gave birth to new power relationships on the continent. Externalizing their rivalries produced conflict overseas in a new age of imperialism, which saw Africa and Asia fall under the domination of the West.

Nationalism overtook liberalism as the dominant force in human affairs after 1850. Nationalists would be less romantic and more hardheaded. The good of the nation and not the individual became the new creed. The state would be deified.

After 1848 – 1849, the middle class ceased to be revolutionary. It became concerned with protecting its hard-earned political power and property rights against radical political and social movements. And the working classes also adopted new tactics and organizations. They turned to trade unions and political parties to achieve their political and social goals.

A great era of human progress was about to begin — material, political, scientific, industrial, social and cultural — shaping of the contours of the world.

4 REALISM AND MATERIALISM (1848-1914)

THE REVOLUTIONARY TRADITION

The era of reaction which had followed the collapse of the Napoleonic regime and the Congress of Vienna (1815) was followed by a wave of liberal and national agitation which was manifested in the Revolutions of 1820, 1825, and 1830.

The liberals, who tended to control the revolutionary agenda in Western Europe, desired constitutional government and the extension of individual freedoms – freedom of speech, press, and assembly. Liberal reforms and programs were advanced in the more economically advanced societies which had significant middle classes. In Central, Eastern, and Southern Europe, nationalism was the primary force for change. The advocates of nationalism sought to dismantle the traditional dynastic political controls which prohibited the formation of genuine nation-states. In addition to these factors, other reformers had succeeded in placing the need for social and economic improvement of the masses on the revolutionary platform; this was especially evident in France and England.

During the 1840s the movement toward revolutionary change was supported by four factors: 1) The failure of the existing regime to address the economic and social problems which accompanied the general economic collapse which occurred during the decade; 2) The regularity of significant food shortages in the major urban centers; 3) The increased popularity of the demands of the liberals and the nationalists; 4) The increasingly radical political, economic, and social proposals advanced by the Utopian Socialists (Charles Fourier, Robert Owen), the Anarchists (Pierre Proudhon), and the Chartists in England.

OUTBREAK AND DEVELOPMENT OF THE REVOLUTIONS OF 1848

France

The once liberal regime of King Louis Philippe (1830 – 1848) became increasingly conservative and oppressive under the leadership of Prime Minister Francois Guizot and the Chamber of Deputies. Guizot's opposition to reforms resulted in the further restriction of individual rights in general and the excessive use of censorship to silence critics of the regime.

The predominantly liberal opposition scheduled a banquet – which was a direct challenge to the regime – for the night of February 22, 1848. Guizot's government refused to sanction the banquet and, as a result, students and working class men took to the streets and violence erupted. In an effort to eliminate further difficulty, Louis Philippe dismissed Guizot; however, on the evening of February 23, 1848, a conflict between government troops and opponents of the regime occurred and over fifty people were killed. Reports of the "massacre" spread quickly and over a thousand barricades were erected. On February 24th, Louis Philippe attempted to develop a strategy which would permit him to remain in power; but, by the end of the day, he abdicated and fled to England.

A provisional government was established which represented the entire spectrum of opposition forces. The principal tasks of the provisional government were (1) to serve as an interim authority, and (2) to arrange for the elections to a National Constituent

Assembly. Among the representatives in the provisional government were Lamartine, a poet, and Louis Blanc, a socialist who was an advocate of National Workshops. During the spring of 1848 national workshops were established to resolve the problem of unemployment.

In April, French citizens voted for representatives to the National Constituent Assembly; the vote indicated that the nation supported the establishment of a republican government but that it was conservative in its economic and social philosophy. The Assembly convened in May and dissolved the national workshops; the result was the confrontation known as The June Days (June 23–27, 1848) during which French troops led by General Louis Eugene Cavaignac suppressed the radicals who wanted to maintain the workshops.

A new constitution was developed and accepted in October 1848. It established the Second French Republic which provided for a president and a single chamber assembly which would be elected on the basis of universal manhood suffrage; the president would serve a four-year term of office. The presidential election was held in December, 1848; Louis Napoleon, nephew of Napoleon I, easily defeated his rivals Cavaignac and Lamartine.

Prussia and the German States

News of the revolt in France resulted in rebellions in Prussia and other German states such as Baden, Bavaria, Hanover, and Saxony. The princes of the lesser states attempted to nullify the more strident demands of the revolutionaries by promising constitutions and appointing liberal ministers. However, King Frederick William IV of Prussia was adamant in his refusal to placate the revolutionaries; consequently, a violent revolution developed in Berlin.

On March 17, 1848, Frederick William IV relented and announced that a Prussian assembly (The Berlin Assembly) would be convened in April, 1848. A constitution would also be developed. Furthermore, he announced that internal reforms would be instituted, and that Prussia would assist in the development of a constitutional revitalization of the German Confederation.

The Frankfurt Assembly, which was a Pan-German assembly interested in the formulation of an integrated union of German states, convened in May 1848. During the next year, the group of liberals and nationalists developed a framework for a united Germany along the lines of the *Kleindeutsch* or Small Germany. This approach to German unification did not incorporate the Austrian Empire because of the great numbers of non-German peoples in that state; the advocates of the *Kleindeutsch* plan opposed the *Grossdeutsch* or Great Germany approach, which would have included Austria, because it violated the principle of national ethnic cohesion. In 1849, Frederick William IV received an offer to lead the new Germany. While interested in pursuing this opportunity, he declined because of the shift in the direction of the revolution; a reaction against the revolution had set in and most of the radical leaders fled the German states.

The Austrian Empire

Revolutionary activity broke out in Vienna on March 13, 1848. Within forty-eight hours, Prince Metternich, the symbol of reaction throughout Europe, resigned as Foreign Minister. Ferdinand I, the Austrian Emperor, acquiesced and granted concessions including a pledge to support the development of a constitution and the extension of individual liberties.

The nationalist ambitions of the Hungarians were advanced by Louis Kossuth. On

March 15, 1848, the Hungarian Diet declared a constitution which established a national assembly based on a limited franchise, specified individual freedoms, eliminated the remnants of the feudal order, and established an autonomous Hungary within the Austrian Empire. On March 31, 1848, the Austrian government accepted these substantive changes.

Czech nationalistic aspirations were manifested with the establishment of a Bohemian Diet in March. Its initial demands concerned universal manhood suffrage, guarantees of basic political and religious rights, and the parity of the Czech and German languages in education and government. On April 8th, Ferdinand I granted these concessions and rendered Bohemia an autonomous state. The further development of Czech nationalism was blurred by the emergency of the Pan-Slavic Congress (June 1848). The leaders of the Pan-Slavic Congress hoped to establish an autonomous government for Czechs, Slovaks, and other Slavs within the Austrian Empire.

The April Decree (April 11, 1848), which was issued by the Hapsburg government, pledged to eliminate the feudal services and duties which were still imposed on the peasants.

Italy

In the Italian peninsula, revolutionary activity broke out in Milan in March 1848 and was directed primarily by nationalists who were interested in expelling the Austrians from Lombardy and Venetia. King Charles Albert of Sardinia and Piedmont capitalized on the revolution by declaring war on Austria. In central Italy, Pope Pius IX expressed support for a unified Italian state. In the Kingdom of the Two Sicilies, an isolated revolt in Palermo, which occurred earlier than the rebellion in Paris, resulted in the granting of a liberal constitution by the reactionary King Ferdinand II.

Throughout Italy the revolution emphasized the cause of Italian nationalism and the re-emergence of Italian pride through the Risorgimento. There was no evidence that the revolution was seriously concerned with the economic and social problems which confronted the Italian peasants.

Austrian Field Marshal Josef Graf Radetzky von Radetz withdrew the Austrian forces to the Quadrilateral, a series of fortresses on the Adige and Mincia. There Radetzky regrouped, and in July 1848, launched a counter-offensive which resulted in the resounding defeat of the Italian forces under Charles Albert at Custozza (July 25, 1848). In 1849 Charles Albert undertook another military initiative but was defeated by Radetzky at Novara (March 23, 1849); Charles Albert abdicated in favor of his son, Victor Emmanuel II.

THE FAILURE OF THE REVOLUTIONS, 1848 – 1849

By the summer of 1848, the revolutionary effort had been spent and the earlier gains of the late winter and spring had been reversed or challenged in many countries. The June Days in France coincided with the dissolution of the Pan-Slavic Congress in Prague by General Alfred Windischgratz. By October, Windischgratz had suppressed the revolution in Vienna, and Radetzky's armies were moving successfully against the Italians. In the fall and winter (1848 – 1849) the revolutions were stifled in France, Prussia, Austria, Italy, and other states.

The failure of the Revolutions of 1848 was due to several major factors. The armed forces had remained loyal to the old leadership and demonstrated a willingness to assist in the suppression of the revolutions. In Western Europe, the revolutionaries were appeased by liberal political reforms. In most instances, the majority of citizens in the

West indicated that they were opposed to radical economic and social change.

In Central Europe, revolutions, which had been led by the middle class, did not express any interest in addressing social and economic problems. When the workers and students demanded social and economic revolution, the middle class became alienated from the revolution which they had led earlier; they desired only political change through the establishment of a constitutional process. This breach within the revolutionary camp was detected and exploited by the old regime.

In Eastern and Southern Europe, the nationalist revolutions lacked organization and, above all, the military capacity to resist the professional armies of the Austrian Empire.

By 1849 the revolutions had been suppressed or redirected. Only in France with the Second French Republic (1848 – 1852) and in Prussia (the Constitution of 1850) did some of the earlier gains endure.

REALPOLITIK AND THE TRIUMPH OF NATIONALISM
Cavour and the Unification of Italy

After the collapse of the revolutionary movements of 1848, the leadership of Italian nationalism was transferred to Sardinian leaders Victor Emmanuel II, Camillo de Cavour, and Giuseppe Garibaldi. They replaced the earlier leaders Giuseppe Mazzini of the Young Italy movement, Charles Albert, the once liberal Pius IX, and V. Gioberti and the Neo-Guelf movement, which a unified Italian state centered on the Papacy. The new leadership did not entertain romantic illusions about the process of transforming Sardinia into a new Italian Kingdom; they were practitioners of the politics of realism, *realpolitik.*

Cavour (1810 – 1861) was a Sardinian who served as editor of Il Risorgimento which was a newspaper that argued that Sardinia should be the basis of a new Italy. Between 1852 and 1861 Cavour served as Victor Emmanuel II's Prime Minister. In that capacity Cavour transformed Sardinian society through the implementation of a series of liberal reforms which were designed to modernize the Sardinian state and attract the support of liberal states such as Great Britain and France. Among Cavour's reforms were the following: 1) The Law on Convents and the Siccardi Law, which were directed at curtailing the influence of the Roman Catholic Church; 2) the reform of the judicial system; 3) the full implementation of the Statuto, the Sardinian constitution which was modeled on the liberal French constitution of 1830; and 4) support for economic development projects such as port and highway construction.

In 1855, under Cavour's direction, Sardinia joined Britain and France in the Crimean War against Russia. At the Paris Peace Conference (1856), Cavour addressed the delegates on the need to eliminate the foreign (Austrian) presence in the Italian peninsula and attracted the attention and sympathy of the French Emperor, Napoleon III.

Cavour and Napoleon III met at Plombiérès (July 20, 1859). The Plombières Agreement stated that in the event that Sardinia went to war with Austria, – presumably after being attacked or provoked – France would provide military assistance to Sardinia, and with victory, Sardinia would annex Lombardy, Venetia, Parma, Modena, and a part of the Papal states. Additionally, the remainder of Italy would be organized into an Italian Confederation under the direction of the Pope, France would receive Nice and Savoy, and the alliance would be finalized by a marriage between the two royal families. The Plombières Agreement was designed to bring about a war with Austria and to assist Sardinia in developing an expanded northern Italian kingdom.

The concept of an Italian confederation under the papacy was contributed by Napoleon III and demonstrates his lack of understanding about the nature of Italian political ambitions and values during this period.

After being provoked, the Austrians declared war on Sardinia in 1859. French forces intervened and the Austrians were defeated in the battles of Magenta (June 4) and Solferino (June 24). Napoleon III's support wavered for four reasons: 1) Prussia mobilized and expressed sympathy for Austria; 2) the outbreak of uncontrolled revolutions in several Northern Italian states; 3) the forcefulness of the new Austrian military efforts; and 4) the lack of public support in France for his involvement and the mounting criticism being advanced by the French Catholic Church, which opposed the war against Catholic Austria.

Napoleon III, without consulting Cavour, signed a secret peace (The Truce of Villafranca) on July 11, 1859. Sardinia received Lombardy but not Venetia; the other terms indicated that Sardinian influence would be restricted and that Austria would remain a power in Italian politics. The terms of Villafranca were clarified and finalized with the Treaty of Zurich (1859).

In 1860, Cavour arranged the annexation of Parma, Modena, Romagna, and Tuscany into Sardinia. These actions were recognized by the Treaty of Turin between Napoleon III and Victor Emmanuel II; Nice and Savoy were transferred to France. With these acquisitions, Cavour anticipated the need for a period of tranquility to incorporate these territories into Sardinia.

Giuseppe Garibaldi and his Red Shirts landed in Sicily (May 1860) and extended the nationalist activity to the south. Within three months, Sicily was taken and by September 7th, Garibaldi was in Naples and the Kingdom of the Two Sicilies had fallen under Sardinian influence. Cavour distrusted Garibaldi but Victor Emmanuel II encouraged him.

In February 1861, in Turin, Victor Emmanuel was declared King of Italy and presided over an Italian Parliament which represented the entire Italian peninsula with the exception of Venetia and the Patrimony of St. Peter (Rome). Cavour died in June 1861.

Venetia was incorporated into the Italian Kingdom in 1866 as a result of an alliance between Bismarck's Prussia and the Kingdom of Italy which preceded the German Civil War between Austria and Prussia. In return for opening a southern front against Austria, Prussia, upon its victory, arranged for Venetia to be transferred to Italy.

Bismarck was again instrumental in the acquisition of Rome into the Italian Kingdom in 1870. In 1870, the Franco-Prussian War broke out and the French garrison, which had been in Rome providing protection for the Pope, was withdrawn to serve on the front against Prussia. Italian troops seized Rome, and in 1871, as a result of a plebiscite, Rome became the capital of the Kingdom of Italy.

BISMARCK AND THE UNIFICATION OF GERMANY

During the period after 1815 Prussia emerged as an alternative to a Hapsburg-based Germany. During the early nineteenth century, Germany was politically decentralized and consisted of dozens of independent states. This multi-state situation had been in place for centuries and had been sanctioned by the Peace of Westphalia in 1648. Prussia had absorbed many of the smaller states during the eighteenth and early nineteenth centuries.

Otto von Bismarck (1810 – 1898) entered the diplomatic service of William I as the Revolutions of 1848 were being suppressed. By the early 1860s Bismarck had emerged as the principal adviser and minister to the King. Bismarck was an advocate of a Prussian-based (Hohenzollern) Germany. During the 1850s and 1860s Bismarck supported a series of military reforms which improved the Prussian army. In 1863 Bismarck joined the Russians in suppressing a Polish rebellion; this enterprise resulted in improved Russian-Prussian relations.

In 1863, the Schleswig-Holstein crisis broke. These provinces, which were occupied by Germans, were under the personal rule of Christian IX of Denmark. The Danish government advanced a new constitution which specified that Schleswig and Holstein would be annexed into Denmark. German reaction was predictable and Bismarck arranged for a joint Austro-Prussian military action. Denmark was defeated and agreed (Treaty of Vienna, 1864) to give up the provinces. Schleswig and Holstein were to be jointly administered by the victors, Austria and Prussia.

Questions of jurisdiction provided the rationale for estranged relations between Austria and Prussia. In 1865, a temporary settlement was reached in the Gastein Convention, which stated that Prussia would administer Schleswig and Austria would manage Holstein. During 1865 and 1866, Bismarck made diplomatic preparations for the forthcoming struggle with Austria. Italy, France, and Russia would not interfere, and Great Britain was not expected to involve itself in a Central European war.

The German Civil War (also known as The Seven Weeks' War) was devastating to Austria. The humiliating defeat at Koniggratz (July 4, 1866) demonstrated the ineptitude of the Austrian forces when confronted by the Prussian army led by General von Moltke. Within two months, Austria had to agree to the peace terms which were drawn up at Nikolsburg and finalized by the Peace of Prague (August 1866).

There were three principal terms. Austria would not be part of any new German state. The Kleindeutsch plan had prevailed over the Grossdeutsch plan. Venetia would be ceded to Italy. Austria would pay an indemnity to Prussia.

In the next year, 1867, the North German Confederation was established by Bismarck. It was designed to facilitate the movement toward a unified German state and included all the German states except Baden, Württemberg, Bavaria, and Saxony; the King of Prussia served as President of the Confederation.

In 1870, the deteriorating relations between France and Germany became critical over the Ems Dispatch. William I, while vacationing at Ems, was approached by representatives of the French government who requested a Prussian pledge not to interfere on the issue of the vacant Spanish throne. William I refused to give such a pledge and informed Bismarck of these developments through a telegram from Ems.

Bismarck exploited the situation by initiating a propaganda campaign against the French. Subsequently, France declared war and the Franco-Prussian War (1870–1871) commenced. Prussian victories at Sedan and Metz proved decisive; Napoleon III and his leading general, Marshal MacMahon, were captured. Paris continued to resist but fell to the Prussians in January 1871. The Treaty of Frankfurt (May, 1871) concluded the war and resulted in France ceding Alsace-Lorraine to Germany and a German occupation until an indemnity was paid.

The German Empire was proclaimed on January 18, 1871 with William I becoming the Emperor of Germany. Bismarck became the Imperial Chancellor. Bavaria, Baden, Württemberg, and Saxony were incorporated into the new Germany.

INTER-EUROPEAN RELATIONS, 1848 – 1878

Since the Napoleonic era the peace in Europe had been sustained because of the memories of the devastation and the disruption caused by the wars of the French

Revolution and Napoleonic Age; the primary structure that maintained the peace was the Concert System. The Concert of Europe was a rather loose and ill-defined understanding among the European nations that they would join together to resolve problems which threatened the status quo; it was believed that joint action would be undertaken to prohibit any drastic alteration in the European system or balance of power. The credibility of the Concert of Europe was undermined by the failure of the powers to cooperate during the revolution of 1848 and 1849. Between 1848 and 1878 the peace among the European powers was interrupted by the Crimean War (1854 – 56) and challenged by the crisis centered on the Russo-Turkish War of 1877 – 78.

THE CRIMEAN WAR

The origins of the Crimean War are to be found in the dispute between two differing groups of Christians (and their protectors) over privileges in the Holy Land. During the 19th century Palestine was part of the Ottoman Turkish Empire. In 1852, the Turks negotiated an agreement with the French to provide enclaves in the Holy Land to Roman Catholic religious orders; this arrangement appeared to jeopardize already existing agreements which provided access to Greek Orthodox religious orders. Czar Nicholas, unaware of the impact of his action, ordered Russian troops to occupy several Danubian principalities; his strategy was to withdraw from these areas once the Turks agreed to clarify and guarantee the rights of the Greek Orthodox orders. The role of Britain in this developing crisis was critical; Nicholas mistakenly was convinced that the British Prime Minister, Lord Aberdeen, would be sympathetic to the Russian policy. Aberdeen, who headed a coalition cabinet, sought to use the Concert of Europe system to settle the question. However, Lord Palmerston, the Home Secretary, supported the Turks; he was suspicious of Russian intervention in the region. Consequently, misunderstandings about Britain's policy developed. In October, 1853, the Turks demanded that the Russians withdraw from the occupied principalities; the Russians failed to respond and the Turks declared war. In February, 1854 Nicholas advanced a draft for a settlement of the Russo-Turkish War; it was rejected and Great Britain and France joined the Ottoman Turks and declared war on Russia.

With the exception of some naval encounters in the Gulf of Finland off the Aaland Islands, this war was conducted on the Crimean peninsula in the Black Sea. In September, 1854, over 50,000 British and French troops landed in the Crimea, determined to take the Russian port city of Sebastopol. While this war has been remembered for the work of Florence Nightengale and the "Charge of the Light Brigade," it was a conflict in which there were more casualties from disease and the weather than from combat. In December 1854, Austria, with great reluctance, became a co-signatory of the Four Points of Vienna which was a statement of British and French war aims. The Four Points specified that (1) Russia should renounce any claims to the occupied principalities, (2) the 1841 Straits Convention would be revised, (3) navigation in the mouth of the Danube River (on the Black Sea) should be internationalized, and (4) Russia should withdraw any claim to having a 'special' protective role for Greek Orthodox residents in the Ottoman Empire. In 1855, Piedmont joined Britain and France in the war. In March 1855 Czar Nicholas died and was succeeded by Alexander II who was opposed to continuing the war. In December 1855, the Austrians, under excessive pressure from the British, French, and Piedmontese, sent an ultimatum to Russia in which they threatened to renounce their neutrality. In response, Alexander II indicated that he would accept the Four Points.

Representatives of the belligerents convened in Paris between February and April 1856. The resulting Peace of Paris had the following major provisions. Russia had to acknowledge international commissions which were to regulate maritime traffic on the Danube, recognize Turkish control of the mouth of the Danube, renounce all claims to the Danubian Principalities of Moldavia and Wallachia (this later led to the establishment of Rumania), agree not to fortify the Aaland Islands, renounce its previously espoused position of protector of the Greek Orthodox residents of the Ottoman Empire, and return all occupied territories to the Ottoman Empire. The Straits Convention of 1841 was revised through the neutralization of the Black Sea. The Declaration of Paris specified the rules which would regulate commerce during periods of war. Lastly, the independence and integrity of the Ottoman Empire were recognized and guaranteed by the signatories.

THE EASTERN QUESTION TO THE CONGRESS OF BERLIN

Another challenge to the Concert of Europe developed in the 1870s with a seemingly endless number of Balkan crises. Once again, the conflict initially involved Russia and Ottoman Turks but it quickly became a conflict with Britain and Russia serving as the principal protagonists. British concerns over Russian ambitions in the Balkans reached a critical level in 1877 when Russia went to war with the Turks.

In 1876, the Turkish forces under the leadership of Osman Pasha soundly defeated the Serbian armies. Serbia requested assistance from the great powers and, as a consequence of the political pressures exercised by the great powers, the Turks agreed to participate in a conference in Constantinople; the meeting resulted in a draft agreement between the Serbs and the Turks. However, Britain quietly advised the Sultan, Abdul Hamid II, to scuttle the agreement, which he did. In June 1877 Russia dispatched forces across the Danube. During the next month, Osman Pasha took up a defensive position in Plevna. During the period of the siege, sympathy in the west shifted toward the Turks, and Britain and Austria became alarmed over the extent of Russian influence in the region. In March 1878, the Russians and the Turks signed the Peace of San Stephano; implementation of its provisions would have resulted in Russian hegemony in the Balkans and dramatically altered the balance of power in the eastern Mediterranean. Specifically it provided for the establishment of a large Bulgarian state which would be under Russian influence; the transfer of Dobrudja, Kars, Ardahan, Bayazid, and Batum to Russia; the expansion of Serbia and Montenegro; and the establishment of an autonomous Bosnia-Herzegovina which would be under Russian control.

Britain, under the leadership of Prime Minister Benjamin Disraeli, denounced the San Stephano Accord, dispatched a naval squadron to Turkish waters, and demanded that the San Stephano agreement be scrapped. The German Chancellor, Otto von Bismarck, intervened and offered his services as mediator.

The delegates of the major powers convened in June and July 1878 to negotiate a settlement. Prior to the meeting, Disraeli had concluded a series of secret arrangements with Austria, Russia and Turkey. The combined impact of these accommodations was to restrict Russian expansion in the region, reaffirm the independence of Turkey, and maintain British control of the Mediterranean. The specific terms of the Treaty of Berlin resulted in the following: 1) recognition of Rumania, Serbia and Montenegro as independent states; 2) the establishment of the autonomous principality of Bulgaria, 3) Austrian acquisition of Bosnia and Herzegovina; and 4) the transfer of Cyprus to Great Britain.

The Russians, who had won the war against Turkey and had imposed the harsh terms of the San Stephano Treaty, found that they left the conference with very little (Kars, Batum, etc.) for their effort. Although Disraeli was the primary agent of this anti-Russian settlement, the Russians blamed Bismarck for their dismal results. Their hostility toward Germany led Bismarck (1879) to embark upon a new system of alliances which transformed European diplomacy and rendered any additional efforts of the Concert of Europe futile.

CAPITALISM AND THE EMERGENCE OF THE NEW LEFT, 1848 – 1914

Economic Developments: The New Industrial Order

During the nineteenth century, Europe experienced the full impact of the Industrial Revolution. The new economic order not only altered the working lives of most Europeans, but also impacted on the very fiber of European culture. The shifts in demography were revolutionary; the process of urbanization was irreversible and the transformation of European values and lifestyle were dramatic. The Industrial Revolution resulted in improving aspects of the physical lives of a greater number of Europeans; at the same time, it led to a factory system with undesirable working and living conditions and the abuses of child labor. While the advantages of industrialism were evident, the disadvantages were more subtle; the industrial working class was more vulnerable than the agrarian peasants because of the fragile nature of the industrial economy. This new economy was based on a dependent system which involved (1) the availability of raw materials, (2) an adequate labor supply, and (3) a distribution system which successfully marketed the products; the distribution system was in itself dependent upon a satisfactory availability of money throughout the economic system. If any one of these requirements was impeded or absent, the industrial work force could be confronted with unemployment and poverty. The industrial system was based fundamentally in developing capitalism which itself was essentially grounded in an appreciation of material culture. The standard of living, neo-mercantilist attitudes towards national power, and the goal of accumulation of wealth were manifestations of this materialism.

As the century progresses, the inequities of the system became increasingly evident. Trade-unionism and socialist political parties emerged which attempted to address these problems and improve the lives of the working class. In most of these expressions of discontent, the influences of Utopian Socialism or Marxism were evident and can be detected readily. Socialism was steeped in economic materialism which had emerged in the eighteenth century and came to dominate the nineteenth and twentieth centuries. Economics was a component in the rise of scientism; by its very nature, it advanced the values of material culture.

Marx and Scientific Socialism

During the period from 1815 to 1848, Utopian Socialists, such as Robert Owen, Saint Simon, and Charles Fourier advocated the establishment of a political-economic system which was based on romantic concepts of the ideal society. The failure of the Revolutions of 1848 and 1849 discredited the Utopian Socialists, and the new "Scientific Socialism" advanced by Karl Marx (1818 – 1883) became the primary ideology of protest and revolution. Marx, a German philosopher, developed a communist philosophic system which was founded on the inherent goodness of man; this Rousseau-influenced position argued that men were basically good but had been corrupted by the artificial institutions (states, churches, etc.) from which they had evolved. Marx stated that the history of humanity was the history of class struggle and that the process of the struggle (the dialectic) would continue until a classless society was realized; the Marxian dialectic was driven by the dynamics of materialism. Further, he contended that the age of the bourgeois domination of the working class was the most severe and oppressive phase of the struggle. The proletariat, or the industrial working class, needed to be educated and led towards a violent revolution which would destroy the institutions which perpetuated the struggle and the suppression of the majority. After the revolution, the people would experience the dictatorship of the proletariat during which the Communist Party would provide leadership. Marx advanced these concepts in a series of tracts and books including *The Communist Manifesto* (1848), *Critique of Political Economy* (1859), and *Capital* (1863 – 64). In most instances, his arguments were put forth in scientific form; Marx accumulated extensive data and developed a persuasive rhetorical style. In the 1860s Marxism was being accepted by many reformers. Marx lived most of his adult life in London where he died in 1883.

The Anarchists

Anarchism emerged in the early 19th century as a consequence of the Industrial Revolution. Its early proponents, William Godwin (1756 – 1836) and Pierre Proudhon (1809 – 65) argued that anarchism, a situation where there would be no property or authority, would be attained through enlightened individualism. Proudhon, in *What is Property* (1840), stated that anarchism would be achieved through education and without violence. After the revolutions of 1848 and 1849, Michael Bakunin, a Russian, stated that violent, terrorist actions were necessary to move the people to revolt against their oppressors; anarchism has been associated with violence since Bakunin's time. A variation of anarchism, called syndicalism, was developed by Georges Sorel in France. Syndicalism, sometimes referred to as anarcho-syndicalism, involved direct economic actions in order to control industries. The strike and industrial sabotage were employed frequently by the syndicalists. Syndicalist influence was restricted to France, Spain (Confederacion Nacional del Trabajo, an organization of several syndicalist unions), and Italy (Filippo Corridoni and the young Benito Mussolini).

The Revisionist Movement

A reconsideration of Marxism commenced before Marx's death in 1883. In that year a group of British leftists organized themselves into the Fabian Society and declared that while they were sympathetic to Marxism – indeed, they considered themselves Marxists – they differed from the orthodoxy on two major points: (1) they did not accept the inevitability of revolution in order to bring about a socialist, i.e. communist society; democratic societies possessed the mechanisms which would lead to the gradual evolution of socialism; (2) the Fabians did not accept the Marxist interpretation of contemporary history; they contended the historical processes endured and were difficult to redirect and reform, while Marxists tended to accept the notion that world revolution was imminent. Sidney and Beatrice Webb, George Bernard Shaw, Keir Hardie, and several others joined in forming the Fabian Society. Later it would split over the Boer War but its members would serve in every Labor ministry.

In Germany the Social Democratic Party (SDP) had been established along the lines of Marxist orthodoxy. In the 1890s, Edward Bernstein (1850 – 1932), who was influenced by the Fabians, redirected the efforts and platform of the SDP toward the revisionist position. Within a few years, the SDP extended its credibility and support to acquire a dominant position in the Reichstag.

The French Socialist Jean Jaures (1859 – 1914) led his group to revisionism; their moderation led to increasing their seats in the Chamber of Deputies and in developing acceptance for their criticisms and proposals during the tumultuous years of the Dreyfus Affair.

While orthodox Marxists (Lenin) denounced the revisionist movement, the majority of socialists in 1914 were revisionists who were willing to use the democratic process to bring about their goals.

BRITAIN AND FRANCE

During the second half of the 19th century, Britain and France enjoyed considerable economic prosperity, experienced periods of jingoistic nationalism, and were confronted with demands for expanding democracy. Great Britain, under the leadership of Lord Palmerston, William Gladstone and Benjamin Disraeli, represented a dichotomy of values and political agendas. On one hand, Britain led Europe into an age of revitalized imperialism and almost unbridled capitalism; on the other hand, Gladstone and the Liberal Party advocated democratic reforms, an anti-imperialist stance, and a program to eliminate or restrict unacceptable working and social conditions. In France, the evolution of a more democratic political order was questioned by the collapse of the Second French Republic and the development of the Second Empire. However, in 1871, the Third Republic was established and the French moved closer to realizing democracy.

The Age of Palmerston

During the period from 1850 to 1865, Lord Palmerston was the dominant political power in Great Britain. Palmerston served in a range of positions including Foreign Secretary, Home Secretary, and Prime Minister. In foreign affairs Palmerston was preoccupied with colonial problems such as the Indian Muting of 1857, troubles in China, and British interests in the American Civil War; Palmerston tended to express little interest in domestic affairs. This period witnessed the realignment of political parties within British politico; the Tory Party was transformed into the Conservative Party under Disreali and the Whig Party became the Liberty Party with Gladstone serving as its new leader. It should be noted that John Bright, a manufacturer, anti-corn law advocate, and leader of the Manchester School, contributed significantly to the development of the Liberal Party. These changes in party organization involved more than appellations. The new structure more clearly represented distinct ideological positions on many substantive issues. The new political structure was facilitated by Palmerston's (the Whig) lack of interest in domestic issues and Lord Derby's (the Tory leader) indifference to political issues; he was preoccupied with his study of the classics and with horse racing.

Until the 1850s the British East India Company managed India for the British government. During this decade a new rifle, the Enfield, was introduced. The procedure for loading the Enfield required that the covering for the cartridges be removed by the teeth prior to inserting them in the rifle. Rumors circulated that the covering was a grease made from the fat of cows and swine; naturally, these rumors alarmed the Hindu and Muslim troops. Troops mutined in Calcutta in 1857 and within a few months over a third of India was in the hands of rebels and Europeans were being killed. A British led force of about 3,000 troops under Sir Hugh Rose suppressed the mutiny which lacked cohesion in its aims, organization, and leadership. By January 1858, Britain had re-established its control of India; the East India Company was dissolved and replaced by the direct authority of London.

During the 1850s and 1860s Palmerston sought to clarify British commercial access to China. In 1858, with the support of French troops, the British army took the Taka Forts on the Peiko River and, in 1860, captured Peking. As a result, China agreed to open Tientsin and other ports to the European powers.

The American Civil War (1861 – 65) curtailed the supply of unprocessed cotton to British mills. The British economy was affected adversely and significant unemployment and factory closings resulted. The American war also led to a discussion within Britain on the fundamental issues of liberty, slavery, and democracy. A crisis between Britain and the United States developed over the Trent Affair (1861) during which a British ship was boarded by American sailors. In the end, the British government and people supported the Union cause because of ideological considerations; even in the areas affected by the shortage of cotton, there was general support for the North.

Disraeli, Gladstone, and the Era of Democratic Reforms

In 1865 Palmerston died and during the next two decades significant domestic developments occured which expanded democracy in Great Britain. The dominant leaders of this period were William Gladstone (1809 – 1898) and Benjamin Disraeli (1804 – 1881). Gladstone, who was initially a Conservative, emerged as a severe critic of the Corn Laws and, as a budgetary expert, became Chancellor of the Exchequer under Palmerston. As the leader of the Liberal Party (to 1895), Gladstone supported Irish Home Rule, fiscal responsibility, free trade, and the extension of democratic principles. He was opposed to imperialism, the involvement of Britain in European affairs, and the further centralization of the British government. Disraeli argued for an aggressive foreign policy, the expansion of the British Empire, and, after opposing democratic reforms, the extension of the franchise.

After defeating Gladstone's effort to extend the vote in 1866, Disraeli advanced the Reform Bill of 1867. This bill, which expanded on the Reform Bill of 1832, was enacted and specified two reforms: 1) There would be a redistribution (similar to reapportionment) of seats which would provide a more equitable representation in the House of Commons; the industrial cities and boroughs gained seats at the expense of some depopulated areas in the north and west. 2) The right to vote was extended to include all adult male citizens of boroughs who paid £10 or more rent annually, and all adult male citizens of the counties who were £12 tenants or £5 leaseholders.

The consequence of this act was that almost all men over 21 years in age who resided in urban centers were granted the right to vote. In 1868, the newly extended electorate provided the Liberals with a victory and Gladstone commenced his first of four terms as Prime Minister.

Gladstone's first ministry (1868 – 1874) was characterized by a wave of domestic legislation which reflected the movement toward democracy. Among the measures which were enacted were five acts:

1) The Ballot Act (1872) which provided for the secret ballot; this act realized a major Chartist demand of the 1830s;

2) Civil Services Reform (1870) which introduced the system of competitive examination for government positions;

3) The Education Act (1870) which established a system of school districts throughout the country, and provided assistance in the organization of school boards,

and for the establishment of schools in poverty stricken regions; free elementary education in Britain would not be realized until 1891,

4) The Land Act (1870) was an attempt to resolve economic and social inequities in Ireland. However, it did not succeed in providing Irish tenants with reasonable safeguards against arbitrary eviction or the imposition of drastic increases in rent, and

5) The University Act (1870) eliminated the use of religious tests which provided a quota of seats in universities for members of the Anglican church.

Between 1874 and 1880 Disraeli served as Prime Minister, and while he was deeply concerned with foreign difficulties, he did succeed in developing the notion of Tory Democracy which was directed at domestic issues. Tory Democracy represented Disreali's views on how the Conservative Party would support necessary domestic action on behalf of the common good.

In 1875, through Disraeli's support, the following measures were passed: 1) Laws which lessened the regulation of trade unions; 2) Food and Drug Act which regulated the sale of these items; 3) Public Health Act which specified government requirements and standards for sanitation; 4) The Artisan's Dwelling Act.

While a few Conservatives, such as Lord Randolph Churchill, attempted to extend the progress of Tory Democracy and to incorporate it permamently within the Conservative program, most of the Conservative Party abandoned this approach after Disraeli's death in 1881.

During his remaining ministries (1880 – 85, 1886, and 1892 – 95), Gladstone was preoccupied with Ireland. However, a further extension of the franchise occurred in 1884 with the passage of the Representation of the People Act which granted the right to vote to adult males in the counties on the same basis as in the boroughs. In 1885 another redistribution of seats in the House of Commons was approved on the ratio of one seat for every 50,000 citizens.

The Second French Republic and the Second Empire

Louis Napoleon became the President of the Second French Republic in December 1848. It was evident that he was not committed to the Republic; in May 1849, elections for the Legislative Assembly clearly indicated that the people were not bound to its continuance either. In this election, the Conservatives and Monarchists scored significant gains; the republicans and radicals lost power in the Assembly. During the three year life of the Second Republic, Louis Napoleon demonstrated his skills as a gifted politican through the manipulation of the various factions in French politics. His deployment of troops in Italy to rescue and restore Pope Pius IX was condemned by the republicans, but strongly supported by the monarchists and moderates. As a consequence of the French military intervention, a French garrison under General Oudinot was stationed in Rome until the fall of 1870 when it was recalled during the Franco-Prussian War.

Louis Napoleon initiated a policy which minimized the importance of the Legislative Assembly, capitalized on the developing Napoleonic Legend, and courted the support of the army, the Catholic Church, and a range of conservative political groups. The Falloux Law returned control of education to the church. Further, Louis Napoleon was confronted with Article 45 of the constitution which stipulated that the president was limited to one four-year term; he had no intention of relinquishing power. With the assistance of a core of dedicated supporters, Louis Napoleon arranged for a coup d'etat on the night of December 1 – 2, 1851. The Second Republic fell and was soon replaced by the Second French Empire.

Louis Napoleon drafted a new constitution which resulted in a highly centralized government centered around himself. He was to have a ten year term, power to declare war, to lead the armed forces, to conduct foreign policy, and to initiate and pronounce all laws; the new Legislative Assembly would be under the control of the president. On December 2, 1852, he announced that he was Napoleon III, Emperor of the French.

The domestic history of the Second Empire is divided into two periods: 1851 to 1860, during which Napoleon III's control was direct and authoritarian, and 1860 to 1870, the decade of the Liberal Empire, during which the regime was liberalized through a series of reforms. During the Second Empire, living conditions in France generally improved. The government instituted agreements and actions which stimulated the movement toward free trade (Cobden-Chevalier Treaty of 1860), improved the efficiency of the French economic system (Credit Mobilier and the Credit Focier, both established in 1852), and conducted major public works programs in French cities with the assistance of such talented leaders as Baron Haussmann, the prefect of the Seine. Even though many artists and scholars (Victor Hugo, Jules Michelet, and Gustav Flaubert) were censored and, on occasion, prosecuted for their works, the artistic and scholarly achievements of the Second Empire were impressive. While Flaubert and Baudelaire, and in music, Jacques Offenbach, were most productive during these decades, younger artists, such as Renoir, Manet, and Cezanne began their careers and were influenced by the culture of the Second Empire. The progressive liberalization of the government during the 1860s resulted in extending the powers of the Legislative Assembly, restricting church control over secondary education, and permitting the development of trade unions. In large part, this liberalization was designed to divert criticism from Napoleon III's unsuccessful foreign policy. French involvement in Algeria, the Crimean War, the process of Italian unification, the establishment of colonial presences in Senegal, Somaliland, and Indo-China (Laos, Cambodia, and Viet Nam), and the ill-fated Mexican adventure (the short-lived rule of Maximilian), resulted in increased criticism of Napoleon III and his authority. The Second Empire collapsed after the capture of Napoleon III during the Franco-Prussian War (1870 – 71). After a regrettable Parisian experience with a communist type of government, the Third French Republic was established; it would survive until 1940.

IMPERIAL RUSSIA

The autocracy of Nicholas I's regime was not threatened by the revolutionary movements of 1848. The consequences of the European revolutionary experience of 1848 to 1849 reinforced the conservative ideology which was the basis of the Romanov regime. In 1848 and 1849, Russian troops suppressed disorganized Polish attempts to reassert Polish nationalism.

Russian involvement in the Crimean war met with defeat. France, Britain, and Piedmont emerged as the victors in this conflict; Russian ambitions in the eastern Mediterranean had been thwarted by a coalition of western European states. In 1855 Nicholas I died and was succeeded by Alexander II (1855 – 1881) who feared the forces of change and introduced reforms in order to remain in power.

Fearing the transformation of Russian society from below, Alexander II instituted a series of reforms which contributed to altering the nature of the social contract in Russia. With the regime in disarray after defeat in the Crimean War, Alexander II, in March 1856, indicated that Russian serfdom had to be eliminated. After several years of formulating the process for its elimination, Alexander II pronounced in 1861 that serfdom was abolished. Further, he issued the following reforms: 1) The serf (peasant) would no longer be dependent upon the lord; 2) all people were to have freedom of movement and were free to change their means of livelihood; and 3) the serf could enter into contracts and could own property.

In fact, the lives of most peasants were not affected by these reforms. Most peasants lived in local communes which regulated the lives of their members; thus, the requirements of commune life nullified the reforms of Alexander II. Another significant development was the creation of the *zemstvos*, which were assemblies which administered the local areas; through the *zemstvos* the Russian rural nobility retained control over local politics. Finally, Alexander II reformed the Russian judiciary system; the new judiciary was to be based upon such enlightened notions as jury trial, the abolition of arbitrary judicial processes, and the equality of all before the law. In fact, the only substantive change was the improvement in the efficiency of the Russian judiciary; however, the reforms did lead to expectations which were later realized.

The reforms of Alexander II did not resolve the problems of Russia. During the 1860s and 1870s criticism of the regime mounted. Moderates called for Russia to proceed along Western lines in a controlled manner in addressing political and economic problems; radicals argued that the overthrow of the system was the only recourse to the problems which confronted the Russian people. Quite naturally, Alexander II and other members of the power structure maintained that Russia would solve its own problems within the existing structure and without external intervention. The economic problems which plagued Russia were staggering. Under the three-field system which was utilized, one third of Russian agricultural land was not being used; the population was increasing dramatically but food protection was not keeping pace. Peasants were allowed to buy land and to live outside of the communes; however, even with the establishment of the Peasants Land Bank (1883), most peasants were unable to take advantage of this opportunity to become property owners. During years of great hardship, the government did intervene with emergency measures which temporarily reduced, deferred, or suspended taxes and/or payments.

While Russian agriculture appeared to have no direction, nor to have experienced any real growth during this period, Russian industry, particularly in textiles and metallurgy, did develop. Between 1870 and 1900, as the result of French loans, the Russian railroad network was expanded significantly. In large part, the expansion of Russian industry resulted from direct governmental intervention. In addition to constructing railroads, the government subsidized industrial development through a protective tariff and by awarding major contracts to emerging industries. From 1892 to 1903 Count S. Y. Witte served as Minister of Finance. As a result of his efforts to stimulate the economy, Russian industry prospered during most of the 1890s. During this same period the government consistently suppressed the development of organized labor. In 1899 a depression broke and the gains of the 1890s quickly were replaced by the increased unemployment and industrial shutdowns; this very difficult situation was aggravated by the outbreak of the Russo-Japanese war in 1904.

The last years of the reign of Alexander II witnessed increased political opposition which was manifested in demands for reforms from an ever more hostile group of intellectuals, the emergence of a Russian populist movement, and attempts to assassinate the czar. Some of the demands for extending reforms came from within the government from such dedicated and talented ministers as D. A. Miliutin, a Minister of War, who reorganized the Russian military system during the 1870s. However, reactionary ministers such as Count Dimitri Tolstoy, Minister of Education, did much to discredit any progressive policies emanating from the regime; Tolstoy repudiated academic freedom and advanced an anti-scientism bias. As the regime matured, greater importance was placed on traditional values. This attitude developed at the same time that nihilism, which rejected romantic illusions of the past in favor of a rugged realism, was being advanced by such writers as Ivan Turgenev in his *Fathers and Sons*.

The notion of the inevitability and desirability of a social and economic revolution was promoted through the Russian populist movement; originally, the populists were interested in an agrarian utopian order in which the lives of all peasants would be transformed into an idyllic state. The populists had no national base of support; government persecution of the populist resulted in the radicalization of the movement. In the late 1870s and early 1880s, leaders such as Andrei Zheleabov and Sophie Perovsky became obsessed with the need to assassinate Alexander II. In March, 1881, he was killed in St. Petersburg when his carriage was bombed; he was succeeded by Alexander III (1881 – 1894) who advocated a national policy based on "Orthodoxy, Autocracy, and Nationalism." Alexander III selected as his primary aides, conservatives such as Count Dimitri Tolstoy, now Minister of the Interior, Count Delianov, Minister of Education, and Constantine Pobedonostev, who headed the Russian Orthodox Church. Alexander III died in 1894 and was succeeded by the last of the Romanovs to hold power, Nicholas II (1894 – 1917). Nicholas II displayed his lack of intelligence, wit, and political acumen, and the absence of a firm will throughout his reign. From assertive ministers to his wife, Alexandra, to Rasputin, Nicholas tended to come under the influence of stronger personalities. The crisis confronting Imperial Russia required extraordinarily effective and cohesive leadership; with Nicholas II, the situation became more severe and, in the end, unacceptable.

The opposition to the Czarist government became more focused and thus, more threatening, with the emergence of the Russian Social Democrats and the Russian Social Revolutionaries; both groups were Marxist. Vladimir Ilyich Ulyanov, also known as Lenin, became the leader of the Bolsheviks, a splinter group of the Social Democrats. Until the impact of the 1899 depression and the horrors associated with the Russo-Japanese war were realized, groups advocating revolutions commanded little support. Even when the Revolution of 1905 occurred, the Marxist groups did not enjoy any political gains. By winter (1904 – 05), the accumulated consequences of inept management of the economy and in the prosecution of the Russo-Japanese War reached a critical stage. A group under the leadership of the radical priest Gapon marched on the Winter Palace in St. Petersburg (January 9, 1905) to submit a list of grievances to the czar; troops fired on the demonstrators and many casualties resulted on this "Bloody Sunday". In response to the massacre, a general strike was called; it was followed by a series of peasant revolts through the spring. During these same months, the Russian armed forces were being defeated by the Japanese and a lack of confidence in the regime became widespread. In June 1905, naval personnel on the battleship Potemkin mutinied while the ship was in Odessa. With this startling development, Nicholas II's government lost its nerve. In October 1905, Nicholas II issued the October Manifesto which called for the convocation of a Duma, or assembly of state, which would serve as an advisory body to the czar; extended civil liberties to include freedom of speech, assembly, and press; and announced that Nicholas II would reorganize his government.

The leading revolutionary forces differed in their responses to the manifesto. The Octobrists indicated that they were satisfied with the arrangements; the Constitutional Democrats, also known as the Cadets, demanded a more liberal representative system. The Duma convened in 1906 and, from its outset to the outbreak of the First World War, was paralyzed by its own internal factionalism which was exploited by the Czar's ministers. By 1907 Nicholas II's ministers had recovered the real power of government. Russia experienced a general though fragile economic recovery which was evident by 1909 and lasted until the war.

THE HAPSBURGS IN DECLINE: AUSTRIA-HUNGARY

After the disruptions of the Revolution of 1848 and 1849, the Austrian government had to address a series of major issues with which it found itself confronted: 1) The issue of German nationalism – the *Kleindeutsch* and the *Grossdeutsch*; 2) the problems associated with the rise of the national aspirations of the ethnic groups which resided in the Balkans; and 3) the management of an empire which was not integrated because of historic tradition and cultural diversification.

During the 1850s the Hapsburg leadership deferred any attempt to resolve these problems, and in doing so, lost the initiative. To the north, Bismarck was developing the Prussian army in anticipation for the struggle with Austria over the future of Germany; in the Balkans, the Hungarians and Czechs, while smarting from the setbacks of 1849, were agitating for national self-determination or, at the least, for a semi-autonomous state. In 1863 and 1864 Austria became involved with Prussia in a war with Denmark. This war was a prelude for the German Civil War of 1866 between Austria and Prussia; Prussia prevailed. The impact of these developments on the Austrian government necessitated a reappraisal of its national policies. Without doubt the most significant development resulting from this reappraisal was the Ausgleich or Compromise, which transformed Austria into the Austro-Hungarian Empire. The Hungarians would have their own assembly, cabinet, and administrative system, and would support and participate in the Imperial army and in the Imperial government. Not only did the Ausgleich assimilate the Hungarians and nullify them as a primary opposition group, it also led to a more efficient government.

During the period from 1867 to 1914, Austria-Hungary continued to experience difficulties with the subject nationalities and with adjusting to a new power structure in Central Europe in which Austria-Hungary was admittedly secondary to Germany. At the same time, it enjoyed a cultural revival in which its scholars (Sigmund Freud, Carl Menger, and Heinrich Friedjung), painters (Hans Makart and Adalvert Stiftor), dramatists (Hugo von Hofmannsthal), and writers (Stefan Zweig and Rilke) were renowned throughout the world.

THE BALKAN STATES AND THE DISINTEGRATION OF THE OTTOMAN EMPIRE

During the period from 1848 to 1914 the influence of the Ottoman Empire was eroded steadily because of its own internal structure and system, the ineptitude of its leaders, the lack of cohesion within the empire, the development of nationalist ambitions among many ethnic groups in the region, and the expansionist policies of Austria-Hungary and Russia in the Balkans, and of Great Britain in the eastern Mediterranean.

By 1914 Rumania, Serbia, Bulgaria, and Montenegro had been established as independent states, Austria had annexed Bosnia and Herzegovina, Britain held Cyprus, and Russia had extended its influence over the new Bulgaria.

ORIGINS, MOTIVES, AND IMPLICATIONS OF THE NEW IMPERIALISM, 1870-1914

During the first seven decades of the 19th century, the European powers did not pursue active imperial expansion. Internal European development preoccupied the powers; colonies were viewed as liabilities because of the direct costs associated with their administration. However, this attitude to extra-European activity began to change in the 1870s and, within the next twenty years, most of the European states were conducting aggressive imperial policies. This sharp departure from previous policy was caused by economic, political, and cultural factors. By the 1870s the European industrial economies had developed to a level where they required external markets to distribute the products which could not be absorbed within their domestic economies. Further, excess capital was available and foreign investment, while with some risk, appeared to offer the promise of high return. Finally, the need for additional sources of raw materials served as an economic rationale and stimulant for imperialism. In part, these economic considerations arose from the existing political forces of the era and, at the same time, motivated the contemporary political leadership to be sympathetic in their reappraisal of imperialism. Politicians were also influenced by the numerous missionary societies which sought government protection, if not support, in extending Christianity throughout the world; British and French missionary societies were vehement in their anti-slavery position. Further, European statesmen, cognizant of the emergence of a new distribution of power in Europe, were interested in asserting their national power overseas through the acquisition of strategic – and many not so strategic – colonies. Disraeli and Salisbury of England, Thiers and Ferry of France, and later Bismarck of Germany were influenced by yet another factor: the European cultural sentiments of the 1870s and 1880s. The writings of John Seeley, Anatole Leroy-Beaulieu and others suggested that the future status of the powers would be dependant upon the extent and significance of their imperial holdings; these thoughts were later amplified by the social and national Darwinists. Exploration and imperial policies were supported by the public throughout the era; national pride and economic opportunities were the factors upon which this popular support was based.

Unlike colonial policies of earlier centuries, the "New Imperialism" of the 1870s was comprehensive in scope and, as Benjamin Disraeli argued in 1872, a call to "greatness" where a nation was to fulfill its destiny. From Disraeli to Kipling to Churchill, there were few leaders who would differ sharply from this view. On the continent, the New Imperialism was opposed most vigorously by orthodox Marxists; even the revisionist groups such as the Social Democratic Party and, during the Boer War, the English Fabian Society, supported imperial policies.

The Scramble for Colonies

The focus of most of the European imperial activities during the late 19th century was Africa. Since the 1850s, Africa had commanded the attention of European explorers such as Richard Burton, Carl Peters, David Livingston, and many others, who were interested in charting the unknown interior of the continent, and, in particular, in locating the headwaters of the Nile. Initially, European interest in these activities was romantic; with John Hanning Speke's discovery of Lake Victoria (1858), Livingston's surveying of the Zambezi, and Stanley's work on the Congo River, Europeans became enraptured with the greatness and novelty of Africa south of the Sahara.

While Disraeli was involved in the intrigue which would result in the British acquisition of the Suez Canal (1875), Britain found itself becoming increasingly involved in establishing itself as an African power. During the 1870s and 1880s Britain was involved in a Zulu War and announced the annexation of the Transvaal, which the Boers regained after their great victory of Majuba Hill (1881) over the British. At about the same time, Belgium established its interest in the Congo; France, in addition to seizing Tunisia, extended its influence into French Equitorial Africa, which was the Ubangui River Basin; and Italy established small colonies in East Africa which would later be extended. During the 1880s Germany became interested in African acquisitions and acquired several African colonies including German East Africa, the Cameroons, Togoland, and German South West Africa. All of these imperial activities heightened tensions among the European powers. Consequently, the Berlin Conference (1884 – 85) was convened. The conference resulted in an agreement which specified the following: 1) The Congo would be under the control of Belgium through an International Association; 2) more liberal use of the Niger and Congo rivers; and 3) European powers could acquire African territory through first occupation and secondly notifying the other European states of their occupation and claim.

Between 1885 and 1914 the principal European states continued to enhance their positions in Africa. Without doubt, Britain was the most active and successful. From 1885 to 1890 Britain expanded its control over Nigeria, moved north from the Cape of Good Hope, and became further involved in East Africa. By this time Salisbury was the leader of the Conservative Party and, when in office, he fostered imperial expansion. Gladstone was still an anti-imperialist and the leader of the Liberal Party; he found the imperialist forces so formidable that he had to compromise his position on occasion when he was Prime Minister. During the 1880s an Islamic revolution under the Mahdi, an Islamic warrior, developed in the Sudan. In 1884 Gladstone sent General Charles Gordon to evacuate Khartoum; Gordon and the city's defenders were slaughtered by the Mahdi's forces in January, 1885. The British found themselves confronted with a continuing native insurrection in the Sudan which was not suppressed effectively until Kitchener's victory at Omdurman in 1898. The French were also quite active during this period; they unified Senegal, the Ivory Coast, and Guinea into French West Africa and extended it to Timbuktu, and moved up the Ubangui toward Lake Chad. While the British had difficulties in the Sudan, the French had to suppress a native insurrection in Madagascar which was prolonged to 1896.

The British movement north of the Cape of Good Hope resulted in a different type of struggle – one that involved Europeans fighting one another rather than a native African force. The Boers had a developed settlement in South Africa since the beginning of the nineteenth century. With the discovery of gold (1882) in the Transvaal, many English Cape settlers moved into the region. The Boers, under the leadership of Paul Kruger, restricted the political and economic rights of the British settlers and developed alternative railroads through Mozambique which would lessen the Boer dependency on the Cape colony. Relations between the British and Boers steadily deteriorated; in 1895, the Jameson Raid, an ill-conceived action not approved by Britain, failed to result in restoring the status of British citizens. The crisis mounted and, in 1899, the Boer War began; from 1899 to 1903, the British and Boers fought a war which was costly to both sides. Britain prevailed and by 1909, the Transvaal, Orange Free State, Natal, and the Cape of Good Hope were united into the Union of South Africa.

Another area of increased imperialist activity was the Pacific, where the islands appealed to many nations. In 1890, the American naval Captain Alfred Mahan published *The Influence of Sea Power Upon History*; in this book he argued that history demonstrated that those nations which controlled the seas prevailed. During the 1880s and 1890s naval ships required coaling stations. While Britain, the Netherlands, and France demonstrated that they were interested in Pacific islands, the most active states in this region during the last twenty years of the 19th century were Germany and the United States. Britain's Pacific interests were motivated primarily in sustaining its control of Australia. The French were interested in Tahiti; after a dispute with France over the Samoan Islands, the islands were split with France, Germany, and the United States. The United States acquired the Philippines in 1898; Germany gained part of New Guinea, and the Marshall, Caroline, and Mariana island chains. The European powers were also interested in the Asian mainland. In 1900, the Boxer Rebellion broke in Peking; it was a native reaction against Western influence in China. An international force was organized to break the siege of the Western legations. Most powers agreed with the American Open Door Policy which recognized the independence and integrity of China and provided economic access for all the powers. Rivalry over China (Manchuria) was a principal cause for the outbreak of the Russo-Japanese War in 1904.

THE AGE OF BISMARCK, 1871 – 1890

The Development of the German Empire

During the period from the establishment of the German Empire in January 1871 to his dismissal as Chancellor of Germany in March 1890, Otto von Bismarck dominated European diplomacy and established an integrated political and economic structure for the new German state. Bismarck established a statist system which was reactionary in political philosophy and based upon industrialism, militarism and innovative social legislation. German adaptation during the *Grundjahre* (the founding years of the new industrial order, 1870 – 1875) was staggering; remarkable increases in productivity and the expansion of industrialization took place during the first twenty years of the German Empire's history.

Until the mid-19th century, Germany consisted of numerous independent states which tended to be identified with regional rather than national concerns; to a large degree, this condition reflected the continuing impact of the Peace of Westphalia (1648). With the unification of Germany, a German state became a reality but the process of integration of regional economic, social, political, and cultural interests had not yet occurred. Bismarck, with the consent and approval of Wilhelm I, the German Emperor, developed a constitution for the new nation which provided for the following:

1) The Emperor would be the executor of state and, as such, establish the domestic and foreign policies; he was also the commander of the armed forces. The Chancellor (similar to Prime Minister) held office at the discretion of the Emperor.

2) A bicameral legislature was established. It consisted of the *Reichstag*; a lower body which represented the nation (the *Volk*); and the Bundesrat, an upper body which represented the various German states. During Bismarck's tenure the *Bundesrat* identified with reactionary conservative positions and served to check any populism which would be reflected in the Reichstag.

During the 1870s and 1880s Bismarck's domestic policies were directed at the establishment of a united strong German state which would be capable of defending itself from a French war of revenge which would be designed to restore Alsace-Lorraine to France. Laws were enacted which unified the monetary system, established an Imperial Bank and strengthened existing banks, developed universal German civil and criminal codes, and required compulsory military service. All of these measures contributed to the integration of the German state.

The German political system was multi-party. The most significant political parties of the era were (1) the Conservatives, which represented the Junkers of Prussia, (2) the Progressives, which unsuccessfully sought to extend democracy through continuing criticism of Bismarck's autocratic procedures; (3) the National Liberals, who represented the German middle class and identified with German nationalism and who provided support for Bismarck's policies; (4) the Center Party (also known as the Catholic Party), which approved Bismarck's policy of centralization and promoted the political concept of Particularism which advocated regional priorities, and (5) the Social Democratic Party (S.P.D.), a Marxist group, which advocated sweeping social legislation, the realization of genuine democracy, and the demilitarization of the German government. Bismarck was unsuccessful in stopping the influence of the Center Party through his anti-Catholic *Kulturkampf* (the May Laws) and in thwarting the growth of the Social Democrats.

In order to develop public support for the government and to minimize the threat from the left, Bismarck instituted a protective tariff, which maintained domestic production, and many social and economic laws which provided social security, regulated child labor, and improved working conditions for all Germans.

European Diplomacy

Bismarck's foreign policy was centered on the primary principle of maintaining the diplomatic isolation of France. After a few years of recovery from their defeat in the Franco-Prussian War, the French were regaining their confidence and publicly discussing the feasibility of a war of revenge to regain Alsace-Lorraine. In 1875, the War-In-Sight-Crisis occurred between the French and Germans. While war was avoided, the crisis clearly indicated the delicate state of the Franco-German relationship. In the crisis stemming from the Russo-Turkish War (1877 – 78), Bismarck tried to serve as the "Honest Broker" at the Congress of Berlin (see Chapter 5). Russia did not succeed at the conference and, incorrectly, blamed Bismarck for its failure. Early in the next year, a cholera epidemic affected Russian cattle herds and Germany placed an embargo on the importation of Russian beef. The Russians were outraged by the German action and launched an anti-German propaganda campaign in the Russian press. Bismarck, desiring to maintain the peace and a predictable diplomatic environment, concluded a secret defensive treaty with Austria-Hungary in 1879. The Dual Alliance was very significant because it was the first "hard" diplomatic alliance of the era. A "hard" alliance involved the specific commitment of military support; traditional or "soft" alliances involved pledges of neutrality or to hold military conversations in the event of a war. The Dual Alliance, which had a five year term and was renewable, directed that one signatory would assist the other in the event that one power was attacked by two or more states.

In 1881, another similar agreement, the Triple Alliance, was signed between Germany, Austria-Hungary, and Italy. In the 1880s, relations between Austria-Hungary and Russia became estranged over Balkan issues. Bismarck, fearing a war, intervened and, by 1887, had negotiated the secret Reinsurance Treaty with Russia. This was a "hard" defensive alliance with a three year term, renewable. Since these were "defensive" arrangements, Bismarck was confident that through German policy, the general European peace would be maintained and the security of Germany ensured through sustaining the diplomatic isolation of France. Bismarck also acted to neutralize the role of Great Britain in European affairs through the implementation of a policy which, in most but not all instances, was supportive of British interests.

In 1888 Wilhelm I died and was succeeded by his son Frederich III, who also died within a few months. Friedrich's son, Wilhelm II (1888–1918), came to power and soon found himself in conflict with Bismarck. Wilhelm II was intent upon administering the government personally and viewed Bismarck as an archaic personality. Early in 1890 two issues developed which led ultimately to Bismarck's dismissal. First, Bismarck had evolved a scheme for a fabricated attempted coup by the Social Democratic Party; his interest was to use this situation to create a national hysteria through which he could restrict the SPD through legal action. Secondly, Bismarck intended to renew the Reinsurance Treaty with Russia to maintain his policy of French diplomatic isolation. Wilhelm II opposed both of these plans; in March 1890, Bismarck, who had used the threat of resignation so skillfully in the past, suggested that he would resign if Wilhelm II would not approve of these actions. Wilhelm II accepted his resignation; in fact, Bismarck was dismissed. The diplomatic developments after 1890 (see Chapter 11) radically altered the alignment of power in Europe. The position of Chancellor of Germany was filled by a series of less talented statesmen including Count von Caprivi (1890 – 94), Prince Hohenlohe (1894 – 1900), Prince Bernhard von Bulow (1900 – 1909), and Chancellor Bethmann-Hollweg.

THE MOVEMENT TOWARD DEMOCRACY IN WESTERN EUROPE TO 1914

Great Britain

Even after the reform measures of 1867 and 1884 to 1885, the movement toward democratic reforms in Great Britain continued unabated. Unlike other European nations where the focus on democracy was limited to gaining the vote, British reform efforts were much more complex and sophisticated and involved social and economic reforms as well as continuing changes in the political process; participation in the system as well as representation were desired by many. During the 1880s and 1890s, new groups emerged which intended to extend the definition of democratic government to embrace new social and economic philosophies of the period. From women's suffrage and the condemnation of imperialism to the redistribution of wealth and the demise of nationalism, these groups represented a broad spectrum of radical and reform ideologies. Among the most significant was the Fabian Society (1883) which advanced a mode of revisionist Marxism and whose members included Sidney and Beatrice Webb, the Scottish politician Keir Hardie (who later led the Labor Party), George Bernard Shaw, H. G. Wells, the historian C. D. H. Cole, and the young Ramsay MacDonald, who became the first Labor Prime Minister. The Fabians argued for evolutionary political transformation which would result in full political democracy and economic socialism. In 1884, the Social Democratic Federation was formed by H. M. Hyndman. In 1893, Keir Hardie established the Independent Labor Party which rapidly became a vocal third party in British politics. The Labor Party attracted trade unionists, socialists, and those who thought that the Conservative and Liberal Parties had no genuine interest in the needs of the general public.

During the early years of the 20th century both the Conservatives and the Liberals advanced more aggressive social and economic programs. The Conservatives, through the efforts of Arthur James Balfour, promoted the Education Act of 1902 which they argued would provide enhanced educational opportunities for the working class. In fact, this act was criticized soundly for not providing what it claimed as its purpose. In 1905, the Liberals under Henry Campbell-Bannerman came to power. The government ministries were staffed by such talented leaders as Herbert Asquith, Sir Edward Grey, David Lloyd George, and Winston Churchill.

The most significant political reform of this long-lived Liberal government was the Parliament Act of 1911 which eliminated the powers of the House of Lords and resulted in the House of Commons becoming the unquestioned center of national power. All revenue bills approved by the House of Commons would automatically become law thirty days after being sent to the House of Lords. If the Lords voted favorably, the law would be enacted earlier. The Lords had no veto power.

Non-revenue bills which were opposed by the Lords would be enacted if passed by three consecutive sessions of Commons. It was not difficult to transform such measures into revenue bills.

Finally, the life-span of Parliament was reduced from seven to five years.

The British political climate during this period was rather volatile. Issues relating to trade unions, Ireland, and women's suffrage tended to factionalize British politics. The Liberal Party, which was in power from 1905 to the early 1920s, came to be institutionalized and in the process came to be identified as "the government." To many, the programs advanced by the Conservative and Labor parties provided the basis for debate and decision. The Liberal Party was withering because it lacked clarity of platform and encapsulated the unrealized domestic goals, the ambiguities of bureaucracy, and the horrors of war.

The most recurring and serious problem which Great Britain experienced during the period from 1890 to 1914 was the "Irish Question." Gladstone, in his final ministry, argued unsuccessfully for Irish Home Rule. In Ireland opposition to British rule and the abuses of British power was evident through the program of the National Land League, which was established in 1879 by Michael Davitt. This organization stimulated and coordinated Irish opposition to British and Irish landlords. The efforts of the National Land League resulted in support for Irish Home Rule. During the 1880s Charles Stewart Parnell led the Irish delegation to the House of Commons. Parnell, through the support of Gladstone, attained some gains for the Irish such as the Land Reform Act and the Arrears Act. In 1890 Parnell became involved in a divorce case and the scandal ruined his career; he died the next year. In 1893 Gladstone devised the Irish Home Rule bill which was passed by the House of Commons but rejected by the House of Lords. The Irish situation became more complicated when the Protestant counties of the north started to enjoy remarkable economic growth from the mid-1890s; they were adamant in their rejection of all measures of Irish Home Rule. In 1914, an Irish Home Rule Act was passed by both the Commons and the Lords but the Protestants refused to accept it; implementation was deferred until after the war.

The Third French Republic

In the fall of 1870, Napoleon III's Second Empire collapsed when it was defeated by the Prussian armies. Napoleon III and his principal aides were captured; later, he abdicated and fled to England. A National Assembly (1871 – 75) was created and Adolphe Thiers was recognized as its chief executive. At the same time, a more radical political entity, the Paris Commune (1870 – 71), came into existence and exercised extraordinary power during the siege of Paris. After the siege and the peace agreement with Prussia, the Paris Commune refused to recognize the authority of the National Assembly. Led by radical Marxists, anarchists, and republicans, the Paris Commune repudiated the conservative and monarchist leadership of the National Assembly; from March to May 1871, the Paris Commune fought a bloody struggle with the troops of the National Assembly. Thousands died and when Paris surrendered, there were thousands of executions – accepted estimates place the number of executions at 20,000 during the first week after Paris fell on May 28, 1871. It was within this historic framework that France began a program of recovery which led to the formulation of the Third French Republic in 1875. The National Assembly sought to (1) put the French political house in order, (2) establish a new constitutional government, (3) pay off an imposed indemnity and, in doing so, remove German troops from French territory, and (4) restore the honor and glory of France. In 1875 a Constitution was adopted which provided for a republican government with a president (with little power), a Senate, and a Chamber of Deputies, which was the center of political power. The politicians and factions which led France during the 1870s and 1880s had to address the dominant forces which served as the dynamic elements of French politics. These forces included the overwhelming influence of the French bourgeoisie (middle class), which was intent upon establishing and sustaining a French republican government; the mounting hostility between the Catholic Church and the French government (anti-clericalism was frequently manifested in the proceedings of the Chamber of Deputies); the unpredictability which accompanied multi-party politics; and, finally, the extreme nationalism which gripped France during these decades and which resulted in continuing calls for a war of revenge against Germany in order to regain Alsace-Lorraine.

During the early years of the Republic, Leon Gambetta (1838 – 1882) led the republicans. Beginning in the 1880s the Third French Republic was challenged by a series of crises which threatened the continuity of the Republic. The Boulanger Crisis (1887 – 1889), the Panama Scandal (1894), and the Dreyfus Affair (1894 – 1906) were serious domestic problems; in all of these developments, the challenge to republicanism came from the right. The sustenance of republicanism through this time of troubles came primarily from (1) the able leadership of the republican government, and (2) the continuing commitment of the bourgeoisie to republicanism. Since the founding of the Third Republic, monarchists and conservatives were interested in overthrowing the regime; however, until the appointment of General Georges Boulanger (1837 – 1891) as Minister of War in 1886, there was no one to lead the anti-republican cause. Boulanger won over the army by improving the basic conditions of military life. His public popularity was high in 1888 and his supporters urged him to conduct a coup; he delayed and by the spring of 1889, the republicans had mounted a case against Boulanger. He was directed to appear to respond to charges of conspiracy; Boulanger broke, fled to Belgium, and committed suicide in 1891. The Boulanger crisis resulted in renewed confidence in the republic; but what popular gains it made were unravelled in 1892 with the Panama Scandal. The French had been involved with the engineering and the raising of capital for the Panama Canal since the 1870s. Early in the 1890s the promoters of the project resorted to the bribery of government officials and of certain members of the press who had access to information which indicated that the work on the canal was not proceeding as had been announced. In 1892 the scandal broke and for months the public indicated that it thought that the entire French government was corrupt. However, by 1893, elections to the Chamber of Deputies resulted in the socialists making notable gains. The monarchists did not attract much public support.

Without a doubt, the most serious threat to the republic came through the Dreyfus Affair. In 1894 Captain Alfred Dreyfus was assigned to the French General Staff. A scandal broke when it was revealed that classified information had been provided to German spies. Dreyfus, a Jew, was charged, tried, and convicted. Later, it was determined that the actual spy was Commandant Marie Charles Esterhazy; however, he was acquitted in order to save the pride and reputation of the army. The monarchists used this incident to criticize republicanism; the republicans countered when Emile Zola took up Dreyfus's cause when he wrote an open letter entitled *J'accuse*, which condemned the General Staff's actions and pronounced Dreyfus's innocence. Leftists supported the Republic and, in 1906, the case was closed when Dreyfus was declared innocent and returned to the ranks. Rather than lead to the collapse of the republic, the Dreyfus Affair demonstrated the intensity of anti-Semitism in French society, the level of corruption in the French army, and the willingness of the Catholic Church and the monarchists to join in a conspiracy against an innocent man. The republicans launched an anti-clerical campaign which included the Association Act (1901) and the separation of church and state (1905).

From 1905 to 1914 the socialists under Jean Juares gained seats in the Chamber of Deputies. The Third French Republic endured the crises which confronted it and, in 1914, enjoyed the support of the vast majority of French citizens.

The Lesser States of Europe

In the Low Countries during the decades prior to 1914, there were differing approaches to extending democracy. An appreciation of democracy was evident in Belgium under the leadership of Leopold I (1865 – 1909) and Albert I (1909 – 1934); during their reigns the franchise was extended, social and economic reforms were introduced, and equity was the basis of the settlement between Flemish and French speaking Belgians. To the north, the Netherlands was slow to adopt democracy. By 1896, only 14% of the Dutch had the vote and it would not be until 1917 that universal manhood suffrage would be enacted.

Denmark experienced a struggle between the old guard represented by Christian IX (1863–1906), who opposed parliamentary government, and the Social Democrats who advocated democratic principles. The Danish Constitution of 1915 provided a basic democratic political system. Sweden, after a decade of debilitating debate, recognized the independence of Norway in 1905; Norway moved quickly toward democracy, granting women the vote in 1907. Sweden, under Gustavus V (1907 – 1950), pronounced a comprehensive democratic system in 1909.

In southern Europe, advocates of democracy did not meet with any substantive success prior to 1914. In Spain, Portugal, and Italy, the monarchist establishments were preoccupied with survival. While an occasional reform was promulgated, there was no intent to move toward full democracy.

EUROPEAN CULTURAL DEVELOPMENTS, 1848 – 1914

The great political and economic changes of this period were accompanied by cultural achievements which included the development of a literate citizenry and substantive innovations in science, literature, art, music and other areas of intellectual activity. In large part, these developments occurred as a reaction against the mechanistic sterility of the scientism and positivism of the age; however, some of the initial achievements, such as Darwin's theories of evolution and natural selection, resulted in extending the exaggerated claims of scientism. From Charles Darwin, Richard Wagner, Friedrich Nietzsche, and Sigmund Freud to Claude Monet, Richard Strauss, Igor Stravinsky, Oscar Wilde, Thomas Mann, and James Joyce, intelligent Europeans of the era pursued many differing, and at times opposing, approaches in their quest for truth and understanding. Many philosophers were critical of the movement toward democracy which they identified with mass culture and political ineptitude. Artists attempted to escape their plight through moving into symbolism with their pen or brush; there, they were free to express their fantasies of hope and despair.

Darwin, Wagner, Freud, and the Emergence of a New Tradition

In 1859, Charles Darwin's (1807 – 1882) *The Origins of the Species* was published; it argued the theory of evolution which had been discussed for more than a generation in Europe. Darwin's contributions to the advocacy of this theory were based (1) on the data which he provided to demonstrate the theory, and (2) in the formulation of a well structured and argued defense of the theory of natural selection (survival of the fittest). The reaction to *The Origins of the Species* was diverse, thorough, and enduring; some discussants were concerned with the implication of the theory on religion, while others were interested in applying aspects of the theory to the understanding of contemporary social problems. Within the Darwinian camp, factions emerged which supported or rejected one or more components of the theory. Samuel Butler and George Bernard Shaw accepted evolution but rejected natural selection; Thomas Huxley was Darwin's most consistent and loyal supporter. Herbert Spencer (1820 – 1903) developed a Social Darwinism which enjoyed extensive acceptance in both scholarly and general circles. One of the obvious consequences of Darwin's theory was that it necessitated a reevaluation of all of the issues relating to man's place in the cosmos. The doctrine of creation was challenged and thus the authenticity of prevailing religion was endangered.

In classical music, the erratic Richard Wagner (1813 – 1883) reflected the incongruities and the harshness of the new age. Wagner developed and imposed an aestheticism that had one fundamental element – it demanded absolute artistic integrity. Wagner shifted styles several times during his career; his *Ring* cycle was centered on German epics and advanced numerous fantasies about the history of the German people.

Sigmund Freud (1856 – 1939) established a new approach to understanding human behavior which was known as psychoanalysis. Freud accepted the impressionist interpretation that reality was not material; rather it was based on moods, concepts, and feelings which shift. In Vienna, Freud developed his concepts that the unconscious was shaped during the formative years, that sexuality was a dominant lifeforce, and that free will may not exist. Freud argued his theories in a formidable body of literature which included the *Origins of Psychoanalysis* and *Civilization and Its Discontents*. The establishment rejected his unorthodox views as threats to religion.

In science itself, new developments challenged the certainty and security of the old science. Max Planck's *Quantum Physics*, Albert Einstein's *Theory of Relativity*, and the impact of the Michelson-Morley Experiment (1887; regarding the measurement of speed; conducted in the United States) led to a new generation of scientists reexamining many of the assumptions of the past.

Impressionism and Symbolism: Forces of the New Art

The turbulence within European cultural life during the fifty years prior to the outbreak of the First World War can be seen most evidently in new attitudes which emerged in art and literature. Not only did the intellectuals find themselves looking for a new intellectual synthesis through which to offer new vision and hope, but they were also liberated from the limitations which had been imposed on their predecessors through a technological breakthrough. The development of photography resulted in artists no longer being required to produce actual representations. Painters were now free to pursue the dictates of their imaginations. Impressionism developed in France during the 1870s; Monet, Manet, Renoir, and others pioneered the new art. Impressionism soon gave way to Post-Impressionism and later Expressionism. At the turn of the century, more radical artistic forms such as Symbolism and Cubism enjoyed notoriety if not general acceptance.

Literature was transformed through the writings of such innovators as Oscar Wilde (*The Picture of Dorian Gray*), Thomas Mann (*Death in Venice*), and the young James Joyce (prior to 1914, *Portrait of the Artist as a Young Man* and *Dubliners*). These writers were interested in discussing the themes which had great personal value and meaning; Joyce will emerge as the most seminal stylist of the twentieth century.

INTERNATIONAL POLITICS AND THE COMING OF THE WAR, 1890 – 1914

During the generation prior to the outbreak of the First World War in the summer of 1914, conflicts and strained relations among the great powers increased in frequency and intensity. There can be no question that the primary factors which contributed to this situation were the heightened nationalism and the cultural materialism of the period.

The Polarization of Europe

In March 1890 Bismarck was dismissed as Chancellor of Germany by the immature, impetuous, and inexperienced Kaiser Wilhelm II. The particular issues which led to Bismarck's fall included the renewal of the Reinsurance Treaty (1887) with Russia and Bismarck's scheme to weaken the role of the Social Democratic Party (SPD) within German politics. With Bismarck's dismissal, the continuing dominance of the German agenda over European affairs was questionable. The intricate alliance system which Bismarck had constructed was directed at maintaining the diplomatic isolation of France.

Germany failed to renew the Reinsurance Treaty with Russia and consequently Russia looked elsewhere to eliminate its own perceived isolation. In 1891 secret negotiations were entered into by the French and Russians. By 1894 these deliberations resulted in the Dual Entente which was a comprehensive military alliance. This agreement was sustained through 1917 and allowed France to pursue a more assertive foreign policy. From the Russian perspective, the fears of isolation and of the development of an anti-Russian combination were abated. Within four years of Bismarck's dismissal, the essential imperative of German foreign policy in the late nineteenth century – the diplomatic isolation of France – was no longer a reality.

In 1895 a new Conservative government came to power in Great Britain. Led by Lord Salisbury, who served as Prime Minister and Foreign Secretary, this government included a wide range of talented statesmen including Joseph Chamberlain, John Morley, Lord Landsdowne, and the young Arthur James Balfour. The Salisbury government was interested in terminating the long-standing policy of "Splendid Isolationism" which had prevailed as Britain's response to European alliances. Salisbury came to argue that the new realities of world politics and economics deemed it advisable for Britain to ally itself with a major power. While coming under general European criticism for its role in the Boer War (1899 – 1902) in South Africa, British representatives approached Berlin in an attempt to develop an Anglo-German alliance. Germany declined the British advances because (1) the Germans were sympathetic to the Boers, (2) the Germans questioned the ability of the British army, (3) they believed that the British would never be able to reach an accommodation with the French or Russians, and (4) Wilhelm II was involved in a major naval building program – this effort would be jeopardized if the Germans were allied to the world's greatest naval power, Britain.

Consequently, Britain pursued diplomatic opportunities which resulted in the Anglo-Japanese Alliance (1902), the Entente Cordiale or Anglo-French Entente (1904), and the Anglo-Russian Entente (1907).

The Anglo-Japanese Alliance of 1902 resulted in the two powers agreeing to adopt a position of benevolent neutrality in the event that the other member state was involved in war. This arrangement was sustained through the First World War.

The Entente Cordiale (1904), which is also known as the Dual Entente or the Anglo-French Entente, was a settlement of long-standing colonial disputes between Britain and France over North African territories. It was agreed that northeast Africa (Egypt and the Anglo-Egyptian Sudan) would be a British sphere of influence and that northwest Africa (Morocco) would be a French sphere of influence. This was a colonial settlement, not a formal alliance; neither power pledged support in the event of war. However, the Entente Cordiale was of critical significance because it drew Britain into the French oriented diplomatic camp.

While Anglo-French relations improved during 1904 to 1905, the historically tense Anglo-Russian relationship was aggravated further through the Russo-Japanese War (1904 – 05). The Dogger Bank Incident resulted in a crisis between these powers when Russian naval ships fired on and sunk several British fishing boats in the North Sea. Britain, which earlier had adopted a sympathetic posture toward Japan, responded by deploying the Home Fleet and curtailing the activities of the Russian fleet. The crisis was resolved when Russia agreed to apologize for the incident and to pay compensation. In 1905 a Liberal government came to power in Britain, and Russia was absorbed in its own revolution which liberalized, at least temporarily, the autocratic regime. Negotiations between these powers were initiated and were facilitated by the French; in 1907 Britain and Russia reached a settlement on their outstanding colonial disputes. They agreed on three points:

1) Persia would be divided into three zones: a northern sector under Russian influence, a southern sector under British control, and a central zone which could be mutually exploited;

2) Afghanistan was recognized as a British sphere of influence;

3) Tibet was recognized as part of China and, as such, was to be free from foreign intervention.

By 1907 France, Britain, and Russia had formed a Triple Entente which effectively balanced the Triple Alliance. While Britain was not formally committed to an alliance system, Sir Edward Grey, British Foreign Minister from 1905, supported secret conversations between British and French military representatives. Thus, in terms of military power and economics, Germany became isolated by 1907.

The Rise of Militarism

During the period after 1890 Europeans began to view the use of military power as not only feasible but also as desirable to bring about a resolution to the increasingly hostile political conditions in Europe. The apparent inability of diplomats to develop lasting settlements supported the further development of this perception. The notion that a major European war was inevitable became acceptable to many.

Within the structure of the European states, militarists enjoyed increased credibility and support. The General Staffs became preoccupied with planning for the anticipated struggle and their plans affected national foreign policies. The Germans, under the influence of General Count Alfred von Schlieffen, developed the Schlieffen Plan by 1905. It was predicated on the assumption that Germany would have to conduct a two front war with France and Russia. It specified that France must be defeated quickly through the use of enveloping tactics which involved the use of German armies of about 1,500,000 men. After victory in the west, Germany would then look to the east to defeat the Russians, who would be slow to mobilize. The French developed the infamous Plan XVII, which was approved by Marshall Joseph Joffre. The French thought that the German attack would be concentrated in the region of Alsace-Lorraine and that the French forces should be massed in that area; the élan of the French soldiery would result in a victory.

The Arms Race

This wave of nationalistic militarism also manifested itself through a continuing arms race which resulted in several threats to the balance of power because of revolutionary technological developments. Field weapons such as mortars and cannons were improved sharply in range, accuracy, and firepower; the machine gun was perfected and produced in quantity. New weapons such as the submarine and airplanes were recognized as having the capacity to be strategic armaments.

In naval weaponry the rivalry between the British and the Germans over capital ships not only exacerbated the deteriorating relationship between the two powers, but also led to restrictions on the national domestic expenditures during peacetime in order to pay for the increasingly costly battleships and cruisers. In 1912, the British-sponsored Haldane Mission was sent to Berlin to negotiate an agreement; the Germans were suspicious and distrustful of the British and were not receptive to any proposal.

Imperialism as a Source of Conflict

During the late 19th century the economically motivated "New Imperialism" resulted in further aggravating the relations among the European powers. The struggle for increased world market share, the need for raw materials, and the availability of capital for overseas investment resulted in enhancing the rivalry among the European nations and, on several occasions, in causing crises to develop. The Fashoda Crisis (1898 –99), the Moroccan Crisis (1905 – 06), the Balkan Crisis (1908), and the Agadir Crisis (1911) demonstrated the impact of imperialism in heightening tensions among European states and in creating an environment in which conflict became more acceptable.

The Fashoda Crisis developed between France and Britain when the French, under the influence of Foreign Minister Theophile Delcasse, ordered Commandant Marchant and a small number of French troops to march across Africa and establish a French "presence" near the headwaters of the Nile. Marchant arrived in Fashoda (now Kodok) in 1898; Fashoda was located on the White Nile, south of Khartoum in the Anglo-Egyptian Sudan. A British army under General Herbert Kitchener, having defeated a native rebel army in the battle of Omdurman, advanced to Khartoum where he learned of the French force at Fashoda. Kitchener marched on Fashoda and a major crisis ensued for months. In the end, the French withdrew and recognized the position of the British in the Anglo-Egyptian Sudan; however, for several months there were serious consideration given to a major war over this colonial issue.

The Moroccan Crisis (1905 – 06) developed when Wilhelm II of Germany travelled to Tangier (March 1905) where he made a speech in support of the independence of Morocco; this position was at odds with that agreed to by the British and the French in the Entente Cordiale. Initially, the German position prevailed because of lack of organization within the Franco-Russian alliance; however, in 1906, at the Algerciras Conference, the German effort was thwarted and the French secured their position in Morocco. Russia, Britain, and even Italy, supported the French on every important issue. German diplomatic isolation—save for the Austrians—became increasingly evident.

The Balkan Crisis of 1908 involved an example of European imperialist rivalry within Europe. Since the Congress of Berlin in 1878, the Austro-Hungarian Empire had administered the Balkan territories of Bosnia and Herzegovina. Austrian influence in this area was opposed by Russia which considered the region as a natural area of Russian influence. Specifically, the Russians hoped to capitalize upon the collapse of the Ottoman Turkish Empire and to gain access to the Mediterranean Sea. In 1908 the decadent Ottoman Empire was experiencing domestic discord which attracted the attention of both the Austrians and the Russians. These two powers agreed that Austria would annex Bosnia and Herzegovina and that Russia would be granted access to the Straits and thus the Mediterranean. Great Britain intervened and demanded that there be no change in the status quo vis-a-vis the Straits. Russia backed down from a confrontation but Austria proceeded to annex Bosnia and Herzegovina. The annexation was condemned by the Pan-Slavists who looked to Russia for assistance; a crisis developed and it appeared that war between Austria and Russia was likely. However, the Russians disengaged from the crisis because of their lack of preparedness for a major struggle and because there were clear indications that Germany would support Austria. The Balkan Crisis was another example of the nature of European rivalries and the rather rapid recourse to sabre-rattling on the part of great powers. Further, it demonstrated that the fundamental regional problem—the developing nationalism among the diverse peoples of the Balkans—was not addressed.

The Agadir Crisis (1911) broke when France announced that its troops would be sent to several Moroccan towns to restore order. Germany, fearing French annexation of all of Morocco, responded by sending the Panther, a German naval ship, to Agadir. After exchanging threats for several weeks, the French and Germans agreed to recognize Morocco as a French protectorate and to transfer two sections of the French Congo to Germany.

An Assassination, and then a War

During the late 19th and early 20th centuries the Ottoman Empire was in a state of collapse. At the same time, Austria and Russia were interested in extending their influence in the region. Further, nationalism among the ethnic groups in the Balkans was rapidly developing. In addition to the Balkan Crisis of 1908 which was mentioned above, the region was involved in the Italian-Turkish War (1911) and the Inter-Balkan Wars of 1912 and 1913.

On June 28, 1914, Archduke Franz Ferdinand, heir to the Austro-Hungarian throne, and his wife were assassinated while on a state visit to Sarajevo, the capital of Bosnia. Their assassin was a radical Serb, Gavrilo Princip, who opposed Franz Ferdinand's plan to integrate the Slavs more fully into the government. The assassination resulted in a crisis between Austria-Hungary and Serbia, and would be the trigger for a series of events that in just two months would envelop Europe in war.

CONCLUSION

Between 1848 and 1914 Europeans experienced revolutionary changes in their culture. These alterations were based on a new sense of reality, and values in which materialism and the notion of human progress were manifested in the pragmatism of the era. Nationalism, science and technology, and the rapid expansion of the population were primary factors which contributed to these changes and to the further expansion of European culture throughout the world. The growth in the European standard of living was uneven. Western Europe developed most comprehensively, Central Europe—especially German urban centers—witnessed remarkable growth during the last decades of the period; and Southern and Eastern Europe lagged behind and, by 1914, the standard of living had not dramatically improved from that of the earlier century. Reaction to these changes varied from the development of Marxism, anarchism, and trade unionism in response to the adverse consequences of capitalism and industrialism, to the emergence of Impressionism, Expressionism, and Symbolism in reaction to the perceived intellectual sterility of mechanistic positivism. Nineteenth century Europe, which was identified with hope, progress, and rationality, gave way to the uncertainty, violence, and irrationality of the twentieth century. Politically, economically, and culturally, Europe between 1848 and 1914 continued the process of accelerated change which had been initiated in the previous century with revolutionary developments in production, and in the fundamental concepts about the relationships of man and the state and of man and the economy.

5 WORLD WAR I AND EUROPE IN CRISIS (1914-1935)

THE ORIGINS OF WORLD WAR I

In August 1914, most of the world's major powers became engaged in a conflict that most people welcomed romantically and believed would last only a few months. Instead, a war of global dimensions evolved that saw the clash of outdated military values with modern technological warfare. A war that most welcomed and that no one seemed to be able to win lasted over four years and resulted in 12 million deaths.

The origins of World War I can be traced to numerous root causes, beginning as far back as the creation of modern Germany in 1871. Achieved through a series of wars, the emergence of this new German state destroyed Europe's traditional balance-of-power, and forced its diplomatic and military planners back to their drawing boards to rethink their collective strategies to maintain proper military and diplomatic balance. In the period between 1871 and 1914, a number of developments took place that heightened tensions between the major powers.

Balance of Power and Europe's Alliance System

One of the major themes in 19th-century Europe's diplomatic arena was an effort by the major powers to organize their international relationships in such a way as to keep any single or collective group of nations from gaining a dominant diplomatic or military advantage on the Continent.

From 1871 to 1890, this balance was maintained through the network of alliances created by the German Chancellor, Otto von Bismarck, and centered on his *Dreikaiserbund* (League of the Three Emperors), which isolated France, and the Dual (Germany, Austria) and Triple (Germany, Austria, Italy) Alliances. Bismarck's fall in 1890 resulted in new policies that saw Germany move closer to Austria, while England and France (Entente Cordiale, 1904), and later Russia (Triple Entente, 1907), drew closer.

Arms Buildup and Imperialism

Germany's dramatic defeat of France in 1870–71 coupled with Kaiser Wilhelm II's decision in 1890 to build up a navy comparable to that of Great Britain created a reactive arms race that haunted Europe. This, blended with European efforts to carve out colonial empires in Africa and Asia—plus a new spirit of nationalism and the growing romanticization of war—helped create an unstable international environment in the years before the outbreak of the World War.

IMMEDIATE CAUSE OF WORLD WAR I

The Balkan Crisis

The Balkans (*balkan* is Turkish for "mountain"), a region which today embraces the former Yugoslavia, Albania, Greece, Bulgaria, and Rumania, was notably unstable. Part of the rapidly decaying Ottoman (Turkish) Empire, it saw two main forces at work: ethnic nationalism among a number of small groups who lived there and intense rivalry between Austria-Hungary and Russia over spheres of influence. Existing friction between Austria and Serbia heated up all the more after Austria annexed Bosnia and Herzegovina in 1908. In 1912, with Russia's blessing, the Balkan League (Serbia, Montenegro, Greece, and Bulgaria) went to war with Turkey. Serbia, which sought a port on the Adriatic, was rebuffed when Austria-Hungary and Italy backed the creation of an independent Albania. Russia, meanwhile, grew increasingly protective of its southern Slavic cousins, supporting Serbia's and Montenegro's claims to Albanian lands. Just weeks after the outbreak of World War I, the new Albanian state collapsed.

THE OUTBREAK OF THE WORLD WAR

Assassination and Reprisals

On June 28, 1914, the Archduke Franz Ferdinand (1863–1914), heir to the Austrian throne, was assassinated by Gavrilo Princip, a young Serbian nationalist. Princip was working for the Serbian Army Intelligence in Sarajevo, then the capital of Bosnia. Austria's rulers felt the murder provided them with an opportunity to move against Serbia and end anti-Austrian unrest in the Balkans. Austria consulted with the German government on July 6 and received a "blank check" to take whatever steps were necessary to punish Serbia. Serbia stood accused of harboring radical anti-Austrian groups like the "Black Hand." On July 23, 1914, the Austrian government presented Serbia with a 10-point ultimatum that required Serbia to suppress and punish all forms of anti-Austrian sentiment there. On July 25, 1914, three hours after mobilizing its army, Serbia accepted most of Austria's terms; it asked only that Austria's demand to participate in Serbian judicial proceedings against anti-Austrian agitators—a demand that Serbia described as unprecedented in relations between sovereign states—be adjudicated by the International Tribunal at The Hague.

The Conflict Expands

Austria immediately broke off official relations with Serbia and mobilized its army. Meanwhile, between July 18–24, Russia let the Austrians and the Germans know that it intended fully to back Serbia in the dispute. France, Russia's ally, voiced support of Russia's moves. Last-ditch attempts by Britain and Germany to mediate the dispute and avoid a general European war failed. On July 28, 1914, Austria went to war against Serbia, and began to bombard Belgrade the following day. At the same time, Russia gradually prepared for war against Austria and Germany, declaring full mobilization on July 30.

Germany and the Schlieffen Plan

German military strategy, based in part on the plan of the Chief of the General Staff, Count Alfred von Schlieffen, viewed Russian mobilization as an act of war. The Schlieffen Plan was based on a two-front war with Russia and France. It was predicated on a swift, decisive blow against France while maintaining a defensive position against slowly mobilizing Russia, which would be dealt with after France. Attacking France required the Germans to march through neutral Belgium, which would later bring England into the war as a protector of Belgian neutrality.

War Begins

Germany demanded that Russia demobilize in 12 hours, and appealed to its ambassador in Berlin. Russia's offer to negotiate the matter was rejected, and Germany declared war on Russia on August 1, 1914. Germany asked France its intentions and Paris replied that it would respond according to its own interests. On August 3, Germany declared war on France. Berlin asked Belgium for permission to send its troops through Belgian territory to attack France, which Belgium refused. On August 4, England, which agreed in 1839 to protect Belgian neutrality, declared war on Germany; Belgium followed suit. Between 1914 and 1915, the alliance of the Central Powers (Germany, Austria-Hungary, Bulgaria, and Turkey) faced the Allied Powers of England, France, Russia, Japan, and in 1917, the United States. A number of smaller countries were also part of the Allied coalition.

THE WAR IN 1914

The Western Front

After entering Belgium, the Germans attacked France on five fronts in an effort to encircle Paris rapidly. France was defeated in the Battle of the Frontier (August 14 – 24) in Lorraine, the Ardennes, and in the Charleroi-Mons area. However, the unexpected Russian attack in East Prussia and Galicia from August 17 to 20 forced Germany to transfer important forces eastward to halt the Russian drive.

To halt a further German advance, the French army, aided by Belgian and English forces, counterattacked. In the Battle of the Marne (September 5 – 9), they stopped the German drive and forced small retreats. Mutual outflanking maneuvers by France and Germany created a battle front that would determine the demarcation of the Western Front for the next 4 years. It ran, in uneven fashion, from the North Sea to Belgium and from northern France to Switzerland.

The Eastern Front

Russian forces under Pavel Rennenkampf and Aleksandr Samsonov, invaded East Prussia and Galicia in mid-August. With only 9 of 87 divisions in the east, the German defense faltered. Generals Paul von Hindenburg and Erich Ludendorff, aided by two corps from the Western Front, were sent on August 23 to revive the Eighth Army in East Prussia.

In the Battles of Tannenberg (August 25 – 31) and Mazurian Lakes (September 6 – 15), the Russian 2nd Army, under Samsonov, met the German Eighth Army. Suffering from poor communications and Rennenkampf's refusal to send the 1st Army to aid him, Samsonov surrendered with 90,000 troops and committed suicide. Moving northward, the German 8th Army now confronted Rennenkampf's 1st Army. After an unsuccessful initial encounter against the Germans, Rennenkampf rapidly retreated, suffering significant losses.

Nikolai Ivanov's Southwest Army group enjoyed some successes against Austro-Hungarian forces in Galicia and southern Poland throughout August. By the end of 1914, they were poised to strike deeper into the area.

The Germans retreated after their assault against Warsaw in late September. Hindenburg's attack on Lodz ten days after he was appointed Commander-in-Chief of the Eastern Front (Nov. 1) was a more more successful venture; by the end of 1914 this important textile center was in German hands.

THE WAR IN 1915

The Western Front

With Germany concentrating on the East, France and England launched a series of small attacks throughout the year that resulted in a few gains and extremely heavy casualties. Wooed by both sides, Italy joined the Allies and declared war on the Central Powers on May 23 after signing the secret Treaty of London (April 26). This treaty gave Italy Austrian provinces in the north and some Turkish territory. Italian attacks against Austria in the Isonzo area towards Trieste were unsuccessful because of difficult terrain, and failed to lessen pressure on the Russians in the East.

The Eastern Front

On January 23, 1915, Austro-German forces began a coordinated offensive in East Russia and in the Carpathians. The two-pronged German assault in the north was stopped on February 27, while Austrian efforts to relieve their besieged defensive network at Przemysl failed when it fell into Russian hands on March 22. In early March, Russian forces under Nikolai Ivanov drove deeper into the Carpathians with inadequate material support.

German forces, strengthened by troops from the Western Front under August von Mackensen, began a move on May 2 to strike at the heart of the Russian Front. They used the greatest artillery concentration of the war at that time as part of their strategy. In June, Mackensen shifted his assault towards Lublin and Brest-Litovsk, while the German XII, X and Niemen armies moved toward Kovno in the Baltic. By August 1915, much of Russian Poland was in German hands.

In an effort to provide direct access to the Turks defending Gallipoli, Germany and Austria invaded Serbia in the early fall, aided by their new ally, Bulgaria. On October 7, the defeated Serbian army retreated to Corfu. Belated Allied efforts to ship troops from Gallipoli to help Bulgaria failed.

Command Changes

Allied frustration resulted in the appointment of Marshal Joseph Joffre as French Commander-in-Chief, and Field Marshal Douglas Haig as British Commander in December 1915.

The Eastern Mediterranean

Turkey entered the war on the Central Power side on October 28, 1914, which prevented the shipment of Anglo-French aid to Russians through the Straits.

The Western stalemate caused Allied strategists to look to the eastern Mediterranean for a way to break the military deadlock. Winston Churchill, Britain's First Lord of the Admiralty, devised a plan to seize the Straits of the Dardanelles to open lines to Russia, take Constantinople, and isolate Turkey. These unsuccessful efforts occured between February 19 and March 18, 1915.

On April 25, Allied forces invaded Gallipoli Peninsula in a different attempt to capture the Straits. Turkish troops offered strong resistance, and forced the Allies (after suffering 252,000 casualties) to begin a three week evacuation that began on December 20, 1915.

The Middle East, 1914 – 1916

In an effort to protect its petroleum interests in the Persian Gulf, an Anglo-Indian force took Al Basrals (Basra) in Southern Iraq in November 1915. The following year, British forces moved north and took Al Kut (Kut al Irnara) from Turkey on September 28. To counter failures on the Western Front, British forces now tried to take Baghdad, but were stopped by the Turks at Ctesiphon on November 22. Turkish forces besieged Al Kut on December 8, and captured it on April 29, 1916. Two-thirds of the 10,000 captured British POW's died of Turkish mistreatment.

THE WAR IN 1916

The Western Front

In order to break the stalemate on the Western Front and drain French forces in the effort, the Germans decided to attack the French fortress town of Verdun.

The Battle for Verdun lasted from February 21 to December 18, 1916. From February until June, German forces, aided by closely coordinated heavy artillery barrages, assaulted the forts around Verdun. The Germans suffered 281,000 casualties while the French, under Marshal Henri Petain, lost 315,000 while successfully defending their position.

To take pressure off the French, an Anglo-French force mounted three attacks on the Germans to the left of Verdun in July, September and November. After the Battle of the Somme (July 1 – November 18), German pressure was reduced, but at great loss. Anglo-French casualties totaled 600,000.

The Eastern Front
Initially, the Allies had hoped for a general coordinated attack on all fronts against the Central Powers. Now efforts centered on relieving pressure at Verdun and on the Italians at Trentino.

Orchestrated by Aleksei Brusilov, The Brusilov Offensive (June 4 – September 20) envisoned a series of unexpected attacks along a lengthy front to confuse the enemy. By late August, he had advanced into Galicia and the Carpathians. The number of enemy troops dead, wounded or captured numbered 1.5 million. Russian losses numbered 500,000.

Rumania entered the war on the Allied side as a result of Russian successes and the secret Treaty of Bucharest (August 17). This treaty specified that Rumania would get Translyvania, Bukovina, the Banat and part of the Hungarian Plain if the Allies won. The ensuing Rumanian thrust into Translyvania was pushed back, and on December 6, a German-Bulgarian army occupied Bucharest as well as the bulk of Rumania.

Central Powers Propose Peace Talks
The death of Austrian Emperor Franz Joseph on November 21 prompted his successor, Charles I, to discuss the prospect of peace terms with his allies. On December 12, the four Central Powers, strengthened by the fall of Bucharest, offered four separate peace proposals based on their recent military achievements. The Allies rejected them on December 30 out of a belief that they were insincere.

War on the High Seas, 1914 – 1916
Britain's naval strategy in the first year of the war was tototally disrupt German shipping world-wide with the aid of the French and the Japanese. Germany sought ways to defend itself and weaken Allied naval strength. By the end of 1914, Allied fleets had gained control of the high seas, which caused Germany to lose control of its colonial empire.

Germany's failure in 1914 to weaken British naval strength prompted German naval leaders to begin to use the submarine as an offensive weapon to weaken the British. On February 4, Germany announced a war zone around the British Isles, and advised neutral powers to sail there at their own risk. On May 7, 1915 a German submarine sank a British passenger vessel, the Lusitania because it was secretly carrying arms. There were 1201 casualties, including 139 Americans.

The United States protested the sinking as a violation of the Declaration of London (1909). After four months of negotiations, Germany agreed not to sink any passenger vessels without warning, and to help all passengers and crew to life boats. Germany shifted its U-boat activity to the Mediterranean.

The main naval battle of World War I was the Battle of Jutland/Skagerrak (May – June 1916). This confrontation pitted 28 British dreadnoughts and 9 cruisers against 16 German dreadnoughts and 5 cruisers. In the end, the battle was a draw, with England losing 14 ships and Germany 11. It forced the German High Sea Fleet not to venture out of port for the rest of the war. Instead, they concentrated on use of the U-boat.

New Military Technology

Germany, Russia, and Great Britain all had submarines, though the Germans used their U-boats most effectively. Designed principally for coastal protection, they increasingly used them to reduce British naval superiority through tactical and psychological means.

By the spring of 1915, British war planners finally awoke to the fact that the machine gun had become the mistress of defensive trench warfare. In a search for a weapon to counter trench defenses, the British developed tanks as an armored "land ship," and first used them on September 15, 1916, in the battle of the Somme. Their value was not immediately realized because there were too few of them to be effective, and interest in them waned. Renewed interest came in 1917.

Airplanes were initially used for observation purposes in the early months of the war. As their numbers grew, mid-air struggles using pistols and rifles took place, until the Germans devised a synchronized propeller and machine gun on its Fokker aircraft in May 1915. The Allies responded with similar equipment and new squadron tactics during the early days of the Verdun campaign in February 1916, and briefly gained control of the skies. They also began to use their aircraft for bombing raids against Zeppelin bases in Germany. Air supremacy shifted to the Germans in 1917.

During the first year of the war, the Germans began to use Zeppelin airships to bomb civilian targets in England. Though their significance was neutralized with the development of the explosive shell in 1916, Zeppelins played an important role as a psychological weapon in the first two years of the war.

In the constant search for methods to counter trench warfare, the Germans and the Allied forces experimented with various forms of internationally outlawed gas. On October 27, 1914, the Germans tried a nose/eye irritant gas at Neuve-Chapelle, and by the spring of 1915 had developed an asphyxiating lachaymatory chlorine gas at the battle of Spres. The British countered with a similar chemical at the battles of Champagne and Loos that fall. Military strategists initially had little faith in gas since its use depended heavily on wind conditions, which could change the direction of the gas at any moment. However, as they desperately struggled to find ways to break the deadlock on the Western Front, they devised tactics and protection methods that enabled them to integrate the use of gas into their strategy.

THE RUSSIAN REVOLUTIONS OF 1917

Two events that would have a dramatic impact on the war and the world were the February and October Revolutions in 1917. The former toppled the Romanov Dynasty and spawned that country's brief flirtation with democracy under the temporary Provisional Government. It collapsed later that year as a result of the October Revolution, which brought Lenin and his Bolshevik faction to power.

Plagued for centuries by a backward autocratic government and a rural serf economy, Russia seemed on the verge of dramatic change after Czar Alexander II (1855 – 1881) freed the serfs in 1861. Emancipation, however, coupled with other important government and social reforms, created chaos nationwide and helped stimulate a new class of violent revolutionaries bent on destroying the Tsarist system. Terrorists murdered Alexander II, which prompted the country's last two rulers, Alexander III (1881 – 1894) and Nicholas II (1894 – 1917) to turn the clock backward politically.

The Russo-Japanese War and the 1905 Revolution

In February 1904, war broke out between Russia and Japan over spheres-of-influence in Korea and Manchuria. Russia's inability to support adequately its military forces in Asia, coupled with growing battlefield losses, prompted a nationwide revolution after police fired on peaceful demonstrators in January 1905. A groundswell of strikes and demonstrations swept the country and neutralized the government, which was on the verge of collapse. Nicholas II survived because he agreed in his October Manifesto (October 30, 1905) to create a constitution, share power with a legislature (Duma), and grant civil rights. This decree defused the crisis and enabled the government to survive and rebuild its political base.

Era of Reaction and Reforms, 1906 – 1912

Once the czar diminished the threat to his throne, and felt more comfortable, he issued the Fundamental Laws (May 6, 1906), which severely limited the power of the Duma. Regardless, over the next eleven years, four growingly conservative Dumas met, and provided a tradition of constitutional governments for the country. This, blended with the emergence of workers' and soldiers' Soviets (councils), and political parties (Kadets, Constitutional Democrats; Octobrists), created an atmosphere of challenge and change for Russia. To counter this mood, the czar appointed Peter Stolypin as Prime Minister (1906 – 1911) to initiate mollifying reforms for the peasants and develop a private agricultural system throughout the country. These efforts, and an industrial boom, influenced Russia's economic potential for the better.

Rasputin and Upheaval, 1912 – 1914

The death of Stolypin in 1911, coupled with a governmental system incapable of dealing with new labor unrest associated with industrial development, brought to the fore a semi-illiterate holy man, Gregorii Rasputin. He seemed to possess powers to save the czar's hemophiliac son, Alexei, and obtained tremendous influence over the royal family.

RUSSIA AT WAR: THE HOME FRONT, 1914 – 1917

Russia's entrance into the World War was met with broad public acceptance and support. Serious problems, however, plagued the government, the military, and the economy that threatened to undermine a military effort that most expected would win the war in a matter of months.

The Military

The draft increased Russia's armed forces from 1,350,000 to 6,500,000 during the war, though the government was only able to equip fully a small percentage of these troops. In addition, the country's military leaders differed on whether to concentrate their efforts on the Austrians or the Germans. While in the field, commanders were handicapped by inadequate communication and maps. As a result, German drives in the spring and summer of 1915 saw Russian spirit collapse as defensive efforts proved ineffective. However, by the end of that year, High Command personnel changes, aided by new industrial output, enabled the Russians to briefly turn the tide of battle.

The Civilian Economy

At first, Russian agricultural production proved adequate for the war's needs, but in time, because of growing labor shortages, production of foodstuffs fell by one-third.

The military only received about one-half of their grain requests because of the collapse of the transportation system. Regardless, by 1917, the country still had enough food for its military and civilian population. Skilled labor shortages, the loss of Poland, and inadequate government planning kept industry from producing the material necessary to supply the military. Consequently, despite a trade surplus in 1914, Russia encumbered a trade deficit of 2.5 billion rubles by 1917 from its Allies.

The Government and the Bureaucracy

As the country's problems mounted, the czar responded by assuming direct command of his army on the front in September 1915, leaving the government in the hands of his wife, Alexandra, and Rasputin. Those in government who appeared critical of the czar's policies were dismissed, and in time the country lost its most effective leaders. The Duma, which was forced to assume more and more leadership responsibilities, formed the Progressive Bloc, a coalition mainly of Kadets and Octobrists, in an effort to try to force the czar to appoint more competent officials. The Czar's refusal to accept this group's proposals led to increasing criticism of his policies. In November 1916, distant relatives of the czar and a Duma member secretly murdered Rasputin.

THE FEBRUARY REVOLUTION

The February Revolution, so named because the Russian calendar at the time was 13 days behind that of the West, was a spontaneous series of events that forced the collapse of the Romanov Dynasty.

Riots and Strikes

Growing discontent with the government's handling of the war saw a new wave of civilian unrest engulf the country. Estimates are that 1,140 such occurrences swept Russia in January and February, which prompted officials to send extra troops into Petrograd (old St. Petersburg) to protect the royal family. Particularly troublesome were food riots. Military and police units ordered to move against the mobs either remained at their posts or joined them.

The Duma

Though ordered by the czar not to meet until April, Duma leaders began to demand dramatic solutions to the country's problems. Its President, M. V. Rodzianko, was in constant consultation with the czar about the growing crisis. On March 12, he informed Nicholas II that civil war had broken out, and that he needed to create a new cabinet responsible to the legislature. Though dissolved on March 11, the Duma met in special session on March 13 and created a Provisional Committee of Elders to deal with the unrest. After two days of discussions, it decided that the czar must give up his throne, and on March 15, 1917, Rodzianko and A. I. Guchkov, leader of the Octobrist Party, convinced the czar to abdicate. He agreed and turned the throne over to his brother, the Grand Duke Michael, who gave it up the following day.

THE PROVISIONAL GOVERNMENT IN POWER (MARCH – NOVEMBER, 1917)

From March through November 1917, a temporary Provisional Government ruled Russia. It tried to move the country towards democracy and keep Russia in the war as a loyal western ally.

Leadership

The principle figures in the new government were Prince George Lvov, a Kadet Party and *zemstvo* leader, who served as Prime Minister and Minister of the Interior; Paul Miliukov, head of the Kadet Party, Foreign Minister; A.I. Guchkov, an Octobrist leader, Minister of War; and Alexander Kerensky, a conservative Socialist Revolutionary and Vice-Chairman of the Petrograd Soviet, Minister of Justice.

Problems

The Provisional Government was made up of middle class and intellectual leaders, and had little contact or sympathy with the problems or concerns of the workers or peasants. Its leaders, particularly Miliukov, felt the government had to remain a loyal ally and stay in the war to maintain its international credibility. Despite pressure to redistribute land, Lvov's government felt that it did not have the authority to deal with this complex issue. Instead, it left the problem to a future Constituent Assembly that would convene within a year. The Provisional Government did, however, implement a number of far-reaching reforms, including full political and religious freedom, election of local officials, an eight hour working day, and legal and judicial changes.

THE PETROGRAD SOVIET

On the eve of Nicholas II's abdication, a "shadow government," the Petrograd Soviet, was formed from among the capital's workers, and took control of the city administration. Briefly, it shared the Tauride Palace with the Provisional Government.

Creation

On March 13, delegates were elected to a Soviet of Worker's Deputies, later renamed the Soviet of Workers and Soldiers Deputies. It was made up of 1,300 representatives, and grew to 3,000 the following week with the addition of military delegates. Because of its size, the Petrograd Soviet created an Executive Committee headed by N.S. Chkeidze, a Menshevik, to make its most important decisions.

Policies

In response to an unsuccessful request to the Provisional Government to absolve soldiers from potentially treasonous actions during the March Revolution, the Petrograd Soviet issued Order No. I (March 14) that granted them amnesty and stated that officers were to be elected by their units. It later issued Order No. II for units throughout the country. These decrees, hesitatingly approved later by the Provisional Government, caused a significant collapse of discipline in the armed forces.

LENIN RETURNS TO RUSSIA

Vladimir Ilyich Ulyanov (Lenin) (1870 – 1924) became involved in revolutionary activity after the execution of his brother for an assassination plot against Alexander III. A committed Marxist, he split with the Menshevik wing of the Russian Social Democratic Party and formed his "Bolshevik" (majority) faction in 1903. Lenin felt the party should be led by a committed elite. He spent much of the period between 1905 and 1917 in exile, and was surprised by the February Revolution. However, with the aid of the Germans, he and some followers were placed in a sealed train and transported from Switzerland via Stockholm to Russia.

The April Theses

On April 16, Lenin arrived at Petrograd's Finland Station and went into hiding. The next day, he proposed his April Theses to the city's Bolshevik leaders, who rejected them. Lenin felt that the Bolsheviks should oppose the Provisional Government and support the theme "All Power to the Soviets." The Soviets, he concluded, should control the government while the war should become a revolution against capitalism, with all soldiers on both sides joining the struggle. In addition, he wanted the country's land, factories, and banks to be nationalized, and the Bolshevik Party should begin to call itself the Communist Party.

THE FIRST COALITION

Paul Miliukov's decision on May 1 to insure the Allies that his country would not sign a separate agreement with Germany and continue to fight until a "decisive victory" was won, caused public demonstrations that forced his resignation and the Lvov government to disavow his note. The Soviet now permitted its members to join the Provisional Government, a new one, known as the First Coalition, and was formed under Prince Lvov that included nine non-socialists and six socialist representatives. Some of its more prominent members were: Alexander Kerensky, who now became Minister of War and the Navy; Victor Chernov, a leading Socialist Revolutionary, now Minister of Agriculture; M. I. Tereshchenko, previously Finance Minister, as Foreign Minister; and H. Tsereteli, the Menshevik leader and head of the Petrograd Soviet, as Minister of Posts and Telegraph. In many instances, the Coalition's new socialist members felt more loyal to the Petrograd Soviet than to the government itself.

THE JULY CRISES

Because of Allied pressure, the Provisional Government decided to mount an offensive on the Eastern Front to counter French military failures and mutinies on the Western Front.

The July Offensive

Kerensky, determined to revive the Russian army, toured the front to rally his forces, and created special "shock" battalions to lead them into battle. On July 1, Russian forces attacked the Austrians in the Lvov area of Galicia and initially scored some successes, though within 12 days the Russian advance was halted, and a week later, Austro-German troops began to push the Russians back. Their retreat turned into a panic and desertions became rampant. The Provisional Government restored the death penalty on July 25 to stop this rupture in discipline, though it did little to stop the army's collapse.

The Second Coalition

In the midst of the July Offensive, the First Coalition collapsed. On July 16, four Kadet members resigned because of the Coalition's decision to grant the Ukraine quasi-federal status, while several days later, Prince Lvov stepped down as Prime Minister over the land question and efforts to strengthen Soviet influence in the Cabinet. Alexander Kerensky became Prime Minister, and twice made cabinet changes between July 25 and August 6. On August 22, he announced that elections for the Constituent Assembly would be on November 25, and that it would open on December 11.

The July Days

Prompted by the failures of the July offensive and the resignation of Kadet ministers from the Cabinet, military units and workers mounted a spontaneous protest against the Provisional Government on July 16. After hesitating, the Bolsheviks agreed to lead the demonstrations, which saw over 500,000 march on the Tauride Palace, demanding that the Petrograd Soviet seize power. The Soviet leaders refused, and on July 18 troops loyal to the Provisional Government put the demonstrations down. Afterwards, the government claimed that Bolshevik leaders were German agents, and tried to arrest them. Many top Bolsheviks went underground or fled abroad.

THE SECOND COALITION AND THE KORNILOV AFFAIR

In an effort to rebuild support for his government, Kerensky decided to call a meeting of delegates representing numerous organizations from throughout the country in late August. The rifts that developed there led to the Kornilov Crisis several weeks later.

The Moscow State Conference (August 26 – 28)

In an effort to find an alternative base of support for the Petrograd Soviet before elections to the Constituent Assembly, Kerensky convened the Moscow State Conference on August 26.

Over 2,000 delegates, representing the Duma, the military, the Soviets, the professions and other groups, met in Moscow. The Bolsheviks opposed the meeting and responded with a general strike.

The conference accentuated the growing difference between Kerensky and the conservatives, who looked to the government's Commander-in-Chief, General Lavr Kornilov, as a leader. Kornilov represented elements who decried the collapse of military discipline and left the Moscow Conference convinced that Kerensky did not have the ability to restore order and stability to the nation and the military.

The Kornilov Affair

The mutual suspicion between Kerensky and Kornilov resulted in a series of indirect, unofficial negotiations between the two that ended in Kornilov's dismissal on September 9. Kornilov responded by ordering his Cossack and "Savage" divisions to march to Petrograd to stop a Bolshevik coup. The Petrograd Soviet rallied to save the revolution, and freed the Bolsheviks from prison to help with defense preparations. Kornilov's coup collapsed, and he surrendered on September 14. Kerensky now became Supreme Commander-in-Chief.

The Third Coalition

On September 14, Kerensky restructured his government as a temporary Directory of Five, and declared Russia a Republic. Thirteen days later, he convened a large gathering of 1,200 representatives from throughout the country to rebuild his power base. From it emerged a Third Coalition government on October 8, that consisted of Socialist Revolutionaries, Mensheviks, Kadets, and ministers without ties to any faction. The conference also decided to establish a Council of the Russian Republic or preparliament with 555 delegates that would open on October 20. The Bolsheviks and other leftists opposed these efforts, which weakened Kerensky's efforts.

THE BOLSHEVIK OCTOBER REVOLUTION

The Kornilov affair and Kerensky's failure to rebuild support for the Provisional Government convinced the Bolshevik's two leaders, Lenin and Leon Trotsky, that now was the time for them to attempt to seize power.

Lenin's Decision to Seize Power

After learning that the II All-Russian Congress of Soviets of Workers and Soldiers Deputies would open on November 7, Lenin began to think of a simultaneous seizure of power, since he was convinced that while the Bolsheviks could dominate that II Soviet Congress, they would not be able to do the same with the Constituent Assembly that was to open later. On October 23 – 24, he returned from Finland to meet with the Party's Central Committee to plan the coup. Though he met with strong resistance, the Committee agreed to create a Political Bureau (Politburo) to oversee the revolution.

Trotsky and the Military Revolutionary Committee

Leon Trotsky, head of the Petrograd Soviet and its Military Revolutionary Committee, convinced troops in Petrograd to support Bolshevik moves. While Trotsky gained control of important strategic points around the city, Kerensky, well-informed of Lenin's plans, finally decided on November 6 to move against the plotters.

The Coup of November 6 – 7

In response, Lenin and Trotsky ordered their supporters to seize the city's transportation and communication centers. The Winter Palace was captured later that evening, along with most of Kerensky's government.

The II Congress of Soviets

The II Congress opened at 11 p.m. on November 7, with Lev Kamenev, a member of Lenin's Politburo, as its head. Over half (390) of the 650 delegates were Bolshevik supporters, and its newly selected 22 member Presidium had 14 Bolsheviks on it. Soon after the II Congress opened, many of the moderate socialists walked out in opposition to Lenin's coup, leaving the Bolsheviks and the Left Socialist Revolutionaries in control of the gathering. Lenin now used the rump Congress as the vehicle to announce his regime.

At the Congress, it was announced that the government's new Cabinet, officially called the Council of People's Commissars (Sovnarkom), and responsible to a Central Executive Committee, would include Lenin as Chairman or head of government, Trotsky as Foreign Commissar, and Josef Stalin as Commissar of Nationalities. The Central Executive Committee of 101 (later 110) delegates would be the government's temporary legislature. The II Congress also issued two decrees on peace and land. The first called for immediate peace without any consideration of indemnities or annexations, while the second adopted the Socialist Revolutionary land program that abolished private ownership of land and decreed that a peasant could only have as much land as he could farm. Village councils would oversee distribution.

THE CONSTITUENT ASSEMBLY

The Constituent Assembly, long promised by the Provisional Government as the country's first legally elected legislature, presented serious problems for Lenin, since he knew the Bolsheviks could not win a majority of seats in it. Regardless, Lenin allowed elections for it to be held on November 25 under universal suffrage. Over 41,000,000 Russians voted. The SR's got 58% of the vote, the Bolsheviks 25%, the Kadets and other parties, 17%. The Assembly was to open on January 18, 1918, though for the next seven weeks, the Bolsheviks did everything possible to discredit the election results. When it convened on January 18 in the Tauride Palace, the building was surrounded by Red Guards and others. The Assembly voted down Bolshevik proposals and elected Victor Chernov, a Socialist Revolutionary, as president. The Bolsheviks walked out. After it adopted laws on land and peace, and declared the country a democratic federal republic, it was adjourned until the next day. When the delegates later returned to the Tauride Palace, they found it surrounded by troops, who announced that the Constituent Assembly was dissolved.

WORLD WAR I: THE FINAL PHASE, 1917 – 1918

In early 1917, the new French commander, General Robert Nivelle, altered the earlier policy of attrition against the Germans, and began to plan distracting Somme attacks with a major assault against the Germans at Champagne. These plans caused friction with Field Marshal Douglas Haig, who had a different strategy and resented serving under Nivelle.

The French Offensive

The Champagne offensive began near Reims on April 16. By May 9, it failed at the second Battle of the Aisne. As a result, a series of mutinies broke out in the French army (May 3 – 20) that forced the replacement of Nivelle for Marshal Henri Petain, who restored order.

The British Offensive

To shore up the failing French battle effort, General Haig began a series of attacks in Flanders on June 7 that resulted in the capture of Messines Ridge the following day. Against French wishes, Haig began a new series of unsuccessful assaults (Third Battle of Ypres from July 31 to November 4) that were designed to capture the Flemish port cities of Ostend and Zeebrugge. These attempts ultimately failed. He did succeed in capturing the Passchendaele Ridge and seriously damaged the strength of the German 4th Army, though his own troops suffered heavy loses.

The Italian Front and the Battle of Caporetto

In response to increased Italian attacks against Austro-Hungary in the Isonzo area in August and September 1917, the German High Command decided to strengthen Central Power resistance with troops from the Eastern Front to defeat the Italians. Consequently, on October 24, a Central Power campaign began at Caporetto, which resulted in an Italian retreat through November 12 and the capture of 250,000 Italians. The loss convinced the Allies to form a Supreme War Council at Versailles to enhance Allied cooperation.

The Tank Battle of Cambrai

From November 20 to December 3, the largest tank battle of the war took place at Cambrai involving 400 British tanks. After breaking through the German Hindenburg Line, a German counter offensive on November 30 pushed the British back.

THE MIDDLE AND NEAR EAST, 1917

Mesopotamia

The British revived their Mesopotamian campaign in 1917 and retook Al Kut on February 23. They captured Baghdad on March 11.

Palestine

British forces in Palestine unsuccessfully attacked Gaza on March 26 – 27, and reassaulted it with the same consequences on April 17 – 19. In the third offensive against Gaza from October 31 to November 7, Turkish forces retreated, which opened the way for a British attack on Jerusalem. While Col. T.E. Lawrence worked to stir Arab passions against the Turks, General Sir Edmund Allenby took Jerusalem on December 9 – 11.

THE U.S. ENTERS THE WAR

American Neutrality

Woodrow Wilson, the American President, issued a declaration of neutrality four days after war broke out in 1914, and offered to work to settle differences between both sides.

The U.S. and Freedom of the Seas

As the war expanded into the Atlantic, Allied efforts to stifle Central Power trade and the German use of the submarine created problems for the United States. In October 1914, President Wilson asked both sides to abide by the Declaration of London (1909) which laid out rules of actions and rights for neutrals and belligerents in war. Germany and its allies agreed to accept its terms because of their inferior naval strength, while the Allied powers refused.

Germany and Submarine Warfare

Throughout the latter part of 1915 and 1916, the U.S. was able to restrict most German submarine activity in the Atlantic because Berlin wanted to avoid any crisis that might bring America into the war. However, the failure of peace initiatives at the end of that year convinced German leaders, who felt their submarine fleet was now capable of a successful full blockade of England, to reinstitute unlimited submarine warfare in the Atlantic on January 31, 1917. Though they knew this policy would probably bring the U.S. into the war, they felt they could defeat Great Britain well before the U.S. could significantly alter its course.

The Zimmerman Telegram

On March 2, British intelligence published the Zimmerman Telegram, a note from the German Foreign Minister to his ambassador in Mexico that ordered him to seek an alliance with that country that would allow Mexico to seize the American Southwest if the U.S. entered the war. The message, which was revealed several days after a number of Americans died on the *Laconia* from a U-boat attack, helped – along with the creation of a democratic Provisional Government in Russia – convince the president and American public opinion that it was now time to enter the war. The United States did enteredthe war on April 6, 1917.

RUSSIA LEAVES THE WAR

One of the cornerstones of Bolshevik propaganda throughout 1917 was a promise to end the war after they had seized power. Once in control, Soviet authorities issued a decree that called for immediate peace "with no indemnities or annexations" at the II Congress of Soviets on November 8, 1917.

The Armistice at Brest-Litovsk

As order collapsed among Russian units along the Eastern Front, the Soviet government began to explore cease fire talks with the Central Powers. Leon Trotsky, the Commissar of Foreign Affairs, offered general negotiations to all sides, and signed an initial armistice as a prelude to peace discussions with Germany at Brest-Litovsk on December 5, 1917.

Trotsky and Initial Peace Negotiations with Germany

Trotsky, who replaced Adolf Joffe as principal delegate soon after talks began, felt he could utter a few revolutionary phrases and close up shop. He was shocked by German demands for Poland, Lithuania and Kurland when negotiations opened on December 22, 1917. This prompted him to return to Moscow for consultations with the Bolshevik leadership.

Soviet Differences Over Peace Terms

Three different perspectives emerged over the German peace terms among the Soviet leadership. One group, led by Nikokai Bukharin, wanted the conflict to continue as a revolutionary war designed to spread Bolshevism. Lenin, however, felt the country needed peace for his government to survive. Western revolution would take place later. Trotsky wanted a policy of no war and no peace.

At a Bolshevik meeting on January 21, 1918, the Soviet leadership barely selected Bukharin's proposal, while the Central Committee overrode this decision on January 24 in favor of Trotsky's proposal.

Negotiations Resume at Brest-Litovsk

Trotsky returned to the peace talks and tried to stall them with his no war, no peace theme. He left Brest-Litovsk on February 10, and eight days later, the Germans responded with broad attacks all across the Eastern Front that met with little Soviet opposition.

The Soviet Response and the Treaty of Brest-Litovsk

On the day the German offensive began, Lenin barely convinced Party leaders to accept Germany's earlier offer. Berlin responded with harsher ones, which the Soviets grudgingly accepted, and were integrated into the Treaty of Brest-Litovsk of March 3, 1918. According to its terms, in return for peace, Soviet Russia lost its Baltic provinces, the Ukraine, Finland, Byelorussia, and part of Transcaucasia. The area lost totalled 1,300,000 square miles and included 62 million people.

THE ALLIED BREAKTHROUGH

By the end of 1917, the Allied war effort seemed in disarray. The French and Italian governments had changed hands in an effort to revive war spirits, while an Anglo-French force arrived to stop the Central advance after Caporetto. To strengthen Allied resolves, the United States declared war on Austro-Hungary on December 6, 1917, while the Allies developed new mining policies to handicap German U-boat movements.

The American Presence: Naval and Economic Support

The United States, which had originally hoped that it could simply supply the Allies with naval and economic support, made its naval presence known immediately and helped Great Britain mount an extremely effective blockade of Germany and, through a convoy system, strengthened the shipment of goods across the Atlantic.

Despite the difficulties of building a military system from scratch, the United States was slowly able to transform its peacetime army of 219,665 men and officers into a force of 2 million. An initial token group, the American Expeditionary Force under General John J. Pershing, arrived in France on June 25, 1917, while by the end of April 1918, 300,000 Americans a month were placed as complete divisions alongside British and French units.

The German Offensive of 1918

Emboldened by their victory over Russia, the German High Command decided to launch an all-out offensive against the Allies in France to win the war.

Strengthened by forces from the Russian front, Erich Ludendorff, the Germans' principal war planner, intended to drive his divisions, which outnumbered the Allies 69 to 33, between the British and the French, and push the former to the Channel.

Beginning on March 21, 1918, Ludendorff mounted four major attacks on the Allied forces in France: Somme (March 21 – April 4), Lys (April 9 – 29), Aisne (May 27 – June 6), and Champagne-Marne (July 15 – 17). The success of the assaults so concerned the Allies that they appointed the French Chief of Staff, Ferdinand Foch, Generalissimo of Allied Forces on April 14. In the third attack on Aisne, the Germans came within 37 miles of Paris. However, the increasing appearance of fresh, though untried American forces, combined with irreplaceable German manpower losses, began to turn the war against the Germans. Four days after the decisive German crossing of the Marne, Foch counterattacked and began to plan for an offensive against the Germans.

The Allied Offensive of 1918

Stirred by the successes on the Marne, the Allies began their offensive against the Germans at Amiens on August 8, 1918. Ludendorff, who called this Germany's "dark day," soon began to think of ways to end the fighting. By September 3, the Germans retreated to the Hindenburg Line. On September 26, Foch began his final offensive, and took the Hindenburg Line the following day. Two days later, Ludendorff advised his government to seek a peace settlement. Over the next month, the French took St. Quetin (October 1), while the British occupied Cambrai, Le Cateau, and Ostend.

On September 14, Allied forces attacked in the Salonika area of Macedonia and forced Bulgaria to sue for peace on September 29.

On September 19, General Allenby began an attack on Turkish forces at Megiddo in Palestine and quickly defeated them. In a rapid collapse of Turkish resistance, the British took Damascus, Aleppo, and finally forced Turkey from the war at the end of October.

On October 24, the Italians began an assault against Austria-Hungary at Vitto Veneto and forced Vienna to sign armistice terms on November 3.

THE ARMISTICE WITH GERMANY

Several days after Ludendorff advised his government to seek peace, Prince Max of Baden assumed the German Chancellorship. On October 4, he asked President Wilson for an armistice, based on the American President's "Fourteen Points" of January 8, 1918. The Allies hesitatingly agreed to support the President's terms, with qualifications, which were given to the Germans on November 5. On November 11 at 11:00 a.m., the war ended on the Western Front.

THE COLLAPSE OF THE GERMAN MONARCHY AND THE CREATION OF THE GERMAN REPUBLIC

The dramatic collapse of German military fortunes had seriously undercut the credibility of the Kaiser, Wilhelm II, and strengthened the hand of the country's politicians. Stimulated by the growing threat of revolution after the German naval rebellion in Kiel on October 28, that had spread to the army, efforts were made to try to get the Kaiser to abdicate in hopes that this would enable Germany to receive better terms from the Allies. The Kaiser fled to army headquarters in Belgium, while on November 9 the Chancellorship was transferred to Friederich Ebert after his fellow socialist leader, Phillip Scheidemann, announced the creation of a German Republic on the same day.

THE PARIS PEACE CONFERENCE OF 1919 – 1920

To a very great extent, the direction and thrust of the discussions at the Paris Peace Conference were determined by the destructive nature of the war itself and the political responsibilities, ideals, and personalities of the principle architects of the settlements at Paris: President Woodrow Wilson of the United States, Prime Minister Lloyd George of Great Britain, Prime Minister/Minister of War Georges Clemenceau of France, and Prime Minister Vittorio Orlando of Italy.

As politicians, they reflected the general mood of victorious Europe's population, who wanted the principal Central Powers, Germany and Austria-Hungary, punished severely for this inhuman calamity. Total losses are not accurately known. Consequently, high and low estimates are given in some categories:

1) France: 1,500,000/1,363,000 dead and 4,797,800/4,660,800 wounded.

2) British Empire: 1,000,000/908,000 dead and 2,282,235/2,190,235 wounded.

3) Italy: 500,000/460,000 dead and 1,737,000/1,697,000 wounded.

4) United States: 116,708/100,000 dead and 104,000/87,292 wounded.

5) Russia: 1,700,000 dead and 7,450,000 wounded.

6) Germany: 2,000,000/1,774,000 dead and 5,368,558/5,142,588 wounded.

7) Austria-Hungary: 1,250,000/1,200,000 dead and 5,820,000/5,770,000 wounded.

WOODROW WILSON AND THE FOURTEEN POINTS

Not handicapped by significant financial or territorial concerns, Wilson idealistically promoted his Fourteen Points that he issued on January 8, 1918 – particularly the last, which dealt with a League of Nations – as the basis of the armistice and the peace settlement. They included 1) Open Covenants of Peace; 2) Freedom of the Seas; 3) Removal of Trade Barriers; 4) Arms Reduction; 5) Settlement of Colonial Claims; 6) Evacuation of Russia; 7) Restoration of Belgium; 8) Return of Alsace-Lorraine to France; 9) Adjustment of Italy's Borders along Ethnic Lines; 10) Autonomy for the Peoples of Austria-Hungary; 11) Evacuation and Restoration of the Balkans; 12) Autonomy for the Non-Turkish Parts of the Turkish Empire; 13) Independent Poland with an Outlet to the Sea; and 14) a League of Nations.

SECRET ALLIED AGREEMENTS CONCLUDED DURING WORLD WAR I

Throughout the war, the Allied powers had concluded a number of secret agreements designed to encourage countries to join their side or as compensation for war efforts. In March 1915, England and France had promised Russia Constantinople, the Straits, and the bordering areas as long as they were openly accessible. In April of the following year, England and France had promised one another, respectively, spheres in Mesopotamia and Palestine, as well as Syria, Adana, Cilia, and southern Kurdistan. The Sykes-Picot Treaty in May 1916 better defined both countries' Arabian spheres. Russia was to have similar rights in Armenia, portions of Kurdistan, and northeastern Anatolia. The Allies gave Italy and Rumania significant territories to encourage them in their war effort in April 1915 and August 1916, while the English promised to support Japan's desire for Germany's Asian possessions. France and Russia agreed to promote one another's claims at a future peace conference, while Arab independence and creation of a Jewish homeland were also promised to others.

PRELIMINARY DISCUSSIONS

The sudden, unexpected end of the war, combined with the growing threat of communist revolution throughout Europe created an unsettling atmosphere at the conference. As a result of the Bolshevik victory in Russia, delegates from the United States, England, France, Italy, and later Japan, hurriedly began informal peace discussions on January 12, 1919. In time, this group was transformed into a Council of Ten, consisting of two representatives from each of these countries. This body conducted most of the significant talks in Paris until March 24, 1919, when the "Big Four" of Wilson (U.S.), Clemenceau (France), Lloyd-George (England), and Orlando (Italy) took over the discussions. Initially, the Allied Powers had hoped for a negotiated settlement with the defeated powers, which necessitated hard terms that would be negotiated down. However, the delays caused by uncertainty over direction at the beginning of the conference, Wilson's insistence that the League of Nations be included in the settlement, and fear of European-wide revolution resulted in a hastily prepared, dictated peace settlement.

France and the Rhineland Conflict

Once talks began among the Big Four, France insisted on the return of Alsace-Lorraine from Germany and the creation of an independent buffer state along the Rhine to protect it from Germany. The United States and Great Britain opposed these claims because they felt it could lead to future Franco-German friction. In return for an Allied guarantee of France's security against Germany, France got the Saar coal mines, and the demilitarization of the Rhine, with portions occupied by the Allies for fifteen years.

German Disarmament

Lloyd-George and Wilson saw German arms reductions as a prelude to a European-wide plan after the conference. They also opposed the draft, though agreed with the French about the need for a small German army.

Reparations

Each of the major powers had differing views on how much compensation Germany should pay for war indebtedness. At British insistence, civilian losses were added to the normal military ones. The "War Guilt" clause, Article 231, was included to justify heavy reparations, while the actual determination of the amount was left to a Reparations Commission.

THE TREATY OF VERSAILLES

The Treaty of Versailles, which was only between Germany and the Allied powers, had fifteen major sections, and almost 450 articles. Any country that ratified it, in turn accepted these terms as well as the League of Nations' Covenant in the first article: 1) Covenant of the League of Nations; 2) Boundaries of Germany; 3) Other Territories of Germany; 4) Germany's Overseas Boundaries and Rights; 5) Germany's Military and Naval Restrictions; 6) Prisoners of War; 7) War Guilt; 8) Reparations; 9) Costs of the War; 10) Customs Agreement and Other Covenants; 11) Aerial Navigation; 12) Freedom of Movement on Europe's Waterways; 13) Labor Organizations; 14) Guarantees; and 15) Mandates for German Colonies and Other General Provisions.

Most Significant Clauses

The treaty's war guilt statements were the justification for its harsh penalties. The former German king, Wilhelm II, was accused of crimes against "international morality and the sanctity of treaties," while Germany took responsibility for itself and for its allies for all losses suffered by the Allied Powers and their supporters as a result of German and Central Power aggression.

Germany had to return Alsace and Lorraine to France and Eupen-Malmedy to Belgium. France got Germany's Saar coal mines as reparations, while the Saar Basin was to be occupied by the major powers for 15 years, after which a plebiscite would decide its ultimate fate. Poland got a number of German provinces and Danzig, now a free city, as its outlet to the sea. Additionally, Germany lost all of its colonies in Asia and Africa.

The German Army was limited to 100,000 men and officers with 12 year enlistments for the former and 25 for the latter. The General Staff was also abolished. The Navy lost its submarines and most offensive naval forces, and was limited to 15,000 men and officers with the same enlistment periods as the army. Aircraft and blimps were outlawed. A Reparations Commission was created to determine Germany's war debt to the Allies, which it figured in 1921 to be $31.4 billion, to be paid over an extended period of time. In the meantime, Germany was to begin immediate payments in goods and raw materials.

German Hesitance to Sign the Treaty

The Allies presented the treaty to the Germans on May 7, 1919, but Foreign Minister Count Brockdorff-Rantzau refused to sign it, precipitating a crisis on both sides. The Germans stated that its terms were too much for the German people, and that it violated the spirit of Wilson's Fourteen Points. After some minor changes were made, the Germans were told to sign the document or face an Allied advance into Germany. The treaty was signed on June 28, 1919, at Versailles.

TREATIES WITH GERMANY'S ALLIES

After the conclusion of the Treaty of Versailles, responsibility for concluding treaties with the other Central Powers fell on the shoulders of the Council of Foreign Ministers and later, the Conference of Ambassadors.

The Treaty of St. Germain (September 10, 1919)

The Allied treaty with Austria legitimized the breakup of the Austrian Empire in the latter days of the war and saw Austrian territory ceded to Italy and the new states of Czechoslovakia, Poland, and Yugoslavia. The agreement included military restrictions and debt payments.

Treaty of Neuilly (November 27, 1919)

Bulgaria lost territory to Yugoslavia and Greece and also had clauses on military limitations and reparations.

Treaty of Trianon (June 4, 1920)

The agreement with Hungary was delayed because of the communist revolution there in 1919 and Rumania's brief occupation of Budapest. Hungary lost two-thirds of its prewar territory in the agreement to Rumania, Yugoslavia, and Czechoslovakia, and became an almost purely Magyar nation. Reparations and military reduction terms were also in the accord.

Treaty of Sevres (August 10, 1920)

Turkey lost most of its non-Turkish territory, principally in the Middle and Near East, and saw the Straits and the surrounding area internationalized and demilitarized. The Turkish revolution of Mustafa Kemal Pasha ultimately saw its terms neutralized, and renegotiated, as the Treaty of Lausanne (July 24, 1923) with Turkey gaining territory in Anatolia, Smyrna, and Thrace.

PROBLEMS OF ALLIED UNITY: JAPAN, ITALY, AND THE U.S.

During and after the meetings in Paris that resulted in the Treaty of Versailles, disputes arose among the Allies that caused friction among them later.

Japan

During the treaty talks, Japan asked for Germany's Shantung Province in China, its Pacific colonies, and a statement on racial equality in the League Covenant. Japan got what it essentially wanted on the first two requests, despite protests from China on Shantung. However, Japan's request for a racial equality clause met strong opposition from the United States and some members of the British Commonwealth, who feared the impact of the statement on immigration. The proposal was denied, principally at the instigation of President Wilson.

Italy

The Italians came to Paris expecting full realization of the secret Treaty of London (1915), plus more. When Orlando proved stubborn on this matter, Wilson appealed directly to the Italian people regarding the issue on April 23, which prompted the Italian delegation to leave the conference temporarily. Italy got the Tyrol, as well as Istria and some Adriatic islands in the Treaty of Rapallo (December 12, 1920). Dalmatia, however, went to Yugoslavia, while Fiume was seized by the Italian patriot/poet Sabhiele D'Annunzio, on September 12, 1919. After a 14-month occupation he departed, leaving its destiny to Italy and Yugoslavia. The Treaty of Rome (January 27, 1924) divided the city between the two, with Italy getting the lion's share of the area.

The United States

Although public and political sentiment was initially in favor of the treaty and its League provisions, Wilson's failure to include Senate representatives in the negotiating, and fear of Presidential usurpation of Congressional war powers created suspicions between Republicans and the President. These suspicions, coupled with concern over the obligations of the United States in future European affairs (particularly those cited in Article X – which would, according to its opponents, give the United States no freedom of choice in deciding whether or not to intervene in world crises) prompted the Senate to reject it twice in 1919 and 1920, though by only seven votes on the latter occasion. The United States concluded a separate peace with Germany in 1921 and never joined the League, though it was active in some of its corollary organizations.

POLITICAL DEVELOPMENTS IN POST-WAR EUROPE, 1918 – 1929

England, 1918 – 1922

Like most other European powers that emerged from the First World War, England had a set of problems unique to its status as a nation absolutely dependent on trade and commerce for its economic well-being.

With the war at an end, the Coalition government of David Lloyd George held the first parliamentary elections since 1910. Known as the "Coupon" or "Khaki" elections, the question of victory, the nature of the settlement with Germany, and the Prime Minister himself were the election's burning issues. Before it took place, the Representation of the Peoples Act granted women over 30 the right to vote. Lloyd George and his Conservative Coalition won a landslide victory (478 seats) while his opponents gained only 87.

Afterwards, England enjoyed an economic boom fueled by government policies and economic production based on pre-war conditions. Unfortunately, government retrenchment, blended with tax increases and over production, resulted in a severe recession by the end of 1921. It began in 1920 with almost 700,000 unemployed by the end of that year and jumped to 2 million within months. Until the Depression, unemployment averaged 12% annually. This resulted in the passage of the Unemployment Insurance Acts (1920, 1922) for workers, and the construction of 200,000 subsidized housing units.

Triggered by the Easter Rebellion of 1916, the extremist Sinn Fein faction gained prominence in Ireland. In 1918, three quarters of its members elected to the British

Parliament instead declared Irish independence in Dublin. This prompted a civil war between the Irish Republican Army and the Black and Tan, England's special occupation forces there. The Lloyd George government responded with a Home Rule division of Ireland with two legislatures, which only the northern six counties accepted. In October 1921, London created the Irish Free State, from which Ulster withdrew, as a part of the British Commonwealth.

Politics, 1922 – 1924

These problems caused the Conservatives to withdraw from Lloyd George's coalition. Andrew Bonar-Law replaced him as head of a new Conservative government, though ill health forced him to resign in 1923, followed briefly by Stanley Baldwin. Continued unemployment and labor problems, coupled with a decline to adopt more protectionistic trade policies resulted in a significant doctrine in support for the Conservatives in the elections of November 1923. Baldwin resigned, followed in office by Ramsey MacDonald, head of the Labour Party. His minority government only lasted nine months, and fell principally because of his efforts to establish formal ties with Russia.

England and Stanley Baldwin, 1924 – 1929

Baldwin entered his second Prime Ministership with a solid electoral victory (411 Seats) and strong Conservative Party backing. The year 1925 marked a turn in the economic crisis, with an increase in prices and wages. The country's return to the gold standard, which made the pound worth too much, affected British trade. In May 1926, a general strike in support of miners who feared a dramatic drop in their already low wages swept the country. Baldwin refused to concede to the miners' demands, broke the strike, and in 1927 sponsored the Trade Unions Act, which outlawed such labor action. On the other hand, the government passed a number of pieces of social legislation that further allowed support for housing construction and expanded pensions through its Widows', Orphans', and Old Age Pensions Act (1925). It also passed new legislation in 1928 that gave women the same voting privileges as men. In foreign affairs, Baldwin cancelled the 1924 commercial agreement with the Soviet Union, and, as a result of Soviet espionage activities, broke formal ties with the USSR in 1927.

FRANCE

The human losses in the war deeply affected France because of a population growth slowdown that had begun in the mid-19th century. Robbed of the flower of its youth, the Third Republic reflected in its political life and foreign policy a country ruled by an aging leadership that sought comfort in its rich past.

The Bloc National, 1919 – 1924

The election of November 1919 represented a momentary shift rightward with the moderate-conservatives winning almost two-thirds of the seats in the Chamber of Deputies. The new government, headed by Premier Alexandre Millerand, was a coalition known as the Bloc National. Aristide Briand replaced Millerand in January 1921, but was removed a year later because of lack of firmness on the German reparations question and was succeeded by Raymond Poincare.

France had borrowed heavily during the war and spent great sums afterwards to rebuild its devastated economy. Unfortunately, it relied on German reparations to fund many of these costs. Problems with these repayments created a financial crisis that saw the French public debt increase accompanied by a steady decline in the value of the franc.

Growing Franco-German differences over Germany's willingness to meet its debt payments created friction between both countries and toppled the government of August Briand. In December 1922, Poincare declared Germany in default on its reparations payments. In January, France and Belgium occupied the Ruhr. Efforts to obtain payments in kind via Franco-Belgium operation of the Ruhr's mines and factories failed because of passive resistance by German workers in the area. The Ruhr's occupiers gained little more financially in payments than they had through normal means, and found the cost of occupation expensive. Consequently, the French government had to raise taxes 20% to cover the cost of the occupation.

The Cartel des Gauches, 1924 – 1926

Poincare's Ruhr occupation policy had divided French voters, while tax increases helped defeat the Bloc National in the May 1924 elections, though it did gain 51% of the popular vote. A Radical/Socialist coalition, the Cartel des Gauches, had majority control of the Chamber. It selected Edouard Herriot, a Radical leader, as Premier, while Millerand continued as President, and Aristide Briand as Foreign Minister. Millerand's interference in policy questions forced his removal on June 10, 1924, with his successor, Gaston Doumergne serving as President until 1931.

France's ailing economy was plagued by a declining franc and inflation. Herriot's efforts to raise direct taxes, force higher levies on the rich, and lower interest rates on government bonds met with radical opposition, which sought indirect tax increases and cuts in government expenditures. Herriot was removed from office on April 10, 1925, and replaced by Paul Painleve, who served for eight months.

Briand, who dominated French foreign affairs until 1932, pursued a policy of reconciliation with Germany and better relations with Europe's other pariah, the USSR. France granted diplomatic recognition to Soviet Russia in 1924, though relations quickly worsened because of the difficulty in getting the tsarist debt question resolved and the Soviets' use of their Paris embassy for espionage activities.

The Union Nationale, 1926 – 1928

The most crucial domestic problem faced by the Carte des Gauches was the declining franc, which by 1926 was only worth one-tenth of its prewar value. Its fall caused a political crisis so severe that the country had six cabinets over a nine month period. Consequently, on July 15, 1926, Briand resigned his premiership, succeeded by Poincare, who formed a Union National cabinet that had six former premiers in it. This coalition was backed by the Radicals as well as Conservatives and centrist parties in the legislature. To resolve the franc problem, the Chamber granted Poincare special authority. Over the next two years, he dramatically raised taxes and was able to get capital that had been taken out of the country reinvested in government bonds or other areas of the economy. By 1928, the franc had risen to 20% of its prewar value, and Poincare was considered a financial miracle worker. Unfortunately, the political and psychological scars left by the crisis would haunt France for two more decades.

WEIMAR GERMANY, 1918 – 1929

The dramatic collapse of the German war effort in the second half of 1918 ultimately created a political crisis that forced the abdication of the King and the creation of a German Republic on November 9.

Provisional Government

From the outset, the Provisional Government, formed of a coalition of Majority and Independent Socialists, was beset by divisions from within and threats of revolution throughout Germany. The first Chancellor was Friedrich Ebert, the Majority Socialist leader. On November 22, state leaders agreed to support a temporary government until elections could be held for a nationally elected legislature, which would draw up a constitution for the new republic.

Elections for the new National Constituent Assembly, which was to be based on proportional representation, gave no party a clear majority. A coalition of the Majority Socialists, the Catholic Center Party, and the German Democratic Party (DDP) dominated the new assembly. On February 11, 1919, the assembly met in the historic town of Weimar and selected Friedrich Ebert President of Germany. Two days later, Phillip Scheidermann formed the first Weimar Cabinet and became its first Chancellor.

On August 11, 1919, a new constitution was promulgated, which provided for a bicameral legislature. The upper chamber, the Reichsrat, represented the Federal states, while the lower house, the Reichstag, with 647 delegates elected by universal suffrage, supplied the country's Chancellor and Cabinet. A President was also to be elected separately for a 7-year term. As a result of Article 48 of the Constitution, he could rule through emergency decree, though the Reichstag could take this authority from him.

Problems of the Weimar Republic, 1919 – 1920

The new government faced a number of serious domestic problems that severely challenged or undercut its authority. Its forced acceptance of the hated Friedensdiktat ("the dictated peace") seriously undermined its prestige, while the unsuccessful, though violent Communist Spartikist Rebellion (January 5 – 11, 1919) in Berlin created a climate of instability. This was followed three months later by the brief communist takeover of Bavaria, and the rightist Kapp Putsch (March 13 – 17, 1920) in the capital the following year.

The territorial, manpower, and economic losses suffered during and after the war, coupled with a $30.4 billion reparations debt, had a severe impact on the German economy and society, and severely handicapped the new government's efforts to establish a stable governing environment.

In an effort of good faith based on hopes of future reparation payment reductions, Germany borrowed heavily and made payments in kind to fulfill its early debt obligations. The result was a spiral of inflation later promoted by the Weimar government to underline Allied insensitivity to Germany's plight, that saw the mark go from 8.4 to the dollar in 1919 to 7,000 marks to the dollar by December 1922. After the Allied Reparations Commission declared Germany in default on its debt, the French and the Belgians occupied the Ruhr on January 11, 1923.

Chancellor Wilhelm Cuno encouraged the Ruhr's Germans passively to resist the occupation, and printed worthless marks which dropped from 40,000 to the dollar in January 1923 to 4.2 trillion to the dollar eleven months later. The occupation ended on September 26, and helped prompt stronger Allied sympathy to Germany's payment difficulties, though the inflationary spiral had severe economic, social, and political consequences.

Weimar Politics, 1919 – 1923

Germany's economic and social difficulties deeply affected its infant democracy. From February 1919 to August 1923, the country had six Chancellors.

In the aftermath of the Kapp Putsch, conservative demands for new elections resulted in a June defeat for the ruling coalition that saw the Democrats (DDP) lose seats to the German National People's Party (DVP) headed by Gustav Stresemann, and the Majority Socialists lose seats to the more reactionary Independent socialists. Conservative Germans blamed the Weimar Coalition for the hated Versailles "Diktat" with its war guilt and reparations terms, while leftist voters felt the government had forgotten its social and revolutionary ideals.

Growing right-wing discontent with the Weimar Government resulted in the assassination of the gifted head of the Catholic Center Party, Matthias Erzberger, on August 29, 1921, and the murder of Foreign Minister Walter Rathenau on June 24, 1922. These were two of the most serious of over 350 political murders in Germany since the end of the war.

The Policies of Gustav Stresemann

The dominant figure in German politics from 1923 to 1929 was Gustav Stresemann, the founder and leader of the DVP. Though he served as Chancellor from August 12 to November 23, 1923, his prominence derives from his role as Foreign Minister from November 1923 until his death on October 3, 1929. He received the Nobel Peace Prize for his diplomatic efforts in 1926.

As Chancellor, Stressmann's felt that the only road to recovery and treaty revision lay in adherence to the Versailles settlement and positive relations with France and its allies. Consequently, on September 26, he ended passive resistance in the Ruhr and began to search for a solution to Germany's reparations payment problem with France. To restore faith in the currency, the government introduced a new one, the Rentenmark, on November 20, 1923, that was equal to 1 billion old marks, and was backed by the mortgage value of Germany's farm and industrial land.

In an effort to come up with a more reasonable debt payment plan for Germany, the Western Allies developed the Dawes Plan that accepted the need for Germany to pay its war debts and blended England's desire for balance with France's needs for repayment assurances. According to its terms, Germany was to begin small payments of a quarter of a billion dollars annually for four years, to be increased if its economy improved. In return, the Allies agreed to help revitalize Germany's ailing economy with a $200 million American loan and withdrawal from the Ruhr.

The crowning achievement in Stresemann's efforts to restore Germany to normal status in the European community was the Locarno Pact, December 1, 1925.

Weimar Politics, 1924 – 1928

Reichstag elections were held twice in 1924. The May 4 contest reflected a backlash against the country's economic difficulties, and saw the Communists win 3,700,000 votes and the Nazis almost 2 million, at the expense of the moderate parties. The December 7 elections were something of a vote on the Dawes Plan and economic revival, and saw the Nazis and the Communists lose almost a million votes apiece.

Following the death of President Ebert on February 28, 1925, two ballots were held for a new President, since none of the candidates won a majority on the first vote. On the second ballot on April 26, the Reichsblock, a coalition of Conservative parties, was able to get its candidate elected. War hero Paul von Hindenburg was narrowly elected against a Centrist coalition and the communists, who had a much smaller showing. Hindenburg, who some conservatives hoped would turn the clock back, vowed to uphold Weimar's Constitution.

The elections of May 20, 1928, saw the Social Democrats get almost one-third of the popular vote which, blended with other moderate groups, created a stable moderate majority in the Reichstag, which chose Hermann Muller as Chancellor. The Nazis, who held 14 Reichstag seats at the end of 1924, lost one, while Communist strength increased.

ITALY

Like other countries that had fought in the World War, Italy had suffered greatly and gained little. Its economy, very weak even before the war broke out, relied heavily upon small family agriculture which contributed 40% of the country's GNP in 1920. Consequently, many of the social, political, and economic problems that plagued the country after the war could not be blamed solely on the conflict itself.

Italian Politics, 1918 – 1919

As a result of growing discontent over the country's troubled economy, the Italian public looked to the parties that offered the most reasonable solutions. Strengthened by universal suffrage, and new proportional representation in Parliament, the Socialists doubled the number of seats to 156 in the Chamber of Deputies in the elections of November 16, 1919. The new Catholic People's Party gained 99 positions. The former party had little faith in the current state, and longed for its downfall, while the latter mixed conservative religious ideals with a desire for political moderation. Most importantly, no strong majority coalition emerged in this or the Parliament elected in May 1921 that was able to deal effectively with the country's numerous problems.

Government of Giovanni Giolitti, 1920 – 1921

From June 9, 1920 until June 26, 1921, Italy's Premier was Giovanni Giolitti, a gifted musician and pre-war figure who had dominated Italian politics between 1901 and 1914. His tactics, to resolve Italy's international conflicts and stay aloof of its domestic conflicts, exacerbated the country's problems. The Socialists took advantage of this atmosphere and promoted a series of strikes and other labor unrest in August and September 1920 that became violent and divided the country and the Socialist movement. Giolitti let the strikes run their course, and worked successfully to lower the government's deficit by 50%.

Benito Mussolini and Italian Fascism

Benito Mussolini, named by his Socialist blacksmith father after the Mexican revolutionary, Benito Juarez, was born in 1883. After a brief teaching stint, he went to Switzerland to avoid military service but returned and became active in Socialist politics. In 1912, he became editor of the Party's newspaper, *Avanti*. Several months after the outbreak of the World War, he broke with the party over involvement in the war, and began to espouse nationalistic ideas that became the nucleus of his fascist movement. He then opened his own newspaper, *Popolo d'Italia* (The People of Italy) to voice his ideas. Mussolini was drafted into military service in 1915, and was badly wounded two years later. After recuperating, he returned to his newspaper, where he blended his feelings about socialism and nationalism with an instinct for violence.

Italy's post-war conflict with its allies at the Paris Peace conference over fulfillment of the terms of the 1915 Treaty of London and the additional request for Fiume played into Mussolini's hands. Mussolini supported the D'Annunzio coup there.

Mussolini, capitalizing on the sympathy of unfulfilled war veterans, disaffected nationalists, and those fearful of communism, formed the Fascio di combattmento (Union of Combat) in Milan on March 23, 1919. Initially, Mussolini's movement had few followers, and it did badly in the November 1919 elections. However, Socialist strikes and unrest enabled him to convince Italians that he alone could bring stability and prosperity to their troubled country.

Fascism's most significant growth came in the midst of the Socialist unrest in 1920. Strengthened by large contributions from wealthy industralists, Mussolini's black-suited Squadristi attacked Socialists, communists, and ultimately, the government itself. Mussolini's followers won 35 seats in the legislative elections in May 1921, which also toppled the Giolitti cabinet.

The center of Fascist strength was in the streets of northern Italy, which Mussolini's followers, through violence, came to control. Mussolini now transformed his movement into the Fascist Party, dropped his socialist views, and began to emphasize the predominance of Italian nationalism.

The resignation of the Bonomi Cabinet on February 9, 1922, underlined the government's inability to maintain stability. In the meantime, the Fascists seized control of Bologna in May, and Milan in August. In response, Socialist leaders called for a nationwide strike on August 1, 1922, which Fascist street violence stopped in 24 hours. On October 24, 1922, Mussolini told followers that if he was not given power, he would "March on Rome." Three days later, Fascists began to seize control of other cities, while 26,000 began to move towards the capital. The government responded with a declaration of martial law, which the king, Victor Emmanuel III, refused to approve. On October 29, the king asked Mussolini to form a new government as Premier of Italy.

Mussolini's Consolidation of Power

Using tactics similar to those of D'Annunzio to seize Fiume earlier, Mussolini built a government made up of a number of sympathetic parties.

Mussolini formed a coalition cabinet that included all major parties except the Communists and the Socialists. After he assured the Chamber of Deputies that his government intended to respect personal liberties but with "dignity and firmness...," it approved his government in a 306 to 116 vote. Nine days later, the Chamber granted him quasi-dictatorial powers for a year.

To enhance his political control of the government, one of Mussolini's assistants, Giacomo Acerbo, successfully introduced a bill to the Chamber on July 21, 1923 (later approved by the Senate) that stated that the party that got the largest number of votes in a national election with a minimum of 25% of the votes cast would control two-thirds of the seats in the Chamber. Mussolini also began to remove non-Fascists from his Cabinet, the Civil Service, and other organs of government. The king kept his throne though Mussolini now became Head of State.

In violence-marred elections on April 6, 1924, the Fascists gained 60% of the popular vote and two-thirds of the Chamber's seats. In response to Fascist campaign tactics, Giacomo Matteotti, a Socialist Chamber member, attacked the Fascists for their misdeeds on May 30. Several days later, Fascist supporters kidnapped and murdered him, provoking his supporters, unwisely, to walk out of the Chamber in protest. Momentarily, Italy was stunned, and Mussolini was vulnerable. The opposition asked the king to dismiss Mussolini, but he refused.

Consolidation of the Dictatorship

On January 3, 1925 Mussolini accepted responsibility for events of the past year. He warned that this instability, caused by his opponents, would be quickly resolved. What followed was a new reign of terror that arrested opponents, closed newspapers, and eliminated basic civil liberties for Italians. On December 24, 1925, the legislature's powers were greatly limited, while those of Mussolini were increased as the new Head of State. Throughout 1926, Mussolini intensified his control over the country with legislation that outlawed strikes and created the syndicalist corporate system. A failed assassination attempt prompted the "Law for the Defense of the State" of November 25, 1926, that created a Special Court to deal with political crimes and introduced the death penalty for threats against the king, his family or the Head of State.

The Fascist Party

In December 1922, Mussolini created a Grand Council of Fascism made up of the Party's principle leaders. In 1928, the Grand Council became the most important organ of government in Italy. The structure of the Fascist Party did not reach final form until November 12, 1932. It was defined as a "civil militia" with the *Duce* (Mussolini) as its head. Its day-to-day affairs were run by the National Directorate headed by a Secretary, with two Vice Secretaries, an Administrative Secretary, and six other members. The Secretary of the National Directorate belonged to the Grand Council. The Party's Provincial Secretaries, appointed by Mussolini, oversaw local Party organizations, the *Fasci di Combattimento*. There were also separate Fascist youth organizations such as the *Piccole Italiane* (under 12) and the *Giovane Italiane* (over 12) for girls; the *Balilla* (8 – 14), the *Avanguardisti* (14 – 18), and the *Giovani Fascisti* (18 – 21) for boys. After 1927, only those who had been members of the *Balilla* and the *Avanguardisti* could be Party members.

The Syndicalist-Corporate System

In an effort to institutionalize his theories about relations between labor and management, Mussolini began to adopt some of the syndicalist theories of his followers. What emerged was a legal superstructure of labor-employer syndicates followed later by a series of government coordinated corporations to oversee the economy.

On April 3, 1926, the Rocco Labor Law created syndicates or organizations for all workers and employers in Italy. It also outlawed strikes and walkouts. Later altered, it created nine syndicate corporations: four for workers and four for employers in each of the major segments of the economy and a ninth for professionals and artists.

On July 1, 1926, Corporations were created to coordinate activities between the worker-employer syndicates, while later that year a Ministry of Corporations came into existence. On February 5, 1934, a Law on Corporations created 22 such bodies that oversaw every facet of the economy, coordinated management-labor relations, and economic production and shipment in every segment of the economy. Each Corporation was overseen by a Minister or other important government or Party official, who sat on the National Council of Corporations that was headed by Mussolini.

Foreign Policy

Some have called the first decade of Mussolini's reign the "time of good behavior." This was more because of his deep involvement in domestic affairs than his creative desire for foreign stability. This, plus the nation's wish for post-war peace and stability saw Italy participate in all of the international developments in the 1920's aimed at securing normalcy in relations with its neighbors.

Because Italy did not receive its desired portions of Dalmatia at the Paris Peace Conference, Italian Nationalist Gabriele D'Annunzio seized Fiume on the Adriatic in the fall of 1919. D'Annunzio's daring gesture as well as his deep sense of Italian national pride deeply affected Mussolini. However, in the atmosphere of detente prevalent in

Europe at the time, he agreed to settle the dispute with Yugoslavia in a treaty on January 27, 1924, which ceded most of the port to Italy, and the surrounding area to Yugoslavia.

In the fall of 1923, Mussolini used the assassination of Italian officials, who were working to resolve a Greek-Albanian border dispute, to seize the island of Corfu. Within a month, however, the British and the French convinced him to return the island for an indemnity.

SOVIET RUSSIA

Soon after the Bolshevik seizure of power, opposition forces began to gather throughout Russia that sought to challenge Soviet authority or use the occasion to breakup the Russian Empire.

Origins of the Russian Civil War, 1918

After Brest-Litovsk, Lenin's government agreed to ship part of a large group of Czech POW's through Vladivostok to the Western Front. On May 14, 1918, a brawl took place between these units and Hungarian POW's at Chelyabinsk in the Urals that led to a Czech rebellion against Soviet authorities and the seizure of the Urals area and eastern Siberia by late summer.

In the spring of 1918, Russia's old war allies had begun to land forces in Russia at major shipping points such as Murmansk, Archangel, and Vladivostok to protect supplies they had sent the Provisional Government. The Czech rebellion stirred the Allied leaders meeting at Paris to upgrade their efforts in Russia to aid the Czechs and other Communist opponents in a limited, and hopefully, non-combative manner. They began to land limited military contingents at the above ports, at Baku and in Odessa to support a victor that would revive the Eastern Front, and to a lesser degree, counterbalance Lenin's threatening communist movement.

Opposition to the Soviet takeover had begun immediately after Lenin's seizure of Petrograd. General M.V. Alexeev had formed a Volunteer Army, whose command was shared and later taken over by General Anton Denikin, who fled to the Don area in early 1918. Another center of White resistance was created first by Socialist Revolutionaries at Omsk, followed later by a government there under Admiral Alexander Kolchak, who was backed by Czech forces and would declare himself Supreme Commander of White forces in the Civil War. In time, most of the major White Commanders would recognize Kolchak's authority. General Eugune Miller created a White opposition outpost at Archangel, and General Nicholas Yudenich another in Estonia.

To meet these threats, Lenin appointed Leon Trotsky as Commissar of War on March 13, 1918, with orders to build a Red Army. By the end of the year, using partial conscription, the new Soviet forces began to retake some of the areas earlier captured by the Whites.

The Russian Civil War, 1919 – 1920

The White forces, constantly weakened by lack of unified command and strategy, enjoyed their greatest successes in 1919, when Deniken, operating from the south, took Kharkov and later Odessa and Kiev. On the other hand, Yudenich was driven from Petrograd, while Deniken lost Kharkov and Kiev. Kolchak had been defeated earlier, and Omsk was taken by November.

By early 1920, White fortunes had begun to collapse. On January 4, Kolchak abdicated in favor of Denikin, and was turned over by his Czech protectors to the Soviets who executed him on February 7. In the meantime, Denikin's capital, Rostov, was taken by the Red Army and his command was taken over later by General Peter Wrangel, whose forces were beaten that fall. Both armies were evacuated from the Crimea.

The Polish-Soviet War, 1920

The new Polish state under Marshal Joszef Pilsudski sought to take advantage of the Civil War in Russia to retake territory lost to Russia during the Polish Partitions in the late 18th century. Polish forces invaded the Ukraine on April 25, and took Kiev two weeks later. A Soviet counteroffensive reached Warsaw by mid-August, but was stopped by the Poles. Both sides concluded an armistice on October 12 and signed the Treaty of Riga on March 12, 1921 that placed Poland's border east of the Curzon Line.

Domestic Policy and Upheaval, 1918 – 1921

In order to provide more food to Russia's cities, the Soviet government implemented a "War Communism" program that centered around forced grain seizures and class war between "Kulaks" (ill-defined middle class peasants) and others. All major industry was also nationalized. These policies triggered rebellions against the seizures that saw the amount of land under cultivation and the total grain produced drop between 1918 – 1921.

The Civil War and War Communism had brought economic disaster and social upheaval throughout the country. On March 1, 1921, as the Soviet leadership met to decide on policies to guide the country in peace, a naval rebellion broke out at the Kronstadt naval base. The Soviet leadership sent Trotsky to put down the rebellion, which he did brutally by March 18.

The New Economic Policy, 1921 – 1927

The Kronstadt rebellion strengthened Lenin's resolve to initiate new policies approved at the X Party Congress that would end grain seizures and stimulate agricultural production. Termed the New Economic Policy (NEP), the government maintained control over the "Commanding Heights" of the economy (foreign trade, transportation, and heavy industry) while opening other sectors to limited capitalist development. It required the peasants to pay the government a fixed acreage tax, and allowed them to sell the surplus for profit. Once the government had resolved the inconsistencies in agricultural and industrial output and pricing, the NEP began to near 1913 production levels. The country remained dominated by small farms and peasant communes. Industrial production also improved, though it was handicapped by outdated technology and equipment which would hinder further output or expansion beyond 1913 levels.

The Death of Lenin and the Rise of Josef Stalin

Vladimir Ilyich Lenin, the founder of the Soviet State, suffered a serious stroke on May 26, 1922 and a second in December of that year. As he faced possible forced retirement or death, he composed a secret "testament" that surveyed the strengths and weaknesses of his possible successor, Stalin, who he feared would abuse power. Unfortunately, his third stroke prevented him from removing Stalin from his position as General Secretary. Lenin died on January 21, 1924.

Josef Visarionovich Dzugashvili (Stalin)(1879 – 1953) was born in the Georgian village of Gori. He became involved in Lenin's Bolshevik movement in his 20's and became Lenin's expert on minorities. Intimidated by the Party's intellectuals, he took over numerous, and in some cases, seemingly unimportant Party organizations after the Revolution and transformed them into important bases of power. Among them were

Politburo (Political Bureau), which ran the country; the Orgburo (Organizational Bureau), which Stalin headed, and which appointed people to positions in groups that implemented Politiburo decisions; the Inspectorate (Rabkrin, Commissariat of the Workers' and Peasants' Inspectorate), also under Stalin's control, which tried to eliminate Party corruption; and the Secretariat, which worked with all Party organs and set the Politburo's agenda. Stalin served as the Party's General Secretary after 1921.

Leon Trotsky

Lev Davidovich Bronstein (Trotsky) (1879 – 1940) was a Jewish intellectual active in Menshevik revolutionary work, particularly in the 1905 Revolution. He joined Lenin's movement in 1917, and soon became his right-hand man. He was Chairman of the Petrograd Soviet, headed the early Brest-Litovsk negotiating team, served as Foreign Commissar, and was father of the Red Army. A brilliant organizer and theorist, Trotsky was also brusque and, some felt, overbearing.

The Struggle for Power, 1924 – 1925

The death of Lenin in 1924 intensified a struggle for control of the Party between Stalin and Trotsky and their respective supporters. Initially, the struggle, which began in 1923, appeared to be betweenthree men. Kamenev, head of the Moscow Soviet, Zinoviev, Party chief in Petrograd and head of the Comintern, and Trotsky. The former two, allied with Stalin, presented a formidable opposition group to Trotsky.

Initially, the struggle centered around Trotsky's accusation that the trio was drifting away from Lenin's commitment to the revolution and "bureaucratizing" the Party. Trotsky believed in the theory of "permanent revolution" that blended an ongoing commitment to world revolution and building socialism with the development of a heavy industrial base in Russia.

Stalin responded with the concept of "Socialism in One Country," that committed the country to building up its socialist base regardless of the status of world revolution.

In the fall of 1924, Trotsky attacked Zinoviev and Kamenev for the drift away from open discussion in the Party and for not supporting Lenin's initial scheme to seize power in November 1917. As a result, Trotsky was removed as Commissar of War on January 16, 1925, while two months later the Party accepted "Socialism in One Country" as its official governing doctrine.

The Struggle for Power, 1925 – 1927

Zinoviev and Kamenev, who agreed with the principles of "Permanent Revolution," began to fear Stalin and soon found themselves allied against him and his new Rightist supporters, Nikolai Bukharin, Alexis Rykov, Chairman of the Council of People's Commisars (Cabinet), and Mikhail Tomsky, head of the trade unions.

The XIV Party Congress rebuffed Kamenev and Zinoviev, and accepted Bukharin's economic policies. It demoted Kamenev to candidate status on the Politburo, while adding a number of Stalin's supporters to that body as well as the Central Committee. Afterwards, Kamenev and Zinoviev joined Trotsky in their dispute with Stalin. As a result, Trotsky and Kamenev lost their seats on the Politburo, while Zinoviev was removed as head of the Comintern.

In early 1927, Trotsky and his followers accused Stalin and the Right of a "Thermidorian Reaction," Menshevism, and further criticized recent foreign policy failures in England and China. Trotsky and Zinoviev lost their positions on the Central Committee, which prompted them to participate in anti-Rightist street demonstrations on November 7, 1927. Both were then thrown out of the Party, followed by their supporters. Trotsky was forced into external exile in Central Asia, while Zinoviev and Kamenev, humiliated and defeated, begged successfully to be allowed to return to the fold.

At the XV Party Congress, Stalin indicated that the Party would now begin gradually to collectivize the country's predominantly small-farm agricultural system. His shocked Rightist allies, now outnumbered by Stalinists on the Politburo, sought an uncomfortable alliance with the defeated Left. Over the next two years, the major old Rightist allies of Stalin, Bukharin, Rykov, and Tomsky, lost their Politburo seats and other Party positions, and ultimately, their Party membership. Brief exile followed in some cases.

Soviet Constitutional Development

Soviet Russia adopted two constitutions in 1918 and 1924. The first reflected the ideals of the state's founders and created the Russian Soviet Federative Socialist Republic (RSFSR) as the country's central administrative unit. An All-Russian Congress of Soviets was the government's legislative authority, while a large Central Executive Committee (CEC), aided by a cabinet or Council of People's Commissars (Sovnarkom) wielded executive power. The Communist Party was not mentioned in the 1918 constitution or in the 1924 constitution. The 1924 document was similar to the earlier one, but also reflected the changes brought about by the creation of the Union of Soviet Socialist Republics (USSR) two years earlier. The CEC was divided into a Council of the Union and a Council of Nationalities, while a new Supreme Court and Procurator was added to the governmental structure. A similar political division was duplicated on lower administrative levels throughout the country. The new constitution also created a Supreme Court and a Procurator responsible to the CEC.

Foreign Policy, 1918 – 1929

Soviet efforts after the October Revolution to openly foment revolution through-out Europe and Asia, its refusal to pay Tsarist debts, and international outrage over the murder of the royal family in 1919 isolated the country. However, adoption of the NEP required more integration with the outside world to rebuild the broken economy.

Russia and Germany, Europe's post-World War I pariahs, drew closer out of necessity. By the early 1920's, Russia was receiving German technological help in weapons development while the Soviets helped train German pilots and others illegally. On April 16, 1922, Soviet Russia and Germany agreed to cancel their respective war debts and to establish formal diplomatic relations.

By 1921, the British concluded a trade accord with the Soviet government and in 1924 extended formal diplomatic recognition to the USSR. Strong public reaction to this move, coupled with the publication of the "Zinoviev Letter" of unknown origin helped topple the pro-Soviet MacDonald government, because the letter encouraged subversion of the British government. Relations were formally severed in 1927 because of Communist support of a British coal mine strike, discovery of spies in a Soviet trade delegation, and Soviet claims that it hoped to use China as a means of hurting England.

The Soviets worked to consolidate their sphere-of-influence acquired earlier in Mongolia, and helped engineer the creation of an independent, though strongly pro-Soviet, People's Republic of Mongolia in 1924.

In China, in an effort to protect traditional Asian strategic interests and take advantage of the chaotic "war lord" atmosphere in China, the Soviets helped found a young Chinese Communist Party (CCP) in 1921. However, when it became apparent that Sun Yat-sen's revolutionary Kuomintang (KMT) was more mature than the infant

CCP, the Soviets encouraged an alliance between its Party and this movement. Sun's successor, Chiang Kai-shek, was deeply suspicious of the Communists and made their destruction part of his effort militarily to unite China.

Founded in 1919, the Soviet-controlled Comintern (Third International or Communist International) sought to coordinate the revolutionary activities of communist parties abroad, though it often conflicted with Soviet diplomatic interests. It became an effectively organized body by 1924, and was completely Stalinized by 1928.

EUROPE IN CRISIS: DEPRESSION AND DICTATORSHIP, 1929 – 1935

England: Ramsay MacDonald and the Depression, 1929 – 1931

Required by law to hold elections in 1929, the May 30 contest saw the Conservatives drop to 260 seats, Labour rise to 287, and the Liberals 59. Ramsay MacDonald formed a minority Labour government that would last until 1931. The most serious problem facing the country was the Depression, which caused unemployment to reach 1,700,000 by 1930 and over 3 million, or 25% of the labor force, by 1932. To meet growing budget deficits caused by heavy subsidies to the unemployed, a special government commission recommended budget cuts and tax increases. Cabinet and labor union opposition helped reduce the total for the cuts (from 78 million to 22 million), but this could not help restore confidence in the government, which fell on August 24, 1931.

The "National Government," 1931 – 1935

The following day, King George VI helped convince MacDonald to return to office as head of a National Coalition cabinet made up of 4 Conservatives, 4 Laborites, and 2 Liberals. The Labour Party refused to recognize the new government and ejected MacDonald and Snowden from the Party. MacDonald's coalition swept the November 1931 general elections winning 554 of 615 seats.

The British government abandoned the gold standard on September 21, 1931, and adopted a series of high tariffs on imports. Unemployment peaked at 3 million in 1932 and dropped to 2 million two years later.

In 1931, the British government implemented the Statute of Westminster, which created the British Commonwealth of Nations, granted its members political equality, and freedom to reject any act passed by Parliament that related to a Dominion state.

The Election of 1935

MacDonald resigned his position in June 1935 because of ill health, and was succeeded by Stanley Baldwin, whose conservative coalition won 428 seats in new elections in November.

France Under Andre Tardieu, 1929 – 1932

On July 27, 1929, Poincare resigned as Premier because of ill health. Over the next three years, the dominant figure in French politics was Andre Tardieu, who headed or played a role in Moderate cabinets.

Tardieu tried to initiate political changes along American or British lines to create a stable two party system that would help France deal with the world economic crisis. He convinced the Laval government and the Chamber to accept electing its members by a plurality vote, though the Senate rejected it. In 1930, the government passed France's most important social welfare legislation, the National Workingmen's Insurance Law. It provided various forms of financial aid for illness, retirement, and death.

The Depression did not hit France until late 1931, and it took it four years to begin to recover from it. At first, however, the country seemed immune to the Depression and the economy boomed. Its manufacturing indices reached a peak in 1929, but began gradually to slide through 1932. The economy recovered the following year, and dropped again through 1935.

Return of the Cartel des Gauches, 1932 – 1934

The defeat of the Moderates and the return of the leftists in the elections of May 1, 1932, reflected growing concern over the economy and failed efforts of the government to respond to the country's problems.

France remained plagued by differences over economic reform between the Radicals and the Socialists. The latter advocated nationalization of major factories, expanded social reforms, and public works programs for the unemployed, while the Radicals sought a reduction in government spending. This instability was also reflected in the fact that there were six Cabinets between June 1932 and February 1934.

The government's inability to deal with the country's economic and political problems saw the emergence of a number of radical groups from across the political spectrum. Some of the more prominent were the Fascist Francistes, the Solidarite Francaise, the "Cagoulards" (Comite Secret d'Action Revoluntionnaire), the Parti Populaire Francaise (PPF) and the Jeunesses Patriotes. Not as radical, though still on the right were the Croix de Feu and the Action Francaise. At the other extreme was the French Communist Party.

The growing influence of these groups exploded on February 6, 1934, around a scandal involving a con-man with government connections, Serge Stavisky. After his suicide on the eve of his arrest in December 1933, the scandal and his reported involvement with high government officials stimulated a growing crescendo of criticism that culminated in riots between rightist and leftist factions that resulted in 15 dead and 1,500 to 1,600 injured. The demonstrations and riots, viewed by some as a rightist effort to seize power, brought about the collapse of the Daladier government. He was immediately succeeded by ex-President Gaston Doumergue, who put together a coalition cabinet dominated by Moderates as well as Radicals and Rightists. It contained six former premiers and Marshal Petain.

Struggle for Stability, 1934 – 1935

The accession of Gaston Doumergue (who had been President from 1924 to 1931) with his "National Union" cabinet, stabilized the public crisis. The new Premier (influenced by Tardieu) used radio to try to convince the public of the need to increase the power of the President, (Albert Lebrum; 1932 – 1940), and to enable the Premier to dissolve the legislature. Discontent with Doumergue's tactics resulted in resignations from his Cabinet and its fall in November 1934.

Between November 1934 and June 1935, France had two more governments under Pierre-Etienne Flandin and F. Bouisson. The situation somewhat stabilized with the selection of Pierre Laval as Premier, who served from June 1935 through January 1936. Laval's controversial policies, strengthened by the ability to pass laws without legislative approval, were to deflate the economy, cut government expenditures, and remain on the gold standard. Laval's government fell in early 1936.

GERMANY

The Young Plan

One of the last accomplishments of Stresemann before his death on October 3 was the Young Plan, an altered reparations proposal that required Germany to make yearly payments for 59 years that varied from 1.6 to 2.4 billion Reichsmarks. In return, the Allies removed all foreign controls on Germany's economy and agreed to leave the Rhineland the following year. Efforts by the conservative extremists to stop Reichstag adoption of the Young Plan failed miserably, while a national referendum on the reactionary bill suffered the same fate.

Germany and the Depression

The Depression had a dramatic effect on the German economy and politics. German exports, which had peaked at 13.5 billion marks in 1929, fell to 12 billion marks in 1930, and to 5.7 billion marks two years later. Imports suffered the same fate, going from 14 billion marks in 1928 to 4.7 billion marks in 1932. The country's national income dropped 20% during this period, while unemployment rose from 1,320,000 in 1929 to 6 million by January 1932. This meant that 43% of the German work force were without jobs (compared to one-quarter of the work force in the U.S.).

The Rise of Adolf Hitler and Nazism.

The history of Nazism is deeply intertwined with that of its leader, Adolf Hitler.

Adolf Hitler was born on April 20, 1889, in the Austrian village of Braunau-am-Inn. A frustrated artist, he moved to Vienna where he unsuccessfully tried to become a student in the Vienna Academy of Fine Arts. He then became an itinerant artist, living in hovels, until the advent of the World War, which he welcomed. His four years at the front were the most meaningful of his life up to that time, and he emerged a decorated corporal with a mission now to go into politics to restore his country's bruised honor.

In 1919, Hitler joined the German Workers Party (DAP), which he soon took over and renamed the National Socialist German Workers Party (NAZI). In 1920, the Party adopted a 25-point program that included treaty revision, anti-Semitism, economic, and other social changes. They also created a defense cadre of the Sturmabteilung (SA), "Storm Troopers," or "brown shirts," which was to help the party seize power. Some of the more significant early Nazi leaders were Ernst Röhm, who helped build up the SA; Dietrich Eckart, first head of the Party paper, the *Volkischer Beobachter*; Alfred Rosenberg, who replaced Eckart as editor of *Volkischer Beobachter* and became the Party's chief ideologist; Hermann Göering, World War I flying ace, who took over the SA in 1922; and Rudolf Hess, who became Hitler's secretary.

The Beer Hall Putsch, 1923

In the midst of the country's severe economic crisis in 1923, the Party, which now had 55,000 members, tried to seize power, first by a march on Berlin, and then, when this seemed impossible, on Munich. The march was stopped by police, and Hitler and his supporters were arrested. Their trial, which Hitler used to voice Nazi ideals, gained him a national reputation. Though sentenced to five years imprisonment, he was released after eight months. While incarcerated, he dictated *Mein Kampf* to Rudolf Hess.

The Nazi Movement, 1924 – 1929

Hitler's failed coup and imprisonment convinced him to seek power through legitimate political channels, which would require transforming the Nazi Party. To do this, he reasserted singular control over the movement from 1924 to 1926. Party districts were set up throughout Germany, overseen by *Gaulieters* personally appointed by Hitler.

They were subdivided into Kreise (districts), and then Ortsgruppen (local chapters). A court system, the *Uschla*, oversaw the Party structure. The Party grew from 27,000 in 1925 to 108,000 in 1929. A number of new leaders emerged at this time, including Joseph Goebbels, who became Party Chief in Berlin and later Hitler's propaganda chief, and Heinrich Himmler, who became head of Hitler's private body guard, the SS (*Schutzstaffel*), in 1929.

Weimar Politics, 1930 – 1933

Germany's economic woes and the government's seeming inability to deal with them, underlined the weaknesses of the country's political system and provided the Nazis with new opportunities.

In March 17, 1930, the alliance of Social Democratic, DVP and other parties collapsed over who should shoulder unemployment benefit costs. A new coalition, under Heinrich Breunig, tried to promote a policy of government economic retrenchment, and deflation, which the Reichstag rejected. Consequently, President Hindenburg invoked Article 48 of the Constitution, which enabled him to order the implementation of Breunig's program. The Reichstag overrode the decree, which forced the government's fall and new elections:

Reichstag Elections of September 14, 1930

The September 14 elections surprised everyone. The Nazis saw their 1928 vote jump from 800,000 to 6.5 million (18.3% of the vote), which gave them 107 Reichstag seats, second only to the Social Democrats, who fell from 152 to 143 seats. Bruenig, however, continued to serve as Chancellor of a weak coalition with the support of Hindenburg and rule by presidential decree. His policies failed to resolve the country's growing economic dilemmas.

Presidential Elections of 1932

Hindenburg's seven year presidential term expired in 1932, and he was convinced to run for reelection to stop Hitler from becoming President in the first ballot of March 13. Hitler got only 30% of the vote (11.3 million) to Hindenburg's 49.45% (18.6 million). Since German law required the new president to have a majority of the votes, a runoff was held on April 10 between Hindenburg, Hitler, and the Communist candidate, Thalmann. Hindenburg received 19.3 million votes (53%), Hitler 13.4 million (37%), and Thalmann 2.2 million votes.

The von Papen Chancellorship

On June 1, Bruenig was replaced by Franz von Papen, who formed a government made up of aristocratic conservatives and others that he and Hindenburg hoped would keep Hitler from power. He held new elections on July 31 that saw the Nazis win 230 Reichstag seats with 37% of the vote (13.7 million), and the Communists 89 seats. Offered the Vice Chancellorship and an opportunity to join a coalition government, Hitler refused. Von Papen, paralyzed politically, ruled by presidential decree. Von Papen dissolved the Reichstag on September 12, and held new elections on November 6. The Nazis only got 30% of the vote and 196 Reichstag seats, while the Communists made substantial gains (120 seats from 89). Von Papen resigned in favor of Kurt von Schleicher, one of the president's closest advisers, as the new Chancellor.

Hitler Becomes Chancellor

Von Papen joined with Hitler to undermine Schleicher, and convinced Hindenburg to appoint Hitler as Chancellor and head of a new coalition cabinet with 3 seats for the Nazis.

Hitler dissolved the Reichstag and called for new elections on March 5. Using Presidential decree powers, he initiated a violent anti-communist campaign that included the lifting of certain press and civil freedoms. On February 27, the Reichstag burned which enabled Hitler to get Hindenburg to issue the "Ordinances for the Protection of the German State and Nation," that removed all civil and press liberties as part of a "revolution" against Communism. In the Reichstag elections of March 5, the Nazis only got 43.9% of the vote and 288 Reichstag seats but, through an alliance with the Nationalists, got majority control of the legislature.

Hitler now intensified his campaign against his political and other opponents, placing many of them in newly opened concentration camps. He also convinced Hindenburg to issue the Enabling Act on March 21 that allowed his Cabinet to pass laws and treaties without legislative backing for 4 years. The Reichstag gave him its full legal approval two days later, since many felt it was the only way legally to maintain some influence over his government.

Once Hitler had full legislative power, he began a policy of *Gleichschaltung* (coordination) to bring all independent organizations and agencies throughout Germany under his control. All political parties were outlawed or forced to dissolve, and on July 14, 1933, the Nazi Party became the only legal party in Germany. In addition, German state authority was reduced and placed under Nazi-appointed *Stattholder* (governors), while the Party throughout Germany was divided into *Gaue* (districts) under a Nazi-selected *Gauleiter*. In addition, non-Aryans and Nazi opponents were removed from the civil service, the court system, and higher education. On May 2, 1933, the government declared strikes illegal, abolished labor unions, and later forced all workers to join the German Labor Front (DAF) under Robert Ley. In 1934 the Reichsrat was abolished and a special People's Court was created to handle cases of treason. Finally, the secret police or GESTAPO (*Geheime Staatspolizei*) was created on April 24, 1933 under Göering to deal with opponents and operate concentration camps. The Party had its own security branch, the SD (*Sicherheitsdienst*) under Reinhard Heydrich.

Hitler Consolidates Power

A growing conflict over the direction of the Nazi "revolution" and the power of the SA *vis a vis* the SS and the German army had been brewing since Hitler took power. Ernst Röhm, head of the SA, wanted his forces to become the nucleus of a new German army headed by himself, while the military, Hitler, and the SS sought ways to contain his growing arrogance and independence. The solution was the violent Röhm purge on the night of June 30, 1934 ("The Night of the Long Knives"), coordinated by the GESTAPO and the SS, that resulted in the arrest and murder of Röhm plus 84 SA leaders, as well as scores of other opponents that Hitler decided to eliminate under the cloud of his purge.

The final barrier to Hitler's full consolidation of power in Germany was overcome with the death of Hindenburg on August 2, 1934. Hitler now combined the offices of President and Chancellor, and required all civil servants and workers to take a personal oath to him as the "Führer of the German Reich and people."

Religion and Anti-Semitism

A state Protestant church of "German Christians" under a Bishop of the Reich, Ludwig Muller, was created in 1934. An underground opposition "Confessing Church" was formed under Martin Niemoller that suffered from severe persecution. On July 8, 1933, the government signed a concordat with the Vatican that promised to allow traditional Catholic rights to continue in Germany. Unfortunately, the Nazis severely restricted Catholic religious practice, which created growing friction with the Vatican.

From the inception of the Nazi state in 1933, anti-Semitism was a constant theme and practice in all *Gleichschaltung* and nazification efforts. Illegal intimidation and harassment of Jews was coupled with rigid enforcement of civil service regulations that forbade employment of non-Aryans. This first wave of anti-Semitic activity culminated with the passage of the Nuremburg Laws of September 15, 1935, that deprived Jews of German citizenship and outlawed sexual or marital relations between Jews and other Germans, thus effectively isolating them from the mainstream of German society.

International Affairs

Hitler's international policies were closely linked to his rebuilding efforts to give him a strong economic and military base for an active, aggressive, independent foreign policy. On October 14, 1933, Hitler had his delegates walk out of the Disarmament Conference because he felt the Allied powers had reneged on an earlier promise to grant Germany arms equality. The Reich simultaneously quit the League of Nations. On January 26, 1934, Germany signed a non-aggression pact with Poland, which ended Germany's traditional anti-Polish foreign policy and broke France's encirclement of Germany via the Little Entente. This was followed by the Saarland's overwhelming decision to return to Germany. The culmination of Hitler's foreign policy moves, though, came with his March 15, 1935, announcement that Germany would no longer be bound by the military restrictions of the Treaty of Versailles, that it had already created an air force (Luftwaffe), and that the Reich would institute a draft to create an army of 500,000 men. Allied opposition to this move was compromised by England's decision to conclude a naval pact with Hitler on June 18, 1935, that restricted German naval tonnage (excluding submarines) to 35% of that for England.

ITALY

Fascist Economic Reforms

Increased economic well-being and growth were the promised results of Mussolini's restructuring of the economic system, while the general goals of the regime were to increase production through more efficient methods and land reclamation, with less dependency upon outside resources.

Efforts to increase the land under cultivation through reclamation projects were handicapped by Mussolini's emphasis on model propaganda projects, though the government had reclaimed 12 million acres by 1938. In fact, the small farmer suffered under these policies, because of Mussolini's quiet support of the larger landowner. In 1930, for example, 87.3% of the population controlled 13.2% of the land. The large farm owners, who made up only 0.5% of the population, controlled 41.9% of the land, while the mid-level farmer, who made up 12.2% of the population, controlled 44.9% of the countryside. Regardless, grain products did increase from 4,479 metric tons in 1924 to 8,184 metric tons in 1938, which enabled the government to cut grain imports by 75%. On the other hand, land needed to produce other agricultural products was used to increase wheat and grain output.

To aid firms affected by the Depression, the government created the I.R.I. (*Instituto per la ricostruzione industriale*) which helped most big companies while smaller unsuccessful ones failed. The result was that the vast majority of Italy's major industry came under some form of government oversight. Italian production figures are unimpressive during this period, with increases for industrial production rising between 1928 and 1935. Steel output dropped, while pig-iron, oil products, and electrical output enjoyed moderate increases in the 1930's.

The overall impact of Mussolini's economic programs saw the country's national income rise 15% from 1925 to 1935, with only a 10% per capita increase during this period. The value of exports dropped from 44,370 million lira in 1925 to 21,750 in 1938 because of the decision in 1927 to peg the lira to an artificially high exchange rate.

Church and State

Until Mussolini's accession to power, the pope had considered himself a prisoner in the Vatican. In 1926, Mussolini's government began talks to resolve this issue, which resulted in the Lateran Accords of February 11, 1929. Italy recognized the Vatican as an independent state, with the pope as its head, while the papacy recognized Italian independence. Catholicism was made the official state religion of Italy, and religious teaching was required in all secondary schools. Church marriages were now fully legal, while the state could veto papal appointments of bishops. In addition, the clergy would declare loyalty to the Italian state. Additionally, the government agreed to pay the Church a financial settlement of 1.75 billion lira for the seizure of Church territory in 1860 – 1870.

A conflict soon broke out over youth education and in May 1931 Mussolini dissolved the Catholic Action's youth groups. The pope responded with an encyclical, *Non abbianio bisogno*, which defended these groups, and criticized the Fascist deification of the state. Mussolini agreed later that year to allow Catholic Action to resume limited youth work.

Foreign Policy

The appointment of Adolph Hitler as Chancellor of Germany in early 1933 provided Mussolini with his most important thrust of diplomatic action since he came to power, while it underlined the currency of fascism as a ruling ideology and strengthened his claim to revision of the 1919 Paris Peace accords.

Since the late 1920's, Mussolini began to support German claims for revision of the Treaty of Versailles to strengthen ties with that country and to counter-balance France, a nation he strongly disliked. These goals were current in his Four Power Pact proposal of March 1933 that envisioned a concert of powers – England, France, Italy, and Germany – that included arms parity for the Reich. French opposition to arms equality and treaty revision, plus concerns that the new consortium would replace the League of Nations, saw an extremely weakened agreement signed in June that was ultimately accepted only by Italy and Germany.

In an effort to counter the significance of France's Little Entente with Czechoslovakia, Yugoslavia, and Rumania, Mussolini concluded the Rome Protocols with Austria and Hungary on March 17, 1934 which created a protective bond of friendship between the three countries.

The first test of the new alliance between Italy and Austria came in July 1934, when German-directed Nazis tried to seize control of the Austrian government. Mussolini, opposed to any German Anschluss with Austria, mobilized Italian forces along the northern Renner Pass as a warning to Hitler. The coup collapsed from lack of direct

German aid.

In response to Hitler's announcement of German rearmament in violation of the Treaty of Versailles on March 16, 1935, France, England, and Italy met at Stresa in northern Italy on April 11 – 14, and concluded agreements that pledged joint military collaboration if Germany moved against Austria or along the Rhine. The three states criticized Germany's recent decision to remilitarize and appealed to the Council of the League of Nations on the matter.

Ethiopia (Abyssinia) became an area of strong Italian interest in the 1880's. The coastal region was slowly brought under Italian control until the Italian defeat at Ethiopian hands at Adowa in 1894. In 1906, the country's autonomy was recognized and in 1923 it joined the League of Nations. Mussolini, driven by a strong patriotic desire to avenge the humiliation at Adowa and to create an empire to thwart domestic concerns over the country's economic problems, searched for the proper moment to seize the country. Acquisition of Ethiopia would enable him to join Italy's two colonies of Eritrea and Somalia, which could become a new area of Italian colonization.

Mussolini, who had been preparing for war with Ethiopia since 1932, established a military base at Wal Wal in Ethiopian territory. Beginning in December 1934, a series of minor conflicts took place between the two countries, which gave Mussolini an excuse to plan for the full takeover of the country in the near future.

Mussolini refused to accept arbitration over Ethiopia, and used Europe's growing concern over Hitler's moves there to cover his own secret designs in Ethiopia. On October 2, 1935, Italy invaded Ethiopia, while the League of Nations, which had received four appeals from Ethiopia since January about Italian territorial transgressions, finally voted to adopt economic sanctions against Mussolini. Unfortunately, the League failed to stop shipments of oil to Italy and continued to allow it to use the Suez Canal. On May 9, 1936, Italy formally annexed the country and joined it to Somalia and Eritrea, which now became known as Italian East Africa.

SOVIET RUSSIA

The period from 1929 to 1935 was a time of tremendous upheaval for the USSR as Stalin tried to initiate major programs of collectivization of agriculture and massive industrial development.

Collectivization of Soviet Agriculture

At the end of 1927, Stalin, concerned over problems of grain supply, ordered the gradual consolidation of the country's 25 million small farms, on which 80% of the population lived, into state-run collective farms.

According to the First Five Year Plan's goals (1928 – 1932), agricultural output was to rise 150% over five years, and 20% of the country's private farms transformed into collectives.

In an effort to link agricultural efficiency with heavy industrial development, Stalin decided by the end of 1929 to rapidly collectivize the country's entire agriculture system. Because of earlier resistance from peasants between 1927 and 1929, Stalin ordered war against the kulak or "middle class" peasant class. Some sources claim that as many as 5 million ill-defined kulaks were internally deported during this period.

The above, combined with forced grain seizures, triggered massive, bloody resistance in the country-side. Though half of the nation's peasants were forced onto collectives during this period, they destroyed a great deal of Russia's livestock in the process. In the spring of 1930, Stalin called a momentary halt to the process, which prompted many peasants to leave the state farms.

Over the next seven years, the entire Soviet system was collectivized, and all peasants forced onto state farms. The two major types of farms were the *sovkhoz*, where peasants were paid for their labor; and the *kovkhoz*, or collective farm, where the peasants gave the government a percentage of their crops and kept the surplus. The three types of *kovkhozs* were the Artel, the most common, where the peasant had a small garden plot; the *toz*, where he owned his tools and animals; and the *commune*, where the state owned everything. One of the most important components of the collective and the state farm system was the Machine Tractor Station (MTS) which controlled the tractors and farm equipment for various government run farms.

Direct and indirect deaths from Stalin's collectivization efforts totaled 14.5 million. Grain production levels did not reach 1928 levels until 1935. It did, though, break the back of rural peasant independence and created a totalitarian network of control throughout the countryside. It also undercut his own base of political support within the Party.

Industrialization

Stalin, concerned that Russia would fall irreparably behind the West industrially, hoped to achieve industrial parity with the West in a decade. At this time, Russia was barely on par with Italy in pig-iron and steel production. To stimulate workers, labor unions lost their autonomy and workers, including impressed peasants, were forced to work at locations and under conditions determined by the state. A special "Turnover" tax was placed on all goods throughout the country to help pay for industrialization.

The industrialization goals of the First Five Year Plan, supported hopefully by a flourishing agricultural system, were to increase total industrial production by 236%, heavy industry by 330%, coal, 200%, electrical output, 400%, and pig-iron production, 300%. Workers were to increase their efforts over 100%. Efficiency was also a hallmark of this program, and production costs were to drop by over a third, and prices by a quarter.

In most instances, the Plan's unrealistic goals were hard to meet. Regardless, steel production doubled, though it fell short of the Plan's goals, as did oil and hard coal output. Total industrial production, however, did barely surpass the Plan's expectations.

The Second Five Year Plan (1933 – 1937) was adopted by the XVII Party Congress in early 1934. Its economic and production targets were less severe than the first Plan, and thus more was achieved. The model for workers was Alexis Stakhanov, a coal miner who met 1400% of his quota in the fall of 1935. A Stakhanovite movement arose to stimulate workers to greater efforts. By the end of the Second Plan, Soviet Russia had emerged as a leading world industrial power, though at great costs. It gave up quality for quantity, and created tremendous social and economic discord that still affects the USSR. The tactics used by Stalin to institute his economic reforms formed the nucleus of his totalitarian system, while reaction to them within the Party led to the Purges.

Party Politics and the Origin of the Purges

The tremendous upheaval caused by forced collectivization, blended with the remnants of the Rightist conflict with Stalin, prompted the Soviet leader to initiate one of the country's periodic purges of the Party. Approved by the top leadership, suspected opponents were driven from Party ranks while Zinoviev and Kamenev were briefly exiled to Siberia. Continued uncertainty over the best policies to follow after the initiation of the Second Five Year Plan ended with the murder at the end of 1934 of

Sergei Kirov, Stalin's supposed heir, and Leningrad party chief. Though the reasons for Kirov's murder are still unclear, his more liberal tendencies, plus his growing popularity, made him a threat to the Soviet leader. In the spring of 1935, the recently renamed and organized secret police, the NKVD, oversaw the beginnings of a new, violent Purge that eradicated 70% of the 1934 Central Committee, and a large percentage of the upper military ranks. Stalin sent between 8 and 9 million to camps and prisons, and caused untold deaths before the Purges ended in 1938.

Foreign Policy, 1929 – 1935

The period from 1929 to 1933 saw the USSR retreat inward as the bulk of its energies were put into domestic economic growth. Regardless, Stalin remained sensitive to growing aggression and ideological threats abroad such as the Japanese invasion of Manchuria in 1931 and Hitler's appointment as Chancellor. As a result, Russia left its cocoon in 1934, joined the League of Nations, and became an advocate of "collective security" while the Comintern adopted Popular Front tactics, allying with other parties against fascism, to strengthen the USSR's international posture. Diplomatically, in addition to League membership, the Soviet Union completed a military pact with France.

INTERNATIONAL DEVELOPMENTS, 1918 – 1935

The League of Nations

Efforts to create some international body to arbitrate international conflicts gained credence with the creation of a Permanent Court of International Justice to handle such matters at the First Hague Conference (1899). At a similar meeting eight years later, concern was expressed over Europe's growing arms race, though no country was willing to give the Permanent Court adequate authority to serve as a legitimate arbitrator. Leon Bourgeois, a French statesman, however, pushed for some sort of strong international peacekeeping body, but no major efforts towards this goal were initiated until 1915, when pro-League of Nations organizations arose in the United States and Great Britain. Support for such a body grew as the war lengthened, and creation of such an organization became the cornerstone of President Woodrow Wilson's post-war policy, enunciated in his "Fourteen Points" speech before Congress on January 8, 1918. His last point called for an international chamber of states to guarantee national autonomy and independence. At the Paris Peace Conference, the major Allied leaders created a Commission for the League to draft its constitution, while the covenant of the League was placed in the Treaty of Versailles.

The Preamble of the League's Covenant

This statement defined the League's purposes, which were to work for international friendship, peace, and security. To attain this, its members agreed to avoid war, maintain peaceful relations with other countries, and honor international law and accords.

The Organization of the League of Nations

Headquartered in Geneva, the League came into existence as the result of an Allied resolution announcing their intentions on January 25, 1919, and the signing of the Treaty of Versailles on June 28, 1919.

The 26 article Covenant determined terms of membership and withdrawal (two-thirds vote to join and two years notice to resign) and means to amend the Covenant (unanimous vote of Council with majority approval from Assembly).

The League's Council originally consisted of five permanent members (France, Italy, England, Japan, and the U.S.), though the U.S. seat was left vacant because the U.S. Senate refused to ratify the Treaty of Versailles. Germany filled the vacancy in 1926. It also had four 1-year rotating seats (increased to 6 in 1922, and raised to 9 seats in 1926). The Council, with each member having one vote, could discuss any matter that threatened international stability, and could recommend action to member states. It also had the right, according to Article 8 of the League Covenant, to seek ways to reduce arms strength, while Articles 10 through 17 gave it the authority to search for means to stop war. It could recommend through a unanimous vote ways to stop aggression, and could suggest economic sanctions and other tactics to enforce its decisions, though its military ability to enforce its decisions was vague. It met four times a year from 1923 to 1929, and then three times annually afterwards.

The League's legislative body had similar debating and discussion authority, though it had no legislative powers. It initially had 43 members, which rose to 49 by the mid-1930's, though six others, including Italy, Germany, and Japan, withdrew their membership during the same period. The USSR, which joined in 1934, was expelled six years later.

The League's judicial responsibilities were handled by the "World Court" that was located at The Hague in The Netherlands. Created in 1921 and opened the following year, it would consider and advise on any case from any nation or the League, acting as an arbiter to prevent international conflict. The court's decisions were not binding: it relied on voluntary submission to its decisions. It initially had eleven judges (later 15) selected for five year terms by the League.

The day-to-day affairs of the League were administered by the General Secretary (Sir Eric Drummond to 1933; J. Avenol afterwards) and his bureaucracy, the Secretariat, which was composed of an international collection of League civil servants.

Lesser known functions of the League dealt with the efforts of its International Labor Organization (I.L.O.) which tried to find ways to reduce labor-management and class tensions; and the Mandates Commission, which oversaw territories taken from the Central Powers and were administered – as a prelude to independence – under mandate from League members. In addition, the League tried to provide medical, economic, and social welfare aid to depressed parts of the world.

THE WASHINGTON CONFERENCE, 1921 – 1922

The first post-war effort to deal with problems of disarmament was the Washington Conference (November 1921 – February 1922). Its participants, which included the major powers in Europe and Asia plus the meeting's sponsor, the United States, discussed a number of problems that resulted in three separate agreements:

The Washington Naval Treaty (Five Power Treaty)

France, Italy, England, the United States, and Japan agreed to halt battleship construction for ten years, while limiting or reducing capital shipping levels to 525,000 tons for the U.S. and England, 315,000 tons for Japan, and 175,000 tons for Italy and France.

The Four Power Treaty

The United States, England, France, and Japan agreed not to seek further Pacific expansion or increased naval strength there and to respect the Pacific holdings of the other signatory powers.

The Nine Power Treaty

To grant China some sense of autonomy not offered at the Paris Peace Conference, an agreement was signed by Japan (after Japan's agreement to return Kiachow to China), the Netherlands, Portugal, Belgium, Italy, France, England, the U.S., and China, , guaranteed China's independence and territorial autonomy.

THE DRAFT TREATY OF MUTUAL ASSISTANCE (1923)

In the ongoing search for ways to encourage continuing disarmament talks and provide security, particularly for France, which continued to worry about future threats from Germany, the League of Nations had set up a Temporary Mixed Commission (TMC) of specialists to study disarmament. The TMC submitted a Draft Treaty of Mutual Assistance to the League Assembly in September 1923 that would enable the Council to determine the guilty nation in the event of a war, and to intervene on the side of the victim. France, Italy, and Japan were the only major states to support the approved treaty. All other important countries rejected it because they were concerned about its regional limitations, its protection for only those that disarmed, and the League's role in such actions, particularly in defining aggression.

THE GENEVA PROTOCOL (1924)

The failure of many important nations to accept the Draft Treaty prompted the British and the French to search for a different solution to the problem of protection for those that disarmed. The result was the Protocol for the Pacific Settlement of International Disputes, or the Geneva Protocol, that stated that the nation that refused to submit to arbitration by the World Court, the League Council, or special arbitrators, would be termed the aggressor. The agreement was tied to a further disarmament conference and a network of regional security pacts. Approved by the Assembly in October 1924, France and its Little Entente allies backed it quickly. England, however, backed by Commonwealth members, disapproved because of the broad commitments involved, which sank any prospect of final approval of the Protocol.

THE LOCARNO PACT (1925)

Failure of the European powers to create some type of international system to prevent aggression was followed by regional efforts prompted by Germany's visionary Foreign Minister, Gustav Stresemann, who in early 1925 approached England and France about an accord whereby Germany would accept its western borders in return for early Allied withdrawal from the demilitarized Rhine area. Stresemann also wanted League membership for his country. While England responded with guarded regional interest, France hesitated. Six months after consultation with its eastern allies, Paris countered with a proposal that would include similar provisions for Germany's eastern borders, secured by a mutual assistance pact between Italy, Great Britain, and France. These countries, along with Belgium, Czechoslovakia, and Poland, met for two months in Locarno, Switzerland, and concluded a number of separate agreements.

Treaty of Mutual Guarantees (Rhineland Pact)

Signed on October 16, 1925, by England, France, Italy, Germany and Belgium, they guaranteed Germany's western boundaries and accepted the Versailles settlement's demilitarized zones. Italy and Great Britain agreed militarily to defend these lines if flagrantly violated.

Arbitration Settlements

In the same spirit, Germany signed arbitration dispute accords that mirrored the Geneva Protocol with France, Belgium, Poland, and Czechoslovakia, and required acceptance of League-determined settlements.

Eastern Accords

Since Germany would only agree to arbitration and not finalize its eastern border, France separately signed guarantees with Poland and Czechoslovakia to defend their frontiers.

Germany Joins the League

The Locarno Pact went into force when Germany joined the League on September 10, 1926, acquiring, after some dispute, the U.S.'s permanent seat on the Council. France and Belgium began to withdraw from the Rhineland, though they left a token force there until 1930.

THE PACT OF PARIS (KELLOGG-BRIAND PACT)

The Locarno Pact heralded a new period in European relations known as the "Era of Locarno" that marked the end of post-war conflict and the beginning of a more normal period of diplomatic friendship and cooperation. It reached its peak, idealistically, with the Franco-American effort in 1928 to seek an international statement to outlaw war. The seed for this new proposal arose on the eve of the tenth anniversary of the American entrance into the World War, and centered around interest in a mutual statement outlawing war as a theme in national policy. In December 1927, Frank Kellogg, the American Secretary of State, proposed that this policy be offered to all nations in the form of a treaty. On August 27, 1928, fifteen countries, including the U.S., Germany, France, Italy and Japan, signed this accord with some minor limitations, which renounced war as a means of solving differences and as a tool of national policy. Within five years, 50 other countries signed the agreement. Unfortunately, without something more than idealism to back it up, the Kellogg-Briand Pact had little practical meaning.

THE WANING SEARCH FOR DISARMAMENT

The Depression did not diminish the desire for disarmament. In fact, it added a new series of problems and concerns that made the search more difficult, and with growing threats of aggression in Asia and Europe, these effortss were destryed.

London Naval Disarmament Treaty

In March 1930, Great Britain and the United States sought to expand the naval limitation terms of the Five Power Treaty of 1922. France and Italy could not agree on terms, while the U.S., England, and Japan accepted mild reductions in cruiser and destroyer strength.

World Disarmament Conference

The starting point for implementation of the 1924 Geneva Protocol was a disarmament conference, which, though envisioned for 1925, did not convene until February 5, 1932. Attended by 60 countries including the USSR and the United States, initial discussions centered around a French proposal that wanted a protective monitoring system and required arbitration before considering disarmament. On the other hand, the U.S. asked for one-third reduction of current treaty shipping strength. Germany countered with demands for arms parity before disarmament. Though this was a front for more complex issues, the Germans left the conference when rebuffed in September 1932, only to be lured back later by a Five Power statement that agreed, in spirit, to Germany's demand. Hitler's accession to power on January 30, 1933, halted any further consideration of this point, which prompted Germany's withdrawal from the conference and the League. This, and France's continued insistence on pre-disarmament security guarantees, neutralized conference efforts, and it closed in failure in June 1934.

LEAGUE AND ALLIED RESPONSE TO AGGRESSION

By 1931, international attention increasingly turned to growing acts or threats of aggression in Europe and Asia, and transformed Europe from a world that hoped for eternal peace to a Continent searching desperately for ways to contain growing aggression.

The League's Lytton Report and Manchuria

On September 19, 1931, the Japanese Kwantung Army, acting independently of the government in Tokyo, began the gradual conquest of Manchuria after fabricating an incident at Mukden to justify their actions. Ultimately, they created a puppet state, Manchukuo, under the last Chinese emperor, Henry Pu Yi. China's League protest resulted in the creation of an investigatory commission under the Earl of Lytton, that criticized Japan's actions and recommended a negotiated settlement that would have allowed Japan to retain most of its conquest. Japan responded by resigning from the League on January 24, 1933.

The Stresa Front

Hitler's announcement on March 15, 1935, of Germany's decisions to rearm and to introduce conscription in violation of the Treaty of Versailles prompted the leaders of England, France, and Italy to meet in Stresa, Italy (April 11 – 14) to discuss a response. They condemned Germany's actions, underlined their commitment to the Locarno Pact, and re-affirmed the support they collectively gave for Austria's independence in early 1934. Prompted by these actions, the League Council also rebuked Germany, and created an investigatory committee to search for economic means to punish the Reich. Great Britain's decision, however, to protect separately its naval strength vis a vis a German buildup in the Anglo-German Naval Treaty of June 18, 1935, effectively compromised the significance of the Stresa Front.

Italy and Ethiopia

By the end of 1934, Italy had begun to create a number of incidents in Ethiopia as a prelude to complete absorption of that country. The Emperor of Ethiopia, Haile Sellasie, appealed directly to the League on the matter in January 1935. Franco-British efforts to mediate the crisis failed, while Ethiopia continued to look to the League to contain Italian aggression. Mussolini was convinced that he could act with impunity when he realizedthat the League was reluctant to do more than make verbal objections to the Italian actions. Consequently, on October 3, 1935, Italy invaded Ethiopia, which prompted the League to declare the former country the aggressor. Ineffective economic sanctions followed on October 19. Independent Anglo-French efforts to halt separately Italian aggression by granting Mussolini most of Ethiopia (with economic predominance) failed in December because of a strong public outcry over the terms. Italy completed its conquest in early May 1935, and annexed Ethiopia on May 9.

6 WORLD WAR II TO THE DEMISE OF COMMUNISM (1935-1996)

THE AUTHORITARIAN STATES

The Soviet Union (U.S.S.R.) and Stalin

The Bolsheviks under Lenin and Trotsky came to power in the revolution of 1917. In a power struggle following the death of Lenin (1924), Josef Stalin won control of the Communist Party and Soviet Government from his rival, Leon Trotsky, who was eventually sent into exile. In 1928 Stalin began to build "socialism in one country." The first and second five-year plans resulted in a degree of centralized control over the nation and its economy unparalleled in history.

The 1936 Constitution was a recognition of the success of socialism. It gave the people civil rights, such as freedom of speech, customary in democracies. In addition it guaranteed a right to work, rest, leisure, and economic security. In fact, these rights were largely ignored by Stalin's government, or they existed only within the limits set by the ruling Communist Party of which Stalin was General Secretary.

Stalin's absolute dictatorship and inability to tolerate any opposition or dissent was revealed to the world by the Great Purge Trials (1936–1938). In 1936, 16 old Bolsheviks—including Gregory Zinoviev (first head of the Communist International) and Lev Kamenev—were placed on trial, publicly confessed to charges of plotting with foreign powers, and were executed. In 1937 Marshal Michael Tukhachevski and a group of the highest-ranking generals were accused of plotting with the Germans and Japanese, and executed after a secret court martial. Other purges and trials followed, including the 1938 trial of Nicolai Bukharin, Alexei Rykov, and other prominent Bolsheviks charged with Trotskyite plots and wanting to restore capitalism.

These events tended to discredit Russia as a reliable factor in international affairs. By the late 1930s the U.S.S.R. presented two images to the world: one a regime of absolute dictatorship and repression exemplified by the Great Purges and the other of undeniable economic progress during a period of world depression. Industrial production increased an average of 14% per annum in the 1930s, and Russia went from 15th to third in production of electricity. The Bolshevik model was, however, one of progress imposed from above at great cost to those below. These impressions help explain the reluctance of British and French leaders throughout the 1930s to rely on the Soviet Union when they had to deal with acts of aggression by Hitler and Mussolini.

Events in Nazi Germany

The Nazi state (Third Reich) was a brutal dictatorship established with Hitler's appointment as Chancellor in 1933. By 1936 Hitler had destroyed the government of the Weimar Republic (established in 1919 at the end of the First World War), suppressed all political parties except the Nazi Party, and consolidated the government of Germany under his control as Fuhrer (leader). Mass organizations such as the Nazi Labor Front and the Hitler Youth were established. The Nazis instituted propaganda campaigns and a regime of terror against political opponents and Jews (who were made scapegoats for Germany's problems). Germany was a police state by 1936. In 1938 the Nazis used the assassination of a German diplomat by a Jewish youth as the excuse for extensive pogroms, or massacres. Scores were murdered and much Jewish property was destroyed or damaged by gangs of Nazi hoodlums. Persecution of the Jews increased in intensity, culminating in the horrors of the war-time concentration camps and the mass murder of millions.

Final control over the armed forces and the foreign office was achieved by Hitler in 1937–1938. He moved against Blomberg (the Minister of War) and Fritsch (the commander-in-chief of the army), taking advantage of the scandals in which they were involved (in the case of Fritsch the accusations were false). Hitler made himself Minister of War and established the High Command of the Armed Forces under his personal representative, General Keitel. At the same time Joachim von Ribbentrop was made Minister of Foreign Affairs, giving the Nazis complete control over the German Foreign Office.

Nevertheless the Nazi regime enjoyed success in part, at least, because it was able to reduce unemployment from 6,000,000 in 1932 to 164,000 by 1938 through so-called four-year plans aimed at rearming Germany and making its economy self-sufficient and free of dependence on any foreign power. The improving economic condition of many, together with Hitler's successes in foreign affairs, gave him a substantial hold over the German people.

By the beginning of World War II Germany had been transformed into a disciplined war machine with all dissent stifled and ready to follow the *Führer* wherever he might lead.

Fascist Italy: The Corporate State

Mussolini's Fascist dictatorship in Italy began with the "March on Rome" in 1922. In the early 1930s Italy suffered from severe economic depression intensified by lack of raw materials and an unfavorable trade balance. In 1935 Mussolini embarked upon the conquest of Ethiopia, and despite condemnation by the League of Nations and unfavorable reactions among the powers, completed the conquest and formally annexed Ethiopia May 9, 1936.

The pattern of Mussolini's dictatorship was that of the "Corporate State." Political parties and electoral districts were abolished. Workers and employers alike were organized into corporations according to the nature of their business. Twenty-two such corporations were established, presided over by a minister of corporations. The corporations and the government (with the balance heavily favoring the employers and the government) generally determined wages, hours, conditions of work, prices, and industrial polices. The structure was completed in 1938 with the abolition of the Chamber of Deputies in the Parliament and its replacement by a Chamber of Fasces and Corporations representing the Fascist Party and the corporations.

Fascism provided a certain excitement and superficial grandeur but no solution to Italy's economic problems. Italian labor was kept under strict control. No strikes were allowed and by 1939 real wages were below those of 1922. Emphasis on foreign adventures and propaganda concerning a new Roman Empire were used to maintain a regime of force and brutality.

Other Authoritarian Regimes

The democratic hopes of those who established independent states in eastern and central Europe following World War I remained unfulfilled in the 1930s. Authoritarian monarchies—military regimes or governments on the fascist model—were established everywhere: Poland by 1939 was under a military regime established by Admiral Horthy, Greece by General Metaxas. Yugoslavia, Rumania, and Bulgaria were ruled by authoritarian monarchies. In Spain General Franco established a fascist dictatorship after the Civil War (1936 – 1939). In Austria the clerical-fascist regime of Kurt Schuschnigg ruled until the *Anschluss* (annexation by Germany) in 1938 and in

Portugal Salazar ruled as dictator.

THE DEMOCRACIES

Great Britain

In Great Britain the Labor Party emerged as the second party in British politics along with the Conservatives. The first Labor government under Ramsey MacDonald governed from January to November, 1924. A second MacDonald cabinet was formed in 1931 but resigned in August because of financial crisis and disagreement over remedies. A national coalition government under Ramsey MacDonald governed from October 1931 to June 1935 when Stanley Baldwin formed a Conservative cabinet. Baldwin was succeeded by Neville Chamberlain (1937–1940) whose government dealt with the problem of German and Italian aggression by a policy of appeasement.

France: The Popular Front

In France a coalition of Radical Socialists, Socialists, and Communists campaigned in 1936 on a pledge to save the country from fascism and solve problems of the depression by instituting economic reforms. The Popular Front government, under Socialist Leon Blum, lasted just over a year. Much reform legislation was enacted, including a 40-hour work week, vacations with pay, collective bargaining, compulsory arbitration of labor disputes, support for agricultural prices, reorganization of the Bank of France, and nationalization of armaments and aircraft industries. Blum was attacked by conservatives and fascists as a radical and a Jew. ("Better Hitler than Leon Blum.") The Popular Front government was defeated by the Senate which refused to vote the government emergency financial powers. Eduard Daladier then formed a conservative government which began to devote its attention to foreign affairs, collaborating with Chamberlain in the appeasement policy. Democracy was preserved from the fascist attacks of the early 1930s, but the Popular Front was not as successful in making permanent changes as might have been hoped, and it was a demoralized and dispirited France that had to meet the German attack on Poland in 1939.

Other Democratic States

Czechoslovakia was the one state of Eastern Europe that maintained a democratic, parliamentary regime. It came under heavy attack from Nazi Germany following the annexation of Austria and was ultimately deserted by its allies, France and Britain, whose leaders forced Czech compliance with the terms of the Munich Agreement of 1938. Switzerland maintained a precarious neutrality throughout the 1930s and World War II with the help of the League of Nations, which freed Switzerland of any obligation to support even sanctions against an aggressor. Sweden also maintained its democratic existence by a firm policy of neutrality. Denmark and Norway were seized by the Germans early in 1940 and remained under German control during World War II. All of the Scandinavian countries were models of liberal democratic government.

CULTURE IN THE LATE 1930S: ENGAGEMENT

The 20th century generally has been one in which there has been a feeling of fragmentation and uncertainty in European thought and the arts. Much of this was due to the discoveries of Freud and Einstein: one emphasizing that much of human behavior is irrational and the other undermining in his theories of relativity the long-held certainties of Newtonian science. The Dutch historian Johan Huizinga noted in 1936 "almost all things which once seemed sacred and immutable have now become unsettled. ... The sense of living in the midst of a violent crisis of civilization, threatening complete collapse, has spread far and wide." (Huizinga, *In the Shadow of Tomorrow*, London, 1936). Intellectuals came increasingly to see the world as an irrational place in which old values and truths had little relevance. Some intellectuals became "engaged" in resistance to fascism and Nazism. Some like Arthur Koestler flirted with communism but broke with Stalin after the Great Purges. Koestler's *Darkness at Noon* (1941) is an attempt to understand the events surrounding those trials. German intellectuals such as Ernst Cassirer and Erich Fromm escaped Nazi Germany and worked in exile. Cassirer, in his *The Myth of the State* (1946), noted that the Nazis manufactured myths of race, leader, party, etc., that disoriented reason and intellect. Fromm published *Escape from Freedom* in 1941 which maintained that modern man had escaped *to* freedom from the orderly, structured world of medieval society but was now trying to escape *from* this freedom and looking for security once again. The artist Picasso expressed his hatred of fascism by his painting of Guernica, a Spanish town subjected to aerial bombardment by the German air force as it intervened in the Spanish Civil War.

Existentialism is the philosophy that best exemplified European feelings in the era of the World Wars. Three 19th-century figures greatly influenced this movement: Kierkegaard, Dostoevski, and Nietzsche. Martin Heidegger (though he rejected the term), Karl Jaspers, Jean-Paul Sartre, and Simone de Beauvoir are four noted figures in 20th-century existentialism, which sought to come to grip with life's central experiences and the trauma of war, death, and evil.

INTERNATIONAL RELATIONS: THE ROAD TO WAR

Several factors need to be understood concerning the events leading to World War II. First, there has been little debate over causes: Germany, Italy, Japan, and the U.S.S.R. were not satisfied with the peace settlement of 1919. They used force to achieve change, from the Japanese invasion of Manchuria in 1931 to the outbreak of war in 1939 over Poland. Hitler, bit by bit, dismantled the Versailles Treaty in central and eastern Europe. Responsibility has also been placed to some degree on Britain and France and even the United States for following a policy of appeasement which it was hoped would satisfy Hitler's demands.

Secondly, Britain and France as well as other democratic states were influenced in their policy by a profound pacifism based on their experience with the loss of life and devastation in World War I and by a dislike of the Stalinist regime in Russia.

Thirdly, while the U.S.S.R. was a revisionist power, it was profoundly distrustful of Germany, Italy, and Japan. The threat to their interests led the Soviet leaders to pursue a policy of collective security through the League of Nations (which they joined in 1934). Only after evidence of Anglo-French weakness did Stalin in 1939 enter an agreement with Hitler. This event, like the Great Purges, only heightened suspicion of Soviet motives and was later to become the subject of debate and recrimination in the Cold War that followed World War II.

Finally, Neville Chamberlain's policy of appeasement was not based on any liking for Hitler, whom he considered "half-crazed," but on a genuine desire to remove causes of discontent inherent in the Versailles settlement and thus create conditions where peace could be maintained. His error lay in his belief that Hitler was open to reason, preferred peace to war, and would respect agreements.

THE COURSE OF EVENTS

Using a Franco-Soviet agreement of the preceding year as an excuse, Hitler, on March 7, 1936, repudiated the Locarno agreements and reoccupied the Rhineland (an area demilitarized by the Versailles Treaty). Neither France (which possessed military superiority at the time) nor Britain was willing to oppose these moves.

The Spanish Civil War (1936 – 1939) is usually seen as a rehearsal for World War II because of outside intervention. The government of the Spanish Republic (established in 1931) caused resentment among conservatives by its programs, including land reform and anti-clerical legislation aimed at the Catholic Church. Labor discontent led to disturbances in industrial Barcelona and the surrounding province of Catalonia. Following an election victory by a popular front of republican and radical parties, right-wing generals in July began a military insurrection. Francisco Franco, stationed at the time in Spanish Morocco, emerged as the leader of this revolt which became a devastating civil war lasting nearly three years.

The democracies, including the United States, followed a course of neutrality, refusing to aid the Spanish government or to become involved. Nazi Germany, Italy and the U.S.S.R. did intervene despite non-intervention agreements negotiated by Britain and France. German air force units were sent to aid the fascist forces of Franco and participated in bombardments of Madrid, Barcelona, and Guernica (the latter incident being the inspiration for Picasso's famous painting which became an anti-fascist symbol known far beyond the world of art). Italy sent troops, tanks, and other materiel. The U.S.S.R. sent advisers and recruited soldiers from among anti-fascists in the United States and other countries to fight in the international brigades with the republican forces. Spain became a battlefield for fascist and anti-fascist forces with Franco winning by 1939 in what was seen as a serious defeat for anti-fascist forces everywhere.

The Spanish Civil War was a factor in bringing together Mussolini and Hitler in a Rome-Berlin Axis. Already Germany and Japan had signed the Anti-Comintern Pact in 1936. Ostensibly directed against international communism, this was the basis for a diplomatic alliance between those countries, and Italy soon adhered to this agreement, becoming Germany's ally in World War II.

Italy, in addition to its involvement in Spain, in 1935 launched a war to conquer the African kingdom of Ethiopia. The democracies chose not to intervene in this case, either, despite Emperor Haile Selassie's plea to the League of Nations. By 1936 the conquest was complete.

In 1937 there was Nazi-inspired agitation in the Baltic port of Danzig, a city basically German to its population, but which had been made a free city under the terms of the Versailles Treaty.

In 1938 Hitler renewed his campaign against Austria which he had unsuccessfully tried to subvert in 1934. Pressure was put on the Austrian Chancellor Schuschnig to make concessions to Hitler, and when this did not work, German troops annexed Austria (the *Anschluss*). Again Britain and France took no effective action, and about six million Austrians were added to Germany.

Hitler turned next to Czechoslovakia. Three million persons of German origin lived in the Sudetenland, a borderland between Germany and Czechoslovakia given to Czechoslovakia in order to provide it with a more defensible boundary. These ethnic Germans (and other minorities of Poles, Ruthenians, and Hungarians) agitated against the democratic government (the only one in eastern Europe in 1938) despite its enlightened minority policy. Hitler used the Sudeten Nazi Party to deliberately provoke a crisis by making demands for a degree of independence unacceptable to the Czech authorities. He then claimed to interfere as the protector of a persecuted minority. In May 1938 rumors of invasion led to warnings from Britain and France followed by assurances from Hitler. Nevertheless in the fall the crisis came to a head with renewed demands from Hitler. Chamberlain twice flew to Germany in person to get German terms. The second time, Hitler's increased demands led to mobilization and other measures towards war. At the last minute a four-power conference was held in Munich with Hitler, Mussolini, Chamberlain and Daladier in attendance. At Munich, Hitler's terms were accepted in the Munich Agreement. Neither Czechoslovakia nor the U.S.S.R. was in attendance. Britain and France, despite the French alliance with Czechoslovakia, put pressure on the Czech government to force it to comply with German demands. Hitler signed a treaty agreeing to this settlement as the limit of his ambitions. At the same time the Poles seized control of Teschen, and Hungary (with the support of Italy and Germany and over the protests of the British and French) seized 7,500 square miles of Slovakia. By the concessions forced on her at Munich, Czechoslovakia lost the frontier defenses and was totally unprotected against any further German encroachments.

In March 1939 Hitler annexed most of the rump Czech state while Hungary conquered Ruthenia. At almost the same time Germany annexed Memel from Lithuania. In April Mussolini, taking advantage of distractions created by Germany, landed an army in Albania and seized that Balkan state in a campaign lasting about one week.

Disillusioned by these continued aggressions, Britain and France made military preparations. Guarantees were given to Poland, Rumania, and Greece. The two democracies also opened negotiations with the U.S.S.R. for an arrangement to obtain that country's aid against further German aggression. Hitler, with Poland next on his timetable, also began a cautious rapproachement with the U.S.S.R. Probably Russian suspicion that the Western powers wanted the U.S.S.R. to bear the brunt of any German attack led Stalin to respond to Hitler's overtures. Negotiations which began very quietly in the spring of 1939 were continued with increasing urgency as summer approached and with it, the time of Hitler's planned attack on Poland. On August 23, 1939, the world was stunned by the announcement of a Nazi-Soviet treaty of friendship. A secret protocol provided that in the event of a "territorial rearrangement" in eastern Europe the two powers would divide Poland. In addition Russia would have the Baltic states (Latvia, Lithuania, and Estonia) and Bessarabia (lost to Rumania in 1918) as part of her sphere. Stalin agreed to remain neutral in any German war with Britain or France.

World War II began with the German invasion of Poland on September 1, 1939, followed by British and French declarations of war against Germany on September 3.

WORLD WAR II

The Polish Campaign and the "Phony War"

The German attack (known as the "blitzkrieg" or "lightning war") overwhelmed the poorly equipped Polish army which could not resist German tanks and airplanes. The outcome was clear after the first few days of fighting, and organized resistance ceased within a month.

In accordance with the secret provisions of the Nazi-Soviet Treaty of August 1939, Russia and Germany shared the Polish spoils. On September 17 the Russian armies attacked the Poles from the east. They met the Germans two days later. Stalin's share of Poland extended approximately to the Curzon Line (a line originally proposed in 1919 and named for the British foreign minister, Lord Curzon, and which was never implemented). Russia also made demands on Finland. Later, in June 1940, while Germany was attacking France, Stalin occupied the Baltic states of Latvia, Lithuania, and Estonia.

Nazi Germany formally annexed the port of Danzig and the Polish Corridor and some territory along the western Polish border. Central Poland was turned into a German protectorate called the Government-General.

Following the successful completion of the Polish campaign, the war settled into a period of inaction on the part of both Germans and the British and French known as the "phony war" or "sitzkrieg." The British and French prepared for a German attack on France and Belgium such as that at the beginning of World War I but failed to take any offensive action. Some peace-feelers were extended by the Germans but met with no success. At sea, a campaign began between the British navy and German submarines which began to prey on Allied shipping. The British were also concerned with finding a way to prevent vital Swedish iron ore from reaching Germany by a route which led over northern Norway and then by ship down the Norwegian coast to German Baltic ports. Any effective blockade would have involved violation of Norwegian territorial waters, however, and this the Chamberlain government was reluctant to do.

The "Winter War" Between Russia and Finland

The only military action of any consequence during the winter of 1939 – 1940 resulted from Russian demands made on Finland, especially for territory adjacent to Leningrad (then only 20 miles from the border). Finnish refusal led to a Russian attack in November 1939. The Finns resisted with considerable vigor, receiving some supplies from Sweden, Britain and France, but eventually by March had to give in to the superior Russian forces. Finland was forced to cede the Karelian Isthmus, Viipuri, and a naval base at Hangoe. Britain and France prepared forces to aid the Finns but by the time they were ready to act the Finns had been defeated.

The German Attack on Denmark and Norway

The period of inactivity in the war in the west came suddenly to an end. On April 8, 1940, the British and French finally announced their intent to mine Norwegian coastal waters to blockade German ships transporting Swedish iron ore. On April 9, as the Norwegians were about to protest this action, the Germans struck. Denmark and Norway were simultaneously attacked. Denmark was quickly occupied. In Norway, German forces landed by air at strategic points with the main forces coming by sea. The British and French responded by sending naval and military forces to Narvik and Trondheim in an effort to assist the Norwegians and to capture some bases before the Germans could overrun the entire country. They were too slow and showed little initiative, and within a few weeks the forces were withdrawn, taking the Norwegian government with them into exile in London.

The Battle of France

On May 10 the main German offensive was launched against France. Belgium and the Netherlands were simultaneously attacked. According to plan, British and French forces advanced to aid the Belgians. At this point the Germans departed from the World War I strategy by launching a surprise armored attack through Luxembourg and the Ardennes Forest (considered by the British and French to be impassable for tanks). As these forces moved towards the Channel coast they divided the Allied armies leaving the Belgians, British Expeditionary Force, and some French forces virtually encircled. The Dutch could offer no real resistance and collapsed in four days after the May 13

German bombing of Rotterdam — one of the first raids intended to terrorize civilians. Queen Wilhemina and her government fled to London. The Belgians, who had made little effort to coordinate plans with the British and French, surrendered May 25th, leaving the British and French in serious danger from the Germans who were advancing to the Channel coast; however, Hitler concentrated on occupying Paris. This provided just enough time for the British to effect an emergency evacuation of some 230,000 of their own men as well as about 120,000 French from the port of Dunkirk and the adjacent coast. This remarkable evacuation saved the lives of the soldiers, but all supplies and equipment were lost including vehicles, tanks, and artillery — a very severe blow to the British Army.

Churchill Becomes British Prime Minister

Even before the offensive against France, on May 7 and 8 an attack was launched in the House of Commons on Prime Minister Chamberlain, prompted by the bungling of the Norwegian campaign but which extended to the whole conduct of the war to that point. Chamberlain, a man of peace who had never properly mobilized the British war effort or developed an effective plan of action, fell from power. A government was formed under Winston Churchill, whose warnings of the German danger and the need for British rearmament all during the 1930s made him Chamberlain's logical successor. The opposition Labor Party agreed to join in a coalition with Clement Attlee becoming deputy prime minister. Several other Laborites followed his lead by accepting cabinet posts. This gave Britain a government which eventually led the nation to final victory but which could do little in 1940 to prevent the defeat of France.

France Makes Peace

Paris fell to the Germans in mid-June. In this crisis Paul Reynaud succeeded Eduard Daladier as premier but was unable to deal with the defeatism of some of his cabinet. On June 16th Reynaud resigned in favor of a government headed by aged Marshal Petain, one of the heroes of World War I. The Petain government quickly made peace with Hitler, who added to French humiliation by dictating the terms of the armistice to the French at Compiegne in the same railroad car used by Marshal Foch when he gave terms to the Germans at the end of the First World War. The complete collapse of France in so short a time came as a tremendous shock to the British as well as to Americans. The failure was not due to treachery or cowardice but to poor morale, a defensive "Maginot" mentality, and a failure on the part of French leaders to think in modern terms or to understand as did the Germans the nature of modern mechanized warfare.

Mussolini chose the moment of French defeat to attack France, declaring war on both France and Britain on June 10th. He gained little by this action, and Hitler largely ignored the Italian dictator in making peace with France.

Hitler's forces remained in occupation of the northern part of France, including Paris. He allowed the French to keep their fleet and overseas territories probably in the hope of making them reliable allies. Petain and his chief minister Pierre Laval established their capital at Vichy and followed a policy of collaboration with their former enemies. A few Frenchmen, however, joined the Free French movement started in London by the then relatively unknown General Charles de Gaulle.

FROM THE FRENCH DEFEAT TO THE INVASION OF RUSSIA

Germany's "New Order" in Europe

By mid-summer 1940, Germany, together with its Italian ally, dominated most of western and central Europe. Germany began with no real plans for a long war, but continued resistance by the British made necessary the belated mobilization of German resources. Hitler's policy included exploiting those areas conquered by Germany. Collaborators were used to establish governments subservient to German policy. These received the name "Quislings" after the Norwegian traitor Vidkun Quisling, who was made premier of Norway during the German occupation. Germany began the policy of forcibly transporting large numbers of conquered Europeans to work in German war industries. Jews especially were forced into slave labor for the German war effort, and increasingly large numbers were rounded up and sent to concentration camps where they were systematically murdered as the Nazis carried out Hitler's "final solution" of genocide against European Jewry. Although much was known about this during the war, the full horror of these atrocities was not revealed until Allied troops entered Germany in 1945.

The Battle of Britain

With the fall of France, Britain remained the only power of consequence at war with the Axis. Hitler began preparations for invading Britain (Operation "Sea Lion"). Air control over the Channel was vital if an invasion force were to be transported safely to the English Coast. The German Air Force (Luftwaffe) under Herman Göring began its air offensive against the British in the summer of 1940. The British, however, had used the year between Munich and the outbreak of war to good advantage, increasing their production of aircraft to 600 per month, almost equal to German production. The Spitfire and Hurricane fighters which were the Royal Air Force's mainstay were designed and produced somewhat later than similar German planes and proved superior. The British had also developed the first radar just in time to be used to give early warning of German attacks. British intelligence was also effective in deciphering German military communications and in providing ways to interfere with the navigational devices used by the German bombers. The Germans concentrated first on British air defenses, then on ports and shipping, and finally in early September they began the attack on London. The Battle of Britain was eventually a defeat for the Germans, who were unable to gain decisive superiority over the British, although they inflicted great damage on both British air defenses and major cities such as London. Despite the damage and loss of life British morale remained high and necessary war production continued. German losses determined that bombing alone could not defeat Britain. Operation "Sea Lion" was postponed October 12th and never seriously taken up again, although the British did not know this and had to continue for some time to give priority to their coastal and air defenses.

Involvement of the United States

The Churchill government worked actively to gain help from the United States, and their efforts obtained a sympathetic response from President Franklin Roosevelt, although in his efforts to enact "measures short of war" to aid Britain he had to deal with strong isolationist sentiment in the United States exemplified by the America First movement. Wendell Willkie, his Republican opponent in the 1940 presidential election, took an identical international position. As early as November 1939 neutrality legislation was amended to lift the ban on the sale of arms to belligerents. Late in 1940, when a crisis developed with respect to protection for British shipping, Roosevelt negotiated an agreement by which Congress was persuaded to transfer to the British 50 World War I destroyers in return for naval bases on British possessions in the Western Hemisphere. In 1941, when British assets in the U.S. had been depleted, the U.S.

president and Congress enacted the Lend-Lease Program to provide resources for continued purchases of weapons and supplies by the British. Later the program was extended to supply Russia and other powers which became involved in the struggle against the Axis. The U.S. also introduced its first peacetime draft and began a tremendous program of military expansion. Bases were obtained in Greenland and Iceland, and American warships began to convoy Allied shipping as far as Iceland. The U.S. was already waging an "undeclared war" against Germany months before the Pearl Harbor attack led to formal American involvement.

Germany Turns East

During the winter of 1940 – 1941, having given up Operation "Sea Lion," Hitler began to shift his forces to the east for an invasion of Russia (Operation "Barbarossa"). The alliance of August 1939 was never harmonious, and German fears were aroused by Russia's annexation of the three Baltic states in June 1940, by the attack on Finland, and by Russian seizure of the province of Bessarabia from Rumania. Russian expansion towards the Balkans dismayed the Germans, who hoped for more influence there themselves. In addition, Hitler's ally Mussolini had, on October 28, 1940, begun an ill-advised invasion of Greece from bases in Albania which the Italians had seized earlier. Within a few weeks the Greeks repulsed the Italians and drove them back into Albania.

The Balkan Campaign

These events prompted Hitler to make demands early in 1941 on Rumania, Bulgaria, and Hungary which led these powers to become German allies accepting occupation by German forces. Yugoslavia resisted and the Germans attacked on April 6th, occupying the state despite considerable resistance. They then advanced to the aid of the Italians in their attack on Greece. Greece was quickly overrun despite aid from the British forces in the Middle East. The Greek government took refuge on Crete some sixty miles off the Greek coast, but that island was also captured from its British garrison. On May 20th German parachute troops and airborne forces established footholds at key points on the island. The defenders were unable to repel the Germans and at the end of May Crete was evacuated by the British, with the Greek government also going into exile in London.

Barbarossa — The Attack on Russia

The German invasion of Russia began June 22, 1941. The invasion force of three million included Finnish, Rumanian, Hungarian, and Italian contingents along with the Germans and advanced on a broad front of about 2,000 miles. In this first season of fighting the Germans seized White Russia and most of the Ukraine, advancing to the Crimean Peninsula in the south. They surrounded the city of Leningrad (although they never managed to actually capture it). Advanced German units came within about 25 miles of Moscow. Government offices were evacuated. In November the enemy actually entered the suburbs, but then the long supply lines, early winter, and Russian resistance (strong despite heavy losses) brought the invasion to a halt. During the winter a Russian counterattack pushed the Germans back from Moscow and saved the capital. Then on December 7th the United States was brought into the war by the surprise Japanese attack on the U.S. naval base at Pearl Harbor, and the entire balance of power in this conflict would ultimately change.

The Far Eastern Crisis

With the coming of the Great Depression and severe economic difficulties,

Japanese militarists gained more and more influence over the civilian government which was unable to control its armed forces — especially the Kwantung army which garrisoned the Japanese-controlled railroad lines in the Chinese province of Manchuria. Believing a policy of expansion and empire-building on the Asian mainland would help solve Japan's difficulties and bring ultimate prosperity, the officers of the Kwantung army engineered an explosion on one of the railroad lines. On September 18, 1931, using this as an excuse, the Japanese occupied all of Manchuria. On July 7, 1937, a full-scale Sino-Japanese war began with a clash between Japanese and Chinese at the Marco Polo Bridge in Peking (now Beijing). An indication of ultimate Japanese aims came on November 3, 1938, when Prince Konoye's government issued a statement on "A New Order in East Asia." This statement envisaged the integration of Japan, Manchuria (now the puppet state of Manchukuo), and China into one "Greater East Asia Co-Prosperity Sphere" under Japanese leadership. In July 1940 the Konoye government was re-formed with General Hideki Tojo (Japan's principal leader in World War I) as minister of war. Japan's policy of friendship with Nazi Germany and Fascist Italy was consolidated with the signing of a formal alliance in September 1940. The war in Europe gave Japan further opportunities for expansion. Concessions were obtained from the Vichy government in French Indochina and Japanese bases were established there.

All of these events led to worsening relations between Japan and the two states in a position to oppose her expansion — the Soviet Union and the United States. Despite border clashes with the Russians, Japan avoided any conflict with that state, and Stalin wanted no war with Japan after he became fully occupied with the German invasion. The United States viewed Japanese activities with increasing disfavor, especially the brutal war against China. A trade treaty was not renewed and exports of scrap metals, oil, etc., necessary to the Japanese war effort, were embargoed by the American government. By 1941 a crisis developed, and although the American government did not know the details at the time, in Japan decisions had already been made that would finally lead to the attack on American naval forces moved to Hawaii as a deterrent to further Japanese expansion. There has been much controversy surrounding the Japanese surprise attack on the Pearl Harbor naval base on December 7, 1941. Here it is sufficient to say that the United States forces were caught off guard and suffered a disastrous defeat which fortunately was not as complete as the Japanese planned. It did, however, put the United States on the defensive for a year or more. In a few weeks Japanese forces were able to occupy strategically important islands (including the Philippines and Dutch East Indies) as well as territory on the Asian mainland (Malaya, with the British naval base at Singapore, and all of Burma to the border of India).

The Japanese attack brought the United States not only into war in the Pacific but also resulted in German and Italian declarations of war which meant the total involvement of the United States in World War II.

The "Turning of the Tide"

The basic strategy for winning the war had been evolved well before Pearl Harbor. Pre-war American strategic planning (the so-called Rainbow plans) provided for several possibilities, always keeping in mind the defense of the Western Hemisphere as the major goal. During 1940 and 1941, as it became more and more apparent that the United States would become involved as an ally first of Britain and then the Soviet Union, plans changed accordingly. A two-front war became increasingly likely, and U.S. strategists decided — with British concurrence — that priority should be given to the war in Europe (a "Germany first" policy), because the danger to both Britain and the U.S.S.R. seemed more immediate than the threat from Japan. As it turned out, the

United States mobilized such great resources that sufficient forces were available to go over to the offensive in the Pacific at the same time European theater requirements were being met and the war against Japan ended only a few weeks after the German surrender.

American involvement in the war was ultimately decisive, for it meant that the greatest industrial power of that time was now arrayed against the Axis powers. The United States became, as President Roosevelt put it, "the arsenal of democracy." American aid was crucial to the immense effort of the Soviet Union. Despite almost unanimous expert opinion that the Russians would collapse under German attack, Roosevelt had his personal assistant Harry Hopkins visit Russia and assess the situation, and based on Hopkins' recommendations Lend-Lease aid was extended to Russia. By 1943 supplies and equipment were reaching Russia in very considerable quantities. Routes were found through the Persian Gulf and overland and also through the Russian Arctic port of Murmansk. The latter route was exceedingly dangerous because of the proximity of German forces based in Norway and on one or two occasions, losses were so great that convoys had to be temporarily suspended until their defenses could be improved. Nevertheless in this modern war where the supply and equipment of vast forces over great distances was a major factor, American industrial strength was decisive.

The Second German Offensive in Russia: Stalingrad

Despite losses that included their richest farm land, one-half of their industry and millions of the population, the Russians not only stopped the Germans and their allies just short of Moscow, but in a winter offensive drove the center German army group back some 80 miles from the capital. Nevertheless, with Hitler in personal control, the German forces launched a second offensive in the summer of 1942. This attack concentrated on the southern part of the front, aiming at the Caucasus and vital oil fields around the Caspian Sea. At Stalingrad on the Volga River the Germans were stopped. There were weeks of bitter fighting in the streets of the city itself. With the onset of winter, Hitler refused to allow the strategic retreat urged by his generals. As a result the Russian forces crossed the river north and south of the city and surrounded 22 German divisions. On January 31, 1943, following the failure of relief efforts, the German commander Paulus surrendered the remnants of his army. From then on the Russians were, with only few exceptions, always on the offensive.

The North African Campaigns

After entering the war in 1940, the Italians invaded British-held Egypt from Libya. In December 1940 the British General Wavell launched a surprise attack. The Italian forces were driven back about 500 miles and 130,000 were captured. Then Hitler intervened, sending General Erwin Rommel with a small German force (the Afrika Korps) to reinforce the Italians. Rommel took command and exploiting the weakness of the British following the dispatch of forces to aid the Greeks, launched a counter-offensive which put his forces on the border of Egypt. Then Rommel in turn had to give up his reserves for the Russian campaign. He managed to recover from a second British attack, however, and by mid-1942 had driven to El Alamein, only 70 miles from Alexandria.

A change in the British high command now placed General Harold Alexander in charge of Middle Eastern forces with General Bernard Montgomery in immediate command of the British Eighth Army. After thorough preparations Montgomery attacked at El Alamein, breaking Rommel's lines and starting a British advance which was not stopped until the armies reached the border of Tunisia.

Meanwhile the British and American leaders, realizing that the forces at their disposal in 1942 would not be sufficient to invade France and start the drive on Germany itself (which was their ultimate goal), decided that they could launch a second offensive in North Africa (Operation "Torch") which would clear the enemy from the entire coast and make the Mediterranean once again safe for Allied shipping. To avoid fighting the French forces which garrisoned the main landing areas (at Casablanca, Oran and Algiers), the Allied command under the American General Dwight Eisenhower, made an agreement with the French commander Admiral Darlan. Darlan did, indeed, assist the Allies to a degree, but there was a loud public outcry in Britain and the U.S. at this alliance with a person who condoned fascism. Darlan was assassinated in December, leading to a struggle for leadership among the French in North Africa, de Gaulle's Free French, the French Resistance and other factions. Roosevelt and Churchill publicly supported senior French officer General Henri Giraud, who had just escaped from imprisonment by the Germans, against the independent and imperious de Gaulle, who was especially disliked by Roosevelt and was not kept informed of the North African operation or allowed to participate. De Gaulle proved his political as well as military talent by completely outmaneuvering Giraud and within a year he was the undisputed leader of all the French elements.

The landings resulted in little conflict with the French and indeed the French forces soon joined the war against the Axis. The Germans and Italians were a different matter, however. Hitler quickly sent German forces under General von Arnim to occupy Tunisia before the Anglo-American forces could get there from their landing points. It was only a matter of time, however, before these forces, together with those commanded by Rommel, were forced into northern Tunisia and forced to surrender. American forces, unused to combat, suffered some reverses at the Battle of the Kasserine Pass, but gained valuable experience. The final victory came in May 1943, about the same time as the Russian victory at Stalingrad.

Winning the Battle of the Atlantic

Another important though less spectacular turning point came in the long, drawn-out battle against German submarines in the North Atlantic. Relatively safe shipping routes across the North Atlantic to Britain were essential to the survival of Britain and absolutely necessary if a force was to be assembled to invade France and strike at Germany proper. At times early in the war the Germans sank ships at a higher rate than the two Allies could replace them, but gradually they began to develop effective countermeasures. New types of aircraft, small aircraft carriers, more numerous and better-equipped escort vessels, new radar and sonar (for underwater detection), extremely efficient radio direction finding, decipherment of German signals plus the building of more ships (including the mass-produced "Liberty Ship" freighter), turned the balance against the Germans despite their development of improved submarines. Again the tide of battle turned by early 1943 and the Atlantic became increasingly dangerous for German submarines .

A Turning Point

Success in these three campaigns — Stalingrad, North Africa, and the Battle of the Atlantic — gave new hope to the Allied cause and made certain that eventually victory would be won. Together with the beginning of an offensive in late 1942 in the Solomon Islands against the Japanese, they made 1943 the turning point of the war.

Allied Victory

At their conference at Casablanca in January 1943 Roosevelt and Churchill developed detailed strategy for the further conduct of the war. The decision to clear the Mediterranean was confirmed, and Sicily was to be invaded to help achieve this purpose. This led almost inevitably to Italy proper. Historians differ as to the significance of the Casablanca decisions. The Italian campaign did knock Italy out of the war and cause Hitler to send forces to Italy that might otherwise have opposed the 1944 landing in Normandy, and it did bring about the downfall of Mussolini and Italian surrender. It also ensured, by using up limited resources such as landing craft, that no second front in France could be opened in 1943 — a fact most unpalatable to Stalin, whose Russian armies were fighting desperately against the bulk of the German army and air force. Also the drawing off of forces from Italy to ensure a successful landing in France made it extremely difficult to achieve decisive victory in Italy and meant a long drawn-out and costly campaign there against skillful and stubborn resistance by the Germans under Marshal Kesselring. Rome was not captured by the Allied forces until June 4, 1944. With a new Italian government now supporting the Allied cause, Italian resistance movements in Northern Italy became a major force in helping to liberate that area from the Germans.

The Second Front in Normandy

At the Teheran Conference, held in November 1943 and attended by all three major Allied leaders (Stalin had previously declined to leave Russia), the final decision reached by Roosevelt and Churchill some six months earlier to invade France in May 1944 was communicated to the Russians. Stalin promised to open a simultaneous Russian offensive.

Despite the claims of General George Marshall and General Sir Alan Brooke (the American and British chiefs of staff, respectively) Roosevelt and Churchill decided on General Dwight Eisenhower, their North African commander, to be supreme commander of the coming invasion. Planning had already been carried for some time under the British General Frederick Morgan when Eisenhower arrived in London to establish Supreme Headquarters Allied Expeditionary Forces (SHAEF) and to weld together an international staff to command the invasion. He proved extremely adept at getting soldiers of several nations to work together harmoniously. British Air Marshal Tedder was his deputy supreme commander and Montgomery initially commanded the ground forces. Included in the invasion army were American, British, Canadian, Polish, and French contingents.

The Normandy invasion (Operation "Overlord") was the largest amphibious operation in history and was preceded by the most elaborate preparations and an enormous buildup of men and supplies. Plans included an air offensive with a force of 10,000 aircraft of all types, a large naval contingent and pre-invasion naval bombardment of the very strong German defenses, a transport force of some 4,000 ships, artificial harbors to receive supplies after the initial landings, and several divisions of airborne troops to be landed behind enemy coastal defenses the night preceding the sea-borne invasion. The landings actually took place beginning June 6, 1944. The first day, 130,000 men were successfully landed. Strong German resistance hemmed in the Allied forces for about a month. Then the Allies, now numbering about 1,000,000, managed a spectacular breakthrough. By the end of 1944 all of France had been seized. A second invasion force landed on the Mediterranean coast in August, freed southern France, and linked up with Eisenhower's forces. By the end of 1944 the Allied armies stood on the borders of Germany ready to invade from both east and west.

The Eastern Front: Poland

Russian successes brought their forces to the border of Poland by July 1944. Russian relations with the Polish government in exile in London, however, had by that time been broken off after the Poles had voiced their suspicions that the Russians and not the Germans might have caused the mass executions of a large number of Polish officers in the Katyn Forest early in the war.

Stalin's armies crossed into Poland July 23, 1944, and three days later the Russian dictator officially recognized a group of Polish Communists (the so-called Lublin Committee) as the government of Poland. As the Russian armies drew near the eastern suburbs of Warsaw, the London Poles (who controlled a large and well-organized resistance movement in Warsaw and who hoped to improve their position by a military effort) on August 1st launched their underground army in an attack on the German garrison. Stalin's forces waited outside the city while the Germans brought in reinforcements and slowly wiped out the Polish underground army in several weeks of heavy street fighting. The offensive then resumed and the city was liberated by the Red Army, but the local influence of the London Poles was now virtually nil. Needless to say, this incident aroused considerable suspicion concerning Stalin's motives and led both Churchill and Roosevelt to begin to think through the political implications of their alliance with Stalin.

Greece, Yugoslavia, and the Balkans

By late summer of 1944 the German position in the Balkans began to collapse. The Red Army crossed the border into Rumania leading King Michael II to seize the opportunity to take his country out of its alliance with Germany and to open the way to the advancing Russians. German troops were forced to make a hasty retreat. At this point Bulgaria saw the light and changed sides. The German forces in Greece, threatened with being cut off, withdrew in October with British forces moving in to take their place. The British hoped to bring about the return of the Greek government in exile from London.

From October 9 – 18, Winston Churchill visited Moscow to try to work out a political arrangement regarding the Balkans and Eastern Europe. (Roosevelt was busy with his campaign for election to a fourth term.) In Moscow Churchill worked out the famous agreement which he describes in his book on World War II. Dealing from a position of weakness, he simply wrote out some figures on a sheet of paper: Russia to have the preponderance of influence in certain countries like Bulgaria and Rumania, Britain to have the major say in Greece, and a fifty-fifty division in Yugoslavia and Hungary. Stalin indicated his agreement. The Americans refused to have anything to do with this "spheres of influence" arrangement.

In Greece Stalin maintained a hands-off policy when the British used military force to impose a settlement there. The Communist-led Greek resistance refused to agree to the return of the Greek government in exile. Fighting between the factions broke out. In December Churchill went to Athens to deal personally with the situation. British forces suppressed the Communist revolt and a regency was established under the Archbishop of Athens to end the political dispute. The British task was much simplified by the fact that Russia gave no support to the Greek Communists but treated Greece as a British sphere of influence.

The German Resistance and the 1944 Attempt to Assassinate Hitler

It was obvious even before the Normandy invasion that Germany was losing the war. Some German officers and civilians had formed a resistance movement. As long as Hitler's policy was successful it had little chance of overthrowing the German dictator. Four years of aerial bombardment, however, had reduced German cities to rubble by early 1944 and virtually destroyed the *Luftwaffe*. The Russians were on the offensive and many German officials did not like to think, after what had happened in Russia, what the Russian armies might do if they reached German soil. Hitler was in direct control of German forces and disregarded professional advice which might have provided a better, less costly defense. Knowing the war was lost after the success of the Normandy invasion, the Resistance plotted to assassinate Hitler. The leaders were retired General Ludwig Beck, Carl Goerdeler (former Mayor of Leipzig), and Count Claus Shenck von Stauffenberg—a much-decorated young staff officer who undertook the dangerous task of actually planting the bomb in Hitler's headquarters on July 20, 1944. Hitler miraculously survived the explosion and launched a reign of terror in reprisal which resulted in imprisonment, torture, and death for anyone even suspected of a connection with the plot. His survival ensured that the war would be fought out on German soil to the bitter end.

Final Questions of Strategy

In General Eisenhower's headquarters there was some dispute over the best way to invade Germany and end the war. Because of the long and rapid drive across France, supplies were insufficient for an immediate broad advance into Germany. Montgomery argued that his forces in the north should be given priority and allowed to push ahead into the North German Plain as the quickest way to end the war. Eisenhower's final decision to reject this and advance on a broad front took into account his fear that some German forces might retreat into mountain areas in southern Germany and in these easily defensible positions, prolong the war.

Before any final attack could be made, however, the Germans launched an offensive of their own beginning December 16. Hitler gathered his last reserves and sent them to attack the Allies in the Ardennes forest region with the goal of breaking through between the Allied forces and driving to the Channel coast. The offensive became known as the Battle of the Bulge. Bad weather for some days made impossible the effective use of Allied air power. The Allied lines held, however, and by the end of the first week of January 1945 the German offensive had been broken and the lines restored. Whether it had any value is open to argument. In Yugoslavia it certainly worked, and Tito (the Communist resistance leader) emerged as head of government and managed to maintain a position of independence not achieved by any other East European country.

The End of the War in Europe

In early spring of 1945 the Allied armies crossed the Rhine. The Americans used a railway bridge at Remagen which they captured just before the Germans had time to destroy it. As the Americans and British and other Allied forces advanced into Germany the Russians attacked from the east. While the Russian armies were fighting their way into Berlin, Hitler committed suicide in the ruins of the bunker where he had spent the last days of the war. Power was handed over to a government headed by Admiral Karl Doenitz. On May 7th, General Alfred Jodl, acting for the German government, made the final unconditional surrender at General Eisenhower's head-quarters near Reims.

The Yalta and Potsdam Conferences

The future treatment of Germany, and Europe generally, was determined by decisions of the "Big Three" (Churchill, Stalin, and Roosevelt). There were two summit meetings attended by all three leaders. Even before the first of these was held at Teheran, Churchill and Roosevelt had met at Casablanca and laid down a basic policy of demanding the unconditional surrender of their enemies. Stalin was agreeable to this.

The first of the major conference convened at Teheran November 28, 1943, and lasted until December 1st. Here the two Western allies told Stalin of the May 1944 date for the planned invasion of Normandy. In turn Stalin confirmed a pledge made earlier that Russia would enter the war against Japan after the war with Germany was concluded. Political questions were barely touched upon. Poland and other topics were raised but not dealt with. Roosevelt reflected the views of his military leaders who were concerned with the quickest ending to the war. Hence he was willing to postpone political decisions on the Balkans and Eastern Europe and concentrate on a second front in France and the shortest road to Berlin. This was agreeable to Stalin since any postponement would only better his position by allowing time for the Red Army to take control of the areas in question. Churchill seems to have had in mind political questions far more than his American colleague (hence his October 1944 visit to Moscow and "spheres of influence" agreement with Stalin referred to above), but as the American participation in the war grew in magnitude, British influence declined, and he had to defer to the wishes of the Americans. It was not softness on communism, as charged by some critics of wartime diplomacy, but rather a desire for a quick military decision, that prompted Roosevelt to cooperate as he did with Stalin despite the fears of Churchill.

The Yalta Conference was the second attended personally by Stalin, Churchill and Roosevelt. It lasted from the 4th to the 11th of February 1945. A plan to divide Germany into zones of occupation, which had been devised in 1943 by a committee under British Deputy Prime Minister Clement Attlee, was formally accepted with the addition of a fourth zone taken from the British and American zones for the French to occupy. Berlin, which lay within the Russian Zone, was divided into four zones of occupation also. Access to Berlin by the Western powers was not as clearly worked out as it should have been.

Such lack of precision was characteristic of other parts of the Yalta agreements as well, leading to future disputes and recriminations between the Western powers and the Russians. Stalin suggested a figure of $20 billion in reparations to be taken from German heavy industry and other assets, and Roosevelt and Churchill agreed this might be a goal but felt it might have to be modified later depending on conditions in Germany. A Declaration on Liberated Europe promised to assist liberated nations in solving problems through elections and by "democratic" means.

In Poland, Churchill and Roosevelt had to allow Stalin to do what he pleased. An eastern frontier was established, corresponding roughly to the old Curzon Line drawn after World War I. Poland, in turn, was allowed to occupy territory in the west up to the line of the Oder and Neisse rivers. These boundaries were not, however, agreed upon as permanent boundaries but might be negotiated later when a peace treaty could be made with Germany. In fact they became permanent when relations between the wartime allies broke down and the Cold War began.

It was agreed that the nucleus of the post-war Polish government would be Stalin's Lublin Committee. The only concession was an agreement to add a number of "democratic leaders" (London Poles), but these, as it turned out, were powerless to affect the course of events and prevent an eventual total takeover of Polish government by the Communists.

In the Far East, in return for his agreement to enter the war against Japan after Germany's defeat, Stalin was promised the southern part of Sakhalin Island, the Kurile

Islands, a lease on the naval base at Port Arthur, a pre-eminent position in control of the commercial port of Dairen, and the use of Manchurian railroads.

There has been much dispute over these concessions and whether they were really necessary. Looking back it is easy to see that Japan was close to defeat, with American and Allied forces near enough to commence a destructive aerial bombardment of Japanese cities and to blockade the main islands. At that time, considering how tenaciously the Japanese had resisted in the various Pacific island campaigns, it was believed that the war might last a considerable time. An invasion of the main islands of Japan was being planned by the American command with estimates of considerable casualties. Any help from the Russians which might pin down the considerable Japanese forces in Manchuria was believed to be extremely desirable. No one could be sure of the secret atomic bomb — which was nearing completion in American laboratories but which had not yet been tested experimentally much less tried in actual combat.

The third summit meeting of the Big Three took place at Potsdam outside Berlin after the end of the European war but while the Pacific war was still going on. The conference began July 17, 1945, with Stalin, Churchill, and the new American President Harry Truman attending. (Roosevelt had died suddenly, shortly after the conclusion of the Yalta meeting.) While the conference was in session, the results of the British general election became known: Churchill was defeated, his place taken by his wartime deputy prime minister, the Labor leader Clement Attlee. The meeting confirmed, in detail, arrangements regarding Germany. A Potsdam Declaration, aimed at Japan, called for immediate Japanese surrender and hinted at the consequences that would ensue if that were not forthcoming. While at the conference, American leaders received the news of the successful testing of the first atomic bomb in the New Mexico desert, but the Japanese were given no clear warning that such a destructive weapon might be used against them.

The Atomic Bomb and the Defeat of Japan

Development of an atomic bomb became a theoretical possibility following the first splitting of uranium atoms by Otto Strassmann and Fritz Hahn at the Kaiser Wilhelm Institute in Berlin just before the war. The news spread quickly and both the British and Americans became concerned that the Germans might develop a weapon based on this principle, and therefore began an effort to build an atomic bomb first. In Britain a research project known as Tube Alloys was begun, and valuable work had been done by the time the United States entered the war. At that point the decision was made to concentrate the work in the United States with its vastly greater resources of power and industrial capacity. The Manhattan Engineering District under Major General Leslie Groves was established to manage the immense research, development, and production effort needed to develop an atomic weapon. By early 1945 it appeared that a weapon would soon be available for testing, and in July the successful test was completed.

President Truman established a committee of prominent scientists and leaders to determine how best to utilize the bomb. They advised the president that they could not devise any practical way of demonstrating the bomb. If it was to be used it had to be dropped on Japan, and President Truman then made the decision to do this. On August 6, 1945, the bomb was dropped by a single plane on Hiroshima and an entire city disappeared with the instantaneous loss of 70,000 lives. In time many other persons died from radiation poisoning and other effects. Since no surrender was received, a second bomb was dropped on Nagasaki, obliterating that city. Even the most fanatical of the Japanese leaders saw what was happening and surrender came quickly. The only departure from unconditional surrender was to allow the Japanese to retain their emperor (Hirohito), but only with the proviso that he would be subject in every respect to the orders of the occupation commander. The formal surrender took place September 2, 1945, in Tokyo Bay on the deck of the battleship *Missouri*, and the occupation of Japan began under the immediate control of the American commander General Douglas MacArthur.

EUROPE AFTER WORLD WAR II: 1945 TO 1953

General Nature of the Peace Settlement

After World War II there was no clear-cut settlement in treaty form as there was after World War I with the Versailles Treaty and other treaties which formed the Paris Peace Settlement of 1919. What planning there was had been done at the series of major wartime conferences between the leaders of Great Britain, the United States, and the Soviet Union. Then, in the years immediately following the German surrender, a series of de facto arrangements were made, shaped by the course of events during the occupation of Germany and the opening years of the so-called Cold War which followed the breakdown of the wartime alliance between the Western powers (Britain, France, and the U.S.) and the Soviet Union.

The Atlantic Charter

Anglo-American ideas about what the postwar world should be like were expressed by Roosevelt and Churchill at their meeting off the coast of Newfoundland in August 1941 in the form of an "Atlantic Charter." This was a general statement of goals: restoration of the sovereignty and self-government of nations conquered by Hitler, free access to world trade and resources, cooperation to improve living standards and economic security, and a peace that would ensure freedom from fear and want and stop the use of force and aggression as instruments of national policy.

Postwar Planning During World War II

At the Casablanca Conference the policy of requiring unconditional surrender by the Axis powers was announced. This ensured that at the end of the war all responsibility for government of the defeated nations would fall on the victors, and they would have a free hand in rebuilding government in those countries. No real planning was done in detail before the time arrived to meet this responsibility. It was done for the most part as the need actually arose.

At Teheran, the Big Three did discuss in a general way the occupation and demilitarization of Germany. They also laid the foundation for a post-war organization — the United Nations Organization — which like the earlier League of Nations was supposed to help regulate international relations and keep the peace and ensure friendly cooperation between the nations of the world.

One possible postwar plan for Germany was initially accepted by Roosevelt and Churchill in September 1944 and then quietly discarded when its impracticality became apparent to all. This was the Morgenthau Plan, named after U.S. Secretary of the Treasury Henry Morgenthau, Jr., who was instrumental in proposing it. This harsh scheme would have largely destroyed Germany as an industrial power and returned it to an agricultural/pastoral economy. Both British and Americans came quickly to realize that Germany could not return to the 18th century before the Industrial Revolution. They also realized that the resources of German heavy industry would be necessary to the recovery and vitality of the rest of Europe. This episode did point up the importance of a healthy German economy to Europe as a whole, and Allied recognition of this.

At the Yalta Conference early in 1945, the Big Three agreed on a number of matters, at least tentatively. The eastern boundary of Poland was set approximately at the old Curzon Line which had been proposed at the end of World War I to run as closely as possible along ethnic lines separating Poles and Russians. Poland was to occupy formerly German territory in the West including the old Polish Corridor, Danzig (Gdansk), and territory up to the Oder and Neisse rivers. Germany was to be disarmed and divided into four zones of occupation: Russian, British, and American, and a zone for France taken from what had been originally agreed to be British and American territory. The principle of German reparations was established but no firm figure was set. Half of the reparations were to go to the Soviet Union.

At Yalta, agreement was also reached with regard to a government for Poland. The Communist Lublin Committee established by Stalin was to be the nucleus of a provisional government with the addition of representatives of other "democratic" elements (*i.e.*, the London Polish Government recognized by Britain and the U.S.). A verbal agreement for the "earliest possible establishment through free elections of governments responsive to the will of the people" cost Stalin little, and there proved to be no way in any event for the other powers to ensure the integrity of such elections if held. The Declaration on Liberated Europe, with its promise of rights of self-determination, provided a false sense of agreement.

The territorial arrangements with regard to Poland and the eastern boundary of Germany, agreed to provisionally at Yalta, were confirmed at Potsdam in July following the German surrender. Although the arrangements were to be provisional pending a formal peace treaty with Germany, they became permanent when no agreement could be reached among the wartime allies on a German treaty.

At Potsdam, agreement was also reached to sign peace treaties as soon as possible with former German allies. A Council of Foreign Ministers was established to draft the treaties. Several meetings were held in 1946 and 1947 and treaties were signed with Italy, Rumania, Hungary, Bulgaria, and Finland. These states paid reparations and agreed to some territorial readjustments as a price for peace. No agreement could be reached on Japan or Germany. In 1951 the Western powers led by the U.S. concluded a treaty with Japan without Russian participation. The latter made their own treaty in 1956. A final meeting of the Council of Foreign Ministers broke up in 1947 over Germany, and no peace treaty was ever signed with that country. The division of Germany for purposes of occupation and military government became permanent with the three Western zones joining and eventually becoming the Federal Republic of Germany and the Russian zone becoming the German Democratic Republic.

Arrangements for the United Nations Organization were confirmed at the Yalta Conference: the large powers would predominate in a Security Council where they would have permanent seats together with several other powers elected from time to time from among the other members of the U.N.O. Consent of all the permanent members was necessary for any action to be taken by the Security Council (thus giving the large powers a veto). The General Assembly was to include all members.

EASTERN EUROPE: 1945 – 1953

The Soviet Union

The ability of the Soviet Union to withstand the terrific pressure of the German invasion and to recover, drive back, and destroy the bulk of the German invaders indicated its great inherent strength. Despite these victories, the Russian government faced tremendous immediate problems. Much of European Russia had been devastated and about 25 million people made homeless. Recovery was achieved using the same drastic, dictatorial methods used by the Communists during the 1930s. Stalin's dictatorship became more firmly entrenched than ever. Any potential opposition was purged. In March 1946 a fourth five-year plan was adopted by the Supreme Soviet intended to increase industrial output to a level 50% higher than before the war. Industrial equipment was collected from areas occupied by the Red Army. In 1947 the state planning commission announced that while goals had not been met in 1946, the yearly goal for 1947 had been surpassed. A bad harvest and food shortage in 1946 had been relieved by a good harvest in 1947, and in December 1947, the government announced the end of food rationing. At the same time a drastic currency devaluation was put through which brought immediate hardship to many people but strengthened the Soviet economy in the long run. As a result of these and other forceful and energetic measures, the Soviet Union was able within a few years to make good most of the wartime damage and to surpass pre-war levels of production. While this was being done at home Stalin pursued an aggressive foreign policy and established a series of Soviet satellite states in Eastern Europe.

The Communization of Eastern Europe

The fate of Eastern Europe (including Poland, Hungary, Rumania, Bulgaria, Czechoslovakia, and the Russian zone of Germany) from 1945 on was determined by the presence of Russian armies in that area. Stalin undoubtedly wanted a group of friendly nations on his western border from which invasion had come twice during his lifetime. The Russian Communists were also determined to support the advance of a communist system similar to that developed in Russia into the countries of Eastern Europe. The presence of the Red Army allowed Russia to do this just as the presence of American forces in Japan determined the postwar course of that nation.

Communization of Eastern Europe and the establishment of regimes in the satellite areas of the Soviet Union occurred in stages over a three year period following the end of the war. The timetable of events varied in each country. Coalitions with other parties existed first, with the Communists forming a front with socialist and peasant parties. Initial measures were taken to punish those who had collaborated with the Nazis during the wartime occupation, on measures such as land reform. Eventually all opposition parties were ousted and in each case the government became one totally dominated by the local Communist party.

Poland: A Test Case

As agreed at Yalta, the Lublin Committee was expanded into a provisional government by the inclusion of Stanislas Mikolajczyk and other leaders from the London Polish government in exile. Communists occupied ministries controlling police, internal affairs, and the military, ensuring that power eventually remained in their control. The Polish Workers (Communist) Party knew it had very little backing among the Polish people who were strongly Catholic and anti-Russian, and they maintained tight control over them from the beginning. Elections agreed to at Yalta were finally held in 1947, but under conditions that made the victory of the Communists inevitable. Mikolajczyk, frustrated in his efforts to influence the government, resigned, went into opposition, and then finally fled the country later in 1947.

Hungary

Toward the end of the war, with German control weakened by defeats at the hands of the Russians, the Hungarian government changed hands and a new regime concluded an armistice on January 20, 1945. Hungary then changed sides and joined the United Nations in the war against Germany. In November 1945 a general election gave victory to the anti-Communist Smallholders Party, whose leader, Zoltan Tildy, formed a coalition government. The government found itself in increasing economic difficulties, and by 1947 the Communists — with Soviet support — began a purge and takeover of the government. In February 1947 Bela Kovacs, secretary general of the Smallholders Party, was arrested and charged with plotting against the Soviet occupation forces. A general election held in August gave the Communists a majority. In January 1948 the Communists engineered a fusion of Communists and Social Democrats into a United Workers Party in which the Communists were dominant. Although the Smallholders Party still held some seats in the cabinet, effective power was in the hands of deputy premier Matyas Rakosi (Communist). A new constitution was promulgated August 7, 1949. The Communist regime was now firmly established and began a program of nationalization of industry followed by a five-year plan of development on the Russian model.

The refusal of the Roman Catholic Church in Hungary to make concessions to the government led to the arrest and trial of Josef Cardinal Mindszenty, who was sentenced in February 1949 to life imprisonment. Other bishops continued their opposition to the government for about two years before they finally took an oath of allegiance to the people's republic in July 1951.

Bulgaria

Postwar developments in Bulgaria were decisively influenced by the Red Army which invaded the country in 1944. The Soviet-sponsored government established in September contained only a few Communists, but they occupied key positions of power. Bulgaria formally capitulated on October 28, 1944, and remained under occupation by the Red Army. An election held in November 1945 gave overwhelming support to a Communist-controlled coalition called the Fatherland Front. In 1946 the Communists made a sweeping purge of the government, executing or removing some 1,500 high-ranking officials of the old regime and many more lesser government officials. A referendum in September formally rejected any restoration of the pre-war monarchy, and later that same month Bulgaria was declared a people's republic.

With considerable government interference, a constituent assembly was elected with a Communist majority. Veteran Communist Georgi Dimitrov returned from Moscow to become premier in February 1947. In that year a Bulgarian Peace Treaty was signed at Paris requiring Bulgaria to pay indemnities and limiting the size of its armed forces. During 1947 the government began a program of nationalization by taking over banks and industries. In December, Soviet forces ended their occupation, leaving behind a firmly entrenched Communist regime which signed a treaty of friendship with the Soviet Union the following year.

Rumania

During the war, Rumania, was governed by a pro-fascist regime which allied the country with the Axis. With Russian armies invading the country, King Michael dismissed the government and accepted armistice terms from the United Nations. The Russians occupied the capital of Bucharest in August 1944. As in other areas of Eastern Europe, a coalition government was first formed with Communists participating along with other parties, but from the beginning the Communists held the real power. In November 1945 a general election took place preceded by a campaign of government violence against opposition parties. During 1947 the leaders of opposition parties such as the National Peasant Party were arrested and sentenced to prison for espionage and treason and their parties dissolved. At the end of the year, King Michael abdicated under Communist pressure. Following elections in 1948, a new constitution was adopted patterned after the Russian model. Relations with Western powers became virtually nil because of accusations of espionage made against Western diplomats. By the end of 1949 Rumania had become completely Communist and a satellite of the Soviet Union.

East Germany

In the Russian zone in Eastern Germany a Soviet satellite state was also established. During the Nazi period, a number of German Communists fled to Moscow. When the Red Army invaded Germany, these exiles returned under the leadership of Wilhelm Pieck and Otto Grotewohl. As relations broke down between the four occupying powers, the Soviet authorities gradually created a Communist state in their zone. Elections in May 1948 resulted in a constituent assembly with a two-thirds majority of Communists. By the end of the month a draft constitution had been approved. On October 7, 1948, a German Democratic Republic was established. Pieck became president and Grotewohl head of a predominantly Communist cabinet. The Soviet military regime was replaced by a Soviet Control Commission. In June 1950 an agreement with Poland granted formal recognition of the Oder-Neisse Line as the boundary between the two states. Economic progress was unsatisfactory for most of the population, and on June 16 – 17, 1953, riots occurred in East Berlin which were suppressed by Soviet forces using tanks. In East Germany a program of economic reform was announced which eventually brought some improvement.

Special Cases

Czechoslovakia is an example of a country whose government tried to remain relatively free and democratic, while at the same time attempted to reach agreement with the Soviet Union that would provide the basis for peaceful coexistence with Russia after the war. The government in exile in London under President Eduard Benes maintained good relations with Moscow during the war. In April 1945 Benes appointed a national front government which was a genuine coalition of parties. The government moved to Prague May 10, 1945. A sweeping purge of those who had collaborated with the Germans was carried out. In addition, on August 3 all those ethnic Germans living in the Sudetenland and elsewhere in the country were deprived of their citizenship and eventually expelled. The period from October 1945 to June 1946 was devoted to choosing a national assembly and establishing a permanent government. Elections held in May 1946 gave the Communists 114 of 300 assembly seats and the Communist Klement Gottwald formed a coalition cabinet. Benes was unanimously re-elected president of the republic. On July 7, 1947, the Czech government decided to accept Marshall Plan aid and to participate in the carrying-out of the plan. At this point Soviet pressure caused the Czech government to break off this policy and withdraw.

The period of genuine coalition government lasted about three years in Czechoslovakia. But here as elsewhere in Eastern Europe, the Communists seized total control of the government, eliminating other political elements. The Communist coup was carried out February 26, 1948. The Communist Party had prepared by infiltrating members into government services and trade unions. With Russian support they then put pressure on President Benes to agree to a cabinet under Klement Gottwald which would be primarily Communist. On March 10 a major obstacle to communization was removed when Foreign Minister Jan Masaryk (son of Thomas Masaryk, founder of the Czech Republic) was killed in a fall from his office window which the authorities reported as suicide. A far-reaching purge in the next several months transformed a democratic Czechoslovakia into a "people's democracy" with a single party government. On May 9 a constituent assembly adopted a new constitution. National elections, in which only a single list of candidates (Communist) appeared on the ballot, confirmed the Communist victory. President Benes resigned June 7 because of ill health and died shortly after on September 3. On June 14, Klement Gottwald became the new president and on January 1, 1949, a Soviet-style five year plan of industrial development began with the aim of making the country independent of the West.

In June 1949 a campaign began against the Roman Catholic Church which as elsewhere in Eastern Europe proved to be a source of opposition to the Communist program. The government formed its own Catholic Action Committee to take control of the local church from Archbishop Joseph Beran and the Catholic hierarchy. On October 14 the government assumed full control of all Catholic affairs. The Catholic clergy were required to swear a loyalty oath to the Communist state.

Czech politics followed a course of increasingly repressive measures paralleling that of Stalin during his last years in the Soviet Union. In 1950 a series of purges were carried out against enemies of the government, including some of its own members who were accused of anti-Soviet, pro-Western activities. Beginning in April, the Czech military was completely reorganized on Soviet lines. In March 1951 further purges were carried out to remove "Titoist" elements (a reference to the Yugoslav Communist leader whose independent policy had earned him the enmity of Stalin). Reports of economic difficulties, including a severe shortage of coal and the failure of a program to collectivize farming, were made public by the government in 1952. Simultaneously, a mass treason trial opened in November. At the trial, Rudolph Slansky, former Czech Communist Party Secretary General, pleaded guilty to treason, espionage, and sabotage.

In Yugoslavia, Marshal Tito and his Communist partisan movement emerged from the war in a strong position because of their effective campaign against the German occupation. Tito was able to establish a Communist government despite considerable pressure from Stalin, and pursue a course independent of the Soviet Union unique among the countries of Eastern Europe.

Elections held November 11, 1945 gave victory to Tito's Communist-dominated National Front. A few days later the Yugoslav monarchy was abolished and the country declared to be the Federal People's Republic of Yugoslavia. A new constitution was adopted January 31, 1946. The new regime was recognized by the Western powers despite its Communist nature and pro-Soviet inclination. Enemies of the new regime were dealt with severely. General Drazha Mihailovich, leader of an anti-Tito wartime resistance movement, was captured, tried, and executed July 17. Archbishop Stepinac, the Catholic leader of Croatia, was arrested on charges of collaborating with the Germans and sentenced to 17 years imprisonment at hard labor.

In 1947 Yugoslavia appeared to follow the lead of the other East European states when it concluded treaties of friendship and alliance with a number of these states and became a founding member of the Communist Information Agency (Cominform) — an organization created to take the place of the old Communist International which had been abolished by Stalin in 1943 as a gesture of goodwill to his wartime allies. In April 1948, Tito announced the start of a five-year plan of development. Tito followed a policy independent of the wishes of Stalin, causing the Russian dictator to try to exert pressure on Yugoslavia and finally to recall Russian advisors and break off relations. On June 28, 1948, the Cominform formally expelled Yugoslavia.

Tito retained the support of his own party, however, when he denied Cominform charges against him at a Congress of the Yugoslavian Communist Party and received a vote of confidence. The dispute continued in 1949 when the satellites of Eastern Europe breaking off economic relations with Yugoslavia. In September the Soviet Union denounced its Treaty of Friendship with Tito's regime. Tito's position was shown to be secure, however, when elections in March 1950 gave overwhelming victory to his People's Front candidates. Tito followed a policy of informal rapprochement with the West. He announced his opposition to Chinese intervention in the Korean War; established diplomatic relations with Greece, and withdrew support from the Communist guerrillas waging war against the government. Tito also made overtures to Italy to repair relations with that country. In November 1951 Tito even went so far as to make an agreement with the United States for the latter to supply equipment, materiel, and services to the Yugoslavian army. In July 1952 the United States agreed to supply tanks, artillery, and jet aircraft to the Yugoslavs despite the fact that Tito — while retaining independence of Stalin — remained staunchly Communist in his government of Yugoslavia.

WESTERN EUROPE: 1945-1953

Italy

In Italy, following the end of hostilities with Germany, the leaders of the Resistance in the north ousted Premier Ivan Bonomi and placed one of their own top leaders, Ferruccio Parri, in power. Parri was the leader of a faction — the Party of Action — which was socialist in its program. Although he was a man of great moral stature, he was a poor administrator and did not appeal to the public. He was left politically isolated when the Socialist leader Pietro Nenni made an alliance with the Communists. Meanwhile, more conservative forces had been gathering strength, and in November 1945, Parri was forced to resign.

The monarchy which had governed Italy since the time of unification in the mid-19th century was now discarded in favor of a republic. On May 9, 1946, King Victor Emmanuel III, compromised by his association with Mussolini's Fascist regime, resigned in favor of his son, who became King Umberto II. His reign was short-lived, for a referendum in June 1946 established a republic. In simultaneous elections for a constituent assembly, three parties predominated: the Social Democrats with 115 members, the Communists with 104, and the Christian Democrats with 207. Under the new regime Enrico de Nicola was chosen president and Alcide de Gasperi formed a new coalition cabinet.

The Christian Democrats and their leader Alcide de Gasperi dominated Italian politics for the next several years. On February 10, 1947, a peace treaty was signed at Paris. Italy paid $350 million in reparations and suffered some minor losses of territory. Trieste, which was in dispute between Italy and Yugoslavia, became a free territory. De Gasperi's government followed a policy of cooperation with the West and kept Italy non-Communist. In April 1948 in the first elections under the new constitution, the Christian Democrats won an absolute majority of seats in the Italian parliament. The issue of communism remained very much alive, and there was considerable Communist-inspired unrest, especially after an attempt was made on the life of the Communist leader Palmiro Togliatti. The Marshall Plan helped stabilize the situation in Italy. In 1948, Italy received $601 million in aid vital to the Italian economy. On April 4, 1949, Italy signed the North Atlantic Treaty and became a member of NATO, firmly allied to the West. The de Gasperi era came to an end in 1953. He won a narrow electoral victory as the head of a coalition in June and resigned July 28 after a vote of no confidence. He died a year later, August 19, 1954.

France

In the last two years of the war, France recovered sufficiently under the leadership of General Charles de Gaulle to begin playing a significant military and political role once again. In July 1944 the United States recognized de Gaulle's Committee of National Liberation as the de facto government of those areas liberated from the German occupation. As the war ended, this provisional government put through a purge of collaborators, including Marshal Petain and Pierre Laval, who had headed the Vichy regime during the war.

In October 1945 elections for a constituent assembly showed the strength of left-wing forces: Communists, 152; Socialists, 151; and the Popular Republican Movement (MRP), 138. De Gaulle, after a period in which he tried to work with the more radical forces, finally resigned in January 1947 and went into retirement. In May 1946 a popular referendum rejected the proposed constitution. In June a new assembly was elected, dominated by the MRP with the Communists second and the Socialists third. A revised constitution was adopted in October establishing a Fourth Republic, very much like the Third, with a weak executive dominated by a strong legislature. This situation resulted in cabinet instability with a series of governments over the next several years. Communist agitation and obstructionism combined with economic difficulties created an increasingly wide split between Communist and non-Communist members of the cabinet which resulted in the exclusion of five Communist members in May 1947.

Meanwhile General de Gaulle had assumed control of a nationwide *Rassemblement du Peuple Français* (RPF) intended to unify non-Communist elements and reform the system of government. For a time the RPF grew in strength at both the local and national level although de Gaulle himself remained out of office. Then, with the lessening of the Communist danger and improvements in the economy, moderates began to oppose what they perceived to be de Gaulle's authoritarian tendencies. By 1953 the RPF had faded from the scene, and de Gaulle returned to retirement.

Economically, France became a welfare state. De Gaulle, during his provisional government, inaugurated this welfare state to associate the working classes with a new spirit of national unity and to deprive the Communists of their propaganda advantage. During the year and a half following de Gaulle's retirement, the three parties (Socialist, Communist and MRP) which dominated politics during that period agreed on a program building on reforms begun during the Popular Front of the 1930s. This program, which included nationalization of coal mines, banking, insurance, gas and electricity as well as allowances for dependent children, was the beginning of a comprehensive system of social security legislation which eventually came to cover more than 50% of the French people.

These changes were accepted by all subsequent regimes as a fait accompli. Although excessively bureaucratic and regulatory, the welfare state did provide a cushion of security for the French population during the period of inflation and economic hardship in the immediate postwar years prior to the advent of the Marshall Plan. The establishment of a national planning office under Jean Monnet was a significant achievement which provided the French government with a framework for guiding economic development which Italy and West Germany lacked. This was important in directing French resources effectively when production began to rise during the prosperous years of the 1950s.

In foreign affairs France played a role in the occupation of Germany. In addition, the Fourth Republic was faced with two major problems abroad when it attempted to assert its authority over Indochina and Algeria. The Indochina situation resulted in a long and costly war against nationalists and Communists under Ho Chi Minh. French involvement ended with the Geneva accords of 1954 and French withdrawal. The Algerian struggle reached a crisis in 1958 which resulted in the return to power of General de Gaulle and the creation of a new Fifth Republic.

Germany

In May 1945, when Germany surrendered unconditionally, the country lay in ruins and faced a tremendous job of recovering economically and politically from the tragic consequences of the Hitler era. About three-quarters of city houses had been gutted by air raids, industry was in a shambles, and the country was divided into zones of occupation ruled by foreign military governors. Economic chaos was the rule, currency was virtually worthless, food was in short supply, and the black market flourished for those who could afford to buy in it. By the Potsdam agreements Germany had lost about one-quarter of its pre-war territory. In addition, some 12 million expelled people of German origin driven from their homes in countries like Poland and Czechoslovakia had to be fed, housed and clothed along with the indigenous population.

Demilitarization, denazification, and democratization were the initial goals of the occupation forces. All four wartime allies agreed on the trial of leading Nazis for a variety of war crimes and "crimes against humanity." An International Military Tribunal was established at Nuremburg to try 22 major war criminals and lesser courts tried many others. The four prosecuting powers gathered massive evidence of the crimes of the Hitler era from captured German archives, interviews, etc., and introduced it into evidence. Most of the defendants were executed, although a few like Rudolf Hess were given life imprisonment. At the time and later, questions were raised concerning the proceedings. Some charges such as the waging of aggressive war and genocide were new to jurisprudence. There was also the question of whether this was not simply "victors' justice." Also, one of the prosecuting powers was the Soviet Union which many felt was guilty of some of the same crimes charged against the Nazi defendants.

The denazification program met with indifferent success. It started out as an effort to investigate everyone who had any connection to the Nazi Party. This included so many that the proceedings became bogged down. It became apparent after a time that not all could be investigated because of the sheer magnitude of the task. Some important Nazi officials were found and punished. Often it was easier to prosecute those less involved, and some important offenders escaped. There was quiet sabotage and a conspiracy of silence by a cynical population. Eventually wider amnesties were granted. The process never officially ended but simply faded away.

The re-establishment of German government in the Western zones met with more success. As relations between the three Western powers and the Soviets gradually broke down in Germany, East and West became separate states. In the West the British and American zones were fused into one in 1946, with the French joining in 1948. Political parties were gradually re-established. First local government was once again run by Germans under close supervision, then gradually more independence was accorded to the Germans to govern themselves at the higher state level. Political parties were authorized by the end of 1945. In January 1946 elections for local offices in the American zone the Christian Democrats were first and the Social Democrats second. Elections in the British and French zones brought the same results.

During 1947 there were two meetings of the Council of Foreign Ministers to work out a peace treaty for Germany. Both failed and the occupying powers began to go their own way in their own zones — the Russians to create a Communist satellite state in East Germany and the British, Americans, and French to create a West German Federal Republic.

In February 1948 a bi-zonal charter granted further powers of government to the Germans in the American and British zones. During 1948 the Allied Control Council (comprised of the military commanders in the four zones) broke down. The Russian delegate walked out of the Council after charging that the three Western powers were undermining four-power cooperation in Germany. Later that year the Russians and East Germans, in an effort to force the Western powers out of their zones in Berlin, began a blockade of the city which was located within the Russian zone. The response was an allied airlift to supply the city, and eventually after some months the blockade was called off.

Meanwhile reconstruction in western Germany proceeded. On June 1, 1948, a six-power agreement of the three Western powers and Belgium, the Netherlands, and Luxembourg was reached, calling for international control of the Ruhr industrial area, German representation in the European Recovery Program (Marshall Plan), and the drafting of a federal constitution for a western Germany.

In April 1949 the three Western powers agreed on an Occupation Statute for Western Germany which gave the Germans considerable autonomy at the national level while reserving wide powers of intervention to the occupying powers. In May a parliamentary council representing the state governments adopted a Basic Law for a Federal Republic of Germany with its capital at Bonn. Elections in August gave the Christian Democrats a slight lead over the Social Democrats, and the next month Konrad Adenauer (Christian Democrat) became Chancellor of the new West German government. Theodore Heuss (Free Democrat) was elected president. For the next 14 years Adenauer (who was 73 at the start) and the Christian Democrats remained in power.

West Germany regained complete independence and sovereignty within a short period of time. As a result of the Korean War (which started in 1950) and fear of Soviet aggression in Europe, the process moved rapidly. West German rearmament was felt by the Western powers to be necessary to the defense of Western Europe. West Germany became firmly allied with the West and eventually with the military organization within NATO.

It should be noted that West German economic recovery had made it the strongest industrial power of Western Europe. Wartime damage to German industry was less than appeared on the surface, and despite early taking of industrial assets as reparations, recovery was rapid once the Marshall Plan came into being. Even the expellees from the east were an asset as they provided extra labor — sometimes skilled. A program of industrial expansion with careful planning and investments, aided by the willingness of the population to accept relatively modest living standards and to work hard, paid dividends. There was little labor strife and for several years no need to provide for military expenditures. By 1950 industrial production surpassed prewar production. All of this made West Germany a great potential asset in the defense of Western Europe.

The possibility of West German rearmament aroused strong protests from the Soviet Union and opposition within West Germany itself from the Social Democrats. Nevertheless, in March 1954 President Heuss signed a constitutional amendment allowing German rearmament. By the end of the year Germany and France had worked out their disagreements over the Saar, and France joined the other Western powers in agreeing to German membership in the Western alliance. On May 5, 1955, West Germany gained sovereign status and joined NATO four days later, and the division of

Germany into two separate states was complete.

Postwar Great Britain

During the war, Great Britain mobilized its resources and more thoroughly and efficiently allocated man power than the Germans. The whole population was affected. Rationing of food and other necessities created hardships which had been shared equally by rich and poor alike. There was little black market activity. During the war the standard of living for the poor had actually risen. No reversal of this equality of sacrifice and opportunity was possible. A program of restoring the balance of trade, directing investment of resources to insure efficiency, and a vast new outlay for social services was agreed on by the parties even before the war ended. As early as 1942 a report known for its author, Sir William Beveridge, proposed "full employment in a free society" and social security "from the cradle to the grave."

As the war ended in May 1945, elections were held that returned a Labor government under Clement Attlee in July. The new government enacted an extensive program increasing unemployment insurance and providing insurance for old age and various contingencies. A comprehensive medical and health service for the entire population was established. Educational facilities were extended, and new planned housing projects built. Efforts were made to rehabilitate depressed areas.

In addition, Labor nationalized the Bank of England, the coal mines, transportation, iron and steel, and utilities (including electricity, gas, and communications). The Conservatives accepted much of this program but centered criticism on Labor's program of nationalizing the "commanding heights" of the economy — especially the iron and steel industry.

In order to complete this extensive series of reforms before its mandate expired in five years, Labor enacted a Parliament bill that reduced the power of the House of Lords to delay legislation from three years to one year. Inheritance and income taxes were sharply increased to pay for the new measures.

Labor found its majority reduced to seven from 148 in the 1950 elections. No further important reform legislation was passed in view of the very slim margin of voting power. In another election, in 1951 a Conservative majority was returned, and Winston Churchill became prime minister again. The new regime immediately reversed the nationalization of iron and steel. Other measures survived, however, especially the universal health care program which proved to be one of the most popular parts of the Labor achievement. The welfare state was permanently established in Britain through the activities of the Labor government. In April 1955 Churchill resigned for reasons of age and health and turned over the prime minister's office to Anthony Eden.

THE MARSHALL PLAN

European recovery from the effects of the war was slow for the first two or three years after 1945. Economic difficulty made for weakness in the face of Communism which, with Russian support, had taken over in Eastern Europe and threatened to take over in Western Europe as well if something was not done. In 1947 in a commencement address at Harvard University, George C. Marshall, the wartime army chief of staff who was now secretary of state under President Truman, proposed an aid program for Western European countries and others if they desired to join. This would revitalize the economies of the European nations and strengthen them to better resist Communism. The European Recovery Program (Marshall Plan) which began the next year showed substantial results in all the Western European countries that took part. By 1950 France and Italy were well above their 1938 levels of production, although population increases of about 10% ate up some of the gains. In Great Britain, Marshall Plan aid was of considerable importance. The most remarkable gains, however, were in West Germany. By early 1949, less than a year after the currency reform in the Western zones, West German production was about 85% of 1936 levels. The country soon experienced gains so great as to constitute what many called an "economic miracle." In Western Europe during the first two years of the Marshall Plan about $8 billion of American aid is estimated to have resulted in an overall expansion of some $30 billion annual output of goods and services.

THE MOVEMENT TOWARD WEST EUROPEAN ECONOMIC UNITY

In May 1951 French Foreign Minister Robert Schuman came forward with the Schuman Plan for a European Coal and Steel Community. This called for a pooling of resources in heavy industry and the elimination of tariffs throughout Western Europe (including France, West Germany, Italy, Belgium, the Netherlands, and Luxembourg). By April 1951 a treaty was signed incorporating the proposals of the Schuman Plan and creating the community from which other steps toward European unity grew (Common Market, General Agreement on Trade and Tariffs, etc.). The five-year period of implementation gave vested interests in each country time to adjust to new conditions.

THE COLD WAR

The question of Poland initiated the breakdown of the wartime alliance between the United States and Britain on the one hand and the U.S.S.R. on the other even before the war ended. It became plain that Stalin intended to install the Communists of the Lublin Committee as a Polish government. All of Eastern Europe was made Communist within two or three years from the end of the war in 1945. There were to be common policies for the whole of Germany, and there was no plan in the beginning to divide the country. However, seemingly irreconcilable differences between the Communist Soviet Union and the Western democracies were present from the beginning of the occupation — differences going back to the revolution in Russia in 1917 which embittered and complicated international relations through the 1920s and 1930s.

World War II was an exception to the rule of general hostility between capitalism and communism. It turned out, however, to be an alliance of expediency only. It therefore broke down when the common enemy was no longer a threat. More fundamental differences came to the fore again and made cooperation difficult if not impossible. In addition, given Stalin's fears and suspicious nature, one should not be surprised at the beginnings of a period of occasional limited conflict and tension short of outright military conflict known as the Cold War. Early in 1946, in a notable speech at Westminster College in Fulton, Missouri, Winston Churchill gave voice to the feelings of many when he announced that "from Stettin in the Baltic to Trieste on the Adriatic, an Iron Curtain has descended across the Continent."

CONFLICT IN GERMANY

After German surrender, the British and American armies withdrew from areas of

Germany and Eastern Europe to within the zones of occupation agreed to in the spring of 1945. A Control Council of allied military governors was created to establish common policies for Germany, but almost immediately there were difficulties with the Russians — a situation made no easier by the fact that there were additional differences between Britain, France, and the U.S. In the Eastern zone the Russians made it plain they intended to Communize the area in the same manner as in Eastern Europe. Early in 1946 they forced through a unification of the Social Democratic party and the Communists in which the Socialists, although originally much stronger, lost any separate identity or ability to influence policy.

The Russians followed their own economic policy, too. Reparations were a cause of recrimination. Figures of $20 billion had been mentioned but not formally agreed to at the wartime conferences with half to go to the Soviet Union. The Western powers had no intention, however, of allowing exports of supplies and equipment from their zones to proceed to a point where they would be forced to import goods just to keep their populations alive and at a minimal standard of living. Eventually the Americans and British halted any further deliveries from their zones to the Russians.

In their own zone the Russians not only dismantled factories and shipped industrial equipment to the Soviet Union but also took reparations from current production, which was specifically forbidden in the Potsdam agreements. The Soviets operated their zone as a single economic entity, violating the agreement that Germany was to be treated as a single unit for purposes of trade. They failed to furnish information and statistical returns for their zone. The Western powers were moved to respond. In May 1946 General Lucius Clay, American military governor, suspended reparations deliveries to the Russian zone in retaliation for Russian intransigence on the Control Council. In December 1946 in a speech at Stuttgart, Secretary of State James Byrnes announced the fusion of the American and British zones into an entity called Bizonia which the French later joined. The Western powers also raised the permitted level of German production and began to move from treating the Germans as conquered enemies to preparing them for a future role as allies of the West.

Breakdown of the Council of Foreign Ministers

Meanwhile, the Council of Foreign Ministers charged with drafting a peace treaty with Germany failed to reach agreement. The Council's last meeting was held November 25 to December 15, 1947, after which it adjourned never to meet again. It had limited successes in arranging treaties with minor states but completely failed to reach any compromise that would unite Germany. Likewise the Allied Control Council broke down. The last meeting was held in March 1948 when the Russian representative, Marshal Sokolovsky, walked out in protest over an Anglo-American invitation to the French to join their zone of Bizonia.

In the same year, Russia and its East German ally precipitated a great crisis in the form of a blockade of the Western sectors of Berlin, which led to the Berlin airlift. Russian action was prompted by a currency reform in the Western zones, but more broadly was aimed at forcing the Western powers to desist from their plan to establish a federal government which would eventually become independent.

THE CONTAINMENT POLICY

There were other areas of Western-Soviet disagreement. Iran, which had been occupied during the war to provide a route for transport of Lend-Lease supplies to Russia, was to be evacuated after the end of hostilities. From 1945 until 1947 Russian forces remained in the north and gave aid to a separatist movement seeking independence from the rest of Iran. Russia also put pressure on Turkey for control of the vital straits from the Black Sea to the Mediterranean — an area long contested by the great powers. In the Far East, the Soviets, although prevented by the American occupation from playing any important role in postwar Japan, did create a Communist regime in North Korea. They had occupied the northern part of the Korean peninsula in the days immediately preceding the Japanese surrender, and they later resisted efforts by the United Nations Organization to reunite the area with South Korea. In addition, the activities of the Chinese Communists (behind which the United States tended to see the machinations of the Soviet Union) and the outbreak of civil war with the Nationalist government under Chiang Kai-shek, did nothing to improve relations.

By 1947 the American government adopted a policy of "containment" to deal with this problem of Soviet Communist expansion. The Truman administration was strongly influenced by the reports of diplomat George Kennan, whose position as counselor at the embassy in Moscow gave him a chance to express his opinion of Russian intentions and how to deal with them. Kennan also wrote in 1947, under the pseudonym of "X", a widely read article entitled "The Sources of Soviet Conduct," published in the influential journal *Foreign Affairs*, in which he suggested a patient but firm, long-term policy of resisting Soviet expansionism. When General George C. Marshall was made secretary of state by President Truman in 1947, he established a Policy-Planning Staff in the State Department and made Kennan the first head.

The Truman Doctrine and aid to Greece

The Truman administration and its successors translated containment into a policy of military alliances, foreign aid, and American bases abroad to ring and contain the Soviet Union militarily, as well as a policy of resisting Communist-inspired wars of "liberation" in unstable areas of the world. The new policy was applied in Greece. In February 1947 the British government made known to Washington that it could no longer give aid to Turkey or to the royalist government installed in Greece by Britain in 1944–1945. The Greek government was experiencing attacks from Communist-led guerillas. On March 12 President Truman spoke to Congress. His message was a clear warning to the Soviet Union. The U.S., he announced, "would support free peoples who are resisting subjugation by armed minorities or by outside pressure." The president asked for $400 million to aid Turkey and Greece. Congress complied, and the aid thus proved effective in Greece.

The Berlin Blockade

Another great crisis, already alluded to, was the blockade of the three Western zones of Berlin — Stalin's answer to the merging of the American and British zones, the currency reform instituted in Western Germany, and his fear that a separate and independent West German state was being created. With the help of Communist East German "People's Police," barriers were raised to any traffic over land from the West to Berlin. President Truman responded with a massive airlift and also by stationing bombers in Britain capable of carrying nuclear weapons. The next year, with the failure of their efforts to drive the Western powers from Berlin, the Russians allowed land traffic to proceed once more. The creation of a West German state could only be countered by the creation of independent Communist East Germany. Neither side pushed the affair to extremes because of the fear of all-out war and the disastrous consequences for all.

The Chinese Civil War and the Establishment
of the People's Republic of China

During World War II the United States followed a policy of trying to bring about cooperation in the war against the Japanese between the Nationalist Government of Chiang Kai-shek and the Communists under Mao Tse-tung. The war ended with the Nationalist government recognized as the legitimate government, but the Communists had a strong position at Yenan in north China and a military force which had proved effective behind enemy lines and was therefore in a good position to compete with the government forces for control of former Japanese-occupied territory. With American help the Nationalists succeeded in garrisoning the cities of Manchuria and other occupied areas, but the Communists controlled much of the surrounding territory. They were able to get additional weapons and supplies from the surrendering Japanese.

The Marshall Mission

The uneasy truce which prevailed during the war almost immediately broke down. The Truman administration sent a diplomatic mission under General George C. Marshall (wartime army chief of staff) to mediate the conflict. Marshall was able to arrange a temporary truce, but even his considerable skill as a mediator proved inadequate to keep the truce from breaking down again into full-scale civil war.

Aid to the Nationalists: the Wedemeyer Mission

Despite the shortcomings of Chiang Kai-shek's regime, and in the atmosphere of the Cold War, the United States believed that it had to aid the Nationalists to prevent a Communist takeover. A mission was sent under General Albert Wedemeyer, supplies and equipment were provided, and loans made to support the Chinese currency and alleviate inflation. All this was to no avail as the Communist forces defeated the Nationalist armies in a series of battles and eventually drove them from the mainland to the island of Taiwan (Formosa). In October 1949, even before the campaign was finally completed, the Communists established the Chinese People's Republic with the capital once again at Peking (Beijing). The Chinese Communist victory was seen at the time by the American government and by many others in the West as a disaster in the Cold War and a defeat for containment.

THE KOREAN WAR

In 1945 the U.S.S.R. declared war on Japan after the dropping of the atomic bomb. During that brief period, Russian armies invaded Manchuria and occupied the northern part of Korea to approximately the 38th parallel. American forces occupied the southern part of Korea at the same time they occupied Japan itself. Agreements were made to divide Korea for administrative purposes along the 38th parallel, and Korea was split into two states: a Communist People's Republic of Korea in the North and a U.N.-backed Republic of South Korea below the 38th parallel. Efforts to unify the country through elections failed. South Korea was allowed to have only a small army equipped with no heavy weapons because of fears that President Syngman Rhee might use such an army to attack the North in his own effort to unify the country. A North Korean Army was created, however, which was supplied with some heavy weapons, such as tanks, by the Russians. By early in 1950 it appeared that the United States, which had withdrawn all its forces to Japan, would not defend South Korea, and the North Koreans were encouraged to launch an invasion and make all Korea Communist.

NSC-68

In the United States the Truman administration had been conducting a general review of the situation created by the Cold War in Europe and elsewhere. The conclusions reached were stated in a secret National Security Council study called NSC-68 which was completed in April 1950. The thesis was that the Soviet Union was an aggressor bent on overrunning Europe and Asia. To counter this, the United States should proceed to develop a thermonuclear (hydrogen) bomb. It should also obtain bases from which it could be delivered against the Soviet Union. United States troops, the document said, should reinforce NATO. Despite obvious reluctance on the part of Europeans who had suffered from German depredations during the war, West Germany should be rearmed. A considerable buildup of American armed forces was proposed with corresponding increases in the military budget. The sudden beginning of the Korean War in June 1950 only confirmed the need for a military program which otherwise might have been difficult to sell to Congress. The U.S. had already in 1947 created a separate Air Force and unified the three services under an overall Department of Defense. Congress also authorized the creation of the Central Intelligence Agency which began to function in the Cold War as not only a collector of intelligence but more and more as a clandestine arm of the government: carrying out secret, often illegal, operations abroad justified as being necessary to combat the clandestine operations of the Soviet Union and its satellites.

The North Korean Invasion

In June 1950 as the North Korean invasion of South Korea got underway, the United States decided on a policy of intervention. Taking advantage of a temporary absence of the Russian delegates, the United States was able to propose intervention and to get U.N. support. Before the war was over, 17 Western or Western-oriented countries had sent contingents to Korea. The South Korean forces, and U.S. forces sent from Japan, supplied most of the U.N. army. General Douglas MacArthur, commander of the occupation forces in Japan, was made overall U.N. commander. After initial defeats and withdrawals, MacArthur carried out an amphibious landing by the newly formed Tenth Corps at Inchon near the South Korean capital of Seoul. This force and the main Eighth Army driving north managed to surround and in a few weeks virtually destroy the invading army.

The Decision to Cross the 38th Parallel

By early fall of 1950 the U.N. forces were back to the 38th parallel and the question arose whether to stop there or continue north and reunify the whole of Korea. Despite warnings against this from the Chinese Communists sent through India, the decision was made to continue north. Some forces had actually reached the Manchurian border when in November the Chinese Communists entered the battle, creating what MacArthur called a new war. Initially surprised by the Chinese attack the U.N. forces were driven back below the 38th parallel again. The commander of the Eighth Army, General Walton Walker, was killed at this time, but under a new commander, General Matthew Ridgway, the army recovered, recaptured Seoul and reached a line approximately at the 38th parallel once again.

During this period of Chinese intervention the Truman administration had been increasingly in conflict with General MacArthur over what should be United States policy. Washington feared that widening the war to China proper might cause intervention by the Russians. In April 1951, after repeated warnings, President Truman relieved MacArthur of his command.

Instead of expanding the war, long and difficult negotiations were begun for an armistice. Eventually, in July 1953 an agreement was signed which still remains in force. No formal peace treaty was ever made, and the Korean War concluded with the situation essentially as it was before the North Korean invasion began. The Korean War prevented the United States from recognizing or establishing formal relations with the Chinese Communist regime (as Great Britain and other European nations had quickly done) until the time of the Nixon administration in the early 1970s.

STRENGTHENING OF NATO

One result of the Korean War was the strengthening of the NATO alliance begun in 1949. A mood approaching panic set in after the North Korean invasion began. The U.S. expressed its fear that NATO would be too weak to resist a possible Russian attack which might come while American forces were engaged in the Far East. The U.S. insisted on a policy of rearming West Germany. Eventually Western European nations accepted West German rearmament but only after agreement to make German forces part of a European defense under NATO control. This policy of military buildup changed the emphasis of foreign aid under the Marshall Plan. In the first two years the aid was primarily economic with few strings attached. Later it became increasingly military aid.

LOSS OF EUROPEAN OVERSEAS EMPIRES

World War II created disruptions that resulted in irresistible pressures for independence in areas overseas against the rule of European powers weakened by that struggle. British, Dutch, French, Portuguese, and Belgian empires in Asia and Africa virtually disappeared in the space of about 15 years following the war. In some instances withdrawal was accomplished by a relatively peaceful transfer of power (as with the British withdrawal from India in 1947), but in other cases the colonial power resisted separation and long, bitter military conflicts resulted. In every case independence created internal problems with which new governments had to struggle, often with violence ensuing and often with foreign intervention.

BRITISH OVERSEAS WITHDRAWAL

Palestine, Israel, and the Arab-Israeli Conflict

Britain received a mandate from the League of Nations following World War I to govern Palestine. Britain had earlier indicated in the Balfour Declaration of November 2, 1917, that it favored the creation of a Jewish "national home" in Palestine. The British position there was complicated by their involvement in the creation of Arab states such as Saudi Arabia and Transjordan, which were adamantly opposed to any Jewish state in Palestine.

Creation of Israel

Following World War II there was a considerable migration of Jews who had survived the Nazi Holocaust to Palestine to join Jews who had settled there earlier. Conflicts broke out with the Arabs. The British occupying forces tried to suppress the violence and to negotiate a settlement between the factions. In 1948, after negotiations failed to achieve agreement, the British, feeling they could no longer support the cost of occupation, announced their withdrawal. Zionist leaders then proclaimed the independent state of Israel and took up arms to fight the armies of Egypt, Syria, and other Arab states which invaded the Jewish-held area. The new Israeli state quickly proved its technological and military superiority by defeating the invaders. Over 500,000 Arabs were displaced from their homes in establishing Israel. Efforts to permanently relocate them failed, and they became a factor in the continued violence in the Middle East.

The Jews of Israel created a modern parliamentary state on the European model with an economy and technology superior to their Arab neighbors. The new state was thought by many Arabs to be simply another manifestation of European imperialism made worse by religious antagonisms.

Further Arab-Israeli Wars

Several further Arab-Israeli wars have served to keep the Middle East in turmoil. In 1956 the Israelis chose the opportunity created by the ill-fated Anglo-French attempt to retake the Suez Canal to launch their own attack on Egypt. Public opinion eventually forced the withdrawal of the British and French, and although the Israelis had achieved military successes, they found themselves barred from use of the Canal by Egypt, which was now in control.

In 1967 the Egyptians closed the Gulf of Aqaba to Israeli shipping, and this together with continued exclusion from the Suez Canal prompted Israel to launch a six-day war against Egypt (and Syria and Jordan, which were allied with Egypt). The Arab forces were badly defeated, and the Israelis occupied additional territory including the Jordanian sector of the city of Jerusalem. An additional million Arabs came under Israeli rule as a result of this campaign.

The Palestine Liberation Organization

Although defeated, the Arabs refused to sign any treaty or to come to terms with Israel. Palestinian refugees living in camps in states bordering Israel created grave problems. A Palestine Liberation Organization (PLO) was formed to fight for the establishment of an Arab Palestinian state on territory taken from Israel on the west bank of the Jordan River. The PLO resorted to terrorist tactics both against Israel and other states in support of their cause.

In October 1973 the Egyptians and Syrians launched an attack on Israel known as the Yom Kippur War. With some difficulty the attacks were repulsed. A settlement was mediated by American Secretary of State Henry Kissinger. The situation has remained unstable, however, with both sides resorting to border raids and other forms of violence short of full-scale war.

The Egyptian Revolution

The British exercised control over Egypt from the end of the 19th century and declared it a British protectorate in December 1914. In 1922 Egypt became nominally independent, and in 1936 an Anglo-Egyptian treaty provided for British forces to withdraw to the Suez Canal Zone where they might keep 10,000 troops. Britain could expand the force in time of war. During World War II the presence of British forces in Egypt, which was the British headquarters in the Middle East, resulted in fighting on Egyptian territory despite efforts by Egypt to remain neutral.

The government under King Farouk did little to alleviate the overriding problem of poverty after the war. In 1952 a group of army officers, including Gamal Abdel Nasser and Anwar Sadat, plotted against the government, and on July 23 the king was overthrown. For a short time the plotters ruled through a figurehead — General

Muhammad Naguib; a Revolutionary Command Council held the real power. Colonel Nasser, the outstanding figure of the group, replaced Naguib as premier in April 1954. A treaty with Britain later that year resulted in the withdrawal of all British troops from the Canal Zone.

The Suez Canal Crisis

Nasser made several agreements in 1955 and 1956 with Communist-bloc nations, establishing trade relations and obtaining weapons. The United States and Britain then withdrew offers of aid in building the Aswan Dam on the Nile River. Nasser in turn nationalized the Suez Canal shortly after the British garrison there had been withdrawn. A crisis ensued when Israeli forces suddenly invaded Egypt. Britain and France, ignoring U.N. attempts to mediate, gave an ultimatum to Israel and Egypt to cease fighting and withdraw from the Canal Zone. When this failed the two powers began a bombardment and invaded the area. Pressure from both the United States and the Soviet Union caused Britain, and then France and Israel to cease fire. A U.N. force was then formed to police the Canal Zone and the cease fire. Eventually foreign forces were withdrawn from Egypt, except that the Israelis remained in possession of the Gaza Strip.

India and Pakistan

British rule in India, the largest and most populous of the colonial areas ruled by Europeans, came to an end in 1947 with a relatively peaceful transfer of power. Pressure for self-government had grown in the 1930s, and the British had granted a constitution, a legislature, trained an Indian civil service, and made other concessions to Indian nationalism. During World War II Britain promised dominion status to India after the war. This did not satisfy the Indian Congress Party, whose leaders wanted full and immediate independence. Complications ensued when Muslim leaders, representing some 100 million Muslims, did not want to live in a state dominated by Hindus and the Congress Party and insisted on a state of their own.

Partition

The British decided to partition the subcontinent into two separate dominions which quickly became independent republics: India — predominantly Hindu with 350 million population, and Pakistan — predominantly Muslim with 75 million population. About 40 million Muslims remained within Indian borders. Independence resulted in bloody rioting between the religious factions, mass expulsions, and the emigration of millions of people. Perhaps a million people lost their lives before the rioting eventually died out. The territory of Kashmir remained in dispute but finally was joined to India in 1975.

India

India under Jawaharlal Nehru and the Congress Party became a parliamentary democracy. Nehru died in 1964. His daughter, Indira Gandhi, became prime minister from 1966 on. The country made economic progress, but gains were largely negated by a population increase to 600 million from 350 million. In 1975 Indira Gandhi was found guilty of electoral fraud. She resorted to force to keep herself in power. When elections were permitted in 1977 she was ousted by the opposition. Eventually her son, Rajiv Ghandi, became prime minister.

Pakistan

Pakistan retained the trappings of democracy with a written constitution and parliamentary form of government, but became in reality a military dictatorship. Gains in population outpaced economic growth as in India. In addition the country was divided into East and West Pakistan separated by 1,000 miles of Indian territory. The two areas had the same religion but different traditions, resulting in a quarrel that led East Pakistan in 1971 to declare itself the independent state of Bangladesh. The Pakistan government in Karachi sent military forces to the east to regain control and bloody fighting ensued. India then intervened militarily, and after defeating the Pakistani army, forced the recognition of an independent Bangladesh.

Malaya, Burma, and Ceylon

Malaya, Burma, and Ceylon were other parts of the British Asian empire that received their independence as did India and Pakistan. All three became members of the British Commonwealth with ties to Great Britain. The Commonwealth, which also includes some former British colonies in Africa, became a significant political grouping associated on an entirely voluntary basis. Malaya suffered nine years of internal strife which delayed independence to 1957 when the Federation of Malaya was created.

THE FRENCH IN INDOCHINA AND ALGERIA

Indochina

Following World War II the French returned to Indochina and attempted to restore their rule there. The opposition nationalist movement was led by the veteran Communist Ho Chi Minh. War broke out between the nationalists and the French forces. Despite materiel aid from the U.S., the French were unable to maintain their position in the north of Vietnam. In 1954 their army was surrounded at Dienbienphu and forced to surrender. This military disaster prompted a change of government in France.

The 1954 Geneva Conference: French Withdrawal

This new government under Premier Pierre Mendes-France negotiated French withdrawal at a conference held at Geneva, Switzerland in 1954. Cambodia and Laos became independent and Vietnam was partitioned at the 17th parallel. The North, with its capital at Hanoi, became a Communist state under Ho Chi Minh. The South remained non-Communist. Under the Geneva Accords, elections were to be held in the South to determine the fate of that area. However, the United States chose to intervene and support the regime of Ngo Dinh Diem, and elections were never held. Eventually a second Vietnamese war resulted with the United States playing the role earlier played by France.

Algeria

Following World War II there was nationalist agitation in Algeria, Tunisia, and Morocco. The French government granted independence to Tunisia and Morocco, but Algeria was considered to be different. It was legally part of metropolitan France. Government there was heavily weighted in favor of the French minority (about 10% of the total population), and the Arab majority had few rights. In 1954 a large-scale revolt of Arab nationalists broke out. The French government began a campaign of suppression lasting over seven years and involving as many as 500,000 troops. Military casualties totaled at least 100,000 Arabs and 10,000 French killed with thousands more civilian casualties. The savage campaign led to torture and other atrocities on both sides.

Army Revolt and Return of General de Gaulle

Egypt and other Arab states gave aid to the Algerian Liberation Front. Algerian terrorists spread the violence as far as Paris itself. The government of the Fourth Republic faced a military and financial burden with no clear end in sight. French Army officers in Algeria and European settlers were adamant, against any concessions, and eventually, under the leadership of General Jacques Massu (in Algeria) and General Raoul Salan (army chief of staff), created a committee of public safety and seized control of government in Algeria. The rebellion threatened to spread to France itself. It led to the downfall of the Fourth Republic and the return to power of General de Gaulle, who established the Fifth Republic with himself as a strong president.

Algerian Independence

De Gaulle moved step by step towards a policy first of autonomy and then independence for Algeria. In a referendum, on January 8, 1961, the French people approved of eventual Algerian self-determination. The army leaders then rebelled, forming a terrorist secret army (the OAS) to oppose de Gaulle's policy with bombings and assassinations. De Gaulle prevailed in the struggle, and in July 1962 French rule ended in Algeria. General Salan (OAS leader) was arrested, tried, and sentenced to life imprisonment. There was a mass exodus of Europeans from Algeria, but most Frenchmen were grateful to de Gaulle for ending the long Algerian conflict.

THE DUTCH AND INDONESIA

During World War II the Japanese conquered the Dutch East Indies. At the end of the war they recognized the independence of the area as Indonesia. When the Dutch attempted to return, four years of bloody fighting ensued against the nationalist forces of Achmed Sukarno. In 1949 the Dutch recognized Indonesian independence but with some ties still with The Netherlands. In 1954 the Indonesians dissolved all ties totally. Sukarno's regime became one of increasing dictatorship thinly disguised by terms like "guided democracy." The constitution was set aside, parliament suspended, and Sukarno became president for life. In 1966 Sukarno was overthrown and replaced by a more stable administration under General Suharto which made more economic and social progress.

THE COLD WAR AFTER THE DEATH OF STALIN

Following Stalin's death, Russian leaders — while maintaining an atmosphere first of tension and then of relaxation in international affairs — appeared more willing than Stalin to be conciliatory and to consider peaceful coexistence among the major competing economic and political systems.

Eisenhower and the 1955 Geneva Summit

In the U.S. the atmosphere also changed with the election of President Dwight Eisenhower; and despite the belligerent rhetoric of Secretary of State John Foster Dulles, conciliatory gestures were not always automatically considered appeasement of the Communists. In 1955 a summit conference of Eisenhower, the British and French leaders, and Khrushchev met at Geneva in an atmosphere more cordial than any since World War II. The "spirit of Geneva" did not last long, however.

The U-2 Incident and Breakup of the Paris Conference, 1960

The United States Central Intelligence Agency developed a high-flying reconnaissance aircraft known as the U-2. Under Eisenhower it was used to make secret flights over the Soviet Union in order to take aerial photographs. At first the Russians were unable to shoot the airplane down, but in 1960 a flight was shot down well inside the Soviet Union. The plane's pilot, Francis Gary Powers, was captured alive. At first the Eisenhower administration denied Russian charges of spying, but then when Khrushchev produced the pilot and remains of the aircraft, they admitted what had happened and accepted responsibility. A summit conference was due to convene shortly in Paris, and an indignant Khrushchev used the occasion to condemn Eisenhower and then break up the meeting.

Kennedy and Khrushchev: The Bay of Pigs Incident

John Kennedy replaced Eisenhower as president of the United States in 1960. He proved to be a "hard liner" in relations with the Soviet Union and a strong opponent of Communism. He inherited the American dispute with Cuban leader Fidel Castro, who had ousted the U.S.-backed, right-wing dictator Fulgencio Battista in January 1959. Castro had dealt with the problem of economic dependency on the U.S. by nationalizing many economic assets — sugar mills, oil refineries, banks — that were American owned. The U.S. retaliated with economic sanctions, and Castro established ties with the Soviet Union, which agreed to buy Cuban sugar and provide goods denied by the U.S. Eisenhower and the CIA then prepared a plan to overthrow Castro using Cuban exiles as an invasion force. Kennedy carried out this plan which resulted in a fiasco at the Bay of Pigs. The Cubans landed, the population did not rise to join them, and the small force was quickly overwhelmed.

Khrushchev and Berlin

After the Berlin Blockade of 1948–1949 Berlin became a symbol of freedom — an oasis of Western influence in the heart of East Germany. Thinking it best to keep Germany divided, Khrushchev tried to exert pressure on the Western powers through Berlin to recognize permanent division of Germany into two states. Late in 1958 he threatened to make unilateral changes in the status of Berlin, but backed down in 1959. In June 1961, following the U-2 incident and breakup of the Paris summit, Khrushchev presented an ultimatum to President Kennedy, threatening to sign a peace treaty with East Germany and then give the new state control over access to Berlin. Shortly after, the East German border was closed and a wall was built through Berlin separating the Russian and Western sectors and preventing any unauthorized travel or communication between them. Despite pressure to take a strong stand, Kennedy simply moved an additional 1,500 American troops to Berlin while accepting the wall rather than risk war.

The Cuban Missile Crisis

In an attempt to protect the Castro regime and to project its power to the borders of the U.S., Khrushchev initiated a policy of installing Russian missiles in Cuba. Aerial reconnaissance revealed this to the American government in October 1962. A 13-day crisis followed. President Kennedy established a "quarantine" of Cuba using the American Navy. (The term quarantine was used because a blockade is an act of war under traditional international law.) Eventually Russian ships, carrying the missiles and nuclear warheads to complete the installation, turned back rather than risk possible war. Khrushchev did obtain an American pledge not to invade Cuba and a commitment to remove American missiles from Turkey, but he had been publicly humiliated. For this and because of the failure of his domestic agricultural development program, his colleagues forced him to retire in 1964.

THE VIETNAM WAR

Before 1954 the conflict in Vietnam involved French armies against the Communist-led nationalist movement. By the 1954 Geneva Accords France withdrew its forces, Vietnam was divided at the 17th parallel, the Communists under Ho Chi Minh held the North, and the South became the Republic of Vietnam with an anti-Communist regime. Elections to unite the country were never held. Instead the United States began to play an ever larger role in South Vietnam, believing that if South Vietnam fell all Southeast Asia would fall like a row of dominos. First Eisenhower, then Kennedy, then Johnson believed this and reacted accordingly, and America's role increased until after 1964 the U.S. was engaged in a full-scale second Vietnam War with the hope of establishing an anti-Communist regime that could "win the hearts and minds of the people" and provide an effective barrier to further Communist expansion. China and the Soviet Union were involved in supporting North Vietnam and the liberation movement mainly by sending supplies and equipment of various kinds. Most NATO countries gave only lukewarm, if any, support to the American war in Vietnam. Eventually public opinion at home brought an end to America's most unpopular war, and Western Europe could breath more easily.

THE CHANGING BALANCE OF POWER

De Gaulle as the Leader of an Independent Europe

After his return to power in France in 1958, General de Gaulle endeavored to make France a leader in European affairs with himself as spokesman for a Europe that he hoped would be a counter to the "dual hegemony" of the U.S. and U.S.S.R. His policies at times were anti-British or anti-American. He vetoed British entry into the Common Market, developed an independent French nuclear force, and tried to bridge the gap between and East and West Europe. Despite his prestige as the last great wartime leader, he did not have great success. Nevertheless Western Europe came into its own as a factor in international affairs.

Detente

The policy of rapprochement interrupted by the Cuban Missile Crisis resumed. Despite the continuing war in Vietnam, Soviet and American leaders exchanged visits. From 1969 on, under President Nixon and National Security Adviser Henry Kissinger, the policy of better relations became known as detente. Negotiations on strategic arms resulted in the SALT I treaty signed during President Nixon's 1972 visit to Moscow. In this spirit of detente, trade between Western Europe and the Soviet Union increased several times. The Soviet Union, faced with agricultural problems, began to purchase large amounts of American grain. In 1975 agreements were reached at Helsinki in Finland between 35 nations for peaceful cooperation. All agreed to accept boundaries in Europe established following World War II, including the Oder-Neisse Line between the German Democratic Republic and Poland.

Nuclear Weapons and the Arms Race

Nuclear weapons were a growing concern in the U.S., the Soviet Union, and other countries—especially those of Western Europe. The enormous destructive power of these weapons had been first revealed when atomic bombs were dropped by the U.S. on Hiroshima and Nagasaki in August 1945. Initial debates on control of nuclear weapons were held in the United Nations at a time when the United States had a monopoly on the atomic bomb. The Soviet Union finally insisted by 1948 that the banning of atomic weapons was of primary importance. No agreement could be reached on inspection procedures, however.

Soon after this the Russians exploded their first atomic bomb. During 1949 and 1950, wars were taking place in Korea, Malaya, and Indochina, and rearmament was the dominant policy, with both the U.S. and the U.S.S.R. starting programs to develop more effective nuclear weapons. These included the hydrogen bomb whose awesome power had to be measured in terms of megatons of conventional explosive.

The war in Korea and the rearmament of West Germany within NATO prevented any serious disarmament negotiations. Europe was divided into separate armed camps: NATO, and the Warsaw Pact led by the Soviet Union. In the next several years the world moved into the age of rocketry, nuclear-powered submarines, and other military products of so-called "high technology." Russia tested its first bomb in 1949. By 1952 the British had tested an atomic bomb. The U.S. successfully developed and tested a thermonuclear weapon (H-bomb) in 1952. In 1953 the Russians exploded a similar weapon. In 1961 the Soviet Union exploded a 60-megaton H-bomb. The French joined the nuclear powers in February 1960. They tested an H-bomb in August 1968. China also became a nuclear power, exploding its first nuclear device in 1964. It fired its first rocket with a nuclear warhead in October 1966 and tested an H-bomb in June 1967. Even Israel and India built reactors with the potential for producing weapons.

The International Arms Trade and Military Expenditures

In the years following World War II, the U.S., the U.S.S.R., and many other countries maintained large standing military establishments—conventional as well as nuclear. An international trade in weapons and military supplies flourished in the 1960s and after with the U.S. and U.S.S.R. as the chief sources of supply. Between 1960 and 1975 the world's annual military expenditures nearly doubled. The U.S. and U.S.S.R accounted for about 60%. In less affluent Afro-Asian nations, spending on weapons expanded and helped contribute to political instability and mistrust. Before World War II, military expenditures are estimated to have been less than 1% of the total world gross national product. In 1983 the figure had risen to 6%.

Agreements on Nuclear Weapons

The radiation and fallout from the various testing programs created a fear that the atmosphere would be poisoned, damage of a genetic nature might be done to plants and animals, and unborn generations of humans might be endangered in ways which were only beginning to be understood. These years prompted the U.S., Britain, and the Soviet Union to sign in April 1963 a treaty to ban nuclear testing in the atmosphere, under water, and in outer space. France and China did not join but went on to develop weapons of their own. The proliferation of nuclear weapons prompted the U.S. and U.S.S.R. also to sign a non-proliferation treaty to which 62 nations subscribed. Among the exceptions were France, China, and West Germany. Following the Cuban Missile Crisis, a direct communications link between Washington and Moscow called the "hot line" was established in order to avoid misunderstandings that might trigger nuclear war. In 1976, in a period of relatively relaxed relations, the two superpowers agreed to limit underground testing to explosions no more than eight times the power of the Hiroshima bomb (the equivalent of 20,000 tons of conventional explosives). Finally, for the first time, in the late 1980s the Russians and the U.S. agreed to limited on-site inspection by outsiders of their tests as well as monitoring of the agreements.

The Space Race and its Implications

A large step was taken toward space exploration during World War II with the development of the German V-2 rocket. German rocket experts were recruited by both the U.S. and U.S.S.R. after World War II. In 1957 the Russians launched the first unmanned satellite to orbit the earth. For a time, they pulled ahead of the U.S. in development of rocket boosters able to put sizable payloads into space. The Russians achieved another first when they put a manned spacecraft into orbit.

Under President Kennedy space exploration was given priority and a goal set of putting a man on the moon by the end of the decade. The U.S. soon caught up with the Russians in the development of large rockets and achieved its goal of sending men to the moon in 1969.

Both nations deployed experimental space stations and unmanned probes of the planets. Many satellites for communication—and some for military purposes such as espionage by aerial photography—were launched in the period after 1960. Some cooperation was achieved when U.S. and Soviet astronauts orbited simultaneously and brought their ships together in outer space. Russia launched space probes to the vicinity of Venus and Mars. Then the U.S. succeeded in landing instruments on the surface of Mars which sent back photographs and other data. Some critics complained of the enormous cost of these activities and of the neglect of problems here on Earth, but others saw future benefits for all resulting.

The military of the U.S. and U.S.S.R. (and other nations to a lesser degree) took advantage of developments in space exploration, rocketry, and related sciences to develop self-propelled missiles of all sizes, including intercontinental ballistic missiles which could carry nuclear warheads across the continents in a matter of minutes. In neither country was an effective anti-missile defense developed; instead, each relied on a policy of deterrence. If the other side knew that its enemy had a missile force capable of surviving any initial attack and returning the attack against the original aggressor then no one would start a nuclear war because of the certainty that they, too, would be destroyed—the theory known as MAD, or mutually assured destruction.

The Reagan Strategic Defense Initiative

To date no sure defense against nuclear attack exists. Extensive civil defense programs are reported to exist in the former Soviet Union, Switzerland, and China which are designed to protect the populace in the event of nuclear attack. It is doubtful if these would prove very effective. Evacuation of civilians from cities that would be targets takes time—more time than would be available.

The alternative was to use missiles to destroy incoming missiles. The U.S. had a program of this sort in the 1950s and 1960s but gave it up in the SALT I agreements. The SALT I agreements also contained an Anti-Ballistic Missile Treaty limiting the use of ABMs. Many experts felt at the time that such a system with its complicated radar and computers simply could not be made effective against incoming missiles. Another development that threatened to overwhelm any conceivable defense was the multiple independently targeted re-entry vehicle—a missile with several warheads, each of which could be aimed independently at a separate target as the missile approached its destination.

The idea of a ballistic missile defense system surfaced again in the U.S. during the presidency of Ronald Reagan. This "Strategic Defense Initiative" quickly became known among its detractors as "Star Wars" (after a popular science fiction movie). The new proposal would rely on platforms in outer space from which particle beams, lasers, and other advanced devices would destroy incoming missiles.

Experts disagreed over the time required to develop and deploy SDI—assuming it could be built. In addition, there was wide disagreement over the vulnerability of such a system to enemy countermeasures In the late 1980s the U.S. Congress had started by funding research for such a system, but the ultimate outcome was uncertain. Reaction in the Soviet Union was predictably negative, and many in the West felt it would simply lead the Soviets to escalate the arms raise once again and invest heavily in weapons to defeat the system.

A NEW ERA BEGINS

Russia after Stalin

Joseph Stalin died in March 1953. His career had been one of undoubted achievements but at tremendous cost. Within Russia, Stalin established a dictatorship unparalleled in history. His ruthlessness and paranoid suspicions grew worse towards the end of his life. Postwar economic reconstruction was accompanied by ideological intolerance and a regime of terror and persecution accompanied by overtones of anti-Semitism. There were indications of a new series of purges coming when Stalin died.

A so-called "troika" consisting of Georgi Malenkov (Chairman of the Council of Ministers), Lavrenti Beria (Stalin's chief of police), and Vyacheslav Molotov (foreign minister) took over government. A power struggle took phce in which the first event was the secret trial and execution of Beria. Eventually a little-known party functionary, Nikita Khrushchev, became Communist Party General Secretary in 1954. Malenkov and Molotov were demoted to lesser positions and eventually disappeared from public view.

Khrushchev's Secret Speech and the Anti-Stalin Campaign

Khrushchev in 1956 delivered a "secret speech" to the 20th Congress of the Communist Party of the Soviet Union. It soon became public knowledge that he had accused Stalin of wholesale "violations of socialist legality" and of creating a "cult of personality." This signified the victory of Khrushchev's policy of relaxing the regime of terror and oppression of the Stalin years. The period became known as "The Thaw" after the title of a novel by Ilya Ehrenburg.

Change occurred in foreign affairs also. Khrushchev visited Belgrade and reestablished relations with Tito, admitting that there was more than one road to socialism. He also visited the United States, met with President Eisenhower, and toured the country. Later, relations became more tense after the U-2 spy plane incident. Khrushchev's policy generally was one where a period of relaxation would be followed by a period of pressure, threats, and tension.

Following the loss of face sustained by Russia as a result of the Cuban Missile Crisis and the failure of Khrushchev's domestic agricultural polices, he was forced out of the party leadership and lived in retirement in Moscow until his death in 1971.

Khrushchev's Successors: Brezhnev, Andropov, and Gorbachev

After Khrushchev's ouster, the leadership in the Central Committee divided power, making Leonid Brezhnev party secretary and Aleksei Kosygin chairman of the council of ministers, or premier. Brezhnev's party position ensured his dominance by the 1970s. In 1977 he presided over the adoption of a new constitution that altered the structure of the regime very little. The same year he was elected president by the Supreme Soviet.

Stalin's successors rehabilitated many of Stalin's victims. They also permitted somewhat greater freedom in literary and artistic matters and even allowed some political criticism. Controls were maintained, however, and sometimes were tightened. Anti-Semitism was also still present, and Soviet Jews were long denied permission to emigrate to Israel. American pressure may have helped to relax this policy in the 1970s when about 150,000 Jews were allowed to leave Russia. Other evidences of continued tight control were the 1974 arrest for treason and forcible deportation of the writer Alexander Solzhenitsyn and the arrest and internal exile for many years of the physicist Andrei Sakharov, who was an outspoken critic of the regime and its violations of human rights.

Brezhnev occupied the top position of power until his death in 1982. He was briefly succeeded by Yuri Andropov (a former secret police chief) and then by Mikhail Gorbachev, who carried out a further relaxation of the internal regime. Gorbachev pushed disarmament and detente in foreign relations, and attempted a wide range of internal reforms known as *perestroika* ("restructuring").

CHANGE IN EASTERN EUROPE

Poland

Khrushchev's speech denouncing Stalin was followed almost immediately by revolts in Poland and Hungary, apparently encouraged by what was happening in Russia. In Poland Wladyslaw Gomulka, previously discredited and imprisoned for "nationalist deviationism," emerged to take over the government. Khrushchev and the Russians decided to tolerate Gomulka, who had wide support. His regime proceeded to halt collectivization of agriculture and curb the use of political terror.

The Solidarity Movement

In the 1980s the trade union movement known as Solidarity and its leader, Lech Walesa, emerged as a political force, organizing mass protests in 1980–1981 and maintaining almost continuous pressure on the government headed by General Wojciech Jaruzelski. Despite government efforts to maintain strong central control and suppress the opposition, the strength of the movement was such that the ruling Communists were forced to recognize the opposition and make concessions.

Hungary

In Hungary in 1956 rioting against the Communist regime broke out and brought Imre Nagy to power. Nagy's policies went too far for the Russians, and Khrushchev intervened forcibly, sending in Russian troops and tanks to replace Nagy with a regime subservient to Moscow under Janos Kadar. The outbreak of the Suez Canal crisis at this time distracted the Western powers from events in Hungary. Despite the immediate political outcome in Hungary, a more flexible economic policy was allowed in Eastern Europe. Collectivization was slowed and a somewhat less restrictive atmosphere resulted even in Hungary.

Intervention in Czechoslovakia, 1968: The Brezhnev Doctrine

Early in 1968 Alexander Dubcek became leader of the Czechoslovakian Communist Party and began a process of liberalization which went further than any other East European country had gone at that time. Kremlin leaders were nervous and in May Premier Aleksei Kosygin went to Czechoslovakia and brought back a reassuring report. However, a manifesto entitled "Two Thousand Words" (issued by Czech intellectuals and calling for even faster reform) and the publication of a draft of rule changes for the Czech Communist Party (allowing an unprecedented range of freedom within the party itself) apparently convinced the Russians to use military force. On August 23 they (together with East Germany, Hungary, Poland, and Bulgaria) sent in troops and established a military occupation. Censorship was reintroduced and changes forced on the country, designed to crush any revolutionary tendency and prevent any democratization. In April 1969 Dubcek was forced out of power and a new regime established under Gustav Husak more compliant with Soviet wishes. Nevertheless, a few changes remained such as the federalization of the country to give equality to the Slovaks.

Continued Change in Eastern Europe

Despite the political limits imposed by the Soviet Union on their East European satellites, economic developments took place during the 1970s and 1980s which eventually led to further liberalization and change in Eastern European countries. The U.S.S.R., short of capital for development, could not supply the needs of East European states, and these began to turn to Western banks. With increasing economic ties and more East-West trade the political situation changed. The Czechs, despite the 1968 intervention, voiced criticism of Soviet missiles on their territory. The Bulgarian government called for making East Europe a nuclear-free zone.

In Rumania, too, change occurred when the government insisted with some success on greater independence in foreign affairs. The Rumanians also resisted Soviet pressure for closer economic ties and greater dependence on the Soviet Union.

CHANGE IN WESTERN EUROPE

NATO and the Common Market

The military pact called the North Atlantic Treaty Organization was originally established in 1948 and strengthened during the early 1950s as a result of the Korean War. It combined armed forces of the U.S., Canada, Portugal, Norway, Iceland, Denmark, Italy, Britain, France, and the Benelux countries (Belgium, the Netherlands, and Luxembourg). Greece and Turkey soon joined. West Germany became a member in 1956 and Spain joined in 1982. It has mainly been an alliance to contain Communism and to protect Western Europe from any threat of Russian attack or subversion.

In addition to NATO, institutions to promote economic unity have been established in the last three decades. Six members (West Germany, France, Italy, and the Benelux countries) formed the European Steel and Coal Community in 1951. Economic collaboration progressed favorably, and in March 1957, inspired chiefly by Belgian Foreign Minister Paul Henri Spaak, two treaties were signed in Rome creating a European Atomic Energy Commission (Euratom) and a European Economic Community (the Common Market)—which eventually absorbed Euratom. The EEC was to be a customs union creating a free market area with a common external tariff with other nations. Toward the outside world the EEC acted as a single bargaining agent for its members in commercial transactions, and it reached a number of agreements with other European and Third World states.

In 1973 the original six were joined by three new members—Britain, Ireland, and Denmark. The name was changed to "European Community." In 1979 there were three more applicants—Spain, Portugal, and Greece. These latter states were less well off and created problems of cheap labor, agricultural products, etc., which delayed their reception as members until 1986. On December 10 and 11, 1991, in the two Treaties of Maastricht (a provincial capital in southeastern Netherlands), the EC members committed to moving toward a new common market—entailing a political and economic union of the 12 nations—that ultimately would have a common currency. The EC today is the world's largest single trading area, with one-fifth of global trade.

Great Britain Since 1951

After the postwar Labor government under Clement Attlee had achieved its major reforms, transforming Britain into a welfare state, it was succeeded by Conservative governments from 1951 to 1964 under Winston Churchill, Anthony Eden, and finally Harold Macmillan. During this period the Conservatives restored truck transportation and iron and steel to private control, introduced some fees into the national health insurance program, and favored private over public development of housing projects. They did not, however, fundamentally alter the social security and health insurance program initiated by Labor, but accepted the welfare state.

Labor returned to power under Harold Wilson from 1964 to 1970. Public housing and slum clearance were again emphasized, the educational system was democratized, free medical services were restored, and social security pensions were increased. A Conservative regime under Edward Heath governed from 1970 to 1974, only to be ousted by Labor once again. Harold Wilson served as Labor prime minister from 1974 to 1976 when he retired to be succeeded by James Callahan. In 1979 the Conservatives returned under the leadership of the first woman prime minister in British history, Margaret Thatcher, whose success in a male-dominated political situation earned her the name "the Iron Lady."

Britain's major postwar problems have been economic. Some $40 billion in foreign investments were liquidated to pay for the British war effort. Thus, investment income was lost after the war, making necessary a considerable expansion of exports to pay for needed imports. There was difficulty in competing for foreign markets. Labor was low in productivity and Britain was outstripped by both West Germany and Japan. Demands for austerity and sacrifice from labor unions to control inflationary pressures resulted in a nationwide coal strike and prolonged work stoppage in 1972. Inflationary pressure increased with the Arab oil embargo and the drastic increase in oil prices during the winter of 1973–1974.

After 1974 Labor changed its policies and sought to cut public expenditures, use public funds for private investment, and limit wage increases. Priority was given to industrial expansion in several key industries with the most promise of growth. Labor for the first time in decades favored the private sector. The pound sterling was devalued from about $4 in 1945 to $1.60 in 1976 to provide more favorable trade conditions. British industry continued to be plagued by poor management and frequent strikes. Imports and pressures for higher wages and welfare benefits continued to fuel inflation.

Relations with Northern Ireland proved a burden to successive British governments. The 1922 settlement had left Northern Ireland as a self-governing part of the United Kingdom. Of 1.5 million inhabitants, one-third were Roman Catholic and two-thirds were Protestant. Catholics claimed they were discriminated against and pressed for annexation by the Republic of Ireland. Activity by the Irish Republican Army brought retaliation by Protestant extremists. From 1969 on, there was considerable violence, causing the British to bring in troops to maintain order. Over 1,500 were killed in the next several years in sporadic outbreaks of violence. Britain could find no solution satisfactory to both sides and the violence continued.

Separatist pressure of a far less violent kind was prevalent in Wales and Scotland. In 1976 Welsh and Scottish regional assemblies were established with jurisdiction over housing, health, education, and other areas of local concern. Budgets, however, remained under the control of London. The Scots were especially motivated to seek change because of the discovery of North Sea oil deposits, much of which lay in Scottish territorial waters.

Under Prime Minister Thatcher in the 1980s the British economy improved somewhat. London regained some of its former power as a financial center. Southern England was prosperous, but the industrial midlands remained in the doldrums with continued widespread unemployment and poverty. In recent years an influx of people from former colonies in Asia, Africa, and the West Indies has caused some racial tensions.

Prime Minister Thatcher has been a partisan of free enterprise. She fought inflation with austerity and let economic problems spur British employers and unions to change for greater efficiency. She received a boost in popularity when Britain fought a brief war with Argentina over the Falkland islands and emerged victorious. She stressed close ties with the Republican administration of Ronald Reagan in the U.S. Her popularity remained undiminished whereas the Labor opposition has been plagued by internal strife. Both the old Liberal party and the new Social Democratic party made gains at the expense of Labor, but neither gained any significant power. A Conservative victory in 1987 elections made Thatcher the longest-serving prime minister in modern British history.

France Under the Fifth Republic

The Fourth Republic established in the wake of World War II suffered from the weaknesses of the Third: a strong legislature and a weak executive leading to competition between factions and instability in government together with problems in trying to maintain French rule in Indochina and Algeria. In June 1958 the Assembly made General de Gaulle premier with six months emergency powers to deal with Algeria and problems posed by a rebellious army.

Under de Gaulle a new constitution was drafted and approved establishing the Fifth Republic with a much strengthened executive in the form of a president with power to dissolve the legislature and call for elections, to submit important questions to popular referendum, and if necessary to assume emergency powers. De Gaulle used all these powers in his eleven years as president.

De Gaulle eventually settled the Algerian problem by granting independence in July 1962. Elsewhere in foreign policy de Gaulle's tenure as first president of the Fifth Republic was marked by an attempt to make France an independent force in world affairs. He saw the struggle as one between powers, not ideologies. France became the world's fourth atomic power in 1960 and developed its own nuclear striking force. De Gaulle refused to follow the lead of either Britain or the U.S. At one time he advocated that Quebec free itself from Canada and at another sided with the Arabs against Israel. Many came to view his foreign policy as quixotic.

In domestic politics de Gaulle strengthened the power of the president by often using the referendum and bypassing the Assembly, as when he secured passage of a constitutional amendment providing for future direct popular election of the president. De Gaulle was re-elected in 1965, but people became restless with what amounted to a republican monarch. Labor became restive over inflation and housing while students objected to expenditures on nuclear forces rather than education. In May 1968 student grievances over conditions in the universities caused hundreds of thousands to revolt. They were soon joined by some 10 million workers who paralyzed the economy. De Gaulle survived by promising educational reform and wage increases. New elections were held June 1968, and de Gaulle was returned to power. Promised reforms were begun, but in April 1969 the president suffered a defeat on a constitutional amendment which he had set up as a vote of confidence. He therefore resigned and died about a year later.

De Gaulle's immediate successors were Georges Pompidou (1969–1974) and Valery Giscard d'Estaing (1974–1981). Both provided France with firm but not particularly radical leadership, and continued to follow an independent foreign policy without De Gaulle's more flamboyant touches.

In 1981 François Mitterand succeeded Giscard d'Estaing. He inherited an economy with troubles. Earlier during the 1970s France had prospered and become the third largest producer of aerospace technology next to the U.S. and the U.S.S.R. Believing prosperity would continue, Giscard d'Estaing's government did not invest sufficiently and allowed wages and social services to increase at high rates. During his first year Mitterand tried to revitalize economic growth, granted wage hikes, reduced the work week, expanded paid vacations, and nationalized 11 large private companies and banks. The aim was to stimulate the economy by expanding worker purchasing power and confiscating the profits of large corporations for public investment. Loans were made abroad to finance this program. When results were poor, these foreign investors were reluctant to grant more credit. Mitterand then reversed his policy and began to cut taxes and social expenditures. By 1984 this had brought down inflation but increased unemployment. The French public generally denounced big government but nevertheless wanted government benefits and services.

Germany After Adenauer: Erhard as Chancellor

The Christian Democrats remained in power after West German independence for two main reasons: (1) prosperity which by the mid-1950s was reaching all classes of Germans, and (2) the unique personality of Chancellor Konrad Adenauer, who kept the country firmly allied with NATO and the West. Christian Democratic victories in 1953 and 1957 showed the public's approval of the laissez-faire policy of Adenauer's economics minister, Ludwig Erhard. Adenauer's long tenure made him the key figure, lessened the importance of parliament, and resulted in much government bureaucracy. Adenauer claimed to want the reunification of Germany, but he insisted on free elections which the Communists of East Germany could not accept, and thus effectively blocked any negotiated solution to the unification problem. Adenauer's last electoral victory was in September 1961. The next year or two the aged Chancellor spent trying to remain in office despite party feeling that he should retire.

In April 1963 the Christian Democrats finally named Erhard to succeed Adenauer. Erhard had quite a different style—treating ministers and department heads as colleagues and equals. There was more of a collegial atmosphere but less drive and vigor, especially in foreign affairs.

By 1966 the Christian Democrats decided on a change. In November 1966 they formed a so-called "great coalition" with the Social Democrats under Willy Brandt. Kurt

Georg Kiesinger became chancellor, and Brandt the Socialist took over as foreign minister. Brandt announced his intention to work step by step for better relations with East Germany, but found that in a coalition of two very dissimilar parties he could make no substantial progress.

In domestic affairs, pressure for change in the German universities led to outbreaks of student violence just before the similar outbreaks among students in France. Early in 1969 Gustav Heinemann (SD) was elected president. An active campaign won the Socialists a gain the Bundestag elections which occurred later in 1969. The Socialists were pined by the Free Democrats and obtained the majority necessary to make Willy Brandt chancellor in October 1969.

Brandt, the former mayor of West Berlin, was Germany's first Socialist chancellor in almost 40 years. In foreign affairs he opened the way for British entry into the Common Market. The German mark was revalued at a higher rate, emphasizing German's true economic strength. Brandt was now able also to move for improved relations with the East (the policy of *Ostpolitik*). He offered improved economic relations to Poland and the U.S.S.R, and in return those states labeled his approach "positive." In the summer of 1970 he negotiated a treaty with the U.S.S.R. in which both parties renounced the use of force in European affairs. Later that year an agreement was made with Poland recognizing the Oder-Neisse line as the legal border between Poland and Germany. Relations improved also with East Germany. Walter Ulbricht retired from government in 1971, and the next year Brandt signed a treaty with East Germany to normalize relations and improve communications. Both states entered the United Nations. The question of whether division was permanent was bypassed.

Elections in November 1972 gave Brandt's coalition a clear victory and a 50-seat majority in the parliament. But there were problems for the chancellor, who had concentrated too much on foreign affairs. Brandt seemed to many too tolerant of disorders among university students. There was criticism also of his sometimes over emotional approach to foreign policy, as in relations with Israel. The discovery of a spy in his immediate office was an excuse for replacing him. Brandt put up little resistance, and Helmut Schmidt (SD) became chancellor in the spring of 1974.

Problems with the economy and the environment brought an end to Schmidt's chancellorship and the rule of the Socialists in 1982. An organization called the Greens, which was a loosely organized coalition of environmentalists alienated from society, detracted from Socialist power. In 1982 the German voters turned to the more conservative Christian Democrats again, and Helmut Kohl became chancellor. The economy continued strong on the whole and the new leadership followed a policy of using German influence to reduce U.S.-U.S.S.R. confrontation and tension.

Italy

Italian politics was plagued with problems caused by lack of common interests among different areas. The Christian Democrats, who were closely allied with the Roman Catholic Church, dominated the national scene. Their organization, though plagued by corruption, did provide some unity to Italian politics by supplying the prime ministers for numerous coalitions.

Italy advanced economically. In the period 1958–1962 the nation moved into the top 10 industrial powers. Natural gas and some oil was discovered in the north and the Po valley area especially benefited.

Unfortunately, business efficiency found no parallel in the government or civil service. Italy suffered from terrorism, kidnappings, and assassinations on the part of extreme radical groups such as the Red Brigades. These agitators hoped to create conditions favorable to the overthrow of the democratic constitution. The most notorious terrorist act was the assassination in 1978 of Aldo Moro, a respected Christian Democratic leader.

In 1983 the Christian Democrats received only about one-third of the popular vote and as a result of this weakness, Bettino Craxi (Socialist) became prime minister at the head of an uneasy coalition which lasted four years—the longest single government in postwar Italian history. After Craxi's resignation, no strong leader emerged.

Spain and Portugal

In the Iberian Peninsula two similar events have been the most important of the postwar era. In Portugal, Europe's longest right-wing dictatorship came to an end in September 1968 when a stroke incapacitated Antonio Salazar, who died two years later. A former collaborator, Marcelo Caetano, became prime minister, and an era of change began. Censorship was relaxed and some freedom was given to political parties.

In 1974 General Antonio de Spinola published his views on the long struggle of Portugal to hold on to its African colonies. This event sparked even more change. Caetano dismissed the general, whose popularity grew nevertheless. In April 1974 the Getano regime was overthrown and a "junta of national salvation" took over, headed by General Spinola. The general proved too conservative and cautious for younger officers, and he was unable to work with the strong forces of the Communist and Socialist parties, which had emerged from secrecy with the collapse of the dictatorship. Spinola retired and went into exile. Portugal went through a succession of governments. Its African colonies of Mozambique and Angola were finally granted independence in 1975. Portugal joined the Common Market in 1986.

In Spain, dictatorship was also brought to an end. Franco, who had been ruler of a fascist regime since the end of the Civil War in 1939, held on until he was close to 70. He then designated the Bourbon prince, Juan Carlos, to be his successor. In 1975 Franco relinquished power and died three weeks later. Juan Carlos proved a popular and able leader and over the next several years took the country from dictatorship to constitutional monarchy. Basque and Catalan separatist movements, which had caused trouble for so long, were appeased by the granting of local autonomy. Spain entered the Common Market in 1986, at the same time as Portugal.

END OF THE COLD WAR AND COLLAPSE OF COMMUNISM

U.S.S.R.: Reforms Lead to Change, 1987–1991

By 1985, when Mikhail Gorbachev became leader of the Soviet Union, that country faced severe economic difficulties. Pollution of rivers, increasing incidence of health problems, a rise in infant mortality in several regions, a decline in industrial production, over-centralization of planning and control, poor worker morale, and the burden of the arms race—all led to pressure for political and economic change. Confidence in central planning and leadership was further undermined and considerable fear generated throughout Europe and abroad by the disaster at the atomic power plant at Chernobyl (which is near Kiev). The reactor's explosion exposed more than 600,000 people to high doses of radiation, according to Leonid Toptunov, a former Soviet scientist.

Gorbachev introduced reforms that had widespread and often unanticipated consequences. Some freedom was allowed for private enterprise, and decentralization of control over industry and agriculture began. Censorship of the media was relaxed and press conferences were held. Gorbachev sought favor with the cultural and scientific elite by bringing back Andrei Sakharov, the noted physicist and dissident, from internal exile. The government also allowed the hitherto proscribed works of Alexander Solzhenitsyn to be openly published. In the area of foreign affairs, a new U.S.-U.S.S.R. agreement on intermediate-range ballistic missiles was reached in 1987.

The most radical of Gorbachev's reforms was to separate the Communist Party from the Soviet government. Between 1988 and 1991 a multi-party democracy with a parliament was introduced, and the Communist Party's monopoly of political life ended. Interest groups became free to organize as political parties, support candidates for office, and solicit votes. A new constitution was adopted in 1988. The new parliament, consisting of a Congress of People's Deputies and a Supreme Soviet, was elected and took office in 1989. In 1990 Gorbachev was elected President.

An unexpected result of Gorbachev's policies of *perestroika* (restructuring) and *glasnost* (openness) was the revival of separatist movements in Eastern Europe and within the multi-national Soviet Union itself. Both Lithuania and Georgia voted for independence from the U.S.S.R.

The Revolution of 1991

In 1991, conservatives and hard-liners attempted a coup d'état against Gorbachev. The revolt was overcome thanks to the determined stand taken by Boris Yeltsin, who headed popular resistance. Although Gorbachev remained in office for a few months more, the real power passed to Yeltsin, and in December—with the dissolution of the U.S.S.R.—Gorbachev resigned and Yeltsin took his place.

Changes Since 1991 Under Yeltsin

The old Soviet Union broke apart once the controls were removed. The Baltic provinces (Latvia, Lithuania, and Estonia) opted for independence, as did the Ukraine and other provinces of the union dominated for so long by the huge Russian Republic. A loose confederation known as the Commonwealth of Independent States emerged, containing 11 of the former Soviet republics. Four— Latvia, Lithuania, Estonia, and Georgia—refused to join.

Economic difficulties associated with the transition to a free economy, the mishandled repression of the Chechnya independence movement, and the forceful dispersal of Yeltsin's parliamentary opponents in 1993 gave ammunition to Yeltsin's opponents. In the 1996 elections, Yeltsin retained office as President despite reports of poor health. Following reelection Yeltsin underwent successful heart surgery, but his health problems and continuing political difficulties made his future as Russia's leader uncertain.

REVOLUTION IN EASTERN EUROPE

Poland

The Solidarity labor movement, led by Lech Walesa (who received the Nobel peace prize in 1983), gained power as the Communist government of General Wojciech Jaruzelski failed to master Poland's economic problems. Power passed to the Polish Parliament, and in the elections held in June 1989, Solidarity won an overwhelming majority. A movement began to transform the state-run economy into one based on market forces. Lech Walesa became President of Poland. By 1993-94, however, economic problems resulted in a Communist majority and a change of administration, but there was no return to the old Communist dictatorship. In 1993, Poland experienced 4% economic growth and appeared to be making a successful transition from a centrally planned to a market economy.

Hungary

Communist leader Janos Kadar was forced out of power in 1987. By March 1990, Hungary had formed a multi-party system and had held free elections that resulted in an overwhelming repudiation of the Communists. As in Poland, the problems of the next four years led to the return of a Communist Social Democratic majority that promised to maintain economic reforms and work for greater social justice.

Czechoslovakia

Communism also met with defeat in Czechoslovakia. Popular demonstrations in Prague in November 1989 resulted in a new government led by the playwright-dissident Václav Havel, who was confirmed in the office of President in elections held in June 1990. Bitter national rivalry caused the nation, created at the end of the first World War, to split into the Czech and Slovak republics on January 1, 1993. Since then, the Czech Republic has experienced relative prosperity, compared with high unemployment and other problems in the Slovak Republic.

The Reunification of Germany

In East Germany, Erich Honecker's government was overthrown in October 1989, and in November the Berlin Wall was breached and removed. In elections held in March 1990, proponents of German reunification won overwhelmingly, and by October, East and West Germany were once again reunited as one country, with its capital at Berlin. By 1995, significant progress had been made in overcoming the problems associated with reunification and a faltering East German economy.

WESTERN EUROPE

Great Britain

The Conservative (or Tory) Party retained power but under changed leadership. Margaret Thatcher, the first woman Prime Minister, differed with her party over Britain's participation in the European Economic Community (the Common Market) and the projected introduction of a common currency. Having lost the support of the Conservatives in Parliament, Thatcher resigned and was replaced by Chancellor of the Exchequer John Major. Under Major's leadership, the Conservatives have had to deal with slow economic growth, unemployment, and racial tensions caused by resentment over the influx of persons from the Commonwealth. In addition, there remains the chronic problem of Northern Ireland, with its Protestant-Roman Catholic animosities; this has been made more difficult by the Irish Republican Army, which has resorted to terrorism and violence to attain unity with Ireland proper. In 1995–96, retired United States Senator George Mitchell assisted in negotiations. So far, no solution has been reached.

France

Socialist President François Mitterand's policies of nationalization and decentralization of the governmental apparatus, put in place by Napoleon almost 200 years earlier, were slowed by conservative resistance to basic change. Slow industrial growth, inflation, and unemployment remained problems. Mitterand lost his Socialist majority in Parliament in 1986, but regained it in 1988. His regime favored close cooperation with the United States and a policy of moderation in domestic affairs. An ailing Mitterand retired at the end of his term in 1995 and died in January 1996.

Italy

By the 1990s, Italian industry and the economy generally had advanced to a point where Italy was a leading center in high-technology industry, fashion, design, and banking. These advances, however, were concentrated around the cities of the north. Southern Italy continued to have problems associated with economic backwardness and poverty.

Political instability has been the mark of Italian politics ever since the end of World War II. Corruption within a system dominated by the Christian Democrats resulted in criminal trials in the 1990s that sent a number of high government officials to prison. In 1993, the electoral system for the Senate of the Italian Parliament was changed from proportional representation to a system that gave power to the party with the majority of votes. The 1994 elections for Parliament brought to power the charismatic, conservative Silvio Berlusconi and his Forzia Italia ("Let's go Italy") movement.

EUROPE'S CHANGING ROLE IN INTERNATIONAL RELATIONS

New Role for NATO?

NATO, which had originated as a Western alliance against the Soviet Union, lost its reason for being with the collapse of the Soviet Union and revolution in Eastern Europe. In his 1996 re-election campaign speeches, U.S. President Bill Clinton suggested that NATO be expanded to include Eastern Europe and that it provide a collective guarantee against any aggression by one power against another. In another area, NATO provided a vehicle for occasional armed intervention in the Balkans in the Bosnian conflict.

Europe and the United Nations

The United Nations continued to play a limited but significant role in world affairs. It served as a vehicle for intervention in disputes between the Arab nations and Israel, in the Sudan, and, more recently, in the Balkans. It has provided humanitarian aid, mediated disputes, and maintained international military units to police peace agreements. In a number of less well-known instances such as telecommunications, international aviation, relief of distress among children, and support of international work in education, the arts, and science, the United Nations and its constituent organizations have played a crucial role.

The Balkan Crisis (Yugoslavia and Its Successor States)

Marshall Tito managed to hold together a nation of six republics with numerous rival ethnic groups, despite difficulties with the economy and in relations with Stalin and the Soviet Union. Even after Tito's death in 1980, the system continued to function for a number of years. But with the turmoil in Eastern Europe and the collapse of the Soviet Union, Yugoslav unity ended in 1991 and various factions took up arms against each other that summer. Slovenes and Croats broke away from Serbian control, and Bosnia and Herzegovina declared independence by the end of the year. Armed conflict broke out between Serbs, Croats, Bosnian Muslims, and other factions and interest groups.

The United Nations sent Cyrus Vance (U.S. Secretary of State under President Carter) and Lord David Owen (a former British Foreign Secretary) to mediate the dispute, but several truces and agreements that had been arranged all broke down. The European states, including Russia, all deplored the strife in the former Yugoslavia. On several occasions NATO intervened with air strikes and economic sanctions against the Serbs, but no agreement could be reached on military action sufficient to force an end to the conflict. In 1995 Richard Holbrooke of the United States negotiated a peace agreement, and in 1996 a multi-national force (which included United States troops for the first time) was sent in to police the agreement and maintain peace.

Europe, the Gulf War, and the Arab-Israeli Peace Movement

In August 1990, in a campaign which met little resistance and lasted only a few days, the army of Saddam Hussein, dictator of Iraq, seized control of its neighbor, Kuwait. The European powers and the United States—seeing a threat to their oil supplies—organized under the leadership of President George Bush. Through the United Nations, they called on Iraq to withdraw, and when this did not occur, an international army led by the United States was mobilized on the border between Kuwait and Saudi Arabia. Even Yeltsin's Russia gave political and economic support. Air strikes against Iraq began in January 1991. When these failed to bring about Iraqi withdrawal from Kuwait, a ground attack by the allied armies, under the command of American General Norman Schwarzkopf, was launched. Iraqi resistance collapsed and in just over four days, the allies had freed Kuwait and driven the Iraqi army back to the Euphrates River. At this point President Bush called a halt to hostilities, and Iraq was forced to give up any claim to Kuwait and to make peace on United Nations terms. Saddam Hussein remained in power, however, and continued to cause difficulties for the United States and its European allies.

The greatest source of instability in the Middle East since World War II has been the continuing conflict between the state of Israel (created by Jews in Palestine in 1948 after British withdrawal) and its Arab neighbors. In 1964, the Palestine Liberation Organization, led by Yassir Arafat, was formed among Arab refugees who had been expelled from their ancestral homes by the Israelis. Its stated goal was the destruction of Israel. By the 1990s, however, possibilities for peace seemed good. By then both Egypt and Jordan had signed peace treaties with Israel. After 50 years of intermittent warfare, the Arab-Israeli struggle was taken to the bargaining table despite resistance from both Arab and Israeli hard-liners. The Palestine Liberation Organization was extended recognition by Israel. In 1993, using the good offices of President Clinton, Prime Minister Itzhak Rabin and PLO leader Arafat concluded agreements for limited self-government for Palestinians in Israel. Despite the assassination of Prime Minister Rabin in 1995 and the election in the spring of 1996 of a more conservative Prime Minister, Benjamin Netanyahu, some progress continued to be made toward a general peace settlement between the Arabs and Israelis.

CULTURAL AND SOCIAL DEVELOPMENTS SINCE WWII

Science and Technology

Advances in science and technology have caused considerable change in the period since World War II. In 1900 there were about 15,000 trained scientists engaged in research and teaching—most in Europe. In the postwar years the figure reached

500,000; in addition to Central and Western Europe, the Soviet Union, the United States, and Japan were heavily involved in scientific research and development of technologies that applied scientific advances to everyday life.

Much of the early work on such devices as rockets, the jet aircraft engine, radar, and the computer was done in England and Germany during and immediately after World War II. The English mathematician Alan Turing was influential in wartime cryptographic work in which machines were developed to discover, by high-speed computation, the random settings of German cipher machines. Significant research on computers was done in places such as the University of Manchester following the war; in the last three decades, however, the lead in computers has been taken by the United States and Japan.

Rapid change occurred in medicine with the development of sulfa drugs, penicillin, cortisone, and antibiotics to cure formerly crippling infections. Vaccines were developed for poliomyelitis (1955) and other diseases. Remarkable developments in surgery included transplantation of vital organs. Research in genetics led to genetic engineering, in which scientists actually learned to create new and different living organisms. Some of this work was done in Europe, but more than ever before the balance was shifting to other areas, including the United States, Russia, and Japan.

In astronomy and space science, Western Europe was unable to match the vast resources of the super powers, but has nevertheless made significant advances. France became a leader in aerospace technology. England became a pioneer in radio astronomy with the work of Sir Bernard Lovell, using the great radio telescope at Jodrell Bank.

After World War II, European countries made extensive use of nuclear reactors for production of electric power. West Germany had the largest nuclear power program in Europe into the late 1970s, but after 1975 built only one more plant because of increasing costs. In Russia, nuclear power stations in recent years have cost up to twice as much as coal-fired plants. With Britain's discovery and exploitation of oil from under the North Sea, the economics of power changed considerably. France maintained its commitment to nuclear power and expected to obtain one-half or more of its power from that source by the year 2000.

The disastrous accident at the reactor at Chernobyl in the Ukraine in April 1986 caused many Europeans to rethink the whole matter of nuclear reactors and public safety. By the late 1980s, given the increasing concern about nuclear accidents and the disposal of radioactive wastes, nuclear power no longer seemed to hold the promise it had in the wake of World War II.

Two technological developments of the highest importance for everyday life were television and the computer. In 1980 there were 33 television sets for every 100 West Germans and 29 for every 100 persons in France. Not the least disturbing thing about television for Europeans was the influx of programs from the U.S.: some 20% of British television and 50% of French television was imported by the 1980s, mainly from the U.S. The ability of television to bring far-away events into the ordinary living room meant an ever-increasing use of the medium to influence politics and other important areas of life in ways just beginning to be studied and understood. The computer has developed from large devices available only for limited use to small personal machines widely available to many people. Its influence on everyday living has been at least as great as that of television.

Religion

In postwar Europe the ecumenical movement among the various branches of the Christian Church has been a notable development. The Second Vatican Council of

1963 supported ecumenicism and called for greater toleration among Christians. Most branches of the Christian Church continued to support traditional beliefs which has meant a continuation of conflict with the teachings of modern science and such philosophies as Marxism. The Roman Catholic Church, in particular, has been outspoken in opposition to nuclear weapons.

Literature and Art

Important work in literature and art has been done in all of the European countries since World War II. Even in Russia, despite censorship, such writers as Pasternak and Solzhenitsyn produced important works that were published abroad, although not in Russia until the political changes of the 1990s. The English writer George Orwell achieved fame for his frightening portrayal of a future totalitarian society in the novel *1984* (published in 1949). Writers such as Frantz Fanon in *The Wretched of the Earth* (published in French in 1961) and Jean-Paul Sartre in his *Critique of Dialectical Reason* condemned colonialism and called attention to the enormous discrepancies between the wealth of Europe and the United States and the underdeveloped nations of the so-called third world.

German writers of the older generation, such as Carl Zuckmayer and Bertholt Brecht, as well as younger writers like Wolfgang Borchert, Günter Grass, and the Swiss Heinrich Böll, produced notable works. Zuckmayer's play, *The Devil's General,* although written in the United States at the end of World War II, gave a remarkable picture of wartime Germany. Grass's novel *The Tin Drum* (1959), also set in Nazi Germany, became a best-seller that was translated into English and other languages.

Censorship in the Soviet Union under Stalin and his successors failed to stifle creativity and criticism. Boris Pasternak's *Doctor Zhivago* was an epic covering the period before, during, and after the 1917 Revolution. Its author, however, was not allowed to leave Russia to accept the Nobel Prize for literature. Alexander Solzhenitsyn's novel *One Day in the Life of Ivan Denisovich* won critical acclaim. A later work, *The Gulag Archipelago,* was a detailed description and indictment of the whole apparatus of forced labor camps run by the secret police during the Stalin era. The author was arrested for treason and forced into exile in 1974.

In film, the work of the Swedish director Ingmar Bergman (*The Seventh Seal, Wild Strawberries*) and the Italians Roberto Rosselini (*Open City*) and Vittorio de Sica (*Bicycle Thief*) attracted attention and critical acclaim. In art the greatest figure was Pablo Picasso, who began work before the first World War and whose productivity in many styles lasted until his death in 1973.

Social and Economic Trends

The high level of economic achievement in Europe and other developed areas by the 1990s did not prevent concern over a variety of issues. Among the most notable were the status of women and the environment. Switzerland was the last advanced Western nation to accord women the right to vote, in 1989. Elsewhere in Europe and Great Britain, women attained legal and political rights at different times. Still, they remained subject to wage and job discrimination.

As a result of scientific research and the activities of environmental groups, the world's leaders became cognizant of potentially severe problems affecting the global environment. Although a United Nations Conference on the Human Environment held in Stockholm in 1972 failed to achieve serious agreements, it did give a lot of publicity to the problems that modern industrialization and increased population have created.

In the 1990s, as Europe, the U.S., and Japan vie for power in the global economy, it remains to be seen if the trend toward European unity—both political and economic—will allow Europe to regain some of its leadership in world affairs.

THE ADVANCED PLACEMENT EXAMINATION IN

European History

TEST 1

THE ADVANCED PLACEMENT EXAMINATION IN

European History
TEST 1

1. Ⓐ Ⓑ Ⓒ Ⓓ Ⓔ	26. Ⓐ Ⓑ Ⓒ Ⓓ Ⓔ	56. Ⓐ Ⓑ Ⓒ Ⓓ Ⓔ
2. Ⓐ Ⓑ Ⓒ Ⓓ Ⓔ	27. Ⓐ Ⓑ Ⓒ Ⓓ Ⓔ	57. Ⓐ Ⓑ Ⓒ Ⓓ Ⓔ
3. Ⓐ Ⓑ Ⓒ Ⓓ Ⓔ	28. Ⓐ Ⓑ Ⓒ Ⓓ Ⓔ	58. Ⓐ Ⓑ Ⓒ Ⓓ Ⓔ
4. Ⓐ Ⓑ Ⓒ Ⓓ Ⓔ	29. Ⓐ Ⓑ Ⓒ Ⓓ Ⓔ	59. Ⓐ Ⓑ Ⓒ Ⓓ Ⓔ
5. Ⓐ Ⓑ Ⓒ Ⓓ Ⓔ	30. Ⓐ Ⓑ Ⓒ Ⓓ Ⓔ	60. Ⓐ Ⓑ Ⓒ Ⓓ Ⓔ
6. Ⓐ Ⓑ Ⓒ Ⓓ Ⓔ	31. Ⓐ Ⓑ Ⓒ Ⓓ Ⓔ	61. Ⓐ Ⓑ Ⓒ Ⓓ Ⓔ
7. Ⓐ Ⓑ Ⓒ Ⓓ Ⓔ	32. Ⓐ Ⓑ Ⓒ Ⓓ Ⓔ	62. Ⓐ Ⓑ Ⓒ Ⓓ Ⓔ
8. Ⓐ Ⓑ Ⓒ Ⓓ Ⓔ	33. Ⓐ Ⓑ Ⓒ Ⓓ Ⓔ	63. Ⓐ Ⓑ Ⓒ Ⓓ Ⓔ
9. Ⓐ Ⓑ Ⓒ Ⓓ Ⓔ	34. Ⓐ Ⓑ Ⓒ Ⓓ Ⓔ	64. Ⓐ Ⓑ Ⓒ Ⓓ Ⓔ
10. Ⓐ Ⓑ Ⓒ Ⓓ Ⓔ	35. Ⓐ Ⓑ Ⓒ Ⓓ Ⓔ	65. Ⓐ Ⓑ Ⓒ Ⓓ Ⓔ
11. Ⓐ Ⓑ Ⓒ Ⓓ Ⓔ	36. Ⓐ Ⓑ Ⓒ Ⓓ Ⓔ	66. Ⓐ Ⓑ Ⓒ Ⓓ Ⓔ
12. Ⓐ Ⓑ Ⓒ Ⓓ Ⓔ	37. Ⓐ Ⓑ Ⓒ Ⓓ Ⓔ	67. Ⓐ Ⓑ Ⓒ Ⓓ Ⓔ
13. Ⓐ Ⓑ Ⓒ Ⓓ Ⓔ	38. Ⓐ Ⓑ Ⓒ Ⓓ Ⓔ	68. Ⓐ Ⓑ Ⓒ Ⓓ Ⓔ
14. Ⓐ Ⓑ Ⓒ Ⓓ Ⓔ	39. Ⓐ Ⓑ Ⓒ Ⓓ Ⓔ	69. Ⓐ Ⓑ Ⓒ Ⓓ Ⓔ
15. Ⓐ Ⓑ Ⓒ Ⓓ Ⓔ	40. Ⓐ Ⓑ Ⓒ Ⓓ Ⓔ	70. Ⓐ Ⓑ Ⓒ Ⓓ Ⓔ
16. Ⓐ Ⓑ Ⓒ Ⓓ Ⓔ	41. Ⓐ Ⓑ Ⓒ Ⓓ Ⓔ	71. Ⓐ Ⓑ Ⓒ Ⓓ Ⓔ
17. Ⓐ Ⓑ Ⓒ Ⓓ Ⓔ	42. Ⓐ Ⓑ Ⓒ Ⓓ Ⓔ	72. Ⓐ Ⓑ Ⓒ Ⓓ Ⓔ
18. Ⓐ Ⓑ Ⓒ Ⓓ Ⓔ	43. Ⓐ Ⓑ Ⓒ Ⓓ Ⓔ	73. Ⓐ Ⓑ Ⓒ Ⓓ Ⓔ
19. Ⓐ Ⓑ Ⓒ Ⓓ Ⓔ	44. Ⓐ Ⓑ Ⓒ Ⓓ Ⓔ	74. Ⓐ Ⓑ Ⓒ Ⓓ Ⓔ
20. Ⓐ Ⓑ Ⓒ Ⓓ Ⓔ	45. Ⓐ Ⓑ Ⓒ Ⓓ Ⓔ	75. Ⓐ Ⓑ Ⓒ Ⓓ Ⓔ
21. Ⓐ Ⓑ Ⓒ Ⓓ Ⓔ	46. Ⓐ Ⓑ Ⓒ Ⓓ Ⓔ	76. Ⓐ Ⓑ Ⓒ Ⓓ Ⓔ
22. Ⓐ Ⓑ Ⓒ Ⓓ Ⓔ	47. Ⓐ Ⓑ Ⓒ Ⓓ Ⓔ	77. Ⓐ Ⓑ Ⓒ Ⓓ Ⓔ
23. Ⓐ Ⓑ Ⓒ Ⓓ Ⓔ	48. Ⓐ Ⓑ Ⓒ Ⓓ Ⓔ	78. Ⓐ Ⓑ Ⓒ Ⓓ Ⓔ
24. Ⓐ Ⓑ Ⓒ Ⓓ Ⓔ	49. Ⓐ Ⓑ Ⓒ Ⓓ Ⓔ	79. Ⓐ Ⓑ Ⓒ Ⓓ Ⓔ
25. Ⓐ Ⓑ Ⓒ Ⓓ Ⓔ	50. Ⓐ Ⓑ Ⓒ Ⓓ Ⓔ	80. Ⓐ Ⓑ Ⓒ Ⓓ Ⓔ
	51. Ⓐ Ⓑ Ⓒ Ⓓ Ⓔ	
	52. Ⓐ Ⓑ Ⓒ Ⓓ Ⓔ	
	53. Ⓐ Ⓑ Ⓒ Ⓓ Ⓔ	
	54. Ⓐ Ⓑ Ⓒ Ⓓ Ⓔ	
	55. Ⓐ Ⓑ Ⓒ Ⓓ Ⓔ	

European History

TEST 1 – Section I

TIME: 55 Minutes
80 Questions

> **DIRECTIONS:** Each of the questions or incomplete statements below is followed by five suggested answers or completions. Select the one that is best in each case.

1. Henry VIII's principal assistant in enhancing monarchial controls during the 1530s was

    (A) Thomas Cranmer.   (D) William Cecil.

    (B) Thomas More.   (E) Thomas Cromwell.

    (C) Thomas Wolsey.

2. The Colloquy of Marburg in 1529

    (A) was an attempt by the Catholic Church to develop a strategy to combat the Protestant movement.

    (B) was a meeting which declared Luther to be an outlaw throughout the Holy Roman Empire.

    (C) was a debate between Luther and Zwingli which resulted in a formal split within Protestantism.

    (D) was an attempt by Charles V to reconcile Luther to the Catholic Church.

    (E) resulted in the fall of Thomas Wolsey as Chancellor of England.

3. English Puritanism developed during the reign of Elizabeth I

    (A) in reaction to the failure of the Elizabethan Religious Settlement to implement the reforms of the Council of Trent.

    (B) because of Elizabeth I's intention to extend Protestant sentiment throughout the realm.

    (C) because of the dissatisfaction with the scope and breath of the Elizabethan Religious Settlement among the Marian Exiles and others who were influenced by Calvinist views.

    (D) as a direct reaction to the Jesuit Mission led by Edmund Campion.

(E)   to maintain the hierarchical and ceremonial aspects of the previous era.

4.   The Petition of Right (1628–29)

(A)   was an attempt by James I to secure additional tax revenues through the Parliament.

(B)   resulted in Parliament voting to execute the Duke of Buckingham.

(C)   was directed at addressing a range of Parliamentary grievances before approving new sources of revenue which were requested by Charles I.

(D)   denounced the left-wing religious policies of Charles I's government.

(E)   was approved by the Addled Parliament.

5.   René Descartes maintained or has been credited with all of the following EXCEPT

(A)   first publication of the discovery of coordinate or analytical geometry.

(B)   developing the science of optics through the laws of refraction of light.

(C)   established as his famous philosophic starting place: "cogito ergo sum" — I think therefore I am.

(D)   the concept of God was unnecessary in his concept of the universe.

(E)   Cartesian Dualism was the link between the physical and spiritual worlds.

6.   The Instrument of Government (1653)

(A)   recognized the demands of the leaders of the Fronde.

(B)   was a plan devised by John Locke for the government of the Carolina policy.

(C)   specified that Charles I was to be executed.

(D)   recognized Scotland and Ireland as free and independent nations.

(E)   established the Protectorate and resulted in Cromwell's designation as Lord Protector.

7.   Henry IV provided French Huguenots with the right to practice their religion through the

(A)   Edict of Potsdam.   (D)   agreement with the Papacy.

(B)   Edict of Fontainebleau.   (E)   Peace of Amiens.

(C)   Edict of Nantes.

8.   During the second half of the 17th century the power of Brandenburg-Prussia was enhanced primarily through the efforts of

(A) Elector Frederick III.   (D) Leopold.

(B) King Frederick I.   (E) Bismarck.

(C) Elector Frederick William.

9. Which of the following thinkers identified most closely with the following statement "renounce notions, and begin to form an acquaintance with things"?

(A) Galileo   (D) Spinoza

(B) Bacon   (E) Boyle

(C) Descartes

10. For several decades during the late 17th century Austria fought on two fronts against which two countries?

(A) Italy and Prussia   (D) Prussia and the Ottoman Empire

(B) England and Russia   (E) France and Italy

(C) France and the Ottoman Empire

11. The Peace of Utrecht

(A) resulted in the political and economic collapse of France.

(B) elevated England to the greatest power in the world.

(C) terminated the Wars of the Age of Louis XIV and restored peace to Europe.

(D) transferred Canada to England.

(E) resulted in the unification of Germany.

12. The Siccardi Law and the Law on Convents were two devices which Cavour utilized to

(A) restrict the influence of the Catholic Church in Piedmont.

(B) attract the support of Bismarck in an alliance directed against France.

(C) pave the way for the entrance of Piedmont into the Crimean War.

(D) enhance his personal relationship with King Victor Emmanuel II.

(E) demonstrate his opposition to the *Syllabus of Errors*.

13. The Reform Bills of 1832, 1867, and 1884–85 in Great Britain resulted in

(A) eliminating child labor abuses in the textile industry.

(B) eliminating the power of the House of Lords.

(C) alleviating the most drastic problems confronting the Irish.

(D) extending the franchise and redistributing the seats in Parliament.

(E) giving the vote to all adults over 21.

14. The Dual Alliance of 1879 may be described as all of the following EX-CEPT

   (A) a defensive pact between Germany and Austria.

   (B) from the German perspective, it was directed at the diplomatic isolation of France.

   (C) from the Austrian perspective, it was directed at Italian encroachment in the Balkans.

   (D) it was renewed through the First World War.

   (E) it addressed German concerns over growing anti-German sentiment in Russia.

15. During the era of the French Revolution, the Thermidorean Reaction

   (A) initiated the Reign of Terror.

   (B) resulted in the dissolution of the National Assembly.

   (C) terminated the Reign of Terror and led to the execution of Robespierre.

   (D) was the direct cause of the rise of Napoleon.

   (E) witnessed the execution of Louis XVI and Marie Antoinette.

16. Which of the following intellectuals did not participate in the Enlightenment?

   (A) Edward Gibbon   (D) Leopold von Ranke

   (B) David Hume   (E) Adam Smith

   (C) Benjamin Franklin

17. The era of the Napoleonic Wars was concluded by the

   (A) Peace of Utrecht.   (D) Congress of Vienna.

   (B) Congress of Berlin.   (E) Peace of Paris.

   (C) Peace of Westphalia.

18. The Decembrist Revolution of 1825 occurred in

   (A) Prussia.   (D) Russia.

   (B) France.   (E) Spain.

   (C) Austria.

19. Charles Fourier, Robert Owen, and Claude Saint-Simon can best be described as

   (A) anarchists.   (B) Marxists.

(C)   advocates of capitalism.   (D)   pre-Marxist socialists.

(E)   revisionists.

20.   The July Revolution in France resulted in the

(A)   development of democracy in France.

(B)   installation of Louis Philippe as king.

(C)   presidency of Louis Napoleon.

(D)   establishment of a republican form of government.

(E)   the withdrawal of Prussian troops.

21.   The map shown here indicates the locations of European revolutions during what year?

(A)   1820

(B)   1830

(C)   1848

(D)   1919

(E)   1825

22.   The Frankfurt Assembly was

(A)   a Pan-German assembly interested in the formulation of an integrated union of German states.

(B)   Bismarck's instrument to bring about a Prussian-dominated Germany.

(C)   a group of German representatives who were concerned primarily with local economic issues.

(D)   an Austrian effort to obstruct Bismarck's plan for German unification.

(E)   a group dedicated to the *Grossdeutsch* plan.

23. The failure of the Revolutions of 1848 may be attributed to all the following factors EXCEPT

   (A) the continuing loyalty of the armed forces to the old leadership.

   (B) the intelligence and cunning of the old leadership in manipulating the revolutionary forces.

   (C) the lack of effective organization among the nationalist revolutionaries in Eastern and Southern Europe.

   (D) the failure of the liberal revolutionaries in Central Europe to address serious social and economic issues.

   (E) the acceptance of political reforms by the liberal revolutionaries in the West at the expense of social and economic considerations.

24. The industrial economy of the 19th century was based upon all of the following EXCEPT

   (A) the availability of raw materials.

   (B) an adequate labor supply.

   (C) the availability of capital.

   (D) a distribution system to market finished products.

   (E) an equitable distribution of profits among all those who were involved in production.

25. Which author advanced the argument that anarchism would be achieved through education and without violence in *What Is Property?*

   (A) William Godwin   (D) Pierre Proudhon

   (B) Michael Bakunin   (E) Charles Fourier

   (C) Georges Sorel

26. The Revisionist Marxist movement

   (A) failed to gain a following during the late 19th century.

   (B) supported the Marxist concept of revolution but differed with numerous other Marxist prescriptions.

   (C) encompassed the Fabian Society, the Social Democratic Party in Germany, and the French Socialist movement led by Jean Jaures.

   (D) was the base upon which Lenin developed his support for the deployment of Communism in Russia.

   (E) never attracted much support except in such Asian societies as China and Vietnam.

27. The New Economic Plan (NEP) was

(A) Lenin's plan to revitalize the Russian economy after the Russian Civil War.

(B) a scheme developed by Trotsky to enhance his control over the Communist Party organization through economic concessions.

(C) Gorbachev's 1989 plan for the restructuring of the Russian economy.

(D) Nicholas II's last attempt to recover political support through economic concessions.

(E) the name given to Stalin's first economic plan which emphasized collective farming and improvements in heavy industry.

28. The Congress of Berlin resulted in all of the following EXCEPT

(A) the recognition of Rumania, Serbia, and Montenegro as independent states.

(B) the realization of Russian war aims in its conflict with the Ottoman Empire.

(C) the transfer of Cyprus from the Ottoman Empire to Great Britain.

(D) the establishment of the autonomous principality of Bulgaria.

(E) Austrian acquisition of Bosnia and Herzegovina.

29. In *Emile* Rousseau

(A) advanced his views on the Social Contract.

(B) called for a "natural" education free of the artificial encumbrances imposed by institutions such as the church.

(C) denounced Voltaire for his pedantic and unproductive lifestyle.

(D) identified with Montesquieu's sympathy for the English constitutional monarchy as a model for a future French government.

(E) advanced his case for atheism.

30. Czar Alexander II of Russia (1855–1881)

(A) established the *zemstvos,* which were assemblies that allowed the Russian rural nobility to maintain control over local politics.

(B) liberated the Russian serfs, thereby improving the political, social, and economic well-being of all Russians.

(C) made a half-hearted effort to reform the Russian judicial system.

(D) reformed the Russian military and curtailed its abuses of the civilian population.

(E) was motivated to reform Russian society not out of fear but because of his genuine desire to improve the condition of all of his people.

31. The Fashoda Crisis

    (A) was a colonial dispute in West Africa between England and France.

    (B) led to the Berlin Convention to settle the problems associated with the "Scramble" for Africa.

    (C) demonstrated that relatively insignificant colonial disputes could bring the great powers to the threshold of general war.

    (D) was concluded when Kitchener's forces defeated the French Force led by Commandant Marchand.

    (E) was caused by the French Foreign Minister, Georges Clemenceau, to divert French public opinion from the Dreyfus Affair.

32. The failure of Wilhelm II's government to continue the Reinsurance Treaty with Russia

    (A) led the Russians to adopt a position of "Splendid Isolationism."

    (B) eventually led to the isolation of Germany.

    (C) resulted in the Austrian-Russian Entente of 1894.

    (D) caused the Russians to undertake a massive naval building program.

    (E) led the Russians to support the establishment of Poland as a buffer state.

33. The Russian Revolution of 1905

    (A) resulted in the abdication of the Czar.

    (B) was immediately suppressed by Nicholas II.

    (C) led to the issuing of the October Manifesto which introduced democratic government to Russia.

    (D) was the primary cause for the defeat of Russia in the Russo-Japanese War.

    (E) led Nicholas II to issue the October Manifesto which called for an advisory assembly (the Duma) to be formed.

34. The Anglo-Russian Entente of 1907

    (A) was a defensive alliance associated with France.

    (B) was a trade agreement which led to improved Anglo-Russian relations.

    (C) was a settlement of colonial disputes involving Persia, Afghanistan, and Tibet.

    (D) is also referred to as the Entente Cordiale.

    (E) was a disarmament agreement involving capital ships.

35. Oscar Wilde's *Portrait of Dorian Gray* and Thomas Mann's *Death in Venice*

    (A) are examples of the romantic literature which dominated the literary scene at the turn of the 20th century.

    (B) embodied a new symbolist direction in literature which addressed themes which were ignored previously.

    (C) emphasized a new sense of realism in literature.

    (D) were representative of a literary movement known as expressionism.

    (E) were not well received by the intellectuals of the era.

36. All of the following statements concerning the Third French Republic are accurate EXCEPT

    (A) the Dreyfus Affair, Panama Scandal, and Boulanger Crisis were serious threats to its continuance.

    (B) the Third French Republic was established in the midst of French defeat in the Franco-Prussian War.

    (C) it was threatened upon its creation by the Paris Commune.

    (D) it established a Constitution in 1875 which provided for a republican form of government.

    (E) it supported an extension of the position of the Catholic Church in French society.

37. The Berlin Conference of 1884–85

    (A) specified that Britain would have control over the Niger and Congo rivers.

    (B) established the principle that an imperial claim had to be supported by occupation and notification to the European powers.

    (C) specified that the Congo would be under Portuguese control.

    (D) supported the dream of Cecil Rhodes for a Cape-to-Cairo railroad under British control.

    (E) established Italian authority in Libya.

38. Bismarck's *Kulturkampf*

    (A) consisted of a series of measures which were intended to eliminate the impact of Marxism in German politics.

    (B) were anti-Catholic laws directed at curtailing the influence of the Center Party.

    (C) was his diplomatic strategy to maintain the diplomatic isolation of France.

(D)   were intended to disrupt the progress of the Social Democratic Party.

(E)   was denounced by Pope Pius X.

39.   The Parliament Act of 1911 included all of the following provisions EXCEPT that the

(A)   life-span of Parliament was reduced from seven to five years.

(B)   revenue bills approved by the House of Commons automatically became law after being sent to the House of Lords.

(C)   House of Lords had no veto power over revenue bills.

(D)   House of Lords could effectively veto non-revenue bills.

(E)   House of Lords could only delay enactment of non-revenue bills.

40.   Who established the Independent Labour Party in 1893?

(A)   Sidney and Beatrice Webb

(B)   George Bernard Shaw

(C)   Keir Hardie

(D)   H. G. Wells

(E)   H. M. Hyndman

41.   The Haldane Mission was a British effort to

(A)   curtail the naval arms race with Germany.

(B)   eliminate colonial disputes with France.

(C)   involve the United States in the war against Germany.

(D)   reestablish British interests in the eastern Mediterranean.

(E)   coordinate its policies with the Low Countries.

42.   All of the following inventions were made after 1830 and expanded the scope of the Industrial Revolution EXCEPT

(A)   Ericsson's screw propeller.

(B)   Faraday's discovery of electromagnetic induction.

(C)   Daguerre's invention of photography.

(D)   Goodyear's rubber vulcanization.

(E)   John Kay's "flying shuttle."

43.   The expansion of the "division of labor" and of "mass production" through the development of standard parts and manufacturing processes were stimulated by

(A)   the institution of bank credit.

(B) the factory system.

(C) competition.

(D) economic imperialism.

(E) local political rivalry.

44. Thomas Malthus, David Ricardo, Nassau Senior, and James Mill have been identified as

(A) positivists.   (D) utilitarians.

(B) romantic idealists.   (E) utopian socialists.

(C) classical economists.

45. Who was the dominant personality at the Congress of Vienna?

(A) Metternich   (D) Talleyrand

(B) Bismarck   (E) Wellington

(C) Alexander I

46. In 1829 the Ottoman Turks were forced to accept the Treaty of Adrianople which

(A) recognized the independence of Bulgaria.

(B) recognized the independence of Greece.

(C) granted Christians access to the Holy Places in Palestine.

(D) permitted Russia to have access to the Mediterranean.

(E) recognized the independence of Serbia.

47. In 1919 the Weimar Republic was challenged by the Communists or Spartacists led by

(A) Ebert.   (D) Michaelis.

(B) Scheidemann.   (E) Erzberger.

(C) Liebknecht and Luxemburg.

48. The League of Nations was successful in resolving all of the following disputes EXCEPT the

(A) Albanian boundary dispute.

(B) Greek-Bulgarian border violation dispute.

(C) Aaland Islands dispute.

(D) Mosul boundary dispute.

(E) Danzig Crisis.

49. The Treaty of Brest-Litovsk

    (A) concluded hostilities between Great Britain and Turkey.

    (B) ended the war between the allies and Hungary.

    (C) concluded hostilities between the allies and Bulgaria.

    (D) was a humiliating agreement which the Russians signed with Germany.

    (E) concluded the war between the allies and the Ottoman Empire.

50. The Locarno Treaty (1925) was a major diplomatic achievement by

    (A) Leon Trotsky.   (D) Benito Mussolini.

    (B) Gustav Stresemann.   (E) Ramsay MacDonald.

    (C) Charles Evans Hughes.

51. As a result of the Easter Rebellion, Eamon DeValera and Arthur Griffith experienced growing support for

    (A) the Irish Republican Army.

    (B) Irish Home Rule.

    (C) their Sinn Fein Movement.

    (D) The Public Safety Act.

    (E) maintaining the British army in Ireland.

52. The Spanish Constitution of 1931

    (A) was an attempt to establish a democratic and secular republic.

    (B) reinforced the monarchy of Alfonso XIII.

    (C) installed Franco as President for life.

    (D) supported the positions of the Church and landowners in Spanish society.

    (E) resulted in the direct intervention of Mussolini's fascist Italy.

53. The Washington and London Naval Conferences

    (A) declared war to be illegal.

    (B) denounced Japanese aggression in China.

    (C) attempted to restrict specific categories of naval weaponry.

    (D) were international efforts designated to end the Chinese Civil War.

    (E) were limited to topics which affected Southeast Asia.

54. The chart which follows indicates that

    (A) nations with large populations were better able to respond to the impact of the Depression than nations with smaller populations.

Number of Persons Employed in 1932 as a Percentage of 1929

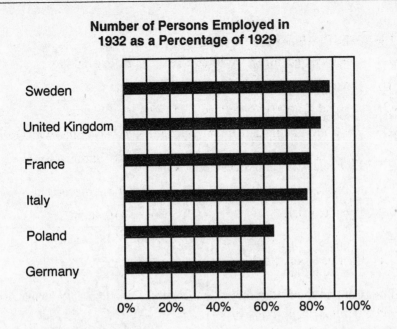

(B)   advanced industrial societies had lower rates of unemployment during this period.

(C)   the post-war economies in Central and Eastern Europe were fragile and subject to rapid deterioration during an economic collapse.

(D)   Sweden and the United Kingdom had the strongest economic systems in the world.

(E)   nations with small populations were better able to respond to the impact of the Depression than nations with larger populations.

55.   The aftermath of the Suez Crisis of 1956 resulted in the fall of

(A)   Charles de Gaulle as President of France.

(B)   Nasser as President of Egypt.

(C)   John Foster Dulles as Secretary of State.

(D)   Anthony Eden as British Prime Minister.

(E)   Pierre Laval as French Premier.

56.   The "Fascintern" was a pact

(A)   directed at subverting the interests of Britain and France.

(B)   between Germany, Italy, and Japan designed to coordinate the development of fascism throughout the world and the defeat of communism.

(C)   between Germany and Italy directed at the Soviet Union.

(D)   between Germany and Russia during the summer 1939.

(E)   whose members stressed the racial superiority of Germans.

57. The Treaty of Rome (1957) established which of the following?

(A) European Free Trade Association

(B) Colombo Plan

(C) Council of Europe

(D) European Economic Community

(E) European Coal and Steel Community

58. The map shows which military deployment?

(A) Plan XVII

(B) Schlieffen Plan

(C) Manstein Plan

(D) German troops during
      the Franco-Prussian War

(E) Ludendorff's
      Spring offensive

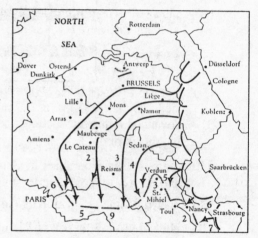

59. What does the following cartoon refer to?

(A)   The continuing cooperation between Hitler and Stalin during the 1930s

(B)   The contradictions inherent in the Russo-German Non-Aggression Pact

(C)   The delight shared by Stalin and Hitler

(D)   The defeat of Czechoslovakia

(E)   The defeat of Finland

60.   The Vienna Summit

(A)   between Kennedy and Khrushchev was disrupted because of the U-2 spy plane crisis.

(B)   between Eisenhower and Khrushchev was disrupted because of the U-2 spy plane crisis.

(C)   between Nixon and Khrushchev was disrupted because of the U-2 spy plane crisis.

(D)   between Kennedy and Khrushchev was focused on nuclear test ban negotiations and the war in Laos; it was followed in the next year by the Cuban missile crisis.

(E)   led to the establishment of NATO.

61.   The Glorious Revolution of 1688–89 resulted in all of the following EXCEPT

(A)   the flight and abdication of James II.

(B)   the passage of the Bill of Rights.

(C)   the elevation of William III and Mary as the monarchs.

(D)   specification that all future monarchs must be members of the Church of England.

(E)   an agreement that in the event of no heirs, the Hanover house would succeed the Stuarts.

62.   In *Hard Times* Charles Dickens depicted an English community which

(A)   was enjoying the fruits of an industrialized-based progress.

(B)   was preoccupied with religious constraints.

(C)   was characterized by difficult personal, class, and environmental adjustments caused by the industrial order.

(D)   prevailed through its repudiation of the Industrial Revolution.

(E)   emphasized British nationalism.

63.   The text of Denis Diderot's *Encyclopedia* was centered primarily on

(A)   theology.   (D)   philosophy.

(B)   technology.   (E)   poetry.

(C)   history.

64. Arnold Toynbee's *A Study of History* and Oswald Spengler's *Decline of the West* advanced a form of history which is described as

(A) narrative.

(B) scientific.

(C) cyclical.

(D) static.

(E) economic determinism.

65. In the following poem, the Hungarian-Swiss Tzara provides a sample of which 20th century literary movement?

"The aeroplane weaves telegraph wires
and the fountain sings the same song,
...
At the rendez-vous of the coachmen the aperitif is orange
but the locomotive mechanics have blue eyes.
The lady has lost her smile in the woods."

(A) Symbolism

(B) Expressionism

(C) Deconstructionism

(D) Dadaism

(E) Idealism

66. Which of the following European intellectuals is not identified with existentialism?

(A) Jean-Paul Sartre

(B) Martin Heidegger

(C) Karl Jaspers

(D) Jacques Maritain

(E) Albert Camus

67. The driving force behind Hegel's dialectic was

(A) nationalism.

(B) racial superiority.

(C) universal reason.

(D) materialism.

(E) religious values.

68. The response of the Catholic Church to the Reformation was delayed because

(A) the Papacy feared the remnants of the Conciliar Movement within the church itself.

(B) Rome wanted to coordinate its policy with secular Catholic leaders.

(C) church leaders thought that the opposition would self-destruct.

(D) the situation did not appear to be that serious from the Roman perspective.

(E) the Church did not possess the monetary resources which were required to confront Protestantism.

69. Since 1950 the Soviet Union has suppressed movements toward more liberal governments in all of the following European countries EXCEPT

    (A) East Germany.   (D) Yugoslavia.

    (B) Poland.   (E) Hungary.

    (C) Czechoslovakia.

70. Who was the first individual to serve as Prime Minister of Great Britain?

    (A) William Pitt   (D) Lord North

    (B) William Gladstone   (E) Robert Walpole

    (C) Lord Palmerston

71. Friedrich Nietzsche advanced his philosophy in which works?

    (A) *Thus Spake Zarathustra* and *The Will to Power*

    (B) *The Golden Bough* and *The Wild Duck*

    (C) *The Return of the Native* and *Jude the Obscure*

    (D) *Civilization and Its Discontents* and *The Riddle of the Universe*

    (E) *The Descent of Man* and *The Weavers*

72. In this painting, entitled "The Eternal City," by the American painter Peter Blume (1937),

    (A) fascist Italy is dominated by the personality of Mussolini.

    (B) fascism in Italy appears to have improved the general condition of the people.

    (C) Mussolini emerges as a benevolent dictator who was genuinely concerned with the condition of the people.

    (D)   presents a sympathetic rendering of the impact of fascism on Italian life and institutions.

    (E)   recounts the March on Rome in 1922.

73.   "Men are born, and always continue free and equal in respect of their rights. Civil distinctions, therefore, can be founded only on public utility." In 1789 these statements were part of

    (A)   the Bill of Rights.

    (B)   the Constitution of the Year III.

    (C)   the Declaration of the Rights of Man and the Citizen.

    (D)   Quesnay's statement on Physiocrat philosophy.

    (E)   *What Is the Third Estate?* by Abbé Siéyès.

74.   During the "June Days" in Paris (1848)

    (A)   conservative monarchists were overwhelmed by the mob.

    (B)   the forces led by Louis Blanc prevailed.

    (C)   the army suppressed the radical revolutionary element.

    (D)   Louis Napoleon came to power.

    (E)   Lamartine was recognized as the primary leader of the revolution movement.

75.   Who led the fight to repeal the Corn Laws (1846)?

    (A)   William Gladstone   (D)   Lord Palmerston

    (B)   Lord Melbourne   (E)   Robert Peel

    (C)   Benjamin Disraeli

76.   In an effort to conduct a successful economic war against Britain, Napoleon created the

    (A)   Bank of France.

    (B)   Confederation of the Rhine.

    (C)   Continental System.

    (D)   Napoleonic Code.

    (E)   Kingdom of the Two Sicilies.

77.   The 1909 budget proposed by Lloyd George advocated

    (A)   progressive income and inheritance taxes.

    (B)   an end to all property taxes.

(C)   drastic reductions in funding for domestic programs.

(D)   drastic reductions in expenditures for weaponry.

(E)   a redistribution of excessive tax revenues.

78.   In this painting, "Guernica" (1937) by Pablo Picasso, the artist rendered his interpretation of

(A)   the chaos caused by the Versailles Peace Conference.

(B)   Hitler's invasion of Poland.

(C)   the impact of the aerial bombardment of a Spanish town by the German Condor Legion during the Spanish Civil War.

(D)   the effect of the depression on French society.

(E)   the fall of France.

79.   What actions by Iraq led to the Persian Gulf War?

(A)   Iraq attacked Israel.

(B)   Iraq continued to persecute the Kurds.

(C)   Iraq invaded Kuwait and seized control.

(D)   Iraq refused to sell oil to the United States.

(E)   Iraq refused to release American hostages.

80.   Who replaced Margaret Thatcher as Prime Minister of Great Britain?

(A)   John Major   (D)   Edward Heath

(B)   George Mitchell   (E)   Robert Owen

(C)   Clement Atlee

European History

TEST 1 – Section II

TIME: Reading Period – 15 minutes
Writing Time for all three essays – 115 minutes

> **DIRECTIONS:** Read over both the Document-Based Essay question in Part A and the choices in Part B during the Reading Period, and use the time to organize answers. All students must answer Part A (the Document-Based Essay Question); and choose TWO questions from Part B to answer.

PART A – DOCUMENT-BASED ESSAY

This question is designed to test your ability to work with historical documents. As you analyze each document, *take into account its source and the point of view of the author*. Write an essay on the following topic that integrates your analysis of the documents. You may refer to historical facts and developments not mentioned in the documents.

Analyze the scope of William Hogarth's criticism of 18th century English society.

Historical Background: William Hogarth (1725–1763) has been recognized as one of England's greatest artists. Hogarth was interested in everyday English life; he wrote "I had rather see the portrait of a dog I know than all the allegories you can show me." Hogarth "felt that art should do more than entertain; it should 'improve the mind' and be 'of public utility.'"

Document 1
"Inhabitants of the Moon"

Some of the Principal Inhabitants of y.ᵉ MOON, as they Were Perfectly Discover'd by a Telescope brought to y.ᵉ Greatest Perfection Since y.ᵉ last Eclipse; Exactly Engraved from the Objects, whereby y.ᵉ Curious may Guess at their Religion, Manners, &c.

Price Six Pence

Document 2
"Chairing the Members"

Document 3
"Gin Lane"

Document 4
"Beer Street"

The initial inscription reads:

Beer, happy Produce of our Isle
    Can sinewy Strength impart,
And wearied with Fatigue and Toil
    Can chear each manly Heart

Document 5
"John Wilkes, Esquire"

PART B – ESSAY QUESTIONS

1. The nature and motivation for warfare in Europe has altered many times during the modern era. Describe, compare, and analyze the motivation for the Wars of Louis XIV and Napoleon.

2. Describe and analyze the causes for the rise of fascism in Germany and Italy.

3. The Stuarts have been held at least partially accountable for the decline of monarchical power in Great Britain. Describe and analyze the justification for such a position.

4. Discuss and analyze the ideological legacy of the French Revolution of 1789.

5. At the Versailles Peace Conference Germany was forced to recognize its responsibility for the First World War. Discuss and analyze the causes which led to the outbreak of the war.

6. Assess the extent to which the overseas empires impacted upon European economic and political life from 1870 to 1914.

THE ADVANCED PLACEMENT EXAMINATION IN

European History

TEST 1 – ANSWERS

1.	(E)	21.	(C)	41.	(A)	61.	(E)
2.	(C)	22.	(A)	42.	(E)	62.	(C)
3.	(C)	23.	(B)	43.	(B)	63.	(B)
4.	(C)	24.	(E)	44.	(C)	64.	(C)
5.	(D)	25.	(D)	45.	(A)	65.	(D)
6.	(E)	26.	(C)	46.	(B)	66.	(D)
7.	(C)	27.	(A)	47.	(C)	67.	(C)
8.	(C)	28.	(B)	48.	(E)	68.	(A)
9.	(B)	29.	(B)	49.	(D)	69.	(D)
10.	(C)	30.	(A)	50.	(B)	70.	(E)
11.	(C)	31.	(C)	51.	(C)	71.	(A)
12.	(A)	32.	(B)	52.	(A)	72.	(A)
13.	(D)	33.	(E)	53.	(C)	73.	(C)
14.	(C)	34.	(C)	54.	(C)	74.	(C)
15.	(C)	35.	(B)	55.	(D)	75.	(E)
16.	(D)	36.	(E)	56.	(B)	76.	(C)
17.	(D)	37.	(B)	57.	(D)	77.	(A)
18.	(D)	38.	(B)	58.	(B)	78.	(C)
19.	(D)	39.	(D)	59.	(B)	79.	(C)
20.	(B)	40.	(C)	60.	(D)	80.	(A)

Detailed Explanations
of Answers

TEST 1

1. **(E)** Thomas Cromwell assisted in the reorganization of the government which enhanced Henry VIII's power during the 1530s. Thomas Cranmer served as the Archbishop of Canterbury; Thomas More was out of favor and was executed for treason concerning Henry VIII's marriage to Anne Boleyn. William Cecil was an aid to Elizabeth I at the end of the 16th century.

2. **(C)** At the Colloquy of Marburg in 1529 Luther and Zwingli failed to concur on such issues as the nature of the Eucharist and the concept of predestination; this resulted in fragmenting Protestantism. (A) was incorrect because the Catholic strategy was centered on the establishment of new religious orders and the decrees and reforms of the Council of Trent. Luther was declared an outlaw by Charles V at the Diet of Worms in 1521. Charles V's attempts to reconcile Luther with the Church were confined to a series of debates which occurred prior to 1521. Thomas Wolsey's fall from power as Henry VIII's principal advisor was not related to the Colloquy of Marburg; it stemmed from the divorce crisis.

3. **(C)** English Puritanism developed during the reign of Elizabeth I because of the dissatisfaction with the scope and breath of the Elizabethan Religious Settlement among the Marian Exiles and others who were influenced by Calvinist views. Obviously, (A) is incorrect because the Council of Trent advanced Catholic doctrines; Elizabeth I was interested in consolidating not extending (B) Protestantism in England; the Jesuit Mission (D) occurred in 1580 and was not related to Puritanism; Puritanism (E) opposed the earlier Catholic forms of worship.

4. **(C)** The Petition of Right addressed perceived constitutional abuses related to the proceedings of the Court of the Star Chamber, a ship's tax, and the quartering of British troops in private dwellings; upon its acceptance by Charles I, additional sources of revenue were provided to alleviate the financial crisis caused by unsuccessful wars against Spain and France. (A) is incorrect because it refers to James I who died in 1625; (B) is false because Parliament did not vote Buckingham's execution — he was murdered in 1628; (D) Charles I's religious policies cannot be labelled left-wing — indeed they were right-of-center and resulted in the charge that Charles I was sympathetic to Catholicism; (E) the

Addled Parliament convened in 1614 and was not connected with the Petition of Right.

5. **(D)** Descartes argued that the reality of God was essential to his concept of the universe. Obviously, Descartes did discover coordinate or analytical geometry, develop the science of optics, used "cogito ergo sum" as his starting place, and contended that his dualism was the link between the physical and spiritual worlds.

6. **(E)** The Instrument of Government of 1653 replaced the Rump Parliament with the Protectorate as the government for the Commonwealth; Cromwell became the Lord Protector and served until his death in 1658. (A) is incorrect because the Fronde was an uprising of French nobility and was unrelated to the Instrument of Government. John Locke's (B) plan for the government of the Carolina Colony was developed during the 1660s and was known as the Framework of Government. (C) Charles I had been executed in 1649 upon the vote of Parliament. Scotland and Ireland (D) were not recognized as free and independent nations during this century.

7. **(C)** The Edict of Nantes of 1598 was issued by Henry IV and allowed the French Huguenots to practice their religion and maintain schools. The Edict of Fontainebleau (B) was issued by Louis XIV in 1685 and revoked the Edict of Nantes. The Edict of Potsdam (A) was decreed by Elector Frederick William of Brandenburg-Prussia in 1686; it invited French Protestants who were fleeing France to settle in Brandenburg-Prussia. The Papacy (D) opposed the Edict of Nantes and all other agreements which tolerated Protestant groups in Catholic countries. The Peace of Amiens (E) was a treaty during the early 19th century.

8. **(C)** Elector Frederick William of Brandenburg-Prussia (1640–88). Elector Frederick III (A) and King Frederick I (B) were the same person; he was the son of Elector Frederick William and did little to enhance the position of his nation. Leopold (D) was the Holy Roman Emperor during the late 17th and early 18th centuries. Bismarck (E) was Chancellor of the German Empire (1871–90).

9. **(B)** Francis Bacon advanced his empiricism during early 17th century. (A) While Galileo accomplished much in the development of science, he did not provide substantive contributions to the philosophy of science. Descartes' *Discourse on Method* (1637) approaches science from a more deductive mathematically-oriented approach; Baruch Spinoza's (D) contributions occurred later and were in mathematics and ethics. In addition to formulating Boyle's Law (concerning gas and temperature), Robert Boyle (E) was a chemist who did much to discredit alchemy during the second half of the 17th century.

10. **(C)** France and the Ottoman Empire. Austria was attacked twice during the period from 1660 to 1685 by the Ottoman Turks and was confronted during

the same time by wars with France. (B) is incorrect because Italy did not exist as a political ally of Austria in the wars against France. (C) is incorrect because England was allied with Austria and Russia was undergoing political crises which were not stabilized until Peter the Great seized power and reformed the government. (D) is incorrect because of Austria's alliance with Prussia and (E) is incorrect because Italy did not exist as a nation-state.

11. **(C)** The Peace of Utrecht terminated the wars of the Age of Louis XIV, restoring peace to Europe. (A) and (B) are incorrect because France, though defeated, was still the most powerful nation in Europe. (D) is incorrect because Canada was not transferred to England until the Treaty of Paris in 1763. (E) is incorrect because the Peace of Utrecht was unrelated to the unification of Germany which occurred in 1871.

12. **(A)** The Siccardi Law and the Law on Convents were two devices which Cavour utilized to (A) restrict the influence of the Catholic Church in Piedmont. They curbed the number of religious orders and limited the number of holy days in Piedmont; these laws were received sympathetically by Liberals but condemned by Conservatives. (B) is incorrect because Bismarck in 1855 did not possess the influence nor entertain interest in pursuing a Prussia-Piedmont alliance directed against France. (C) is incorrect because Cavour's decision to join Britain and France in the Crimean War against Russia was not connected to these two domestic laws. (D) Cavour enjoyed the support of Victor Emmanuel II and did not initiate these laws for personal political gain. (E) Pope Pius IX's *Syllabus of Errors* was published in 1864 — many years after these enactments and after Cavour's death.

13. **(D)** The Reform Bills of 1832, 1867, and 1884-85 in Great Britain were significant milestones in the development of democracy in Great Britain and resulted in (D) extending the franchise and redistributing the seats in Parliament. In addition to extending the vote to most men over the age of 21. These measures redistributed the seats in Parliament; this action eliminated many "rotten boroughs" and provided the industrialized cities of the Midlands with Parliamentary representation. Efforts to eliminate child labor abuses were embodied in a series of enactments including the Factory Act of 1833. The influence of the House of Lords was not curtailed until the passage of the Parliament Bill of 1911. The myriad of political, economic, and social ills which confronted the Irish were not resolved in the 19th century. In 1918 all men over 21 and women over 30 were given the right to vote; women over 21 were enfranchised in 1928.

14. **(C)** From the Austrian perspective, the Dual Alliance was directed at Russian — not Italian — encroachment in the Balkans. The Dual Alliance (1879) was a defensive pact between Austria and Germany which was renewed through the First World War, and addressed German concerns over the diplomatic isolation of France and growing anti-German sentiment.

15. **(C)** The Thermidorean Reaction of July 1794 (C) terminated the Reign of Terror and led to the execution of Robespierre. The Reign of Terror was initiated by the June Days of 1793 when the radical Jacobins overthrew the Girondins; the National Assembly was dissolved in 1791 when the Legislative Assembly was formed; Napoleon did not come to power until the *coup d'état* of Brumaire in 1799; Louis XVI and Marie Antoinette were executed by vote of the Convention prior to the seizure of that institution by the radical Jacobins.

16. **(D)** Leopold von Ranke, the 19th century German historian, was not a contributor to the Enlightenment. Englishman Edward Gibbon (*The Decline and Fall of the Roman Empire*) and Scots David Hume (*History of England* and many works in philosophy) and Adam Smith (*Wealth of Nations*) were contributors. Benjamin Franklin, a major force in the American revolution, was a multi-faceted genius of the Enlightenment.

17. **(D)** The Congress of Vienna concluded the wars of the Napoleonic era. The Peace of Utrecht (1713) concluded the War of the Spanish Succession; the Congress of Berlin (1878) terminated the Russo-Turkish War of 1877–78; The Peace of Westphalia closed the Thirty Years' War; and the Peace of Paris (1856) ended the Crimean War.

18. **(D)** The Decembrist Revolution of 1825 occurred in Russia. Prussia, France, Austria, and Spain did not experience any revolutions during 1825; when most of Europe underwent revolution in 1848, Russia and Great Britain did not experience any such activity.

19. **(D)** Charles Fourier, Robert Dawn, and Claude Saint-Simon can best be described as pre-Marxist socialists; some authorities identify them as Utopian Socialists. Anarchism was introduced by Pierre Proudhon in *What is Property?*; Marx and Engels developed Scientific Socialism, or Marxism; and the term *revisionists* is applied to Marxists who differ with one or more of the basic Marxian notions. All of these individuals and groups were opposed to capitalism.

20. **(B)** Louis Philippe was installed as King of France as a result of the liberal July Revolution of 1830. While Louis Philippe and his advisors were "liberal" at the beginning of the reign, they were not democrats (A) and became increasingly conservative. The July Revolution established a constitutional monarchy, not a republic (D). Louis Napoleon was elected President of France in 1848 (C). The withdrawal of Prussian troops (E) was not related to the July Revolution.

21. **(C)** The map indicates the revolutions which occupied Europe during 1848. The revolutions of 1820 (A), 1825 (E), and 1830 (D) were not as significant nor as widespread as the revolutions of 1848. In 1919 revolutions (usually attempts by Marxists) occurred in Berlin and several other cities in central and eastern Europe.

22. **(A)** The Frankfurt Assembly was a Pan-German assembly interested in the formulation of an integrated union of German states; the representatives were interested in the *Kleindeutsch* (Small Germany) not the (E) *Grossdeutsch* (Big Germany). Bismarck (B) was not in power during the history of the Frankfurt Assembly (1849–50); the primary interest of the delegates (C) was political not economic unification. The Austrians (D) had little influence in the Frankfurt Assembly.

23. **(B)** The failure of the Revolutions of 1848 cannot be attributed to the intelligence and cunning of the old leadership in manipulating the revolutionary forces. Indeed, the old guard proved to be rather inept and did not indicate any inspired leadership when the revolutions broke; there was a sense of inevitably concerning the revolutions which led to despair and initial compliance with the revolutionary demands. It was only after the revolutionary leaders made a series of errors (A) (C) (D) and (E) that the old regime found itself able to restore itself to power.

24. **(E)** The industrial economy of the 19th century was not based upon an equitable distribution of profits among all those who were involved in production. Marxists and other critics of capitalism condemned the creed of capitalists and the abhorrent conditions of the industrial proletariat. Raw materials, a constant labor supply, capital, and an expanding marketplace were critical elements in the development of the industrial economy.

25. **(D)** Pierre Proudhon (D) advanced a justification for anarchism in *What is Property?* in which he asserted that change could be realized through education and non-violence. William Godwin's (A) *Enquiry Concerning Social Justice* argued for a utopia based upon the perfectibility of all individuals. Michael Bakunin (B) was an anarchist who attacked Marx and his philosophy. Georges Sorel (C) founded an anarchist variation known as Syndicalism. Charles Fourier (E) was a Utopian Socialist.

26. **(C)** The Revisionist Marxist movement encompassed the Fabian Society (Sidney and Beatrice Webb, George Bernard Shaw, Keir Hardie, et al.), the Social Democratic Party (Eduard Berstein), and the French socialist movement led by Jean Jaures. Revisionist Marxism gained a significant following (A) during the late 19th century; it opposed the Marxist imperative of revolution; Lenin was an orthodox Marxist and opposed (D) the revisionists; most Asian Marxists did not identify with the revisionist movement.

27. **(A)** The New Economic Plan (NEP) was Lenin's plan (1921) to revitalize the Russian economy after the Russian Civil War. It was not (B) a scheme by Trotsky to control the Communist Party, nor (D) Nicholas II's last attempt to recover political support through economic concessions. Obviously, it was not (C) Gorbachev's 1989 plan for the restructuring of the Russian economy although there are valid points of comparison between the 1921 and 1989 schemes.

Stalin's first economic plan (E) was known as the first Five-Year Plan; it resulted in a long-term commitment to collectivization and the expansion of Russian heavy industry.

28.   **(B)**   The Congress of Berlin (1878) did not result in the realization of Russian war aims in its conflict with the Ottoman Empire. The Russians wanted to establish a large Bulgarian state, gain access to the Mediterranean Sea, and extend their control in the Black Sea and eastern Balkan areas. A small, autonomous principality of Bulgaria (D) was established; Rumania, Serbia, and Montenegro were recognized as independent states (A); Cyprus (C) was transferred to Great Britain; and Austria acquired Bosnia and Herzegovina (E).

29.   **(B)**   In *Emile* Rousseau (B) called for a "natural" education free of the artificial encumbrances imposed by institutions such as the church. His view on the social contract (A) was advanced separately; Rousseau did not (C) denounce Voltaire for his pedantic and unproductive lifestyle; nor did Rousseau in *Emile* identify with (D) Montesquieu's sympathy for the English Constitutional monarchy. Since the concept of God was essential in Rousseau's thought, he did not advance his case for atheism (E).

30.   **(A)**   Czar Alexander II of Russia (1855–1881) (A) established the *zemstvos* which were assemblies that allowed the Russian rural nobility to maintain control over local politics. Alexander II's Emancipation of the Serfs (1861) did not (B) improve the political, social, and economic well-being of the Russian serfs. However, Alexander II did (C) make substantive improvements in the Russian judiciary; he did not (D) reform the Russian military. Alexander II was motivated (E) by fear of the masses, not out of any genuine desire to improve the condition of the Russian people.

31.   **(C)**   The Fashoda Crisis (1898–99) between Great Britain and France demonstrated that relatively colonial disputes could bring the great powers to the threshold of a general war. Fashoda was in East Africa not (A) West Africa; the Berlin Convention was held during 1884–85, more than a decade prior to the crisis; no major military engagement (D) occurred during the Fashoda crisis. Delcasse (E) was the French leader during the Fashoda affair.

32.   **(B)**   The failure of Wilhelm II's government to continue the Reinsurance Treaty with Russia eventually led to the isolation of Germany. Russia was not interested in any (A) isolationist or non-aligned position; the German action contributed to the formation of the (C) Franco-Russian Entente or Dual Entente of 1894 — Austria was allied with Germany. Russia was opposed to (E) an independent Poland because such a development would result in a loss of territory; while the Russian navy expanded slightly during this period, the Russian economy was not able to (D) support a massive naval building program.

33. **(E)** The Russian Revolution of 1905 led Nicholas II to issue the October Manifesto which called for an advisory assembly (the Duma) to be formed. It did not (A) result in the abdication of the Czar (he would resign in March, 1917), nor was it (B) suppressed by Nicholas II. The October Manifesto was not (C) democratic in nature; the Revolution of 1905 occurred (E) after Russian forces were being defeated in the Russo-Japanese war. The death in the war was a factor which stimulated the revolution.

34. **(C)** The Anglo-Russian Entente of 1907 was a settlement of colonial disputes involving Persia, Afghanistan, and Tibet; Persia was divided into three zones, Afghanistan was recognized as a British sphere of influence, and Tibet was recognized as part of China. No defensive (A) alliance between Britain, France, and Russia was signed prior to 1914; the Anglo-Russian Entente was not a reciprocal trade agreement (B) nor did it involve naval disarmament (E). (D) The Entente Cordiale refers to the Anglo-French agreement of 1904.

35. **(B)** Oscar Wilde's *Portrait of Dorian Gray* and Thomas Mann's *Death in Venice* embodied a new symbolists' direction in literature which addressed themes which were ignored previously; these themes include fantasies relating to the perpetual "youth" in exchange for the soul, and homosexuality. These works and others of this vintage could not be (A) construed as examples of romantic literature in the literary tradition of romanticism nor can they be categorized as examples of the (C) new sense of realism in literature or examples (D) of any expressionist literary movement. Both of these works were applauded by intellectuals at the time of their publication.

36. **(E)** The Third French Republic did not support an extension of the Catholic Church in French society. Quite to the contrary, the policies of the Third French Republic tended to restrict the influence of the Catholic Church; on occasion, the policies can be described accurately as anti-clerical. The (A) Dreyfus Affair, Panama Scandal, and Boulanger Crisis were serious threats to the continuance of the Third French Republic which had been established (B) in the midst of the French defeat in the Franco-Prussian War (1870–71). During the spring, 1871, the Paris Commune (C) threatened the new republic but the Commune collapsed. In 1875 (D) a constitution was adopted which formalized the establishment of the Third French Republic.

37. **(B)** The Berlin Conference of 1884–85 established the principle that an imperial claim had to be supported by occupation and notification to the European powers. The Berlin Conference, which was directed at curtailing the growth of Britain's Empire, did not (A) specify that Britain would have control over the Niger and Congo rivers, nor did it support (D) the dream of Cecil Rhodes for a Cape-to-Cairo railroad under British control. Further, the conference did not (C) specify that the Congo would be under Portuguese control; it turned the Congo over to Belgium. Italy obtained Libya during the first decade of the 20th century.

38. **(B)** Bismarck's *Kulturkampf* were anti-Catholic laws directed at curtailing the influence of the Center Party. While Bismarck opposed the popularization of Marxist principles (A) through the Social Democratic Party (D), he utilized other devices to restrict that party's growth and influence. The *Kulturkampf* had nothing to do with the centerpiece of Bismarck's foreign policy — (C) maintaining the diplomatic isolation of France. While the Papacy condemned the *Kulturkampf*, it was not led by Pope Pius X who became the Pontiff during the early 20th century.

39. **(D)** The Parliament Act of 1911 did not permit the House of Lords to effectively veto non-revenue bills. In addition to a brief delay in the event of a veto by the House of Lords, the House of Commons could redraft the measure and transform it into a revenue bill immediately. The Act did (A) reduce the life span of a Parliament from seven to five years; obviously, the House of Lords (C) has no veto power over revenue bills.

40. **(C)** The Independent Labour Party was established in 1893 by Keir Hardie, a Scottish socialist member of Parliament. Sidney and Beatrice Webb (A) and George Bernard Shaw (B) were socialists and founders of the Fabian Society. H. G. Wells (D) and H. J. Hyndman (E) were other left-wing political spokesmen during the late 19th century.

41. **(A)** The Haldane Mission was a British effort (1912) to curtail the naval arms race with Germany. It had no relation to a (B) colonial dispute with France, (C) involving the United States in the war against Germany, (D) reestablishing British interests in the Eastern Mediterranean, or (E) coordinating British policies with the Low Countries.

42. **(E)** John Kay's "flying shuttle" was made during the 18th century. Ericsson's screw propeller (A), Faraday's discovery of electromagnetic induction (B), Daguerre's invention of photography (C), and Goodyear's rubber vulcanization process (D) all appeared after 1830.

43. **(B)** The expansion of the "division of labor"' and of "mass production" through the development of standard parts and manufacturing processes were stimulated by (B) the factory system. While the (A) institution of bank credit and (B) competition were important elements in the development of capitalism, they did not stimulate the "division of labor" or "mass production." (D) Economic imperialism will be a byproduct of the system; (E) local political rivalry — although different than in the past — was not directly related to this development.

44. **(C)** Thomas Maltus, David Ricardo, Nassau Senior, and James Mill have been identified as classical economists. None of these individuals could be described as (E) utopian socialists, (A) positivists, or (B) romantic idealists; James Mill was associated with the (D) utilitarians.

45. **(A)** The dominant personality at the Congress of Vienna was Metternich. Alexander I (C), Talleyrand (D), and Wellington (E) attended the Congress but none of them could be considered as dominant. (B) Bismarck was an essential statesman a half century after the close of the Congress of Vienna.

46. **(B)** In 1829 the Ottoman Turks were forced to accept the Treaty of Adrianople which (B) recognized the independence of Greece. Bulgarian independence (A) would not be recognized until the Congress of Berlin in 1878. Serbian independence (E) was not recognized fully until the 1880s. The (C) Christian right of access to the Holy Places in Palestine was a factor in the origins of the Crimean War (1854), and Russian access to the Mediterranean was a constant item on the agenda of East Mediterranean affairs until it was realized in 1967.

47. **(C)** In 1919 the Weimar Republic was challenged by the Communists or Spartacists led by (C) Karl Liebknecht and Rosa Luxemburg. (A) Ebert, (B) Scheidemann, (D) Michaelis, and (E) Erzberger were all involved — some critically — with the emergence and development of the Weimar Republic.

48. **(E)** The League of Nations succeeded in resolving the Albanian boundary dispute between Greece, Italy, and Yugoslavia in 1921, the (B) Greek-Bulgarian dispute of 1926, the (C) Aaland Islands dispute between Sweden and Finland in 1931, and the (D) Mosul Boundary dispute between Great Britain and Turkey in 1926. However, the League of Nations had no success in resolving the Danzig Crisis (E) between Germany and Poland (supported by Britain and France) in 1939.

49. **(D)** The Treaty of Brest-Litovsk (March, 1918) was (D) a humiliating agreement which the Russians signed with Germany. The Treaty of Neuilly (C) concluded hostilities between the allies and Bulgaria; the Treaty of Trianon (B) ended the war between the allies and Hungary; the Treaty of Sèvres (E) ended the war between the allies and the Ottoman Empire. There was no formal separate treaty concluding hostilities between Great Britain and Turkey.

50. **(B)** The Locarno Treaty (1925) was a major diplomatic achievement by Gustav Stressmann, the German Foreign Minister. Leon Trotsky (A) was being ousted from power by Stalin and forced to flee the Soviet Union; (C) Charles Evan Hughes was the American Secretary of State at this time — in 1924, Hughes was instrumental in the development of the Dawes Plan; (D) Benito Mussolini was in power and his government was involved in the Locarno negotiations; and (E) Ramsay MacDonald was the leader of the Labour Party in Great Britain.

51. **(C)** As a result of the Easter Rebellion, Eamon DeValera and Arthur Griffith experienced growing support for their Sinn Fein Movement. They were not directly involved with (A) the Irish Republican Army, or the old (B) Irish

Home Rule movement; they opposed (D) the Public Safety Act and (E) maintaining the British army in Ireland.

52. **(A)** The Spanish Constitution of 1931 was an attempt to establish a democratic and secular republic. King Alfonso XIII, (B) fled the country; Franco (C) would not seize power until his victory in the Spanish Civil War in 1939; the 1931 Constitution undermined (D) the positions of the Church and the landowners in Spanish society. Mussolini's Italy (E) would not be involved until the outbreak of the Spanish Civil War in 1936.

53. **(C)** The Washington (1921–22) and London (1930) Naval Conferences attempted to restrict specific categories of naval weaponry. The Kellog-Briand Pact (1927) declared (A) war to be illegal; the Japanese aggression in China (B) began in 1931 after the London Naval Conference; the Chinese Civil War (D) did not begin until 1927 — long after the close of the Washington Conference; and, while Southeast Asia (E) was a major item on the agenda of these conferences, the limitations on naval weaponry cannot be construed as a regional issue.

54. **(C)** The chart indicates that the post-war economics in Central and Eastern Europe were fragile and subject to rapid deterioration during an economic collapse.

55. **(D)** The aftermath of the Suez Crisis of 1956 resulted in the fall of Anthony Eden as British Prime Minister. Eden had succeeded Churchill in 1955 but his tenure as Prime Minister was cut short by his support of an interventionist action in Egypt; the United States condemned the joint British-French-Israeli action. Charles deGaulle (A) became President of the Fourth French Republic in 1958; Gamel Abdel Nasser remained as President of Egypt until his death in 1970; John Foster Dulles held the position as the American Secretary of State until his death in 1959; Pierre Laval was a leader of the Third French Republic and the Vichy Regime — he was executed as a collaborator after the Second World War.

56. **(B)** The "Fascintern" was a pact between Germany, Italy, and Japan designed to coordinate the development of fascism throughout the world and the defeat of communism. While one may argue that the Fascintern was intent upon (A) subverting the interests of Britain and France, these countries were not specified. It was obviously not (D) an agreement between Germany and Russia (not to be confused with the Russian-German Nonaggression Pact of 1939), nor did the pact specify the racial superiority of Germans (E) — neither the Italians nor the Japanese were inclined to accept such a provision. (C) is incorrect because Japan was omitted.

57. **(D)** The Treaty of Rome (1957) established the European Economic Community. The European Free Trade Association (A), the Colombo Plan (B), the Council of Europe (C), and the European Coal and Steel Community (E)

were all significant events in the recovery of Europe after the Second World War. The European Economic Community will expand to include most of the western European nations.

58.   **(B)**   The map indicates the Schlieffen Plan, which was developed in 1905 and deployed in August 1914 upon the outbreak of the First World War. Plan XVII (A) was the French plan which was based on the assumption that the Germans would attack in eastern France; the French hoped to seize Alsace and Lorraine. The Manstein Plan (C) was the German military strategy devised by General Erich von Manstein that led to the collapse of France during May-June 1940. The map surely does not indicate the movement of German troops during the Franco-Prussian war in 1870–71, nor Ludendorff's Spring Offensive in 1918.

59.   **(B)**   The "Rendezvous" (1939) by British cartoonist David Lou referred to the contradiction inherent in the Russo-German Nonaggression Pact. It does not refer to (D) Czechoslovakia, (E) Finland, or (C) any delight shared by Stalin and Hitler, both of whom suspected each other's motives.

60.   **(D)**   The Vienna Summit (1961) between Kennedy and Khrushchev was focused on nuclear test ban negotiations and the war in Laos; it was followed in the next year by the Cuban missile crisis. Many analysts make a direct connection between the Vienna Summit and the Cuban missile crisis because Khrushchev departed from the meeting convinced that Kennedy was weak and that his presidency provided opportunities for Soviet expansion. (A), (B), and (C) are incorrect because the U-2 plane crisis broke up the Paris Summit between Eisenhower and Khrushchev. (E) NATO was established in 1949.

61.   **(E)**   The Glorious Revolution of 1688–89 did not result in an agreement that in the event of no heirs, the Hanover house would succeed the Stuarts. Such an arrangement was specified in the Act of Succession of 1701, a year before William III's death and the succession of Queen Anne. She survived all her children. Upon her death in 1714, George I became the first Hanoverian King of England.

62.   **(C)**   In *Hard Times*, Charles Dickens depicted an English community that (C) was characterized by difficult personal, class, and environmental adjustments caused by the industrial order. Certainly, Dickens' portrait of English industrial life during the 1850s did not indicate that (A) the people were enjoying the fruits of industrial-driven progress, that the people of Coketown were (B) preoccupied with religious constraints, that this society (D) repudiated the industrial order, nor a society that (E) emphasized British nationalism.

63.   **(B)**   The text of Denis Diderot's *Encyclopedia* was centered primarily on (B) technology. While history (C) and philosophy (D) were important elements, technological innovations and science were emphasized in this profusely illustrated work. Theology (A) and poetry (E) were not given much attention.

64.   **(C)**   Arnold Toynbee's *A Study of History* and Oswald Spengler's *Decline of the West* advanced a form of history which is described as (C) cyclical. Both Toynbee and Spengler approached history from the perspective of human institutions being organisms — born, develop, mature, grow old, and die.

65.   **(D)**   In the poem, the Hungarian-Swiss Tzara provides a sample of a 20th century literary movement known as Dadaism. This post-World War I literary episode was a reaction against the order which led to the war and its horrors; Dadaism, which was short-lived, contributed to the emergence of surrealism. Symbolism (A) was the appellation given to the wider literary movement and which was addressed in Edmund Wilson's *Axel's Castle*. Expressionism (B) and (E) idealism are terms which relate to many facets of art — both literary and other. Deconstructionism (C) is a term which applies to post-1950 literary values and criticism.

66.   **(D)**   All of the listed European intellectuals identified with existentialism except Jacques Maritain. Maritain, a Christian humanist, advanced a persuasive Neo-Thomism in a broad range of studies including *Man and the State*. Sartre (A), Heidegger (B), Jaspers (C), and Camus (E) were leading proponents of varying forms of existentialism.

67.   **(C)**   The driving force behind Hegel's dialectic was universal reason — the Hegelian God. Marx will identify materialism (D) as the key historical force. Hegel's philosophy has been used, and manipulated, by those who identify with (A) nationalism, (B) racial superiority, and, to a much lesser extent, (E) religious values.

68.   **(A)**   The response of the Catholic Church to the Reformation was delayed because the Papacy feared the remnants of the Conciliar Movement with the church itself. The Conciliar Movement, which was clearly evident at the Council of Constance (1414) and later at the Councils of Basel and Florence, was a tradition in the Roman Catholic Church which asserted that authority within the church resided in the assembly of bishops; it was a challenge to the concept of Petrine Supremacy and the authority of the Papacy. Rome (B) had little interest in coordinating its policy with secular leaders, although the early support of Charles V and Henry VIII was well received. By the 1530s most intelligent Church leaders did not (C) think that Protestantism would self-destruct or that (D) the situation was not a serious crisis. The monetary situation of the Church (E) was not relevant to taking a position against Protestantism.

69.   **(D)**   Since 1950 the Soviet Union has suppressed movements toward more liberal governments in East Germany (A), Poland (B), Czechoslovakia (C) and Hungary (E) but not Yugoslavia (D). Marshall Tito's Yugoslavia developed a position of independence from the Soviet Union during the 1950s; its approach to Communism was more innovative and resulted in a more fluid economic

system. The Soviet Union's suppression of liberalism in East Germany and Poland (1953), Hungary (1956), and Czechoslovakia (1968) was violent and followed by the installation of pro-Soviet regimes.

70. **(E)** The first individual who served as Prime Minister of Great Britain was Robert Walpole who initiated the Cabinet system of government between 1721 and 1740; an absence of monarchial leadership on the part of George I and George II resulted in the need for a new entity to provide executive leadership. William Pitt (A) and Lord North (D) led governments during the 18th century; Palmerston (C) and Gladstone (B) were prominent Prime Ministers during the second half of the 19th century.

71. **(A)** Friedrich Nietzsche advanced his philosophy in such works as (A) *Thus Spake Zarathustra* and *The Will to Power*. (B) *The Golden Bough* was written by Sir James Frazer, an English anthropologist, and *The Wild Duck* was a play by Henrik Ibsen. (C) *The Return of the Native* and *Jude the Obscure* were by Thomas Hardy. (D) *Civilization and Its Discontents* was by Sigmund Freud and *The Riddle of the Universe* was by the biologist, Heinrich Haeckel. (E) *The Descent of Man* was by Charles Darwin and *The Weavers* was by Gerhard Hauptmann.

72. **(A)** In the painting "The Eternal City," the American painter Peter Blume portrays a (A) fascist Italy which is dominated by the personality of Mussolini. Obviously, the painting does not depict (B) how fascism in Italy improved the general condition of the people, (C) Mussolini as a benevolent dictator, (D) a sympathetic rendering of the impact of fascism on Italian life and institutions, nor does it (E) recount the March on Rome in 1922.

73. **(C)** "Men are born, and always continue free and equal in respect of their rights. Civil distinctions, therefore, can be found only on public utility." In 1789 these statements were part of (C) the Declaration of the Rights of Man and the Citizen which was passed by the National Assembly in France. The English Bill of Rights (1689) was a consequence of the Glorious Revolution which resulted in William and Mary coming to power. The Constitution of the Year III (1795) established the Directory in France; it was a government which was advised by experts or intellectuals. In *What Is the Third Estate?* (1788) Abbé Siéyès maintained that the Third Estate of the Estates-General was in fact a "National Assembly" and representative of the national sovereign power.

74. **(C)** During the "June Days" in Paris (1848) the (C) army suppressed the radical revolutionary element. The workers who had identified with or had been supported by the National Workshop Program (Louis Blanc) were opposed to the conservative policies of the new elect Assembly; they revolted and were suppressed by military units which were loyal to the government. Obviously, this situation indicates that (A) and (B) were incorrect responses. (D) Louis Napoleon

did not come to power until the subsequent elections for the presidency of the Second French Republic. (E) Lamartine was a poet and republican leader who enjoyed support during the Winter and Spring of 1848; thereafter, Lamartine's influence declined.

75. **(E)** The repeal of the Corn Laws (1846) in England was led by (E) Robert Peel who was the Prime Minister during the 1840s. While William Gladstone (A), Benjamin Disraeli (C), and Lord Palmerston (D) were prominent political leaders, they did not determine the decision on the Corn Laws' repeal. The repeal of these measures alleviated the burden on the general population by removing restrictions which raised the price of grain. Lord Melbourne (B) was Prime Minister during the 1830s.

76. **(C)** In an effort to conduct a successful economic war against Britain, Napoleon created the (C) Continental System. Its primary goal was the economic isolation of Britain through the closing of European markets for British goods. Earlier, Napoleon established (A) the Bank of France to consolidate the French national economy; the (D) Napoleonic Code was a codification and reform of French law. The (B) Confederation of the Rhine was supported by Napoleon and was intended to decentralize German states. The (E) Kingdom of the Two Sicilies appeared earlier.

77. **(A)** The 1909 budget proposed by Lloyd George advocated (A) progressive income and inheritance taxes. This liberal budget was designed to tax those who could afford it — the wealthy class, and to raise revenues for defense and domestic social programs. (B) Property taxes did not cease nor were there drastic reductions in funding for (C) domestic programs or (D) weapons. Obviously, the 1909 budget did not specify a (E) redistribution of excessive tax revenues.

78. **(C)** In this painting entitled "Guernica" (1937), Pablo Picasso portrayed (C) the impact of the aerial bombardment of a Spanish town by the German Condor Legion during the Spanish Civil War. Both German and Italian military "volunteers" assisted Franco's fascist forces in the struggle against the republicans.

79. **(C)** Iraq invaded Kuwait, controlling the entire country. Kuwait is a major supplier of oil to the United States and Western Europe. (D) is incorrect because Iraq did not attempt to boycott sales of oil to the U.S. or any other country, though the invasion of Kuwait destabilized a region that is among the chief suppliers of oil to the world. Iraq did threaten Israel (A) and launched Scud missiles into Israel, but this happened after the war had begun. Though Iraq did at the time and later continued to persecute the Kurdish minority (B), this was not the reason for the invasion of the multinational coalition. Iraq released Americans (E) in its territory before the war began.

80. **(A)** John Major replaced "the Iron Lady" as Great Britain's Prime Minister. George Mitchell (B) is a former United States Senator whom President Clinton dispatched on a mission to Northern Ireland to find avenues for reconciliation between Roman Catholics and Protestants. Clement Atlee (C) served as British Prime Minister from 1945-1951, granting independence to India, Pakistan, Burma, and Ceylon, and giving up British control over Egypt and Palestine. Edward Heath (D) was British Prime Minister from 1970-1974. Choice (E), Robert Owen (1771-1858), was a Welsh social reformer.

Sample Answer to Document-Based Question

Eighteenth century English urban life has been viewed as violent and on occasion, almost out of control. William Hogarth was perhaps the most significant social critic of the century; rather than direct his artistic interest and talent to the common portrait paintings of the period or replicating the neo-classicism which was popular on the continent at that time, Hogarth addressed serious social issues in a format which appealed to a larger audience.

In "Chairing the Members" Hogarth criticized the method of 'electing' members of Parliament during the mid-eighteenth century. The procedure led to corruption and abuse and resulted in reforms during the next century. Hogarth was concerned — indeed, he was outraged — by the detachment of the British establishment from the problems which plagued the general populace. In "Inhabitants of the Moon" Hogarth accused the establishment — the monarchy, the church, and the courts — of corruption and exploitation. In "Gin Lane" and "Beer Street" Hogarth condemned the massive consumption of cheap gin and urged people to drink beer; the gin business was riddled with corruption and resulted in excessive profits for the gin brokers and those who financed its production. In "John Wilkes, Esquire" Hogarth found an advocate for political reform; Wilkes was elected repeatedly to the House of Commons but ultimately was tried for his radical views.

Hogarth's social criticisms did not resolve the ills of 18th century but they enhanced awareness of the problems. Later, with reformers such as Bentham, Mill, and Wilberforce, reforms would be implemented which eliminated many of these abuses.

Sample Answers to Essay Questions

1.   For more than 50 years (1660–1715) the policies of Louis XIV dominated European history. Through the War of Devolution, the Dutch War, the War of the League of Augsburg, and the War of the Spanish Succession, Louis XIV attempted to establish personal control over Western and Central Europe. To Louis XIV war was a means to demonstrate his greatness and to acquire a significant place in history. While Napoleon entertained similar personal notions and a vision of the greatness of France, the Napoleonic wars differed from those of Louis XIV because there was an ideological consideration — the revolution — which motivated the French to support his policies. Further, the Napoleonic wars involved a proportionately higher number of "citizens" than did the military enterprises of Louis XIV.

During the last four decades of the 17th century Louis XIV's France enjoyed a position of hegemony over European affairs. The War of Devolution, which was related to property claims in small towns in the Spanish Netherlands, resulted in the establishment of an alliance, anchored with Great Britain and the

Netherlands, against France. The British and the Dutch feared that unless Louis XIV was contained that he would establish such an overwhelming base of power that he would alter the balance of power and eliminate the sovereignty of many nations by destroying the European equilibrium. In the Dutch War, the War of the League of Augsburg, and the War of the Spanish Succession, the European powers responded to French aggression through the establishment of coalitions. The success of the coalitions maintained the balance of power and, in the end, not only thwarted Louis XIV's aspirations but also demonstrated that France was basically isolated. States as diverse as Britain, Austria, the Netherlands and Prussia joined to preserve their independence. At the Peace of Utrecht in 1713–14 France was still recognized as the greatest European power; however, France did not achieve its goals and was in fact defeated in the War of the Spanish Succession and had to make concessions to the coalition victors.

The Napoleonic Wars (1799–1815) constituted a more serious threat to the European political structure than did the wars of Louis XIV. Napoleon carried with him the liberal ideology and reforms of the French Revolution; the French revolutionary tradition was viewed as more dangerous than the might of the French armies. Upon achieving victory, Napoleon not only would establish French control over the defeated state or region; but he would also introduce political and economic reforms which threatened the basis of the old order's power. Legal reforms in Spain, economic reforms in the German states, and other similar developments rendered the Napoleonic Wars much more complex than earlier struggles. The other nations of Europe responded to French power and the revolution through resurrecting the coalition concept which had prevailed against Louis XIV. From the outbreak of resistance in Spain in 1808 to the defeat in Russia (1812–13) and the devastation of French defeat at Waterloo in June, 1815, the coalition against Napoleon succeeded in suppressing this second French attempt to alter the European political system.

In the wars of Louis XIV many of the coalition members were motivated by dynastic considerations; Britain and the Netherlands were clearly motivated by national values. During the Napoleonic period, the coalition was generally motivated by nationalism, although dynastic priorities were not absent. In Central and Southern Europe nationalism prevailed over the revolutionary tradition; however, in spite of efforts to suppress this tradition, it would reappear in the Revolutions of 1820, 1830, and 1848.

2.   While the development and support of fascism in Germany and Italy had many parallel or similar experiences, the causes for the rise of fascism in each of these nations was unique.

When Adolph Hitler became the German Chancellor in January, 1933, the fascist movement achieved a victory which only a few years before was considered well beyond its reach. Beginning in 1919 the Nazi Party adopted the fascist corporate approach to government, which viewed the state as a entity in its own right; the state was more important than the individuals who resided in it. German fascism was romantic, militaristic, highly nationalistic, and espoused a racist totalitarianism which was fundamentally anti-democratic. During the 1920s

Hitler and his Nazi Party were considered radical dissidents who never would come to power; the Weimar Republic continued to enjoy the support of the German people until the impact of the Depression which began to devastate the German economy in 1930. The fascist success in Germany can be attributed to (1) the continuing economic and social crisis caused by the Depression, (2) the inability of the Weimar Republic to advance a credible policy to alleviate the widespread distress, (3) the organization of the Nazi Party, (4) the continuing humiliation from defeat in the war, and (5) the charisma of Adolph Hitler. Through Hitler's direction the Nazis gained a significant base of strength in the German *Reichstag* from which he was able to demand a place in the new Hindenberg government in 1933. Once in power Hitler moved quickly to consolidate his position; he passed the Enabling Act which gave him dictatorial powers and purged Germany of his political enemies.

The rise of fascism in Italy via Benito Mussolini can be attributed to a number a number of factors, including (1) the failure to obtain the expected gains for Italy's involvement and sacrifices during the First World War, (2) the postwar economic collapse, (3) "1919ism" — the fear of Bolshevism, (4) the ineptitude of the centrist Italian parties in handling the political and economic crisis which gripped Italy after the war, and (5) the opportunistic Mussolini. During the war Italians had entertained thoughts that they would acquire colonies and great power status as a result of their involvement with the allies; at the Versailles Conference and in the subsequent treaty it was evident that these goals were not realized. At the same time Britain and the United States ceased making loans after the armistice; this action resulted in a financial crisis in Italy which was aggravated by the rapid demobilization of the Italian army, high unemployment, and inflation. "1919ism" was the Italian Red Scare, the fear that the economic crisis would provide the Bolsheviks with an opportunity to initiate a revolution; this anxiety resulted in polarizing Italian society with the wealthy classes identifying with order and the preservation of their own interests. During the chaotic period from 1918 to 1922, the Italian political system proved unable to resolve the crisis; Italian political parties were not able to overcome their own party factionalism and sustain a durable coalition government. Into this void of leadership stepped Mussolini, a flamboyant and egocentric demagogue who promised to reestablish order and a sense of national pride to Italy. Mussolini's seizure of power — the March on Rome (1922) — was not opposed.

3.   When James I assumed the throne upon the death of Elizabeth I in 1603, the monarchy in Britain was a strong executive position which was restricted by the English constitutional concept of the "King in Parliament." By the time that Queen Anne — the last Stuart — died in 1714, the alignment of English domestic political power had shifted. While there were many factors which led to this alteration, the Stuart monarchs contributed to this erosion of monarchical power through inept leadership and policies which did not consider the English historical tradition nor the forces which were current during the 17th century.

James I (1603–25) alienated Parliament by asserting his support for royal absoluticism and the "Divine Right of Kings." During his reign, James convened few Parliaments and those which were held were confrontational — the Addled Parliament of 1614 is a good example. Further, James I did not address the continuing religious crisis which centered on Puritanism; the Hampton Court Conference reinforced the Anglican status quo and led to a loss of support for James among the Puritans. James I's personal life did not enhance his public reputation; his purported bisexuality, his awkward physical appearance, and his Scots accent rendered him "unkingly" to many. Charles I (1625–49) succeeded his father and found himself involved with unsuccessful and costly foreign enterprises in Spain and France; in 1628, the King's favorite, the Duke of Buckingham, was assassinated and Charles I was forced to convene a Parliament for funds to pay his debts caused by the foreign wars. Parliament forced Charles to sign the Petition of Rights which was an statement of grievances; Charles pledged not to improperly collect the ships' tax, not to abuse the use of martial law as it related to the public billeting of troops, and to respect the writ of habeas corpus. After Parliament provided the funds, Charles I decided to rule without a Parliament — from 1629 to 1640 no Parliament sat. During this period Charles I and his aid, Archbishop William Laud, attempted to suppress Puritanism throughout the country. In 1637 Charles I and Laud extended this policy in Scotland; the Scottish reaction led to war and reluctantly, in the spring of 1640, Charles I summoned what became known as the Short Parliament — it lasted for only three weeks. The suppressed Parliamentary and Puritan forces demanded that Charles I meet their demands before they would grant funds to raise an army; Charles I dissolved the Short Parliament. With the Scottish problem becoming more acute, Charles summoned the "Long" Parliament in the fall of 1640 — it sat for years. Between 1640 and 1660 English politics were in a state of flux; the English Civil War, the execution of Charles I, the establishment of the Commonwealth and the Protectorate, and the Restoration of the Stuarts in the person of Charles II transpired during those decades. The Parliament was strengthened and the monarchy weakened as a result of these development. The monarchy which was restored in 1660 was a modified and restricted executive force.

In 1688 and 1689 another constitutional crisis gripped the nation. James II, a Catholic, had a male heir and baptized the child a Catholic. Faced with the likelihood of having a series of Catholic monarchs over a Protestant nation, Tory and Whig politicians in Parliament arranged for William and Mary to replace James II who later fled the nation. This Glorious Revolution was formalized with the Bill of Rights in April 1689 which stipulated that the Parliament, through its control of finances, was the dominant force in English politics. The monarch was still very significant and exercised considerable power; however, the power enjoyed by the great Tudor monarchs, Henry VIII and Elizabeth I, would not be seen again.

4.   Any attempt to reflect upon the ideological legacy of the French Revolution of 1789 must be preceded by a brief review of the intellectual forces which impacted on the revolution and the ideology which was manifested during the revolution. The revolution which broke in France in 1789 and continued for the next decade was ideologically motivated by the political and philosophic con-

cepts which were advanced during the Enlightenment — the Age of Reason. While many varying sentiments emerged during the 18th century, there was a common ideological basis: 18th century intellectuals were interested in developing a rationally based human society which was free from the assumptions of the past and which would advanced human progress. One of the best sources on this topic is Keith M. Baker's *Inventing the French Revolution*.

During the revolution itself, there was a great debate over how to realize these goals. This debate, which continued long after the revolutions were suppressed, was one of the major ideological legacies of the French Revolution — an open and public dialogue on issues of concern. It anticipated an environment which fostered intellectual activity; the anti-intellectualism of the past would be replaced. During the 19th century attempts were made to curtail the freedom of speech through varying forms of censorship; the July Ordinances and the later actions of Francois Guizot in the 1840s were examples of this censorship. Freedom of speech or debate was the underlying component of the radical philosophic tradition which emerged from the French Revolution. Another major factor which endured was the revision of the notion of humanity which developed during the revolutionary period. The thoughts of Rousseau, Montesquieu, and others and the historic experience of the revolution influenced Marx, Proudhon, and John Stuart Mill in the 19th century as well as Sartre, Freud, and others in the 20th century as they attempted to develop an understanding of humanity and the individual. The notion of the role and rights of "the people" were altered; the last vestiges of the medieval order were struggling to survive. Related to the changing concept of "the people," was a broadening of the idea of the "nation." Further no longer would man be viewed primarily in a religious context; humankind was to be examined and measured within a political, economic, or social context.

Finally, any consideration of the ideological legacy must include comments on the "cult of progress." While J. B. Bury and others have considered this issue, the impact of the "concept of progress" as a consequence of the French Revolution must be revised continually. Further, the interrelationship of "progress" with other developments such as racism, democracy, and totalitarianism. The French Revolution of 1789 initiated a global revolutionary tradition which was not limited to France or Europe.

5.   While Germany was forced to agree with the infamous War Guilt clause (Article 231) of the Versailles Treaty, the outbreak of the First World War involved many diverse factors which renders any assignment of specific national guilt a rather futile undertaking. The immediate circumstances which led to the outbreak of the war were focused on the diplomatic crisis of the summer of 1914; the Austrians, with German support, reacted to the assassination of Archduke Franz Ferdinand by directing an ultimatum at Serbia, which was supported by Russia. The alliance systems were deployed and the war was underway by early August.

The causes which led to this situation were (1) the polarization of Europe into two armed camps, (2) imperialism, and (3) militarism and the arms race. Since Bismarck's dismissal in 1890 the European diplomatic situation had become more complex; by 1907, it was clear that two separate and opposing groups of nations existed. In 1890 Germany failed to renew the Reinsurance Treaty with Russia; within four years, the Russians entered into the Dual Entente with France which terminated the key element in Bismarck's foreign policy, the diplomatic isolation of France. During the late 1890s Germany rebuffed British overtures for an alliance; this rejection resulted in the British entering into the Anglo-Japanese alliance (1902), the Anglo-French Entente (or Entente Cordiale) (1904), and the Anglo-Russian Entente (1907). While these arrangements did not obligate Britain to any direct military action in the event of war, they did affiliate Britain with the French oriented diplomatic system. This affiliation was evident during the Algerciras Conference in 1906. Germany and Austria-Hungary were isolated.

Imperialistic rivalries contributed to a increasingly hostile environment among the European powers. From the Fashoda Crisis of 1898–99 to the First and Second Moroccan Crises and the continuing Balkan conflicts, the European powers found themselves in conflict with one another — frequently over areas that were unrelated to their national security or interests. This conflicting environment was exacerbated by the growing influence of the military within European governments. A sense of the "inevitably" of war led the great powers to develop war plans such as the German Schlieffen (1905) and the French Plan XVII (1912). These developments implied that a military resolution to a crisis was acceptable; there was dissatifaction with the "indecisive" nature of diplomatic settlements. Further aggravating this militarism was the impact of technology on weaponry. During the two decades immediately prior to the outbreak of the war, improvements and innovations in weapons were revolutionary. The development of new classes of capital ships with enhanced ranges and armament, the revolution in artillery, and innovations in field weapons such as the machine gun and in the quality of repeating rifles resulted in an arms race which directed funds away from domestic needs.

In the summer of 1914 the mediation efforts which had worked on previous occasions failed and Europe stumbled into a war for which it had longed prepared. While Germany must be faulted for William II's "Blank Cheque" to the Austrians, most of the major powers were responsible for contributing to an situation in which a general war was acceptable. The causes for this war and, in many incidents, most wars are to be found in the mentality of the age which permits nations to adopt confrontational policies and procedures.

6.   From Disraeli's call for a "New Imperialism" in the early 1870s to 1914, the European powers participated in the most reckless and active era of colonial expansion. Bolstered by economic need, aspects of social Darwinism, and the zealousness of militant Christianity and European nationalism, the European powers participated in the "Scramble for Africa," for a position in China, and for Pacific islands. Considerable resources were expended in the acquisition and maintenance of these colonial empires; the conseqences of imperialism resulted in national and domestic political rivalries and mixed economic results.

From the perspective of the impact of imperialism on the relations between nation-states, one can divide this era into two chronological periods: before and after the Berlin Convention of 1884–85. This meeting established the principle that any claim to a territory had to be supported by occupation and notification to the other European powers of the claim; this was intended to regulate colonial claims and to limit the expansion of the British Empire. Throughout the entire era, imperialism resulted in conflicts between the European powers; the Afghan wars, the Fashoda crisis, the Venezuelan dispute, the Boer War, the First and Second Moroccan Crises, and the Libyan crisis illustrate the extent and frequency of these conflicts. Further, imperialism emerged as a domestic political issue in Britain, France, Germany, Italy, and Belgium. In England, Disraeli and his Conservative Party supported imperial expansion and involved the nation in a series of colonial wars including the Ashanti and Zulu wars. Disraeli's Liberal rival was William Gladstone, an espoused anti-imperialist. Gladstone found that it was extremely difficult to maintain his anti-imperialist position during his four tenures as Prime Minister; this was due to international and national political factors. Thus, Gladstone found himself despatching General Charles Gordon to the Sudan and then sending an expeditionary force to rescue Gordon. Within England the Fabian Society was consistently anti-imperialist until the Boer War when the Fabians were factionalized over British involvement in South Africa. In Germany and France liberal and socialist political parties opposed the imperialist policies advanced by the rightist and conservative governments and parties.

European economic life was stimulated by the increased trade which resulted from imperialism and the establishment of colonies. Not only did the European powers acquire new sources of raw materials, but also — and more importantly in most instances — they acquired new markets where they could distribute their finished goods. Domestic industries which provided transport or products associated with transport and new settlements profited from the expansion. At the same time, imperial activities diverted capital away from domestic investments and programs; some contend that the Western European economies possessed excess capital during this period which could not be absorbed by the domestic economies. Another negative economic factor was the continuing costs associated with the administration and defense of colonies; this involved human as well as financial resources. It appears that the immediate economic impact was positive but that the long-term result was negative. It should also be noted that the economic gains during the early decades of this period resulted in deferring consideration of domestic economic problems which affected the working classes.

THE ADVANCED
PLACEMENT EXAMINATION IN

European
History

TEST 2

THE ADVANCED PLACEMENT EXAMINATION IN

European History

TEST 2

1. (A) (B) (C) (D) (E)
2. (A) (B) (C) (D) (E)
3. (A) (B) (C) (D) (E)
4. (A) (B) (C) (D) (E)
5. (A) (B) (C) (D) (E)
6. (A) (B) (C) (D) (E)
7. (A) (B) (C) (D) (E)
8. (A) (B) (C) (D) (E)
9. (A) (B) (C) (D) (E)
10. (A) (B) (C) (D) (E)
11. (A) (B) (C) (D) (E)
12. (A) (B) (C) (D) (E)
13. (A) (B) (C) (D) (E)
14. (A) (B) (C) (D) (E)
15. (A) (B) (C) (D) (E)
16. (A) (B) (C) (D) (E)
17. (A) (B) (C) (D) (E)
18. (A) (B) (C) (D) (E)
19. (A) (B) (C) (D) (E)
20. (A) (B) (C) (D) (E)
21. (A) (B) (C) (D) (E)
22. (A) (B) (C) (D) (E)
23. (A) (B) (C) (D) (E)
24. (A) (B) (C) (D) (E)
25. (A) (B) (C) (D) (E)

26. (A) (B) (C) (D) (E)
27. (A) (B) (C) (D) (E)
28. (A) (B) (C) (D) (E)
29. (A) (B) (C) (D) (E)
30. (A) (B) (C) (D) (E)
31. (A) (B) (C) (D) (E)
32. (A) (B) (C) (D) (E)
33. (A) (B) (C) (D) (E)
34. (A) (B) (C) (D) (E)
35. (A) (B) (C) (D) (E)
36. (A) (B) (C) (D) (E)
37. (A) (B) (C) (D) (E)
38. (A) (B) (C) (D) (E)
39. (A) (B) (C) (D) (E)
40. (A) (B) (C) (D) (E)
41. (A) (B) (C) (D) (E)
42. (A) (B) (C) (D) (E)
43. (A) (B) (C) (D) (E)
44. (A) (B) (C) (D) (E)
45. (A) (B) (C) (D) (E)
46. (A) (B) (C) (D) (E)
47. (A) (B) (C) (D) (E)
48. (A) (B) (C) (D) (E)
49. (A) (B) (C) (D) (E)
50. (A) (B) (C) (D) (E)
51. (A) (B) (C) (D) (E)
52. (A) (B) (C) (D) (E)
53. (A) (B) (C) (D) (E)
54. (A) (B) (C) (D) (E)
55. (A) (B) (C) (D) (E)

56. (A) (B) (C) (D) (E)
57. (A) (B) (C) (D) (E)
58. (A) (B) (C) (D) (E)
59. (A) (B) (C) (D) (E)
60. (A) (B) (C) (D) (E)
61. (A) (B) (C) (D) (E)
62. (A) (B) (C) (D) (E)
63. (A) (B) (C) (D) (E)
64. (A) (B) (C) (D) (E)
65. (A) (B) (C) (D) (E)
66. (A) (B) (C) (D) (E)
67. (A) (B) (C) (D) (E)
68. (A) (B) (C) (D) (E)
69. (A) (B) (C) (D) (E)
70. (A) (B) (C) (D) (E)
71. (A) (B) (C) (D) (E)
72. (A) (B) (C) (D) (E)
73. (A) (B) (C) (D) (E)
74. (A) (B) (C) (D) (E)
75. (A) (B) (C) (D) (E)
76. (A) (B) (C) (D) (E)
77. (A) (B) (C) (D) (E)
78. (A) (B) (C) (D) (E)
79. (A) (B) (C) (D) (E)
80. (A) (B) (C) (D) (E)

European History

TEST 2 – Section I

TIME: 55 Minutes
80 Questions

DIRECTIONS: Each of the questions or incomplete statements below is followed by five suggested answers or completions. Select the one that is best in each case.

---

1. Renaissance Humanism was a threat to the Church because it

    (A) espoused atheism.

    (B) denounced scholasticism.

    (C) denounced neo-Platonism.

    (D) emphasized a return to the original sources of Christianity.

    (E) advanced an amoral philosophy.

2. *Defense of the Seven Sacraments* was a tract

    (A) written by Thomas More in which the Church is attacked because of its sacramental theology.

    (B) written by Zwingli which argued that the Eucharist was a symbolic reenactment of the Last Supper.

    (C) in which Luther called upon the German nobility to accept responsibility for cleansing Christianity of the abuses which had developed within the Church.

    (D) written by Henry VIII in which the Roman Catholic Church's position on sacramental theology was supported.

    (E) in which Thomas Cranmer argued that the Edwardian Prayer Book was justified by the sacraments.

3. Erasmus of Rotterdam was the author of

    (A)   *The Praise of Folly.*   (D)   *The Prince.*

    (B)   *The Birth of Venus.*   (E)   *Don Quixote.*

    (C)   *Utopia.*

4. The Henrician reaffirmation of Catholic theology was made in the

    (A)   Ten Articles of Faith.

    (B)   Six Articles of Faith.

    (C)   Forty-two Articles of Faith.

    (D)   Act of Supremacy.

    (E)   Act of Uniformity.

5. The Peace of Augsburg

    (A)   recognized that Lutheranism was the true interpretation of Christianity.

    (B)   recognized the principle that the religion of the leader would determine the religion of the people.

    (C)   denounced the Papacy and Charles V.

    (D)   resulted in the recognition of Lutheranism, Calvinism, and Catholicism.

    (E)   authored the seizure of all Church property in German states.

6. The Catholic Counter-Reformation included all of the following EXCEPT

    (A)   the *Index of Prohibited Books.*

    (B)   the Council of Trent.

    (C)   a more assertive Papacy.

    (D)   the establishment of new religious orders.

    (E)   a willingness to negotiate non-doctrinal issues with reformers.

7. Where did the Saint Bartholomew's Day Massacre occur?

    (A)   France   (B)   England

(C) Spain   (D) The Netherlands

(E) The Holy Roman Empire

8. The Price Revolution of the 16th century was caused by

(A) the establishment of monopolies.

(B) the importation of silver and gold into the European economy.

(C) a shortage of labor.

(D) the wars of religion caused by the Reformation.

(E) an unfavorable balance of trade.

9. The Peace of Westphalia (1648)

(A) transferred Louisiana from France to Britain.

(B) recognized the independence of the Netherlands.

(C) recognized the unity of the German Empire.

(D) was a triumph of the Hapsburg polity to unity.

(E) recognized the primacy of Russia in the Baltic.

10. Sir Isaac Newton's intellectual synthesis was advanced in

(A) *Principia.*   (D) *Three Laws of Planetary Motion.*

(B) *Discourse on Method.*   (E) *The Prince.*

(C) *Novum Organum.*

11. Richelieu served as "Prime Minister" to

(A) Louis XII.   (D) Louis XIII.

(B) Henry IV.   (E) Francis I.

(C) Louis XIV.

12. In the Edict of Fontainebleau, Louis XIV

(A) abrogated the Edict of Nantes.

(B) abrogated the Edict of Potsdam.

(C) announced his divorce from Catherine de Medici.

(D) denounced Cardinal Mazarin.

(E) initiated the War of the Spanish Succession.

13. In order to seize the Russian throne, Peter the Great had to overthrow his sister

(A) Theodora.   (D) Catherine.

(B) Natalia.   (E) Elizabeth.

(C) Sophia.

14. Peter the Great's principal foreign policy achievement was

(A) the acquisition of ports on the Black Sea.

(B) the acquisition of ports on the Baltic Sea.

(C) the Russian gains in the three partitions of Poland.

(D) the defensive alliance with England.

(E) the defeat of France in the Great Northern War.

Unemployment
(Numbers in thousands & percentage of appropriate work force)

	Germany		Great Britain	
1930	3,076	15.3	1,917	14.6
1932	5,575	30.1	2,745	22.5
1934	2,718	14.9	2,159	17.7
1936	2,151	11.6	1,755	14.3
1938	429	2.1	1,191	13.3

15. The chart above indicates

(A) that Germany and Great Britain recovered from the Depression at about the same level and rate.

(B) that Hitler's Germany reduced unemployment at a remarkable rate during the period from 1936 and 1938.

(C)   that Britain was complacent about its double-digit unemployment during the 1930s.

(D)   that the German economic system was superior to that of Great Britain.

(E)   none of the above.

16.   A moderate proposal which called on France to adopt a political system similar to Great Britain was an element espoused by Montesquieu in

(A)   *The Social Contract.*

(B)   *The Spirit of the Laws.*

(C)   *The Encyclopedia.*

(D)   *The Declaration of the Rights of Man and the Citizen.*

(E)   *Two Treatises on Civil Government.*

17.   Which of the following chronological sequences on the French Revolution is correct?

(A)   Directory, Consulate, Legislative Assembly

(B)   Legislative Assembly, Convention, Directory

(C)   Convention, Consulate, Directory

(D)   National Assembly, Convention, Directory

(E)   Consulate, Empire, Directory

18.   Thomas Hobbes' political philosophy can be most clearly identified with the thought of which of the following?

(A)   Rousseau   (D)   Montesquieu

(B)   Voltaire   (E)   Robespierre

(C)   Quesnay

19.   Who was the most important enlightened political ruler of the 18th century?

(A)   Catherine the Great   (D)   Frederick the Great

(B)   Louis XV   (E)   Joseph II

(C)   Maria Theresa

20. The reaction to the Peterloo Massacre was characteristic of the conservative policies advanced by the British government under

    (A) George Canning.   (D) Lord Liverpool.

    (B) Robert Peel.   (E) Horatio Hunt.

    (C) Lord Melbourne.

21. The Factory Act of 1833

    (A) established the five-day work week in Britain.

    (B) eliminated child labor in the mining of coal and iron.

    (C) required employers to provide comprehensive medical coverage for all employees.

    (D) alleviated some of the abuses of child labor in the textile industry.

    (E) specified that pregnant women could not work in environmentally unsafe conditions.

22. The Anglo-French Entente (also known as the Entente Cordiale)

    (A) was a defensive treaty directed at containing German expansion in Europe.

    (B) was a defensive treaty directed at containing German expansion overseas.

    (C) resolved Anglo-French colonial disputes in Egypt and Morocco.

    (D) was a 19th century agreement which ended the diplomatic isolation of Britain.

    (E) was an agreement to finance the building of the Trans-Siberian railroad.

23. Who was the most prominent British advocate for the abolition of slavery during the early 19th century?

    (A) William Pitt the Younger

    (B) the Duke of Wellington

    (C) William Wilberforce

    (D) William Wordsworth

    (E) William Blake

24. English Utilitarianism was identified with the phrase

    (A) all power to the people.

    (B) from each according to his labor, to each according to his need.

    (C) universal reason.

    (D) the greatest good for the greatest number.

    (E) collectivistic nationalism.

25. An economic philosophy identified with "bullionism" and the need to maintain a favorable balance of trade was

    (A) Utopian Socialism.   (D) Syndicalism.

    (B) Marxism.   (E) Mercantilism.

    (C) Capitalism.

26. Which British Prime Minister was associated closely with the Irish Home Rule bill?

    (A) Benjamin Disraeli   (D) Joseph Chamberlain

    (B) William Gladstone   (E) Robert Peel

    (C) Lord Salisbury

27. The Balfour Declaration (1917)

    (A) denounced the use of chemicals by the Germans on the Western Front.

    (B) was a pledge of British support for the future.

    (C) was a mediation effort to resolve the Anglo-Irish crisis.

    (D) was an attempt to persuade the United States to abandon its neutrality.

    (E) repudiated the notion of war aims involving territory and compensation.

28. The Boulanger Crisis

    (A) was a left-wing attempt engineered by Leon Gambetta to overthrow the Third French Republic.

(B) involved a financial scandal associated with raising funds to build the Panama Canal.

(C) was caused by a right-wing scheme to overthrow the Third French Republic and install General Georges Boulanger as the political leader.

(D) broke when the Dreyfus scandal became known to the French press.

(E) resulted in the monarchists gaining a majority in the Chamber of Deputies.

29. All of the following were plots against Elizabeth I EXCEPT

(A) the Babington Plot.

(B) the Throckmorton Plot.

(C) the Ridolfi Plot.

(D) the Rising of the Northern Earls.

(E) the Wisbech Stirs.

30. The map below indicates the partition of Africa in what year?

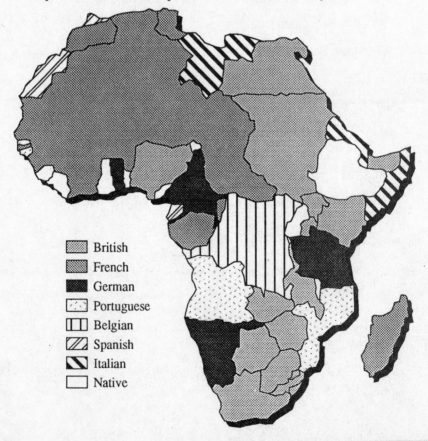

British
French
German
Portuguese
Belgian
Spanish
Italian
Native

(A) 1815   (D) 1960

(B) 1914   (E) 1848

(C) 1870

31. The French essayist Montaigne was representative of which intellectual movement?

(A) Enlightenment   (D) Utopian Socialism

(B) Baroque   (E) Symbolism

(C) Positivism

32. The Hundred Days was

(A) the label given to the reactionary period which followed the Manchester riots in Britain.

(B) an unsuccessful attempt by Napoleon to restore himself as a credible European leader.

(C) the worst phase of the Reign of Terror.

(D) a period which witnessed British defeats in Africa and the Low Countries.

(E) the reactionary phase of the Revolutions of 1848.

33. Jeremy Bentham, James Mill and John Stuart Mill were

(A) Positivists.   (D) Utopian Socialists.

(B) Romantic Idealists.   (E) early advocates of Marxism.

(C) Utilitarians.

34. The Russian blockade of Berlin in 1948–49 was a reaction to

(A) the unification of the British, French, and American zones into West Germany.

(B) the Truman Doctrine.

(C) the Marshall Plan.

(D) the formation of NATO.

(E) the Chinese revolution.

35. The Revolutions of 1848 reflected the interest of all of the following EXCEPT

    (A)   the Liberals.   (D)   the middle class.

    (B)   the Utopians.   (E)   the Marxists.

    (C)   the Nationalists.

36. In the "April Theses" Lenin

    (A)   challenged the policies of the Provisional Government.

    (B)   outlined a plan for a Russian class war after the Revolution of 1905.

    (C)   denounced the revisionist elements within socialism.

    (D)   called for continuing the war against Germany.

    (E)   designated Kerensky as his successor.

37. Mazzini's Roman Republic was

    (A)   instrumental in the unification of Italy in 1870.

    (B)   was suppressed by the armies of Charles Albert.

    (C)   was suppressed by units of the French army.

    (D)   was suppressed by the Swiss Guard.

    (E)   approved in Cavour's plan for a unified Italy.

38. The Schleswig-Holstein question was a contentious issue between

    (A)   Prussia and Sweden.

    (B)   Austria and Prussia.

    (C)   Prussia and Russia.

    (D)   Prussia and the Netherlands.

    (E)   Prussia and Great Britain.

39. Who was the leader of the Hungarians during the Revolutions of 1848?

    (A)   Windischgratz   (D)   Radetsky

    (B)   Louis Kossuth   (E)   Castlereagh

    (C)   Metternich

40. The Dogger Bank Incident resulted in a diplomatic crisis between which two countries?

    (A) Great Britain and France

    (B) France and Germany

    (C) Great Britain and Russia

    (D) Russia and France

    (E) Belgium and France

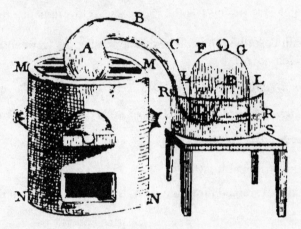

41. The above drawing represents

    (A) the "Leyden Jar."

    (B) the Stephen Gray experiment which demonstrated that electricity could be conducted by means of threads.

    (C) the "Phlogiston" theory.

    (D) Lavoisier's Apparatus for the Decomposition of Air.

    (E) Franklin's device for the processing of alcohol.

42. "1919ism" identifies the

    (A) economic crisis after the First World War.

    (B) the post-war euphoria.

    (C) hysteria known as the Red Scare.

    (D) triumphs of fascism in Italy.

    (E) horrors associated with the Russian Civil War.

43. The Dawes Plan

    (A) was an international proposal to outlaw war.

    (B) was a reparations plan designed to eliminate the friction which led to the Ruhr Crisis.

    (C) was denounced by Gustav Stresemann.

    (D) was a permanent reparations settlement which survived until the 1930s.

    (E) resulted in the dismemberment of Czechoslovakia.

44. Thomas Mann described the collapse of a prosperous German commercial family in which novel?

    (A) *Death in Venice*

    (B) *The Magic Mountain*

    (C) *Buddenbrooks*

    (D) *Lady Chatterley's Lover*

    (E) *Mario and the Magician*

45. Arthur Koestler examined the situation of the victims of the Stalinist purges in

    (A) *Revolt of the Masses.*

    (B) *The Myth of the State.*

    (C) *Darkness at Noon.*

    (D) *Escape from Freedom.*

    (E) *The Treason of the Intellectuals.*

46. The rise of fascism in Germany can be attributed to all of the following EXCEPT

    (A) the failure of the Weimar Republic to address the crisis caused by the Depression.

    (B) the effective organization of the Nazi Party.

    (C) the charisma of Adolph Hitler.

    (D) the lingering humiliation of defeat in the First World War.

    (E) the policies of Gustav Stresemann.

47. The sketch shown below is of

(A) Richard Arkwright's water frame.

(B) the spinning jenny which was invented by James Hargreaves.

(C) Eli Whitney's cotton gin.

(D) James Watt's silk-making machine.

(E) Franklin's paper-making machine.

48. In *A Study of History* a religious-based philosophy of history is advanced by

(A) Oswald Spengler.

(B) William McNeill.

(C) Arnold Toynbee.

(D) T. S. Eliot.

(E) Christopher Dawson.

49. In order "To overcome nothingness ... individuals must define life for themselves and celebrate it fully, instinctively, heroically." This statement reflected the philosophy of which of the following?

(A) Ernst Cassirer

(B) Jacques Maritain

(C) Fredrich Nietzsche

(D) Paul Tillich

(E) Karl Barth

50. In 1968, who led Czechoslovakia's "Prague Spring" — an attempt to develop "socialism with a human face"?

    (A) Havel

    (B) Marshall Tito

    (C) Erich Honecker

    (D) Lech Walesa

    (E) Alexander Dubcek

51. In 1834 German states (excluding Austria) agreed to eliminate tariffs between the states through a customs union known as the

    (A) *Furstenstaat.*

    (B) The Confederation of the Rhine.

    (C) The Frankfurt Assembly.

    (D) *Zollverein.*

    (E) Hanseatic League.

52. "Do you not hear them repeating unceasingly that all that is above them is incapable and unworthy of governing them; that the present distribution of good throughout the world is unjust; that property rests on a foundation which is not an equitable foundation? ... I believe that we are at this moment sleeping on a volcano." Alexis de Tocqueville made these remarks to

    (A) the American Senate in 1838.

    (B) the Chamber of Deputies in 1848.

    (C) the court of Charles X in 1830.

    (D) the new leaders of the Third French Republic in 1871.

    (E) none of the above.

53. In *English Constitution* (1867) an argument was advanced which contended that the British Cabinet system of government was superior to the American constitutional system. Who wrote this book?

    (A) Walter Bagehot

    (B) Robert Southey

    (C) Thomas Carlyle

    (D) John Henry Newman

    (E) John Ruskin

54. A late Renaissance reformer who maintained that "the Hermetic philosophy, with its mystical approach to God and nature, held the key to true wisdom," was

(A) Descartes.

(B) Montaigne.

(C) Francis Bacon.

(D) Giordano Bruno.

(E) Newton.

55. The maps below indicate changes in the western border of Russia between what years?

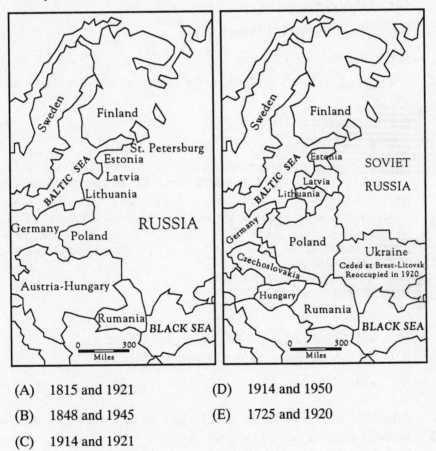

(A) 1815 and 1921

(B) 1848 and 1945

(C) 1914 and 1921

(D) 1914 and 1950

(E) 1725 and 1920

56. Britain established direct authority over India after the suppression of the

(A) Opium Wars.

(B) Boxer Rebellion.

(C) Sepoy Mutiny.

(D) assassination of Gandhi.

(E) Warren Hastings affair.

57. Which of the following African societies was not under European rule by 1914?

(A) The Congo
(D) Angola

(B) South Africa
(E) Ethiopia

(C) Nigeria

58. The British policy of "Splendid Isolationism" was terminated with the

(A) Anglo-French Entente.
(D) Second Moroccan Crisis.

(B) Anglo-Russian Entente.
(E) Boer War.

(C) Anglo-Japanese Alliance.

59. The Versailles Treaty resulted in the formation of several new nations including

(A) Yugoslavia and Hungary.
(D) Austria and Germany.

(B) Poland and Greece.
(E) Austria and Italy.

(C) Poland and Italy.

60. Article 231 of the Versailles Treaty

(A) is known as the "War Guilt" clause and established Germany's responsibility for the war.

(B) established the new nation of Poland.

(C) denounced all secret treaties.

(D) established the League of Nations.

(E) resulted in the decentralization of Germany.

61. After 1945 the policies of the Soviet Union resulted in all of the following EXCEPT

(A) the continuing development of Soviet military power.

(B) a slow demobilization from a war economy.

(C) consistency in the exercise of power by the Communist Party.

(D) a general improvement in the standard of living.

(E) extensive influence in the United Nations during the years immediately following the Second World War.

62. The pessimism which permeated the works of intellectuals between the First and Second World Wars was evident in works by all of the following EXCEPT

   (A)   T. S. Eliot.

   (B)   William Butler Yeats.

   (C)   Johan Huizinga.

   (D)   Carl Gustav Jung.

   (E)   Herbert Spencer.

63. In bringing about a centralized Italy, who was Cavour's most significant non-Italian ally?

   (A)   Bismarck

   (B)   Napoleon III

   (C)   Palmerston

   (D)   Franz Joseph

   (E)   Queen Victoria

64. Syndicalism was a manifestastion of anarchism which was founded by

   (A)   Kropotkin.

   (B)   Sorel.

   (C)   Bakunin.

   (D)   Sidney Webb.

   (E)   Mazzini.

65. The achievements of the Jacobins included all of the following EXCEPT

   (A)   abolition of slavery.

   (B)   the franchise given to all adult males.

   (C)   adoption of the metric system.

   (D)   decreeing the law of the maximum — fixed prices on essentials and raised wages.

   (E)   distribution of all land among the peasants.

66. The British working class demonstrated unity during the

   (A)   demonstrations by anarchists prior to the First World War.

   (B)   movements towards female suffrage.

   (C)   General Strike of 1926.

(D)   post-World War I recession.

(E)   depression which occurred after the Napoleonic Wars.

67.   During the late 1930s efforts to perpetuate the Third French Republic were centered in the Popular Front which was under the leadership of

(A)   Pierre Laval.   (D)   Marcel Deat.

(B)   Léon Blum.   (E)   Marc Bloch.

(C)   Philippe Pétain.

68.   In 1938 the Austrian Republic was incorporated formally into the Third Reich through the

(A)   Nuremburg Laws.   (D)   Munich accord.

(B)   military conquest.   (E)   occupation of the Rhineland.

(C)   *Anschluss.*

69.   Karl Marx believed in all of the following EXCEPT

(A)   the importance of the role of the Communist Party.

(B)   the dialectic view of history.

(C)   materialism was the driving force of history.

(D)   the importance of gaining power through legal means.

(E)   that private property was a primary cause of economic, social, and political distress.

70.   The definitive "Whig" interpretation of British history was advanced in the 19th century by

(A)   David Hume.   (D)   John Stuart Mill.

(B)   Edward Gibbon.   (E)   Jeremy Bentham.

(C)   Thomas Babington Macaulay.

71.   The following map indicates the thesis advanced by H. Mackinder in 1904 that

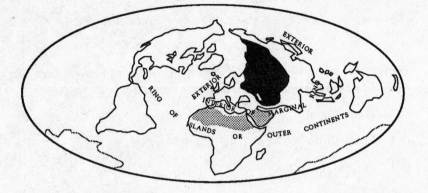

(A) the continental part of Eurasia forms the world heartland and constitutes a potential threat for sea powers.

(B) only a combined Anglo-American-Russian alliance could prevent German world domination.

(C) the theory advanced by Alfred Mahan in *The Influence of Sea Power Upon History* was correct.

(D) sea powers must dominate land powers through containment.

(E) the Southern Hemisphere is as significant as the Northern Hemisphere.

72. German isolation was evident at the

(A) Portsmouth Conference.   (D) Congress of Berlin.

(B) Algerciras Conference.   (E) World Peace Conference.

(C) Berlin Convention.

73. The map shown on the following page indicates

(A) the political boundaries in the Near East in 1960.

(B) the political boundaries in the Near East during the Presidency of Gamel Nasser in Egypt.

(C) the partition of the Ottoman Empire after the First World War.

(D) The scope of the European colonial holdings in the Near East after 1945.

(E) the status of the Ottoman Empire after the Congress of Berlin.

74. The *Marriage of Figaro, Don Giovanni,* and *The Magic Flute* were operas by

    (A) Franz Joseph Haydn.

    (B) Wolfgang Amadeus Mozart.

    (C) Johann Sebastian Bach.

    (D) George Frederick Handel.

    (E) Henry Purcell.

75. The drawing shown here by Karl Arnold appeared in *Simplicissimus* (July, 1924) and was entitled *Neue Typen: Der Rassemensch* —*New Types: The Racial Man* or *The Man of Breeding*). It was a critical comment on

    (A) the Prussian Junkers who condemned the Versailles Treaty.

    (B) the anti-Semites who supported Hitler and the emerging Nazi Party.

    (C) German capitalism.

    (D) German social decadence.

    (E) the ineptitude of the Social Democratic Party.

76. All of the following were reforms initiated by William Gladstone EXCEPT the

    (A) Education Act of 1870.   (D) Irish Land Act.

    (B) Ballot Act of 1872.   (E) Reform Bill of 1867.

    (C) Civil Service Reform of 1870.

77. The notion that "civilization was not the product of an artificial, international elite ... but the genuine culture of the common people, the *Volk*" was advanced by

    (A) Chateaubriand in *The Genius of Christianity*

    (B) Georg Wilhelm Hegel in *Reason in History*

    (C) Giuseppe Verdi in *Don Carlo*

    (D) William Wordsworth in *Lyrical Ballads*

    (E) Johann von Herder in *Ideas for a Philosophy of Human History*

78. Enclosures were required

    (A) to reinforce the concept of private property.

    (B) to eliminate continuing boundary disputes.

    (C) to permit scientific farming.

    (D) to assist in accurate property tax collections.

    (E) to permit the newly rich to acquire property.

79. What were the three Soviet Baltic provinces that broke away from the U.S.S.R. in 1991?

    (A) Ukraine, Lithuania, Estonia

    (B) Latvia, Lithuania, Estonia

    (C) Poland, Czechoslovakia, Hungary

    (D) Lithuania, Chechnya, Georgia

    (E) Serbia, Bosnia, Croatia

80. Who led the Polish Solidarity movement?

    (A) Lech Valesa

    (B) Wojciech Jaruzelski

    (C) Boris Yeltsin

    (D) Pope John Paul II

    (E) Janos Kadar

European History

TEST 2 – Section II

TIME: Reading Period – 15 minutes
Writing Time for all three essays – 115 minutes

DIRECTIONS: Read over both the Document-Based Essay question in Part A and the choices in Part B during the Reading Period, and use the time to organize answers. All students must answer Part A (the Document-Based Essay Question); and choose TWO questions from Part B to answer.

PART A – DOCUMENT-BASED ESSAY

This question is designed to test your ability to work with historical documents. As you analyze each document, *take into account its source and the point of view of the author.* Write an essay on the following topic that integrates your analysis of the documents. You may refer to historical facts and developments not mentioned in the documents.

Analyze the rivalry between Benjamin Disraeli and William Gladstone which dominated English politics from the late 1860s to 1880.

Historical Background: During the late 1860s the political rivalry between the Conservative Benjamin Disraeli and the Liberal Gladstone blossomed and continued until Disraeli's death in 1881. This period witnessed the extension of the franchise, a wide range of domestic legislation, and a debate on imperialism.

Document 1
"Hoity-Toity"

Document 2
Letter from Queen Victoria to William Gladstone — May 6, 1870

...The circumstances respecting the Bill to give women the same position as men with respect to Parliamentary franchise gives her an opportunity to observe that she had for some time past wished to call Mr. Gladstone's attention to the mad & utterly demoralizing movement of the present day to place women in the same position as to professions — as *men*;—& amongst others, in the *Medical Line* ....

The Queen is a women herself—& knows what an anomaly her *own* position is:—but that can be reconciled with reason & propriety tho' it is a terribly difficult & trying one. But to tear away all the barriers wʰ surround a woman, & to propose that they shᵈ study with *men*—things wʰ cᵈ not be named before them—certainly not *in a mixed* audience—wʰᵈ be to introduce a total disregard of what must be considered as belonging to the rules & principles of morality.

The Queen feels so strongly upon his dangerous & unchristian & unnatural *cry* & movement of "women's rights,"—in wʰ she knows Mr. Gladstone *agrees*; (as he sent her that excellent Pamphlet by a Lady) that she is most anxious that Mr. Gladstone & others shᵈ take some steps to check this alarming danger & to make whatever use they can of her name.

She sends the letters wʰ speak for themselves.

Let woman be what God intended; a helpmate for a man—but with totally different duties & vocations.

Document 3
"The Conservative Programme"

Document 4
"The Colossus of the World"

Document 5
"On the Dizzy Brink"

Document 6
"A Bad Example"

PART B – ESSAY QUESTIONS

1. Using the Glorious Revolution of 1688, the French Revolution of 1789, and the Russian Revolution of 1917, discuss and analyze the nature and scope of the revolutionary tradition in modern Europe.

2. Describe and analyze the impact of the Counter-Reformation on European history.

3. Describe and analyze the characteristics of fascism.

4. Describe and compare the origins and proposals of the utopian socialists, the marxists, the anarchists, and the revisionists during the 19th century.

5. Describe and analyze the development of democracy in Great Britain during the 19th and 20th centuries.

6. Describe and compare the unification of Germany and Italy during the 19th century.

THE ADVANCED PLACEMENT EXAMINATION IN

European History

TEST 2 – ANSWERS

1.	**(D)**	21.	**(D)**	41.	**(D)**	61.	**(E)**
2.	**(D)**	22.	**(C)**	42.	**(C)**	62.	**(E)**
3.	**(A)**	23.	**(C)**	43.	**(B)**	63.	**(B)**
4.	**(B)**	24.	**(D)**	44.	**(C)**	64.	**(B)**
5.	**(B)**	25.	**(E)**	45.	**(C)**	65.	**(E)**
6.	**(E)**	26.	**(B)**	46.	**(E)**	66.	**(C)**
7.	**(A)**	27.	**(B)**	47.	**(B)**	67.	**(B)**
8.	**(B)**	28.	**(C)**	48.	**(C)**	68.	**(C)**
9.	**(B)**	29.	**(E)**	49.	**(C)**	69.	**(D)**
10.	**(A)**	30.	**(B)**	50.	**(E)**	70.	**(C)**
11.	**(D)**	31.	**(B)**	51.	**(D)**	71.	**(A)**
12.	**(A)**	32.	**(B)**	52.	**(B)**	72.	**(B)**
13.	**(C)**	33.	**(C)**	53.	**(A)**	73.	**(C)**
14.	**(B)**	34.	**(A)**	54.	**(D)**	74.	**(B)**
15.	**(B)**	35.	**(E)**	55.	**(C)**	75.	**(B)**
16.	**(B)**	36.	**(A)**	56.	**(C)**	76.	**(E)**
17.	**(B)**	37.	**(C)**	57.	**(E)**	77.	**(E)**
18.	**(B)**	38.	**(B)**	58.	**(C)**	78.	**(C)**
19.	**(D)**	39.	**(B)**	59.	**(A)**	79.	**(B)**
20.	**(D)**	40.	**(C)**	60.	**(A)**	80.	**(A)**

Detailed Explanations
of Answers
TEST 2

1. **(D)** Renaissance Humanism was a threat to the Church because it (D) emphasized a return to the original sources of Christianity — the Bible and the writings of the Fathers of Church. In that light, the humanists tended to ignore or denounce the proceedings of Church councils and pontiffs during the Middle Ages. While many Renaissance humanists denounced scholasticism, there was no inherent opposition to it and many retained support of the late Medieval philosophy. Renaissance humanism did not espouse atheism nor did it advance an amoral philosophy; it tended to advance a neo-Platonism through the writings of such individuals as Pico Della Mirandola and Marsiglio.

2. **(D)** The *Defense of the Seven Sacraments* was a tract (D) written by Henry VIII in which the Roman Catholic Church's position on sacramental theology was supported. This 1521 publication repudiated Luther's views on the sacraments which were advanced in pamphlets during the preceding year. While some earlier authorities have asserted that the real author of the tract was Thomas More (A), contemporary scholarship has affirmed that, while More no doubt provided assistance, authorship should be attributed to Henry VIII. Zwingli (B) did maintain that the Eucharist was a symbolic reenactment of the Last Supper but he did not write this tract. Obviously, Luther (C), to whom it was directed, and Cranmer (E), who came to prominence during the next decade, were not the authors.

3. **(A)** Erasmus of Rotterdam was the author of (A) *The Praise of Folly* which was a criticism of the ambitions of the clergy. *The Birth of Venus* (B) was not a literary work. Thomas More was the author of *Utopia* (C); Niccolo Machiavelli wrote (D) *The Prince*; and Cervantes was the author of *Don Quixote*.

4. **(B)** The Henrican reaffirmation of the Catholic Theology was made in the (B) Six Articles of Faith of 1539. In response to mounting criticism and the vague (A) Ten Articles of Faith (1536) and the dissolution of the monasteries, Henry VIII retreated from the movement toward Protestantism. The (D) Act of Supremacy and (E) Act of Uniformity were passed by the Reformation Parliament to decree and enforce Henry VIII's authority over the Church in England.

The Forty-Two Articles of Faith (E) was a statement of Protestant doctrines developed by Thomas Cranmer during the early 1550s.

5.   **(B)**   The Peace of Augsburg (1555) (B) recognized the principle that the religion of the leader would determine the religion of the people; it was a major victory for Lutheranism and a defeat of the Hapsburg aspirations to effectively control the Holy Roman Empire. Lutheranism (A) was not recognized as the true interpretation of Christianity nor did it (E) authorize the seizure of all Church property in German states. Calvinism (D) was not recognized until the Peace of Westphalia in 1648; (C) Charles V and the Papacy were negotiators in formulating the Peace of Augsburg.

6.   **(E)**   The Catholic Counter-Reformation did not include (E) a willingness to negotiate non-doctrinal issues with reformers; indeed, the Catholic Church considered all confrontational issues to be doctrinal. The Council of Trent (B) was convened in three sessions from 1545 to 1564 and reaffirmed traditional Catholic doctrines; new religious orders (D) such as the Jesuits and Oratorians appeared; the papacy (C) became more assertive as can be seen in the issuing of the *Index of Prohibited Books* in 1558-59.

7.   **(A)**   The St. Batholomew's Day Massacre occurred in 1572 in (A) France; it was the work of Queen Catherine De Medici and involved the execution of thousands of French Huguenots during the subsequent months. Obviously, this event did not transpire in (B) England, (C) Spain, (D) the Netherlands, or (E) the Holy Roman Empire.

8.   **(B)**   The Price Revolution of the 16th century was caused by (B) the importation of silver and gold into the European economy; the influx of specie from Latin America resulted in eliminating the scarcity of money — the result was a general fourfold increase in prices. The establishment of monopolies (A) and the maintenance of a favorable balance of trade (E) were important elements in 17th century mercantilism. While there were occasional labor shortages (C) and the wars of religion (D) did not disrupt economic activities, these developments did not have any substantive impact on the price revolution.

9.   **(B)**   The Peace of Westphalia (1648) (B) recognized the independence of the Netherlands and Switzerland. Louisiana (A) was not transferred to Britain; Sweden not Russia (E) was recognized as the primary power in the Baltic; and the Hapsburg plan (D) and (C) for a unified central Europe was destroyed.

10.   **(A)**   Sir Isaac Newton's intellectual synthesis was advanced in (A) *Principia* in 1687; he established scientism as a credible alternative to preceding intellectual approaches and methods. *Discourse on Method* (B) was written by René Descartes in 1637; *Novum Organum* (C) was a work by Francis Bacon which addressed the issue of empiricism; Kepler developed the Three Laws of Planetary Motion (D); and *The Prince* was written by Machiavelli.

11. **(D)** Richelieu served as "Prime Minister" to (D) Louis XIII. For over two decades during the turbulence of the Thirty Years' War and the LaRochelle crisis with the Huguenots, Cardinal Richelieu administered France for Louis XIII. Henry IV (B) was Louis XIII's father; Louis XIV (C) was his son. Louis XII (A) and Francis I (E) were earlier French monarchs.

12. **(A)** In the Edict of Fontainebleau (1685), Louis XIV (A) abrogated the Edict of Nantes of 1598 in which Henry IV had to extend some religious liberties to French Protestants. Fontainebleau directed that all Frenchmen would conform to Catholicism. The Edict of Potsdam (1686) (B) was issued by Elector Frederick William of Brandenburg-Prussia; it invited French Protestants to migrate to Brandenburg. (E) The War of the Spanish Succession commenced in 1702; the Fontainebleau decree was not related to (C) Catherine De Medici or (D) Cardinal Mazarin.

13. **(C)** In order to seize the Russian throne, Peter the Great had to overthrow (1689) his sister (C) Sophia. His mother, (B) served as regent until 1694 when Peter took over the government. Catherine (D) and Elizabeth (E) were Russian leaders in the 18th century. (A) Theodora was not a Romanov ruler.

14. **(B)** Peter the Great's principal foreign policy achievement was (B) the acquisition of ports on the Baltic Sea. Peter's victory over Sweden (E) in the Great Northern War — Peace of Nystadt, 1721 — provided Russia with direct access to the Baltic and then to the Atlantic. His efforts to acquire ports on the Black Sea (A) were not realized; later Catherine the Great would expand in this area at the expense of the Ottoman Turks. The partitions of Poland (C) occurred after Peter's death; Russia did not enter into any alliance with England (D) during this period.

15. **(B)** This chart indicates (B) that Hitler's Germany reduced unemployment at a remarkable rate during the period from 1936 to 1938; the fascist economic controls facilitated this development. (A), (C), (D) are incorrect; the German economy was not "superior" to Britain's nor was Britain content with excessive unemployment — while there is much to criticize about the manner in which the Labour and Conservative parties handled economic recovery, one must remember that free economies are naturally more difficult to direct than state controlled economic systems.

16. **(B)** A moderate proposal which called on France to adopt a political system similar to that of Great Britain was an element espoused by Montesquieu in (B) *The Spirit of the Laws. The Social Contract* (A) was written by Jean Jacques Rousseau; *The Encyclopedia* (C) was by Denis Diderot; *The Declaration of the Rights of Man and the Citizen* (D) was produced by the National Assembly in August, 1789; and John Locke wrote *Two Treatises on Civil Government.*

17. **(B)** The correct chronological sequence is (B) Legislative Assembly

(1791–92), Convention (1792–95), and Directory (1795–99). The National Assembly existed from 1789 to 1791; the Consulate from 1799 to 1804; and the Empire from 1804 to 1814.

18. **(B)** Thomas Hobbes' political philosophy can be most clearly identified with the thought of (B) Voltaire. Voltaire maintained that Enlightened Despotism would be the best form of government for France; this position concurs with the Hobessian view that people need to be governed, not government by the people; (C) Quesnay's program was similar though not as directly related. (A) Rousseau, (D) Montesquieu, and (E) Robespierre entertained political theories which were more revolutionary in the context of sovereign power and the exercise of that power.

19. **(D)** The most prominent enlightened political ruler of the 18th century was (D) Frederick the Great of Prussia. He had a genuine interest in enlightened government and introduced a wide range of reforms. Catherine the Great (A) of Russia considered herself enlightened but her barbarism did not support that claim. Louis XV (C) and Maria Theresa (C) were opposed to the thought of the enlightenment; Maria Theresa's son, Joseph II (E), introduced some reforms but became a reactionary after the outbreak of the French Revolution.

20. **(D)** The reaction to the Peterloo Massacre was characteristic of the conservative policies advanced by the British government under (D) Lord Liverpool. While George Canning (A) and Robert Peel (B) were involved in the government, they were not very influential at this time. Melbourne (C) became Prime Minister during the 1830s; Horatio Hunt (E) was the radical who spoke to the crowd at St. Peter's Field, Manchester, prior to the riot.

21. **(D)** The Factory Act of 1833 (D) alleviated some of the abuses of child labor in the textile industry. The five-day work week (A) did not become a reality until the 20th century; reforms in the use of children in mining and heavy industry (B) were not implemented until later in the 19th century; employers were never required (C) to provide comprehensive medical coverage for all employees; this measure made no provision for the special treatment of (E) pregnant women.

22. **(C)** The Anglo-French Entente (also known as the Entente Cordiale) (C) resolved Anglo-French colonial disputes in Egypt and Morocco; northeast Africa (Egypt and the Sudan) was recognized as a British sphere of influence, northwest Africa (Morocco and Algeria) was recognized as a French sphere of influence. This arrangement was not (A) directed at German expansion in Europe or (B) overseas; it was signed in 1904 and therefore was not (D) a 19th century agreement; the Trans-Siberian railroad had been funded by French loans during the 1880s and 1890s, it was not mentioned in this agreement.

23. **(C)** The most prominent British advocate for the abolition of slavery

during the early 19th century was (C) William Wilberforce. While Wordsworth (D) and Blake (E) were sympathetic to abolitionism, they were not in the fore-front of opposition to slavery. William Pitt the Younger (A) and Wellington (B) were preoccupied with the Napoleonic Wars.

24.   **(D)**   English Utilitarianism was identified with the phrase (D) "the great-est good for the greatest number." Jeremy Bentham, James Mill, and John Stuart Mill were prominent Utilitarians. "All power to the people" and "From each according to his labor, to each according to his need" (B) were elements in Lenin's rhetoric. "Universal reason" (C) is identified with Georg Wilhelm Hegel; and "collectivistic nationalism" is associated with Johann Fichte.

25.   **(E)**   Mercantilism was an economic philosophy identified with "bullion-ism" and the need to maintain a favorable balance of trade. Utopian Socialism (A) was an early 19th century philosophy which emphasized the need for a more equitable distribution of wealth; (B) Marxism and (D) Syndicalism were leftist approaches to economics and politics. (C) Capitalism was the developing condi-tion in which mercantilism operated.

26.   **(B)**   The British Prime Minister who was associated closely with Irish Home Rule was (B) William Gladstone. Gladstone maintained through his four ministries that one of his principal tasks was "to pacify Ireland." Robert Peel's (E) career was over before the Irish crisis broke during the second half of the 19th century. Benjamin Disraeli (A), Lord Salisbury (B), and Joseph Chamber-lain (D) were not particularly interested or sympathetic to the Irish.

27.   **(B)**   The Balfour Declaration (1917) (B) was a pledge of British support for the future establishment of a Jewish state. It was not related to (A) the German use of chemicals, (C) the Anglo-Irish crisis stemming from the Easter Rebellion, (D) American neutrality, or (E) war aims.

28.   **(C)**   The Boulanger Crisis (C) was caused by a right-wing scheme to overthrow the Third French Republic and install General Georges Boulanger as the political leader; it was supported by monarchists and other rightist enemies of the republic. It was not (A) a left-wing scheme, nor was it related to the (B) Panama Canal or (D) the Dreyfus Affair. When the crisis failed, the monarchists did not (E) gain a majority of seats in the Chamber of Deputies.

29.   **(E)**   While the (A) Babington Plot, (B) the Throckmorton Plot, (C) the Ridolfi Plot, and (D) the Rising of the Northern Earls were attempts to overthrow Elizabeth I, the Wisbech Stirs of the late 1590s was a controversy among Catho-lics over control of the outlawed English Catholic Church.

30.   **(B)**   The map indicates the partition of Africa in (B) 1914 after most of the European powers had participated in establishing colonial empires.

31. **(B)** The French essayist Montaigne was representative of an intellectual movement known as (B) Baroque which was an intellectual quest for a new synthesis; it was caused by the chaos of the Reformation/Counter-Reformation era. The Enlightenment (A) developed in the 18th century and constituted an elaboration on the new scientific snythesis which emerged during the 17th century. (C) Positivism, (D) Utopian Socialism, and (E) Symbolism were 19th century intellectual movements.

32. **(B)** The Hundred Days (1815) was (B) an unsuccessful attempt by Napoleon to restore himself as a credible European leader. The Hundred Days concluded in June, 1815 at the Battle of Waterloo when Wellington's army defeated Napoleon. Obviously, the Hundred Days did not relate to (A) the reactionary period in Britain following the Manchester riots, (C) the Reign of Terror, (D) British defeats in Africa and the Low Countries, or (E) the collapse of the Revolutions of 1848.

33. **(C)** Jeremy Bentham, James Mill and John Stuart Mill were (C) Utilitarians who argued the case "the greatest good for the greatest number." Auguste Comte established (A) Positivism; Fichte and Hegel were German Romantic Idealists (B); Robert Owen and Charles Fourier were Utopian Socialists (D); and the only early advocates of Marxism (E) were Karl Marx and Friedrich Engels.

34. **(A)** The Russian blockade of Berlin in 1948–49 was a reaction to (A) the unification of the British, French, and American zones into West Germany. While the (B) Truman Doctrine was directed at preventing communist victories in Greece and Turkey, and the Marshall Plan (C) was designed to assist in accelerating the economic recovery of Europe, they were not the direct causes of the blockade. NATO (D) was formed after the blockade began and the Chinese Communist (E) victory did not occur until October 1949.

35. **(E)** Marxist interests were not reflected during the Revolutions of 1848 because Marxism was still in the process of development; while the *Communist Manifesto* was written at this time, it was not distributed widely and had no impact on the revolution. *Das Kapital* was not completed until the 1860s. The Liberal (A) desire for constitutional government, the radical economic alternatives of the Utopian Socialists (B), the nationalists (C) call for self-determination, and the enfranchisement of the middle class (D) were all evident during the revolutions of 1848.

36. **(A)** In the "April Theses" (1917) Lenin (A) challenged the policies of the Provisional Government; Lenin was opposed (D) to continuing the war against Germany. (B) is incorrect because the "April Theses" were not related to the 1905 revolution; Lenin denounced the revisionists in *What Is to Be Done?* in 1902; he did not support Kerensky (E) as his successor — Kerensky had fled to Western Europe.

37. **(C)** Giuseppi Mazzini's (1805-1872) idealistic Young Italy movement was originally supported by both Pope Pius IX and Charles Albert, the king of Sardinia. But the failure of the Revolutions of 1848 and the Roman Republic (of which Mazzini was one of the leaders) convinced the pope to abandon his support. The pope's control over the Papal States was restored through intervention by the French Army, which suppressed Mazzini's government.

Mazzini's actions had no positive effects of the later unification of Italy in 1870 (A); Charles Albert himself was defeated by an Austrian army following the pope's denunciation of the 1848 liberal movements (B); the Swiss Guard played no real role in the Roman Republic's suppression (D); and Camillo Benso di Cavour's (1810-1861) pragmatic understanding of the political forces at work during the period contrasted sharply with Mazzini's idealism.

38. **(B)** The Schleswig-Holstein question was a contentious issue between (B) Austria and Prussia during the 1860s; it was a contributing factor to the outbreak of the German Civil War (1866) between these powers. Bismarck manipulated the crisis to create a favorable situation for Prussia. Neither Sweden (A), Russia (C), the Netherlands (D), nor Great Britain (E) were involved critically with the Schleswig-Holstein issue.

39. **(B)** The leader of the Hungarians during the Revolutions of 1848 was (B) Louis Kossuth who advanced the nationalist aspirations of the Hungarian people and identified with liberal constitutional reforms. Windischgratz (A) dissolved the Pan-Slavic Congress in Prague in June, 1848; Metternich (C) was the conservative Austrian Foreign Minister who was removed during the early weeks of the 1848 revolution in Vienna. (D) Radetsky defeated the army of Charles Albert of Piedmont and thus thwarted aspirations for Italian unification in 1848. (E) Castlereagh was the British Foreign Secretary during the Congress of Vienna in 1815.

40. **(C)** The Dogger Bank Incident resulted in a diplomatic crisis (1904) between (C) Great Britain and Russia. Russian naval units in the North Sea attacked British fishing boats — mistaking them for Japanese ships. Britain, which adopted a position of benevolent neutrality to Japan at the outbreak of the Russo-Japanese war due to its obligations under the Anglo-Japanese treaty of 1902, threatened to go to war with Russia. Russia apologized for the incident and paid compensation to the victims. France (A), Germany (B), and Belgium (E) were not involved in the incident.

41. **(D)** The drawing represents (D) Lavoisier's Apparatus for the Decomposition of Air. The Leyden Jar (A) was a means of storing electricity and was used by Benjamin Franklin (E) in his kite experiment. While Stephen Gray did make contributions to the science of electricity (B) and the erroneous Phlogiston theory (C) was toppled during this period, they were not related to the illustration.

42. **(C)** "1919ism" identifies the (C) hysteria known as the Red Scare; there

was widespread concern the Bolsheviks would take over many of the European governments after the First World War. This concern was aggravated by the economic (A) consequences of the post-war era and the turbulence in Central, Southern, and Eastern European politics. The Russian Civil War did not conclude until 1921 (E); Mussolini did not come to power in Italy until 1922 (D).

43.   **(B)**   The Dawes Plan (B) of 1924 was a reparations plan designed to eliminate the friction which led to the Ruhr Crisis. The Kellogg-Briand Pact (1927) was (A) an international proposal to outlaw war. Stresemann (C) supported the Dawes Plan to gain the withdrawal of French and Belgian troops from the Ruhr Valley. The Dawes Plan was not permanent (D); in 1929, it was replaced by the Young Plan. The Munich agreement of 1938 (E) resulted in the dismemberment of Czechoslovakia.

44.   **(C)**   Thomas Mann described the collapse of a prosperous German commercial family in (C) *Buddenbrooks* which was published in 1901. Mann also wrote *Death in Venice* (A), *The Magic Fountain* (B), and *Mario the Magician* (E); *Lady Chatterley's Lover* was written by D. H. Lawrence (D).

45.   **(C)**   Arthur Koestler examined the situation of the victims of the Stalinist purges in (C) *Darkness at Noon* which was published in 1941. Through the central character, Rubashov, Koestler described the plight of the Old Bolsheviks. *The Revolt of the Masses* (1930) (A) was written by José Ortega y Gasset. *The Myth of the State* (1946) was the last work by Ernst Cassier; *Escape from Freedom* (1941) was written by Erick Fromm; and *The Treason of the Intellectuals* (1927) was by Julien Benda, a French critic.

46.   **(E)**   The rise of fascism in Germany (1933) cannot be attributed to the policies of Gustav Stresemann who died in 1929. Stresemann was one of the few able leaders to emerge during the Weimar Republic; he did much to restore German prestige and establish stability in Central Europe. The (A) failure of the Weimar Republic to address the crisis caused by the Depression, the (B) effective organization of the Nazi Party, the (C) charisma of Adolph Hitler, and (D) lingering humiliation of defeat in the First World War were factors which contributed to the rise of fascism in Germany.

47.   **(B)**   The sketch is of the spinning jenny which was invented by James Hargreaves.

48.   **(C)**   In *A Study of History* a religious based philosophy of history was advanced by (C) Arnold Toynbee. William McNeill (B) wrote *The Rise of the West*; Oswald Spengler (A) wrote *The Decline of the West;* T. S. Eliot (D) and Christopher Dawson (E) were influenced significantly by religion and religious values.

49.   **(C)**   In order "To overcome nothingness. ... individuals must define life for themselves and celebrate it fully, instinctively, heroically." This statement reflected the philosophy of (C) Fredrich Nietzsche. Ernst Cassier was a German philosopher who wrote *The Myth of the State*; he defended rationalism and interpreted Nazism as the triumph of "mythical thinking." (B) Jacques Maritain was a French philospher who advanced Neo-Thomism is works such as *Man and the State*. Paul Tillich (D) and Karl Barth (E) developed Protestant-based philosophies.

50.   **(E)**   In 1968 Czechoslovakia's "Prague Spring' — an attempt to develop "socialism with a human face" was led by (E) Alexander Dubcek. Havel (A) is a dissident Czech playwrite who later became President of Czechoslovakia. (B) Marshall Tito was the post-war leader of Yugoslavia; (C) Erick Honecker was the leader of East Germany during the 1970s and 1980s; and Lech Walesa (D) is the Polish labor and political reformer.

51.   **(D)**   In 1834 German states (excluding Austria) agreed to eliminate tariffs between the states through a customs union known as the (D) *Zollverein*. The *Furstenstaat* (A) was a term which indicated the "state of the prices," the decentralized German political condition established by the Peace of Westphalia in 1648. The Confederation of the Rhine (B) was organized by Napoleon as a means of administering German states and maintaining the decentralized German political situation. The Frankfurt Assembly (C) emerged in 1848 as part of the revolutionary movement; it was interested in a unified Germany. The Hanseatic League (E) was a medieval organization of German and other North Sea and Baltic governments.

52.   **(B)**   In January, 1848 — only weeks prior to the outbreak of the February revolution in Paris — Alexis de Tocqueville addressed (B) the Chamber of Deputies with the remarks quoted in the question. In this statement de Tocqueville addressed the concerns of French liberalism during 1848 — the need to open the political system to the people and the urgency of the economic crisis caused by a maldistribution of wealth. De Tocqueville did not (A) address the United States Senate in 1838, (C) the court of Charles X in 1830, or (D) the new leaders of the Third French Republic in 1871.

53.   **(A)**   In *English Constitution* (1867) an argument was advanced which contended that the British Cabinet system of government was superior to the American constitutional system; this book was written by (A) Walter Bagehot. Robert Southey (B) (1774–1843) was an historian who wrote biographies of Nelson and Wesley. Thomas Carlyle (C) (1795–1881) wrote a wide range of historical works including *The French Revolution, Oliver Cromwell's Letters and Speeches*, and *History of Frederick the Great*. John Henry Newman (D) (1801–1890) was a prominent Catholic leader and author of several books including *Apologia pro Vita Sua* and *The Idea of a University*. John Ruskin (E) (1819–1900) was a critic of art and architecture.

54. **(D)** Giordano Bruno (D) (1548–1600) was a late Renaissance reformer who maintained that "the Hermetic philosophy, with its mystical approach to God and nature held the key to true wisdom." Descartes (A), who argued for the necessity of God, looked for an order in the cosmos which could be understood by mathematics. Montaigne (B) was a Baroque philosopher and essayist. Francis Bacon (C) asserted that the empirical method was the only approach to understanding nature. Sir Isaac Newton published *Principia* in 1687 and advanced a new intellectual synthesis which is the basis of scientism.

55. **(C)** The maps indicate changes in the western border of Russia between (C) 1914 an 1921. These changes were associated with developments and decisions which were caused by the First World War, the Russian Revolution, and the rise of nationalism in eastern Europe — the creation of Poland and other new nation states.

56. **(C)** Britain established direct authority over India after the suppression of the (C) Sepoy Mutiny of 1857. This mutiny, which was caused directly by a violation with Islamic practices, had its roots in the manner in which the East India Company had administered the colony. The (A) Opium Wars (1840s) involved Britain in a series of minor conflicts with Asian princes over the distribution of opium. The Boxer Rebellion (1899–1900) was an anti-foreign outburst against foreign influence in China; it resulted in the siege of the foreign legations in Beijing and the use of a multi-national force to raise the siege. The assassination of Gandhi in January 1948 occurred after Britain had withdrawn from India; India had become a free nation and held dominion status in the British Commonwealth of Nations. The Warren Hastings Affair (E) was a scandal which involved British management of India during the late 18th century.

57. **(E)** By 1914 only (E) Ethiopia of the nations listed was independent of foreign rule. The Congo (A) was under Belgian authority; South Africa (B) and Nigeria (C) were part of the British Empire; and (D) Angola was administered by Portugal.

58. **(C)** The British policy of "Splendid Isolationism" was terminated with the (C) Anglo-Japanese Alliance of 1902; it specified that each nation would adopt a position of benevolent neutrality in the event that the other was attacked by another state. This agreement which was maintained through the First World War preceded the (A) Anglo-French Entente (1904), the (B) Anglo-Russian Entente (1907), and the (D) Second Moroccan Crisis (1911). The Boer War (D) preceded the Anglo-Japanese accord.

59. **(A)** The Versailles Treaty resulted in the formation of several new nations including (A) Yugoslavia and Hungary; Yugoslavia was a new kingdom which was based on an expanding Serbia; Hungary came from the Austro-Hungarian Empire which was dissolved. (B) and (C) are incorrect because while Poland was a new state in 1919, both Italy and Greece had existed previously.

(D) and (E) are incorrect because Germany and Italy both existed earlier; Austria was a new nation which emerged from the Austro-Hungarian Empire.

60.   **(A)**   Article 231 of the Versailles Treaty (A) is known as the "War Guilt" clause and established Germany's responsibility for the war; the case for reparations was based on the assignment and the acceptance of guilt. While (B) the establishment of Poland, (C) the denounciation of secret diplomacy, and (D) the establishment of the League of Nations were provided for in other clauses of the treaty, the Versailles agreement did not (E) result in the decentralization of Germany.

61.   **(E)**   After 1945 the policies of the Soviet Union resulted in (A) the continuing development of Soviet military power, (B) a slow demobilization from a war economy, (C) consistency in the exercise of power by the Communist Party, and (D) a general improvement in the standard of living. The Soviet Union did NOT (E) enjoy extensive influence in the United Nations during the years immediately following the Second World War; the American influence at the United Nations was sustained through the 1960s when the Soviets did gain considerable influence in the international assembly, especially among the new developing nations of the Third World.

62.   **(E)**   The pessimism which permeated the works of intellectuals between the First and Second World Wars was evident in the works of (A) T. S. Eliot ("The Waste Land," 1922), (B) William Butler Yeats ("The Second Coming," 1919), (C) Johan Huizinga (*In the Shadow of Tomorrow*, 1936), and (D) Carl Gustav Jung (*Modern Man in Search of a Soul*, 1933). The correct response is (E) Herbert Spencer, the social Darwinist and advocate of progress of the 19th century.

63.   **(B)**   Cavour's most significant non-Italian ally in bringing about a centralized Italy was (B) Napoleon III, Emperor of the French. Napoleon III was influenced by Cavour's remarks at the Paris meeting which closed the Crimean War and in 1858 and 1859 became an ally of Piedmont; consequently, Piedmont seized Lombardy from Austria. Bismarck (A) assisted Italy in gaining Venetia in 1866 but Cavour was dead by that time. Neither the British Prime Minister Lord Palmerston (C), Queen Victoria (E), nor the Austrian Emperor Franz Joseph (D) provided substantive support to Cavour or to the cause of Italian unification.

64.   **(B)**   Syndicalism was a manifestation of anarchism which was founded by (B) Georges Sorel, a French radical. Syndicalism, which was based on control of trade unions and dissident political groups, gained some success in France, Spain and Italy. (A) Prince Peter Kropotkin and (C) Michael Bakunin were Russian anarchists who espoused a comprehensive anarchist philosophy and strategy. Sidney Webb (D) was a founder of the Fabian Society, a revisionist, and a member of the London Municipal government during the 20th century. (E) Mazzini advanced a liberal nationalism which influenced pre-1848 groups — Young Italy, Young Germany, and the Pan-Slavic movements.

65.   **(E)**   Among the achievements (some of which were short-lived) of the Jacobins were (A) the abolishment of slavery, (B) giving the franchise to all adult males, (C) adaption of the metric system, and (D) decreeing the law of the maximum which fixed prices on essentials and raised wages. The Jacobins did not succeed in the (E) distribution of all land among the peasants.

66.   **(C)**   The British working class demonstrated unity during the (C) General Strike of 1926. This labor action was initiated as a dispute in the coal industry and it quickly became a demonstration of the dissatisfaction of the laboring class. Such working class unity was not discernible in (A) demonstrations by anarchists prior to the First World War, (B) during the movement towards female suffrage, the (D) post-World War I recession, or even during the devastating (E) depression which occurred after the Napoleonic Wars.

67.   **(B)**   During the late 1930s efforts to perpetuate the Third French Republic were centered in the Popular Front which was under the leadership of (B) Léon Blum. Pierre Laval (A) and Philippe Pétain (C) did not have confidence in the republic and were moving to the right. Marc Bloch (E) was an historian who contributed to the establishment of the *Annales* school. Marcel Deat (D) was a French "Neo-Socialist" — a fascist.

68.   **(C)**   In 1938 the Austrian Republic was incorporated formally into the Third Reich through the (C) *Anschluss*. This action realized the hopes of the advocates of the *Grossdeutsch* plan for a greater Germany. The (A) Nuremburg Laws were the racial laws passed by Hitler regime during the mid-1930s. While German troops occupied Austria, there was no (B) military conquest. The Munich accord took place in September, 1938 and involved the future of Czechoslovakia. The (E) occupation of the Rhineland occurred earlier; it was Hitler's first violation of the Versailles Treaty.

69.   **(D)**   Karl Marx believed in (A) the importance of the role of the Communist Party in leading the revolution and educating the people, (B) the dialectic view of history, (C) materialism as the driving force of history, and (E) that private property was a primary cause of economic, social, and political distress. Marx did NOT believe in (D) the importance of gaining power through legal means; indeed, to gain power in such a manner would corrupt the new government because it did not abolish all vestiges of the old regime — a comprehensive and total revolution was needed.

70.   **(C)**   The definitive "Whig" interpretation of British history was advanced in the 19th century by (C) Thomas Babington Macaulay. Macaulay argued that the rise of Parliament and the corresponding decrease of monarchial power was the central, continuing, and positive theme of British political history. David Hume (A) *Constitutional History of England* and Edward Gibbon (B) *Decline and Fall of the Roman Empire* were English historians of the 18th century. (E) Jeremy Bentham established English Utilitarianism and (D) John Stuart Mill *On*

Civil Government and *On Liberty*, while identified as a Utilitarian, was a multi-faceted political philosopher and reformer of the 19th century.

71. **(A)** The map indicates the thesis advanced by H. Mackinder in 1904 that (A) the continental part of Eurasia forms the world's heartland and constitutes a potential threat for sea powers. Mackinder and other geopoliticians influenced many policy makers during this period; later, during the 1930s, Mackinder will abandon this thesis because of technology and economic trends. (D) A consequence of Mackinder's thesis may have been that sea powers must dominate land powers through containment; such a conclusion would have been supported by (C) the American strategist Alfred Mahan who wrote *The Influence of Sea Power Upon History*. Obviously, Mackinder did not contend that (B) only a combined Anglo-American-Russian alliance could prevent German world domination or that (E) the Southern Hemisphere is as significant as the Northern Hemisphere.

72. **(B)** German isolation was evident at the (B) Algerciras Conference in 1906. At this Spanish conference, which was called to resolve the First Moroccan Crisis, Germany found itself opposed by France, Russia, and Great Britain as well as by a number of lesser powers; only Austria-Hungary supported the German position. The (A) Portsmouth Conference resolved the Russo-Japanese war; the (C) Berlin Convention (1884–85) established principles for the colonization of Africa and settled the issue of the Congo; the (D) Congress of Berlin (1878) terminated the Russo-Turkish War of 1877–78; and the (E) World Peace Conference(s) were non-confrontational meetings prior to the First World War.

73. **(C)** The map indicates the partition of the Ottoman Empire after the First World War. The further emergence of new nations from colonies and the independence of Israel in 1948 render (A), (B), and (D) incorrect. The Congress of Berlin (E) occurred in 1878 and did not result in any substantive changes in the boundaries of the Near East except for Britain obtaining the island of Cyprus.

74. **(B)** *The Marriage of Figaro, Don Giovanni*, and *The Magic Flute* were operas by (B) Wolfgang Amadeus Mozart. Franz Joseph Haydn (A), Johann Sebastian Bach (C), and George Frederick Handel (D) were major 18th century composers; Henry Purcell (E) was the great English Baroque composer of the 17th century.

75. **(B)** The drawing, *Neue Typen: Der Rassemensch* by Karl Arnold (July 1924) was a critical commentary on (B) the anti-Semites who supported Hitler and the emerging Nazi Party. Obviously, (A), (C), (D), and (E) are incorrect responses.

76. **(E)** While William Gladstone initiated (A) the Education Act of 1870, the (B) Ballot Act of 1872, the (C) Civil Service Reform of 1870, and (D) the Irish Land Act of 1870, he was not responsible for (E) the Reform Bill of 1867. That measure was enacted under the leadership of Gladstone's Conservative rival, Benjamin Disraeli.

77. **(E)** The notion that "civilization was not the product of an artificial, international elite … but of some genuine culture of the common people, the *Volk*" was advanced by (E) Johann von Herder in *Ideas for a Philosophy of Human History*. Herder influenced Fichte, Hegel (B), and other German nationalists and intellectuals. William Wordsworth's (D) *Lyrical Ballads* did not advance such a direct political and national theme; the conservative (A) Chateaubriand emphasized the role of Divine intervention and the human response to religion in *The Genius of Christianity*. Such sentiments are not reflected in Verdi's *Don Carlo*.

78. **(C)** Enclosures were required (C) to permit scientific farming. Other devices were available to (A) reinforce the concept of private property, (B) eliminate continuing boundary disputes, and (D) assist in accurate property tax collections. (E) Permission for newly rich to acquire property was not a consideration.

79. **(B)** Latvia, Lithuania, and Estonia were the three Baltic provinces that broke away from the Soviet Union in 1991. Ukraine broke away from the Soviet Union about the same time as Latvia, Lithuania, and Estonia, but it is not a Baltic state (A). Poland, Czechoslovakia, and Hungary (C) were never part of the Soviet Union. As of 1996, Chechnya was fighting a war to gain independence from Russia. Georgia broke away from the Soviet Union about the same time as other states, but it is not a Baltic state (D). Serbia, Bosnia, and Croatia (E) were formed with the break-up of Yugoslavia, not the Soviet Union.

80. **(A)** The leader of Poland's Solidarity movement was Lech Walesa, who would go on to be elected Poland's president. Jaruzelski (B) was Poland's last Communist leader; Yeltsin (C) became the Russian president in 1991, and Kadar (E) was the Hungarian Premier between 1956 and 1958 and again between 1961 and 1965. Pope John Paul II (D) is the current head of the Roman Catholic Church.

Sample Answer to Document-Based Question

Between the passage of the Reform Bill of 1867 and the death of Benjamin Disraeli, Disraeli and William Gladstone were the leaders of the Conservative and Liberal parties respectively. They were classic rivals who attacked one another on every possible occasion and who appeared to prosper as a result of the antagonism. During the early 1870s Gladstone initiated a series of reforms which included the Education Act of 1870, the Ballot Act of 1872, and reforms of the military and municipal governments. Disraeli characteristically denounced the reforms as absurd or for not going far enough in resolving a particular problem. In 1872 Disraeli in his famous "Crystal Palace Speech" introduced the concept of the New Imperialism; Disraeli advocated British imperialism and Gladstone emerged as the staunch anti-imperialist.

Punch magazine capitalized on this personal rivalry during the 1870s in scores of cartoons. In its cartoons *Punch* sought to attack those people and institutions which took themselves too seriously; no topic or issue — except the person of Queen Victoria — was immune from ridicule. In "Hoity-Toity!!!" the lingering issue of the Alabama claims crisis with the United States was held up for scorn. In the second document, the letter from Victoria to Gladstone, the Queen advances the argument of her class in her opposition to extending the vote to women and in providing women with an equal opportunity in the professions. In "The Conservative Programme" *Punch* attacked Disraeli for being evasive in describing the domestic policies and programs of the Conservative Party. This criticism was targeted at Disraeli because of the absence of specific Conservative programs; this was especially noticeable when compared to the apparently endless list of Gladstone's proposals which was ridiculed in "The Colossus of Words" in 1879. Disraeli daring was the subject of "On the Dizzy Brink" when the Conservative leader appeared politically vulnerable in 1878. Within a few months Disraeli nullified his critics when he emerged as the victor at the Congress of Berlin (June-July, 1878) which settled the Russo-Turkish War of 1877–78. The final cartoon "A Bad Example" was critical of both Disraeli and Gladstone for their personal attacks on one another. In spite of their antagonism, Britain was well served by its two most distinguished prime ministers of the second half of the 19th century.

Sample Answers to Essay Questions

1.   The concept of "revolution" and "the revolutionary tradition" cannot be defined uniformly within the context of modern European history except in the most general terms. The notion of "revolution" was transformed from the political, Glorious Revolution of 1688 in Great Britain, to the mostly, but not exclusive, politicial French Revolution of 1789, and to the political, economic, and social Russian Revoltion of 1917. The revolutionary tradition in modern

European history has been extended or broadened since the 17th century to include most aspects of human activity; however, even in the revolutions in Eastern Europe in 1989, the orientation was basically political. The notion that political change will serve to correct problems — many of which are economic and social rather than political in nature — has been sustained for 300 years.

The Glorious Revolution of 1688 resulted in the installation of William and Mary and, in April 1689, the enactment of the Bill of Rights. This measure established the primacy of Parliament in controlling the revenues of the government; the monarch was still influencial but was clearly limited in power. This "revolution" was basically non-violent; it was a revolution which was conducted by consensus within the aristocracy. The Glorious Revolution was political — constitutional — in scope and intent; economic and social issues were considered only in the light of the political settlement. The French Revolution of 1789 (which includes the subsequent developments of the next decade) was much more complex. To most of the participants the revolution was political; but there were some (the Jacobins) who were intent upon extending the revolution to all aspects of French and European culture. Redistribution of land, eliminating the power of the church, and the adoption of a new calendar were some of the more radical aspects of this movement. The concept of "Citizen" which emerged was based on democratic and egalitarian notions which were not evident during the Glorious Revolution; during the hundred years between the these two revolutions, two major developments occurred which affected the scope and definition of the revolution: namely, the Enlightenment and the Industrial Revolution. During the following century (the 19th century) the Industrial Revolution continued to develop and democracy emerged in western Europe. The Communist Russian Revolution of 1917, while still fundamentally political in process was cultural in intent; it attempted to remedy the abuses which afflicted humanity by establishing a new order which was based on justice and equality through a state of classlessness. The Russian Revolution, after a turbulent civil war, commanded the support of the Russian people through the party for the next 70 years.

2.　　The Counter-Reformation or the Catholic Reformation was the reaction of the Roman Catholic Church to the Reformation. It was composed of several distinct developments which had varying impacts on European history; however, the general impact of the Counter-Reformation was negative because the Church identified with the old order and adopted a defensive ideological position which solidified doctrines and the precepts of the Church. This was anti-intellectual and resulted in the Church being identified as a remnant of the medieval order rather than as an active power in the shaping of modern European society.

The Roman Church was slow to react to the Lutheran Reformation because of the fear that the conciliar movement within the church would reassert itself. The conciliar movement, which maintained that ultimate power in the church resided in the bishops meeting in council — not the Papacy, was evident during the 15th century at the Councils of Constance, Florence, and Basel. During the 1520s and 1530s, other than decrees of excommunication and the like, the response of the church was limited to the establishment of new religious orders.

Among these orders were the Theatines, the Oratorians, and the Jesuits; they were intended to create a new, more positive image of the Catholic clergy and generally stressed the pastoral needs of the people. The Jesuits were founded by Ignatius Loyola, a retired Spanish miltary officer; this order would serve the interests of the Papacy and regain the people and territory which had been lost because of Protestantism. Reinforced by pledges of loyalty and by a deteriorating position, Rome convened the Council of Trent in 1545; this Council would meet in three sessions from 1545 to 1564 and constitute the most important component of the Counter-Reformation. Traditional church doctrines on the sacraments and an elite ordained priesthood were reaffirmed; the Council of Trent formalized the split within Christendom — doctrinal determinations rendered any compromise with Protestant leaders impossible. During 1558–59 the Papacy decreed that it established the *Index of Prohibited Books* (1559–1967) which listed works which were contrary to church teaching; Catholics, under pain of sin, were directed to refrain from these books. During the late 16th century and for the next two centuries, the Roman church relied on the Inquisition to enforce its doctrines and to defend the Church's interests.

The anti-intellectual and reactionary characteristics of the Counter-Reformation continued to dominate Catholic thought and policy until the 20th century. Pope Pius IX denounced most aspects of modern culture in *Syllabus of Errors* in 1864; at the First Vatican Council (1870–71) the doctrine of papal infallibility was adopted. During the first decade of the 20th century Pope Pius X denounced "modernism." Within the context of European history, the Counter-Reformation was equated frequently with authoritarianism and the medieval order.

3.   The characteristics of fascism include (1) the corporate view of society, (2) nationalism, (3) romanticism, (4) totalitarianism, (5) militarism, and (6) racism. The ideology of fascism developed during the late 19th and early 20th centuries as a reaction to the perceived failure of democratic governments to address the mounting social and economic problems of the period. Fascism was opposed to individualism and to the Marxist view of history and Communism. In many ways, fascism was ideologically connected to German romantic idealism and other conservative philosophies of the early 19th century.

In the fascist model the state's (nation, *volk*) interests have primacy over individual desires and rights; there are no individual rights which are "sacred" that must be respected. The state is an organic corporate entity which must be sustained by the labors of the people; individuals are assets as long as they are making a positive contribution to the historic progress of the state. National pride and patriotism are more than demonstrations of civic responsibility, they are essential virtues in this ideology which is based on romanticism. Rather than emphasizing the value of reason and rational processes, fascists were more interested in a society based on faith, intuition, and deep conviction. The fascist implementation of these sentiments rendered their approach fundamentally anti-intellectual; they maintained deep-rooted suspicion of all intellectuals. Another characteristic of fascism was totalitarianism; the fascist revolution would by necessity be comprehensive and affect every aspect of human activity. For the sake of the whole, each individual must comply with the regulations which were established and implemented by an authoritarian elite which had been provided with legitimate and unquestionably valid historic insight and knowledge. Since the state was an organism, it had to demonstrate regularly through military action that it was growing and strong; a nation that was preoccupied with peace-at-any-cost was decadent and invited attack by younger, more virile nations. Fascism was also characterised by racism. While many historians, such as Hannah Arendt (*The Origins of Totalitarianism*) have argued successfully that racism was inter-woven with the totalitarianism of the modern age, it is extremely important to note that racism was an integral component of fascism. Fascist societies in Germany, Italy, Spain, Japan, Brazil, Argentina, and elsewhere advanced racist positions which were based on hatred and which were anti-intellectual and untenable; nonetheless the ideology of racism was one of the most visible and pernicious characteristics of fascism.

Fascism was an assault on freedom, on the value of the individual, on rationality, and on democracy. It was an anti-modernist force which was reactionary and which was rendered more dangerous than the dictatorships of the past because of technology and the manipulation of mass culture.

4.   During the 19th century several political and economic alternatives to capitalism were developed in response to the negative consequences of the Industrial Revolution, the lingering sentiments associated with the French Revolution, and the absence of participatory governments.

The Utopian Socialists emerged early in the 19th century under the leadership of Charles Fourier, Robert Owen, and Claude Saint-Simon. They were interested in alleviating the distress associated with the industrial revolution and un-regulated urban life in general. They maintained that employers who provided for the economic and social well-being of their employees would be rewarded through increased productivity. Further, community-held businesses would prosper because all participants had a stake in the success of the effort. The Utopian Socialists had a rather naive understanding of history and the forces which were current during their own time — they underestimated the depth of human greed and they failed to appreciate that many Europeans did not entertain any sense of "economic" responsibility to their employees. Several attempts at establishing utopian communities were undertaken by Robert Owen; several achieved initial success and survived for several decades.

The tactics and the philosophy of the utopian socialists were discredited by the failure of the revolutions of 1848. Marxism, or scientific socialism, emerged as a "realistic" alternative to utopian socialism. In many works such as *The Communist Manifesto, Critique of Political Economy*, and *Das Capital* Karl Marx argued that one must understand that history was in fact a struggle — the dialectic — in which "the people" had been suppressed; material culture or economics was the driving force of Marx's dialectic. The future progress of humanity demanded that a violent revolution occur in which all aspects of *bourgeoisie* culture would be destroyed — churches, governmental institutions, capitalism, etc. After a period known as "the dictatorship of the proletariat" (led by the Communist Party), the people would overthrow the party and enter into a "classless society." The Marxist philosophy attracted the support of many intellectuals and reformers during the second half of the 19th century. While most accepted his conceptual arguments, many Marxists departed from Marx on the necessity of revolution. These "evolutionists", or revisionists, contended that revolution was not required when the people could elect a marxist government to implement the revolutionary reforms. Among the revisionists were Sidney and Beatrice Webb, Keir Hardie, and George Bernard Shaw (who were all involved in the formation of the Fabian Society in Great Britain), Edward Berstein who led the Social Democratic Party (SDP) in Germany, and the French socialist Jean Jaures. The revisionist approach was denounced by Lenin in *What is to be Done?* (1902).

Anarchism was a political philosophy which was originated by the French radical Pierre Proudhon who wrote *What Is Property*? immediately prior to the revolutions of 1848. Proudhon and the Russian anarchists Michael Bakunin and Prince Peter Kropotkin envisioned a simple society along Jacobin lines; individuals would live in harmony and equality after the artifical structures (religion, nations, etc.) had been eliminated. The people would rise in general revolution after their oppressors. Unlike the Marxists who were literate-oriented, the anarchists placed their hopes with the common uneducated people. Anarchism attracted considerable support, especially in Southern Europe.

5.   The process of the democratization of British politics during the 19th and 20th centuries was as much a reaction to changing economic and social conditions as it was to a commitment to the "concept of democracy." The Industrial Revolution led to expanding the urban population and increased literacy; these factors in turn led to a political awareness which had to be directed through political reforms.

In 1832, under the leadership of Earl Grey, the first of several measures was enacted which began the process of extending the franchise. The Reform Bill of 1832 added freemen who paid 10 shillings rent per year to the electoral rolls; further, it redistributed Parliamentary seats by eliminating so-called "rotten boroughs" which were over-represented, and by creating new seats for the industrial communities of the Midlands. In the 1860s both the Conservatives and the Liberals recognized the need to extend the process further; in 1867, under Prime Minister Benjamin Disraeli, the Reform Bill of 1867 gave the vote to almost all males living in urban centers; it also redistributed Parliamentary seats. The Reform Bills of 1884–85, during Gladstone's ministry, resulted in giving the vote to all men and in redistribution of seats based on population shifts. The movement for female suffrage emerged during the second half of the 19th century and was led by dedicated women such as Sylvia and Christabel Pankhurst. Their efforts and those of many others did not result in female suffrage until after the First World War; in the initial measure women over the age of 30 were given the same voting rights as men who were 21 years old, in 1928, the Flapper Act resulted in reducing the age for women to 21.

Another important measure in the process of democratization was the Parliament Act of 1911. This measure removed the effective veto power of the House of Lords and recognized that the nation was represented in the House of Commons. As a result of the Parliament Act the House of Commons had complete control over all revenue measures; the House of Lords could delay the enactment of non-revenue measures for three weeks. If a non-revenue measure was significant, it could be redrafted as a revenue statue and enacted immediately.

The process of extending democracy in Great Britain was relatively peaceful. While demonstrations and an occasional riot occurred, there was no general insurrection as was the case on the continent during the same period.

6. The unification movements in Germany and Italy paralleled one another during the period from 1850 to 1870. Both efforts were based on expanding an existing state; both involved domestic adjustments and international conflicts; and both movements capitalized upon national sentiments which had been expressed during the revolutions of 1848. The architect of German unification was the Prussian Otto von Bismarck; Italian unification was supported by Camillio Cavour, Napoleon III, Giuseppe Garibaldi, and King Victor Emmanuel II.

During the revolutions of 1848 many German statesmen and intellectuals had anticipated that Prussia would be the nucleus of a new Germany. While that goal was not realized at that time, Prussia emerged in the 1850s and 1860s as an aggressive state which was interested in consolidating its position in north central Europe. Under the leadership of William I and Bismarck Prussia introduced a constititutional government in 1850, domestic political and legal reforms during the 1850s, and expanded its army. During the early 1860s Prussia was allied with Austria in a brief war (1863) with Denmark over the provinces of Schleswig and Holstein; as a result of the Danish defeat the provinces came under the joint administration of the victors. In turn, this led to a situation which Bismarck exploited in his preparations for the showdown with Austria. With guarantees of Italian participation on a southern front and of French neutrality, Bismarck fabricated a crisis to which the Austrians responded by declaring war. The German Civil War of 1866 resulted in the humiliating defeat of Austria. Bismarck did not exact any territory from Austria; it was evident that Prussia was the preeminent power in Central Europe. In 1867 Bismarck established the North German Confederation as a means of transforming Prussia influence into a German State. During the summer 1870 a diplomatic crisis developed between France and Prussia over the "Ems Despatch." Arguing that William I had been insulted by French diplomats in discussions relating to the Spanish succession, Bismarck created a crisis which led to a French declaration of war. The Franco-Prussian War of 1870–71 resulted in the defeat of France, the surrender of Napoleon III, the end of the Second French Empire, Prussian occupation of much of France, and, in January 1871, the establishment of the German Empire.

In 1848 Italian unification was supported by King Charles Albert of Sardinia-Piedmont. After initial successes, his forces were defeated by the Austrians. In Rome Mazzini's ill-fated Roman Republic was overthrown by French troops and an increasingly conservative Pope Piux IX was restored to power.

During the 1850s Camillio Cavour, who served as Prime Minister to Victor Emmanuel II, emerged as the leader of an expanded Sardinian state, which it was anticipated would result in a unified Italy. Cavour attracted the support of European liberals through a range of social, constitutional, and economic reforms; Sardinia was a participant with Britain and France in the Crimean War against Russia. In 1856 at the Paris Peace Conference, Cavour spoke on the need to establish an Italy which was governed by Italians — a direct attack on the continuing Austrian control of Lombardy and Venetia. His remarks were received sympathetically by Napoleon III, the French Emperor who had been raised in Italy. In 1858 Cavour and Napoleon III signed the secret Plombières Agreement which pledged French support in driving the Austrians from the two provinces if the Austrians declared war. Cavour construed a crisis and the Austrians obliged by declaring war (1859). As a result of this brief war, Sardinia obtained Lombardy but Austria retained Venetia. Cavour died shortly thereafter. In 1860 Garibaldi and an army of 1,000 men landed in Sicily and within three months seized control of the Kingdom of the Two Sicilies. This new acquisition was incorporated into a Sardinian-dominated Italian Confederation. In 1866 the Italians acquired Venetia in return for their participation in the German Civil War. Italian unification was realized in the fall of 1870 when Italian forces, capitalizing on the withdrawal of the French garrison (Franco-Prussian War), seized Rome — the Patrimony of St. Peter.

THE ADVANCED PLACEMENT EXAMINATION IN

European History

TEST 3

THE ADVANCED PLACEMENT EXAMINATION IN

European History
TEST 3

1. Ⓐ Ⓑ Ⓒ Ⓓ Ⓔ
2. Ⓐ Ⓑ Ⓒ Ⓓ Ⓔ
3. Ⓐ Ⓑ Ⓒ Ⓓ Ⓔ
4. Ⓐ Ⓑ Ⓒ Ⓓ Ⓔ
5. Ⓐ Ⓑ Ⓒ Ⓓ Ⓔ
6. Ⓐ Ⓑ Ⓒ Ⓓ Ⓔ
7. Ⓐ Ⓑ Ⓒ Ⓓ Ⓔ
8. Ⓐ Ⓑ Ⓒ Ⓓ Ⓔ
9. Ⓐ Ⓑ Ⓒ Ⓓ Ⓔ
10. Ⓐ Ⓑ Ⓒ Ⓓ Ⓔ
11. Ⓐ Ⓑ Ⓒ Ⓓ Ⓔ
12. Ⓐ Ⓑ Ⓒ Ⓓ Ⓔ
13. Ⓐ Ⓑ Ⓒ Ⓓ Ⓔ
14. Ⓐ Ⓑ Ⓒ Ⓓ Ⓔ
15. Ⓐ Ⓑ Ⓒ Ⓓ Ⓔ
16. Ⓐ Ⓑ Ⓒ Ⓓ Ⓔ
17. Ⓐ Ⓑ Ⓒ Ⓓ Ⓔ
18. Ⓐ Ⓑ Ⓒ Ⓓ Ⓔ
19. Ⓐ Ⓑ Ⓒ Ⓓ Ⓔ
20. Ⓐ Ⓑ Ⓒ Ⓓ Ⓔ
21. Ⓐ Ⓑ Ⓒ Ⓓ Ⓔ
22. Ⓐ Ⓑ Ⓒ Ⓓ Ⓔ
23. Ⓐ Ⓑ Ⓒ Ⓓ Ⓔ
24. Ⓐ Ⓑ Ⓒ Ⓓ Ⓔ
25. Ⓐ Ⓑ Ⓒ Ⓓ Ⓔ

26. Ⓐ Ⓑ Ⓒ Ⓓ Ⓔ
27. Ⓐ Ⓑ Ⓒ Ⓓ Ⓔ
28. Ⓐ Ⓑ Ⓒ Ⓓ Ⓔ
29. Ⓐ Ⓑ Ⓒ Ⓓ Ⓔ
30. Ⓐ Ⓑ Ⓒ Ⓓ Ⓔ
31. Ⓐ Ⓑ Ⓒ Ⓓ Ⓔ
32. Ⓐ Ⓑ Ⓒ Ⓓ Ⓔ
33. Ⓐ Ⓑ Ⓒ Ⓓ Ⓔ
34. Ⓐ Ⓑ Ⓒ Ⓓ Ⓔ
35. Ⓐ Ⓑ Ⓒ Ⓓ Ⓔ
36. Ⓐ Ⓑ Ⓒ Ⓓ Ⓔ
37. Ⓐ Ⓑ Ⓒ Ⓓ Ⓔ
38. Ⓐ Ⓑ Ⓒ Ⓓ Ⓔ
39. Ⓐ Ⓑ Ⓒ Ⓓ Ⓔ
40. Ⓐ Ⓑ Ⓒ Ⓓ Ⓔ
41. Ⓐ Ⓑ Ⓒ Ⓓ Ⓔ
42. Ⓐ Ⓑ Ⓒ Ⓓ Ⓔ
43. Ⓐ Ⓑ Ⓒ Ⓓ Ⓔ
44. Ⓐ Ⓑ Ⓒ Ⓓ Ⓔ
45. Ⓐ Ⓑ Ⓒ Ⓓ Ⓔ
46. Ⓐ Ⓑ Ⓒ Ⓓ Ⓔ
47. Ⓐ Ⓑ Ⓒ Ⓓ Ⓔ
48. Ⓐ Ⓑ Ⓒ Ⓓ Ⓔ
49. Ⓐ Ⓑ Ⓒ Ⓓ Ⓔ
50. Ⓐ Ⓑ Ⓒ Ⓓ Ⓔ
51. Ⓐ Ⓑ Ⓒ Ⓓ Ⓔ
52. Ⓐ Ⓑ Ⓒ Ⓓ Ⓔ
53. Ⓐ Ⓑ Ⓒ Ⓓ Ⓔ
54. Ⓐ Ⓑ Ⓒ Ⓓ Ⓔ
55. Ⓐ Ⓑ Ⓒ Ⓓ Ⓔ

56. Ⓐ Ⓑ Ⓒ Ⓓ Ⓔ
57. Ⓐ Ⓑ Ⓒ Ⓓ Ⓔ
58. Ⓐ Ⓑ Ⓒ Ⓓ Ⓔ
59. Ⓐ Ⓑ Ⓒ Ⓓ Ⓔ
60. Ⓐ Ⓑ Ⓒ Ⓓ Ⓔ
61. Ⓐ Ⓑ Ⓒ Ⓓ Ⓔ
62. Ⓐ Ⓑ Ⓒ Ⓓ Ⓔ
63. Ⓐ Ⓑ Ⓒ Ⓓ Ⓔ
64. Ⓐ Ⓑ Ⓒ Ⓓ Ⓔ
65. Ⓐ Ⓑ Ⓒ Ⓓ Ⓔ
66. Ⓐ Ⓑ Ⓒ Ⓓ Ⓔ
67. Ⓐ Ⓑ Ⓒ Ⓓ Ⓔ
68. Ⓐ Ⓑ Ⓒ Ⓓ Ⓔ
69. Ⓐ Ⓑ Ⓒ Ⓓ Ⓔ
70. Ⓐ Ⓑ Ⓒ Ⓓ Ⓔ
71. Ⓐ Ⓑ Ⓒ Ⓓ Ⓔ
72. Ⓐ Ⓑ Ⓒ Ⓓ Ⓔ
73. Ⓐ Ⓑ Ⓒ Ⓓ Ⓔ
74. Ⓐ Ⓑ Ⓒ Ⓓ Ⓔ
75. Ⓐ Ⓑ Ⓒ Ⓓ Ⓔ
76. Ⓐ Ⓑ Ⓒ Ⓓ Ⓔ
77. Ⓐ Ⓑ Ⓒ Ⓓ Ⓔ
78. Ⓐ Ⓑ Ⓒ Ⓓ Ⓔ
79. Ⓐ Ⓑ Ⓒ Ⓓ Ⓔ
80. Ⓐ Ⓑ Ⓒ Ⓓ Ⓔ

European History

TEST 3 – Section I

TIME: 55 Minutes
80 Questions

DIRECTIONS: Each of the questions or incomplete statements below is followed by five suggested answers or completions. Select the one that is best in each case.

---

1. "...there is no place for industry...no arts; no letters; no society; and which is the worst of all, continual fear, and danger of violent death; and the life of man, solitary, poor, nasty, brutish, and short." This quotation from Thomas Hobbes' *Leviathan* (1651) described the concept known as

   (A) natural rights.

   (B) state of nature.

   (C) social contract.

   (D) reason of state (raison d'état).

   (E) nationalism.

2. Which one of the following would most likely oppose *laissez-faire* policies in 19th century Europe?

   (A) Factory owner

   (B) Liberal

   (C) Free trader

   (D) Socialist

   (E) Middle-class businessman

3.   The painting above by François Dubois, an eyewitness, describes the massacre on St. Bartholomew's Day of 1572 of

(A)   Dutch nobility.

(B)   German peasants.

(C)   French Calvinists.

(D)   Spanish Catholics.

(E)   English merchants.

4.   Which one of the following was a characteristic of the peace settlements at the end of World War I?

(A)   Division of Germany into two parts

(B)   Expansion of the territory of the Ottoman Empire

(C)   The emergence of the Soviet Union as a significant part of the European diplomatic system

(D)   The long-term stationing of American troops in Europe

(E)   Germany was required to pay reparations

5.   All of the following are characteristics of Renaissance humanism EXCEPT

(A)   sanctity of the Latin texts of scriptures.

(B)   belief that ancient Latin and Greek writers were inferior to later authors.

(C)   rejection of Christian principles.

(D)   it functioned as a primary cause of the Reformation.

(E)   accomplished scholarship in ancient languages.

6.   The October Manifesto of Tsar Nicholas II promised all of the following EXCEPT

(A)   a Duma.   (D)   a fair, democratic voting system.

(B)   political reforms.   (E)   full civil liberties.

(C)   a Russian parliament.

7.   Ferdinand and Isabella's policies of Spanish nationalism led to the expulsion, from Spain, of large numbers of Spanish

(A)   Protestants.   (D)   Calvinists.

(B)   Catholics.   (E)   monks.

(C)   Jews.

8.   During the Thirty Years' War, the Lutheran movement was saved from extinction by the military intervention of which foreign monarch?

(A)   French king, Philip the Fair

(B)   English king, Henry VIII

(C)   Swedish king, Gustavus Adolphus

(D)   Austrian Emperor, Charles V

(E)   Spanish king, Philip II

9.   All of the following were significant economic trends in Germany during the 1920s EXCEPT

(A)   large amounts of money leaving the country to pay reparations.

(B)   periods of high inflation.

(C)   a very stable currency (the mark).

(D)   periods of high unemployment.

(E)   the German government placed large amounts of paper money in circulation.

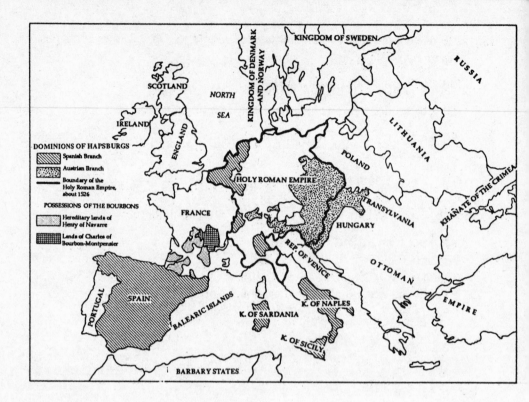

10. The map above depicts Europe around

   (A) 1800.   (D) 1950.

   (B) 1500.   (E) 1900.

   (C) 1700.

11. Which European nation failed to establish an African colony when its expeditionary force was overwhelmingly defeated by a native force at Adowa, Ethiopia in 1896?

   (A) Italy.   (D) Britain.

   (B) Belgium.   (E) Austria

   (C) Portugal.

12. "Sturm und Drang" was a significant period in the career of

   (A) Rousseau.   (D) Stendahl.

   (B) Goethe.   (E) Kant.

   (C) Mill.

13. All of the following were characteristics of the Positivism of August Comte EXCEPT

   (A) belief in a three-stage view of history.

   (B) belief that all knowledge must be scientifically verified.

   (C) achievement of Progress and Order through a government of major scientists and philosophers.

   (D) a new Religion of Science.

   (E) admiration for science and technology.

14. Which one of the following best characterizes the relationship between the Commercial Revolution and the Italian Renaissance?

   (A) The Commercial Revolution caused Europeans to concentrate on their own continent, to the exclusion of the rest of the world.

   (B) The Commercial Revolution was a result of the Italian Renaissance.

   (C) The new merchant class of the Commercial Revolution was more interested in the secular world and less interested in religion.

   (D) There is no connection.

   (E) The Commercial Revolution enriched Italian farmers.

15. "Imperialism emerged as a development and direct continuation of the fundamental properties of capitalism....imperialism is the monopoly stage of capitalism."

   The writer quoted above would most likely accept which of the following statements as true?

   (A) Imperialism was caused by European advances in science and technology.

   (B) A desire for national prestige drove Europeans into a race to gain colonies.

   (C) Imperialism was a natural and predictable result of the growth of capitalism.

   (D) A country with an advanced capitalistic system might become the "colony" of another country.

   (E) Imperialism fed the egos of the smaller, less powerful nations of Europe.

16. "Intendants" were

    (A) secret letters of arrest.

    (B) courts where secret trials were held.

    (C) censors employed by Louis XIV.

    (D) secret emissaries of the pope.

    (E) regional government agents in France.

17. The early 20th century pacifist and winner of the Nobel Peace Prize for her book *Lay Down Your Arms* (1889) was

    (A) Tirpitz.   (D) von Bethmann-Hollweg.

    (B) Luxemberg.   (E) Cosima Wagner.

    (C) von Suttner.

18. When the heir to the Austrian throne was assassinated in August, 1914, and the Russian government responded to the ensuing crisis by mobilizing its troops, Germany followed its obligations under the Triple Alliance and declared war on Russia. Which of the following countries did Germany invade first?

    (A) Russia   (D) Britain

    (B) Austria-Hungary   (E) Italy

    (C) France

19. According to the graph shown on the following page, which one of the following statements is true?

    (A) Industrial production had a greater impact than agricultural production in Britain in 1800.

    (B) Agricultural production had a greater impact than industrial production in Germany in 1900.

    (C) Agriculture became less significant in Britain and Germany by 1900.

    (D) Britain produced fewer industrial products than Germany.

    (E) During the period shown, industrial production was an insignificant part of the British economy.

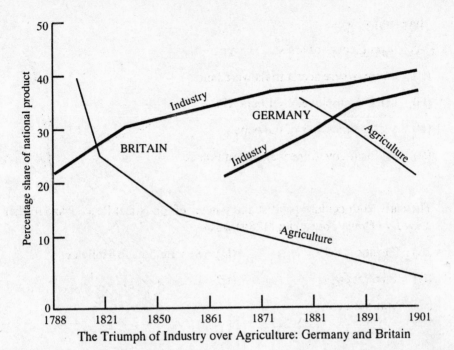

The Triumph of Industry over Agriculture: Germany and Britain

20. During the Reformation, Anabaptism drew its membership mostly from the ranks of the

    (A) nobility.   (D) businessmen.

    (B) middle class.   (E) Army officers.

    (C) peasants.

21. All of the following were part of the Counter-Reformation EXCEPT

    (A) the Index.   (D) the Council of Trent.

    (B) the Augsburg Confession.   (E) the Society of Jesus.

    (C) the Inquisition.

22. This drawing below by Isaac Newton illustrates his experiments with

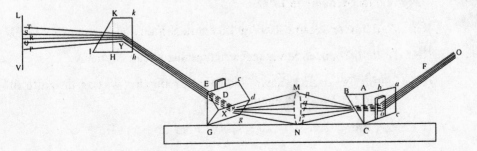

(A) fluids.

(D) gravity.

(B) energy.

(E) gases.

(C) light.

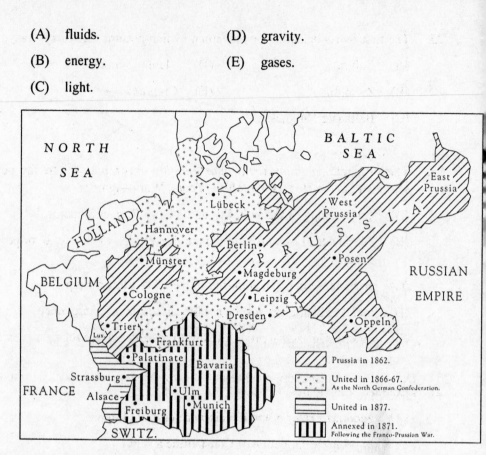

23. According to the map above, Prussia

(A) held territory in both eastern and western Germany before 1870.

(B) assumed control of Alsace-Lorraine after 1866.

(C) annexed Bavaria to Prussia in 1866.

(D) was able to unite all of Germany in 1866.

(E) occupied more territory than the Austrian Empire.

24. Which of the following forms of government would most likely win the approval of a *politique*?

(A) Secular government in which religion plays no role

(B) Theocracy

(C) Parliamentary government

(D) Huguenot government

(E) Government based on the ideas of Pope Innocent III

25. The first Swiss leader of the movement which became Calvinism was

    (A) Calvin.   (D) Menno Simons.

    (B) Zwingli.   (E) Cranmer.

    (C) Balthasar Hubmeier.

26. The principle of *cuius regio, eius religio*—incorporated into the peace settlement at the close of the Thirty Years' War—signified

    (A) a weakening of the authority of the Holy Roman Emperor.

    (B) the power of monarchs to dictate the religion of their state or principality.

    (C) an increase in papal authority in the Holy Roman Empire.

    (D) increased authority for the nobility in religious controversies.

    (E) that religion was a private matter to be decided by each individual.

27. Lorenzo Valla gained fame for

    (A) becoming ruler of the Renaissance city of Florence.

    (B) proving the Donation of Constantine a fraud.

    (C) his inventions.

    (D) challenging the authority of Voltaire.

    (E)   helping to unify Italy.

28. The "Commenda" was a commercial contract involving a merchant and

    (A) a serf.   (D) merchant-adventurers.

    (B) bankers.   (E) his local monarch.

    (C) an artisan.

29. The "Weber thesis" attempted to explain the connections between the rise of Calvinism and the rise of

    (A) absolute monarchies.   (D) Anglicanism.

    (B) capitalism.   (E) Lutheranism.

    (C) the nation-state.

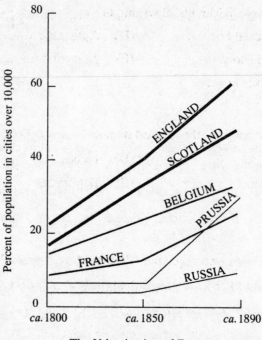

The Urbanization of Europe

30. According to the graph above, which was the most urbanized part of Europe in the 19th century?

(A) Eastern Europe   (D) Central Europe

(B) Prussia   (E) The British Isles

(C) France

31. The Fronde were directed primarily against

(A) the power of French landlords.

(B) the authority of the absolute monarchy.

(C) the influence of the nobility.

(D) the wealth of the church.

(E) the poverty of the peasants.

32. "Anxiety, or the idea of anxiety, permeates modern thought in all its aspects. You find it almost everywhere you look: in Freudian psychology, in the philosophy of existentialism, in poetry and the novel, in the language of religion...and...of course, in contemporary political movements."

This passage is an example of writing in

(A)   intellectual history.   (D)   diplomatic history.

(B)   social history.   (E)   political history.

(C)   economic history.

33.   "The greatest good for the greatest number" was a belief of

(A)   Marx.   (D)   Freud.

(B)   Bentham.   (E)   DeMaistre.

(C)   Mill.

34.   All of the following are true about the Nazi-Soviet pact of 1939 EXCEPT

(A)   it was also known as the Molotov-Ribbentrop Pact.

(B)   it was a nonaggression pact.

(C)   it was signed shortly before the beginning of World War II.

(D)   it protected the sovereignty of Poland.

(E)   it was an agreement between governments which were thought to be ideological enemies.

35.   Prussia's acquisition of the Rhineland area of Germany at the Congress of Vienna proved to be a significant development because

(A)   the Rhineland became a buffer zone between Germany and France.

(B)   most German industry developed in the area.

(C)   it proved to be a very fertile agricultural area.

(D)   in military terms, it was the easiest part of Germany to defend.

(E)   it was welcomed by France.

36.   A long-term trend which was a basic cause of World War I was

(A)   the decline of the Ottoman Empire.

(B)   the rise of Poland.

(C)   Italian interest in the Balkans.

(D)   Russian refusal to become involved in the Balkans.

(E)   a decline in nationalist sentiment in Europe.

37. The Wars of the Roses advanced the cause of absolutism in England by

    (A) strengthening the English economy.

    (B) weakening the older nobility.

    (C) weakening the power of the church.

    (D) increasing the number of nobility in the realm.

    (E) stimulating English exploration of North America.

38. The English author of *Utopia* (1516) was

    (A) More.   (D) Cromwell.

    (B) Tyndale.   (E) Spenser.

    (C) Molière.

39. Henry VIII of England was awarded the title of "Defender of the Faith" by the pope for his

    (A) appointment of Thomas Cranmer as Archbishop of Canterbury.

    (B) criticisms of Lutheranism.

    (C) wars against Charles V.

    (D) participation in the Crusades.

    (E) financial support of the papacy.

40. Elizabeth I of England attempted to quiet religious controversies in her realm through a compromise creed of faith known as the

    (A) Act of the Six Articles.   (D) Toleration Decree.

    (B) Test Act.   (E) League of Augsburg.

    (C) Thirty-Nine Articles.

41. Which of the following was most influential in the spread of Protestantism in 16th century Europe?

    (A) The universities   (D) Lectures

    (B) The Holy Roman Emperors (E) Monarchical authority

    (C) The printing press

42. Which one of the following *philosophes* opposed Voltaire's concept of Enlightened Despotism?

    (A) Condorcet   (D) d'Holbach

    (B) Montesquieu   (E) Helvetius

    (C) Diderot

43. The first German attempt at democracy was known as the

    (A) First German Republic.   (D) Weimar Republic.

    (B) Second Empire.   (E) Bismarckian empire.

    (C) Third Reich.

44. A group which reacted to the Industrial Revolution by smashing machinery was known as the

    (A) Utopian Socialists.   (D) Chartists.

    (B) Levellers.   (E) Union of Welfare.

    (C) Luddites.

45. According to the map below, which of the following was not part of Napoleon's "Grand Empire"?

EXTENT OF NAPOLEONIC POWER, 1812

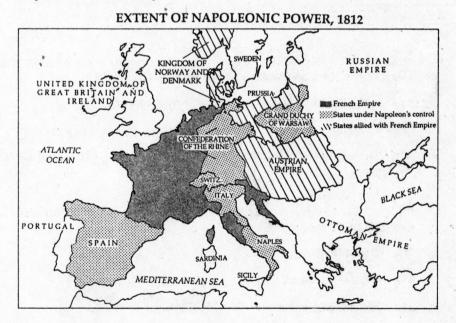

(A) Most of Germany   (D) The Netherlands

(B) Spain   (E) France

(C) Austria

46. The term "Utopian Socialism" was coined by

(A) Fourier.   (D) Renan.

(B) Marx.   (E) Lenin.

(C) Guizot.

47. The novel *Sybil* (1845), which surprised many readers by expressing sympathy for the working class in the 19th century, was written by

(A) George Sand.   (D) Gladstone.

(B) Disraeli.   (E) Clemenceau.

(C) Wordsworth.

48. The primary problem of France when Charles DeGaulle became president of the nation during the 1950s was

(A) to increase French participation in the North Atlantic Treaty Organization (NATO).

(B) to settle the Algerian problem.

(C) the recovery from the devastation of World War II.

(D) to end the occupation of France by German forces.

(E) the deficit budgets of the French government.

49. The "Humiliation of Olmuetz" was the result of an Austrian and Prussian dispute over

(A) Poland.

(B) territory.

(C) reparations.

(D) the Zollverein.

(E) the border between the two countries.

50. "Existence precedes essence" was coined in the 20th century by

    (A) Nietzsche.   (D) Benda.

    (B) Kierkegaard.   (E) Sartre.

    (C) Gasset.

51. The Vienna Circle is generally associated with the movement known as

    (A) Existentialism.   (D) Structuralism.

    (B) Logical Positivism.   (E) Impressionism.

    (C) Marxism-Leninism.

52. The "stream of consciousness" as a method of narrative fiction was developed by

    (A) W. B. Yeats.   (D) Samuel Beckett.

    (B) Virginia Woolf.   (E) Bertolt Brecht.

    (C) Henrik Ibsen.

53. The "Sick Man of Europe," which British and French foreign policy sought to preserve in the 19th century, was

    (A) the Russian Empire.   (D) the Ottoman Empire.

    (B) Poland.   (E) the Austrian Empire.

    (C) Switzerland.

54. Which of the following was partitioned and annexed by three powerful neighbors in the late 18th century?

    (A) Italy   (D) Sweden

    (B) Poland   (E) Spain

    (C) Finland

55. Which one of the following was true about the European middle class in the 19th century?

    (A) Its political influence decreased throughout the century

(B) It was most sizable in Russia

(C) It called for government aid to business

(D) It held great wealth in the form of land

(E) It espoused liberalism

56. The Defenestration of Prague was a cause of which war?

(A) War of the Spanish Succession

(B) Hundred Years' War

(C) War of Jenkins Ear

(D) Thirty Years' War

(E) War of Austrian Succession

57. "Paris is worth a Mass" was said by

(A) Henry VIII.   (D) Henry IV.

(B) Louis XVIII.   (E) Louis Philippe.

(C) Louis XIV.

58. Which of the following is a reasonable conclusion from the graph shown here?

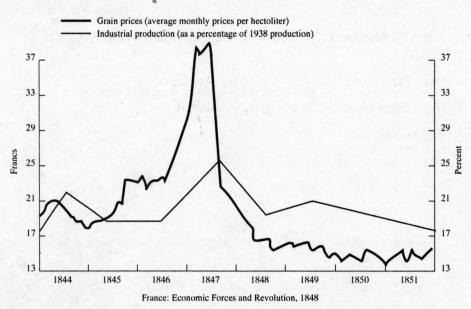

France: Economic Forces and Revolution, 1848

(A) There was no connection between grain prices and industrial production.

(B) High grain prices were a factor in the revolution of 1848 in France.

(C) Industrial production and grain prices sometimes declined in tandem.

(D) High industrial production caused grain prices to rise.

(E) Declining industrial production caused grain prices to fall.

59. "We Italians then owe to the Church of Rome and to her priests for our having become irreligious and bad; but we owe her still a greater debt... that the Church has kept and still keeps our country divided."
This passage expresses the opinion of

(A) Luther.   (D) Machiavelli.

(B) Calvin.   (E) Dante Alighieri.

(C) Pope Boniface VIII.

60. Hohenzollern authority in ruling Prussia depended on the cooperation and support of the

(A) bankers.   (D) constitution.

(B) Junkers.   (E) intellectuals.

(C) courts.

61. James II's statement "No bishop, no king" was a defiant reply to (the) English

(A) Parliament.   (D) Anglicans.

(B) Catholics.   (E) nobility.

(C) Calvinists.

62. This Soviet poster of 1930 was an attack on

    (A) militarism.

    (B) war.

    (C) religion.

    (D) capitalism.

    (E) pacifism.

63. The most powerful ruler of the time of the Reformation — who held the title of Holy Roman Emperor, King of Spain, and Emperor of Austria— was

    (A) Maria Theresa.   (D) Henry VIII.

    (B) Charles V.   (E) William the Silent.

    (C) Philip the Fair.

64. Which social group was the major beneficiary of the Corn Laws in early 19th century Britain?

    (A) Nobility   (D) Small farmers

    (B) Middle class   (E) Industrialists

    (C) Businessmen

65. Which novel satirized obsolete standards of feudalism and chivalry?

    (A) *Tom Jones*   (D) *Emile*

    (B) *Candide*   (E) *War and Peace*

    (C) *Don Quixote*

66. "Mother died today...or maybe yesterday. I can't be sure." These are the first words of a 20th century novel by

    (A) Joyce.   (D) Sartre.

    (B) Grass.   (E) Malraux.

    (C) Camus.

67. Which of the following best characterizes the attitude of 19th century Russian Slavophils?

    (A) All Slavs should be united under a single government.

    (B) All western influences should be rejected.

    (C) Westernization should not be allowed to destroy the distinctive aspects of Slavic culture.

    (D) Russia should have no role in the leadership of the Slavic nations.

    (E) Russia should become completely westernized.

68. During the first half of the 19th century, which of the following tended to hold down population growth in Ireland?

    (A) Bloody Sunday   (D) The Home Rule issue

    (B) The Peterloo Massacre   (E) Industrialization

    (C) The Potato Blight

69. All of the following were characteristics of Russia when Peter the Great assumed the throne EXCEPT

    (A) a weak nobility.

    (B) a split in the Russian Orthodox church.

    (C) lack of access to the Baltic and Black Seas.

    (D) limited contact with the rest of Europe.

    (E) an economy based on agriculture.

70. Which of the following best characterizes the Zimmerman telegram of World War I?

    (A) It led to a German invasion of Belgium.

    (B) It became a cause of the Franco-Prussian war of 1870.

(C)   It suggested that Mexico help the German government.

(D)   It was a German ultimatum to Poland.

(E)   It was a major reason for Britain's entry into the war.

71.   The painting above, by Salvador Dali, illustrates the 20th century style of painting known as

(A)   Dadaism.   (D)   surrealism.

(B)   the Fauvres.   (E)   impressionism.

(C)   cubism.

72.   The principle that "form follows function" was a basic tenet of the 20th century school of architecture known as

(A)   the Oxford Movement.   (D)   the Jacobins.

(B)   the Bauhaus school.   (E)   neo-Romanticism.

(C)   the Bloomsbury circle.

73.   All of the following are preconditions for the Industrial Revolution EXCEPT

(A)   an adequate road system.

(B)   a failing agricultural system.

(C)   adequate raw materials.

(D)   a spirit of entrepreneurship.

(E)   a source of financing to build factories.

74.   Which one of the following statements best characterizes the Babylonian Captivity?

(A)   The Jewish people were forced to live in Babylon as slaves.

(B)   The papacy was dominated by the French monarchy.

(C)   Martin Luther was kidnapped by sympathetic noblemen.

(D)   Galileo was forced to bow to church authority.

(E)   Papal lands were annexed by the new government of a united Italy in 1870.

75.   Keynesianism (the economic doctrines of the 20th century British economist John Maynard Keynes) teaches that during times of economic downturns governments should

(A)   practice austerity.

(B)   increase taxes.

(C)   create budget deficits.

(D)   institute wage and price controls.

(E)   nationalize major industries.

76.   The establishment of French absolutism was primarily the work of royal ministers such as Richelieu and

(A)   Mazarin.   (D)   Montesquieu.

(B)   Colbert.   (E)   LaMettre.

(C)   Walpole.

77.   The agreement that provided for increased European economic unity is known as the

(A)   Treaty of Versailles.   (D)   Potsdam Treaty.

(B)   Maastricht Treaties.   (E)   Treaty of Paris.

(C)   Geneva Accords.

78. Which of the following best characterizes Burke's *Reflections on the Revolution in France*?

    (A) It condemned the French Revolution as a source of radical ideas used in the American Revolution.

    (B) It praised the French Revolution as a sincere attempt to spread liberty and promote equality.

    (C) It condemned the violence and anarchy of the French Revolution.

    (D) It praised the French Revolution and condemned the American Revolution.

    (E) It condemned all revolutions.

79. A 19th century novel which asserted the superiority of science to traditional ways of thinking was

    (A) *Les Misérables* by Hugo.

    (B) *Crime and Punishment* by Dostoyevsky.

    (C) *Degeneration* by Nordau.

    (D) *Frankenstein* by Shelley.

    (E) *Fathers and Sons* by Turgenev.

80. Which was the last advanced Western nation to grant women the right to vote, in 1989?

    (A) Sweden   (D) Switzerland

    (B) France   (E) Ireland

    (C) Spain

European History

TEST 3 – Section II

TIME: Reading Period – 15 minutes
Writing Time for all three essays – 115 minutes

DIRECTIONS: Read over both the Document-Based Essay question in Part A and the choices in Part B during the Reading Period, and use the time to organize answers. All students must answer Part A (the Document-Based Essay Question); and choose TWO questions from Part B to answer.

PART A – DOCUMENT-BASED ESSAY

This question is designed to test your ability to work with historical documents. As you analyze each document, take into account the source and the point of view of the author. Write an essay on the following topic that integrates your analysis of the documents. You may refer to historical facts and developments not mentioned in the documents.

Analyze the nature and causes of the Great Fear in the French Revolution of 1789, and assess the validity of the following statement about the Great Fear.

"The Great Fear can be explained by the economic, social, and political circumstances prevailing in France in 1789…(it) gathered the peasants together; allowed them to achieve the full realization of their strength and reinforced the attack already launched against (feudalism)…it played its part in preparations for the (revolution) and on these grounds alone must count as one of the most important episodes in the history of the French nation."
—Georges Lefebvre, *The Great Fear of 1789*

Historical Background: The Great Fear began in the Spring of 1789, when peasants throughout the rural areas of France armed themselves in response to rumors of aristocratic plots and roving bands of brigands. Peasants mistakenly attacked other peasants; much of the violence was directed against local noblemen. The violence and anarchy of the Great Fear gained the attention of both royal ministers and the National Convention of the revolution. Both groups moved to release the peasants from their remaining obligations under feudalism.

Document 1
Background of the French Revolution

FRENCH POPULATION IN 1789
TOTAL: from 22,000,000 to 25,000,000

First Estate   Clergy .... 100,000 to 130,000

Second Estate   Nobility .... 400,000 or fewer

Third Estate   { *Upper Bourgeoisie
*Bourgeoisie
Urban Proletariat   }   5,250,000, more or less*
Peasantry .... 16,250,000 to 21,500,000

* All bourgeois did not live in cities and towns. Many–especially doctors, lawyers and *rentiers* (those living on income from investments)–lived in the country or in small villages. Total *urban* population was surely less than 4,000,000 and perhaps as low as 2,000,000.

Document 2
"The first cause is the small yield of this year's harvest which in some districts did not even produce the quantities of a normal year...Second, the rains and inundations of 1787, the hail and drought of 1788...Third, the usury...the closing of granaries by landed proprietors...Fourth, private sales from the granaries...Fifth, the lack of supplies at the market place..."
—Report to the Paris parliament on the increases in grain prices, December, 1788.

Document 3
"The backwardness of France is beyond credibility. From Strasburg hither, I have not been able see a newspaper...well dressed people are now talking of the news of two or three weeks past, and plainly by their discourses know nothing of what has been passing. The whole town of Besançon has not been able to afford me the *Journal de Paris*, nor of any other paper that gives certain of the transactions of the states; yet it is the capital of a province, large as half a dozen English counties, and containing 25,000 souls...No one paper has been established in Paris for circulation in the provinces..."
—Arthur Young, English tourist, July 17, 1789.

Document 4
"...information in France (is not so) diffusive as I imagined. Of the active citizens...nearly half, particularly in the country, can neither write nor read."
—William Taylor, English tourist, June, 1790.

Document 5

" ...(to the south of Romily) rumors said that brigands had appeared in the canton; they had been seen going into the woods. The tocsin was sounded and three thousand men gathered to hunt down these alleged brigands...but the brigands were only a herd of cows."

—From a report in the *Journal de Troyes*, a newspaper, July 28, 1789.

Document 6

(Jacques Turgot, one of the finance ministers of King Louis XVI, made a concerted attempt to institute administrative and economic reforms during his brief tenure. Some of the reforms abolished the last feudal obligations of the peasants, including the corvée, which required the peasants to provide free labor for public works or other tasks as directed by the nobility.)

"We have noted with pain that...works have been executed, for the most part, by means of the corvées required of our subjects...while they have been paid no wages for the time they are so employed...The weight of this obligation does not fall, nor can it ever fall, anywhere else than upon the poorest part of our subjects, upon those who have no property other than their hands and their industry, upon the peasants, the farmers. The landowners, almost all of whom are...exempt, contribute but very little."

—From a decree of Turgot abolishing the corvée, 1776.

Document 7

"The high price of corn has occasioned many insurrections in some of the provincial towns, and particularly at Rheims and Vendôme: at St. Quentin a barge laden with 2,000 sacks of the above-mentioned commodity belonging to the very rich individual of the place, who was accused in the neighboring villages of having made his fortune by entirely engrossing the article, was seized upon by the populace and the whole of the cargo was thrown into the river."

—Lord Dorset to Lord Carmarthen, British nobility, March 19, 1789.

Document 8

"In the early Spring of 1789...the Duc d'Orléans was very popular in Paris. The previous year he had sold many paintings from the fine collection in his palace, and it was generally believed that the eight millions raised by the sale had been devoted to relieving the suffering of the people during the hard winter which had just ended. In contrast, whether rightly or wrongly, there was no mention of any charitable gifts from the royal princes or from the king and queen...Nor did the king ever show himself. Hidden away at Versailles or hunting in the nearby forests, he suspected nothing, foresaw nothing, and believed nothing he was told."

—*Escape from Terror: the Journal of Madame de la Tour du Pin* (ed. and trans. Felice Harcourt, Folio Society, 1979),p. 79.

Document 9

"One hundred and fifty chateaux…have already burned. What should I say about the atrocities, the murders committed against the noblemen? A nobleman who was paralyzed, and left on a funeral pile…They burned the feet of another so that he would give up his title-deeds."

—Marquis de Ferrières, French nobleman, deputy of the Estates-General, Memoirs, July 1789.

Document 10

"The National Convention, after hearing the report of its committee on public safety, decreed that all persons who spread false news or cite terror in the provinces, arouse the citizens, or cause disturbances and trouble, shall be brought before the extraordinary tribunal and punished as counter-revolutionary…It was not necessary that there should be uprisings and disturbances; only news that might lead to these."

—Durand deMaillane, historian, from his *History of the National Convention* (1820).

(The National Convention subsequently abolished all feudal obligations.)

Cartoon of a French peasant supporting representatives of the nobility and clergy, while the peasant's grain is eaten by doves and rabbits which were reserved by law for the sport of the nobility.

PART B – ESSAY QUESTIONS

1. Assess and analyze the extent to which the English Civil War and Glorious Revolution of 1688 advanced the cause of constitutionalism in England in the 17th century.

2. Describe and assess the role of the British policy of "splendid isolation" in balance-of-power diplomacy in 19th century Europe.

3. Describe and compare the political beliefs of the 18th century French *philosophes* Voltaire and Montesquieu.

4. Describe and analyze the effects of the Industrial Revolution on European society in the 19th century.

5. Assess and analyze the extent to which the peace settlements in Europe at the end of World War I became causes of World War II.

6. Describe and compare the major doctrines of the three prominent groups of the Protestant Reformation—Lutheranism, Calvinism, and Anabaptism.

THE ADVANCED PLACEMENT EXAMINATION IN

European History

TEST 3 – ANSWERS

1.	**(B)**	21.	**(B)**	41.	**(C)**	61.	**(C)**
2.	**(D)**	22.	**(C)**	42.	**(B)**	62.	**(C)**
3.	**(C)**	23.	**(A)**	43.	**(D)**	63.	**(B)**
4.	**(A)**	24.	**(A)**	44.	**(C)**	64.	**(A)**
5.	**(E)**	25.	**(B)**	45.	**(C)**	65.	**(C)**
6.	**(D)**	26.	**(B)**	46.	**(B)**	66.	**(C)**
7.	**(C)**	27.	**(B)**	47.	**(B)**	67.	**(C)**
8.	**(C)**	28.	**(D)**	48.	**(B)**	68.	**(C)**
9.	**(C)**	29.	**(B)**	49.	**(D)**	69.	**(A)**
10.	**(B)**	30.	**(E)**	50.	**(E)**	70.	**(C)**
11.	**(A)**	31.	**(B)**	51.	**(B)**	71.	**(D)**
12.	**(B)**	32.	**(A)**	52.	**(B)**	72.	**(B)**
13.	**(D)**	33.	**(B)**	53.	**(D)**	73.	**(B)**
14.	**(C)**	34.	**(D)**	54.	**(B)**	74.	**(B)**
15.	**(C)**	35.	**(B)**	55.	**(E)**	75.	**(C)**
16.	**(E)**	36.	**(A)**	56.	**(D)**	76.	**(A)**
17.	**(C)**	37.	**(B)**	57.	**(D)**	77.	**(B)**
18.	**(C)**	38.	**(A)**	58.	**(C)**	78.	**(C)**
19.	**(C)**	39.	**(B)**	59.	**(D)**	79.	**(E)**
20.	**(C)**	40.	**(C)**	60.	**(B)**	80.	**(D)**

Detailed Explanations
of Answers
TEST 3

1. **(B)** Although "quotation" questions may ask the name of the author or the book title, this question requests more than factual recall. It requires an ability to recognize the main idea of the passage—to read the quotation and understand its philosophic implications. Knowledge of the terminology of 17th century writers is also helpful. Hobbes' *Leviathan* described early human society (the "state of nature") as an anarchic "war of all against all." For self-protection, citizens agreed among themselves to form the first government, an agreement termed by Hobbes the "social contract." It is especially important to read the quotation carefully, since two of the answers (B) and (C) are from the *Leviathan*; you may be misled into choosing (C) because you have studied the *Leviathan* in a class and the "social contract" sounds familiar. If the correct answer is not apparent after a second reading of the quotation, it may at least be possible to eliminate the other two answers. The concept of natural rights, incorporated into the French Declaration of the Rights of Man and the Bill of Rights to the United States Constitution, was summarized by John Locke as the idea that human beings are born "free, equal, and independent." "Reason of state" was the justification used by French statesmen such as Cardinal Richelieu to defend measures to create a centralized absolute monarchy in France. Answer (E), nationalism, is not only incorrect but also irrelevant to this question.

2. **(D)** *Laissez-faire* (from the French *laissez-nous faire*, leave us alone), described the economic outlook of 19th century liberals, many of whom were businessmen or industrialists who sought an end to government regulation of business. Proponents of *laissez-faire* envisioned an era of free economic activity in Europe without tariff barriers ("free trade"). Thus factory owners, liberals, and free traders" were all supporters of *laissez-faire*. Not so 19th-century socialists, who saw *laissez-faire* as an obstacle to even minimal measures to help the working class, such as government safety inspections of factories. This question tests both your knowledge and your analytical skills. It requires that you draw inferences or conclusions from the information given. It also requires an understanding of terminology (liberals, free traders and middle-class businessmen), as well as an ability to analyze the implications of *laissez-faire* for groups such as factory owners and socialists. If you realize that at least two of the answers are virtually

the same (for example, liberals and free traders), these answers may be eliminated. Since only (A) and (D) are left as possible answers, the chances of a successful guess have increased to 50%. Because only .25 point is subtracted for incorrect answers, guessing is recommended when one, and especially two, of the answers may be eliminated.

3. **(C)** The St. Bartholomew's Day Massacre in Paris of French Calvinists, often termed "Huguenots", led to a civil war in France (the War of the Three Henries) and the first Bourbon monarch (Henry IV). When dealing with questions based on illustrations (paintings or drawings), it is important to look for explicit details or other information in the question and in the illustration itself, since it is usually not possible to arrive at a correct answer by eliminating answers. The clues in this case are in the question rather than in the painting. If the primary clue is not sufficient ("St. Bartholomew's Day"), there is a secondary clue in the obviously-French name of the painter. Do not be misled by the use of the term "French Calvinists" instead of the name "Huguenots", which is the term usually used by textbook writers; the use of the term "French Calvinists" is another detail testing your knowledge and understanding of European history.

4. **(A)** At first glance this question appears to test only the memorization of facts, but another look will show that it also requires understanding of the diplomatic situation in Europe around 1920. The correct answer may require some thought, since there was no political division of Germany into two governments, as happened at the end of World War II. The "division of Germany into two parts" refers to the "Polish Corridor", created by the peacemakers in order to give Poland an "outlet to the sea." The "Polish Corridor", a strip of fomerly-German land ceded to Poland in order to provide access to the port city of Danzig, isolated eastern Prussia from the remainder of Germany. It may be possible to arrive at the correct answer by analyzing the other four answers and eliminating them; each is untrue. The end of World War I brought the final collapse of the Ottoman Empire and its reduction to the borders of modern Turkey. The newly Communist government of Russia, which came to power in 1917, was ostracized by the other great powers when the war ended. Answer (D) may be tempting because the United States left large numbers of troops in Europe after World War II. This question refers to World War I, however. The United States withdrew from Europe both militarily and diplomatically after that war, preferring to return to "normalcy." Under the terms of the Treaty of Versailles, Germany was required to pay reparations.

5. **(E)** This question is partly knowledge-based, but it also requires an understanding of the principles of Christian Humanism and an ability to analyze what ideas they would disapprove (A) and (C) and approve (E). Renaissance Humanism, also known as Christian Humanism, combined studies of ancient languages with a zeal to make the Scriptures available in the local languages. Virtually all Christian Humanists translated portions of the Scriptures into European languages, using the Latin text which was the sole version available during the

Middle Ages. Very few Christian Humanists were connected with the Reformation; the most famous of them, Erasmus of Rotterdam, criticized laxness within the Catholic church but refused to join with the Protestant reformers.

6. **(D)** Although the tsar's manifesto succeeded in calming and ending the Revolution of 1905, the document's promises of reforms contained a loophole: no mention was made of election procedures for the promised Duma, or parliament. When Nicholas II called the Duma into session after the revolution of 1905, he instituted voting procedures which gave considerably heavier representation to the wealthy and to districts around Moscow, which were considered the most loyal to the government.

7. **(C)** While this question calls for fact retention, it also requires an ability to analyze the implications of their policies—unless the answer is apparent upon first reading. The first monarchs of a united Spain, Ferdinand and Isabella achieved that unity by gaining control of the remaining Muslim sections of southern Spain. In an effort to promote cultural unity and establish a national identity, they defined Spanish nationalism in terms of their understanding of orthodox Catholicism. Those not fitting their definition of orthodoxy were condemned as disloyal or subversive. Two particular groups, Jews and Muslims who had converted to Christianity but retained Muslim customs or dress, were forced into exile by Spanish authorities.

8. **(C)** The diversity of monarchs listed in the answers should indicate that guessing is a possiblity. Two were devout Catholics (D) and (E), while a third (A) predates the Reformation by almost 200 years. During the Thirty Years' War, when Catholic forces from southern Germany and Austria were close to pushing Lutheran forces into the Baltic sea, the Lutheran convert Gustavus Adolphus intervened in Germany, saving the Lutheran cause. Adolphus was himself killed during a key battle.

9. **(C)** Answers (B) and (C) are opposites; high inflation almost always affects the value of a country's currency. If you recognize this conflict, it will become apparent that one of these two answers is the correct answer. If necessary, it is worthwhile guessing, since your odds are 50% and only .25 point is deducted for an incorrect guess.

10. **(B)** On the map several areas of Europe are depicted with dark shading. These areas are the lands controlled by the Hapsburgs in the 16th century. Answer (C) is incorrect, since Spain was lost by the Hapsburgs in the 1600s. A further clue: the large size of the Ottoman Empire, covering the entire Balkan peninsula, precludes any answer after about 1870.

11. **(A)** The mention of Ethiopia may bring Italy to mind. If not, a possible guess is indicated if you are able to remember Mussolini's invasion of Ethiopia during the 1930s. The sole European nation to have its plans to establish an

African colony in the late 19th century blocked by a native African force, Italy for some time regarded the incident a national humiliation. The incident was one of several reasons the Italian dictator Mussolini gave for his successful military takeover of Ethiopia in 1935.

12. **(B)** Knowledge-based questions such as this are not usually susceptible to successful guessing, since the other answers cannot be eliminated unless you know as least two or three of them well. As a young man, the German poet Goethe anticipated elements of Romanticism, and his youthful writings, such as *The Sorrows of the Young Werther* (1774), exhibited some Romantic characteristics. This period is often termed his "Sturm und Drang" (storm and stress) period.

13. **(D)** Comte, an early 19th century writer, based his system of Positivism on the belief that history was entering a third, scientifically-oriented stage. In this new era, only statements that might be scientifically verified were to be considered knowledge. A committee of scientists and philosophers would govern, creating "Progress and Order." Religion would be considered outdated.

14. **(C)** Here two different developments (the Commercial Revolution and Italian Renaissance) are tied, and you are asked to explain the connection. The correct answer requires memory retention, understanding of terminology, and an ability to analyze the social and economic connections between the two developments. The Commercial Revolution describes the expansion of trade and the establishment of a broad system of joint-stock companies and banks in pre-Renaissance Italy. The new merchants of the Commercial Revolution held few ties to the earlier Middle Ages. They established new towns in Italy, such as Florence; they preferred "worldly" reading material on topics such as etiquette and politics; and for some time their new towns held no cathedrals or even smaller churches. In effect, the Commercial Revolution created a new, secular middle class which financed much of the artistic and literary work of the Italian Renaissance. The other answers are either incorrect or irrelevant.

15. **(C)** Although knowledge of terminology is a great help, in this question careful reading and analyzing of the implication of statements is essential. This quotation, from Vladimir Lenin, father of the Soviet Revolution of 1917, is part of his argument that capitalism held internal contradictions which would lead to its self-destruction; a major contradiction was the uncontrolled race for colonies. [Source: Lenin, *Imperialism: The Highest Stage of Capitalism* (New York: International Publishers, 1934)]

16. **(E)** In their work to strengthen the French absolute monarchs, royal ministers Cardinals Mazarin and Richelieu placed government agents, or intendants, in areas throughout France, where they acted as both the "king's ears" and as collectors of revenue. The move established a "royal presence" in major areas of the country. Answers (A) (*lettres de cachet*) and (B) were other steps taken to strengthen absolutism in France.

17. **(C)** The first woman to be awarded the Nobel peace Prize, Bertha von Suttner, an Austrian, gained wide attention for her book, which contributed to the founding of Peace Societies in Austria and Germany. Admiral Tirpitz represented the opposite pole; he masterminded Germany's plans, beginning in the 1890s, to create a German navy to rival the British navy. Rosa Luxemberg, a German Marxist, was killed during a failed revolutionary attempt in Germany in 1919. Theobald von Bethmann-Hollweg was the chancellor of Germany during the early stages of World War I. Cosima Wagner was the influential wife of composer Richard Wagner.

18. **(C)** This question deals with a complex situation at the start of the war. It requires analytical thinking, an understanding of a complex chain of events, and some knowledge of terminology (although the key term—"Schlieffen Plan"—does not appear in the question). Answer (A) may be eliminated, since such an obvious answer is unlikely to be the correct one on an advanced test. During frequent renewals of the Triple Alliance during the late 19th century, Germany was consistently pushed by Austria to make increasingly specific and secret promises of aid to Austria in the event of war. According to one German promise, a Russian mobilization was to lead to a German declaration of war. German military planners, however, were worried about a two-front war, to both the east (Russia) and west (France). A commission working under the German Count Alfred von Schlieffen produced the famous Schlieffen Plan, which required that Germany immediately invade the weaker country of the two in overwhelming numbers, with the goal of quickly defeating the weaker country. The writers of the Schlieffen Plan assumed the weaker nation was France.

19. **(C)** Of the first three answers, the only one that is a correct interpretation of the graph is (C). Answer (D) may or may not be true, but the graph (which indicates percentage shares of national product) does not provide the kind of information required to decide.

20. **(C)** This question is a thorough test of your knowledge of the Reformation, since it asks about the social basis of a Protestant group. Some answers may be eliminated, if you already know the social bases of Calvinism and Lutheranism. Each of the three major Protestant groups—Lutheran, Calvinist, and Anabaptist—relied in major ways on particular social elements. Although Lutheranism drew support from a broad social spectrum, Luther himself was forced to rely on sympathetic members of the nobility of the Holy Roman Empire in order to defend Lutheranism against the Holy Roman Emperor. Calvinism held special appeal for the new middle class, particularly business elements. Anabaptism drew most of its membership from the peasantry in western Germany and the Low Countries.

21. **(B)** If the "Augsburg Confession" is not recognized at first glance, attempt to eliminate the other answers. All of the other terms are part of the Counter-Reformation. Once again, terminology is important. Pope Paul III called

the Council of Trent into session in 1545 as a means of revitalizing and reforming parts of the church. The Council approved restrictions on the reading material of ordinary Catholics (the Index), commissions to investigate the spread of Protestantism (which is what the Inquisition was originally designed to do), and a new group to combat the spread of Protestant ideas (the Society of Jesus, or Jesuits). The Augsburg Confession was a compromise confession of faith written by Luther's friend Philip Melanchthon in a vain attempt to reconcile Protestant and Catholic princes in the Holy Roman Empire.

22. **(C)** In answering this question, study the drawing carefully. The prism-shaped objects are indeed prisms, splitting light entering from the right into a spectrum, recombining it, and splitting it again. Answer (D) may attract those who do not study the drawing, since Newton formulated laws of gravity and motion; carefully looking at the drawing should allow you to avoid this mistake.

23. **(A)** As shown by the variously marked areas of the map, Prussia was able to unite most of northern Germany in 1867 and combine it with Prussian land in both eastern and western Germany. Answers (B), (C), (D) and (E) will be ruled out by a careful study of the map.

24. **(A)** The *politiques*, who emerged from the French civil war of religion (the War of the Three Henries) as the leading political group in France, argued that government should be based purely on political principles. Religion in politics was seen an an obstacle to good government. Answers (B) (government by religious leaders), (D), and (E) might be eliminated, since they represent an opposite viewpoint. A *politique* might accept answer (D), but parliamentary government developed only later in France was irrelevant to the central concerns of the *politiques*.

25. **(B)** The wording of the question ("first Swiss leader") indicates that the easy answer—Calvin—must be incorrect. If the correct answer is unknown, it may be possible to eliminate answer (D), who was the best-known Anabaptist leader. Answer (C) is a lesser-known Anabaptist and (E) is the name of the Archbishop of Canterbury who helped Henry VIII create the Church of England. Before the French lawyer John Calvin assumed the leadership of the movement which would bear his name, Calvinism was known as "Zwinglism." It leader, Ulrich Zwingli, created a religious community in Switzerland before his death in a battle with Swiss Catholic armies.

26. **(B)** Questions such as this underline the importance of not only understanding terminlogy but also its implications. Short of knowing Latin, a reasonable approach to this question would be to identify which answers were not results of the Thirty Years' War. The Thirty Years' War ended with a compromise settlement which allowed local monarchs or princes in the Holy Roman Empire to dictate the religious denomination of their area. Dissenters among their subjects were expected to convert or to move to another territory.

27. **(B)** In this case, it is not enough to be able to name a Christian Humanist or explain the ideas of the Christian Humanist. This question tests the depth of your knowlege about Christian Humanism and the Renaissance. Even if you can identify Valla, the correct answer also requires that you know a particular term ("Donation of Constantine"). The Donation was a document which canon (church) lawyers used against Holy Roman emperors who challenged papal authority. Ostensibly a signed document in which the Roman emperor Constantine acknowledged papal superiority in both the religious and temporal (nonchurch) realms, the Donation was proved a fraud by Valla on the basis of Latin usage not appropriate for its date and for references to historical events which occurred at a later date.

28. **(D)** Italian economic success during the Renaissance was partly the result of ingenious devices which Italian merchants created to lessen the risks involved in long-distance travel and trade on the treacherous and frequently stormy Mediterranean sea. The commenda freed the merchant himself from dangerous journeys; it was a contract between the merchant who furnished goods for sale and a "merchant-adventurer" who agreed to take the goods to distant locations and return with the proceeds. The merchant-adventurer was generally paid one-third of the resulting profits. If the term "commenda" is unknown the clue "Italian Renaissance" may lead to the realization that answer (A) is unlikely. If you are unable to eliminate more answers, however, guessing may not prove profitable.

29. **(B)** Answering this question requires more than terminolgy, since it also asks for an understanding of the implications of the Weber thesis. Note, however, that some answers appear unlikely. Answers (A) and (C) were in development before the rise of Calvinism. Anglicanism should seem an unlikely choice, since it was restricted to only one part of Europe and was a result of the political and personal desires of King Henry VIII. Weber, an early 20th century German sociologist, theorized that a mutually helpful relationship existed between Calvinism and capitalism because they both were based on common virtues such as industriousness, thrift, etc. Answer (E) is simply incorrect.

30. **(E)** This question requires that you not only interpret the graph correctly but also use your knowledge of history and geography. The two most urbanized areas (England and Scotland) are major parts of the British Isles.

31. **(B)** Beginning with terminology ("identify the Fronde"), this question asks for an analysis of the purpose of these periodic revolts by the nobility of France. A phenomenon of largely the 16th and 17th centuries, they were regarded as threats to royal authority by monarchical ministers Mazarin and Richelieu, who suppressed them ruthlessly. Most ended when Louis XIV involved the most powerful members of the nobility in sterile and useless ceremonial lives at his palace of Versailles.

32. **(A)** Intellectual historians study the role of ideas and intellectuals in his-

tory. Do not let the quotation intimidate you; read the quotation and note what kind of subject matter is involved. For a careful reader, the answer is not difficult.

33. **(B)**   Jeremy Bentham, who used this slogan to describe his philosophy of Utilitarianism, believed that one of the unsettled tasks remaining from the Enlightenment was the creation of a new, nonreligious system of morality that would be socially beneficial. His "moral calculus" sought to create a system of morality and laws that would reward the obedient with pleasure and criminals with painful emotions. Note that answer (A) is an attempt to mislead you; it seems a plausible answer, but is not the correct one. DeMaistre was an early 19th century French conservative writer and a Romantic.

34. **(D)**   When the Soviet dictator Joseph Stalin changed policies and decided to seek accommodation with Hitler's Germany in 1939, a Nazi-Soviet nonagression pact was negotiated by foreign ministers Ribbentrop and Molotov. It contained a secret provision providing for invasion of Poland by both countries and partition of Poland between them. This question demands a detailed knowledge of the pact, even if the answer is to be arrived at by elimination. If you are able to eliminate two or three of the answers, guessing is indicated.

35. **(B)**   Relinquished by Austria because its distance from Vienna had made it difficult to defend against Napoleon Bonaparte, the Rhineland was awarded by the Congress of Vienna to Prussia, which had sought territorial rewards for its role in defeating the French emperor. After 1850, the Rhineland, with its supplies of coal and iron ore and its location along the Rhine river, became the major industrial area of Germany. This questions asks for the significance and implications of a geographical change. One possible way to arrive at the correct answer is to try to recall other incidents involving the Rhineland in German history. If you can remember that the French invaded the area in 1923 to take control of industrial centers there, you may realize that answer (B) must be correct.

36. **(A)**   Although the war began as a result of the assassination of the heir to the Austrian throne and an ensuing dispute between Austria and Serbia, the background to these events was the steady decline of the Ottoman Empire, which at one time had controlled most of the Balkan peninsula. The resulting power vacuum allowed Austrian expansion into the Balkans, a development which created friction with new nations in the peninsula such as Serbia. Questions such as these test your breadth of knowledge and your analytical skills. Textbooks frequently designate the causes of the First World War as being trends such as secret alliances or yellow journalism; background events such as the decline of the Ottoman Empire are generally implicit.

37. **(B)**   The English Wars of the Roses (named for the flowers appearing on rival family crests) of the late 15th century exhausted and impoverished much of the English nobility, allowing the family which emerged victorious in the wars,

the Tudors, to create a more powerful monarchy. The Tudors created new nobility by rewarding loyal followers with titles and land, thus making much of the nobility a service class dependent on the monarch's good will and generosity. In this question the emphasis is upon your understanding of terminology (absolutism) and the impact of historical events: what were the results of the Wars of the Roses? In approaching the question, consider which of the answers would have increased monarchical authority; all of the other answers are either irrelevant or would have weakened the monarchy.

38. **(A)** More's *Utopia* was not the first imaginary society of the future—Plato wrote about an equally famous utopia—but it gained much attenton with its portrait of an ideal society where wars were avoided by bribes or assassinations, where a council of families ruled instead of a monarch, and where religious disputes were avoided by requiring only three simple, uncontroversial religious beliefs of all citizens. If the answer is not known at first, consider that the question contains a clue: the author is English. Answer (C) (a French playwright) may be eliminated. Cromwell was a famous Puritan leader, and Tyndale an English Biblical scholar. Spenser was an English poet of the Elizabethan era.

39. **(B)** One of the ironies of history was that Henry, who would split the Church of England from the Roman Catholic church because of the pope's refusal to sanction a "divorce" from Henry's first wife, had earlier written a leaflet severely criticizing Luther's doctrines. The title, awarded by a grateful pope, is still used by British monarchs. A key phrase in the question is "awarded by the pope", suggesting that Henry had been of service to the Church. Charles V was a devout Catholic, and the pope would not have pleased by attacks on Charles' authority. Cranmer leaned toward Protestantism. The Crusades occurred several centuries before Henry's reign. Answer (E) is irrelevant and, after Henry's break with the papacy, untrue.

40. **(C)** By the time of Elizabeth's reign, the Church of England created by her father Henry VIII was torn between high church (leaning toward Catholic forms of worship) and low church (leaning toward Protestant forms) members as well as early Calvinists. Her ministers persuaded Parliament that religious peace might be restored by the Thirty-Nine Articles, a broad creed of faith. The Act of the Six Articles was a law requested by Elizabeth's father, Henry VIII, retaining six of the Roman Catholic sacraments in the new Church of England. Test Acts and Toleration decrees were royal and parliamentary documents dealing with the issue of religious qualifications for government office holders. The War of the League of Augsburg was one of the many wars of Louis XIV of France.

41. **(C)** Movable type printing came into use shortly before the Reformation, and it made possible the production of cheap leaflets, and Biblical translations on a large scale. The question asks you to make a judgment—the "most influential." Answer (B) may be eliminated quickly. The military power of Charles V, Holy Roman Emperor during the Reformation, was an obstacle to the spread of Protestantism.

42. **(B)** The *philosophes* were the leading writers of the French Enlightenment of the 1700s. Voltaire turned to the idea of Enlightened Despotism because he was personally and intellectually opposed to rule by the nobility in France. The alternative to rule by the nobility, he reasoned, was rule by a monarch educated in the advanced outlook of the *philosophes*. Montesquieu, one of the few *philosophes* from the noble class, argued in his *Spirit of Laws* (1748) that power needed to be limited in government. His solution, a separation of powers between different elements of the government, was in reality a scheme to increase the power of the noblility at the expense of the monarch. The same idea emerged, with a different meaning, in the United States Constitution.

43. **(D)** The Weimar Republic (1920-1933), created by three parties in the German Reichstag in the wake of World War I, was never fully accepted by most Germans who saw it as weak and an expedient measure to seek better peace terms from the American president Woodrow Wilson and his European allies. The Republic was ended by Adolf Hitler, who was legally appointed chancellor of the Republic in January, 1933. Hitler called his government the Third Reich ("Reich" meaning "empire"). Although basic fact retention may be of help here, the question also tests your understanding of the significance of the Weimar Republic. Answer (B) may be eliminated (a democracy is unlikely to be called an "empire"). Answers (C) and (E) may be eliminated as well, if you realize that "Reich" means "empire," or that the "Third Reich" was the title of Hitler's German government.

44. **(C)** The Luddites, a largely British phenomenon, were workers who believed that early machines threatened their livelihood. Mobs of Luddites invaded factories and newspaper offices, attempting to vandalize the offending machines. The Levellers appeared in 17th century England; most sought an egalitarian society. Utopian Socialists were early 19th century thinkers who attempted to devise plans to mitigate the social evils of the Industrial Revolution. Chartism, a 19th century movement, circulated mass petitions in attempt to convince the British parliament to expand the right to vote. The Union of Warfare, led by army officers, attempted to overthrow the Russian tsarist government in the Decembrist Revolt of 1825. Note that this question attempts to test how precise your knowledge is by listing two names that sound similar (Luddites and Levellers); Levellers may even sound like a more plausible name for people who destroyed machinery.

45. **(C)** Of the areas mentioned, only Austria is part of the dotted area ("allied with Napoleon"). A straightforward exercise in map reading, this question illustrates the importance of careful reading: the word "not" is the key part of the question.

46. **(B)** Karl Marx presented his own socialism as "scientific," based on a grasp of the scientific laws of economics and history. He ridiculed earlier socialists who had sought to help the working class by rolling back the Industrial

Revolution, generally through Utopian communities or through government sponsored workshops. Fourier was an example. Guizot was a leading French politician in the reign of Louis Philippe (1830-1848). Renan was a 19th century French linguist, historian, and writer on early Christianity. Although he was a Marxist, Lenin did not coin the term "Utopian Socialism."

47. **(B)** Disraeli's *Sybil* symbolized his social concerns and his desire to modernize the British Conservative party, which he led. Disraeli sought to move the party away from its exclusive reliance on the British nobility, broadening its platform to attract the middle and working classes. George Sand (pseudonym of Baroness Dudevant) was a novelist. William Wordsworth was a prominent British Romantic poet. Gladstone, leader of the opposition Liberal party, was Disraeli's great political rival in the years 1866-1881. Clemenceau was the leader of France during World War I.

48. **(B)** DeGaulle, a World War II hero, came to power as a result of a crisis caused by independence riots in Algeria, where a native population pushed for independence while a sizable French population clamored for continued ties with France. After granting Algerian independence, DeGaulle steered France on an independent course in Europe, insisting on the withdrawal of NATO bases from the country while continuing to cooperate with NATO.

49. **(D)** After the Congress of Vienna (1814-1815), which reduced the number of states and independent cities in Germany to 39, Prussia and Austria both aspired to unite the country under their leadership. In 1834, Prussia formed the Zollverein, a tariff-free union, with several of the German states. It aggressively moved to expand the Zollverein throughout Germany. Fearing a backdoor unification under Prussian leadership, Austria threatened war. During a meeting between diplomats of the two countries at Olmuetz, Prussia backed down. If these facts are not known, there is probably no way to arrive at a successful guess for a question such as this.

50. **(E)** Sartre, one of the most prominent of the French existentialists, coined the phrase which gave the movement its name. Benda and Gasset may be eliminated; the first was the author of a book (*The Betrayal of the Intellectuals*) which argued that intellectuals had lost objectivity by becoming too involved in world affairs; the latter was notable for his warnings during the 1920s and 1930s that democracy signified a levelling of culture to mass tastes. Nietzsche and Kierkegaard may be tempting answers, since both are forerunners of Existentialism, but they lived during the 19th, and not the 20th, century.

51. **(B)** The Vienna Circle, which denotes a loosely organized group of individuals in 1920s and 1930s Vienna, sought to redefine philosophy to make it more precise and more useful to the natural sciences. The result, often termed "logical positivism" or "linguistic analysis," was formulated by individuals such as Ludwig Wittgenstein and Rudolf Carnap. It had nothing to do with Marxism

or Existentialism. Structuralism, intially a part of lingustic studies, has spread into many fields in the 20th century; in language studies, it describes the belief that many languages share common structures because language is based on common traits in the human mind. Impressionism describes a school of artists in the second half of the 19th century.

52. **(B)** Although many 20th century writers experimented with the stream of consciousness method—in which a story is told from an uniterrupted flow of one individual's thoughts and conscious experiences—the writer who used the method almost exclusively was Virgina Woolf. Perceptive test takers may note that she is the only novelist in the group of names. Yeats was a poet. Beckett, Ibsen, and Brecht were playwrights.

53. **(D)** Fearing a general European war if the Ottoman Empire collapsed and neighboring European states bickered over the division of the spoils, both Britain and France sought to protect the Empire. The two nations were the instigators of the Crimean War in the 1850s, regarding an invasion of southern Russia as the only way to halt Russian pressure on the Ottoman Empire. If the answer is not clear on first reading, some may be eliminated (Poland, which did not exist as an independent nation in the 19th century, and Switzerland, which has not been part of the European diplomatic system). A clue is furnished by the mention of Britain and France, since the correct answer has to be an area where they shared a common interest or concern.

54. **(B)** While this question mentions the lesser-known countries of Finland and Sweden, which you may not be able to eliminate since their history is not general knowledge, at least some of the answers may be eliminated. Part of northern Italy was held in the 19th century by a powerful neighbor (the Austrian Empire), but it was not divided among its neighbors. If you realize that there was no partition of Spain, the correct answer may be arrived at by guesswork and elimination.

55. **(E)** A question which requires both fact retention and analysis, this question must contain four untrue statements and one true one. The impact of the middle class grew throughout the century (thus answer (A) is untrue), and its size was greatly expanded by the Industrial Revolution (thus answer (B) is untrue). Its *laissez-faire* ideology was the opposite of answer (C) and, as a product of the Industrial Revolution, it did not hold its wealth in the form of large amounts of land, as the old nobility did.

56. **(D)** This fact-based question contains a major clue (the Defenestration of Prague) which refers to an incident in which a group of young men were pushed out of a window at Prague in the early 17th century. If that term is not known, it may be possible to use knowledge of the other wars to eliminate them. The War of the Spanish Succession won for Louis XIV of France the right to put a branch of his Bourbon family on the throne of Spain. The Hundred Years' War ended

English control over much of France. The War of Jenkins Ear involved England and Spain in a war over trading rights in the Caribbean in the 1700s. In the War of the Austrian Succession, Frederick the Great challenged Maria Theresa's right to the Austrian throne. The location of the "Defenestration" (in central Europe) may make it possible to eliminate answers (A), (B), and (C).

57. **(D)** All but answer (A) are French monarchs; the correct answer is the furthest back in history and, possibly, the least known. A Huguenot, Henry of Navarre, agreed to help end France's major religious war (the War of the Three Henries in the 16th century) by becoming both a Catholic and monarch (Henry IV). (The quotation signifies his commitment to national interests). If at least two answers are eliminated (say, the English king Henry VIII and Louis Philippe, a 19th century French monarch), it is worthwhile guessing, since only .25 point is deducted for an incorrect answer.

58. **(C)** From the information given in the graph, the only statement that is reasonable is (C) (from late 1847 to 1851). The other statements may or may not be true, but the graph does not give sufficient information to test them.

59. **(D)** A careful reading and understanding of the passage is essential. Because this passage is critical of papal involvement in politics, it is possible to eliminate answer (C). Answer (A) may sound tempting but, once again, the "obvious" answer is incorrect; Luther was German, and not Italian. Of the remaining answers, it may be possible to arrive at answer (D) because you have previously read Machiavelli and know of his strong criticisms of papal involvement in Italian politics.

60. **(B)** This question relies on not only knowledge but also understanding of the social system in Prussia—the German state which united all of Germany in 1870. The Prussian Junkers, whose income came largely from huge landed estates in eastern Prussia, provided the major civil servants and army leadership for the Hohenzollerns (the Prussian ruling family); they were found in prominent German positions as late as World War II. Prussia had no constitution until 1850. Answer (C) might be partially correct, since the Junkers often were judge and jury on their own landed estates and filled significant Judicial posts, but it is not the best answer. In the 19th century, middle class German businessmen and bankers saw the Junkers as political rivals, since the Junkers pushed for tariff and tax policies which favored agriculture over industry.

61. **(C)** At the Hampton Court conference of 1610, James II issued this response to English Calvinists who wanted to eliminate the system of bishops (which they saw as obstacles to Calvinist-oriented reforms in the Church of England).

62. **(C)** Although a large cannon barrel looms large in the poster, below it is a cross and a man in clerical garments. Not only are answers (A) and (B) the

same—indicating that they should be eliminated—but the purpose of the cannon barrel appears to be to accuse religion of hypocrisy (of sanctioning war while preaching love and peace). Answer (D) is for those who do not study the poster carefully; it seems plausible but is not the correct answer.

63. **(B)** The Hapsburg family, with Austria as its base, also held the crown of Spain until that throne was gained by the French Bourbons in the War of the Spanish Succession (1701-1714). Their power and wealth allowed them to place many of their sons in the position of Holy Roman Emperor. Charles V's powerful base allowed him to block Henry VIII's "divorce" from his first wife, Catherine of Aragon, an aunt of Charles; it also made him the leader of military efforts to exterminate early Protestantism. Since Philip the Fair was a French king, Henry VIII was an English monarch and William the Silent was a leader in the Dutch struggle for independence from Spain during the 16th and early 17th centuries, they may be eliminated.

64. **(A)** This question draws on knowledge-based analytical skills, requiring both a knowledge of the Corn Laws and an ability to analyze their social impact. Passed by the British Parliament during the Napoleonic Wars, when goods were frequently in short supply, the Corn Laws applied to grain grown within Britain. In times when the supply of grain was low, the tariff on foreign grain increased dramatically. The laws guaranteed that the owners of farms and farm lands, mainly the nobility, would make a fortune during times of food shortage. Businessmen and industrialists objected to the laws because they restricted foreign trade, since other countries could not sell their agricultural products to Britain in order to buy British factory-made goods. Thus answers (B) through (E) are incorrect.

65. **(C)** Miguel Cervantes' *Don Quixote* is the story of a errant and aged Spanish knight whose semihumorous misadventures are parodies of medieval standards of chivalry. Tom Jones is an 18th century novel describing the adventures of a young Englishman. *Candide* is a satirical story by the 18th century French *philosophe* Voltaire. *Emile*, by the late 18th century French political and social writer Rousseau, details his criticisms of the education of children in his time. *War and Peace*, by the Russian writer Tolstoy, describes aristocratic life in Russia during the Napoleonic Wars.

66. **(C)** Camus' portrait of an alienated, emotionally uninvolved "hero" emerged at the beginning of his novel *The Stranger*, probably the most popular novel associated with the Existentialist movement (although Camus rejected the label Existentialist). Although knowledge of the other authors may be of some help, this question is almost entirely based upon fact rentention. Andre Malraux was a 20th century French writer and public official.

67. **(C)** This question illustrates the importance of knowing the exact meaning of terminology. The Slavophiles did not reject western influences for Russia, but

many wanted to retain the distinctiveness of Russian culture. Thus (B) and (E) are incorrect. Answers (A) and (D) refer to the movement named Pan Slavism, which was a different movement from Slavophilism. Pan Slavists wanted to unite all Slavs (which includes most of the people of eastern Europe) under a single nation, generally Russia. But not all Slavophiies espoused Pan Slavism, or vice versa.

68. **(C)** The question calls for analytical abilities, since the correct answer is usually not described in textbooks as a means of population control. To arrive at the correct answer, you must analyze the probable effects of the Potato Blight, a disease which destroyed much of the major food crop of Ireland during the 1830s and 1840s. Of the remaining answers, one (A) occurred in Russia in the early 20th century. In the Peterloo Massacre (B), an army unit charged into a crowd of citizens demonstrating for expansion in the number of people who could vote in Great Britain in 1819. "Home Rule" (D) does apply to Ireland, but was the name of the political issue, debated in the British parliament in the late 19th century, of whether to grant Ireland limited self-government. (E) is simply incorrect.

69. **(A)** By the time Peter ascended the throne, the power of the boyars, the original Russian nobility, had been weakened by previous tsars such as Ivan IV ("the Terrible"), but they still wielded considerable influence. The other statements are all true. The Russian church had been split in the 1600s by liturgical disputes; Russia did not win access to either sea until the reign of Peter, who opened the way to the Baltic; and Russian contact with the west had been of a limited nature.

70. **(C)** The question offers a vital clue—that the Zimmerman telegram was sent during World War I. It may be easy to confuse it with the "Ems telegram" or the "Ems Dispatch" that the German chancellor Otto von Bismarck cleverly edited in 1870, thus causing France to declare war on Prussia. The Zimmerman telegram, sent from the German foreign office to the government of Mexico, suggested that Mexico take military or other actions to divert the United States from becoming militarily involved in Europe. In the event of a German victory in the war, Mexico might be rewarded by regaining California, Texas, and other parts of the United States which were originally Mexican territory. Answer (E) is incorrect; Britain entered the war mainly because of the German army invasion of France by marching through neutral Belgium.

71. **(D)** It is likely that a question about art will appear on the test. Occasionally only the painting itself will be a clue to the correct answer, although in this case the name of the artist is also given and points the way to surrealism, which many of Dali's paintings typified. Surrealism, popular during the 1920s and 1930s in Europe, often produced bizarre, dream-like images of great emotional power. If you cannot eliminate one or two of the answers, it may be best to pass this question by. The Fauvres ("wild beasts") emerged during the 1890s, producing paintings of strong color and intensity, sometimes based on African or Cen-

tral American art. Dadaism has been described as "antiart" protesting the meaninglessness of World War I. Cubist art often tried to portray articles as if seen from several points of view simultaneously. Impressionism was a 19th century movement.

72. **(B)**   The Bauhaus school, which flourished in 1920s Germany and was brought to the United States by German emigrees during the 1930s, reacted against the opulence of the earlier Victorian age. The skyline of many large American cities demonstrates the continuing influence of this school. Of the other answers, the Oxford Movement was a "high church" movement in the 19th century Anglican church. The Bloomsbury circle was a literary group in 1920s Britain. The Jacobins were the leaders of France during the "Reign of Terror" of the French Revolution of 1789. Neo-Romanticism in architecture tends to favor a less austere and more ornamental style than the Bauhaus school.

73. **(B)**   Britain, the first nation into the Industrial Revolution, held the advantages of coal and iron ore deposits, a good road system, and a nobility which was willing to underwrite the risky venture of opening factories ("entrepreneurship"). You may be able to eliminate these answers. If not, you may arrive at answer (B) by a process of analysis. The Agricultural Revolution, which increased farm yields but placed many small farmers out of work, created a large labor supply for the factories. Plus, financing for many early factories came from a nobility which owned most of the land and depended, at least initially, on farm income.

74. **(B)**   The closest to a "trick" question you may encounter, this item deals with a topic which appears on achievement tests with some frequency, perhaps because answer (A) may appear very tempting. During the early 14th century, Pope Boniface VIII was kidnapped by henchmen of King Philip the Fair of France. The following century—-when the popes were forced to live at Avignon, France under domination of the French monarchy—was termed "the Babylonian captivity" by papal defenders who compared it to the Jewish people's experience. You should not be tempted to select (A), because this is, after all, a test in European history. The remaining answers are true events, but are moot or irrelevant for this question.

75. **(C)**   For this fact question, you must not only know the facts about Keynes but also understand the logic of his economic system. Without this understanding, your chances of selecting the correct answer are slight, since the correct answer may appear to be the least likely. Keynes asserted that governments should spend more money during economic crises—even to the point of running deficits—in order to "prime the pump" of the economy.

76. **(A)**   Another fact-based question, this one assumes that you already are able to identify Richelieu; the question tests the depth of your knowledge of political history. Mazarin followed Richelieu as chief royal minister in France and continued his policies. Of the remaining answers, Walpole was the first

British prime minister; Colbert was a finance minister in France; Montesquieu and LaMettre were 18th century French *philosophes.*

77. **(B)** The Maastricht Treaties marked the agreement in 1991 among members of the European Community to begin measured steps toward an economic and political union that would ultimately have its own currency.

78. **(C)** When somewhat complicated answers appear, as in this case, it is important to read the answers carefully, since the misreading of one word (such as "not") may cause you to pick an incorrect answer. Like many Englishmen, Burke was sympathetic with the French Revolution's aims during its early stages but later, when he wrote the book, he was appalled at the violence of the revolution. Since the American Revolution occurred before the French Revolution, answer (A) is not possible. Answer (D) gives Burke's opinion in reverse.

79. **(E)** *Fathers and Sons* is probably not one of the better known books of the century, and there may even be a temptation to choose *Frankenstein* (a book which suggests that there may be evil in human tinkering with nature). The best clue to the correct answer is the title *Fathers and Sons,* a title which suggests generational conflict. The other answers simply do not fit the description in the question. Hugo's book was a novel of social justice. Dostoyevsky's work was a psychological novel, and *Degeneration* was an alarmist warning that human evolution might proceed backwards.

80. **(D)** Switzerland became the last advanced Western nation to grant women the right to vote, in 1989. Other nations in the West granted women this right at various other times.

Sample Answer to Document-Based Question

In the myriad of events which shaped the French Revolution of 1789, much attention has been given to occurrences in the capital city of Paris, where mobs in the streets weakened a royal government already under attack from an increasingly restive middle class. Less attention has been given to the reactions of the French peasants, or small farmers, whose grievances and concerns emerged during a period of anarchy and violence called the Great Fear.

The restiveness of the French peasants had been aggravated by both natural and political events. Three years of substandard harvests had contributed to economic misery in the rural areas of France. As grain prices rose, the peasants complained about the burden of their remaining feudal obligations. These included the corvée, the necessity of providing free labor for public works projects or other tasks as assigned by the local nobility.

It was not surprising that peasant grievances were initially directed against the nobility they saw as contributing to their misery. Rumors of aristocratic plots swept the countryside, including rumors of food horders among a greedy nobility. Some of the first violence of 1789 was in the rural areas, where peasants took control of local granaries and attacked members of the nobility.

The situation appeared to worsen because of lack of accurate information. An English observer noted the lack of rural newspapers. Word of mouth became the source of information. The most common rumor was that bands of brigands were operating in the area. Responding to such rumors, organized groups of armed peasants sometimes attacked other groups of peasants by mistake. In one case, the band of brigands turned out to be a herd of cows.

At the very least, such sporadic violence demonstrated the decline of the old regime: the decline of royal control in the rural areas of France. There were signs that peasant unhappiness was increasingly directed against the monarchy itself. It was noted that, although some noblemen contributed their personal funds to buy food for the peasants, the king made no appearance in the countryside, nor did he comment on events. The king remained a distant figure, hunting wildlife that the peasants were forbidden to hunt.

Although the leaders of the revolution in Paris were from the middle class, the Great Fear obviously had considerable impact. When King Louis XVI called the Estates General into session in 1789, the Third Estate—consisting of a middle class minority and an overwhelming peasant majority—emerged as the dominant group in France. When the Third Estate was transformed into a National Convention, the Convention became so alarmed by the Great Fear that it made rumormongering a criminal offense. Later, the Convention acknowledged one of the major concerns of the peasants by abolishing the remaining feudal obligations in France.

While the peasants were less educated and sophisticated than the middle class politicians who led France during the revolution, they clearly had an impact on events. The Great Fear united the peasants and made them aware of their own power.

In their own disorganized way, the peasants had made the end of feudalism one of the great achievements of the Revolution.

This essay 1) uses documents in a careful way, even quoting some indirectly; 2) has a clear introduction and conclusion; 3) centers each paragraph around a single theme or idea; 4) cites specific examples; 5) includes "outside" information; and 6) clearly addresses itself to the topic. All but point 1) are also demonstrated in the following essays as well.)

Sample Answers to Essay Questions

1.   Other Europeans sometimes regarded the English as a country of madmen during the 17th century, when the English overthrew two monarchs, even executing one. Yet the English Civil War and the Glorious Revolution of 1688 were singular constitutional events, pushing England ahead of the rest of Europe in terms of political development.

Both events transferred some elements of royal power to the English Parliament, which had existed since the 13th century; In the years since, the relationships between kings and Parliament had not always been smooth. The Tudor monarchs of the 16th century had handled Parliament with skill, using a mixture of compromise, guile, bribes, and cleverness to maintain royal authority. Their successors, the Stuarts, proved less successful in dealing with Parliament. Parliament tried to outlaw Roman Catholic advisers to James I by passing a Test Act, which required that high civil servants be members of the Church of England. When James tried to nullify the Test Act with his own Toleration Decree, Parliament cut his funding. Like other Stuart monarchs, James relied on subsidies from foreign monarchs.

Charles I continued the Test Act-Toleration Decree cycle. He also tried to combat the growing Calvinist (Puritan) presence in the Church of England. Many Puritans became Anglicans when Elizabeth I instituted the Thirty-Nine Articles, a broad creed of faith designed to quiet religious controversy within the Church of England. When Civil War broke out in 1641, the king was confronted with two armies: the army of Parliament and the army of the Puritans.

Charles' defeat and execution at the end of the war did not directly advance constitutionalism, since the following years of Puritan rule were neither successful nor favorable to the growth of parliamentary power. Oliver Cromwell personally ruled for a time as Lord High Protector. Upon his death, parliament chose to restore the monarchy by inviting Charles II to rule.

While Charles II avoided reopening old wounds, his successor, James II returned to the cycle of Test Acts and Toleration decrees. The resulting Glorious Revolution saw James flee the country and Parliament once again placed in a position to select a new monarch. Their choices—James' daughter Mary and her Dutch husband—conceded considerable amounts of royal power to parliament. For example, they agreed to a Bill of Rights banning royal interference in court proceedings and guaranteeing freedom from arbitrary arrests. The events of 1688 finally established the sovereignty of Parliament.

The political violence and chaos of the 17th century brought changes to

England that France would undergo a century later. The unwritten English constitution had been considerably revised, and Parliament had become a sovereign, significant presence in the English political system.

2.   During the century between the Congress of Vienna and World War I, balance-of-power diplomacy helped Europe to avoid a continent-wide war. The primary reason for the success of this diplomacy was the British policy of "splendid isolation", meaning no permanent alliances and freedom to join with other nations temporarily to block expansionist or threatening moves by other European states. Britain came to "splendid isolation" through circumstances rather than design. At the Congress of Vienna, the British representative Castlereagh stood apart from the other diplomats on the issue of restoring all monarchs removed from their thrones by Napoleon Bonaparte. Castlereagh feared such actions would lead to future revolutions and instability on the European continent. When the great powers sent French troops to suppress a Spanish revolt of 1820, Castlereagh responded by withdrawing Britain from membership in the Quadruple Alliance formed at Vienna. For the rest of the century, other British diplomats proudly followed the policy of "splendid isolation", accepting Castlereagh's view that the continental powers were not to be trusted.

     One of the first results was a British suggestion to the United States government, proposing that the two countries issue a joint declaration that the time had passed for European nations to establish colonies in North or South America. The United States declined—memories of the American Revolution and War of 1812 were strong—but the American President James Monroe later issued essentially the same declaration. Only one major attempt was made by a European power during the century to establish a colony in North America, an unsuccessful Austrian attempt to make a colony of Mexico during the United States Civil War. The real "enforcer" of the Monroe Doctrine, however, was the British navy, whose presence astride the Atlantic ocean was the most significant deterrent to foreign adventurers by continental powers.

     Throughout the 19th century, British foreign policy worked to limit expansionist plans by the other great powers. A common target was Russia. British policy sought to block Russian designs in Afghanistan; the same applied to Persia, where Britain had its own colonial interests. Objecting to Russian "bullying" of the Ottoman Empire on the issue of Russian Orthodox monasteries in the Empire, Britain and France sent troops to southern Russia in the Crimean War. When a Russo-Turkish war of 1877 ended with a treaty which the British prime minister Disraeli regarded as too favorable for Russia, he led the other European powers in successfully demanding revisions more favorable to the Ottoman Empire.

     After 1870, the rise of new European nations, plus British difficulties in the Age of Imperialism, led the British government to seek allies. The appearance of a powerful and united Germany in the center of Europe was one reason, although the German chancellor Bismarck played the role of "honest broker"' in continental disputes. Yet his successor as leader of Germany, Emperor William II, alarmed the British government by his plans to construct a German navy rivaling the British fleet.

During the Boer War in South Africa, British military actions were widely criticized in Europe, and Britain had no allies to speak up in its defense.

The end of "splendid isolation" came in 1902, when Britain cautiously allied itself with non-European Japan. From 1904 through 1907, Britain became a member of the Triple Entente with France and Russia, one of the two major alliances of World War I.

The driving force in balance of power diplomacy in 19th century Europe, "splendid isolation" helped maintain the 100-year European peace of 1815-1914, when Europe became, for a time, the dominant economic and military force in the world.

3.   Although the French *philosophes* of the 18th century shared a common outlook on many issues, they often differed on the practical steps to achieve their goals. Such was the case with Voltaire and Montesquieu, two of the best-known writers on the political issues of the period.

Although he was educated in Jesuit schools, Voltaire became a determined opponent of both religious influence in French politics and the political power of the French nobility. Voltaire's hatred of the nobility was partly personal, the result of a court case where he was found guilty of slandering a nobleman and went into self-imposed exile in England for a time. More importantly, Voltaire regarded the nobility as the greatest obstacle to changes and reforms sought by many of the *philosophes*.

As a privileged class, the nobility would, Voltaire believed, always oppose the social and political reforms which the *philosophes* thought would create a better environment for nurturing future generations. These included the establishment of a new, simplified religion (Deism), which Voltaire expected the nobility to oppose because most high clergy were from the ranks of the aristocracy.

Voltaire placed his hopes for achieving such reforms in the French monarchy, which he saw as the only alternative to rule by the nobility. Educated in the ideas and outlook of the *philosophes*, monarchs would become Enlightened Despots who would force reforms upon their subjects in a "revolution from above."

Montesquieu approached politics from an entirely different perspective. A member of the French nobility, Montesquieu shared the other *philosophes'* quest to find objective, semiscientific methods to improve their society. His major work, the *Spirit of Laws*, sought to define the factors which explained why the French government was so different from other governments, such as the government of Turkey.

Montesquieu regarded the growth of the absolute monarchy in France as a sign of decline. He particularly objected to the king's attempts to restrict the authority of the *parlements*, the French courts traditionally controlled by the nobility. Opposing Enlightened Despotism, Montesquieu instead wrote of the importance of maintaining a separation of powers in government. The idea was applicable outside of France—it appeared in the United States Constitution—but within France it signified a way to nullify royal authority.

Starting from similar principles, Voltaire and Montesquieu produced very different political solutions for France, solutions which would be made moot by the French Revolution of 1789. Their writings demonstrate the wide range of diverse ideas produced by the French Enlightenment.

4.   By the end of the 19th century, the Industrial Revolution had helped to make Europe the dominant economic and military power in the world. It also, however, had created major social problems as European countries became increasingly urbanized, a large but vulnerable working class emerged, and a burgeoning and increasingly affluent middle class demanded its share of political power.

Although the Industrial Revolution stretched from the mid-1700s, when Britain entered the industrial age, until the early 20th century, when industrialization emerged in Russia, the sufferings of the working class became obvious as early as the 1830s. Early factories were only marginally profitable, and they paid subsistence wages, required long hours of work, and frequently shut down for several months because managers had miscalculated demands for their products. Until Britain began regulating working hours in the 1830s, men might work up to 15 or 16 hours a day, women 12 to 14, and children 10. A British parliamentary commission discovered in the early 1830s that children who worked in mines frequently had one leg that grew shorter than another, because the children carried burlap sacks of coal generally on the same side of their body.

The middle class—whose occupations included the financing of the factories (banks), the management of the factories, or selling factory products—generally showed little concern for the working class. It is often observed that the middle class showed little social conscience, preferring to promote its own political agenda of gaining the right to vote for middle class males and increasing the authority of parliaments or legislatures. In Britain, the self-proclaimed "Workshop of the World" in the 19th century, the middle-class liberals also envisioned a "free-trade" world, where manufactured goods would be sold throughout the world without tariff barriers.

As new factories led to the rise of new cities and the rapid growth of existing urban centers, there was also growth in social problems such as illegitimacy and prostitution. The famous "Victorian Code" of the century, with its stern code of sexual conduct, was probably an attempt to both combat and cover up such problems.

Since middle class liberals preferred to ignore the problems of the working classes, movements to help the working class grew up outside the umbrella of liberalism. Movements to help the workers were labeled socialism. In the first half of the century, most socialists were Utopian Socialists, who preferred to return Europe to pre-industrialist days. Some, such as Charles Fourier, preferred to establish communities where factories were unnecessary. Karl Marx rejected Utopian Socialism because he saw the Industrial Revolution as a great industrial advance; the problem, as he saw it, was the ownership of the factories and the small percentage of profits going to the workers.

Industrialization came first to western European countries (Britain and France), proceeded to central Europe (Germany and Italy), and emerged last in the easternmost nation of Russia. Some of the nations where the Industrial Revolution occurred later appeared to have special problems in adjusting to industrialization. In Germany, the Junker class, a noble class whose wealth was based on large-scale farming in eastern Germany, forced the middle class to share power with it until nearly World War II. In Russia, writers named the Slavophiles saw industrialization as a western influence that threatened to destroy the uniquely Russian traits of the country. In fact the communist revolution of 1917 marked the triumph of the opposite school, the westerners.

While the Industrial Revolution made Europe for a time the preeminent continent in the world, it also was the cause of much social suffering, class division, and cultural confusion.

5.   Described by wartime propaganda as the "war to end all wars," World War I was followed by peace settlements which promoted bitterness and disillusionment in Europe. In this way, the settlements may have themselves become causes of World War II.

Three treaties ended the war—the Treaty of Versailles with Germany and the Treaties of St. Germain and Neuilly with Austria and the Ottoman Empire. The Treaty of Versailles was criticized within Germany as the "imposed treaty," so called because it was not the treaty promised when Germany asked for a cease fire in November of 1918. Germany had been promised a negotiated treaty, but the Treaty of Versailles, written by Germany's enemies, had been forced upon Germany with the choice of signing the treaty or resuming hostilities.

Already embittered by a continuing British naval blockade of Germany in 1919, after the war ended—which, rightly or wrongly, was blamed by many Germans as the cause of starvation in the country—Germans were especially unhappy with some parts of the treaty. The German army was limited to 100,0000 men; training was prohibited in tanks and planes; and Germany was required to pay an unspecified amount of reparations. To many Germans it appeared their nation was being blamed for starting the war and for all destruction resulting from the war.

The Treaty of Versailles opened the way for politicians such as Adolf Hitler, who argued that Britain and France were not to be trusted and their democracies were not to be emulated. Although Hitler's National Socialist party was never able to garner more than 34% of the vote, he probably spoke for many Germans when he dismissed the German government formed after the war, the Weimar Republic, as an expedient and weak government formed in hopes of gaining easier peace terms from Woodrow Wilson and his allies.

In order to convince many Germans that military force was necessary to roll back the hated treaty, Hitler also could point to two other parts of the peace settlements. Germany had lost much of mineral-rich Silesia to the recreated Poland, even though the majority of Silesians had chosen, in a referendum, to remain with Germany. Hitler also exploited the issue of the "Polish Corridor," a strip of formerly-German land awarded to Poland in order to give the Poles an outlet to the sea.

The treaties with Austria and the Ottoman Empire allowed the victorious allies to create a series of new nations in eastern Europe. The new nations were not particularly stable, struggling with internal divisions and bickering with their neighbors over borders and territory. In his book *Mein Kampf*, Hitler, an Austrian, looked at these areas as a natural direction for future German expansion.

Disillusionment over the peace settlement was not restricted to Germany. Britain and France had been promised a collective security agreement with the United States by Woodrow Wilson. When the United States, instead, withdrew from the European diplomatic system after the war, both European nations struggled to find new ways to make themselves secure. By the 1930s, many British citizens and some French citizens had come to believe that the Treaty of Versailles had been too harsh. The result, unfortunately, was a tendency to view Hitler as a mere statesman with valid grievances who needed to be "appeased."

It would be inaccurate to say the treaties at the end of World War I became the major causes of World War II. The major causes lay in the personality and ideas of Adolf Hitler. By helping Hitler's rise to power, and by failing to establish a stable diplomatic system to block him, the treaties were, however, a factor.

6.   United on a major principle—the preeminence of Scriptures over theological or papal authority—the three Protestant groups of the Reformation differed in significant ways on the implications of the Scriptures.

The two major doctrines of Martin Luther became part of most Protestant theology, although not necessarily by the names that Luther used. Like most Protestants of the Reformation, Luther found the New Testament letters of St. Paul a source of inspiration. St. Paul's statement that "the just shall live by faith" led to Luther's doctrine of "justification by faith". Arguing (somewhat erroneously) that Roman Catholic doctrines held that "good works" could compensate for sins, Luther taught that human sin was too great to be balanced out by good deeds. In his doctrine of "justification by faith," the emphasis was upon God's grace and upon salvation given in return for individual faith.

Luther's portrayal of individuals alone before God's judgment, penitent and seeking salvation, led to his other doctrine which became widely accepted within Protestantism: the priesthood of the believer. Rejecting priests as unnecessary intermediaries, most Protestants viewed their ministers as having no special status except as pastors to a congregation.

Calvinism was distinctive for its doctrine of Predestination. The doctrine of Predestination had been considered and rejected by St. Augustine, and few other groups in Protestantism gave it much attention. John Calvin made it a central theme in his *Institutes of the Christian Religion*. Popular Calvinism added the idea that God would not allow the "elect of God" to suffer in this life; "success" became the sign of salvation. For some, success in business became a mark of salvation.

Anabaptism, which largely drew its membership from the peasantry, tended to hold that belief should be based on the Scriptures alone. Although Anabaptist beliefs tended to vary from congregation to congregation, and from town to town, Anabaptists were generally less educated than other Protestants and regarded with suspicion any ideas or doctrines not clearly articulated in the Scriptures.

One area of major difference between the three Protestant groups of the Reformation was in their attitudes toward the Eucharist, or communion. Luther believed that Christ was present during communion, but he tended to reject the Catholic belief that Christ was present in the elements of communion, the bread and wine. Calvinists and Anabaptists were likely to regard Communion as a memorial service, without the physical presence of Christ.

In sum, while the three major groups of the Protestant Reformation drew different lessons from Scripture, they found agreement in their outlooks on the role of the churches and the relationship of sinners to God.

THE ADVANCED
PLACEMENT EXAMINATION IN

European
History

TEST 4

THE ADVANCED PLACEMENT EXAMINATION IN

European History

TEST 4

1. Ⓐ Ⓑ Ⓒ Ⓓ Ⓔ
2. Ⓐ Ⓑ Ⓒ Ⓓ Ⓔ
3. Ⓐ Ⓑ Ⓒ Ⓓ Ⓔ
4. Ⓐ Ⓑ Ⓒ Ⓓ Ⓔ
5. Ⓐ Ⓑ Ⓒ Ⓓ Ⓔ
6. Ⓐ Ⓑ Ⓒ Ⓓ Ⓔ
7. Ⓐ Ⓑ Ⓒ Ⓓ Ⓔ
8. Ⓐ Ⓑ Ⓒ Ⓓ Ⓔ
9. Ⓐ Ⓑ Ⓒ Ⓓ Ⓔ
10. Ⓐ Ⓑ Ⓒ Ⓓ Ⓔ
11. Ⓐ Ⓑ Ⓒ Ⓓ Ⓔ
12. Ⓐ Ⓑ Ⓒ Ⓓ Ⓔ
13. Ⓐ Ⓑ Ⓒ Ⓓ Ⓔ
14. Ⓐ Ⓑ Ⓒ Ⓓ Ⓔ
15. Ⓐ Ⓑ Ⓒ Ⓓ Ⓔ
16. Ⓐ Ⓑ Ⓒ Ⓓ Ⓔ
17. Ⓐ Ⓑ Ⓒ Ⓓ Ⓔ
18. Ⓐ Ⓑ Ⓒ Ⓓ Ⓔ
19. Ⓐ Ⓑ Ⓒ Ⓓ Ⓔ
20. Ⓐ Ⓑ Ⓒ Ⓓ Ⓔ
21. Ⓐ Ⓑ Ⓒ Ⓓ Ⓔ
22. Ⓐ Ⓑ Ⓒ Ⓓ Ⓔ
23. Ⓐ Ⓑ Ⓒ Ⓓ Ⓔ
24. Ⓐ Ⓑ Ⓒ Ⓓ Ⓔ
25. Ⓐ Ⓑ Ⓒ Ⓓ Ⓔ

26. Ⓐ Ⓑ Ⓒ Ⓓ Ⓔ
27. Ⓐ Ⓑ Ⓒ Ⓓ Ⓔ
28. Ⓐ Ⓑ Ⓒ Ⓓ Ⓔ
29. Ⓐ Ⓑ Ⓒ Ⓓ Ⓔ
30. Ⓐ Ⓑ Ⓒ Ⓓ Ⓔ
31. Ⓐ Ⓑ Ⓒ Ⓓ Ⓔ
32. Ⓐ Ⓑ Ⓒ Ⓓ Ⓔ
33. Ⓐ Ⓑ Ⓒ Ⓓ Ⓔ
34. Ⓐ Ⓑ Ⓒ Ⓓ Ⓔ
35. Ⓐ Ⓑ Ⓒ Ⓓ Ⓔ
36. Ⓐ Ⓑ Ⓒ Ⓓ Ⓔ
37. Ⓐ Ⓑ Ⓒ Ⓓ Ⓔ
38. Ⓐ Ⓑ Ⓒ Ⓓ Ⓔ
39. Ⓐ Ⓑ Ⓒ Ⓓ Ⓔ
40. Ⓐ Ⓑ Ⓒ Ⓓ Ⓔ
41. Ⓐ Ⓑ Ⓒ Ⓓ Ⓔ
42. Ⓐ Ⓑ Ⓒ Ⓓ Ⓔ
43. Ⓐ Ⓑ Ⓒ Ⓓ Ⓔ
44. Ⓐ Ⓑ Ⓒ Ⓓ Ⓔ
45. Ⓐ Ⓑ Ⓒ Ⓓ Ⓔ
46. Ⓐ Ⓑ Ⓒ Ⓓ Ⓔ
47. Ⓐ Ⓑ Ⓒ Ⓓ Ⓔ
48. Ⓐ Ⓑ Ⓒ Ⓓ Ⓔ
49. Ⓐ Ⓑ Ⓒ Ⓓ Ⓔ
50. Ⓐ Ⓑ Ⓒ Ⓓ Ⓔ
51. Ⓐ Ⓑ Ⓒ Ⓓ Ⓔ
52. Ⓐ Ⓑ Ⓒ Ⓓ Ⓔ
53. Ⓐ Ⓑ Ⓒ Ⓓ Ⓔ
54. Ⓐ Ⓑ Ⓒ Ⓓ Ⓔ
55. Ⓐ Ⓑ Ⓒ Ⓓ Ⓔ

56. Ⓐ Ⓑ Ⓒ Ⓓ Ⓔ
57. Ⓐ Ⓑ Ⓒ Ⓓ Ⓔ
58. Ⓐ Ⓑ Ⓒ Ⓓ Ⓔ
59. Ⓐ Ⓑ Ⓒ Ⓓ Ⓔ
60. Ⓐ Ⓑ Ⓒ Ⓓ Ⓔ
61. Ⓐ Ⓑ Ⓒ Ⓓ Ⓔ
62. Ⓐ Ⓑ Ⓒ Ⓓ Ⓔ
63. Ⓐ Ⓑ Ⓒ Ⓓ Ⓔ
64. Ⓐ Ⓑ Ⓒ Ⓓ Ⓔ
65. Ⓐ Ⓑ Ⓒ Ⓓ Ⓔ
66. Ⓐ Ⓑ Ⓒ Ⓓ Ⓔ
67. Ⓐ Ⓑ Ⓒ Ⓓ Ⓔ
68. Ⓐ Ⓑ Ⓒ Ⓓ Ⓔ
69. Ⓐ Ⓑ Ⓒ Ⓓ Ⓔ
70. Ⓐ Ⓑ Ⓒ Ⓓ Ⓔ
71. Ⓐ Ⓑ Ⓒ Ⓓ Ⓔ
72. Ⓐ Ⓑ Ⓒ Ⓓ Ⓔ
73. Ⓐ Ⓑ Ⓒ Ⓓ Ⓔ
74. Ⓐ Ⓑ Ⓒ Ⓓ Ⓔ
75. Ⓐ Ⓑ Ⓒ Ⓓ Ⓔ
76. Ⓐ Ⓑ Ⓒ Ⓓ Ⓔ
77. Ⓐ Ⓑ Ⓒ Ⓓ Ⓔ
78. Ⓐ Ⓑ Ⓒ Ⓓ Ⓔ
79. Ⓐ Ⓑ Ⓒ Ⓓ Ⓔ
80. Ⓐ Ⓑ Ⓒ Ⓓ Ⓔ

European History

TEST 4 – Section I

TIME: 55 Minutes
80 Questions

DIRECTIONS: Each of the questions or incomplete statements below is followed by five suggested answers or completions. Select the one that is best in each case.

---

1. All of the following statements are true about the 18th century French philosopher Voltaire EXCEPT

   (A) he admired the British political system.

   (B) he was an atheist.

   (C) he believed that religious considerations had biased the French judicial system.

   (D) he favored Enlightened Despotism.

   (E) he wrote a novel as a reply to the German philosopher Leibniz.

2. Which one of the following statements best characterizes the Russian *strelski*?

   (A) They comprised an elite military group, with great influence in Russian politics.

   (B) As intellectuals, they were an important group at court.

   (C) They were the leaders of the Decembrist revolt of 1825.

   (D) As church leaders, they contributed to the myth of Holy Russia.

   (E) They were foreigners who chose to live in Russia.

3. The Abbé Sièyés exerted a major influence on the French Revolution through his book

   (A) *Essay on Human Understanding.*

(B)   *What Is to Be Done?*

(C)   *The Progress of the Human Mind.*

(D)   *The Third Estate.*

(E)   None of the above

4.   With papal encouragement, Spain in 1494 agreed to recognize that one other nation had valid claims to parts of South and Central America. Which nation was it?

(A)   Great Britain   (D)   Italy

(B)   Portugal   (E)   France

(C)   Austria

5.   A major result of Pride's Purge (1648) was to

(A)   rid Parliament of opposition to Puritanism.

(B)   give Oliver Cromwell virtual control of Parliament.

(C)   ban all Puritans from Parliament.

(D)   add to the number of Puritans in high office.

(E)   create a Republic.

6.   All of the following statements about the Edict of Nantes are true EXCEPT

(A)   it banned Huguenot military forces and fortresses.

(B)   it promoted religious toleration.

(C)   it guaranteed freedom of worship for French Calvinists.

(D)   it followed a major civil war in France.

(E)   it was revoked by Louis XIV.

7.   Which one of the following statements best characterizes the differences between John Locke's "state of nature" and Rousseau's "state of nature"?

(A)   Locke called for reform; Rousseau was satisfied with the status quo.

(B)   Rousseau's "state of nature" did not have political connotations.

(C)   Rousseau's "state of nature" was one of economic equality.

(D)   Locke's "state of nature" ended with a "social contract," while Rousseau's did not.

(E)   Locke's "state of nature" was a violent and dangerous society.

8.   All of the following were achieved during the Prussian Era of Reform, 1806-1821, EXCEPT

(A)   improvements in the number and quality of Prussian soldiers.

(B)   the abolition of serfdom.

(C)   the end of the Junker monopoly on landholding.

(D)   universal manhood suffrage.

(E)   reform of the state bureaucracy.

9.   Which one of the following statements best explains the political and military decline of Poland by the late 18th century?

(A)   A lack of a parliamentary system

(B)   The liberum veto

(C)   The impact of religious wars in Poland

(D)   The selection of any Polish monarchs from the ranks of the nobility

(E)   The strength of the Polish monarchy

10.   During the Third French Republic, 1875-1945, which one of the following describes a famous political crisis centered around the accusations of treason against a French military officer?

(A)   The Irish Question   (D)   The Dreyfus Affair

(B)   The Panama Canal Scandal   (E)   The "Daily Telegraph Affair"

(C)   The Zabern Affair

11.   The Risorgimento was the name of

(A)   the emergence of a prosperous Europe from the ashes of World War II.

(B)   the movement to unify Italy.

(C)   the high cultural achievements of the Italian Renaissance.

(D)   Napoleonic rule in Italy.

(E)   the movement to unify Germany.

12.   The cause of the Crimean War included British and French objections to

(A)   Russian foreign policy toward the Ottoman Empire.

(B)   Austrian foreign policy in the Balkans.

(C)   the aggressive foreign policy of the Ottoman Empire.

(D)   Austrian occupation of northern Italy.

(E)   the foreign policy of Bismarck.

13.   Robert Walpole was notable for

(A)   being the first English prime minister.

(B)   his work to perfect the steam engine.

(C)   his leadership of the British trade union movement.

(D)   his work as a physicist.

(E)   his novels.

14.   In the post-World War II period, which one of the following Soviet writers was not allowed to travel to Stockholm to receive his Nobel prize for literature?

(A)   Shostakovitch   (D)   Brezhnev

(B)   Pasternak   (E)   Prokofiev

(C)   Beria

15.   All of the following statements about Eastern Europe from 1945 to 1960 are true EXCEPT

(A)   all Eastern Europe nations were subservient to the Soviet government.

(B)   Eastern European nations rejected the Marshall Plan.

(C)   there was a revolt in Hungary.

(D)   there was a revolt in East Germany.

(E)   almost all of the nations of Eastern Europe were militarily allied with the Soviet Union.

16. Which one of the following was a major reason for the failure of attempts to unite Germany and Austria in 1934?

    (A) The German government rejected the plan.

    (B) Austria threatened war if the plan was implemented.

    (C) Mussolini was opposed to the merger.

    (D) Britain and France opposed the merger.

    (E) Hitler opposed uniting the two countries.

17. Among the issues advocated by the Action Française of Charles Maurras was

    (A) opposition to monarchies.

    (B) anti-Semitism.

    (C) a smaller French army.

    (D) loyalty to the Third French Republic.

    (E) parliamentary government.

18. The following map depicts the late 18th century partitions of

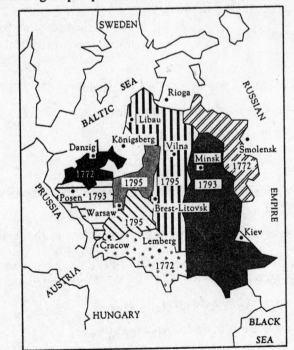

(A) Hungary.   (D) Russia.

(B) Austria.   (E) France.

(C) Poland.

19. The Locarno treaties of the mid-1920s committed

(A) Britain and France to defend Poland.

(B) the Soviet Union to respect the borders of its Eastern European neighbors.

(C) the League of Nations to intervene in the Soviet Union.

(D) Germany to make changes in its borders only by peaceful means.

(E) the United States to protect the borders of France.

20. All of the following are characteristics of the Romantic movement EXCEPT

(A) focus on emotion or intuition over reason.

(B) rejection of the study of history as useless.

(C) admiration for the Enlightenment.

(D) glorification of the Middle Ages.

(E) glorification of folk culture.

21. Which of the following would a Fabian Socialist most likely approve?

(A) Adam Smith's *Wealth of Nations*

(B) Government-owned utilities

(C) *Laissez-faire* policies

(D) An increase in the budget for the British navy

(E) Government subsidies to private corporations

22. Before 1870, which one of the following fit Metternich's description of a "geographic expression"?

(A) France   (D) Spain

(B) Britain   (E) Germany

(C) Russia

23. In 1820, freedom of the press and student activities were suppressed throughout Germany as part of the

    (A) Charter of 1814.   (D) Carlsbad Decrees.

    (B) Declaration of the Rights of Man.   (E) Schlieffen Plan.

    (C) Holy Alliance.

24. The "King's Friends" was used by King George III to

    (A) finance Hessian soldiers in the American Revolution.

    (B) attempt to control Parliament.

    (C) prevent revolutions in Britain.

    (D) weaken royal authority.

    (E) finance early British factories.

25. "By pursuing his own interest (every individual) frequently promotes that of society more effectively than when he really intends to promote it. I have never known much good done by those who affected to trade for the public good."

    This passage expresses the opinion of

    (A) Thomas Malthus in *Essay on Population.*

    (B) Adam Smith in *Wealth of Nations.*

    (C) Karl Marx in *Das Kapital.*

    (D) Charles Darwin in *Origin of Species.*

    (E) Jane Austen in *Pride and Prejudice.*

26. The First Estate in the Estates-General was

    (A) the nobility.   (D) the clergy.

    (B) the middle class.   (E) the factory owners.

    (C) the peasants.

27. Which of the following was a result of the Civil Constitution of the Clergy?

    (A) The clergy were given a privileged position in the Estates-General.

    (B) The church was made a department of the French state.

    (C) The clergy were condemned to execution during the Reign of Terror.

    (D) The office of bishop was abolished.

    (E) The church was made completely independent from the state.

28. Which one of the following is a description of the Charter of 1814?

    (A) A grant of land

    (B) A constitution

    (C) An anti-parliamentary tirade

    (D) A proclamation of religious freedom

    (E) A proclamation establishing a national bank in France

29. Locke's *Two Treatises on Civil Government* approved of revolution provided that

    (A) the revolution was not violent.

    (B) the government has violated property rights.

    (C) the poor are oppressed.

    (D) the government has not held elections.

    (E) the government is a monarchy.

30. The Clarendon Code, enforced in England from 1661 through 1665,

    (A) attempted to reestablish Puritan rule in England.

    (B) was approved by the new monarch, Charles II.

    (C) excluded Catholics and Presbyterians from high office.

    (D) required English colonies to trade only with the mother country.

    (E) was a document favoring religious toleration.

31. The "idols" of Francis Bacon, as explained in his *Novum Organum*, were

    (A) strict standards of scientific accuracy.

    (B) impediments to clear scientific thinking.

    (C) religious objects.

    (D) famous scientists.

    (E) political objectives.

Part of the text in the illustration reads
"So soon as a coin in coffer rings,
The soul into heaven springs."

32. The individual depicted on the horse in the picture above is

    (A) Calvin.   (D) Luther.

    (B) Tetzel.   (E) Henry VIII.

    (C) Boniface VIII.

33. In transforming the Roman Catholic church in his realm into the Church of England, Henry VIII

    (A) ended the Catholic sacraments.

    (B) disbanded the monasteries.

    (C) brought Protestant influences into the church.

    (D) radically altered the religious doctrines of the church.

    (E) strengthened the authority of the pope over English churches.

34. In the final stages of the Thirty Years' War, Cardinal Richelieu of France sent aid to

    (A) the Catholic Austrian Hapsburgs.

    (B) the Protestant monarchs of the Dutch Republic and Sweden.

    (C) the Catholic Spanish Hapsburgs.

    (D) Russia.

    (E) Prussia.

35. Which slogan best describes the proclaimed policy of the Soviet Union during the late 1950s and early 1960s toward the capitalist nations of the world?

    (A) "V for Victory"   (D) "Peace, Land, and Bread"

    (B) "The Third Force"   (E) "Peace in Our Time"

    (C) "Peaceful Coexistence"

36. Which one of the following was NOT part of the early years of the Cold War?

    (A) Berlin blockade

    (B) Atomic monopoly by the United States

    (C) Soviet occupation of Eastern Europe

    (D) Rearmament of Germany

    (E) A Communist government was established in Poland.

37. The author of the *Decline of the West* (1918) was

    (A) Mann.   (D) Proust.

    (B) Spengler.   (E) Beckett.

    (C) Joyce.

38. Stalin's policy of "Socialism in One Country" required the Soviet Union to avoid

    (A) industrialization.   (D) wars.

    (B) factories.   (E) government-controlled economy.

    (C) a large working class.

39. According to the ideas of Karl Marx, the LAST of the major European powers to have a proletarian revolution was supposed to be

    (A) Britain.   (D) Germany.

    (B) Italy.   (E) Russia.

    (C) France.

40. The "gap theory" was used by the German politician Bismarck to end the

    (A) Corn Law Crisis.   (D) Crimean War.

    (B) Army Bill Crisis.   (E) Boulanger Crisis.

    (C) Revolution of 1848.

41. Which of the following was most closely associated with the Reign of Terror during the French Revolution of 1789?

    (A) Danton   (D) Lafayette

    (B) The Jacobins   (E) Clemenceau

    (C) The Duke of Brunswick

42. "I dissent from those who are unwilling that the sacred Scriptures should be read by the unlearned and translated into the vulgar tongue, as though Christ had taught such subtleties that they can scarcely be understood even by a few theologians...."

This passage expresses the opinion of

(A)   Ignatius Loyola.   (D)   Erasmus of Rotterdam.

(B)   Machiavelli.   (E)   Robert Boyle.

(C)   Galileo Galilei.

43.   The Enclosure movement of the 17th and 18th centuries

(A)   attempted to reunite all Christians in one church.

(B)   sought to group factories closely together for maximum efficiency.

(C)   fenced in public land for private use.

(D)   sought to ban trade with nations outside of Europe.

(E)   sought to ban emigration from Europe to North America.

44.   Although he was a Roman Catholic, which one of the following individuals was most like Calvin in his efforts to reform the church and society?

(A)   Savonarola   (D)   Lavoissier

(B)   Ignatius Loyola   (E)   Charles V

(C)   Thomas More

45.   During the 16th and 17th centuries, all of the following represented challenges to royal authority EXCEPT

(A)   the parliaments.   (D)   Puritans.

(B)   New Model Army.   (E)   the Roundheads.

(C)   the palace of Versailles.

46. The emblem shown above was that of

   (A) Frederick the Great.   (D) Charles XII.

   (B) Peter the Great.   (E) Philip II.

   (C) Louis XIV.

47. In terms of political and military power, the major losers from the rise of Peter the Great's Russia were

   (A) Portugal and the Dutch Republic. (D) Italy and Spain.

   (B) Sweden and Poland.   (E) Britain and France.

   (C) Austria and Prussia.

48. The Royal Society of London, founded in 1662, was one of the first

   (A) societies dedicated to geographic exploration.

   (B) groups to stage Shakespearean plays.

   (C) literary clubs.

   (D) scientific societies.

   (E) political clubs.

49. Before he became president of Czechoslovakia, Václav Havel was known as a dissident and a

    (A) shipyard worker.   (D) soldier.

    (B) filmmaker.   (E) poet.

    (C) playwright.

50. "Écrasez l'infame," Voltaire's slogan of "crush the infamous thing," called for the suppression of

    (A) the church.   (D) censorship.

    (B) immorality.   (E) French universities.

    (C) the French monarchy.

51. Rousseau's concept of the ideal government was centered on

    (A) the general will.   (D) abolition of the government.

    (B) a strengthened monarchy. (E) a strengthened army.

    (C) a theocracy.

52. Which of the following issues made the most important contribution to the defeat of Italy's Christian Democratic party?

    (A) Poverty throughout the country

    (B) Chronic food shortages

    (C) Political corruption and instability

    (D) Religious conservatives in the party alienated many Italians

    (E) Italy's support of the United States during the Persian Gulf War

53. "Behold, an immense people united in a single person; behold this holy power, paternal, and absolute; behold the secret cause which governs the whole body of the state, contained in a single head; you see the image of God in the king, and you have the idea of royal majesty..."

   This passage by the French bishop Bossuet illustrates the concept of

   (A) sovereignty.

   (B) absolutism.

   (C) divine right.

   (D) papal authority.

   (E) parliamentary government.

54. The Pugachev rebellion was a threat to the power of

   (A) Frederick the Great.

   (B) Mussolini.

   (C) Catherine the Great.

   (D) Peter the Great.

   (E) Louis XIV.

55. Which of the following best characterizes the Table of Ranks of Peter the Great of Russia?

   (A) It separated the Russian population into distinct classes.

   (B) It set educational and performance levels for civil servants.

   (C) It required the nobility to serve in the Russian army.

   (D) It legalized serfdom.

   (E) It established a Russian parliament.

56. In the "Diplomatic Revolution" of 1756

   (A) Prussia became an ally of Britain.

   (B) Austria became an ally of Britain.

   (C) France fought Austria.

(D)   the Holy Roman Empire was abolished.

(E)   the Austrian government was overthrown by a popular revolt.

57.   A primary factor in the influence of the *sans-culottes* in the French Revolution of 1789 was

(A)   their admiration for the monarchy.

(B)   their large military forces.

(C)   their alliance with the Jacobins.

(D)   their lack of concern for economic issues.

(E)   their contempt for the middle class.

58.   The British Chartist movement of the 19th century drew much of its support from the

(A)   nobility.   (D)   workers.

(B)   middle class.   (E)   factory owners.

(C)   small farmers.

59.   During the revolutions of 1848, attempts to unite Germany under the leadership of the Prussian monarch were made by

(A)   the royal ministers of Prussia.

(B)   a national parliament at Frankfurt.

(C)   the Prussian king.

(D)   the king's relatives.

(E)   the Prussian army.

60.   *"We don't want to fight,*
      But, by jingo, if we do,
      We've got the ships,
      We've got the men,
      We've got the money too."

This saying, popular with British crowds reacting to tense British-Russian relations in 1877, gave rise to the term

(A)   chauvinism.   (D)   jingoism.

(B)   rule Britannia.   (E)   Fortress of Democracy.

(C)   Workshop of the World.

61.   Italy was unified in 1870 under the leadership of the Italian state of

(A)   Sicily.   (D)   Venetia.

(B)   Piedmont.   (E)   Tuscany.

(C)   Corsica.

62.   During the Persian Gulf War, what action did Russia take?

(A)   Russia supported Iraq by selling arms.

(B)   Russia supported Iraq with troops and weapons.

(C)   Russia supported Iraq diplomatically, but not materially.

(D)   Russia supported the international army led by the United States.

(E)   Russia remained neutral.

63.   "After reports of the renunciation by the Hereditary Prince of Hohenzollern had been officially transmitted...to the Imperial Government of France, the French Ambassador presented to His Majesty the King...the demand...that His Majesty the King would obligate himself for all future time never again to give his approval to the candidacy of the Hohenzollerns should it be renewed."

This passage is from the text of

(A)   the Fourteen Points.   (D)   the British Constitution.

(B)   the Treaty of Versailles.   (E)   the Congress of Berlin.

(C)   the Ems Telegram.

64.   The Paris Commune, established at the close of the Franco-Prussian war of 1870, was suppressed by

(A)   the Prussian army.   (D)   the Spanish army.

(B)   the French army.   (E)   the British army.

(C)   the Russian army.

65.   All of the following were characteristics of the Second Industrial Revolution EXCEPT

(A)   emergence of major steel industries.

(B)   large growth of the textile industry.

(C)   emergence of the German chemical industry.

(D)   application of electricity to industrial production.

(E)   the widespread use of oil.

66.   In World War II, the Battle of Britain was fought largely as a

(A)   naval battle.   (D)   diplomatic battle.

(B)   land battle.   (E)   submarine battle.

(C)   air battle.

67.   The map on the following page illustrates the

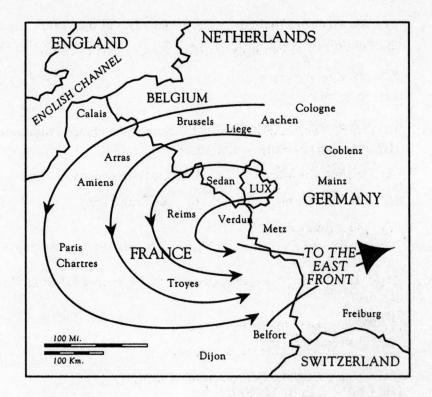

(A) Maginot Line.   (D) "soft underbelly of Europe."

(B) Schlieffen Plan.   (E) French defenses in World War I.

(C) German invasion of France in 1940.

68. The earliest form of Communism in the Soviet Union was called

(A) Marxist-Leninism.   (D) War Communism.

(B) Socialism in One Country. (E) Strength through Unity.

(C) Let a Thousand Flowers Bloom.

69. The term "iron curtain," used to describe Soviet-dominated areas of Eastern Europe, was coined in the late 1940s by

(A) Churchill.   (D) Khrushchev.

(B) de Gaulle.   (E) Stalin.

(C) Adenauer.

70. The advice that the German government gave to the Austro-Hungarian government during the early days of World War I is often characterized as

    (A) cautious.

    (B) a "blank check."

    (C) uncertainty.

    (D) warnings for Austria-Hungary to act carefully so it would not lose support from Germany.

    (E) concern that Austria-Hungary would act recklessly.

71. The founder of psychoanalysis, Sigmund Freud, often named psychological conditions after

    (A) famous scientists.   (D) ancient myths.

    (B) friends.   (E) members of his family.

    (C) mathematical terms.

THE CHANGE IN NATIONAL POPULATIONS AT THE TURN OF THE CENTURY (POPULATION IN MILLIONS)

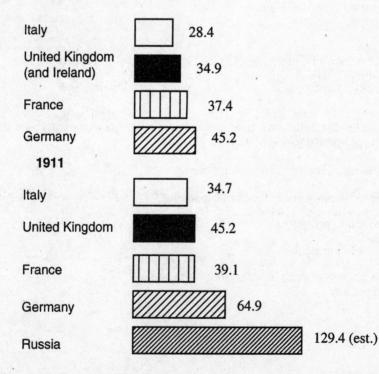

1881

Italy — 28.4

United Kingdom (and Ireland) — 34.9

France — 37.4

Germany — 45.2

1911

Italy — 34.7

United Kingdom — 45.2

France — 39.1

Germany — 64.9

Russia — 129.4 (est.)

72. All the following statements are reasonable conclusions about the graph shown on the previous page EXCEPT

    (A) the United Kingdom gained more people than France.

    (B) the United Kingdom gained more people than Italy.

    (C) in percentage terms, Russia experienced the greatest population growth.

    (D) Germany gained more people than France.

    (E) much of Europe was experiencing a population growth.

73. Which of the following describes an important trend in Britain during the Depression of the 1930s?

    (A) Interest rates rose rapidly.

    (B) Unemployment remained high.

    (C) Property values rose.

    (D) National industrial production was at an all-time high.

    (E) Military spending increased rapidly.

74. The United Nations was originally envisioned in a document known as the

    (A) Truman Doctrine.   (D) Brussels Pact.

    (B) Atlantic Charter.   (E) Treaty of Rapallo.

    (C) Molotov Plan.

75. Which one of the following factors stimulated the growth of fascism in Europe during the 1920s and 1930s?

    (A) Free trade among European nations

    (B) The development of cheaper armaments

    (C) Economic prosperity

    (D) Fear of communism

    (E) The growth of parliamentary governments

76. The Nuremberg trials were

    (A) mass purges in the Soviet Union.

    (B) trials of war criminals.

    (C) the trials which placed Hitler in prison as a young man.

    (D) trials of manufacturers who were war profiteers in World War I.

    (E) trials of German army officers who conspired to kill Hitler during World War II.

77. A primary element in National Socialist ("Nazi") ideology was the belief in

    (A) the equality of all Germans.

    (B) democratic elections.

    (C) the need for *Lebensraum*.

    (D) the need to restrain nationalist feelings.

    (E) peaceful cooperation among nations to prevent war.

78. Which of the following best characterizes the beliefs of St. Simon (1760-1825)?

    (A) Admiration for industrialization

    (B) Fear of modern trends

    (C) Admiration for religion

    (D) Rejection of the usefulness of science

    (E) Concern that Europe was in decline

79. *"Nature and nature's law lay hid in night,*
    God said, 'Let Newton be,' and all was light."

    This passage, which is from a poem praising science and Newton, was written by

    (A) Tennyson.   (D) Wordsworth.

    (B) Yeats.   (E) Zola.

    (C) Pope.

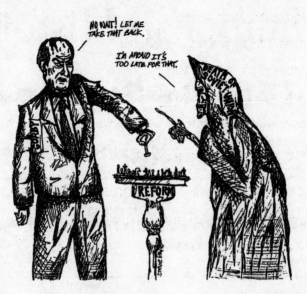

Steve Raper

80. The political cartoonist is most strongly making the point that

    (A) Gorbachev never really favored either *glasnost* or *perestroika*.

    (B) Gorbachev's reforms were implemented too slowly to be effective.

    (C) Gorbachev believed that the Russian Republic would be better off economically and militarily by leaving the Soviet Union.

    (D) once implemented, reform measures proved difficult for the CPSU to control.

    (E) the attempted August 1991 coup pushed Gorbachev into moves with which he was not comfortable.

European History

TEST 4 – Section II

TIME: Reading Period – 15 minutes
Writing Time for all three essays – 115 minutes

DIRECTIONS: Read over both the Document-Based Essay question in Part A and the choices in Part B during the Reading Period, and use the time to organize answers. All students must answer Part A (the Document-Based Essay Question) and choose TWO questions from Part B to answer.

PART A – DOCUMENT-BASED ESSAY

This question is designed to test your ability to work with historical documents. As you analyze each document, take into account the source and the point of view of the author. Write an essay on the following topic that integrates your analysis of the documents. You may refer to historical facts and developments not mentioned in the documents.

Analyze the nature of the Peterloo Massacre of 1819, and assess the validity of the following statement about the event.

"Peterloo...proved to be a watershed. A nice, neat little massacre occurring within a quarter of an hour. No long drawn-out horror to numb the sensibilities. Not too many casualties, but sufficiently occasioned, with sabres slashing, children screaming, and horses trampling, to shock....(it) galvanized the middle-class Radicals, prodded the Whigs, and stiffened the Government into action."
—Joyce Marlow, *The Peterloo Massacre*

Historical Background: The Peterloo Massacre occurred during a time of turmoil and tension in Great Britain. The Napoleonic Wars had ended just four years before. Food prices were rising, and some blamed the Corn Laws, which the Tories had passed through parliament during the Napoleonic Wars. By imposing large tariffs on foreign grain during times of shortage, the Corn Laws were designed to increase food prices and benefit the nobility financially. Only the very wealthy—almost all nobility—voted for the elected house of Parliament, the House of Commons. Middle-class orators who were demanding the expansion of the electorate cited the Corn Laws as an example of the evils of the nobility's monopoly of Parliament. As new industrial cities arose, orators also complained about the "rotten boroughs" (election districts which were over-represented in Parliament because their population had declined). In 1819, one of the middle-class orators promoting expansion of the electorate, Henry Hunt, called for a rally to be held at St. Peter's Field in the relatively new, industrial city of Manchester. Despite its rapid growth, Manchester did not have a representative in Parliament. Local authorities, fearing violence, sent local militia and an army cavalry unit into the crowd. In the ensuing panic, a number of people in the crowd were killed and many injured. This event was later dubbed the "Peterloo Massacre."

Document 1

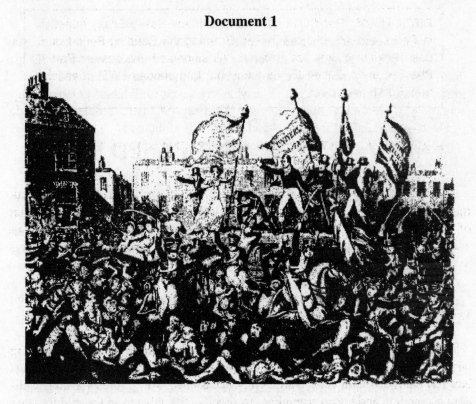

Contemporary drawing of the Peterloo Massacre.

Document 2

"(They should) take the liberty to recommend to those poor fellows, the language of whose petition breathed throughout every line a feeling of despondency and forlorn hope...to seek a redress of their manifold grievance...He advised them to give up all ideas of leaving the country...to join with the great body of people who...had embarked in a firm and constitutional way to reform the House of Commons, and never were either to the right or left until Annual Parliaments, Universal Suffrage, and Election by Ballot shall be established in the land."

—J. T. Saxton, radical reform leader, to the distressed weavers of Manchester in June 1819.

Document 3

"...we are unsound in the vitals...,that's the seat of the mischief—the Constitution's become rotten at the core—Corruption's at the very helm of the state; it sits and rules in the very House of Commons; this is the source, the true and the only one of all our sufferings—what the remedy, then? Why, reform—a radical and complete constitutional reform; we want nothing but this...to mend our markets and give every poor man plenty of work and good wages for doing it."

—From a letter to the *Manchester Mercury* in August 1819.

Document 4

"'We are very well as we are,' says the hereditary Lord, who squanders away his 30,000 British pounds a year in every species of debauchery and dissipation...'We are very well as we are,' say the Representatives and Aristocratical Proprietors of Rotten Boroughs. But what say seven millions of persons in this country who are totally *unrepresented?* What say the liberal minded—the independent—the friends of freedom—and the friends of thought?"

—From an article in the *Manchester Gazette,* December 16, 1818.

Document 5

"You will meet on Monday next, friends, and by your *steady, firm, and temperate* deporting, you will convince all your enemies, that you feel you have an *important* and *imperious public duty* to perform. Our Enemies will seek every opportunity to...excite a riot, that they may have a pretence for Spilling our Blood....Come, then, friends, to the meeting with no other Weapon but that of a self approving conscience; determine not to suffer yourself to be irritated or excited, by any means whatsoever, to cause any breach of the public peace."

—Statement by Hunt, announcing the rally at St. Peter's Field.

Document 6

(Local authorities stationed themselves in buildings near the rally to observe the crowd; after the rally had begun, they ordered the local militia (the Yeomanry) and an army cavalry unit, both of which were waiting in nearby streets, to move into the crowd to maintain order.)

"At first (the movement of the Manchester Yeomanry) was not rapid, and there was some show of an attempt to follow their officer in regular succession, five or six abreast; but they soon increased their speed...they had long been insulted with taunts of cowardice, (and) continued their course, seemed to vie with each other which should be first...As the cavalry approached the dense mass of people they used their utmost efforts to escape; but so closely were they pressed in opposite directions by the soldiers, the special constables,... and their own immense numbers, that immediate escape was impossible...On the arrival (of the troops)...a scene of dreadful confusion ensued."

—Account of the Rev. Edward Stanley, an eyewitness.

Document 7
LIST OF THE DEAD AT "PETERLOO"

Thomas Ashworth. Sabred and trampled.

John Ashton. Sabred and trampled on by the crowd.

Thomas Buckley. Sabred and trampled.

James Crompton. Trampled on by the cavalry.

William Fildes. Two years old. Ridden over by the cavalry.

Sarah Jones. No cause given.

John Lees. Sabred.

Arthur O'Neill. Inwardly crushed.

Martha Partington. Thrown into a cellar and killed.

John Rhodes. Died several weeks later.

Joseph Ashworth. Shot.

William Bradshaw. No cause given.

William Dawson. Sabred and crushed.

Edmund Dawson. Died of sabre wounds.

—From a list compiled from many sources by a modern historian.

Document 8

"The inscriptions upon the flag are "Parliaments Annual, Suffrage Universal." I cannot say that I see anything wrong in either of these. 'Unity Strength.' 'Liberty and Fraternity.' Now are these...calculated to produce dissatisfaction and contempt and hatred to His Majesty's Government?

—Justice Bayler, defense attorney, at the trial of Hunt, describing banners at the St. Peter's Field rally.

Document 9

"The results of yesterday will bring down the name of Hunt and his accomplices...With a fractious perverseness...they have set open defiance upon the timely warning of the magistrates...and daringly invited the attendance of a mass of people which may be computed at near 100,000....Yesterday's proceedings showed that the Revolutionary attempts of this base Junto was no longer to be tolerated."

—From one of the first newspaper accounts of the massacre, in the *Manchester Mercury,* August 17, 1819.

Document 10

(The Peterloo Massacre was regarded as a civil insurrection by the Tories in Parliament, who used their majority to force through Parliament a series of laws restricting basic liberties, the Six Acts. The rival Whigs opposed the Six Acts and tended to see the incident as evidence of popular discontent and proof of the need for electoral reform.)

"He felt himself bound to recommend to the House, if it wished to avoid civil dissension, if it wished to avoid the greatest of all evils, the shedding of English

blood by English hands, to examine fairly and freely into the state of representation...."
—From a speech by a Whig member of Parliament, December 1819.

Document 11

"For many months, we had suffered the terrors of siege, having enemies
within as well as without; and when we went to bed at night, we knew not, but
that our town would be in flames before morning....Who shall complain of
Peterloo, when the *organized terrors of months of slavery and fear* had driven us
to make a desperate stand for all, which Britons can value."
—A Tory speaker defending the authorities' handling of the crowd.

Document 12

"...it must be admitted that taxation is ponderous, and that the middle class
are like enough to fall into the state of the lower, and the lower into a state of
starvation. But what can Reform, or any other nostrum of political agitation do
here? We are suffering the effects of the late war and bad harvests, and must wait
patiently until the tide turns. It is absurd to attribute such calamities to borough-
mongering and the Bourbons."
—Lord Gatliffe to Lord Farington, June 5, 1819 (The Bourbons were the
French ruling family).

Document 13

"The policy which is meant to suppress or fetter discussion is...doubtful; for
the best vent for passion...is the freedom of using angry words."
—A Whig comment on the Six Acts, from an article in the *London Times*.

Document 14

(Among those expressing disapproval of the Six Acts was the young Tory Robert
Peel, later to be prime minister of England. During the 1820s, Peel and other
"reform" Tories would convince Parliament to approve legal and other reforms.)

"Do you not think that the tone of England...is more liberal...than the policy
of the government? Do you not think there is more a feeling, becoming daily
more general...in favor of some undefined change in the role of governing the
country...?"
—Robert Peel, Letter of 1819.

Document 15

(The Tories controlled Parliament until 1831. During an election in 1829, the
Duke of Wellington, campaigning for the Tories, was greeted by signs bearing
the words "Remember Peterloo." By the time of major national elections in 1831,
the Whigs had committed themselves to expanding the electorate. When they
won, they passed legislation giving the suffrage to half of the adult middle-class
males, beginning a process that continued throughout the century.)

"Peterloo was Tory justice, and is what they would repeat should they ever come to power again."

—From a Liberal party pamphlet directed against the Conservative party (formerly called the Tories) in the election of 1874.

PART B – ESSAY QUESTIONS

1. Describe and compare the policies of mercantilism and *laissez-faire*.

2. Describe and analyze why the debate over a sun-centered versus earth-centered solar system was the primary controversy of the Scientific Revolution.

3. Assess and analyze how problems in the World War II alliance of the United States, Great Britain, and the Soviet Union helped lead to the Cold War.

4. "The French Enlightenment" was a fountainhead of humanitarian and libertarian principles; it articulated grievances and sought alternatives. The German Enlightenment was more abstract and less practical."

    Analyze and assess the validity of this statement, citing specific individuals.

5. Describe and assess the importance of primogeniture in creating a distinctive social structure in Great Britain, as compared to continental European nations such as France.

6. Louis XIV (reigned 1643-1715) was France's most famous absolute monarch, while Napoleon III (reigned 1851-1870), a nephew of Napoleon Bonaparte, became emperor of France in an army-direct coup d'état and ruled in conjunction with a two-house legislature.

    Starting with the portraits shown on the following page, analyze similarities and differences in the nature and style of these two monarchies.

THE ADVANCED PLACEMENT EXAMINATION IN

European History

TEST 4 – ANSWERS

1.	(B)	21.	(B)	41.	(B)	61.	(B)
2.	(A)	22.	(E)	42.	(D)	62.	(D)
3.	(D)	23.	(D)	43.	(C)	63.	(C)
4.	(B)	24.	(B)	44.	(A)	64.	(B)
5.	(B)	25.	(B)	45.	(C)	65.	(B)
6.	(A)	26.	(D)	46.	(C)	66.	(C)
7.	(C)	27.	(B)	47.	(B)	67.	(B)
8.	(D)	28.	(B)	48.	(D)	68.	(D)
9.	(B)	29.	(B)	49.	(C)	69.	(A)
10.	(D)	30.	(C)	50.	(A)	70.	(B)
11.	(B)	31.	(B)	51.	(A)	71.	(D)
12.	(A)	32.	(B)	52.	(C)	72.	(C)
13.	(A)	33.	(B)	53.	(C)	73.	(B)
14.	(B)	34.	(B)	54.	(C)	74.	(B)
15.	(A)	35.	(C)	55.	(B)	75.	(D)
16.	(C)	36.	(D)	56.	(A)	76.	(B)
17.	(B)	37.	(B)	57.	(C)	77.	(C)
18.	(C)	38.	(D)	58.	(D)	78.	(A)
19.	(D)	39.	(E)	59.	(B)	79.	(C)
20.	(C)	40.	(B)	60.	(D)	80.	(D)

Detailed Explanations
of Answers
TEST 4

1. **(B)** "Exclusion" questions, which ask you to identify the single answer which does not fit with the others, may be approached in two different ways. One approach is to identify the single answer that is false; the other is to eliminate all true answers. Although he criticized Christianity as "superstition" and believed that religious bias caused French Huguenots to be unjustly convicted of crimes, Voltaire retained God in his philosophy. His version of religion, Deism, envisioned God as a creator of the universe; a minimal number of simple religious beliefs were to be part of Deism, in order to avoid constant theological arguments. The remaining answers are true: Voltaire favored the reform of French society from "above" by the monarch (Enlightened Despotism); during a brief stay in England, he wrote a book praising the English political system; and he wrote his cynical and skeptical book *Candide* as a reply to the German philosopher Leibniz, who insisted that this is the best of all possible worlds.

2. **(A)** The *strelski*, or Moscow guards, created and toppled tsars; the nobility sought their favor. Peter the Great destroyed the *strelski* after a revolt in 1698. With some knowledge of Russian history, one or two of the other answers may be eliminated. Answer (C) is not likely, since the date of the Decembrist revolt places it much too late in Russian history.

3. **(D)** Sièyés' *The Third Estate* sought to use a military coup d'état to create a strong, but unelected, executive. The book suggested goals that Napoleon Bonaparte later accomplished. *What Is to Be Done?* was the title of Vladimir Lenin's book detailing the path to proletarian revolution in Russia. In his *Essay on Human Understanding*, John Locke argued that human personality is formed entirely by the environment, rather than by innate or preconceived ideas. *The Progress of the Human Mind*, by the philosopher Condorcet, argued that human perfectibility was possible and that "nature has set no limits to our hopes."

4. **(B)** Portuguese navigators played a role in the explorations of the New World. If this fact is not known, there are other possible approaches. Consider clues that you may already know: Portuguese is the language of Brazil, the

largest nation in South America. Some elimination may also be done: (D) is obviously incorrect, since there was no united Italy until 1870.

5. **(B)** Pride's Purge, named for the colonel who carried it out, occurred after the English Civil War of the 1640s, which was won by a faction of the Puritans (the Congregationalists) under Oliver Cromwell. All opponents of Cromwell were removed from Parliament, including Puritans who belonged to the other faction, the Presbyterians. Only about 50 supporters of Cromwell were left in Parliament. The remaining answers are untrue or simply not applicable.

6. **(A)** Here is another example of an "exclusion" question. The Edict of Nantes was issued by Henry IV, France's first Bourbon monarch, after France's major religious war. A Huguenot, Henry became monarch by promising to convert to Roman Catholicism. The war left France exhausted, and convinced many that religious issues should be kept strictly separate from political issues. Thus there was support for the Edict, which guaranteed the Huguenots freedom of worship and the right to have their own fortresses in the countryside. Louis XIV, the most powerful of the French monarchs and a devout Catholic, later revoked the Edict, asserting that the right of Huguenots to have their own fortresses was a violation of his royal sovereignty.

7. **(C)** Locke envisioned the "state of nature" as a time of relative peace and harmony. The "social contract," by which the first government was established, was necessary only because certain tasks, such as road building, might be done only collectively. Rousseau also used the term "social contract," but his "state of nature" was a time of economic equality; insisting that "property is theft," Rousseau argued that economic inequality began when human beings began to place value on objects that might be hoarded, such as gold or precious stones (unlike food, which was perishable).

8. **(D)** Although the first three answers plus answer (E) were achieved during the Era of Reform—including abolition of much of the power of the Junkers, the nobility which owned the large farm estates in eastern Prussia—the monarchy did not institute universal manhood suffrage (all adult males being allowed to vote) until 1850. Even then, the votes of the wealthy "counted" for much more than the middle class or the poor.

9. **(B)** A major cause was the failure of the Polish parliament, the Diet, to function effectively. The liberum veto, which allowed any member to force adjournment by objecting to the topic under discussion, made the Diet ineffective. The other answers are either not applicable or untrue. Poland had no religious wars. The Polish nobility, deeply split among themselves, often selected foreigners as monarchs rather than pick someone from their own ranks. Thus answer (E) is also incorrect; Poland had more problems with weak monarchs than with overly assertive monarchs.

10. **(D)**   The first 30 years of the Third French Republic were tumultuous, as Monarchists bitterly tried to gain control of the Republic. When doubts began to surface over the guilt of Alfred Dreyfus, a military intelligence officer convicted by a Royalist-controlled court martial of passing military secrets to Germany, the rival Republicans were able to use the issue to destroy Royalist credibility in France. As for the other answers, the Irish Question signified British debates over pacifying unhappy Ireland in the 19th century, when all of Ireland was part of Britain. The Zabern Affair described the shooting of demonstrators in the Alsace-Lorraine section of Germany by a German army unit in 1913. The Panama Canal scandal was another attempt of Royalists to turn public opinion to their side; it concerned financial scandals in a failed French project to build the canal. In the "Daily Telegraph Affair," the German Emperor William II was embarrassed by a controversy over the publication of comments which he made to a British newspaper reporter.

11. **(B)**   The Risorgimento, or "resurgence," began early in the 19th century with Italians such as Mazzini, who sought a unified and liberal Italy, with a parliament elected by universal suffrage. Note that answer (E) requires you not only to know that the term Risorgimento refers to national unification but also to identify the correct country.

12. **(A)**   The war began when Britain and France objected to what they saw as Russian bullying of the Ottoman Empire in a dispute over monasteries in the Holy Land. Austria tried to stay neutral for much of the war; during the 19th century, the weakening Ottoman Empire tended to avoid aggressive foreign policies. Answer (E) is incorrect because Bismarck did not come to power until nearly a decade after the Crimean War.

13. **(A)**   Since the first two Hanoverian monarchs of the 1700s had little interest in government, Parliament increasingly assumed royal powers. Although he did not have the actual title of "prime minister," Walpole in fact assumed that role by first, representing the largest faction in Parliament and second, taking the responsibility to explain the monarch's point of view in parliamentary debates.

14. **(B)**   Pasternak was forbidden to receive the prize personally after the publication of his novel *Dr. Zhivago*, which included critical comments about the 1917 communist revolution. Shostakovitch and Prokofiev were Soviet composers; Beria a head of the KGB, the secret police; and Brezhnev a ruler of the Soviet Union during the late 1960s and 1970s.

15. **(A)**   Under the leadership of Marshall Tito, a communist and World War II hero, Yugoslavia refused to follow Soviet directives after World War II. This "exclusion" question may also be answered by identifying the remaining answers as true. Eastern European nations were forbidden by the Soviet government to participate in the Marshall Plan. A revolt in East Germany in 1953 was suppressed by the country's government, and a Hungarian revolt of 1956 was put

down by the Soviet army. Almost all Eastern European nations were militarily allied with the Soviet Union through the Warsaw Pact.

16. **(C)**   Although Britain and France were not in favor of the attempts, their opposition had little impact on Hitler's attempts to unite Germany with the country that was his birthplace, Austria. The significant opposition came from Mussolini, who worried that the Italian minority in Austria would be mistreated by a racially-minded Nazi government. The two countries were united in 1938 when Hitler and Mussolini reached a private understanding. Note the importance of the date ("1934") in the question.

17. **(B)**   Nurtured during the early years of the Third French Republic, when Royalists in France bitterly tried to gain control over the state, the Action Française advocated an authoritarian government with a strengthened military. The organization, a pre-fascist movement, also advocated anti-Semitism.

18. **(C)**   The major clues are the date (which tests historical knowledge) and the geography of the map (which tests your knowledge of geography in history). Note that the word "Poland" does not appear on the map. Of the incorrect answers, all but France also appear on the map, and there may be a tendency to select one of them.

19. **(D)**   A series of two-nation treaties, the Locarno treaties included a German-French understanding in which Germany accepted its post-World War I borders. The treaties cleared the way for German membership in the League of Nations. Despite promises made by the American President Woodrow Wilson, the United States withdrew from the European diplomatic system after the war.

20. **(C)**   In general, the Romantics regarded the Enlightenment as an era which worshipped cold, mechanical Reason and failed to appreciate the variety and spontaneity of human experiences. While the Enlightenment philosophers thought history might furnish lessons for morality and government, the Romantics emphasized history as an emotional experience. The Middle Ages were particularly admired, to the point that replicas of castles and "new" ruins of buildings were constructed during the Romantic era. In contrast to the cosmopolitan atmosphere of the French Enlightenment, many Romantics championed the worth of individual nations and cultures.

21. **(B)**   The Fabian Socialists were a largely British movement which attracted the support of notables such as George Bernard Shaw and H. G. Wells. Led by Sydney and Beatrice Webb, they called for increasing the public ownership of private industry, even to the point of state ownership. Such changes, they insisted, were to come peacefully.

22. **(E)**   Until 1866-1870, Germany was divided into a multitude of states that

at one point totaled more than 300. Because most of the other European states, unlike Germany, had developed strong national monarchies, many of them had been unified much earlier.

23. **(D)** Prussia and Austria, the two largest German states, combined in 1820 to issue the Carlsbad Decrees, which established a system of press censors and university inspectors. The goal was to suppress liberal movements. The other answers are not applicable. The Charter of 1814 was France's second constitution. It was issued by Louis XVIII, the first monarch after the Napoleonic period, in hopes of guaranteeing his acceptance by the French people. The Holy Alliance was formed at the Congress of Vienna and required the great powers to conduct their diplomacy according to the principles of Jesus Christ. The Declaration of the Rights of Man was issued during the French Revolution of 1789. The Schlieffen Plan was a German military plan, implemented in World War I, for an invasion of France.

24. **(B)** After his predecessors, the first two Hanoverian monarchs of the 1700s, virtually ignored Parliament, George III was a more serious monarch. Parliament, which had assumed much of the king's powers during the period of weakened monarchs, resisted. The formation of such a faction of supporters in Parliament, the "king's friends," was intended to give the throne a group of dedicated spokesmen and admirers within the parliamentary system.

25. **(B)** Smith's book, which appeared in 1776, opposed mercantilism and predicted that the greatest prosperity would be reached when individuals were free to pursue their own selfish interests without government interference or regulation.

26. **(D)** A product of the Middle Ages, the Estates-General reflected the society of that time. The clergy were preeminent, the nobility were the Second Estate, and the Third Estate comprised the remainder of the population (the peasants and middle class). Factory owners, non-existent in the Middle Ages, were present in the Estates-General only as part of the Third Estate.

27. **(B)** Passed by the National Assembly during the French Revolution, the Civil Constitution of the Clergy reflected the anticlericalism of many revolutionaries. It denied papal power to appoint bishops or other clergy, substituting popular election instead, and made them salaried officials of the state. While some clergy perished in the Reign of Terror, there was no direct connection between these events and the Civil Constitution. Note that answer (E) flatly contradicts answer (B), suggesting that one of these two is the correct answer.

28. **(B)** The Charter was the first constitution issued by a monarch. It created a two-house legislature that helped govern the country, in different forms, throughout the century. As mentioned in the explanation for Question No. 23, the monarch, Louis XVIII, issued the document to insure popular acceptance of his rule.

29. **(B)** Locke approved of a revolution carried through by the educated and propertied, provided that the monarch has violated property rights. In the case of James II, ousted in the Glorious Revolution of 1688, Locke believed that his government had extracted "forced loans" from prominent citizens in order to underwrite government expenses. American forefathers copied the phrase "life, liberty, and the pursuit of happiness" from Locke, although in Locke's words it was originally "life, liberty, and the right to property."

30. **(C)** Directed against Charles II, the monarch who restored the Stuart monarchy after the period of Puritan rule in England, the Code was passed by Parliament in an attempt to deny Charles the right to appoint close Catholic friends as his advisers.

31. **(B)** Bacon's book asserted that scientists ideally should be clear-minded thinkers, untouched by religious or political biases or philosophical preconceptions. He listed a series of biases or preconceptions which might be obstacles to scientific work, terming them "idols." Answer (C) is too obvious an answer to consider seriously.

32. **(B)** The picture depicts the sale of indulgences in early 1500s Germany by the Dominican monk Tetzel. The incident angered Luther and set him on the path which led to the Reformation. The wording of the question may mislead you by causing you to examine the picture for major clues. This approach is not likely to be helpful. The real clues are in the "jingle," which you may even remember from a history course. If you do, the question then asks for something more: the name of the monk who sold indulgences in Luther's part of Germany.

33. **(B)** Henry's break with the papacy was personal, centered around his desire to "divorce" his first wife because she had not produced a male heir to the throne. The sole change Henry desired was a transfer in the major authority of the church from the pope to himself (thus answer (E) is incorrect). He retained six of the church's sacraments with the Act of the Six Articles and resolutely opposed Protestant influences, keeping a close eye on his Archbishop of Canterbury, who favored Protestantism. In order to persuade many of the nobility to accept his changes, Henry dissolved the Roman Catholic monasteries and distributed their wealth among influential noblemen.

34. **(B)** During Europe's final religious war, and one of its most destructive—rivalling the damage to Germany at the end of World War II—the Hapsburgs sought to destroy Protestantism in Europe and advance Hapsburg interests. Operating on the principle of raisons d'état ("reasons of state"), Richelieu, although a Catholic Cardinal, decided that his country's best interests lay in weakening the rival Hapsburgs. He chose to do so by sending aid to Protestant forces, at least until he believed it necessary for France to intervene in the war directly.

35. **(C)**   Khrushchev, ruler of the Soviet Union after the death of Stalin, proclaimed the superiority of the Soviet system and predicted a continued competition with capitalism, but he added that the struggle would be peaceful. Answer (A) was a World War II slogan of the Allies fighting Germany and Italy. Answer (B) was the slogan during the 1960s of the French president Charles DeGaulle, who predicted increasing European independence from the "superpowers" of the United States and the Soviet Union. Answer (D) was one of Lenin's slogans in pre-revolutionary Russia. "Peace in Our Time" was the prediction made by the British Prime Minister Chamberlain in 1938 following the Munich conference over the fate of Czechoslovakia.

36. **(D)**   One possible approach to this "exclusion" question is to try to identify which answer was not true of the post World War II period. Germany, divided into non-Communist and Communist states, was not allowed to have an army until non-Communist West Germany joined the North Atlantic Treaty Organization in 1955 and Communist East Germany joined the corresponding Warsaw Pact. An alternate approach is to determine that answers (A) through (C), plus answer (E), were true of the postwar period, leaving (D) as the correct answer by elimination.

37. **(B)**   Spengler portrayed history as a series of cycles in which civilizations rose and decayed. His assertions that Western culture was nearing the end of its cycle found a large audience after World War I among embittered Germans who spoke of building a new, nondemocratic and, in some cases, a racist, civilization. While this question appears to require exact knowledge of the book involved, the key to the question is the types of writers represented. Only Spengler was an expository writer; all of the others were literary writers. Thomas Mann was Germany's most famous novelist in the years between World War I and World War II. Joyce's *Ulysses* (1921) has been termed the most influential English novel of the century. Proust pioneered the "stream of consciousness" method of writing in his autobiographical *Remembrance of Things Past* (1913-1927). Beckett, an Irish playwright, became famous for plays such as *Waiting for Godot* (1953).

38. **(D)**   Although at first glance this appears to be a knowledge-based question, it actually requires an ability to analyze your knowledge and to understand the implications of Stalin's policy. "Socialism in One Country," primarily a plan to industrialize Russia through five-year plans, required husbanding all national resources for domestic use; attempts to aid foreign communist parties and attempts to foment revolution in other European nations were to be abandoned. The policy, however, also required avoiding wars or foreign alliances which might lead to war.

39. **(E)**   A test of the thoroughness of your knowledge of Marx' ideas and your ability to analyze the implications of your knowledge, this question focuses on the fact that Marx believed revolution to be a logical outcome of the growth of

capitalism. The most industrialized nations would have the first large proletarian classes, and thus also have the first revolutions. Nations which had not yet begun to industrialize would have revolutions last; Marx, in fact, ridiculed the large peasant class in Russia, which he believed would be innately opposed to major change.

40. **(B)** The question asks for knowledge of terminology ("gap theory") but adds a major clue ("Bismarck"). Since the country in which the Army Bill Crisis occurred is not identified, you must know that term as well. Bismarck was brought to power in Prussia by the crisis, which was a stalemate between the Prussian king and his legislature over reforms of the Prussian army. Bismarck solved the stalemate by insisting that the Prussian constitution contained a "gap": there was no mention of what was to be done if such a logjam developed. Since the king had granted the constitution, Bismarck insisted that the monarch might ignore the liberals in the legislature and follow his own judgment. Answer (E) (the name of a political crisis in France during the 1880s) is designed to tempt those who know that the "gap theory" solved a crisis but are not certain of the name of the crisis.

41. **(B)** The answer is a choice between (A) and (B). (C) (the name of a brother of King Louis XVI), (D) (a member of the French nobility sympathetic to the revolution), and (E) (the head of the French government during World War I) are irrelevant. Danton was, in fact, a politician who was a victim of the Reign of Terror and of the dominant political faction of the time, the Jacobins.

42. **(D)** A test of your historical knowledge and ability to apply it, this question cites a quotation that illustrates the Christian Humanists' interest in translating the Bible from Latin into the local languages of Europe. The only Christian Humanist listed in the answers is Erasmus. Loyola was founder of the Society of Jesus, or Jesuits; Machiavelli was a political writer during the Italian Renaissance; Galileo was a scientist during the Scientific Revolution; and Robert Boyle was one of the first prominent European physicists and chemists.

43. **(C)** During the 1600s and early 1700s, when prices for wool rose significantly, the nobility sought grazing land for large herds of sheep. In Western Europe, and especially in England, public lands and small farms were fenced in ("enclosed") to create large grazing territories. Answers (A) and (D) attempt to sound plausible for those who do not know the Enclosure Movement. Answer (B) may be tempting for those with only a slight knowledge of the movement since, in England, the Enclosure Acts threw peasants out of work and thus created a source of cheap labor for the early factories.

44. **(A)** In late 15th century Florence, the monk Savonarola decried worldly influences in church and society, insisting that while the church itself could not be corrupt, the leaders of the church might be corrupted. His efforts to enforce repentance and ban sinful influences are reminiscent of Calvin's Geneva.

45. **(C)** In this case, the problem is to identify the opposition or challenges to royal authority—and then to identify the single answer which represents the opposite, a development or event which strengthened absolutism. Four of the five answer choices may be eliminated because they attempted to weaken monarchies—the parliaments (French courts controlled by the nobility, and frequent platforms for opposing royal power); the New Model Army (the name for the army of Oliver Cromwell, the victor over Charles I in the English Civil War); the Puritans themselves, major opponents of Charles in that war; and the Roundheads, the term used to describe the military opposition to Charles. Only Louis XIV's palace of Versailles, where many of the French nobility lived and became involved in useless ceremonial lives, helped strengthen absolutism. Note that this question mixes events in two countries (France and England), requiring you to use "comparative history."

46. **(C)** The emblem of Louis XIV in front of the sun, with the sun's rays visible around his head, symbolizes his title of "the Sun King." The remaining answers—the 18th century Prussian monarch Frederick, the late 16th and 17th century rulers Peter of Russia and Charles of Sweden, and the 16th century Spanish monarch Philip II are not applicable.

47. **(B)** Peter's reforms, and his creation of a Russian navy based on the Baltic Sea, challenged the power of Sweden, which saw Peter's construction of a new capital city in northeastern Russia as a direct challenge. By Peter's reign, Poland had already declined considerably from the late 1400s when a union of Poland and Lithuania had stretched from the Baltic Sea almost to the Black Sea.

48. **(D)** The wars of religion in Europe had the ironic effect of stimulating interest in science, which some Europeans argued was less emotional and less likely to lead to warfare. The 17th century saw the establishment of scientific societies in most European nations.

49. **(C)** The correct answer is (C). Havel worked as a playwright.

50. **(A)** An example of a question which requests knowledge of a particular kind of terminology—slogans—this question asks for your understanding of Voltaire's outlook and the major target of his writings. If enough is known about Voltaire, some answers may be eliminated; since Voltaire favored (and helped coin the name) Enlightened Despotism, answer (C), for example, is not correct. Answer (D) sounds plausible, but is not the correct answer.

51. **(A)** Rousseau's political ideas remain the subject of much debate, but it is clear that he believed that political problems might be solved through the "general will," an amorphous idea which his interpreters have variously described as a democratic majority or government by a fascist oligarchy. Answer (B) summarizes Voltaire's position; (C) a theocracy, which means rule by church elites, would have been rejected by virtually all leading French thinkers of Rousseau's

day.

52. **(C)**   The correct answer is (C). Political corruption and instability were the central causes of the downfall of the Christian Democrats in the 1990s. Corruption landed a number of them in jail, and the party had never been able to maintain a stable ruling coalition in the Italian Parliament for the duration of the entire post-war period. Though the economic status of southern Italy lagged that of the prosperous North, poverty (A) was not widespread in Italy; food shortages (B) were not a problem for Italy; the Christian Democrats, despite their name, were a centrist and largely secular political party (D), and Italy did indeed support the U.S. during the Persian Gulf War (E), a fact unrelated to the fortunes of the Christian Democrats.

53. **(C)**   This question demands both knowledge of terminology and careful reading skills. Answers (A) through (C) are so closely related that a second reading of the passage is recommended in order to distinguish between them. Although the passage deals with sovereignty and may be used to defend an absolute monarch, the last part of the passage ("You see the image of God in the king...") makes clear that the writer is using "divine right" to justify monarchies. "Divine right of kings" was the name given to arguments that monarchs held their throne by divine authority: God had seen that they were born into the royal family, God had safeguarded them to adulthood, and God had preserved their health. Another side of the argument was that revolution was contrary to God's will. Answer (D) is an attempt to test those who see the word "God" in the passage but otherwise do not read it carefully.

54. **(C)**   Claiming to be Catherine the Great's dead husband, Emelyan Pugachev led a large peasant rebellion from 1773 through 1775, nearly toppling Catherine, who had gained the throne by arranging for the murder of her husband. The central, or eastern-European sounding, name of "Pugachev" is a clue that answer (B) is probably incorrect.

55. **(B)**   The Table of Ranks set educational and training standards for Russian high civil servants, almost all of whom were nobility; promotion was also based on the same criteria. It was part of Peter's attempt to supplement the old boyar nobility with a new, service-based nobility beholden to the tsar.

56. **(A)**   In 1756, Britain, which for some time had been allied with Austria, signed an alliance with Austria's great rival, Prussia. That event led to a new French-Austrian alliance the same year.

57. **(C)**   A mixed, largely middle class group which included shopkeepers and artisans, the *sans-culottes* (meaning "those without kneebreeches," a reference to their refusal to wear the fine clothes of the upper classes) hated the food shortages and rising food prices of the early stages of the revolution. Their discontent focussed on the social inequalities in France; in the National Assembly, their

representatives joined with the Jacobins to create a bare, one-vote majority favoring the execution of King Louis XVI.

58. **(D)** Convinced that liberalism spoke for the middle class, many workers joined the Chartist movement, which during the 1830s and 1840s presented several mass petitions to Parliament demanding the abolition of property qualifications for voting, secret ballots, universal suffrage, and payment for members of Parliament.

59. **(B)** Although Prussia would later unite Germany through wars, the Prussian king rejected the crown of united Germany when it was offered by a national assembly, the Frankfurt Parliament, during the revolution of 1848. The reason he gave was that he refused to accept the crown from the hands of revolutionaries. A careful look at the answers will show that answer (B) is distinctively different from the other three, indicating that it is either the correct answer or a ploy to tempt those who know nothing about the topic. Answer (E) is a plausible-sounding, but incorrect, answer.

60. **(D)** Jingoism, taken from the word "jingo" in the second line of the saying, came to mean emotional, mindless nationalism. The other answers are attempts to create plausible alternatives. For example, British citizens proudly boasted in the 19th century that their nation, the most highly industrialized in the world at the time, was the "Workshop of the World."

61. **(B)** Camillo Cavour, the diplomat who planned most of the steps of Italian unification, was royal minister for the kingdom of Piedmont in northwest Italy. The role of Prussia in unifying Germany is much better known, but Piedmont basically played the role of Prussia in Italy and Cavour played the role of Bismarck. Sicily was part of a southern Italian monarchical state until Italy was unified. Corsica is a Mediterranean island south of France. Venetia, in northeast Italy, was largely held by Austria from 1815 to 1867. The region of Tuscany, in northwest Italy, played a lesser role in unification than did Piedmont.

62. **(D)** The correct choice is (D). Russia backed the international force led by the United States. Since this army was mobilized against Iraq because of Saddam Hussein's invasion of Kuwait, any choice indicating Russian neutrality or support for Iraq would, by inference, have to be dismissed.

63. **(C)** The Ems Telegram was a carefully edited version of a telegram which the Prussian king sent to Bismarck in 1870. The Spanish throne was vacant, and a young member of the Prussian ruling family (the Hohenzollerns) had been asked to become the new monarch of Spain. The French Emperor Napoleon III vigorously opposed this arrangement, seeing it as an attempt to encircle France with German monarchs. Rather than risk war, the Prussian king withdrew the "Hohenzollern candidacy" to the Spanish throne. When Napoleon III ordered the French ambassador to obtain the king's promise that the situation would not

recur, the king reported this conversation to Bismarck through a telegram. In order to anger France and cause Napoleon III to declare war, Bismarck edited the telegram—overemphasizing the insulting nature of the French ambassador's demand—and released it to the press. The Fourteen Points of Woodrow Wilson, summarizing American war aims in World War I, and the Treaty of Versailles, the main treaty to end World War I, are later in history. Answer (D) should not be tempting; the British constitution is unwritten. During the Congress of Berlin of 1878 (a diplomatic conference), the great powers of Europe successfully pressured Russia to soften a harsh treaty it had forced on the Ottoman Empire.

64. **(B)** Answer (A) appears too obvious, and it is. When the French government, which had moved to the city of Bordeaux, signed a peace agreement with Prussia in 1871, the city of Paris, which was under siege by Prussia, refused to accept the surrender. A separate government in Paris, the Commune, spoke of nationalizing banks in order to finance continued resistance to the German invaders. French troops loyal to the government suppressed the Commune, but the event left a trauma among much of the French middle class, which feared that radicalism was growing in France.

65. **(B)** The term "Second Industrial Revolution" describes an economic shift in the second half of the 19th century when steel, electricity, oil, and chemicals became important parts of industrialization, supplementing the steam, iron, and textiles which had been central to the First Industrial Revolution. The one item in the answers that belongs to the First, rather than the Second, Industrial Revolution is textiles.

66. **(C)** The Battle of Britain was the name given to the period in 1940 and 1941 when German planes ceaselessly bombed England, beginning with the bombing of air bases and expanding to day-and-night bombing of the city of London. Most of the German Luftwaffe, or air force, was lost in the battle; some historians believe the outcome prevented a German invasion attempt.

67. **(B)** The Schlieffen Plan, a German army contingency plan first formulated in the 1870s, called for a quick defeat of France in the event of a future European war. The plan was a solution to the German generals' nightmare of a future two-front war; after a French surrender, the German army would be prepared to fight Russia. The words "to the east front" show that this map does not describe events in World War II, since the German invasion of France in that war preceded their invasion of Russia. The Maginot Line describes a series of fortifications the French built along their border with Germany during the 1920s. Answer (D) was the name of Winston Churchill's belief that Germany was vulnerable to invasion through Southern Europe.

68. **(D)** Believing that the Russian revolution of 1917 had prepared Russia for full Marxism, the country's new leader, Lenin, attempted to create a society which would be as close to an ideal Marxist society as possible. War Communism (1918-1921), so called because Russia was in the midst of a civil war between Marxists and monarchists, attempted to eliminate management from factories and place the farmers on a basic salary. The system was replaced with a more capitalistic one (the New Economic Policy) in 1921, partly because War Communism contained no incentives to encourage farmers and workers to increase their production.

69. **(A)** Invited to deliver a speech at a small Missouri college, Churchill predicted a long era of ideological struggle between the Soviet Union and the "free world." Answer (D) may be eliminated immediately; Khrushchev was ruler of the Soviet Union during the late 1950s and early 1960s, following some 25 years of Stalin's rule. Adenauer was the head of the West German government during the 1950s.

70. **(B)** In urging Austria-Hungary to deal with Serbia quickly while public sympathy still lay with Austria (which had lost its heir to the throne in an assassination), Germany failed to exercise any kind of restraint on Austro-Hungarian actions. Some historians have characterized Germany's advice as a "blank check" which implied that Germany would support whatever actions Austria-Hungary took.

71. **(D)** Freud thought that many of the problems he analyzed in human behavior had already been portrayed in ancient Greek myths and plays. An example was the "Oedipus complex," named after a tragic play about a man who unknowingly murders his father and marries his mother.

72. **(C)** Answer (C) is not a reasonable conclusion because the graph indicates growth in actual numbers ("population in millions") rather than percentages. The percentage of growth for Russia cannot be calculated since the graph does not give the numerical population of Russia at the start of the period (1881).

73. **(B)** As late as 1937, Britain still had 1.5 million persons unemployed. The other answers are all untrue. Property values, production, and interest rates fell, and depression-time Britian was ill-prepared to cope with the rise of Hitler's Germany.

74. **(B)** The product of a meeting off the coast of Newfoundland in 1941 between British prime minister Churchill and the American President Roosevelt, the Atlantic Charter listed joint war aims in World War II, including the goal of a United Nations. The Truman Doctrine was a pledge to "contain" Communism by the American president of the same name. The Molotov Plan was a Soviet counterpart to the Marshall Plan of economic aid to postwar Europe. The Brussels Pact laid the groundwork for the NATO alliance after World War II. The Treaty

of Rapallo, signed during the 1920s, established diplomatic ties between Weimar Germany and the new communist government of Russia.

75. **(D)** Fascist leaders often portrayed themselves as the only alternative to the spread of communism across Europe. The Depression helped bring fascist leaders such as Hitler to power and also caused European nations to enact protectionist policies, leading to a marked decline in trade in Europe. Fascism tended to gain support in nations without a tradition of successful parliamentary government.

76. **(B)** At the end of World War II, former Nazi leaders were placed on public trial in Nuremberg as war criminals guilty of crimes against humanity. The other answers are irrelevant [(A) and (C)] or untrue (there were no major European trials of alleged "war profiteers" at the end of World War I); or simply incorrect (the trials of army officers who conspired against Hitler were not named the "Nuremburg trials)."

77. **(C)** Answers (A), (B), (D), and (E) are the opposite of Nazi beliefs. A common theme in Nazi speeches and writings was the need to capture additional living space (*Lebensraum*) for the German people.

78. **(A)** A forerunner of August Comte, the founder of the philosophy of Positivism, St. Simon believed that industrialization, aided by science, would bring a wondrous new age to Europe. Despite the religious sound of his name, Answer (C) is incorrect.

79. **(C)** Pope, an 18th century writer, is an example of popular fascination with Newton's work and with the emergence of science in particular. Answer (A) may be eliminated since Tennyson, a 19th century poet, used his poems to express doubts about the lack of humane values in science and nature.

80. **(D)** The correct answer is (D). By 1990, Gorbachev attempted to slow down some aspects of *glasnost* and *perestroika*. However, the influence of the media and more moderate elements of the CPSU continued to push for reform. As Gorbachev was increasingly viewed as "politically irrelevant" following the August 1991 coup attempt, he signed the dissolution agreement for the Soviet Union on December 25, 1991, and resigned political office.

Sample Answer to Document-Based Question

Although it was not a large "massacre" by modern standards, the Peterloo Massacre of 1819 proved to be a significant event in British political history, leading to repressive legislation, dividing Tories from Whigs, helping convert the Whigs to the cause of electoral reform, and remaining a political issue for years to come.

Some facts are undisputed; others will probably never be resolved. The Napoleonic Wars left suffering in their wake and exacerbated social problems in Britain. During the wars, the British nobility, who controlled Parliament, had passed the Corn Laws, which were designed to enrich the nobility in time of food shortage. Although great shortages had not yet developed, this example of the use of Parliament for the economic ends of the nobility disturbed many in the British middle class.

The middle class also was excluded from Parliament. Voting was open— and oral—and restricted to a small number of the wealthy, almost all nobility. The years immediately after 1815 saw the rise of a number of public speakers who demanded the expansion of the suffrage—the right to vote—to encompass the middle class. Some went further, demanding annual parliaments or voting rights for all adult males. Among the latter group was Henry Hunt, a so-called "radical reformer."

Hunt and his colleagues planned a protest meeting on a farm field—St. Peter's Field outside of the industrial city of Manchester. The selection of Manchester was deliberate. Like many new industrial cities, Manchester was growing rapidly, but it lacked representation in Parliament. On the other hand, many older and formerly prosperous cities, such as the port city of Dover, had fallen on hard times and lost population. Yet Dover had representation in Parliament. Cities such as Dover, with undeserved representation, were termed "rotten boroughs."

Exactly what happened remains a matter of dispute. Hunt had issued a proclamation to the public before the rally, urging a peaceful demonstration and implying that conservative forces might try to provoke the crowd into violence. There appears to be no evidence that the crowd was violent; but the local authorities, fearful of a crowd estimated at 100,000, sent the local militia (the Manchester Yeomanry) into the crowd. They were followed by an army calvary unit. What followed next is unclear; some say that the soldiers were provoked, and others that they were out of control. People were trampled and slashed with sabres. The number of dead was small—by a modern historian's account, about 14. But the injuries of the dead appear to confirm that they were killed by a the militia or army, rather than trampled by an unruly crowd. Almost all of the dead were "sabred."

Conservatives in Britain, particularly the Tories, saw the Peterloo incident as a popular riot, a possible forerunner of a revolution like the recent French experience. Radical reformers saw brutality by the authorities against peaceful protesters. They were eventually joined in that view by many Whigs. Some Tories such as Robert Peel, later a famous Tory reformer, seemed to agree that the incident had been handled poorly by local authorities. The Whig-Tory split widened when the Tories, who controlled Parliament, passed the Six Acts, a series of repressive laws which suppressed civil liberties.

The course of repression did not serve the Tories well, During the 1820s, reformers such as Peel tried an alternative approach—recognizing that such incidents indicated popular unrest about injustices in the British system. Peel convinced Parliament to reform the British legal and police system during the 1820s.

The Peterloo incident may have helped make expansion of the electorate a key concern of the Whigs. During the late 1820s, when the Tory Duke of Wellington campaigned, he was met by signs that read "Remember Peterloo." When the Whigs won election in 1831—with their name changed to the Liberal Party—they pledged to expand the right to vote. Only half of the male members of the middle class was given the right to vote by the Whigs, but it was a start of a process which continued throughout the century. The Peterloo issue was alive as late as the 1870s, when a Liberal party pamphlet reminded voters of "Tory Justice."

A seemingly minor political incident became a seminal and festering issue in British politics, focussing the attention of the Whigs on electoral reform and providing them with a continuing political issue against the Tories or Conservatives.

Sample Answers to Essay Questions

1.   Mercantilism, an economic policy developed during the age of absolute monarchies, and *laissez-faire,* preeminent during the era of industrialization and the rise of the middle class, were virtually completely opposite economic policies. Yet each was popular during its own time, largely for reasons connected with the political and economic conditions of the eras.

In many ways, mercantilism, popular during the late 17th and 18th centuries, represented an attempt to extend the powers of absolutism to trade and colonies. Assuming that resources were strictly limited and that European nations would engage in a prolonged struggle to control those resources, the ministers of European monarchs attempted to tie the economies of their colonies closely to that of the mother nation. Colonies were to function as both a market for the mother country's products and also as a source of raw materials.

Mercantilist policies seldom functioned as hoped, as illustrated by the case of Britain, which had begun to gather an extensive colonial empire. North American industries frequently wanted to produce their own versions of products made in Britain, but royal ministers promoted legislation to prevent such colonial competition. Raw materials were also, at times, available more cheaply from other nations than from Britain's own colonies.

The problems involved in mercantilism were obvious by the time Adam Smith published his *Wealth of Nations* in 1776. Smith argued for an era of economic freedom, where individuals might pursue their own economic self-interest without government regulation or limitation. The result, he believed, would be economic expansions that would create new resources. His book coincided with the early stages of the Industrial Revolution, and Britain, far ahead of the rest of Europe in industrialization by the early 1800s, liked the idea of a tariff-free Europe, an era of "free trade."

The middle class, growing rapidly in size as industrialization proceeded, also liked the *laissez-faire* idea of keeping government separate from business. Building on the ideas of Thomas Malthus, who argued that the food supply increased much more slowly than the population, the Scottish economist Ricardo produced the iron law of wages: wages to the working class might not be increased in real terms. Wage hikes would only produce inflation—and no real improvement for the workers.

Ricardo's work seemed to demonstrate that natural economic law kept the working class in dire straits, and not economic exploitation. His work probably soothed the consciences of any middle-class business people who feared government regulation of factories. Yet it illustrated a basic contradiction in *laissez-faire* ideas: Smith argued that resources were not finite but might be expanded by free economic activity, while Ricardo argued that there was only a limited amount of wealth.

2.   Starting from the basic premise that the old, Earth-centered view of the solar system had become too complicated, scientists during the Scientific Revolution gradually moved to the Copernican version of a sun-centered solar system. In the process, the Copernican system challenged church authority, helped the newer inductive reasoning triumph over the deductive reasoning of the Middle Ages, and became a testing ground for the emergence of scientific methods.

During the Middle Ages, the earth-centered view had met the requirements of Scholasticism, the medieval system of deductive logic and knowledge which emphasized reliance on church authorities. Where church authorities had not written on a problem, an outside—even pagan—author might be approved. The earth-centered system of the second-century Greek-Egyptian astronomer Ptolemy was given church approval partly because it seemed to conform to Scriptures—where the sun was described as moving backward—but also because it illustrated the supreme medieval irony: human beings were sinful and wretched but also important enough to be at the center of not only the solar system but the entire universe.

In the 16th century, the Polish astronomer Copernicus pointed to the increasing complexity of the Ptolemaic system as a reason to consider alternatives. As a high official in the Catholic church, Copernicus merely suggested alternative hypotheses. His work, however, began a process in which facts gained through observation were assembled into alternative theories; "induction" replaced deduction.

When the Italian Galileo used his observations with a telescope to support the Copernican system, he fell victim to church discipline in a famous trial. His work on inertia, however, and upon the speed of falling bodies, however, led to research by others. The Central European astronomer Kepler added to the Copernican trend by producing three laws of planetary motion which favored the Copernican view. Devoutly religious, however, Kepler believed that he was functioning, not as a critic of religion, but as a prophet discovering the mysteries of God's creation.

The work of Newton illustrated the importance of mathematics for scientific work, producing another scientific "principle" to oppose church authority. Newton's work on gravity virtually confirmed the Copernican system, which could not be proved by methods involving observations and experiments. Gravity, for Newton, was a property of all matter and was strongest in the largest bodies. His work implied that the most massive object in the solar system, the sun, would have to be at the center of the system. Newton arrived at his answers through mathematics, but others saw the virtues of inductive thinking revealed in the triumph of the Copernican view. While writers like Descartes praised deduction, Francis Bacon insisted that the new scientific method of induction would solve all of the of riddles of nature in perhaps a century.

The Copernican controversy became central to the Scientific Revolution because it combined so many elements in the emergence of science—the replacement of deductive reasoning (to some degree) by induction, the emergence of the scientific method as an "authority" in itself, and calls for the freedom of scientists to pursue their work without theological restrictions. Few other developments in the Scientific Revolution were quite so broad and far-reaching.

3.   Thrust into World War II by the actions of fascist Germany and Japan, the three major or non-fascist powers—the United States, Britain, and the Soviet Union—discovered during the course of the war that the sole point of total agreement among them was their opposition to the totalitarian governments they were fighting.

Some historians have referred to the alliance as the "Accidental Alliance," the alliance created, not by a common outlook of its members, but by the events of the war. Britain had been brought into the war by the German attack on Poland; the Soviet Union had entered because Hitler, wanting to impress on Britain how isolated it was, had sent German troops into the Soviet Union; and the United States had entered the war because of an attack by Japan, Germany's ally, on an American naval installation in Hawaii.

While the United States and Britain shared a common language and similar forms of government, the Soviet Union had little in common with its allies. Relations between the Soviet Union and British government had been particularly cool. During the 1930s, when the aggressive diplomacy of Hitler had been met with general British-French acquiescence, Stalin appeared to believe that this "appeasement" was a deliberately anti-Soviet policy. Documentary evidence is lacking—Stalin's archives are not available to historians of either east or west—

but Stalin appeared to believe that the British hoped to use Hitler, an avowed anti-Communist, to rid the world of Communism. Stalins' suspicions may have deepened when a Soviet observer who attended the Munich conference of 1938 was rebuffed by Britain and France when he suggested a collective security agreement against Germany. Possibly this rebuff explains the Soviet government's decision to sign a nonaggression pact with Germany in 1939, shortly before the German invasion of Poland. But the pact contained a provision for a de facto partition of Poland between Germany and the Soviet Union. In effect, Stalin cleared the way for the start of World War II. The British government, which went to war to defend the sovereignty of Poland, did not forget Stalin's role in the events of 1939. The British prime minister Winston Churchill was especially suspicious of his Soviet ally, particularly when the Soviet Union announced formation of a Polish communist government in exile to replace the civilian government which had fled to London.

Representing a country that had remained distant from prewar European diplomacy, the American President Roosevelt took a more tolerant view of Stalin, whom he termed "Uncle Joe." Roosevelt worked with Churchill to solve a problem which arose when the two leaders decided to delay a landing in France until landings and victories were assured in North Africa and Italy. Stalin had been demanding a "second front" in France to relieve pressure on Soviet troops. In an attempt to assure Stalin that no separate peace would be signed with Hitler—that a German victory in the Soviet Union would not end the struggle— both men issued a proclamation that their nations would not leave the war until unconditional surrender by Germany. Despite the conciliatory offer, Stalin refused to declare war against Japan. In fact, the Soviet Union would declare war against Japan only three days before the war ended, and only after two atomic bombs had been dropped on Japanese cities.

By the time of the Normandy landings in mid 1944, German troops were retreating from the territory of the Soviet Union. Stalin appeared to believe that victory over Germany had been achieved almost entirely by his troops; the landing of his allies in France might be a mopping up operation. Stalin's ambitions in Eastern Europe loomed large. When the Soviet army approached Warsaw, the Polish underground revolted against the German rulers of the city. The Soviet advance halted just long enough for the Germans to eliminate this politically active group of Poles.

The conferences at Yalta and Potsdam at the end of the war have been criticized for ceding Eastern Europe to Stalin, but they largely recognized what had already happened to that area, which was occupied by Soviet troops. For the British—who had gone to war to preserve Poland—the loss of that nation was particularly bitter. A Winston Churchill speech in 1946 coined the term "iron curtain" and pointed to the major issue of the Cold War: the Soviet domination of Eastern European nations which had enjoyed a brief period of self-determination between 1919 and 1939.

The total reasons for Soviet occupation of Eastern Europe are probably mixed and complex. Fear of a resurgent Germany, desire for a buffer zone against a future German invasion, use of opportunities to spread Communist revolutions—it is difficult to sort out which played the major role. It is clear, however, that the tensions and suspicions among the antifascist allies of World War II laid no basis for their cooperation in the post-war world. Instead, they appeared to guarantee division between the two sides once World War II had ended.

4.   Although the Enlightenment is often portrayed as a single historical period, there were actually three Enlightenments—English (late 1600s), French (1700s), and German (second half of 1700s). Each was a response to the particular conditions prevailing in those nations; not surprisingly, each produced somewhat different solutions.

All three tended to agree on basic tenets. All three favored Reason—the common ability of human beings to interpret nature logically and to find common, logical solutions to their problems. All three tended to reject intolerance, unjustified biases, and dogmatic religion. There was also a shared admiration of natural science, not surprising considering that the Scientific Revolution had occurred in the previous two centuries.

The French Enlightenment was a very cosmopolitan period, focussed on issues which the philosophes believed to be of concern to all mankind. A major reason was because the philosophes, most of whom lived in Paris, were of several nationalities. Baron d'Holbach, champion of materialism, was German; Beccaria, who argued that the purpose of the law was not to impress God's will but to bring the greatest happiness of greatest number, was Italian. It is said that the first appearance of the word "humanity" was in the French language during this period.

Nevertheless, purely French conditions had a significant influence. Voltaire's call for a secular French society, and his condemnation of Christianity as superstition and prejudice, reflected the traditional intolerance shown to religious minorities in France by the state. French Huguenots, who had gained freedom of worship and the right to bear arms by the Edict of Nantes, lost these when Louis XIV revoked the edict in 1685. Voltaire himself deplored the the French army's destruction of the Huguenot city of Port Royal. The most famous court case in which he became involved, the Calas case, concerned a Huguenot father found guilty of murdering a son who, it was said, desired to convert to the Roman Catholicism of his fiancée.

In order to achieve a secular society, the philosophes became reformers, proposing specific social arrangements or solutions. *Candide* showed Voltaire's reformist bent, since it was written in angry reaction to the German philosopher Leibniz' statement that this is the best of all possible worlds. Voltaire did not reject religion entirely; he kept God as a Creator in his own Deism, in which there were to be no complicated doctrines to nurture theological arguments. God the creator sounded suspiciously like Newton's portrait of God as the "clockwinder" of the universe.

The same faith in secular reform drove Diderot to publish his famous

Encyclopedia; led Voltaire and others to believe that Enlightened Despots might reform their countries in a "revolution from above"; and caused Rousseau, who in some ways was a philosophe and in some ways was not, to seek citizen participation in government through his idea of the "general will."

None of the philosophes were scientists, but it was clear that they envisioned a universe and society governed by immutable and rational laws. While it would be difficult to tie the philosophes directly to the French Revolution, it appears they made criticisms of the French government and society respectable in their country.

Conditions in Germany were quite different. Germany was, according to a famous saying, a "geographic expression" which contained more than 300 states, many with their own petty monarch. The major religious war in Germany had ended in 1648 with arrangements which allowed each monarch to dictate the official religious denomination of his area. While the French absolute monarchs of the 1700s imposed censorship in an almost half-hearted way, German petty monarchs included religious authority in their sovereignty. The German middle class, smaller in numbers than the French middle class, did not challenge monarchical power the way the French had. Observers commented about the subservience of the German burgher; the spirit of reform was lacking.

The two major German figures of the Enlightenment, Leibniz and Kant, admired natural science, but their attitudes toward it were quite different from the French philosophes'. Leibniz tended to be interested in rationalism, and he, along with Newton and the French mathematician Descartes, is given credit for the discovery of calculus. Yet Leibniz rejected Newton's theory of gravity and was unimpressed with the experimental work that led to that theory or that seemed to confirm that theory.

Kant also was interested in Reason, but his emphasis was on the ability of the mind, through Reason, to shape reality. Kant had been appalled at the work of the Scottish philosopher Hume, who seemed to challenge the validity of science by demonstrating that "cause and effect" was always assumed in science but could not be proven. Kant sought to demonstrate that the mind operated in such a way that "cause and effect" was always perceived; while "cause and effect" might not be proven, the mind operated in a regular and consistent ways, according to its own internal laws. His *Critique of Pure Reason* was an attempt to rescue science from philosophical skepticism. It also attempted to lay the basis for a new, nonreligious morality; the "categorical imperative" was a moral rule that was logically self-evident.

Monarchical authority intervened when Kant, in his subsequent book, *Critique of Practical Reason*, speculated that while the existence of God might not be proven, belief in God was a practical necessity. After the appearance of the book, he was commanded by the Prussian monarch to halt his commentaries on religious matters. Perhaps this incident is one reason why Kant, when writing of the ideal state, wrote in terms of abstractions rather than specifics, and entirely avoided reform proposals.

More likely, the German Enlightenment, and Kant, reflected the domination of German monarchs over matters of free thought and religion, as well as the deferential attitude of the German middle class toward monarchs and nobility. Kant's ideal state was a state which met certain abstract philosophic criteria, rather than a state which was judged on the basis of specific, practical results, such as prosperity or free speech.

The future direction of German thought was evident in two traits seen in Kant: (1) his "inwardness," or emphasis on the internal workings of the mind, and (2) his attempts to define the ideal government on theoretical rather than practical grounds. Beginning with German Idealism in the early 19th century, German thinkers were often accused of being much more abstract than French or British counterparts, of emphasizing internal freedom over external rights, and of justifying the status quo more than challenging it. That trend appeared to be clear as early as the German Enlightenment.

Despite their shared belief in similar qualities such as Reason, the German and French Enlightenments were quite different periods. The French Enlightenment sought to strengthen humanitarian impulses such as toleration and to encourage free thought and criticism. Such traits were lacking in the German Enlightenment, which spoke of the "ideal" than the "real."

5.   Although the practice of primogeniture was no longer legally required in Great Britain after the Renaissance, it was continued by many noble families as a matter of tradition. In this way it exerted a significant impact on British society and politics.

Primogeniture required that upon the death of a nobleman, the title and land passed only to one child—the eldest son, or to his male heir if he was not alive. If the eldest son was not living and had left no heir, the title and landed estate went to the next eldest son. The remaining noble children might inherit wealth, but not the title or the landed estate of the family.

At first glance it might be assumed that the system would guarantee the continuation of feudalism, since it derived from the medieval system of overlords, who often passed their positions down through families. It did result, in Britain, in the preservation of the landed estates and the wealth of noble families. Significantly, however, it created a distinctively British class, the gentry, the titleless sons and daughters of the nobility. The gentry might often have great wealth—they might inherit wealth other than the estate. For those who found their own success in business, their wealth might conceivably be greater than that of the family member who inherited the title and the estate.

The gentry class proved to have a distinctive impact on Britain. Because they were less tied to family tradition than the major family heir, they felt less loyalty to the monarch and were more likely to act independently of the throne. In the English Civil War of the 1640s, the gentry were prominent in the armies opposing Charles I; many were found in the Puritan forces. The existence of the gentry may also explain the greater openness of the British nobility to the world, as compared to continental nobility. One reason why Britain entered the Industrial Revolution before other European nations was because of the willingness of some noblemen to finance the first factories. It is likely that the British nobility became more involved in business through their relatives, the gentry. In fact, the British nobility was much less isolated from the remaining elements of their society than their continental cousins. The famous Victorian Compromise—by which middle class and nobility in 19th century Britain shared political power and preserved a role for the nobility in the political system—was a probable result of primogeniture.

While primogeniture was used on the continent, its implementation was much less systematic than in Britain. Only one other nation, Hungary, developed a gentry. As a result, the nobility in countries like France were as a group less prosperous. By the time of the French Revolution of 1789, landed estates had been divided between so many children and grandchildren in France that many noble families were in real financial distress. The French peasants of 1789 were not the only Frenchmen in financial straits.

Without a gentry class of relatives to serve as windows to the outside world, the continental nobility tended to stay more isolated from new financial and economic developments. French noblemen were likely to be isolated from business, regarding real labor as being degrading and unworthy—except in the case of hobbies like rose gardening. Isolated from society in a way their English counterparts were not, the French nobility found it more difficult to comprehend, and compromise with, the middle class and its demands for constitutional government. French conservatives like Chateaubriand and DeMaistre saw in past ages the only forms of society that God approved, whereas the English conservative Burke insisted only that change be measured and not rashly done.

Although it was an archaic and rapidly-disappearing tradition, primogeniture—by giving Britain special advantages in the era of constitutionalism and industrialization—was a major reason why Britain, more than any other European state in the 19th century, represented the nation of social and political reform.

6.   Although paintings and drawings of monarchs are often enigmatic—since it is not always clear whether they reveal the artist's real assessment of the subject or are intended as propaganda—illustrations such as these are often useful and revealing.

The painting of Louis XIV, France's "Sun King," portrays a great and noble figure who embodied the "glory" he sought for France. Louis' lavish, almost sumptuous lifestyle at his palace of Versailles is evident in the curtains and in Louis' own robes, which bear the *fleur de lis,* or lily, symbolic of Bourbon monarchs. There is a touch of vanity in the stilted and somewhat delicate pose. The overall impression is worshipful, a suitable approach for a monarch who convinced much of the French upper nobility that it was a special honor to live with him at Versailles.

The sword is a curious touch. Perhaps it signifies his status as an absolute monarch who wielded powers of life and death over his subjects. It may also signify the iron hand of a monarch whose ministers created a highly centralized government by using measures such as imprisonment without formal arrest or court proceedings.

The sword may also be an attempt to indicate the strong will and energy of a monarch who carried out numerous wars to advance French interests in Europe. If so, if makes Louis appear to be a more active military man than he actually was, since he left the conduct of wars to his generals and engineers.

Two elements often associated with Louis are missing from the portrait. First, there are no emblems of his self-promoted role as "Sun King." Second, although the portrait appears to show strength and determination, there is no sign of the religiously intolerant monach who ruthlessly suppressed Jansenism in France and forced most Huguenots into exile with his revocation of the Edict of Nantes.

The illustration of Napoleon III is a marked contrast to that of the "sun king." The portrait is both austere and vague. The one definite impression is that he was a military leader, but this is probably a touch of propaganda. Napoleon III exploited the name of his famous uncle, but he himself lacked a military reputation. In 1859, during an invasion of Italy, Napoleon III was so sickened by a tour of a battlefield that, within days, he withdrew his forces from Italy. His lack of a strong military record, plus his ineptness as a young Romantic revolutionary, led to rumors that he was not truly a Bonaparte—that his mother and father had been separated for 10 months before his birth.

The vagueness and austerity of the picture reflects Napoleon III's style of rule. Unlike Napoleon Bonaparte, Napoleon III did not hold unchallenged power. He had relied on the support of the army to reach the throne; his empire included a two-house legislature. In many ways he was like the "bourgeois king," Louis Philippe (reigned 1830-1848), who attempted to rule in a style befitting the rapidly rising middle class. Napoleon III believed that government existed in order to guarantee prosperity for its citizens, and the middle and working classes did benefit from rising incomes during his reign. His appearance in the illustration as a conscientious, hard-working monarch is reminiscent of the image cultivated by another monarch associated with the middle class, Queen Victoria.

The austerity of the portrait is a bit surprising, however, for a man whose wife, Eugenie, was the fashionsetter for her time. Napoleon III also desired to be remembered in history for his rebuilding and beautification of central Paris. Of course, the rebuilding was also motivated by practical considerations. The new broad avenues made it very difficult for revolutionaries to build barricades, and the new circular plazas facilitated the movement of artillery by the French army in an emergency.

The lack of detail in the portrait is also appropriate for an emperor who could play the role of political cameleon and who, in 1860, found it necessary to alter his style of rule. During the 1850s, when he played the role of an authoritarian monarch who allowed the legislature to discuss only the matters he had approved, elections for the legislature gradually began turning against the Emperor's stable of parties. From 1860 through 1870, he was the "Liberal Emperor," attempting to retain his popularity by removing restrictions on the legislature and the press.

Unlike Louis XIV, Napoleon III was never really an absolute monarch. His portrait attempts not to overwhelm the viewer but to impress the viewer with his competence. The differences between the two portraits reflect the wide gaps between their reigns. The contrast is between a serenely confident monarch and a monarch who was attempting, very late in European history, to ignore the tides of history and the trends toward constitutional and parliamentary government in Europe.

THE ADVANCED PLACEMENT EXAMINATION IN

European History

TEST 5

THE ADVANCED PLACEMENT EXAMINATION IN

European History
TEST 5

1. Ⓐ Ⓑ Ⓒ Ⓓ Ⓔ
2. Ⓐ Ⓑ Ⓒ Ⓓ Ⓔ
3. Ⓐ Ⓑ Ⓒ Ⓓ Ⓔ
4. Ⓐ Ⓑ Ⓒ Ⓓ Ⓔ
5. Ⓐ Ⓑ Ⓒ Ⓓ Ⓔ
6. Ⓐ Ⓑ Ⓒ Ⓓ Ⓔ
7. Ⓐ Ⓑ Ⓒ Ⓓ Ⓔ
8. Ⓐ Ⓑ Ⓒ Ⓓ Ⓔ
9. Ⓐ Ⓑ Ⓒ Ⓓ Ⓔ
10. Ⓐ Ⓑ Ⓒ Ⓓ Ⓔ
11. Ⓐ Ⓑ Ⓒ Ⓓ Ⓔ
12. Ⓐ Ⓑ Ⓒ Ⓓ Ⓔ
13. Ⓐ Ⓑ Ⓒ Ⓓ Ⓔ
14. Ⓐ Ⓑ Ⓒ Ⓓ Ⓔ
15. Ⓐ Ⓑ Ⓒ Ⓓ Ⓔ
16. Ⓐ Ⓑ Ⓒ Ⓓ Ⓔ
17. Ⓐ Ⓑ Ⓒ Ⓓ Ⓔ
18. Ⓐ Ⓑ Ⓒ Ⓓ Ⓔ
19. Ⓐ Ⓑ Ⓒ Ⓓ Ⓔ
20. Ⓐ Ⓑ Ⓒ Ⓓ Ⓔ
21. Ⓐ Ⓑ Ⓒ Ⓓ Ⓔ
22. Ⓐ Ⓑ Ⓒ Ⓓ Ⓔ
23. Ⓐ Ⓑ Ⓒ Ⓓ Ⓔ
24. Ⓐ Ⓑ Ⓒ Ⓓ Ⓔ
25. Ⓐ Ⓑ Ⓒ Ⓓ Ⓔ

26. Ⓐ Ⓑ Ⓒ Ⓓ Ⓔ
27. Ⓐ Ⓑ Ⓒ Ⓓ Ⓔ
28. Ⓐ Ⓑ Ⓒ Ⓓ Ⓔ
29. Ⓐ Ⓑ Ⓒ Ⓓ Ⓔ
30. Ⓐ Ⓑ Ⓒ Ⓓ Ⓔ
31. Ⓐ Ⓑ Ⓒ Ⓓ Ⓔ
32. Ⓐ Ⓑ Ⓒ Ⓓ Ⓔ
33. Ⓐ Ⓑ Ⓒ Ⓓ Ⓔ
34. Ⓐ Ⓑ Ⓒ Ⓓ Ⓔ
35. Ⓐ Ⓑ Ⓒ Ⓓ Ⓔ
36. Ⓐ Ⓑ Ⓒ Ⓓ Ⓔ
37. Ⓐ Ⓑ Ⓒ Ⓓ Ⓔ
38. Ⓐ Ⓑ Ⓒ Ⓓ Ⓔ
39. Ⓐ Ⓑ Ⓒ Ⓓ Ⓔ
40. Ⓐ Ⓑ Ⓒ Ⓓ Ⓔ
41. Ⓐ Ⓑ Ⓒ Ⓓ Ⓔ
42. Ⓐ Ⓑ Ⓒ Ⓓ Ⓔ
43. Ⓐ Ⓑ Ⓒ Ⓓ Ⓔ
44. Ⓐ Ⓑ Ⓒ Ⓓ Ⓔ
45. Ⓐ Ⓑ Ⓒ Ⓓ Ⓔ
46. Ⓐ Ⓑ Ⓒ Ⓓ Ⓔ
47. Ⓐ Ⓑ Ⓒ Ⓓ Ⓔ
48. Ⓐ Ⓑ Ⓒ Ⓓ Ⓔ
49. Ⓐ Ⓑ Ⓒ Ⓓ Ⓔ
50. Ⓐ Ⓑ Ⓒ Ⓓ Ⓔ
51. Ⓐ Ⓑ Ⓒ Ⓓ Ⓔ
52. Ⓐ Ⓑ Ⓒ Ⓓ Ⓔ
53. Ⓐ Ⓑ Ⓒ Ⓓ Ⓔ
54. Ⓐ Ⓑ Ⓒ Ⓓ Ⓔ
55. Ⓐ Ⓑ Ⓒ Ⓓ Ⓔ

56. Ⓐ Ⓑ Ⓒ Ⓓ Ⓔ
57. Ⓐ Ⓑ Ⓒ Ⓓ Ⓔ
58. Ⓐ Ⓑ Ⓒ Ⓓ Ⓔ
59. Ⓐ Ⓑ Ⓒ Ⓓ Ⓔ
60. Ⓐ Ⓑ Ⓒ Ⓓ Ⓔ
61. Ⓐ Ⓑ Ⓒ Ⓓ Ⓔ
62. Ⓐ Ⓑ Ⓒ Ⓓ Ⓔ
63. Ⓐ Ⓑ Ⓒ Ⓓ Ⓔ
64. Ⓐ Ⓑ Ⓒ Ⓓ Ⓔ
65. Ⓐ Ⓑ Ⓒ Ⓓ Ⓔ
66. Ⓐ Ⓑ Ⓒ Ⓓ Ⓔ
67. Ⓐ Ⓑ Ⓒ Ⓓ Ⓔ
68. Ⓐ Ⓑ Ⓒ Ⓓ Ⓔ
69. Ⓐ Ⓑ Ⓒ Ⓓ Ⓔ
70. Ⓐ Ⓑ Ⓒ Ⓓ Ⓔ
71. Ⓐ Ⓑ Ⓒ Ⓓ Ⓔ
72. Ⓐ Ⓑ Ⓒ Ⓓ Ⓔ
73. Ⓐ Ⓑ Ⓒ Ⓓ Ⓔ
74. Ⓐ Ⓑ Ⓒ Ⓓ Ⓔ
75. Ⓐ Ⓑ Ⓒ Ⓓ Ⓔ
76. Ⓐ Ⓑ Ⓒ Ⓓ Ⓔ
77. Ⓐ Ⓑ Ⓒ Ⓓ Ⓔ
78. Ⓐ Ⓑ Ⓒ Ⓓ Ⓔ
79. Ⓐ Ⓑ Ⓒ Ⓓ Ⓔ
80. Ⓐ Ⓑ Ⓒ Ⓓ Ⓔ

European History
TEST 5 – Section I

TIME: 55 Minutes
80 Questions

> **DIRECTIONS:** Each of the questions or incomplete statements below is followed by five suggested answers or completions. Select the one that is best in each case.

1. "…I have heard him say, that after his Booke of the *Circulation of the Blood* came out, that he fell mightily in his Practice, and that it was believed by the Vulgar that he was crack-brained."

   This excerpt, taken from an account by John Aubrey, describes

   (A) Paracelsus.

   (B) Galvani.

   (C) Lorenzo Valla.

   (D) William Harvey.

   (E) Francis Bacon.

2. The phrase "Cogito ergo sum" ("I think, therefore I am"), reflecting the process of logical deduction, is associated with

   (A) Hugo Grotius.

   (B) Jean Bodin.

   (C) Galileo.

   (D) Joseph Dalton Hooker.

   (E) René Descartes.

3. Known as the "Prince of the Humanists," in such works as *In Praise of Folly* he criticized the clergy and abuses that he saw in the Christian Church. His given name was

   (A) Petrarch.

   (B) Desiderius Erasmus.

   (C) Agricola.

   (D) Pico della Mirandola.

   (E) Pierre d'Ailly.

4. The 16th century religious wars that had plagued France were largely ended with the

   (A) accession of Louis XI.

   (B) Edict of Nantes.

   (C) Massacre of St. Bartholomew's Day.

   (D) Treaty of Cateau-Cambresis.

   (E) resolution of the Hapsburg-Bourbon conflict by the Peace of Augsburg.

5. The German sociologist Max Weber advanced the thesis that a significant result of the Protestant Reformation was that

   (A) Protestantism, particularly Calvinism, fostered capitalism.

   (B) Luther's strong support of the German peasant class weakened his appeal in southern Germany.

   (C) a close alliance evolved between Luther and the leaders of the Anabaptist movement.

   (D) it greatly enhanced Europe's overseas exploration.

   (E) Protestant opposition to usury hampered the growth of industry in Germany.

6. Had Pope Alexander VI's Treaty of Tordisillas been observed

   (A) England would have remained Catholic.

   (B) the Dutch would have traded the Cape Colony for Brazil.

   (C) Spain and Portugal would have dominated the overseas world.

   (D) England would have received the Ohio Valley in exchange for French holdings in the Caribbean.

   (E) Switzerland would have remained under the control of the Hapsburgs of Austria.

7. The Portuguese explorer Vasco da Gama was the first European to

   (A) circumnavigate the globe.

   (B) reach the southernmost tip of Africa.

   (C) reach Japan and trade with the people of that land.

(D)   touch upon the coast of Brazil.

(E)   find an all-water route to India.

8.   "All are not created on equal terms, but some are preordained to eternal life, others to eternal damnation; and, accordingly, as each has been created for one or the other of these ends, we say that he has been predestined to life or death..."

This statement reflects an essential view of

(A)   Thomas Hobbes.   (D)   the Council of Trent.

(B)   John Calvin.   (E)   Ulrich Zwingli.

(C)   Martin Luther.

9.   "The state of the monarchy is the supremest thing upon the earth; for kings are not only God's lieutenants upon earth, and sit upon God's throne, but even by God himself they are called gods..."

This concept of the status of monarchy would best reflect the view of

(A)   Frederick the Great.   (D)   William III of England.

(B)   John Locke.   (E)   Joseph II of Austria.

(C)   James I Stuart.

10.   During the French Revolution the most powerful member of the Committee of Public Safety was

(A)   Maximilien de Robespierre. (D)   Gracchus Babeuf.

(B)   Georges Danton.   (E)   the Marquis de Lafayette.

(C)   Napoleon Bonaparte.

11.   The principle of territoriality (the right of the legitimate ruler to determine the faith of his subjects) was embodied in the

(A)   Edict of Nantes.

(B)   Peace of Augsburg.

(C)   Six Articles of Henry VIII.

(D)   *Spiritual Exercises* of Ignatius Loyola.

(E)   doctrinal pronouncements of the Council of Trent.

12. A *philosophe* of 18th century France would

    (A) strongly advocate the nationalistic aspirations of the monarchy.

    (B) ridicule the idea of progress.

    (C) support the political theories earlier advocated by Thomas Hobbes.

    (D) oppose religious intolerance and superstition.

    (E) reject the mechanistic view of the world advanced by earlier scientists.

13. The "Great Fear" that swept through the French countryside in 1789 had its origin in

    (A) the movement of the armies of Prussia and Austria on Paris.

    (B) that the leaders of the "Reign of Terror" in Paris were preparing to extend it to all of France.

    (C) that brigands were attacking villages and burning crops.

    (D) that the execution of the French king would lead England to declare war on France.

    (E) that the overthrow of the Jacobins would result in a restoration of the monarchy.

14. Come forth into the light of things,
    Let Nature be your teacher...
    Enough of Science and of Art
    Close up those barren leaves
    Come forth, and bring with you a heart
    That watches and receives

    Such a view would most likely be expressed by a

    (A) deist.   (D) disciple of Diderot.

    (B) follower of Rousseau.   (E) philosophe.

    (C) physiocrat.

15. The thesis that "population, when unchecked, increases in a geometrical ratio...subsistence only arithmetically, was advanced in the *Essay on Population* by

    (A) Saint-Simon.   (B) Thomas Malthus

(C)   Jeremy Bentham.   (D)   Henri Bergson.

(E)   Herbert Spenser.

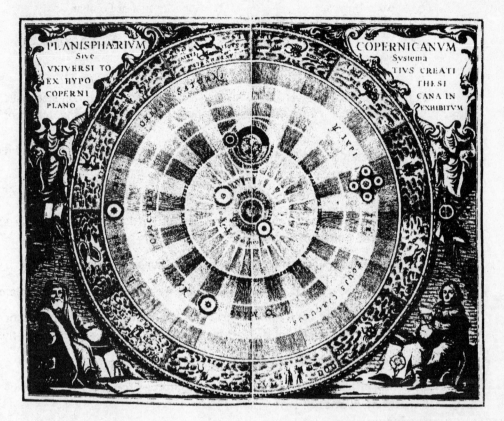

16.   The illustration above, an early depiction of Copernicus's concept of the universe, indicates that he was in error

(A)   in that he still retained the medieval concept of placing heaven at the outermost reaches of the universe.

(B)   by retaining Ptolemy's geocentric theory.

(C)   by adhering to the view that the orbits of the planets are circular.

(D)   in that he failed to take into consideration the advances which had been made by Kepler.

(E)   by rejecting the heliocentric theory.

17.   "If votes are taken by order, five million citizens will not be able to decide anything for the general interest, because it will not please a couple of hundred thousand privileged individuals. The will of a single individual will veto and destroy the will of more than a hundred people".

This complaint, voiced on the eve of the meeting of the Estates General in 1789, was expressed by

(A)   Abbe Siéyès.

(D)   the Marquis of Pombal.

(B)   Jacques Necker.

(E)   a leader of the *emigrés* faction.

(C)   Anne Robert Turgot.

18.   As a consequence of the English "Glorious" or "Bloodless" Revolution of 1688–89,

(A)   the Hanoverian dynasty came to the throne.

(B)   Oliver Cromwell was overthrown.

(C)   Anglicanism was proclaimed the faith of the state.

(D)   Charles I Stuart was executed.

(E)   the principle of constitutional monarchy was firmly established.

19.   All of the following have been advanced as explanations for the coming of the French Revolution EXCEPT

(A)   the desire of the middle class for a greater voice in government.

(B)   an inefficient and corrupt government aroused the anger of a mass of the French people.

(C)   the nobility of France sought to enhance their power.

(D)   a majority of the French populace desired to replace the monarchy with a republic.

(E)   the activities of the philosophes had weakened faith in traditional values and institutions.

20.   "Man is born free; and everywhere he is in chains...How did this change come about? I do not know. What can make it legitimate? That question I think I can answer."

These words began the famous work, treating the nature of the social contract, by

(A)   Edmund Burke.

(D)   Ferdinand de Lesseps.

(B)   Jean Jacques Rousseau.

(E)   Denis Diderot.

(C)   John Locke.

21. Following the execution of King Charles I Stuart, England was governed by

    (A) William and Mary.

    (B) Mary Tudor.

    (C) the Lord Protector Oliver Cromwell.

    (D) the "Old Pretender."

    (E) his son Charles II.

22. All of the following statements about Cardinal Richelieu are true EXCEPT that he

    (A) sought to weaken the power of the nobility.

    (B) waged war on the French Protestants.

    (C) deprived the Huguenots of their religious rights.

    (D) supported the German Protestants in their struggle with the Hapsburgs.

    (E) supported Gustavus Adolphus in his military operations in Germany.

23. "Whereas you...in the year 1615 were denounced to this Holy Office for holding as true the false doctrine taught by many, that the sun is the center of the world and immovable, and that the earth moves, and also with a diurnal motion...."

    This was the charge brought against

    (A) Nicholas Copernicus.   (D) Tycho Brahe.

    (B) Johannes Kepler.   (E) Anton van Leeuwenhoek.

    (C) Galilei Galileo.

24. According to the mercantilist theory, colonies

    (A) should receive their independence as soon as they were economically self-sufficient.

    (B) were a military burden to the mother country.

    (C) should be encouraged to develop their own industry.

    (D) were strongest if allowed to trade freely with other countries.

    (E) should serve as markets and sources of raw materials for their mother country.

25. "I believe in the equality of man; and I believe that religious duties consist in doing justice, loving mercy, and endeavoring to make all our fellow creatures happy…All national institutions of churches, whether Jewish, Christian, or Turkish, appear to me no other than human inventions, set up to terrify and enslave mankind, and monopolize power and profit."

This view would best reflect the attitudes of a

(A) Quietist.

(D) Jensenite.

(B) Deist.

(E) follower of Michael Servetus.

(C) Hutterite.

26. Martin Luther believed that the problem of personal sin had its solution in

(A) good works.

(B) acceptance of the doctrine of predestination.

(C) justification by faith.

(D) an inner awakening to the spirit of God.

(E) adherence to the teachings of the Church councils.

27. In 1995-1996, retired United States Senator George Mitchell assisted in negotiations between

(A) Great Britain and the Irish Republican Army.

(B) Israel and the Palestine Liberation Organization.

(C) Serbia and Bosnia.

(D) East and West Germany.

(E) Slovakia and the Czech Republic.

28. Peter the Great's purpose in building the city of St. Petersburg was

    (A)   to escape the influence of Mongol forces in Moscow.

    (B)   the establishment within Russia of a region free of serfdom.

    (C)   to throw off the powerful pressures of the monks of the Greek Ortho-
          dox Church.

    (D)   to hasten the Westernization of Russia.

    (E)   to create a defensive barrier against the aggression of the Poles.

29. A major figure in the Age of Exploration, Prince Henry the Navigator of
    Portugal sponsored

    (A)   the exploration of the west coast of Africa.

    (B)   the establishment of colonies in Brazil.

    (C)   Hernando Cortez's conquest of the Maya.

    (D)   the creation of an important trading post in Goa.

    (E)   the earliest efforts to discover a Northwest Passage.

30. The Thirty Years' War

    (A)   began when the Bohemians attempted to place a Catholic on the
          throne.

    (B)   served to promote German unity.

    (C)   did not involve France.

    (D)   resulted in the expulsion of the Ottoman Turks from the Balkans.

    (E)   saw Danish troops fighting on the side of the German Protestants.

31. "The prince is to the nation he governs what the head is to the man; it is his duty to see, think, and act for the whole community, that he may procure it every advantage of which it is capable. He must be active, possess integrity, and collect his whole powers, that he may be able to run the career he has commenced."

    This concept of the obligations of the ruler would best reflect the views of

    (A)   Peter the Great.   (D)   Louis XIV.

    (B)   James I Stuart.   (E)   Bishop Bossuet.

    (C)   Frederick the Great.

32. The War of the Roses was a dynastic conflict between the house of York and that of the

    (A)   Hanoverians.   (D)   Stuarts.

    (B)   Lancastrians.   (E)   Plantangenets.

    (C)   Windsors.

33. Kepler's contribution to the Scientific Revolution was his

    (A)   presentation of sound mathematical proof supporting Ptolemy's geocentric theory.

    (B)   demonstration that the planets move at a constant speed.

    (C)   demonstration that the surface of the moon was not smooth.

    (D)   proving mathematically that the orbits of the planets are elliptical.

    (E)   demonstration of the errors in the astronomical measurements of Tycho Brahe.

34. "That the pretended power of suspending the laws, or for execution of laws, by regal authority, without the consent of Parliament is illegal....That the raising or keeping of a standing army within the kingdom in the name of peace, unless it be with the consent of Parliament, is against the law."

    The first English monarch to accept and rule in accordance with these decrees was

    (A)   George I.   (D)   Charles II.

    (B)   William III.   (E)   Henry VIII.

    (C)   Queen Anne.

35. The Protestant Reformation

    (A) represented a rejection of many aspects of primitive Christianity.

    (B) weakened nationalistic feelings.

    (C) tended to strengthen the power of secular rulers.

    (D) resulted in the first Christian missionaries seeking converts in the Far East.

    (E) served to weaken the hold of spiritual beliefs on the minds of Europeans.

36. In his *An Essay Concerning Human Understanding*, John Locke held that human knowledge was derived from

    (A) heredity and faith.

    (B) conscience and emotions.

    (C) intuition and moral law.

    (D) environment and reason.

    (E) divine inspiration and innate perception.

37. All of the following are correctly matched EXCEPT

    (A) Pizarro—conquest of the empire of the Incas.

    (B) Coronado—early exploration of the American Southwest.

    (C) Balboa—exploration of the Mississippi Valley.

    (D) Cortez—conquest of the Aztecs.

    (E) Bartholomeu Diaz—reaches the southernmost tip of Africa.

38. The map-graph on the following page indicates that the greatest advance in the speed of travel between A.D. 1500 and 1700

    (A) resulted from the development of roads through the passes of the Alps.

    (B) brought Venice into closer contact with the capital of the Byzantine Empire.

    (C) was within the Italian peninsula.

    (D) was in overland travel to Eastern Europe.

    (E) was in areas accessible by sea.

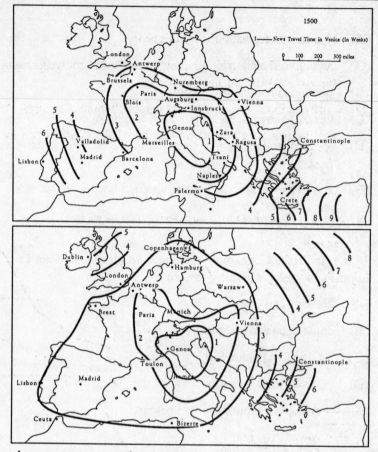

39. "The only way to erect such a common power as may be able to defend them from the invasion of foreigners and the injuries of one another, and thereby secure them in such sort as that by their own industry and by the fruits of the earth they may nourish themselves and live contentedly, is to confer all their power and strength upon one man, or upon one assembly of men, that they may reduce all their wills by plurality of voices unto one will..."

This theory of government reflected the view of

(A) John Locke.

(B) Jean Bodin.

(C) John Napier.

(D) Baron de Montesquieu.

(E) Thomas Hobbes.

40. A conclusion which might be drawn from the graphs shown on the following page is that

(A) Russia on the eve of the First World War, had still failed to develop her industrial base.

(B)   France was on the decline industrially.

(C)   economic factors may have entered into the mounting antagonism between Great Britain and Germany.

(D)   Austrian industrial growth was lagging behind even small Belgium.

(E)   the unification of Germany had had little impact upon the industrial growth of that country.

INDUSTRIAL PRODUCTION (THOUSANDS OF METRIC TONS)

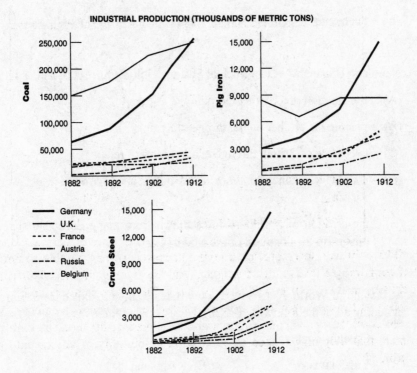

41.   In the wake of the failure of the Beer Hall Putsch, Hitler determined that

(A)   it would be necessary to recruit officers from the regular army.

(B)   he had to eliminate the paramilitary groups around him who frightened the conservative, middle class of Germany.

(C)   Bavaria was not a suitable region in which to build his political power.

(D)   the way to achieve political power was not through force but through the democratic elections and party politics.

(E)   it was necessary to form an alliance with the Social Democratic Party.

42. The Decembrist Revolution of 1825 was

(A) an effort of liberal Russian army officers to introduce governmental reforms.

(B) the initial attempt of Italian nationalists to bring about the unification of that land.

(C) an early example of the growing Pan-Slavic movement in the Balkans.

(D) a movement on the part of the Norwegians to win independence from Denmark.

(E) successful in gaining Belgian independence from Holland.

43. Napoleon Bonaparte's "Continental System," initiated in 1806, had as its goal

(A) the creation of a unified Germany.

(B) placing his brother on the throne of Spain.

(C) the defeat of Britain through economic warfare.

(D) a military alliance of those states under his control to wage war on Russia.

(E) the creation of a military force drawn from many European states to undertake the conquest of the Middle East.

44. At the end of World War I several new states came into existence in Europe, including all of the following EXCEPT

(A) Czechoslovakia. (D) Finland.

(B) Yugoslavia. (E) Albania.

(C) Estonia.

45. The defacing of the political poster, as seen in the illustration on the following page, was a prelude to

(A) the failed Nazi attempt to overthrow the Weimar Republic in 1923.

(B) the Munich Conference.

(C) the Nazi annexation of Austria in 1938.

(D) Hitler's occupation of the Rhineland.

(E) the seizure of Danzig.

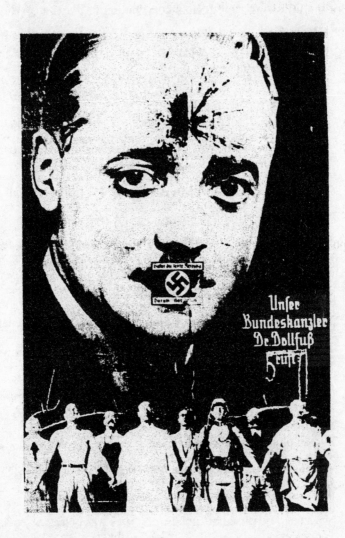

Unfer
Bundeskanzler
De.Dollfuß
heute

46. A concept of Bolshevism, advanced by Lenin, but NOT to be found in the writings of Marx is

   (A) that the industrial class, exploited by the bourgeoisie, will rise in rebellion and overthrow their oppressors.

   (B) that there is a need for an elite cadre to control the "dictatorship of the proletariat," giving impetus and direction to the revolution.

   (C) that control of society throughout the ages has rested in the hands of those who control the tools of production.

   (D) the concept of economic determinism.

   (E) the view that the existing governments, mere tools of the dominant economic class, would not sincerely act on behalf of the working class.

47. All of the following were factors contributing to the rise of Hitler to power EXCEPT

   (A) German anger over what was viewed as the unfair terms of the Treaty of Versailles.

   (B) the failure of the Weimar Republic to solve the economic problems confronting the nation.

   (C) the struggle between the Social Democrats and Communists.

   (D) mounting German fears of a remilitarized France.

   (E) the political machinations of von Papen.

48. Lenin's New Economic Policy (NEP), introduced in 1921, was designed to

   (A) bring about the rapid industrialization of the Soviet Union.

   (B) restore limited economic freedom.

   (C) collectivize Russian agriculture through the establishment of communes.

   (D) set five-year goals.

   (E) speed up the process of nationalization of industry.

49. The German philosopher Friedrich Nietzsche saw Western civilization as

   (A) placing too much stress upon rational thinking.

   (B) requiring a reorientation based upon Christian morality.

   (C) weakened because not enough emphasis was placed on social morality.

   (D) requiring that greater stress be placed upon political democracy.

   (E) placing too much emphasis on elitist elements in society.

50. The Treaty of Nanking (1842) ended a conflict between Great Britain and Manchu China which had its origin in

   (A) British concern over Russian penetration of Korea.

   (B) opium smuggled into China from British India.

   (C) the activities of Chinese pirates in the South China Sea.

   (D) Chinese expulsion of British diplomats from Peking.

   (E) the attacks of Chinese on Christian missionaries and Chinese converts.

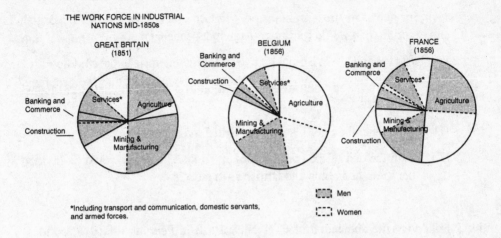

THE WORK FORCE IN INDUSTRIAL
NATIONS MID-1850s

*Including transport and communication, domestic servants, and armed forces.

51. On the basis of the charts above, it is clear that for the countries represented, in the mid-19th century

(A) women were still largely excluded from the labor force in industrialized states.

(B) in Great Britain the role of women in agriculture was on the decline.

(C) construction remained solely a male occupation.

(D) in France and Belgium mining and manufacturing were increasing steadily.

(E) women had yet to participate in banking and commercial activities in Great Britain.

52. The Sudeten question which led to the calling of the Munich Conference of 1938 centered on

(A) Hitler's introduction of German troops into the demilitarized Rhineland.

(B) ethnic Germans in the western regions of Czechoslovakia.

(C) territory disputed between Germany and Poland.

(D) the free city of Danzig.

(E) the unification of Germany and Austria.

53. The Balfour Declaration, issued during World War I, stated that

   (A) in return for their military cooperation against the Turks, the British and French would recognize Arab independence.

   (B) France and Great Britain had no territorial interests in the Middle East.

   (C) Britain viewed with favor the creation of a Jewish homeland in Palestine.

   (D) Egypt and the Suez Canal were British protectorates.

   (E) with the end of the conflict former Turkish holdings would be divided between the French and British as mandates.

54. Following the abdication of Czar Nicholas II in February of 1917, political power in revolutionary Russia passed into the hands of

   (A) Vladimir Lenin.   (D) Joseph Stalin.

   (B) Leon Trotsky.   (E) Admiral Kolchak.

   (C) Alexander Kerensky.

55. The immediate spark igniting World War I was the

   (A) invasion of Belgium by the German army.

   (B) assassination of Archduke Francis Ferdinand.

   (C) Austrian annexation of Bosnia-Herzegovina.

   (D) announcement of Italy's decision to ally with France.

   (E) joint Russo-Serbian attack on Austria.

56. A major consequence of the Sepoy or Indian Mutiny was that

   (A) Great Britain annexed all of India.

   (B) the East India Company was dissolved and its authority assumed by the British government.

   (C) the Thugges of the country were severely repressed.

   (D) native Indians were no longer permitted to serve in the military.

   (E) Indians were not allowed to hold positions in the Indian Civil Service.

57. As a consequence of the Russo-Japanese War,

    (A) Russia was forced to sell Alaska to the United States.

    (B) Russia and Japan divided Korea.

    (C) Japan annexed Manchuria.

    (D) China was forced to cede her Maritime Provinces, including Vladivostok, to Russia.

    (E) Russia abandoned her interests in Manchuria.

58. As a result of the Crimean War, Russia

    (A) gained control of the Black Sea.

    (B) was confronted with a revolution.

    (C) saw the introduction of a number of important reforms.

    (D) tightened control over the serfs.

    (E) introduced a national Duma, or parliament.

59. Social Darwinism provided theoretical support for all of the following EXCEPT

    (A) economic individualism.   (D) cosmopolitanism.

    (B) militarism.   (E) imperialism.

    (C) the growth of big industry.

60. Viewing history and the evolution of civilizations in biological terms, he believed that the West had entered a stage of decline. He was

    (A) Oswald Spengler.   (D) Leander Jameson.

    (B) Sidney Webb.   (E) Vincenzo Lombardi.

    (C) Karl Peters.

GERMAN ELECTIONS TO THE WEIMAR ASSEMBLY AND REICHSTAG, 1919-1933
(Number of seats obtained by the major parties, arranged with the Left at the top, the Right at the bottom)

	Jan. 1919	June 1920	May 1924	Dec. 1924	May 1928	Sept. 1930	July 1932	Nov. 1932	Mar. 1933
Communists	—a	2	62	45	54	77	89	100	81
Independent Socialists	22	81	—b						
Social Democrats	163	112	100	131	152	143	133	121	125
Democrats	74	45	28	32	25	14	4	2	5
Center	71	68	65	69	61	68	75	70	74
People's party	22	62	44	51	45	30	7	11	2
Nationalists	42	66	96	103	78	41	40	51	52
Nazis			38	20	12	107	230	196	288

a—The Communist party boycotted the elections to the Weimar constituent assembly.

b—In these and succeeding elections the Independent Socialists had merged with the Social Democrats.

61. The chart above indicates that

   (A)   the Nazi Party benefited the most politically from the Great Depression.

   (B)   a coalition of the moderates in 1933 could have halted Hitler's gaining control of the German state.

   (C)   in the 1920s the major threat to the Social Democrats' power came from the Center.

   (D)   the French-Belgian occupation of the Ruhr resulted in loss of support for the Communists.

   (E)   the economic recovery the Weimar Republic experienced in the mid-1920s substantially helped the Nazis win support.

62. The threat of a communist revolution in Germany in the days following the end of World War I was seen in the

   (A)   the activities of the Frei Korps.

   (B)   efforts of the socialist leaders of the Weimar Republic.

   (C)   Spartacist movement.

   (D)   Munich Beer Hall Putsch of 1923.

   (E)   actions of Bela Kun.

63. In his philosophical view there existed beneath the conscious intellect a "will," a force that is the real conduct of human behavior. He was

    (A) Arthur Schopenhauer.   (D) Samuel Smiles.

    (B) Max Weber.   (E) Herbert Spenser.

    (C) Emile Durkheim.

64. What was the original purpose of NATO?

    (A) To provide a peaceful resolution in the Balkans

    (B) To provide an army to enforce United Nations decisions

    (C) To protect Europe from Soviet aggression

    (D) To work to protect human rights throughout the world

    (E) To protect Israel from Arab aggression

65. A significant difference between the problem created for the Austro-Hungarian empire by Czech nationalism and that of the Serbs was that

    (A) the Serbs were more politically advanced than the Czechs.

    (B) a majority of the Serbs were willing to accept autonomy within the Dual Monarchy, while the Czechs sought complete independence.

    (C) the Czechs could look to Germany for support.

    (D) an independent Serbian state existed to encourage their ethnic kinsmen within the Dual Monarchy.

    (E) a majority of Czechs were concerned with their cultural rights rather than independence.

66. In the course of World War I Britain was faced with a serious rebellion on the part of her subjects in

    (A) the Union of South Africa.   (D) Palestine.

    (B) India.   (E) Cyprus.

    (C) Ireland.

67. Attacking the society of his day for its conformity and subjugation to what he deemed a Christian "slave" morality, he longed for the strong individuals who could overthrow current values and through disciplined struggle and sacrifice achieve their "wholeness."

    (A)   Karl Barth   (D)   Soren Kierkegaard

    (B)   Friedrich Nietzche   (E)   Paul Tillich

    (C)   Jean-Paul Sartre

68. Werner Heisenberg's contribution to 20th century science was

    (A)   the development of the "Big Bang" theory regarding the origin of the universe.

    (B)   the theory of plate techtonics and continental drift.

    (C)   to raise serious questions regarding the ability of the scientist to know, in fact, the way things actually are.

    (D)   the discovery of the oldest known *homonic* at that time, at a site in East Africa.

    (E)   the invention of the radio telescope.

69. In the works of Arthur de Gobineau and Houston Stuart Chamberlain were concepts which contributed significantly to the

    (A)   development of existentialism.

    (B)   doctrines of the National Socialist Workers Party.

    (C)   economic doctrines of Neo-Mercantilism.

    (D)   policy of appeasement pursued by France and Great Britain in the 1930s.

    (E)   Dadaist movement.

70. 1. Open covenants openly arrived at…diplomacy shall proceed always frankly and in the public view.

2. Absolute freedom of navigation...alike in peace and war.

3. Adequate guarantees...that national armaments will be reduced to the lowest point consistent with domestic safety.

The statements above constitute a portion of those found in the

(A)   Atlantic Charter.   (D)   McMahon Letters.

(B)   Treaty of Versailles.   (E)   Kellogg-Briand Pact.

(C)   Fourteen Points of Woodrow Wilson.

71. In 1958, Charles de Gaulle came to power in France in the midst of a crisis provoked by

(A)   the popular debate as to the policy to be pursued in the conduct of conflict in Indo-China.

(B)   widespread riots on the part of French university students.

(C)   the issue of French membership in NATO.

(D)   controversy over the struggle being waged against Algerian nationalists.

(E)   the question of French membership in the Common Market.

72. The philosopher José Ortega y Gasset, reflecting the mood of pessimism which was prevalent among many intellectuals following World War I, argued that

(A)   Western civilization was destined to give way to that of Asia.

(B)   modern technology, particularly that in the military area, would lead to the annihilation of European society.

(C)   the only solution to the problems confronting European society was submission to totalitarian rule.

(D)   the greatest threat to the highest achievements of Western civilization was to be found in the rise of the masses.

(E)   the cultural dominance that was held by Europe had passed into the hands of the people of the New World.

73.   In France of the 1930s, the activities of organizations such as the *Croix de Feu* and *Action Française* served as evidence of the

(A)   threat to government stability from the political left.

(B)   increasing tendency toward isolationism on the part of the French people.

(C)   strong popular support in France for the Republican cause in Spain.

(D)   existence in France of a strong fascist element.

(E)   widespread popular backing for the Popular Front of Leon Blum.

74.   "Aside from the demoralizing effect on the world at large, and the possibilities of disturbances as a result of the desperation of the people concerned... it is logical that the United States should do whatever it is able to do to assist in the return of normal economic health in the world, and without which there can be no political stability and no assured peace."

These sentiments, expressed in the course of a speech given on June 5, 1947, reflected the program subsequently established by

(A)   Winston Churchill.   (D)   Franklin D. Roosevelt.

(B)   George C. Marshall.   (E)   John Foster Dulles.

(C)   Dwight D. Eisenhower.

75.   A major scientific breakthrough came in the 1950s with the work of James D. Watson and Francis H. C. Crick in

(A)   the area of artificial intelligence.

(B)   the field of biological inheritance and DNA molecules.

(C)   viral infections.

(D)   the nature and origin of Black Holes.

(E)   discovery of holes in the Earth's ozone layer and the danger of global warming.

76. The decision of the French, British, and Israelis to launch an invasion of Egypt in 1956 was the result of the

    (A) formation of the United Arab Republic as a prelude to a coordinated attack on Israel.

    (B) Egyptian announcement that they would permit the Soviet navy to use the naval facilities of the port of Alexandria.

    (C) Russia's announcement that it would assist Egypt in the construction of the Aswan Dam in return for military bases.

    (D) plans of Nasser to nationalize the Suez Canal.

    (E) Egyptian support of the communist rebels of North Yemen.

77. What accident caused Europeans to rethink expansion of nuclear power?

    (A) Three Mile Island

    (B) Chernobyl

    (C) The atomic bombing of Nagasaki and Hiroshima

    (D) Bhopal

    (E) North Korea

78. The Brezhnev Doctrine held that

    (A) Russia had an obligation to aid Communist revolutions anywhere in the world.

    (B) each country had the right to pursue its own road to communism.

    (C) the development of the agricultural section of the Russian economy should take precedence over heavy industry.

    (D) Communist countries had the right to intervene in the internal affairs of other Communist countries.

    (E) Jewish dissidents in the Soviet Union would henceforth be permitted to leave the country.

79. The Korean War began when

    (A) Communist China sent troops across the Yalu River into North Korea.

    (B) General Douglas MacArthur was named head of the United Nations forces in Korea.

    (C) the Communist Peoples Democratic Republic of North Korea invaded South Korea.

    (D) United States forces were sent into South Korea to crush a Communist insurrection supported by the Soviet Union.

    (E) the Republic of Korea invaded North Korea.

80. In 1956, Soviet troops brutally crushed a movement to democracy in

    (A) Yugoslavia.   (D) Czechoslovakia.

    (B) Poland.   (E) Hungary.

    (C) Afghanistan.

European History

TEST 5 – Section II

TIME: Reading Period – 15 minutes
Writing Time for all three essays – 115 minutes

> **DIRECTIONS:** Read over both the Document-Based Essay question in Part A and the choices in Part B during the Reading Period, and use the time to organize answers. All students must answer Part A (the Document-Based Essay Question), and choose TWO questions from Part B to answer.

PART A – DOCUMENT-BASED ESSAY

This question is designed to test your ability to work with historical documents. As you analyze each document, take into account the source and the point of view of the author. Write an essay on the following topic that integrates your analysis of the documents. You may refer to historical facts and developments not mentioned in the documents.

The view expressed by the author of Document 1 has long influenced historians of Imperialism, accepted by many, and subjected to modification or rejection by others. Utilizing the documents presented here, evaluate its validity or possible weaknesses.

Document 1
Analysis of the actual course of modern Imperialism has laid bare the combination of economic and political forces which fashions it. The forces are traced to the sources in the selfish interests of certain industrial, financial, and professional classes seeking private advantages out of a policy of imperial expansion.
—J. A. Hobson, anti-imperialist economist, *Imperialism, A Study*, 1902

Document 2
"Our connection with them [the Malay States] is due to the simple fact that seventy years ago the British government was invited, pushed, and persuaded into helping the rulers of certain states to introduce order into their disorderly, penniless, and distracted households by sending trained British civil servants to advise the rulers in the art of administration and to organize a system of govern-

ment which would secure justice, freedom, safety for all, with the benefits of what is known as civilization."

–Frank Swettenham, British Colonial Official, circa 1869

Document 3

"No one acquainted with the actual state of society in the West Indies...can doubt that, if they were left, unaided by us, to settle amongst themselves in whose hands power should be placed, a fearful war of colour would probably soon break out,...and civilization would be thrown back for centuries."

–Lord Grey, Head, British Colonial Office, 1853

Document 4

"Everyone will admit...the value of that commerce which penetrates to every part of the globe; and many of these colonies give harbours and security to that trade, which are most useful in times of peace, but are absolutely necessary in time of war."

–Lord John Russell, British Prime Minister, 1850

Document 5

"If persons, knowing the risks they run, owing to the disturbed state of these countries, choose to hazard their lives and properties for sake of large profits which accompany successful trading, they must not expect the British Government to be answerable if their speculation proves unsuccessful."

–Governor, Straits Settlements, circa 1860

Document 6

"Let us endeavour to strike our roots into the soil by the gradual introduction and establishment of our own principles and opinions; of our laws, institutions, and manners; above all, as the source of every other improvement, of our religion, and consequently of our morals."

–William Wilberforce, British Statesman/Humanitarian, circa 1825

Document 7

"The position of Russia in Central Asia is that of all civilized states which are brought into contact with half-savage nomad populations possessing no fixed social organization."

"In such cases, the more civilized state is forced in the interest of the security of its frontier, and commercial relations, to exercise a certain ascendancy over her turbulent and undesirable neighbors. Raids and acts of pillage must be put down. To do this, the tribes of the frontier must be reduced to a state of submission. This result once attained, these tribes take to more peaceful habits, but are in turn exposed to the attacks of the more distant tribes against whom the State is bound to protect them."

–Prince Gorchakov, Russian Foreign Minister, 1864

Document 8

Onward Christian Soldiers, on to heathen lands,
Prayer-books in your pockets, rifles in your hands
Take the glorious tidings where trade can be done:
Spread the peaceful gospel—with a Maxim gun.
   –Henri Labouchère, Anti-Imperialist Editor, *Pioneers' Hymn*, 1893

Document 9

"Throughout the Century of Peace…man's mind had become open to the truth, had become sensible to the diversity of species, had become conscious of Nature's law of development…The stern logic of facts proclaimed the Negro and Chinaman below the level of the Caucasian, and incapacitated from advance towards his intellectual standard. To the development of the White Man, the Black Man and the Yellow must ever remain inferior, and as the former raised itself higher and yet higher, so did those latter seem to sink out of humanity and appear nearer and nearer to the brutes."
   –W. D. Hay, Social Darwinist author, *Three Hundred Years Hence*, 1881

Document 10

"At this time, as you know, a warship cannot carry more than fourteen days worth of coal, no matter how perfectly it is organized, and a ship which is out of coal is a derelict on the surface of the sea, abandoned to the first person who comes along. Thus the necessity of having on the oceans provisions stations, shelters, ports for defense and revictualizing. And it is for this that we needed Tunisia, for this that we needed Saigon, and the Mekong Delta, for this that we need Madagascar, that we are at Diego-Suarez and Vohemar and will never leave them. Gentlemen, in Europe as it is today…a policy of peaceful seclusion or abstention is simply the highway to decadence."
   –Jules Ferry, French Imperialist, speech to French National Assembly, 1883

Document 11
Population (in millions)

	Great Britain	Russia	France	Germany	Italy
1796		29			
1800	10-9			24-5	18-1
1801			27-3		
1830	16-5			29-6	
1831			31-9		
1850	20-9			35-4	23
1851			35-8		
1858		67			
1870	26-2			40-9	26-6
1871			36-1		
1897		129			
1900	37			56-4	32-4
1901			39		
1910	40-8				
1911			39-2		34-8
1914		142		67-8	
1921	42		39-2		38-4

Document 12
"We stand on nationalism in our belief that the unfolding of economic and political power by the German nation abroad is the prerequisite for all far-reaching social reforms at home."

–Manifesto of the *Nationalsozialer Verein*, 1897

Document 13

THE NEW AFRICAN MISSION.

Rev. Mr. Fun : "THIS, DEARLY BELOVED BROTHER, IS OUR CIVILISATION. A TEMPTING PICTURE, IT IS NOT?"

Document 14

"Nations may be roughly divided between the living and the dying...For one reason or another—from the necessities of politics or under the pretence of philanthropy—the living nations will gradually encroach on the territory of the dying, and the seeds and the causes of conflict among civilized nations will speedily appear."

–Lord Salisbury, British Minister, 1898

Document 15

"...No doubt there will remain people like the aged savage who in his old age went back to his savage tribe and said that he had 'tried civilization for forty years, and it was not worth the trouble,' but we not take account of the mistaken ideas of unfit men and beaten races."

–Walter Bagehot, *Physics and Politics*, 1869

Document 16

"Early in November [1897] several Ministers, including myself, received a memorandum drawn up by Count Muraviov. It pointed out that the occupation of Kiao-Chow by the Germans offered a favourable occasion for us to seize one of the Chinese ports, notably Port Arthur...He pointed out that these ports had an enormous strategical importance."
–Count Witte, Russian Finance Minister, *Memoirs*

Document 17

Take up the White Man's burden—
Send forth the best ye breed—
Go bind your sons to exile—
To serve your captives' need;
To wait in heavy harness,
On fluttered folk and wild—
Your new-caught, sullen peoples,
Half-devil and half-child.
–Rudyard Kipling, Imperialist poet, 1893

Document 18

"An Empire such as ours requires as its first condition an Imperial Race—a race vigorous and industrious and intrepid. Health of mind and body exalt a nation in the competition of the universe. The survival of the fittest is an absolute truth in the conditions of the modern world."
–Lord Rosebery, former British Prime Minister, *The Times*, 1900

Document 19

"In order to save the 40,000,000 inhabitants of the United Kingdom from a bloody civil war, we colonial statesmen must acquire new lands to settle the surplus population, to provide new markets for the goods produced by them in the factories and mines. The Empire, as I have always said, is a bread and butter question. If you want to avoid civil war, you must become imperialists."
–Cecil Rhodes, South African Statesman and Apostle of Imperialism, 1895

PART B – ESSAY QUESTIONS

1. In the course of the17th century "absolutistic" regimes spread, with varied degrees of success, across much of Continental Europe. Why? What were the conditions and forces at work to make this form of government desirable—or at least seem desirable?

2. Discuss the complaints and aspirations of the various social classes in France on the eve of the French Revolution.

3. The peoples of Europe, convinced that their nations' causes were just, entered World War I in August of 1914 enthusiastically, in the belief that victory would be theirs by Christmas. What went wrong? Why did they, civilian and military alike, have such a mistaken concept of the nature of modern warfare? What changes had taken place in previous decades to so dramatically alter the nature of warfare?

4. At the outset of the Age of Exploration and Discovery it was the nations of the Iberian Peninsula—Portugal and Spain—that led the way. Why? What particular circumstances, advantages, motives, favored these states taking the lead?

5. Karl Marx made a number of assertions regarding how the governments would respond to the industrialization of society and expanding capitalism. Discuss the basic theses upon which he predicated these assertions and the specific nature of these assertions. Having done this, discuss Marx's record as a "prophet," indicating the extent to which his predictions proved valid.

6. The late 19th and early 20th centuries saw the long-held concept of the fundamental rationality of man come under attack: there were those who perceived man as being driven by forces other than those of a conscious (i.e., rational) nature. Discuss the reasons for this intellectual, yet anti-rational movement, and indicate some of its leading spokesmen.

THE ADVANCED PLACEMENT EXAMINATION IN

European History

TEST 5 – ANSWERS

1.	**(D)**	21.	**(C)**	41.	**(D)**	61.	**(A)**
2.	**(E)**	22.	**(C)**	42.	**(A)**	62.	**(C)**
3.	**(B)**	23.	**(C)**	43.	**(C)**	63.	**(A)**
4.	**(B)**	24.	**(E)**	44.	**(E)**	64.	**(C)**
5.	**(A)**	25.	**(B)**	45.	**(C)**	65.	**(D)**
6.	**(C)**	26.	**(C)**	46.	**(B)**	66.	**(C)**
7.	**(E)**	27.	**(A)**	47.	**(D)**	67.	**(B)**
8.	**(B)**	28.	**(D)**	48.	**(B)**	68.	**(C)**
9.	**(C)**	29.	**(A)**	49.	**(A)**	69.	**(B)**
10.	**(A)**	30.	**(E)**	50.	**(B)**	70.	**(C)**
11.	**(B)**	31.	**(C)**	51.	**(E)**	71.	**(D)**
12.	**(D)**	32.	**(B)**	52.	**(B)**	72.	**(D)**
13.	**(C)**	33.	**(D)**	53.	**(C)**	73.	**(D)**
14.	**(B)**	34.	**(B)**	54.	**(C)**	74.	**(B)**
15.	**(B)**	35.	**(C)**	55.	**(B)**	75.	**(B)**
16.	**(C)**	36.	**(D)**	56.	**(B)**	76.	**(D)**
17.	**(A)**	37.	**(C)**	57.	**(E)**	77.	**(B)**
18.	**(E)**	38.	**(E)**	58.	**(C)**	78.	**(D)**
19.	**(D)**	39.	**(E)**	59.	**(D)**	79.	**(C)**
20.	**(B)**	40.	**(C)**	60.	**(A)**	80.	**(E)**

Detailed Explanations
of Answers
TEST 5

1. **(D)** William Harvey, an English physician and experimentalist, advanced the view in 1628 that the blood circulated and the heart acted as a pump. Paracelsus was a 16th century physician who attacked the long accepted theories of "humors" as a source of disease (A). Lorenzo Valla, a Renaissance humanist, demonstrated that the "Donation of Constantine" was a forgery (C). Galvani was an 18th century anatomist and experimenter with electricity (B). Francis Bacon (1561–1626) was an ardent advocate of the inductive approach to scientific research (E).

2. **(E)** René Descartes was a 17th century French geometer and mathematician and a proponent of deductive reasoning. Hugo Grotius was a Dutch legal theorist in the area of international law (A). Jean Bodin was a 16th century French *politique* and advocate of religious toleration (B). Galileo was a famed Renaissance physicist and astronomer (C). Joseph Dalton Hooker was a 19th century British botanist (D).

3. **(B)** Desiderius Erasmus, a Dutch humanist of the Northern Renaissance, was a strong critic of abuses within the Church, but was not a supporter of the Reformation launched by Luther, who had been influenced by him. Petrarch was a leading literary figure in the early Renaissance in Italy (A). Agricola was a 16th century scientist in the field of mining technology (C). Mirandola was a Renaissance humanist (D). Pierre d'Ailly, bishop of Cambrei and Puy and Chancellor of the University of Paris, was a leading figure in the Conciliar Movement of the 14th and 15th centuries (E).

4. **(B)** Enacted by King Henry IV, the Edict of Nantes granted limited religious and political autonomy to the Huguenots. Louis XI came to the throne following the Hundred Years' War in the 15th century (A). The St. Bartholomew's Day Massacre was an incident, inaugurating the bloodiest phases of the Religious Wars (C). The Treaty of Cateau-Cambresis (1559) ended the Hapsburg-Valois conflict (D).The Peace of Augsburg was a settlement between German Protestants and Catholics in the Reformation (E).

5.   **(A)**   A 19th century German sociologist, Weber advanced the theory of the "Protestant work ethic" and its significance in the emergence of capitalism. Luther supported neither the south German peasants (B), who demonstrated "revolutionary" tendencies in the early days of the Reformation nor the Anabaptists (C): indeed, he called for their extermination. The Reformation, if anything, deterred Protestant involvement in overseas exploration (D), a movement Catholic Portugal and Spain had already inaugurated. The Protestants took a more lenient view towards usury than did the medieval church (E).

6.   **(C)**   The treaty (1494) established a line of demarcation, with Portugal to have all lands to the east of it, and Spain all those to the west. England had nothing to do with the treaty, nor did she or other nations pay any heed to it (A). The Dutch did not gain control of the Cape region of South Africa until the 17th century (B), while the Ohio Valley was not to be penetrated for several centuries (D). The treaty had nothing to do with the Swiss, who by the end of the 15th century had largely gained their independence from the Hapsburgs (E).

7.   **(E)**   Vasco da Gama reached the port of Calicut on the Malabar coast of India in 1497. Bartholomeu Dias reached the tip of Africa in 1488 (B), while Magellan of Spain was the first to circumnavigate the globe (A) (actually it was his captain, del Cano, as Magellan was slain in the Philippines). Portuguese seamen reached Japan in 1530 (C), while Cabral landed in Brazil (D) in 1500 (although there is slight evidence that other Portuguese explorers landed there earlier).

8.   **(B)**   This statement is an example of the doctrine of "Double Predestination," a core element in Calvin's teachings. Thomas Hobbes (A) was a political writer in 17th century England and the author of the *Leviathan*. While the doctrine of predestination had long been a concept in Christianity, neither Luther (C), the Catholic Council of Trent (D), nor Zwingli (E) placed the great emphasis on it seen in Calvin's works.

9.   **(C)**   This statement reflects the doctrine of the "Divine Right of Monarchy," a theory held by the early Stuart monarchs of England. Neither Frederick the Great (A) nor Joseph II of Austria (E), both "Enlightened Despots," would have written or spoken in such terms, while William III of England (D), king by selection of the Parliament, would also have been hesitant to claim such power. John Locke (B), an outspoken exponent of "constitutional monarchy," would have rejected such an idea out-of-hand.

10.   **(A)**   One of the "Twelve who Ruled" on the Committee of Public Safety, Robespierre was its most articulate spokesman. None of the other men was ever a member of the committee: Lafayette (E), a moderate aristocrat, fled France before it came to power; Babeuf (D), a "communist" revolutionary, was executed by the Directory, while Napoleon (C) did not rise to prominence in France until

after its fall. Danton (B), a leading figure in the early days of the revolution, fell victim to the "Terror" inaugurated by the Committee.

11. **(B)** The Peace of Augsburg was a religious accord reached among the German princes in 1155. The Edict of Nantes (1595) ended the religious wars in France (A). The Six Articles (1534) defined heretical acts in the eyes of the Anglican Church (C). The *Spiritual Exercises* (D) was a manual written by the founder of the Jesuits. The Council of Trent (1545–64) was a part of the Catholic Counter-Reformation (E).

12. **(D)** The *philosophes* of the Age of Reason strongly opposed religious intolerance and what they viewed as irrational superstition of religious beliefs. Cosmopolitan in outlook and generally anti-monarchial (A), they were convinced of mankind's ability to progress (B), and were strongly under the influence of earlier scientists and their concept of the universe (E).

13. **(C)** Rumors had spread among the peasants that the monarch and aristocracy intended to crush them through the use of brigands. Prussia and Austria were not at war with France in 1789 (A), nor had the king been executed (D), nor the Jacobin "Terror" begun (B).

14. **(B)** The poem reflects a romantic view, questioning the merits of science and extolling nature and the emotions. The other answers refer to men or movements which were strongly influenced by reason and science and had little regard for the "sentiments of the heart."

15. **(B)** Thomas Malthus was an 18th century forerunner in the field of human demography. Saint-Simon (A) was a prominent utopian socialist of the early 19th century, Bentham (C) the founder of Utilitarianism. Bergson (D) was a social philosopher of the late 19th century, the advocate of the *élan vital*, and Spenser (E) was an ardent Social Darwinist.

16. **(C)** The fact that the orbits were elliptical was determined by Kepler after the death of Copernicus. Copernicus's theory rejected both the medieval (A) and Ptolemaic (B) concept of the universe while advancing the heliocentric theory (E). Kepler's work (D) was conducted after the death of Copernicus.

17. **(A)** The quotation is from his pamphlet "What is the Third Estate?", a strong argument against the Estates General voting "by the order." Necker (B) and Turgot (C) had passed from the political scene by 1789, while Pombal (D) was a Portuguese statesmen. The *emigrés* or aristocrats generally favored voting by the order (E).

18. **(E)** The new monarchs, William and Mary, were required to accept the "Bill of Rights" and, in essence, the ultimate authority of Parliament. The

Hanoverian dynasty (A) only assumed the throne on the death of Queen Anne (1714), while Cromwell (B) died a natural death nearly three decades prior to 1688. Anglicanism was proclaimed the religion of England in the reign of Henry VIII in the early 16th century (C).

19. **(D)** The *cahiers* or list of grievances of 1789 indicated that a majority of the French people wanted the monarchy reformed, not abolished. All of the other complaints or demands have been advanced as probable factors in the coming of the Revolution.

20. **(B)** These are the opening words of Rousseau's *Social Contract*. Locke (C) was an earlier English statesman, political theorist, and scientist, while Burke (A) was an English politician and the author of *Reflections on the Revolution in France*. Diderot (E) was a philosophe of the Age of Reason and the editor of the monumental *Encyclopedie*. De Lesseps (D) was the architect and builder of the Suez Canal.

21. **(C)** Cromwell governed as a virtual military dictator following the execution of Charles I. Tudor (B) reigned in the mid-16th century, while William and Mary came to the throne in 1688 (A). The "Old Pretender," the son of the banished James II, never reigned (D). Charles II, son of Charles I, came to the throne in 1661 following the death of Cromwell (E).

22. **(C)** While waging war on the French Protestants (Huguenots) and depriving them of certain political and military privileges, he did not deny their religious rights. His major goal was the enhancement of the power of the crown, which meant weakening the influence of the aristocracy and that of the Hapsburgs through aid to the German Protestants and King Gustavus Adolphus in the Thirty Years' War.

23. **(C)** This is a passage from the notes of the Inquisition trial of Galileo for advancing his astronomical views. Copernicus (A), Kepler (B), and Brahe (D), all astronomers, were dead by 1615, while the Dutchman Leeuwenhoek (E) was the first man to use the microscope to observe microorganisms.

24. **(E)** The utilization of colonies as "feeders" of raw materials to the mother country, and closed markets to the finished products of the mother country, was a standard concept of the mercantile system. There was no desire to see colonies gain their independence (A) in the mercantile system, to develop their own industry (C), nor to be permitted to trade with other countries (D), both or all of which would serve as competition to the mother country. Colonies, as in the case of the American holdings of England, were customarily expected to defend themselves (B).

25. **(B)** The words, those of Thomas Paine, reflect a deistic, almost agnostic,

religious outlook. All other groups, regardless of their sectarian views, would hold a more traditional view of religion and, specifically, of Christianity.

26. **(C)** Justification by faith constituted the central pillar of the Lutheran faith. All other concepts noted were either rejected by Luther or viewed as of secondary importance.

27. **(A)** The correct answer is (A). Former United States Senator Mitchell went to assist in negotiations between the British and the Irish Republican Army at the request of U.S. President Bill Clinton, who himself was cheered by large crowds when he travelled to strife-torn Northern Ireland in 1996 to champion the cause of peace between Roman Catholics and Protestants.

28. **(D)** He specifically spoke of the city as his "window to the West," the avenue through which Western trade and technology would flow into Russia. When Peter came to the Russian throne, the power of the Mongols had already been broken (A) and he was to weaken that of the Orthodox Church (C) through means not related to the establishment of St. Petersburg. Poland was on a marked path of decline (E) and he tightened the controls on the serfs (B) rather than loosening them.

29. **(A)** In the first half of the 15th century his seamen explored the west coast of Africa as far south as the Cape Verde Islands. Brazil (B) was first discovered by the Portuguese seamen in 1500, four decades after Prince Henry's death, while Goa (D), in India, was also established by the Portuguese some time after his passing. Cortez, in the service of Spain, conquered the Aztecs (C), not the Mayas, and Portugal's explorations were directed southward, not to the northwest (E).

30. **(E)** The Danes briefly entered the conflict to support the German Protestants and, if possible, acquire territory. The roots of the war were to be found in the attempt of the Bohemians to place Frederick II of the Palatinate, a Calvinist, on the throne (A). Rather than promoting German unity (B), the struggle resulted in continued division. France throughout the conflict supported the German Protestants and their allies (E). The war did not involve the Ottomans, who were driven from the Balkans only in the 19th century (D).

31. **(C)** The role of the prince is seen as a "career," not a God-given right: this was the concept held by the Enlightened Despots, of whom Frederick the Great, whose words these are, was a prime example. All of the other monarchs and individuals noted were strong advocates of the concept of "divine right" monarchy.

32. **(B)** The Lancastrians triumphed in the person of Henry VII, a Tudor in 1485. The Hanoverians (A) and Windsors (C), actually the same dynasty (its German name was changed in World War I), came to the throne with the death of Queen Anne in 1713, the Stuarts (D) on the death of Elizabeth I in 1603, while the Plantangenets (E) were a medieval dynasty.

33. **(D)** By abandoning Copernicus's concept of circular orbits, Kepler demonstrated the validity of the former's heliocentric theory. He proved the error of Ptolemy's theory (A) and demonstrated that the speed of the planets in their orbits varies in relation to their distance from the sun (B). It was Galileo who, using a telescope, saw for the first time the rough surface of the moon (C). Kepler utilized many of the measurements of Brahe, his former employer (E).

34. **(B)** The words are from the English Bill of Rights, accepted by King William before he came to the throne in 1688. George I (A) and Anne (C), coming to the throne after the enactment of the Bill of Rights, accepted it, while Charles II (D) and Henry VIII (E) reigned earlier (and probably would have rejected it).

35. **(C)** Religious conformity increasingly became a means by which the power of the prince was enhanced. Protestants tended strongly to look to the primitive Christian Church and community for what they saw as correct guidance (A). Nationalistic feelings were an integral aspect of the Reformation (B), while the religious enthusiasm of Europeans assumed near-fanatic proportions (E). The practice of sending missionaries to the Eastern lands can be seen almost from the time of the crucifixion (D).

36. **(D)** Man's mind, a "blank tablet" at birth, gained knowledge only through sensory perception and reflection on the knowledge so acquired. Locke rejected any sources of knowledge other than the information he gained through his sensory contacts with the world about him and his integration of that knowledge through his powers of reasoning.

37. **(C)** Balboa was the first European to gaze on the waters of the Pacific. All other matches are correct.

38. **(E)** The seaports of Ceuta, Lisbon, Brest, London, and Copenhagen, formerly six or more days of travel from Venice, have been brought within three days of travel time. Travel times to all of the other regions, primarily overland, have remained virtually unaltered.

39. **(E)** The concept, that of "absolutism," was supported by Hobbes in his work the *Leviathan*. John Locke (A), in his *Two Treatises on Civil Government*, clearly rejected such a concept. Bodin (B) and Montesquieu (D), French political theorists of the 16th and 18th centuries respectively, would also have rejected

such a concept of absolutism. Napier (C) was a scientist, the deviser of logarithms.

40. **(C)** By 1902 Germany had surpassed Great Britain, in some cases markedly, in basic industrial production, a fact that created increasing tension between the two states. Russia (A), if not one of the major industrial powers of Europe, had established a base. France (B), if not as productive as Germany or England, was increasing its production, as was Austria (D). Clearly German unification in 1871 led to an explosion in her industrial growth (E).

41. **(D)** It was to be through the electoral process that the Nazis gained power. Hitler gained the somewhat qualified support of the aristocratic officer corps only after attaining power (A). His first paramilitary backing, the SA or "Storm Troopers," were broken by Hitler only in 1935 (B). He continued to work out of Bavaria until the early 1930s (C), while he was always in opposition to the SD Party (E).

42. **(A)** The revolutionaries were a small group of young Russian army officers who had been stationed in post-revolutionary France. The Italian unification movement (B) only resorted to open revolt in the 1840s; the Pan-Slavic movement (C) also emerged later than 1825. In 1825 Norway was a part of Sweden (D), and the Belgians gained their independence from Holland in 1832 (E).

43. **(C)** It was designed to exclude England from all trade with the Continent. Joseph Bonaparte was placed on the Spanish throne in 1809 (B). France had little desire to see a unified Germany (A), although the "Redaction of 1803" did reduce the number of German states to 39. He was allied with Russia in 1806 (D), going to war with her only in 1812. After his earlier activities in Egypt, he undertook no further military operations in that region (E).

44. **(E)** Albania came into existence in the 19th century. Estonia (C) and Finland (B) came into existence in the wake of the Russian Revolution, Czechoslovakia (A) with the breakup of the Austro-Hungarian Empire, and Yugoslavia (B) with the unification of various Slavic states.

45. **(C)** Dr. Dollfuss, the individual portrayed on the defaced poster, was chancellor of Austria. He was murdered by Austrian Nazis in 1933, five years before the *Anchluss*, or German annexation of Austria. Hitler's target in 1923 was basically the Bavarian government, not the Weimar Republic (A). The Munich Conference (B) was the prelude to the seizure of the Sudetenland and eventually all of Czechoslovakia. The German military occupied the demilitarized Rhineland in 1935 (D), while Danzig (E) was seized in the opening days of World War II.

46. **(B)** The idea that an elite cadre was necessary to give leadership to the

anticipated revolution was that of V. I. Lenin. For Marx, such a revolution was inevitable as the condition of the working class grew intolerable (A). Since, in Marx's view, the "capitalist class," controlling the "modes" or tools of production, dominated society (C), including government (E), they would not permit the state to aid the working class. "Economic Determinism" (D) is a concept at the core of Marxism.

47. **(D)** France, having constructed the Maginot Line, was inclined to assume a defensive stand in the 1930s. German bitterness of the Treaty, the "Diktat," was deep (A), while the economic failures of the Weimar Republic (B), together with its association with the "Diktat," hurt it in the eyes of the Germans. As the Communist influence arose at the expense of the SDs, many Germans felt the Nazis represented the only alternative (C). Von Papen (E) aided Hitler in gaining the office of chancellor in the belief that he could "control" him.

48. **(B)** Introduced in the face of falling production and popular discontent, the NEP allowed greater economic freedom in the hope of increasing production. The First Five-Year plan (D), linked to the collectivization of agriculture (C) and the effort to expand industry greatly (A), was introduced in the late 1920s by Stalin. The NEP represented a "step back" from nationalization of industry (E).

49. **(A)** He placed great emphasis on man utilizing his inner "will," an intuitive, irrational force. Highly contemptuous of Christian "slave mentality," (B) contemporary moral standards (C), and democracy (D), he called for an elite "superman" who depended on his "will" to lead society (E).

50. **(B)** The war it ended was the "First Opium War," begun when Chinese officials sought to halt the importation of opium. The Russian threat (A) had not yet emerged at the time of the war, while British officials (D) had not yet been permitted to enter Peking. Attacks on Christian missionaries (E) only came later in the 19th century. Piracy was as much a problem for the Chinese as it was for the British (C).

51. **(E)** The pie chart for Great Britain indicates women had not yet broken into the ranks of banking and commerce. In each of the three charts women are seen to represent a factor in all areas except banking and commerce in England.

52. **(B)** Hitler demanded that the large ethnic German population in the Sudentenland be united with Germany. The unification of Germany and Austria (the *Anschluss*) had already occurred (E), as had the occupation of the Rhineland (A). Danzig (D) became the center of a territorial dispute between Germany and Poland in 1939 (C).

53. **(C)** Issued in 1917, it recognized the Zionist aspirations to establish a homeland in the Holy Land. Recognition of the Arab desire for independence (A)

came in the so-called McMahon Letters. The French and British did have territorial interests in the Near East (B), as indicated by the secret Skyes-Picot Treaty (E). Egypt and the Canal (D) were already under British control before the war.

54. **(C)** While Prince Lvov briefly headed the Provisional Government that sought to control Russia following the February Revolution, the figure most closely associated with that failed government was Kerensky. While Lenin (A), together with Trotsky (B) and Stalin (D), were active in this period, they came to real power only with the revolution of October 1917. Kolchak (E) was a leader of one of the anti-Bolshevik White Russian armies.

55. **(B)** The assassination of the archduke and his wife in Sarajevo on June 28, 1914 led to an Austrian ultimatum to Serbia which, in turn, resulted in the outbreak of hostilities. The German invasion of Belgium (A) after the war had started led to England's entry into the conflict. Bosnia-Herzegovina had been annexed earlier (C). Italy joined France (D) in 1915. The Russian and Serbian armies attacked only after the war had broken out (E).

56. **(B)** The British East India Company, which had earlier lost its trade monopoly, was dissolved and replaced by the authority of the British government in those areas it had controlled. The British never formerly annexed all of India (A), many regions remaining under the nominal control of local princes. The cult of Thugge (C) had been eliminated earlier. Indians constituted the bulk of the Indian Army (D) and served in the civil service (E), though not in higher positions.

57. **(E)** With her defeat in the war, Russian interests in the Far East were abandoned for the time being. The Japanese did not annex Manchuria (C) until 1931, while in 1910 they annexed all of Korea (B). Russia had sold Alaska (A) earlier and also acquired the Maritime Provinces (D) from China at an earlier date.

58. **(C)** Alexander II began a series of reforms, including the emancipation of the serfs. Russia had acquired access to the Black Sea earlier (A), in the reign of Catherine the Great, while a Duma (E) was established in 1905. There was no revolution in the years immediately following the Crimean War (B), the first occurring in 1905.

59. **(D)** Social Darwinism tended to be highly nationalistic rather than cosmopolitan. With utilization of the concept of "survival of the fittest" derived from Darwin's theories, all of the other activities mentioned could be justified.

60. **(A)** Oswald Spengler was the German author of *The Decline of the West*, a pessimistic view of the future of Western civilization. Sidney Webb (B) was a British socialist while Karl Peters (C) and Leander Jameson (D) were imperialists in Africa. "Vincenzo" Lombardi (E) is better known as the late Vince Lombardi, noted coach of the Green Bay Packers professional football team.

61. **(A)**   The elections of 1928, prior to the onset of the Depression, saw the Nazis as the smallest party of those represented on the chart; by 1933, they were the largest. A union of all the parties represented on the chart for March 1933 would still not have outvoted the Nazis (B). The major threat to the SDs in the 1920s came either from the Independent Socialists, the Nationalists, or the Nazis (C). The French-Belgian occupation of the Ruhr (D), occurring in 1923, boosted the Communist representation in the Assembly notably, while the Weimar Republic's subsequent economic recovery (E) hurt the Nazis.

62. **(C)**   The Spartacists, led by Rosa Luxemberg, seized control of Berlin for a week in January 1918, hoping to inaugurate the communist revolution in Germany. They were crushed by Frei Korps units. The Frei Korps (A), composed of ex-German soldiers, were largely politically conservative or reactionary. The socialists (B), who gained control of the Weimar Republic from the outset, were anti-communists. The Beer Hall Putsch (D), led by Hitler, was rabidly anti-communist. Bela Kun (E), a communist, was active in Hungary, not Germany.

63. **(A)**   A German philosopher of the early 19th century, Schopenhauer believed man was driven by the "will," an inner, irrational and creative force. Weber (B) and Durkheim (C) were sociologists of the late 19th century, Spenser (E) a strong advocate of Social Darwinism, as was Smiles (D).

64. **(C)**   NATO, the North Atlantic Treaty Organization, was founded in 1949 to protect Europe from Soviet aggression. Following the collapse of the Soviet Union, U.S. President Clinton suggested that NATO provide a collective guarantee against any aggression by one power against another. Though NATO, among other international groups, has sought a solution to the Balkan crisis (A), this was not its founding purpose. Choice (B) is not the best answer because while NATO countries have supplied troops for U.N. missions, such activity is not part of NATO's charter. Choice (D) is incorrect because although NATO members have generally supported human rights, they have usually considered preventing expansion of Soviet influence their primary objective. Finally, NATO nations' support of Israel (E) has been inconsistent, and never part of NATO's overall objective.

65. **(D)**   Serbia was extremely active in stirring up the nationalistic feelings of Serbs living within Austrian territory, an activity that contributed greatly to the coming of World War I. The Czechs were, in fact, more advanced politically than the Serbs (A). Both wanted independence (B) and (E). Germany, as a close ally of the Austrians, was not inclined to support the Slavic Czechs (C).

66. **(C)**   The Sinn Fein, the nationalist party in Ireland, broke out in open revolt at Easter of 1916. It was crushed. All of the other regions remained loyal during the war.

67. **(B)**   The future hope of mankind, Nietzsche believed, lies with the strong-

willed individual who would be guided by his inner, "creative" will. Barth (A), Tillich (E), and Kierkegaard (D) were theologians, while Sartre (C) was a post-World War I exponent of existentialism.

68. **(C)** Heisenberg's "uncertainty principle" stated that no fixed model of the atoms of a given element was possible, only an approximation. The "Big Bang" theory (A) is the result of the work of a number of astronomers, among the earliest of whom were Lemaitre and Gamow, while the same is true of the geological theory of plate tectonics (B)—the German Alfred Lothar Wegener being among the earliest to conceive of Continental drift. Claims as to who has discovered the oldest homonid (D) are contested between several anthropologists. Richard Leakey is among the leading claimants. The first major radio telescope was constructed under the supervision of Sir Bernard Lovell (E).

69. **(B)** Both men, one a Frenchman, the other English, were ardent racists, believing firmly in the superiority of the German "race." Existentialism (A) as a philosophy developed largely after their deaths, as did the Dadaist art movement (E). They wrote little or nothing in the area of economics (C), and they died prior to 1930.

70. **(C)** These are three of the "Fourteen Points" of Woodrow Wilson which he tried to make the basis of the treaty ending World War I. The Atlantic Charter (A) was an agreement stating the vision of the post-war world signed by Churchill and Roosevelt. The Treaty of Versailles (B), ending World War I, did not incorporate any of the Fourteen Points. The McMahon Letters (D) related to Anglo-Arab relations during the First World War, while the Kellogg-Briand Pact (E) was an international agreement of the 1920s.

71. **(D)** De Gaulle came to power in the midst of the bitter conflict between the French and Algerian nationalists. By the time de Gaulle came to power, the French had withdrawn from Indo-China (A), the other questions arose subsequent to his assuming power.

72. **(D)** He envisioned that society was sinking to a level of mediocrity as the vision of mass education set in. The other issues did not greatly concern him or did not reflect the central thrust of his argument.

73. **(D)** These political factions were ardently reactionary and to a degree pro-Nazi. Far to the right, they were opposed to Leon Blum (E), and the leftist Republicans of Spain were inclined to look to Nazi Germany as an ally. They never achieved political power.

74. **(B)** The speech, made by Secretary of State George C. Marshall, marked the inauguration of the idea of the Marshall Plan designed to bring about the economic rehabilitation of Europe following World War II. It was firmly sup-

ported by the other statesmen noted, save Roosevelt, who had died in 1945.

75. **(B)** The men were joint discoverers of the so-called Double Helix. The other scientific discoveries were not associated with Watson and Crick.

76. **(D)** Israel invaded Egypt after Nasser attempted to nationalize the Suez Canal. The invasion was a failure, largely due to the pressure put on the invaders by the United States and the United Nations. The other diplomatic activities on the part of Egypt, while occurring, were not related to the invasion.

77. **(B)** The explosion at the Chernobyl nuclear power plant near Kiev caused Europeans to rethink expansion of nuclear power: One former Soviet scientist, Leonid Toptunov, has reported that more than 600,000 people received high doses of radiation—and their names have been entered in a medical register for the rest of their lives—because of the 1986 accident. Three Mile Island (A), in Middletown, Pa., was the site of a nuclear power plant accident in 1979 that resulted in the release of small amounts of radioactive gases through the plant's venting system and the formation of a hydrogen gas bubble in the reactor's containment vessel. The atomic bombing of Nagasaki and Hiroshima (C), Japan, was carried out by the United States at the end of World War II. In 1984, Bhopal (D), India, was the site of a massive chemical plant explosion and poisonous gas leak.

78. **(D)** This right of intervention was clearly seen in the invasion of Czechoslovakia by the Warsaw Pact States. The idea of assisting communist revolutions around the world (A) has been asserted from an early period, while the idea of communist states having the right to pursue their own path (B), such as Yugoslavia or China, did not set well with most Soviet leaders. Even today, the rights of dissident Jews to emigrate is not wholly free (E).

79. **(C)** The North Koreans launched a surprise attack on the South Koreans. The Chinese entry into the war (A) came only when it had been underway for many months, as did the naming of MacArthur (B) to head the United Nations' forces, which came into the struggle only after it had broken out (D).

80. **(E)** All of these states except Yugoslavia have been invaded by Soviet troops, but in 1956 it was Hungary's turn.

Sample Answer to Document-Based Question

J. A. Hobson, an economist and publicist with a brilliant mind, had a great impact both in his own day and subsequent decades upon the study of Imperialism and its roots. Among those he influenced were V. I. Lenin, who drew upon him heavily for his work *Imperialism, the Highest Stage of Capitalism*, the major Marxian discussion of the subject. However, in his own day and, to a greater extent, in recent years, scholars have raised questions regarding his conclusions. There are to be seen in these documents a number of the assertions, attitudes, and claims held by prominent statesmen and intellectuals of the Age of Imperialism which seem, if not to wholly discredit Hobson's views, to raise questions as to whether they alone can account for the colonial expansion of Europe in the 19th century.

In Document 2 there is seen the assertion by an English official familiar with the colonial scene that the impetus for the penetration of a region did not always come from the European governments themselves: rather, there were native elements within countries or regions that welcomed foreigners. In this case, according to the English official, princes of the Malaysian regions found it desirable to draw upon British expertise in organizing their relatively primitive governments along more efficient lines. It is possible to demonstrate that there were in many other areas of Africa and Asia native elements who found contact with Europeans advantageous. Thus in many lands merchants, seeking to expand their own trade, found in the Europeans a ready market. Document 5 also indicates that it was not always the home government, in this case England, which pushed or even supported the economic penetration of the backward regions: if merchants wished to trade in areas of instability they did so at their own risk and should expect no assistance from their own governments. Admittedly, both documents pre-date the great Age of Imperialism, an age in which, in the wake of intensified economic competition among the major states of Europe, gunboat diplomacy became more common.

Much has been written about the White Man's Burden as a factor in European Imperialism. This concept, eulogized in Kipling's poems (Document 17) held it was a virtual obligation of Westerners, possessing a superior civilization, to bring the benefits of that civilization—or at least those aspects of it that they could absorb—to the backward peoples of Asia and Africa. This moralistic view was early seen in the writings of William Wilberforce, a statesman and humanitarian who had demonstrated his real concern for mankind in his ardent struggle to end slavery in all English holdings and, indeed, worldwide. Certainly many of those Europeans who were involved in the colonial regions of the globe were sincere in their efforts to improve the welfare of their subjects. The activities of the British in India in seeking to eradicate suttee (i.e., widow burning), the cult of thuggee, and to improve food production and health services provides evidence of this. It could be argued, however, that this paternalistic attitude, if beneficent, still maintained the colonial peoples as subjects. Once established in a colony, it was possible to argue, not without some justification, that the continued presence of the civilizing influence of the Europeans was necessary to prevent the natives from falling back into a state of anarchy and near-barbarism (Document 3). Clearly there were those who, opposed to imperialism, questioned this humanitarianism as nothing more than a cloak to conceal more selfish motives. Thus Documents 8 and 13 portray the missionary as little more than the vanguard of a nation's political and economic interests.

It is clear that as the 19th century advanced, this paternalistic attitude for man took a less humane twist as the impact of Social Darwinism was felt. Now, rather than a humanitarian duty, the subjugation of backward peoples was seen as a natural part of the struggle for the survival of the fittest (Documents 9, 14, 15, and 18) in which the needs of the weak need not be taken into consideration. There is evident, too, a strong element of racism, for the white race is destined to triumph over the inferior black and yellow races. In Document 14, there is the suggestion that the struggle in the colonial sphere is also becoming one in which the Western states themselves are in a mounting and, in Social Darwinistic terms, natural struggle in which the stronger, living nations will overcome the weaker, dying Western states.

Clearly it was not always solely or even primarily economic advantages that the colonial powers sought in imposing their rule on the peoples of Asia and Africa. Bases for strategic purposes were often a goal (Documents 4, 10, 16). As the maritime and naval expansion of Europe took place, this became all the more true. While it might be argued that such harbors and fortified sites were utilized to enhance and expand a nation's economic interests, it is also true that they served as protection against potential threats from other European powers. British expansion into the inhospitable and costly Northwest Territories was due more to a perceived threat from Russia to India than from visions of economic gain. Clearly, a Russian foreign minister found it logical to justify his country's expansion into central Asia on the basis of the threat presented by the semi-civilized peoples of that region.

Documents 11, 12, and 19 provide evidence of yet two more explanations which have been advanced to explain, if not justify, Europe's imperialistic surge. Document 11 indicates that Eastern Europe, in the course of the 19th century, experienced a large growth in its population. To the leaders of many of these countries this growth seemed to demand that a safety valve be found for the surplus population. To many the solution lay in the establishment of overseas colonies. This argument was seen in the claims of Cecil Rhodes, virtually the personification of Imperialism (Document 19) and in the claims of many German advocates of colonial expansion that *Lebensraum* (living space) represented a logical solution to their expanding population. Documents 12 and 19 provide yet a second motive for the acquisition of colonies: they were necessary for the economic vitality of the mother country, not solely to provide profits for Hobson's "certain industrial, financial, and professional classes," but, rather, for the working class of the nation in general. It would, in the view of the *Nationalsozialer Verein* Manifesto, contribute to social reform in Germany, while Rhodes, more dramatically, argued that it was the only alternative to civil war in England.

To argue that Hobson was wrong in arguing for the significance of economic factors in the 19th century surge of European Imperialism would be in error, for it is obvious that many of the documents presented here do take note of the role of that factor, even though it might not be the central idea discussed. It would be correct however, as many scholars have done, to insist that to explain a major movement in history such as Imperialism on the basis of mono-causation is in error. Any such movement is the consequence of the interaction of numerous forces. Even where one force such as economics may be of paramount importance, it can and often is multi-faceted: profits derived from the colonial world certainly benefited certain of the capitalist elements in the state: but such prosperity could also serve the interests of the masses and make them no less eager for colonial expansion. Nor is it possible to contend that there were no Imperialists who were not motivated by truly humanitarian sentiments rather than solely visions of profit, or a statesman who was not concerned with the defense of his country rather than financial gain for privileged elements in his nation. Great historical movements are too complex to have simple, singular explanations.

Sample Answers to Essay Questions

1.   The efforts of European princes to bring the affairs of their states more firmly under their control had their origins both in internal elements which constituted, or were seen as constituting disruptive forces threatening their realm's stability and strength and, at the same time, changes in the nature of relations between states.

Internally, many states were, in the wake of the Reformation, confronted with the pressure of religious groups which, although in the minority, were extremely militant in their desire to gain recognition of their particular form of Christianity. France in the mid-16th century had been torn apart by conflicts which, in part, had their origins in the bitter conflict between Calvinist Huguenots and the predominant Catholic population. In the 16th and 17th centuries too, England and Germany endured, to varying degrees, bitter struggles having their roots at least in part in the clash of Catholic and Protestant sects. The answer to many princes was uniformity, the imposition on the state's population of one faith, that of the prince. The dissenters' choices were generally limited—accept the state religion, suffer persecution, or flee. Although Cardinal Richelieu, unable to tolerate the special political and military privileges the Huguenots received as a result of the Edict of Nantes, crushed them on the battlefield, he did not deprive them of their religious rights. Such an act of toleration, however, was relatively rare for the age: King Louis XIV, in persecuting the Huguenots for their religious beliefs, was far closer to the norm. Even the recognized church was sometimes seen as a potential threat: such was the case in France, where the feared loyalty of Catholic ecclesiasts to Rome led to French monarchs seeking to bring their churchmen more firmly under their control in the form of the Gallican Church.

Religious groups were not the only elements in the states of Europe that were seen as threats to stability. The aristocracy of Europe had emerged from the medieval period possessing many privileges and rights which acted as significant obstacles to the exercise of princely power. Jealous of their privileged position, they were determined to retain and, provided the opportunity, to expand it. They were willing to endanger the security of their country in order to do so, as was demonstrated both in the course of the French Religious Wars and, in the mid-17th century, the Fronde, a revolt on the part of aristocratic elements aimed at curtailing the trend toward centralization initiated by Richelieu and Mazarin.

Nor were religious and aristocratic groups the only potentially disruptive elements in society, for in many states there were other virtually autonomous elements enjoying rights which exempted them from the complete control of the state. Such was the case with the Comuneros, an urban bourgeois movement crushed by Charles V, a Hapsburg in 1523.

In addition to the instability generated by various internal forces, changes in the nature of relations between states served to enhance the presumed need for concentrating power in the hands of a central administration, controlled by the prince. Competition become more intense and, for at least a few states, had assumed a "global" nature. If a nation was to survive, much less thrive, it had to be able to defend itself and, if the opportunity presented itself, to take advantage of its neighbors. Such ability was to a large extent dependent on the existence of a strong military establishment. As armies grew larger—Louis XIV maintained a standing army of 400,000—the costs entailed in maintaining them, together with the expense of extensive fortifications, arsenals, supply depots, transportation facilities, and administrative support systems necessary to sustain them increased steadily. This, in turn, demanded more effective control of the state's revenues and, equally important, increasing those revenues as much as possible. The fiscal affairs of the state consequently entailed the expansion and centralization of the necessary organs of state. Moreover, in an age of expanding commercial activities, the economic well-being of the state was seen as requiring close state involvement in every facet of its economic activity. Mercantilism, the economic side of absolutism, was oriented toward strengthening the economic vitality of the state at the expense of one's enemies or possible enemies.

These various threats, internal and external, to the state's well-being led many to conclude that the only solution was to vest ultimate and absolute power in the hands of the prince, one whose concern would be for the welfare of the entire nation, not simply one class or element. Such was the argument advanced by Thomas Hobbes in his *Leviathan*, where he argued that the alternative to placing sovereignty in the hands of one man was, in essence, anarchy. Such was the power Louis XIV envisioned when he proclaimed "I am the state."

2. When one initially contemplates the classes of pre-Revolutionary France there is a tendency to think of the "Three Estates" and to envision each as a monolithic unit, with the attitudes and aspirations of its individual members in

general accord. This was, in fact, not the case. As the Estates General met in the summer of 1789, sharp divisions within each of the estates developed which placed elements of each in disagreement.

The "First Estate," the clergy, is an excellent example of this discord. Constituting one percent of the population, the church held one-third of the land. It was from these, and from the annual tithe imposed upon the annual production of land tilled by laymen, that it derived its major revenues, a yearly income perhaps one-half that of the monarchy. Rather than paying a tax upon this great wealth, the church gave only a "free gift," an insignificant amount in relation to its revenue. Not all clergy enjoyed equal wealth, however, and, far from being a unified group, they were actually splintered into several factions. The primary division was the great prelates—archbishops, bishops, and abbots—and the urban and village priests. Drawn overwhelmingly, if not solely, from the aristocracy, interests of the upper clergies were linked to that class and with the protection of their own privileged position. While there were undoubtedly those who took their ecclesiastical duties seriously, many were content to relegate their duties to subordinates and enjoy the pleasures of Paris or Versailles. The urban and villages curés, in contrast, were drawn from the bourgeoisie. Laboring for their flocks, they were increasingly angered at the lifestyle of the higher clergy and the many abuses they saw. While a majority of the village priests remained committed to the doctrines of the church, many urban priests, having fallen under the influence of the *philosophes* were questioning those doctrines.

The "Second Estate," the aristocracy, was also split into several factions. The Nobles of the Sword, hereditary aristocrats, enjoyed virtual exemption from taxes and held a monopoly on army commissions and high ecclesiastical posts. They desired to retain and expand their privileged status and to extend their political influence. The Nobles of the Robe were aristocrats who had acquired their title through purchase. Generally wealthier than the Nobles of the Sword and holding key government posts, they were among the most ardent defenders of the monarchy and, like their hereditary counterparts, envisioned extending their control over the throne and reenforcing their status. Not all aristocrats were wealthy, for the *hobereaux*, the "little falcons," were little better off than the average peasant. Possessing feudal and manorial rights which permitted them to impose levies on the peasantry, they did so with increasing vigor, to the growing hatred of the peasants.

The "Third Estate," constituting ninety-eight percent of the population, presented the greatest diversity of aspirations and complaints. While the wealthy bourgeoisie, men involved in commerce or the professions, might envision one day entering the ranks of the aristocracy, they, like all bourgeoisie, found the social arrogance of the aristocracy abhorrent. It was among them, and among the middle class, that the criticisms of the *Ancien Régime* and the calls for reform raised by the *philosophes* took hold. The wealth and arrogance of the higher clergy and the aristocrats, the regime's ineffective foreign policy, the presumed corruption of the administration, the inequity of the tax system, the mercantilist and guild systems, even the basic concepts of Christianity were attacked and calls for reform made by them. Well-educated, articulate, and well aware of their significant contribution to the economic life of France, above all they wanted a greater voice in the political life of the country.

The peasantry of France were, on the whole, better off than those elsewhere, serfdom having virtually disappeared in the country. Their complaints, however, were many. A severe land shortage led them to covet the lands of the church and aristocracy. There was anger over an unequal and onerous tax system, with its income, land, and poll taxes and the despised *gabelle* or salt tax, the burden of which fell particularly heavily upon them. Hated even more was the imposition of manorial and feudal levies. While a majority of the peasantry remained loyal to the church and their village priests, they, too, held the higher clergy in contempt. Even those peasants who held land were constantly confronted with the threat of disaster in the face of droughts, while their incomes in the best of times hardly kept up with the rising inflation; for those who had no land, poverty was a constant companion.

For the lower classes in the cities, a group that had not found a collective voice, the complaints were many: low wages, high unemployment, social degradation, and hunger, to name but a few.

The *cahiers*, or list of grievances, drawn up on the eve of the Revolution expressed the wishes of many in society, and particularly the middle class: personal freedom for all citizens, freedom of expression, an end to a harsh and unequal system of justice, a greater voice in the affairs of government. They called for reform of the monarchy, not its overthrow—that would only come later.

3.   Europe, in the summer of 1914, had seen but three major international conflicts in the century since the defeat of Napoleon Bonaparte. These conflicts, the Austro-Prussian, Franco-Prussian, and Crimean Wars had been relatively clean wars—relatively short and characterized more by the glamour of battle—cavalry charges and colorful uniforms—rather than bloodshed. Even the costly futility of the "Charge of the Light Brigade" was surrounded with jingoistic glory rather than the reality of the carnage it represented. Beyond this, the peoples of the major powers knew only of conflicts waged in the remote Balkans or the colonial regions of the world by professional soldiers or backward peoples. Few people, including the professional military, seemed to perceive that the nature of warfare had seen any changes since 1850, changes resulting from the industrialization of Europe, advances in transportation and military technology, the massive mobilization of the manpower of Europe, and the enhanced ability of governments to utilize propaganda to martial the minds and energy of the masses to a cause.

The Industrial Revolution had seen a tremendous increase in the manufacturing capabilities of Europe. This increase was seen not only in consumer goods but in the weapons of war. A true arms race had engulfed the nations of the Continent in the second half of the 19th century as arms, munitions, ever-larger guns and ships rolled off the assembly line. These were readily available to any nation possessing the financial resources to acquire them and believing, rightly or wrongly, that it required them to defend their honor. Moreover, not only were arms in greater supply than ever before, they were of a greater destructive nature than any previously used by man.

Not only were the arms present in abundance, the same was true of the men to use them. Following the Franco-Prussian War many states, emulating the obviously efficient Prussian military system, adopted national military service: the consequence was that by 1914 these states had millions of men under arms or in reserve ready to take up arms.

Beyond the mere presence of millions of men prepared to take up arms, there had come into existence a mind-set which seemed to both justify and indeed glorify war. Drawing upon the doctrines of Social Darwinism, there were those who argued that the battlefield was the ultimate proving ground upon which the merit of men and of their culture was tested: the strong survived, the weak perished. Further, as the people of Europe became more literate and as newspapers—as a consequence of the technological advances such as the rotary press, the linotype, and cheap paper from wood pulp—sprang up in ever increasing numbers, governments were not slow in using them for propaganda purposes. Through the press it was possible to inculcate in the peoples' minds the idea that their nation's cause was always correct. Nationalism, assuming the role of a secular religion, dictated that one must be prepared to fight and, if necessary, die, for the Motherland.

It was with this fanaticism that Germans, Frenchmen, Austrians, Russians, and others, after several decades of international tension, joyously marched to war in August of 1914, determined to defeat the foe in a "short little conflict." The realities of modern warfare quickly became clear: above all was the fact that the defensive tactics and tools of war had negated the possibility of a rapid and successful offensive war. Even a momentary breakthrough of the enemies' lines was rapidly closed as reserve troops could be quickly moved up via railroads to close the breach. As the western front settled down to trench warfare, the machine gun, barbed wire, endless barrages of heavy artillery, and poison gas demonstrated that sheer courage or even manpower could not bring victory: it was a lesson that cost millions of lives. On the eastern front, the Russian fate demonstrated the inadequacy of numbers if a nation lacked the industrial base to support them. Nor were the civilians spared, for even if they were not in the line of march of the armies engaged in battle, they could be made to suffer through blockades of food supplies as the submarines roved the seas or zeppelins or bombers struck from above.

The result was that, rather than the "quick little war" all of the combatants had anticipated, Europe waged a horrible struggle for four years—years which cost ten million and more lives, both military and civilian, billions of dollars in property, and four empires. Victory, if it could be called that, came in the end not, as the result of military triumph on the battlefield, but through attrition.

4.   Initially Portugal, and soon after, Spain, took the lead in overseas exploration in the 14th century, exploration which culminated in the discovery of both an all-water route to the Far East and the New World. Both states enjoyed several advantages arising from their geographical and political circumstances as well as scientific and technological advances achieved by them. To these factors must be added that of strong motivational forces which had their origins in economic and spiritual factors.

Clearly, their geographical location, particularly that of Portugal, provided easy access to the Atlantic and provided greater familiarity with its waters. Geography played a role in that both Iberian states, distant from Venice, which held a virtual monopoly on trade with the Near East, paid a heavy price for items of both a luxury nature and those essentials which were obtained from the Near East and regions further east. In addition to the economic motive, the peoples of Portugal and Spain were driven by an extremely strong one of an ideological nature, that of the spirit of the crusader. For centuries they had been involved in an ongoing crusade against the Moslems for control of their countries. It was only in 1492 that the Spanish, with the fall of the Moslem stronghold of Grenada, had reclaimed their land. This prolonged struggle had several consequences. On one hand it tended to weld the Christians of the two states into a more unified force under their respective monarchs. No less important, it instilled in them the mentality of the crusader: exploration and discovery was, for them, also a mission of faith, an opportunity to hunt down the Moslem—or any non-Christian they might encounter—and convert or destroy them.

Long before the voyages of Vasco da Gama of Portugal, or Spain's Columbus, penetration of the Atlantic had begun. In 1270 the Portuguese seaman Malocello reached the Canaries, while in 1290 the Genoese Dorio and Vivaldo set out to explore the west coast of Africa, a voyage from which they never returned. Knowledge of these earlier activities, together with spiritual, economic, and scientific motives, were clearly united in the person of Prince Henry the Navigator, the third son of King John I of Portugal. A crusader himself, early in the 15th century he established a base at Sagres in southern Portugal, a primitive research and development laboratory: for nearly forty years he dedicated himself to the dual mission of taking the conflict to the Moslems and, closely linked to that mission, exploration of the west coast of Africa. To facilitate this venture he assembled an array of experts in the area of marine science and technology: chart-makers, sea captains, shipbuilders, and instrument makers, men predominantly from Venice and Genoa, but also from Scandinavia—almost certainly drawing upon the knowledge of men of that region regarding the long existing colonies established by Norsemen in Iceland and Greenland and perhaps even the brief effort to establish a colony on the mainland of North America—and Germany, as well as Jewish scholars, Arabs from North Africa, and native tribesmen from West Africa. Under Prince Henry's leadership these men assembled a pool of knowledge regarding the waters about Africa, and began to construct superior navigation instruments and a better type of sea-going vessel, the caraval. Most important, Prince Henry regularly dispatched his sea captains to penetrate the waters of the Atlantic. In 1418 the Madeira Islands and in 1427 the Azores were discovered. His seamen also began to gradually make their way down the west coast of Africa: in 1433 Cape Bojador was reached and, in 1445, Cape Verde. These discoveries resulted in the establishment of a brisk trade with the region. Before his death in 1460 his seamen had sailed as far as the Senegal and Gambia rivers and discovered the Cape Verde Islands. Portuguese exploration continued after his death and, by 1488, Bartolomeu Dias reached the Cape of Good Hope at the southernmost tip of Africa. Nine years later Vasco da Gama sailed to Calicut on the Malabar Coast of India and, by 1513, Portuguese merchant seamen were penetrating the Spice Islands of the East Indies and had reached Canton in China. By this time, of course, the voyage of Columbus for Spain had revealed a "New World" to the West. There is some evidence, by no means conclusive, that seamen sailing for Portugal, sailed to Greenland and perhaps Newfoundland as early as the 1470s, and perhaps to Brazil by that time or even earlier.

The advantages of location and motive were not the only ones enjoyed by the peoples of the Iberian Peninsula. They were early unified states and, as such, able to throw more firmly the support of the government behind the effort to explore, as seen in the activities of Prince Henry, and Queen Isabella of Spain's support of Columbus. In sharp contrast, the other main regions of Western Europe were involved in either internal conflict or wars among themselves. The Hundred Years' War raged between France and England until 1453, after which France was occupied first, with rebuilding its strength, and then conflicts in Italy and internal religious strife throughout much of the 16th century. Meanwhile, England was first plunged into the War of the Roses and then had problems related to its own Reformation. Germany and Italy, lacking unity and frequently involved in wars and the interference of the more powerful states, were in no position to exploit the opportunities that had been revealed by the Portuguese and Spanish, while Holland, England and France could do so gradually. By that time Spain and Portugal had established vast overseas empires.

5.   At the heart of Marx's concept of history was the theory of economic determinism: it was the economic structure of a given society and, more important, who controls the means of production that determined its religious, artistic, and political orientation: its superstructure—its intellectual, cultural, and political concepts—were designed to serve and protect the interests of those who controlled the all-important economic substructure. History, he contended, had passed through several phases which had seen society based primarily upon slave labor and then upon the labor of serfs. History, he argued, was the unveiling of "class struggle," the struggle between those who controlled the means of production and those whose labor they exploited. In his day, he held, in a number of states as well—at least in those which had become industrialized—that society's economic foundation was built upon industrial "wage slaves" who were increasingly controlled and exploited by the capitalist class.

In this industrial society, he maintained, it was inconceivable that governments would act on behalf of the working class, for governments were simply a derivative of the economic foundation and under the thumb of that segment of society which controlled that base—in this case the capitalist. Clearly, he held, for the capitalist class to permit governments to act in the interests of the workers, and thus against their own, was inconceivable. The condition of the wage slave, already wretched, would grow worse as the capitalist class, seeking to maintain and enhance their own profits in an increasingly competitive world, would steadily exploit the workers more and more. Further, the ranks of the middle class would be steadily thinned as, losing in the struggle to obtain a share of the ever-diminishing profits available, they were themselves driven down to the status of wage slaves. When the conditions of the working class became intolerable, they would rise in a great, violent revolution, overthrowing the capitalist class, and take into their own hands possession of the modes of production (i.e., the machines and tools of industry). At this point in time a one class society or, in Marx's terms, a classless society would come into existence and, as there was no longer a ruling class requiring coercion, the state would also cease to exist: mankind would enter a golden age characterized only by material abundance and the elimination of crime, greed, and war.

Marx's vision of the future appealed to many, worker and intellectual alike, and as it gained dedicated followers, terrified the middle and upper classes and the governments of most nations. Yet it became clear that the historical developments which Marx held to be inevitable were not occurring. Governments—or at least significant elements within them—did begin to intervene on the behalf of the working class. In England this was due to a number of different factors. The development of a two-party system, each party competing for votes, saw a gradual extension of the franchise to an ever larger percentage of the population. Beginning in 1832, fifteen years before publication of *The Communist Manifesto* and thirty-five years before *Das Kapital*, this trend was applied to the middle class and by the early 1900s virtually every adult male had the right to vote. No less important, the working class, forming political parties, gained an increasing voice in Parliament, thus allowing pressure for the enactment of pro-labor legislature. Long before this, however, numerous laws were passed which served to ease the admittedly wretched conditions of the working classes in the early stages of the Industrial Revolution. Whether these reforms stemmed from truly humanitarian motives, elements within the "ruling class," or from clashes of interest among that class—as between the landowners and industrialists—the state did intervene. In Germany, Bismarck, concerned over the perceived threat of socialism, created the first state socialism from above. While state intervention came slowly and often begrudgingly, it did come and, moreover, the condition of the working class in much of western Europe gradually improved while the ranks of the middle class, rather than thinning, expanded.

In the face of the seeming failure of Marx's predictions as to the fate of the industrial-capitalistic states, Marxists and others sought an explanation. The most ardently argued was that through the exploitation of colonial peoples—imperialism—capitalism gained exorbitant profits, some of which were allowed to sift down to the working class, easing their condition and temporarily, but only temporarily, delaying the inevitable workers' revolution. The merits of this argument are still debated by Marxists and non-Marxists alike. Perhaps the most obvious failure of Marx's prophecies was the fact that when the workers' revolution did occur, it was in a state with little industrial development and that the state, far from withering away, became stronger, indeed, totalitarian, with a clear ruling class—the Communist elite.

6.　From the Scientific Revolution of the 16th and 17th centuries onward, European society had witnessed the steady expansion of man's knowledge of the physical world about him and, through the technological application of this knowledge, of his material world. While there had been those, such as the romantics of the early 19th century, who had questioned the true worth of reason as against the sentiments found in the heart and expressed alarm over the dehumanization of the individual, science and technology continued to advance even more rapidly and, in so doing altered the face of much of Western Europe and, at the same time, brought marked changes in the social structure and intellectual atmosphere of that region. These advances, bringing increasing creature comfort and economic betterment, an economic betterment that even encompassed increasing numbers of the working classes, seemed to reinforce the vision of the 18th century *philosophes* in the unending progress to be achieved through the application of reason and the tools of science.

As the 19th century drew to a close there were those who, if not questioning the achievements of science and technology in the past, or doubting that in the future they would continue to expand man's knowledge and benefit him and society materially, challenged what they saw as an extension of science into areas outside its proper sphere—areas related to human activities. Not unlike the romantics, they opposed what they saw as the virtual deification of science and reason and the deterministic, mechanistic concept of the universe—and man—the scientist seemed to be erecting. The impact of industrialization, urbanization, and capitalism were also seen as but a few of the elements of the age which were serving to subordinate the individual in the morass of the masses of industrial society, and to remove the human element from culture. The era of the *fin de si`ecle* saw those who sought to point out this peril and, in some cases, provide alternatives.

Friedrich Nietzche held that the masses possessed a "herd mentality," were ensnared by Christianity, (a "slave religion"), traditional morality, and bourgeois materialism, and were unable to break free of the decadent cultural malaise of mediocrity of the age. A basic cause of this decadence, he maintained, was the excessive development of the rational faculty at the expense of a creativity which he felt came only from the spontaneity of intuition or "will," a malady he traced back to Socrates and Plato. The hope for the future, he felt, rested in those superior individuals who, drawing upon an "inner will to power," an inner, primitive life force, could free himself of the bonds of slave morality and reason and release a fundamental, inner creativity.

A similar vision of an inner, non-rational, intuitive life force was to be seen in the *élan vital* of Henri Bergson, a vital impetus which he perceived as a non-mechanistic explanation for mankind's evolution in the past and the true hope for future progress. Samuel Butler, seeing science as having evolved into a virtual religion dominated by priest-like scientists, spoke of free will, spontaneity, and cunning—in a force having its origin not in man's consciousness or reason but in an inner spiritual subconscious level of man's mind, as the truly creative force advancing civilization.

This perception of man being driven by irrational, animal forces, having their roots in its subconscious being, appeared to receive scientific support in the work of Darwin, with his emphasis upon man's primitive, animal origins. Even more so, Sigmund Freud, in arguing that man's consciousness—rationality as traditionally understood—was hardly more than veneer concealing a subconscious world of repressed sexuality and neuroses of which he had little or no knowledge or control, reinforced the vision of man's fundamental irrationality.

Science itself was advancing theories which tended to disturb the stable, orderly Newtonian "world machine" which for nearly two centuries had constituted a basic cornerstone in man's vision of the universe. The work of Einstein, Planck, and Heisenberg served to alter, if not destroy, the perception of absolutes which man had come to believe existed on the basis of classical Newtonian physics: space, time, motion, and matter became less certain in the mind of man, as did science's ability to ever find absolute solutions in all spheres of knowledge.

The doubts raised regarding the true merit of reason as a beneficial guide for civilization and, indeed, whether man was in fact, truly rational, gave rise to new literary and artistic schools which sought to penetrate and reveal the subconscious, inner reality of the human spirit. It contributed, too, although it was not the sole source, to the new totalitarian political concepts, as seen in the Nazi utilization of their grossly distorted version of Nietzche's superman.

THE ADVANCED
PLACEMENT EXAMINATION IN

European
History

TEST 6

THE ADVANCED PLACEMENT EXAMINATION IN

European History

TEST 6

1. Ⓐ Ⓑ Ⓒ Ⓓ Ⓔ
2. Ⓐ Ⓑ Ⓒ Ⓓ Ⓔ
3. Ⓐ Ⓑ Ⓒ Ⓓ Ⓔ
4. Ⓐ Ⓑ Ⓒ Ⓓ Ⓔ
5. Ⓐ Ⓑ Ⓒ Ⓓ Ⓔ
6. Ⓐ Ⓑ Ⓒ Ⓓ Ⓔ
7. Ⓐ Ⓑ Ⓒ Ⓓ Ⓔ
8. Ⓐ Ⓑ Ⓒ Ⓓ Ⓔ
9. Ⓐ Ⓑ Ⓒ Ⓓ Ⓔ
10. Ⓐ Ⓑ Ⓒ Ⓓ Ⓔ
11. Ⓐ Ⓑ Ⓒ Ⓓ Ⓔ
12. Ⓐ Ⓑ Ⓒ Ⓓ Ⓔ
13. Ⓐ Ⓑ Ⓒ Ⓓ Ⓔ
14. Ⓐ Ⓑ Ⓒ Ⓓ Ⓔ
15. Ⓐ Ⓑ Ⓒ Ⓓ Ⓔ
16. Ⓐ Ⓑ Ⓒ Ⓓ Ⓔ
17. Ⓐ Ⓑ Ⓒ Ⓓ Ⓔ
18. Ⓐ Ⓑ Ⓒ Ⓓ Ⓔ
19. Ⓐ Ⓑ Ⓒ Ⓓ Ⓔ
20. Ⓐ Ⓑ Ⓒ Ⓓ Ⓔ
21. Ⓐ Ⓑ Ⓒ Ⓓ Ⓔ
22. Ⓐ Ⓑ Ⓒ Ⓓ Ⓔ
23. Ⓐ Ⓑ Ⓒ Ⓓ Ⓔ
24. Ⓐ Ⓑ Ⓒ Ⓓ Ⓔ
25. Ⓐ Ⓑ Ⓒ Ⓓ Ⓔ

26. Ⓐ Ⓑ Ⓒ Ⓓ Ⓔ
27. Ⓐ Ⓑ Ⓒ Ⓓ Ⓔ
28. Ⓐ Ⓑ Ⓒ Ⓓ Ⓔ
29. Ⓐ Ⓑ Ⓒ Ⓓ Ⓔ
30. Ⓐ Ⓑ Ⓒ Ⓓ Ⓔ
31. Ⓐ Ⓑ Ⓒ Ⓓ Ⓔ
32. Ⓐ Ⓑ Ⓒ Ⓓ Ⓔ
33. Ⓐ Ⓑ Ⓒ Ⓓ Ⓔ
34. Ⓐ Ⓑ Ⓒ Ⓓ Ⓔ
35. Ⓐ Ⓑ Ⓒ Ⓓ Ⓔ
36. Ⓐ Ⓑ Ⓒ Ⓓ Ⓔ
37. Ⓐ Ⓑ Ⓒ Ⓓ Ⓔ
38. Ⓐ Ⓑ Ⓒ Ⓓ Ⓔ
39. Ⓐ Ⓑ Ⓒ Ⓓ Ⓔ
40. Ⓐ Ⓑ Ⓒ Ⓓ Ⓔ
41. Ⓐ Ⓑ Ⓒ Ⓓ Ⓔ
42. Ⓐ Ⓑ Ⓒ Ⓓ Ⓔ
43. Ⓐ Ⓑ Ⓒ Ⓓ Ⓔ
44. Ⓐ Ⓑ Ⓒ Ⓓ Ⓔ
45. Ⓐ Ⓑ Ⓒ Ⓓ Ⓔ
46. Ⓐ Ⓑ Ⓒ Ⓓ Ⓔ
47. Ⓐ Ⓑ Ⓒ Ⓓ Ⓔ
48. Ⓐ Ⓑ Ⓒ Ⓓ Ⓔ
49. Ⓐ Ⓑ Ⓒ Ⓓ Ⓔ
50. Ⓐ Ⓑ Ⓒ Ⓓ Ⓔ
51. Ⓐ Ⓑ Ⓒ Ⓓ Ⓔ
52. Ⓐ Ⓑ Ⓒ Ⓓ Ⓔ
53. Ⓐ Ⓑ Ⓒ Ⓓ Ⓔ
54. Ⓐ Ⓑ Ⓒ Ⓓ Ⓔ
55. Ⓐ Ⓑ Ⓒ Ⓓ Ⓔ

56. Ⓐ Ⓑ Ⓒ Ⓓ Ⓔ
57. Ⓐ Ⓑ Ⓒ Ⓓ Ⓔ
58. Ⓐ Ⓑ Ⓒ Ⓓ Ⓔ
59. Ⓐ Ⓑ Ⓒ Ⓓ Ⓔ
60. Ⓐ Ⓑ Ⓒ Ⓓ Ⓔ
61. Ⓐ Ⓑ Ⓒ Ⓓ Ⓔ
62. Ⓐ Ⓑ Ⓒ Ⓓ Ⓔ
63. Ⓐ Ⓑ Ⓒ Ⓓ Ⓔ
64. Ⓐ Ⓑ Ⓒ Ⓓ Ⓔ
65. Ⓐ Ⓑ Ⓒ Ⓓ Ⓔ
66. Ⓐ Ⓑ Ⓒ Ⓓ Ⓔ
67. Ⓐ Ⓑ Ⓒ Ⓓ Ⓔ
68. Ⓐ Ⓑ Ⓒ Ⓓ Ⓔ
69. Ⓐ Ⓑ Ⓒ Ⓓ Ⓔ
70. Ⓐ Ⓑ Ⓒ Ⓓ Ⓔ
71. Ⓐ Ⓑ Ⓒ Ⓓ Ⓔ
72. Ⓐ Ⓑ Ⓒ Ⓓ Ⓔ
73. Ⓐ Ⓑ Ⓒ Ⓓ Ⓔ
74. Ⓐ Ⓑ Ⓒ Ⓓ Ⓔ
75. Ⓐ Ⓑ Ⓒ Ⓓ Ⓔ
76. Ⓐ Ⓑ Ⓒ Ⓓ Ⓔ
77. Ⓐ Ⓑ Ⓒ Ⓓ Ⓔ
78. Ⓐ Ⓑ Ⓒ Ⓓ Ⓔ
79. Ⓐ Ⓑ Ⓒ Ⓓ Ⓔ
80. Ⓐ Ⓑ Ⓒ Ⓓ Ⓔ

European History
TEST 6 – Section I

TIME: 55 Minutes
80 Questions

DIRECTIONS: Each of the questions or incomplete statements below is followed by five suggested answers or completions. Select the one that is best in each case.

---

1.   The Northern Renaissance differed from the Renaissance in Italy in that

   (A)   it lacked the strong financial foundation provided by the city-states of Italy.

   (B)   while attaining triumphs in the architectural area, it did not demonstrate the artistic glory seen in the south.

   (C)   it placed a greater emphasis upon religious piety.

   (D)   it drew more heavily on the Byzantine tradition via contacts with the Russian Orthodox Church.

   (E)   it reflected more strongly the influence of contacts with the civilizations of the New World.

2.   "...It is, then, much safer to be feared than to be loved ...for touching human nature, we may say in general that men are untruthful, unconstant, dissemblers, they avoid dangers and are covetous of gain. While you do them good, they are wholly yours... but when (danger) approaches, they revolt."

   Such was the lesson taught to rulers by

   (A)   Lorenzo Valla.   (D)   Hugo Grotius.

   (B)   Machiavelli.   (E)   Johan Huizinga.

   (C)   Montaigne.

3. The monarch who, by invading Italy in the 1490s, upset the balance of power in that region was

    (A) Charles V Hapsburg.   (D) Ferdinand of Spain.

    (B) Henry VII of England.   (E) Suleiman the Magnificent.

    (C) Charles VIII of France.

4. As a consequence of the English War of the Roses

    (A) English territorial holdings in France were lost.

    (B) Anglicanism was proclaimed the state religion.

    (C) the Tudor dynasty came to the throne.

    (D) monasticism in England was abolished.

    (E) the kingdoms of England and Scotland were unified.

5. The specific abuse that Luther addressed in his "Ninety-Five Theses" was

    (A) simony.

    (B) the sale of indulgences.

    (C) clerical marriage.

    (D) lay investiture.

    (E) recognition of secular authority.

6. All of the following were factors in the success of Luther's religious movement EXCEPT

    (A) the printing press.

    (B) German nationalism.

    (C) his alliance with German princes.

    (D) widespread concern in Germany over the political intentions of the Hapsburg emperor.

    (E) his support of the new concepts of the universe resulting from the ideas of Copernicus and other scientists.

7.   The basic idea of mercantilism was

   (A)   to acquire colonies.

   (B)   the promotion of social welfare through increased economic activity.

   (C)   to gain access to raw materials.

   (D)   the maintenance of a favorable balance of trade in order to increase the country's holdings in gold and silver.

   (E)   pursuit of a policy of *laissez faire* to maintain an equitable balance of trade.

8.   Perhaps the most significant reason for the weakness of New France in comparison with the British holdings in North America was that

   (A)   the Indian tribes tended to be much more favorably inclined to the British.

   (B)   the population of England was much larger, permitting more settlers to migrate to its New World colonies.

   (C)   the French government maintained a highly restrictive immigration policy.

   (D)   French explorers failed to penetrate the interior and construct forts.

   (E)   the ardent missionary activities of French missionaries alienated the Indians.

9.   Under the domestic system in England

   (A)   shipbuilding was made a state monopoly.

   (B)   spinning and weaving of yarn and cloth was done in the workers' homes.

   (C)   factory workers were prohibited from joining unions.

   (D)   farmers expanded the use of crop rotation and fertilization.

   (E)   the immigration of foreign workers was expanded to take advantage of the skills of French textile workers.

10.   The *Asiento*, granted to the English in the Peace of Utrecht, gave them

   (A)   possession of Gibraltar.

(B)   the exclusive right to sell African slaves in the Spanish colonies of the New World.

(C)   permission to trade freely in the Spanish islands of the Caribbean.

(D)   the French island of Guadaloupe.

(E)   the territory of Florida.

FRANCE

11.   The map of France above, showing the boundaries of the local governments together with that country's immediate neighbors, would have been familiar to which of the monarchs listed below?

(A)   Louis XIV   (D)   Louis Napoleon III

(B)   Louis Philippe   (E)   Henry IV

(C)   Napoleon Bonaparte

12. Holding that man's life in a "state of nature" was "solitary, poor, nasty, brutish, and short, strong," absolutistic government (to bring order out of chaos) was advocated by

    (A) Thomas Hobbes.

    (B) John Milton.

    (C) William Blackstone.

    (D) Baron d'Holbach.

    (E) Jacques Bossuet.

13. All of the following states were militarily involved in the Thirty Years' War EXCEPT

    (A) Sweden.

    (B) Austria.

    (C) France.

    (D) Denmark.

    (E) England.

14. As a consequence of the Great Northern War, Peter the Great

    (A) replaced his insane half-brother Feodor as czar of Russia.

    (B) drove the Turks from the northern shores of the Black Sea.

    (C) extended Russian holdings into central Siberia.

    (D) gave Russia a "window to the West" on the Baltic Sea.

    (E) destroyed the political influence of the *streltsy* and Old Believers religious sect.

15. One of the main failures of the Peace of Augsburg (1555) was

    (A) it left Italy disunited and a prey of the great powers.

    (B) it did not provide for recognition of the Calvinists.

    (C) by recognizing the rights of the Anabaptist, it introduced a radical religious faction into Germany.

    (D) it allowed France too many special privileges in Germany.

    (E) the powers of the emperor were not clarified.

16. The theory of the separation of powers was most clearly enunciated in the works of

    (A) Voltaire.

    (B) Montesquieu.

(C)   Jean Jacques Rousseau.   (D)   John Locke.

(E)   Thomas Hobbes.

17.   While "Puritanism" encompassed a number of religious groups, its core was based upon the doctrines of

(A)   Martin Luther.   (D)   John Huss.

(B)   Jacob Hutter.   (E)   Michael Servetus.

(C)   Zwingli and Calvin.

18.   The second enclosure movement, occurring in England in the 18th century, was designed to

(A)   stimulate the growth of industrialization.

(B)   strengthen the mining industry.

(C)   replenish the forests of the country.

(D)   increase and consolidate crop lands.

(E)   expand lands available for sheep-raising.

19.   The map below indicates that

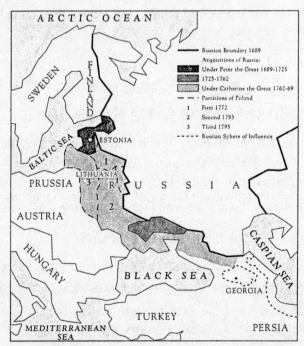

(A) prior to the reign of Peter the Great, Russia was completely shut off from access to the open seas.

(B) prior to 1800, the greatest acquisition of territory occurred during the reign of Catherine the Great.

(C) during the reign of Peter the Great, Russia gained access to the waters of the Mediterranean Sea.

(D) Peter the Great's expansion in the south was limited to the establishment of ports on the Black Sea.

(E) the partitions of Poland saw Russia gain the greatest share of the spoils.

20. A vocal element in the French Revolution, the *sans-culottes* were

(A) impoverished peasants.

(B) the urban and village priests.

(C) the urban working class.

(D) nobles forced to flee to the safety of the German states.

(E) opponents of the Civil Constitution of the Clergy.

21. Those members of the Estates General who took the famous Tennis Court Oath swore to

(A) overthrow Louis XVI.

(B) establish a republic.

(C) draft a constitution for France.

(D) break the ties between the French church and the papacy.

(E) establish the principle of complete religious toleration in France.

22. Obsessed with the idea of his sinfulness, Luther finally came to the conclusion that

(A) salvation was to be found in good works.

(B) it was by faith, and faith alone, that humans can be justified in the sight of God.

(C) as Christ had humbled himself on the cross, so man must humble himself in life to attain benefits in afterlife.

(D)   the sacraments of Baptism and the Eucharist were instruments essential to obtaining God's grace.

(E)   without absolute adherence to the guidance provided by the clergy, man had no hope of salvation.

23.   Which of the following statements is FALSE? Scientific research conducted in the 17th and 18th centuries

(A)   assumed an international scope as governments supported scientific inquiry, hoping new discoveries would have immediate and practical application.

(B)   laid firm foundations in physics, chemistry and medicine as independent and rapidly expanding disciplines.

(C)   was centered primarily in the major universities, which were richly endowed by merchants and entrepreneurs.

(D)   was stimulated by the belief that the comprehension of and harnessing of the laws of nature would benefit mankind.

(E)   received the encouragement of rulers who saw the practical value of discoveries to the mercantilistic policies of their states.

24.   The Thirty Years' War was brought to an end by the

(A)   Battle of White Mountain.   (D)   Edict of Restitution.

(B)   Treaty of Tilsit.   (E)   Treaty of Westphalia.

(C)   death of Gustavus Adolphus.

25.   The battle waged between Generals Wolfe and Montcalm on the Plains of Abraham determined

(A)   that the Stuart dynasty would never again rule England.

(B)   the fate of France's North American empire.

(C)   that Austria had lost control of Silesia to the Prussians.

(D)   the ultimate victor in the War of the Spanish Succession.

(E)   whether France or Great Britain would have paramount influence in India.

26. All of the following statements are in accord with the theories of the Deists EXCEPT

(A) absolute standards of good and evil do not exist: good simply results in pleasure, evil in pain.

(B) God does not respond to individual petitions to intervene with the laws of nature on their behalf.

(C) God should be perceived as the prime mover, the source of the laws of nature which are comprehensible to the mind of man.

(D) the concept of divine predestination is in opposition to the human dignity reason bestows upon the individual.

(E) the individual possesses the freedom and rational ability to determine what is good and evil and to choose between them.

27. Ecumenicism, which has characterized the Catholic Church since the Second Vatican Council in 1963, is best described as

(A) a call for dogmatic adherence to church teachings.

(B) increasing evangelic activity.

(C) tolerance among Christians.

(D) constituting missionary work.

(E) encouraging less church involvement in politics.

28. An important source of labor for the new factories of an industrialized England was the

(A) consequence of the abolition of serfdom.

(B) importation of slaves.

(C) influx of new immigrants.

(D) workers left unemployed as a result of the second enclosure movement.

(E) indentured laborers.

29. The Portuguese gained control of Brazil as a colony as a consequence of

    (A) the need for it as a base on the route to India.

    (B) the Treaty of Tordesillas.

    (C) the fact that the Spanish mistakenly believed it to be of no value.

    (D) Spain ceding it to Portugal in return for the Philippine Islands.

    (E) the Treaty of Utrecht.

30. The English Navigation Acts were designed to

    (A) restrict the number of vessels constructed to prevent overbuilding.

    (B) establish regulations for safer travel.

    (C) ensure that vessels carried sufficient insurance to safeguard investors.

    (D) weaken Dutch trade and encourage that of England.

    (E) permit English ships to violate the monopolistic practices of the Spanish.

31. Which of the following statements about the mid-18th century is most accurate?

    (A) The British controlled the trade in all of India.

    (B) The Chinese had begun to realize the technological advantages enjoyed by the West.

    (C) The Moslems had begun to enjoy a political renaissance.

    (D) The English had begun to break into the monopoly that the Spanish had previously enjoyed in Japan.

    (E) West African rulers prevented European control of the slave trade in Africa.

32. Russian national development was thwarted for two centuries by

    (A) disunity among the various branches of the Russian people.

    (B) the subjection to the Ottoman Turks.

    (C) the Golden Horde.

    (D) the excessive influence of the Russian Orthodox Church.

    (E) the domination of the Teutonic Knights.

33. The Royal Society of London is most logically associated with

    (A) the Scientific Revolution.

    (B) James II Stuart of England.

    (C) efforts to bring the Christian faith to the natives of Africa.

    (D) financing the establishment of colonial settlements in British North America.

    (E) supporting commercial activities in the Far East.

34. "It appears then that wages are subject to a rise or fall from two causes: First, the supply and demand of labourers. Secondly, the price of the commodities on which the wages of labour are expanded...With a population pressing against the means of subsistence, the only remedies are either a reduction of people or a more rapid accumulation of capital."

    These words are best associated with

    (A) Jeremy Bentham.   (D) Robert Peel.

    (B) David Ricardo.   (E) David Hume.

    (C) Robert Owen.

35. The Levellers were

    (A) anti-industrial woolen weavers deprived of their jobs by mechanization.

    (B) radical religious revolutionaries of the 17th century who sought social and political reform.

    (C) landowners in 19th century England opposed to the imposition of duties on imported grain.

    (D) followers of Gracchus Babeuf.

    (E) the armed supporters of Oliver Cromwell.

36. Historical research indicates that the long-term consequence of the Industrial Revolution for the working class was to

    (A) reduce their standard of living by removing them from their agricultural roots.

    (B) increase the length of their workday.

    (C) reduce the financial contribution of women to the family income.

    (D) increase their standard of living.

    (E) leave their standard of living at about the same level, but deprive them of the advantages provided by rural life.

37. Catherine the Great

    (A) introduced reforms easing the burden on the serfs.

    (B) inaugurated the Slavophile movement.

    (C) annexed the Maritime Provinces of Manchu China.

    (D) extended Russia's territorial holdings at the expense of the Crimean Tatar.

    (E) reduced the power of the nobility.

38. All of the following were causes of Gorbachev's reform of the Soviet Union EXCEPT

   (A) Environmental problems

   (B) Increasing health problems among Soviet citizens

   (C) Decline in industrial production

   (D) Increasing oil prices

   (E) Over-centralization of the economy

39. Edmund Burke

   (A) believed that revolutionary change would benefit all people.

   (B) strongly advocated the use of military force to crush the American Revolution.

   (C) proposed uprooting political institutions that were not as useful as they had been in the past.

   (D) advocated evolution rather than revolution.

   (E) in 1783 wrote his *Reflections* on the American Revolution.

40. The most dominant figure at the Congress of Vienna was

   (A) Talleyrand.   (D) Czar Alexander II.

   (B) Metternich.   (E) Baron von Stein.

   (C) Viscount Castlereagh.

41. The most serious error made by the statesmen assembled at the Congress of Vienna was

   (A) initiating a conflict with the Ottoman Turks.

   (B) restoring Louis XVIII to the throne of France.

   (C) ignoring the nationalistic and democratic sentiments alive in Europe.

    (D)   ceding Denmark to Norway.

    (E)   imposing the Carlsbad Decrees on Prussia.

42.   Czar Alexander II undertook all of the following reforms EXCEPT

    (A)   emancipation of the serfs.

    (B)   establishment of a national Duma or Parliament.

    (C)   relaxation of press censorship.

    (D)   the creation of local *zemstovos* or provincial assemblies.

    (E)   expansion of educational opportunities.

43.   A common element among the revolutionary movements that swept through Europe in 1848 was

    (A)   unity of purpose among middle-class liberals and urban workers.

    (B)   rejection of ethnic rivalry in the name of nationalistic aspirations.

    (C)   coordinated and timely action on the part of experienced leaders.

    (D)   initial success as a result of the hesitation of governmental leaders to use their superior forces.

    (E)   no fear of the intervention of external, foreign forces.

44.   The reign of Napoleon III ended when he

    (A)   was forced to resign as a consequence of his Mexican fiasco.

    (B)   was driven from France in the wake of the violence of the Paris Commune of 1871.

    (C)   was assassinated in 1870.

    (D)   surrendered to Prussian troops at Sedan.

    (E)   allowed the British to gain control of the Suez Canal.

45. In 1902, in response to what it viewed as threats to its colonial interests, Great Britain entered into a defensive alliance with

    (A) Italy.   (D) France.

    (B) Russia.   (E) Germany.

    (C) Japan.

46. All of the following statements about the outset of World War I are true EXCEPT

    (A) the idea of conflict was enthusiastically received by the general public in all lands.

    (B) few, including military men, anticipated the nature of the war that erupted.

    (C) socialist politicians in every country opposed their governments' decision to enter the war.

    (D) each side was convinced its cause was just.

    (E) the Austrian effort was hampered by ethnic disunity.

47. The political cartoon illustrated below, appearing in a French newspaper of 1902, suggests

    (A) Japan's military aggression in China was a threat to Western economic interests.

    (B) China was a target of Russian imperialism.

    (C)   Japan was running a great risk challenging Russian power in the Far East.

    (D)   Russia was planning to invade Japan.

    (E)   an alliance between Japan and Russia would threaten French interests in China.

48.   World War I saw the use of all the following weapons of war EXCEPT

    (A)   machine guns.   (D)   incendiary bombs.

    (B)   flame throwers.   (E)   tanks.

    (C)   poison gas.

49.   A powerful pacificistic work, the horrendous nature of warfare in the First World War was depicted in a famous novel by

    (A)   Günter Grass.   (D)   Arthur Koestler.

    (B)   John Steinbeck.   (E)   Erich Maria Remarque.

    (C)   D.H. Lawrence.

50.   Which of the following statements about totalitarianism is FALSE?

    (A)   It frequently had a cult leader as head of state.

    (B)   It demanded absolute commitment to its ideology.

    (C)   It had no connections with 19th century ideologies.

    (D)   Extreme nationalism was a primary element of its ideology.

    (E)   Its political structure was monolithic, one party alone being tolerated.

51.   War "as an instrument of national policy" was renounced by those nations that signed the

    (A)   Locarno Treaties.   (D)   Lytton Commission Report.

    (B)   Kellogg-Briand Pact.   (E)   Treaty of Rapallo.

    (C)   Versailles Peace Treaty.

52. The Truman Doctrine was designed to

    (A) assist in the economic reconstruction of post-World War II Japan.

    (B) assist with military advisors and aid any country threatened by communism.

    (C) prevent a conflict between Greece and Turkey as a consequence of their dispute over Cyprus.

    (D) supply and maintain direct contact with Berlin during the blockade of that city by the Russians from June 1948 to May 1949.

    (E) seek a peaceful solution to the conflict between India and Pakistan over Kashmir.

53. The Mau Mau were

    (A) fanatical anti-Zionist followers of the Grand Mufti of Jerusalem.

    (B) Basque separatists using terrorist tactics against the post-Franco government of Spain.

    (C) a terrorist government fighting the British in Kenya.

    (D) followers of the Congolese radical Patrice Lamumba.

    (E) early opponents of the policy of apartheid in South Africa.

54. All of the following nations have had a woman as head of state since World War II EXCEPT

    (A) India.   (D) Pakistan.

    (B) England.   (E) Israel.

    (C) France.

55. All of the following statements regarding Great Britain's economic status following World War I are true EXCEPT that

    (A) many of her overseas investments had been liquidated.

    (B) her industrial plant was growing antiquated.

    (C) as a result of immigration, she experienced a labor shortage.

    (D) there was a sharp rise in the cost of living.

    (E) the United States, Canada, and Germany were strong industrial rivals.

56. The late former President François Mitterand of France was a member of what political party?

(A) Conservative

(B) Labor

(C) Communist

(D) Socialist

(E) Christian Democratic

57. "Take up the White Man's burden
Send forth the best you breed
Go bind your sons to exile
To serve your captives' need"

Thus wrote the poet laureate of imperialism,

(A) Cecil Rhodes.   (D) W.B. Yeats.

(B) Rudyard Kipling.   (E) Thomas Arnold.

(C) Leander Jameson.

58. The French fought bitterly against the Algerian rebels because

(A) having lost their Indo-Chinese holdings, de Gaulle was determined they would not lose Algeria.

(B) Algeria was a significant source of oil for France.

(C) the French viewed Algeria as an integral part of France.

(D) the French feared the existence of a communist state so close to their country.

(E) there were no significant anti-imperialist feelings in France.

59. The mandate system established following World War I

   (A) was only applied to former German colonies.

   (B) served to weaken European imperialism since all mandates were promised their independence in ten years.

   (C) involved only France and Great Britain.

   (D) quickly was the source of unrest in the Near East.

   (E) was not accepted by the League of Nations.

60. In the years of its existence only one country was expelled from the League of Nations. This country was

   (A) Japan, as a consequence of its aggression against China.

   (B) Nazi Germany, in the wake of its attack on Austria.

   (C) the Soviet Union, following its invasion of Finland.

   (D) Italy, for its assault on Ethiopia.

   (E) the regime of Francisco Franco, as a result of his brutal crushing of the Spanish Republicans.

61. Europeans demonstrated a greater interest in Africa's interior after 1850 as a result of

   (A) the fact that it was no longer possible to obtain sufficient slaves in the coastal regions.

   (B) medical advances which made it easier for them to live there.

   (C) growing concern over the expanding influence of the Moslems in central Africa.

   (D) the opportunities for economic territorial gain in Asia were fading.

   (E) the successful independence movements in Latin America had closed off its markets to Europe.

62. **ARTICLE III**

    It being obviously necessary and desirable, that British subjects should have some port whereat they may careen and refit their Ships, when required, and keep stores for that purpose, His Majesty the Emperor of China cedes to Her Majesty the Queen of Great Britain, etc., the Island of Hongkong, to be possessed in perpetuity by her Britannic Majesty...

    The statement above is derived from the treaty ending the

    (A) Boxer Rebellion.

    (B) Sepoy Rebellion.

    (C) Russo-Japanese War.

    (D) First Opium War.

    (E) Tai-ping Rebellion.

63. In the early 1930s Stalin altered the Soviet Union's foreign policy

    (A) when he sought closer ties with Nazi Germany.

    (B) by increasing the revolutionary activities of the Comintern world-wide.

    (C) by drawing Russia into isolation.

    (D) through seeking closer cooperation with the western democracies.

    (E) by withdrawing from the League of Nations.

64. By the close of the 19th century virtually all of Africa had been cut up into colonial holdings by the great powers of Europe, there remaining few independent nations. Those few states which retained their independence are designated on the map on the following page by which marking?

    (A) 1

    (B) 2

    (C) 3

    (D) 4

    (E) 5

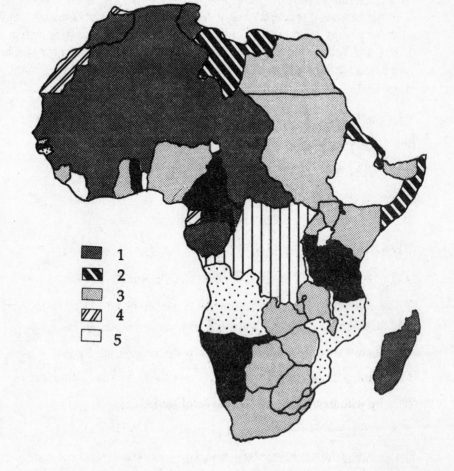

▓	1
▨	2
▒	3
▨	4
☐	5

65. "I say to the House as I said to Ministers who have joined this government, 'I have nothing to offer but blood, toil, sweat, and tears.' We have before us an ordeal of the most grievous kind. We have before us many, many months of struggle and suffering."

So spoke

(A) Otto von Bismarck   (D) Sir Edward Grey

(B) Georges Clemenceau   (E) Franklin D. Roosevelt

(C) Winston Churchill

66. Wladyslaw Gomulka, Alexander Dubcek, and Marshal Tito all had in common the fact that they

(A) stood in opposition to de-Stalinization.

(B) abandoned socialism.

(C)   saw their countries occupied by Soviet troops under the Brezhnev Doctrine.

(D)   came into confrontation with the Soviet Union.

(E)   supported Mao Tze-tung in his conflict with Stalin.

67.   Since the end of the Second World War, separatist movements have led to violence in

(A)   Northern Ireland, Spain, and Yugoslavia.

(B)   Spain, Greece, and Holland.

(C)   Northern Ireland, Holland, and Portugal.

(D)   Greece, Yugoslavia, and Spain.

(E)   Portugal, Greece, and Northern Ireland.

68.   The name of Auschwitz will always stand as a reminder of the

(A)   betrayal of the Czechs to Hitler by the French and British in 1939.

(B)   "Final Solution."

(C)   rapid defeat of French military forces by the Nazis in 1940.

(D)   Nazi annexation of Austria in 1938.

(E)   courageous, if futile, Warsaw uprising of 1945.

69.   Economic aid from the United States for the reconstruction of Europe following World War II was announced in 1947 by

(A)   Adlai Stevenson.   (D)   Dwight D. Eisenhower.

(B)   George Kennen.   (E)   John Foster Dulles.

(C)   George C. Marshall.

70.   Which of the following is closely associated with the name of Lech Walesa?

(A)   *Glasnost*   (D)   Soviet dissidents

(B)   The Red Brigade   (E)   The Hungarian Uprising of 1956

(C)   Solidarity

71. The Soviet desire to reduce the level of international tensions during the Khrushchev era stemmed from his

    (A) conviction that Stalin had wholly misunderstood the intentions of the United States.

    (B) desire to create in the West a false sense of security in preparation for the "final, inevitable triumph" of international communism.

    (C) belief that the forces of Western capitalism were too strong to overcome.

    (D) desire to move the Soviet Union away from the basic doctrines of Marxism-Leninism toward true "democratic socialism."

    (E) need to strengthen his position within the Soviet Union and avert the disintegration of the Communist bloc in Eastern Europe.

72. The fact that the Nationalist Socialists were able to gain sufficient electoral support in the early 1930s to come to power was due, in part, to the anger generated by the Treaty of Versailles and the

    (A) Communist efforts to seize power by force.

    (B) triumph of Mussolini in Italy.

    (C) achievements of Gustav Stresemann.

    (D) inflation of the 1920s and depression of the early 1930s.

    (E) ardent support they received from the much-revered President Hindenburg.

73. The Green Party in West Germany is closely associated with

    (A) the interests of the country's influential agricultural bloc.

    (B) the resurgence of Neo-Nazism.

    (C) a strong environmentalist element in German society.

    (D) the leading elements seeking the reunification of East and West Germany.

    (E) a revived Pan-Germanic movement.

74. The Franco-Algerian conflict resulted in

    (A) a confrontation between the United States and the Soviet Union.

    (B) the intervention of NATO as a "peace keeping" force.

    (C)   France being compelled to withdraw her military from French Indo-China.

    (D)   the fall of the Fourth French Republic.

    (E)   reaffirmation of French political control over the region.

75.   Which of the following books may be said to have been the most influential expression of post-World War II European pessimism?

    (A)   *Red and Black*

    (B)   *The Decline of the West*

    (C)   *Arms and the Man*

    (D)   *Foundations of the Nineteenth Century*

    (E)   *1984*

76.   Factors which have contributed to the rapid rise in world population in recent decades include all of the following EXCEPT

    (A)   a reversal in the traditional balance between births and deaths.

    (B)   medical advances eliminating or reducing earlier great plagues.

    (C)   the absence of any truly effective contraceptives.

    (D)   opposition of Third World leaders to either sterilization or birth control devices on the basis of the view these are actually a subtle form of Western genocide.

    (E)   marked declines in infant mortality.

77.   A significant feature in the capitalist global economy in recent decades has been

    (A)   the increasingly low rate of profits.

    (B)   the transfer of jobs from the Third World nations to the countries of the First World.

    (C)   the rise of multi-national corporations.

    (D)   an inability to produce sufficient consumer goods to meet the ever mounting demand.

    (E)   a resistance of the advanced nations to supply the much needed capital to those countries designated as "backward."

78. The most significant stimulus to colonial revolt against the West was

    (A) the voluntary decision of the Dutch to abandon their holdings in the Indonesian area following World War II.

    (B) Great Britain's abandonment of its colonial holdings in favor of the creation of the Commonwealth of Nations in the 1930s.

    (C) the military defeat of Western powers by a non-Western country in World War II.

    (D) the decision of the French to abandon her colonies in 1945.

    (E) the example of Hitler standing up to Great Britain and France.

79. The Baltic states have demanded independence from the Soviet Union on the basis that

    (A) they were illegally annexed by Stalin in 1939.

    (B) the Russians had not withdrawn their troops from those countries at the end of World War II as they had pledged to at the Yalta Conference.

    (C) they have no historical link with Russia.

    (D) they are ethnically distinct from the Slavic Russians.

    (E) they wish reunification with the now unified Germany.

80. The theory of history advanced by Marx appealed to many of the working class largely because

    (A) the *Communist Manifesto* held out the vision of the unity of the working class worldwide.

    (B) it placed heavy emphasis upon the bonds of nationalistic sentiment so close to the hearts of the working class.

    (C) it held out the vision of a near-utopian society for the proletariat in the wake of the inevitable revolutionary process.

    (D) it provided the vision of a revolutionary-minded leadership in the form of the communist cadre.

    (E) its vision of the alliance of the working and middle class gave promise of ultimate triumph over the capitalist class.

European History

TEST 6 – Section II

TIME: Reading Period – 15 minutes
Writing Time for all three essays – 115 minutes

DIRECTIONS: Read over both the Document-Based Essay question in Part A and the choices in Part B during the Reading Period, and use the time to organize answers. All students must answer Part A (the Document-Based Essay Question); and choose TWO questions from Part B to answer.

PART A – DOCUMENT-BASED ESSAY

This question is designed to test your ability to work with historical documents. As you analyze each document, take into account the source and the point of view of the author. Write an essay on the following topic that integrates historical facts and developments not mentioned in the documents.

The last four centuries, centuries which saw the evolution of the national State in its modern form, have produced almost endless debates as to the rights and obligations of the individual citizen in relation to the State and the nature of the State itself. On the basis of the concepts advanced in the documents present here, discuss the diverse and changing views related to the citizen and the State which they reveal.

Document 1

The Great Leviathan or State, Frontispiece to *Leviathan* by Thomas Hobbes, 1651

Document 2

"The state of monarchy is the supremest thing upon earth; for kings are not only God's lieutenants upon earth, and sit upon God's throne, but even by God Himself they are called gods...they may make and unmake their subjects, they have power of raising and casting down, of life and of death, judges over all their subjects and in all causes and yet accountable to none but God only."

—James I of England, Speech before Parliament, 1609

Document 3

"Princes are gods and participate somehow in divine independence...There is only God who may judge over their judgements and their persons...The prince may correct himself when he knows that he has done evil, but against his authority there is no remedy other than his own authority...The prince as prince is not regarded as an individual; he is a public personage...Let God withdraw His hand, and the world will fall into nothing; let authority cease in the realm, and all will be in confusion."

—Jacques-Bénigne Bossuet, circa 1660

Document 4

"The only way to erect such a common power, as may be able to defend them [the people] from the invasion of foreigners, and the injuries of one another, and thereby to secure them in such sort, as that by their own industry, and by the fruits of the earth, they may nourish themselves and live contentedly; is to confer all their power and strength upon one man, or upon one assembly of men...there can happen no breach of covenant on the part of the sovereign; and consequently none of his subjects, by any pretence of forfeiture, can be freed from his subjection..."

—Excerpt from *Leviathan* by Thomas Hobbes, 1651

Document 5

"A man, as has been proved, cannot subject himself to the arbitrary power of another; and having, in the state of Nature, no arbitrary power over the life, liberty, or possession of another, but only so much as the law of Nature gave him for the preservation of himself and the rest of mankind, this is all he doth, or can give up to the commonwealth, and by it to the legislative power, so that the legislative can have no more than this. Their power in the utmost bounds of it is limited to the public good of society. It is a power that hath no other end but preservation, and therefore can never have a right to destroy, enslave, or designedly to impoverish the subjects..."

—John Locke, *Two Treatises on Civil Government*, 1690

Document 6

"Government cannot be good, if it does not have sole power...There cannot be two powers in one state...It is a great fortune for the prince and for the state when there are many philosophers to impress their teachings on the minds of men...The philosophers have no special interest, and are able to speak only in favor of reason and the public interest...The happiest thing that can happen to men, is for the prince to be a philosopher...He furthers the development of reason."

—Voltaire, "The Voice of the Sage and of the People," 1750

Document 7

"[The prince] ought often to recollect he himself is but a man, like the least of his subjects. He is only the first servant of the state, who is obliged to act with probity and prudence; and to remain as totally disinterested as if were each moment liable to render an account of his administrations to his fellow citizens."

—Frederick II, King of Prussia, "Duties of a Prince," 1781

Document 8

"To the end, therefore, that the social compact should not prove an empty form, it tacitly includes this engagement, which only can enforce the rest, *viz.* that whosoever refuses to pay obedience to the general will, shall be liable to it by the force of the whole body...It is agreed that what an individual alienates of

his power, his possession, or his liberty, by the social compact, is only such parts of them whose use is of importance to the community; but it must be confessed also, that the sovereign is the only proper judge of this importance."
—J. J. Rousseau, *Social Contract*, 1762

Document 9

"[The liberties of Englishmen constitute an] entailed inheritance derived to us from our forefathers, and to be transmitted to our posterity as an estate specially belonging to people of this kingdom...A partnership in all art, a partnership in every virtue, and in all perfection. As the ends of such a partnership cannot be obtained in many generations, it becomes a partnership not only between those who are living, but between those who are living and those who are to be born."
—Edmund Burke, *Reflections on the Revolution in France*, 1790

Document 10

"Love your country. Your country is the land where your parents sleep, where is spoken that language in which the chosen of your heart blushing whispered the first word of love; it is the home that God has given you, that by striving to perfect yourselves therein, you may prepare to ascend to Him. It is your name, your glory, your sign among the people. Give it your thoughts, your counsels, your blood. Raise it up, great and beautiful as it was foretold by our great men."
—Giuseppe Mazzini, circa 1840

Document 11

"The citizen body is sovereign in the sense that no individual, no faction, no association can arrogate to itself a sovereignty not delegated to it by the people. But, there is a part of human life which necessarily remains individual and independent, and has the right to stand outside all social control. Where the independent life of the individual begins, the jurisdiction of the sovereignty ends. Rousseau failed to see this elementary truth, and the result of his error is that the *control social*, so often invoked in favor of liberty, is the most formidable ally of all despotisms."
—D. Constant, *Cours de politique constitutionnelle*, 1839

Document 12

"The sole end for which mankind is warranted, individually or collectively, in interfering with the liberty of action of any of their numbers, is self-protection...the only purpose for which power can be rightfully exercised over any member of a civilized community, against his will, is to prevent harm to others. His own good, either physical or moral, is not sufficient warrant. He cannot rightfully be compelled to do or forebear because it will be better for him to do so, because it will make him happier, because, in the opinion of others, to do so would be wise, or even true...No society in which these liberties are not,

on the whole, respected, is free. The only freedom which deserves the name, is that of pursuing our own good in our own way, so long as we do not attempt to deprive others of theirs, or impeding their efforts to obtain it."
—John Stuart Mill, *On Liberty*

Document 13
"The State is in the first instance power, that it may maintain itself; it is not the totality of the people itself, as Hegel assumed in his deification of the State—the people is not altogether amalgamated with it; but the State protects and embraces the life of the people, regulating it externally in all directions. On principle it does not ask how the people is disposed; it demands obedience: its laws must be kept, whether willingly or unwillingly...When the State can no longer carry out what it wills, it perishes in anarchy...History wears thoroughly masculine features; it is not for sentimental natures or for women. Only brave nations have a secure existence, a future, a development; weak and cowardly nations go to the wall, and rightly so."
—Heinrich von Treitschke, *Lectures on Politics*, circa 1880

Document 14
"It is that in all places people of the same race, the same language, the same religion, and the same customs regard each other as brothers and work for independence and self-government, and organize a more perfect government to work for the public welfare and to oppose the infringement of other races."
—Liang Ch'i-ch'ao, "The Renovation of the People," 1902

Document 15
"What is the significance of this revolution? Its significance is, in the first place, that we shall have a soviet government, without the participation of bourgeoisie of any kind. The oppressed masses will of themselves form a government. The old state machinery will be smashed into bits and in its place will be created a new machinery of government by the soviet organizations. From now on there is a new page in the history of Russia, and the present, third Russian revolution shall in its final result lead to the victory of Socialism."
—V.I. Lenin, Petrograd, November 1917

Document 16
"The State is only a means towards an end. Its highest aim is the care and maintenance of those primeval racial elements which create the beauty and dignity of a higher civilization...The dead mechanism [of the old State] must be replaced by a living organism based on the herd instinct, which appears when all are of one blood...One must never forget it: the majority can never replace the leader. It [the majority] is not only stupid but cowardly. You cannot get the wise man out of a hundred fools, and a heroic decision cannot come out of a hundred cowards."
—Adolf Hitler, *Mein Kampf*, 1924

PART B – ESSAY QUESTIONS

1. "The Crimean War, 1852–1856, was one of the silliest wars ever fought; yet its consequences were extraordinarily important for Russia and for Europe as a whole..."
—William H. McNeill, *A History of the World Community*

   Discuss, briefly, the origins of this "silly war" and, having done so, indicate the "extraordinarily important" consequences of it on Russia and Europe.

2. The Reformation inaugurated by Martin Luther was primarily a religious protest. At the same time it unleashed or soon gave rise to a number of other diverse protests and calls for change in areas which, while related to social, political, and economic issues rather than spiritual matters, were advanced by religious groups. Discuss, giving specific examples of the various protests or calls for change.

3. Historians frequently speak of the "Old Imperialism," that of the period between roughly 1500 and 1750, and the "New Imperialism" of the late 19th and early 20th centuries. Compare and contrast these, indicating differences and similarities that may have existed and the reasons for changes which might have occurred.

4. The Scientific Revolution of the 16th and 17th centuries was more than simply an advance in man's understanding of the physical world. It marked the inauguration of revolutions in man's perception of and relations with that world, with society, and with his fellow man: it was, in essence, a social, cultural, intellectual, and political revolution. Discuss.

5. A question which has long intrigued historians is that of the "hero"—the "great man" in history. Is history shaped by the "strong man," the dynamic individual, or are such individuals simply a product of their times—the consequence of the political, social, cultural, etc., conditions of the age? With this question in mind, assess the rise of Adolf Hitler to dominance in Germany. Was his ascent to power inevitable, or simply a consequence of the times?

6.   The Agricultural and Industrial Revolutions of the 18th and early 19th centuries dramatically altered the economic base of English society. They also brought marked changes in its social and political structure and its demographic face. Discuss, giving specific examples of the changes wrought.

THE ADVANCED PLACEMENT EXAMINATION IN

European History

TEST 6 – ANSWERS

1.	**(C)**	21.	**(C)**	41.	**(C)**	61.	**(B)**
2.	**(B)**	22.	**(B)**	42.	**(B)**	62.	**(D)**
3.	**(C)**	23.	**(C)**	43.	**(D)**	63.	**(D)**
4.	**(C)**	24.	**(E)**	44.	**(D)**	64.	**(E)**
5.	**(B)**	25.	**(B)**	45.	**(C)**	65.	**(C)**
6.	**(E)**	26.	**(A)**	46.	**(C)**	66.	**(D)**
7.	**(D)**	27.	**(C)**	47.	**(C)**	67.	**(A)**
8.	**(C)**	28.	**(D)**	48.	**(D)**	68.	**(B)**
9.	**(B)**	29.	**(B)**	49.	**(E)**	69.	**(C)**
10.	**(B)**	30.	**(D)**	50.	**(C)**	70.	**(C)**
11.	**(C)**	31.	**(E)**	51.	**(B)**	71.	**(E)**
12.	**(A)**	32.	**(C)**	52.	**(B)**	72.	**(D)**
13.	**(E)**	33.	**(A)**	53.	**(C)**	73.	**(C)**
14.	**(D)**	34.	**(B)**	54.	**(C)**	74.	**(D)**
15.	**(B)**	35.	**(B)**	55.	**(C)**	75.	**(B)**
16.	**(B)**	36.	**(D)**	56.	**(D)**	76.	**(C)**
17.	**(C)**	37.	**(D)**	57.	**(B)**	77.	**(C)**
18.	**(D)**	38.	**(D)**	58.	**(C)**	78.	**(C)**
19.	**(B)**	39.	**(D)**	59.	**(D)**	79.	**(A)**
20.	**(C)**	40.	**(B)**	60.	**(C)**	80.	**(C)**

Detailed Explanations
of Answers

TEST 6

1. **(C)** The piety of the Northern Renaissance was reflected in the writings of the Christian humanists such as Erasmus and Thomas à Kempis and the religious art of Dürer. Like the Southern or Italian Renaissance, the Renaissance in the north had a strong financial basis (A), that of the wealth of the commercial enterprises of southern Germany, the Flemish region, and the Hansa cities. Both its architectural (B) and artistic achievements were significant. There was little Byzantine influence (D), nor was there any indication of New World influences (E).

2. **(B)** Author of, among other works, *The Prince*, a realistic, albeit cynical look at the manner in which the ruler should govern his Renaissance state, Lorenzo Valla (A) was a humanist scholar of the Italian Renaissance who demonstrated that the "Donation of Constantine" was a forgery; Montaigne was a significant French humanist and philosopher of the late 16th century (C); while Grotius (D) was a Dutch legal theorist who wrote on international law, particularly as it related to warfare. Huizinga (E) was a modern historian of the early modern period.

3. **(C)** In 1494, at the invitation of the duke of Milan, Charles invaded Italy, initiating a conflict with the Hapsburgs which was to last 65 years. Charles V Hapsburg (A) did not come to the imperial throne until 1519, while Henry VII of England (B) was occupied with domestic problems. Suleiman (E) was not involved in Italy while Ferdinand (D), having dynastic interests in Italy, initially opposed the French invasion.

4. **(C)** The Tudor dynasty was established in the person of Henry VII. England lost its holdings in France (A) at the end of the Hundred Years' War in 1453, while Anglicanism (B) was proclaimed the religion of England during the reign of Henry VIII and the monastic establishments were abolished (D) during the same reign. England and Scotland were unified (E) only in the first decade of the 18th century.

5. **(B)** The activities of the Dominican Tetzel and his unbridled commercialism in the sale of indulgences prompted Luther to act. The other issues noted, while at various times severe problems within the church, were not of immediate concern to Luther when he posted the "Ninety-Five Theses."

6. **(E)** Copernicuss views were only published *after* Luther's death. All of the other factors mentioned were significant in contributing to the ultimate success of the religious protest inaugurated by Luther in the German area.

7. **(D)** Mercantilism might be envisioned as economic warfare in which one nation sought to gain an advantage over another through the acquisition of wealth in terms of precious metal. Items (A), (B), and (C), while facets of mercantilism, were secondary and contributory to the main goal of the acquisition of wealth. *Laissez faire* economics (E) were diametrically in opposition to the fundamental principles of mercantilism.

8. **(C)** France applied very rigid religious and political restrictions on those permitted to migrate to the New World. The Indians, in contact with the French and British, overwhelmingly supported the French (A). France's population was larger than that of England (B). The French explorers and merchants penetrated the interior to a much greater extent than the English (D) and their missionaries were generally more successful in their relations with the Indians (E).

9. **(B)** Raw wool was distributed to the workers, frequently peasants, who spun and wove it in their own homes. The domestic system was not related to ship construction (A) which was not under any circumstances a state monopoly. The true factory had not yet appeared in the textile industry, though when it did unions (C) were long prohibited. It was not related to agricultural practices (D) and had little or no relation to the admission of foreign workers (E).

10. **(B)** The Royal African Company of Great Britain received the right to provide slaves for a period of thirty years. Gibraltar was ceded to England in the Treaty of Utrecht (A). Spain did not grant Britain a free hand to trade in her Caribbean holdings (C), nor were Guadaloupe (D) or Florida (E) involved in the Treaty of Utrecht.

11. **(C)** As the map demonstrates that France has been divided into over eighty "departments," it could not represent France prior to the Revolution, since that division was one of the achievements of the National Assembly. Nor could it represent France after 1806, for the Holy Roman Empire, which came to an end in that year, is shown as still existing.

12. **(A)** The phrase is from Hobbes' major work, *The Leviathan*. John Milton (B), an English poet and Cromwell's secretary, was the author of *Paradise Lost*; Blackstone was a leading English legalist (C); d'Holbach was a French

philosophe (D); and Bossuet was an advisor of King Louis XIV and an ardent defender of the theory of divine right monarchy (E).

13. **(E)** Sweden, France, Austria, and Denmark were all involved militarily in the conflict. England, involved in the struggle between the Stuarts and Puritans, remained aloof.

14. **(D)** Defeating Sweden in the conflict, Peter gained control of extensive areas of the southern shores of the Baltic Sea and built the city of St. Petersburg. Peter's half-brother (A) was Alexis. Although he sought to gain access to the Black Sea, Peter failed to defeat the Turks (B), an achievement later of Catherine the Great. The push across the vastness of Siberia (C) had been carried out earlier, while the defeat of the *streltsy* (palace guards) and Old Believers (E) was unrelated to the Great Northern War.

15. **(B)** The Peace of Augsburg related only to those of the Catholic and Lutheran faiths. The Peace of Augsburg did not touch upon either Italy (A) or France (D), while no mention was made of the Anabaptists (C), a sect persecuted by all major religions. The powers of the emperor *were* clearly defined (E).

16. **(B)** In his *Spirit of the Laws* he divided the functions of government into the executive, judicial, and legislative bodies. The other men all wrote on the subject of government, their views ranging from favoritism of absolutistic government (Hobbes) to democracy (Rousseau), but none focused specifically on the issue of separation of power as did Montesquieu.

17. **(C)** Calvin's religious beliefs, giving rise to such sects as the Calvinists, Puritans, and Presbyterians, drew upon the foundation in Geneva laid by Zwingli. Luther (A) rejected a number of the doctrines of "Puritanism," particularly that of predestination. Hutter (B) was an Anabaptist, while Huss (D) and Servetus (E) were pre-Reformation religious reformers.

18. **(D)** By forcing smaller peasants from the land, hitherto open fields were consolidated into larger, more efficiently operated farms. Indirectly, through the creation of a large labor pool, the enclosure movement contributed to industrialization (A) and as a result of that, the increased need for coal, iron, and other metals (B), but this was not the primary objective, nor was reforestation (C). The *first* enclosure movement of an earlier period was designed to benefit the raising of sheep (E).

19. **(B)** Catherine's military victories at the expense of the Crimean Tatars, together with the extensive territories gained at the expense of the Poles in three partitions of their country, achieved a significant expansion of her country's holdings. Russian access to ports on the Mediterranean remained markedly limited by Turkish control of the Dardanelles well into the 20th century (C). Prior to

Peter the Great, direct assess to open waters in European Russia was limited to Archangel on the White Sea (Arctic Ocean). While Peter the Great attempted to expand toward the Black Sea, he was unsuccessful (D). On the basis of the information provided on the map, it is impossible to determine the extent of Russia's share of the partition.

20. **(C)** *Sans-culottes*–without the breeches"–associated with the clothing of the upper classes and aristocracy. Opponents of the Civil Constitution of the Clergy (E), which included many peasants (A) and priests (B), were simply viewed as counter-revolutionaries, while those nobles who fled the violence of the revolution for safety in the German region (D) were designated as emigres.

21. **(C)** Proclaiming themselves a national assembly, they swore not to disband until they had established a constitution for the country. The other objectives noted only came as the revolution gained momentum.

22. **(B)** For Luther, ultimate salvation rested in the individual's faith in the promise of salvation given by Christ. Good works (A) were of secondary importance to Luther, while Baptism and the Eucharist (D), perceived of as being of importance, were also secondary to faith, as was humility (C). Luther placed emphasis upon the guidance of the Bible, not that of the clergy (E), which could conceivably err.

23. **(C)** The universities, tending to be dominated by the church, did not provide the proper atmosphere for scientific research. All of the other statements regarding the role of and attitude toward scientific investigation are valid.

24. **(E)** Negotiated over a period of five years, the treaty was finally signed on October 24, 1648. The Treaty of Tilsit (B), involving France, Prussia, and Russia, was signed during the Napoleonic Wars. Gustavus (C) was killed during the course of the Thirty Years' War, but it continued on for several years. The Battle of White Mountain (A) occurred at the outset of the conflict. The Edict of Restitution (D), relating to the restoration of ecclesiastical estates, was signed in 1629.

25. **(B)** Fought on the outskirts of Quebec, Canada, in 1759, the battle led to the annexation of virtually all French holdings in North America by the British in the Treaty of Paris in 1763. The defeat of the Stuarts in the Battle of Culloden, April 16, 1746, basically ended their efforts to reclaim the English throne (A). In the course of the Seven Years' War, Austria did, in fact, lose Silesia to Prussia, but in a struggle distinct from that between Britain and France (C). The War of the Spanish Succession (D) occurred a half century earlier. The struggle for India (E), waged between Clive and Dupleix, was decided at the Battle of Plassey.

26. **(A)** The Deists, if having reservations about the doctrines of the estab-

lished religions, did believe that there existed basic standards of what was right and wrong. Perceiving God as the prime creator and mover (C), they believed that, having established the natural laws by which man should act (D), did not intervene in his everyday life (B). Man, possessing reason, should learn to live in conformity (E) with those natural laws.

27. **(C)** Ecumenicism, one of several important reforms of the Roman Catholic Church of the Second Vatican Council, is a call for toleration among Catholics as well as cooperation among Christian denominations. While choices (B), increasing evangelic activity, and (D), missionary work, might seem plausible, there is no direct link with ecumenicism. Preaching dogma (A) runs counter to this idea, and choice (E), less church involvement in politics, again unconnected to ecumenicism, is a statement that's also belied by the Roman Catholic Church's outspoken opposition to nuclear weaponry, among other issues.

28. **(D)** The second enclosure movement, seeking the consolidation of small farm holdings for efficiency, saw many peasants driven from the land, thus creating a significant labor pool. Serfdom (A) had basically disappeared from England many decades earlier. Slavery (B) was disappearing as an institution from England, while neither immigration (C) nor indentured labor (E) represented a significant source of labor.

29. **(B)** The Treaty, enacted by Pope Alexander VI in 1494, divided the world between the Spanish and Portuguese. At the request of the Portuguese the original line drawn down the Atlantic Ocean was moved westward, thus including a section of Brazil. Since this occurred prior to the official discovery of Brazil, it has been theorized that the Portuguese already knew of its existence. It was not on the Portuguese route to the East (A). The Spanish were not aware of its existence when the Portuguese claimed it (C) and (D). The Treaty of Utrecht (E) ended the War of the Spanish Succession several centuries later.

30. **(D)** The Navigation Acts were fundamentally laws designed to strengthen England's economy and foreign trade. They were initially designed to weaken that of Holland, in the mid-17th century the most powerful mercantile state in Europe. While designed to enhance England's trade, they did not legalize infringing upon Spain's monopolistic trade system—infringement which, in fact, had long been undertaken by English merchants.

31. **(E)** While Europeans, particularly England, were in a dominant position in the transportation of slaves to the New World and elsewhere, within Africa itself, native rulers, together with Moslem slave traders, held control. While having obtained a paramount position in India by the mid-18th century, she did not control all of India (A), many regions remaining under the rule of local princes. The Chinese (B) were very slow in perceiving technological advantages enjoyed by the West, becoming aware of them only well into the 19th century. Japan had isolated herself from virtually all Western trade from the early 17th century (D),

while the Moslem world (C) was in political decline.

32. **(C)** The Mongols, conquering much of Russia in the mid-13th century, dominated much of that land as the Golden Horde well into the 14th century when, at the Battle of Kulikovo in 1380, Dmitri Donskoi turned the tide against the Tatars. The Ottoman Turks (B) long remained a threat and obstacle to Russian expansion, but in the southern regions. The Russian Orthodox religion (D) served as a strong unifying force among the Russians (A). The Teutonic Knights (E) were defeated by Alexander Nevski in 1242.

33. **(A)** Founded during the reign of Charles II Stuart (B), the Royal Society was dedicated to scientific investigation. The Royal Society was not involved directly in religious (C), colonial (D), or economic activities (E).

34. **(B)** The words are derived from Ricardo's writings on the so-called "Iron Law of Wages." Jeremy Bentham (A) was the founder of the Utilitarian school of social philosophy; Robert Peel was an important English politician and reformer of the early 19th century (D); David Hume was an English *philosophe* of the 18th century (E), while Robert Owen was an English utopian socialist (C).

35. **(B)** Among other reforms they sought were the vote for virtually every male adult and parliamentary elections every year. The Luddites, opposing mechanization which they saw as threatening their livelihood, sought to destroy machines (A). English landowners (C) generally approved of duties to protect their agricultural interests. Babeuf (D), a proto-Communist of revolutionary France, had a handful of followers known as the Society of Equals. The Levellers were opponents of Cromwell (E).

36. **(D)** While it was a gradual improvement, studies have shown that an improvement in the conditions of the working class in European industrial societies did take place. The standard of living in agrarian society, it has been shown, was not necessarily superior to that of the industrial worker (A). While hours were perhaps increased initially, laws gradually cut the hours of labor (B). Women's financial contribution (C) tended to increase as their numbers in the labor force mounted.

37. **(D)** Through her military activities, Catherine added extensively to Russian territory in the Crimean and Black Sea areas. While imposing ever greater restrictions on the serfs (A), she enhanced the privileges of the nobles (E). The Slavophile movement (B), like the expansion of Russia to Vladivostok (C), was a later development in Russian history.

38. **(D)** By the 1980s, the political, economic, and enviromental climate of the Sovet Union was precarious. Oil prices actually remained fairly stable during the period leading up to Gorbachev's reforms. The totalitarian regimes that preceded Gorbachev (A) had allowed environmental problems to proliferate, one consequence of which was increasing health problems for Soviet citizens (B). Declin-

ing industrial production made it difficult for the Soviet Union to compete with the West in developing arms and providing its citizens with a level of industrial output to which Western Europeans and Americans had become accustomed (C). This was due in part to an over-centralized economy (E) that provided no incentives for factory managers and industrial entities to become more efficient.

39. **(D)** In his *Reflections on the Revolution in France* he spoke out for evolutionary, not revolutionary, change. Opposed to the radical changes taking place in France (A), he saw the American Revolution (E) as the result of a natural, evolutionary process and held that the colonials should be allowed to go free without a struggle (B). Institutions (C) such as the French monarchy, if not attuned to the times, should be reformed, not simply destroyed.

40. **(B)** Metternich of Austria was to be the dominant statesman of continental Europe for 33 years, the so-called "Coachman of Europe." The other statesmen noted, while present at Vienna, played roles secondary to that of Metternich, in whose shadow they stood.

41. **(C)** Much of the 19th century was to see revolutionary violence stemming from nationalistic and liberal aspirations thwarted by the decisions made at Vienna. The decisions reached at Vienna did not touch upon the Ottomans (A). Louis (B), overall, did not prove a bad king. Norway was ceded to Sweden at Vienna (D), while the Carlsbad Decrees (E) were passed several years after the Congress of Vienna (1819).

42. **(B)** The Duma was established in Russia only in 1905 by Czar Nicholas II. All of the other reforms noted were part of the program of Alexander II.

43. **(D)** The Austrians in Italy and their own country were slow to react to the revolutionary violence in its initial stages, as were the Prussian and French rulers. Class conflict (A), ethnic rivalries (B), and lack of strong unity among the revolutionary elements (C) tended to characterize the revolutionary movements. Fear of external intervention (E), as occurred in Hungary, where Russian troops intervened, was not uncommon.

44. **(D)** In the defeat of his country in the course of the Franco-Prussian War, he surrendered with a large part of the French army at Sedan and, abdicating, fled the country. He survived the failure of his imperialist policy in Mexico (A) and fled the country prior to the outbreak of the Paris Commune (B). The British gained control of the Suez Canal (E) in 1882, after Napoleon III's fall.

45. **(C)** The Anglo-Japanese Alliance of 1902 was, from the British point of view, designed primarily to protect India against a perceived Russian threat. England's alliance with Russia (B) and France (D) came in response to the Dual Alliance (Germany (E) and Austria), while she formed an alliance with Italy (A) only in the course of World War I (1915).

46. **(C)**   Socialists, except for the most radical, generally strongly supported the national interests of their own countries during the conflict. All of the other statements are true.

47. **(C)**   The cartoon depicts the kimono-clad Japanese as walking a tight-wire (or in this case a wobbly bamboo pole) clearly arousing the ire of the Russian bear. There are no indications in the cartoon of the nature of the risk Japan was running or of any outside power being involved in the affair.

48. **(D)**   Incendiary bombs were introduced in the course of World War II. All of the other weapons were utilized in World War I.

49. **(E)**   *All Quiet on the Western Front* is recognized as one of the great anti-war novels of the 20th century. Steinbeck (B), Koestler (D), and Grass (A), novelists of the Depression and World War II eras, did not treat the first World War with the intensity of Remarque, although Grass did deal with World War II. Lawrence (D) dealt more with human relations and sexuality.

50. **(C)**   The ultra-nationalistic, elitist, and racial theories, to name a few elements of the fascist movement, all had strong roots in diverse 19th century ideologies. The cult leader (A) (i.e., Der Fuehrer, Il Duce, etc.), the monolithic party (E) ultra-nationalism (D), and the demand for absolute loyalty (B), were all elements of the fascist movement.

51. **(B)**   An international accord of the Locarno Era, it was signed by a score of nations in 1928 with the overly optimistic idea of "outlawing warfare." The Locarno Treaties (A) were a series of international accords signed in 1925, including a guarantee of Germany's western borders and a mutual defense accord between France, Poland, and Czechoslovakia. The Treaty of Versailles (C) ended World War I between Germany and the Allies. There were two Treaties of Rapallo (E), one in 1920 between Italy and Yugoslavia which made Fiume a free state and ceded Zara to Italy, the second in 1922 between Germany and the Soviet Union cancelling the former's reparation payments. The Lytton Commission Report (D) dealt with Japanese aggression in Manchuria in 1931.

52. **(B)**   The Truman Doctrine was introduced primarily as a result of the perceived threat of communist supported insurgents seeking to overthrow the established Greek government. It had nothing to do with the economic rebuilding of Japan (A), the conflict over the Kashmir region (E) or the subsequent conflict between Turks and Greeks on the island of Cyprus (C). The supplying of Berlin (D) was essentially a matter of food, not a military crisis.

53. **(C)**   The Mau Mau—terrorists to some, freedom fighters to others—fought to end English control of Kenya. The Grand Mufti (A), having widespread support among the Arabs, was the founder of the Moslem Brotherhood. The other movements referred to were, and in some cases continue to be, internal struggles for greater freedom or complete independence.

54. **(C)** France has not had in the modern era a woman who served either as premiere or president, the two principal executive offices. All of the other nations have at one time or another had a woman as their chief executive officer: India—Nehru; England—Thatcher; Pakistan—Buto; Israel—Meir.

55. **(C)** With the discharge of tens of thousands of soldiers and the general industrial slump that occurred in the years following the end of the war, Great Britain's problem was one of severe unemployment, not a labor shortage. All of the other statements regarding Great Britain's economic situation are true.

56. **(D)** Mitterand, who died in 1996, was a Socialist. France's Conservative Party is headed by Jacques Chirac (A). While France has a Communist Party, it has not been very significant in French politics since the end of the 1980s (C). Labor (B) and Christian Democratic (E) are party names associated with other countries.

57. **(B)** The excerpt is from the poem "The White Man's Burden" by Kipling, one of the great apostles of English imperialism. Cecil Rhodes (A) was a South African gold and diamond magnate, statesman, and a great practitioner of imperialism, while Jameson (C) was his agent in his efforts to gain control of the Transvaal from the Boers. Yeats (D) was a British poet, Arnold (E) a literary critic.

58. **(C)** Algeria, long the home of many thousands of French from metropolitan France, was recognized as a department of metropolitan France, hence viewed as an integral part of that nation.

59. **(D)** The Arabs, formerly under Ottoman domination, felt they had been deprived of the independence promised them when they were placed under mandates. Also, the struggle between Zionist and Arab claims in Palestine quickly erupted. Ottoman lands (A) as well as German were taken. The term of the mandate holdings varied (B). Japan, South Africa, and the United States also received mandates (C). The mandates were technically under the supervision of the League (E).

60. **(C)** The Soviet Union was the only nation to be expelled from the League, this for her "Winter War" with Finland. Germany, Japan, and Italy walked out of the League, while Franco did not represent the legal Spanish government.

61. **(B)** Long viewed as a graveyard of Europeans, medical advances—particularly the introduction of quinine—reduced the peril of disease greatly. By the mid-19th century the demand for slaves was diminishing greatly as Britain waged a struggle for the abolition of slavery (A). Islam (C), as a religion, had long been present in parts of central Africa, but did represent a particular incentive to European imperialism. Both Asia (D) and Latin America (E) continued to provide ample opportunities for European economic and territorial imperialism.

62. **(D)**   The excerpt is from the Treaty of Nanking (1842) ending the First Opium War and seeing the island of Hong Kong ceded to England. The Tai-ping Rebellion (E) was an internal rebellion in China in the mid-19th century, while the Sepoy Rebellion (B) occurred in India at approximately the same time. The Russo-Japanese War (C) and the Boxer Rebellion (A) took place in the first decade of the 20th century and neither directly involves Great Britain or touched upon control of Hong Kong.

63. **(D)**   Frightened by the rise of an aggressive Japan and Germany, Stalin sought closer relations with anti-fascist (A) governments in the West. Stalin's actions represented an attempt to break with the isolation of Russia (C) which had previously existed. To win favor with the West, the Comintern was dissolved (B). Formerly not a member of the League of Nations, the Soviet Union was admitted to that organization in 1934 (E).

64. **(E)**   Liberia and Abyssinia were the only independent nations in Africa in 1900. 1, British; 2, Italian; 3, Belgian; 4, Spanish.

65. **(C)**   The excerpt is from a speech made by Winston Churchill in the days immediately following the evacuation of British military forces from Dunkirk. Otto von Bismarck (A), the "Iron Chancellor," was the chancellor of Prussia in the second half of the 19th century, Clemenceau was the premiere of France during the First World War (B), Sir Edward Grey was England's foreign minister during that conflict (D), while Roosevelt was the president of the United States (E) from 1934 to 1945.

66. **(D)**   Gomulka (Poland) Dubcek (Czechoslovakia), and Tito (Yugoslavia) all came into confrontation with the Soviet Union. None were great supporters of Stalinism (A), though none rejected socialism (B). Yugoslavia, unlike the other two countries, never experienced occupation by Soviet troops (C) nor were they supporters of Mao of China (E).

67. **(A)**   Northern Ireland has been the scene of a blood struggle on the part of those Irish Catholics who wish unification with the Republic of Ireland, while the Basques in Spain and Croats of Yugoslavia have also carried on terrorists activities directed at separatism. Greece, Portugal, and Holland have experienced no such movements.

68. **(B)**   Auschwitz was one of the most notorious of the Nazi death camps where the murder of tens of thousands of Jews and others was carried out by the Nazis. The Munich Conference is associated with the sell-out of Czechoslovakia (A); the *Anschluss* was the annexation of Austria (D). No specific, one-word terms are associated with either the French (C) or Polish (E) defeats.

69. **(C)**   Marshall, Secretary of State in 1947, enunciated the so-called

Marshall Plan. Stevenson (A), governor of Illinois, was a presidential candidate on the Democratic slate in 1952; he was defeated by Eisenhower. Kennen (B) was an important official with the State Department; Eisenhower (D) was supreme commander of the Western Allied forces in the invasion of Europe in World War II and twice president of the United States, and Dulles (E) was Secretary of State under Eisenhower.

70. **(C)** Walesa founded and went on to lead the Solidarity movement in Poland and was later elected his nation's president. *Glasnost* (A) is the term applied to the reform movement led by Gorbachev in the Soviet Union; the Red Brigade (B) is a radical leftist terrorist group active in Western Europe. Imre Nagy (E) is associated with the failed efforts of the Hungarians to pursue a course of domestic policy independent of the Soviet Union in 1956, while no one individual stands out as the leader of the Soviet dissidents (D).

71. **(E)** Strains were already beginning to show on the domestic scene of the Soviet Union, particularly in the area of consumer goods, as they were in terms of the Soviet's relations with her satellite states. Khrushchev, although he initiated the de-Stalinization campaign, had no doubts, at least openly expressed, regarding the superiority of the Soviet system or the certainty of the Marxist-Leninist theory of history.

72. **(D)** Germany was severely hit by the Depression and many of the middle and upper class, fearing Communism, turned to Hitler seemingly as the only alternative. The Communists, like Hitler, sought power through the ballot box (A). Mussolini's rise to power (B), occurring a decade earlier, had little or no effect on the situation in Germany. Stresemann (C), who had pulled Germany to her feet after the disastrous depression of 1923, had actually set back Hitler's political aspirations. President Hindenburg (E) loathed Hitler.

73. **(C)** The Green Party has led a strong environmentalist drive in West Germany, holding that the extensive, and unchecked, industrialization of the country was destroying the atmosphere and landscape. Neither Neo-Nazi (B) nor Pan-Germanic (E), the Green Party's attitude toward German reunification (D) or agricultural (A) policies do not represent its primary goals.

74. **(D)** Amid tremendous agitation generated by those who either favored maintaining a firm hold on Algeria or those who opposed doing so, the Fourth French Republic fell and Charles de Gaulle came to power. Neither the Soviet Union, the United States (A) nor NATO (B) became involved in the conflict; and France, which had already withdrawn from Indo-China (C) when the Algerian struggle erupted, was in the end forced to recognize the independence of that region.

75. **(B)** The author of the work, Oswald Spengler, was convinced that Western

civilization had reached its zenith and was entering a stage of rapid decline. G.B. Shaw's *Arms and Man* (C), Stendahl's *Red and Black* (A), and H.S. Chamberlain's *Foundations of the Nineteenth Century* (D, were all written prior to the First World War. Orwell's *1984* (E) deals with a futuristic totalitarian state.

76. **(C)** Numerous contraceptive devices have been developed in the years since the end of World War II and have been available to a significant portion of the world's population. All of the other factors mentioned have contributed significantly to the ballooning global population.

77. **(C)** The world of high finance and commercial and industrial activity has tended to become dominated by the great international corporations. None of the other statements regarding post-World War II are valid.

78. **(C)** The victories won by the Japanese in the early days of World War II, bringing as they did the humiliation of colonial peoples' former Western masters together with the establishment of puppet—but native—governments, was an extremely significant factor in the rise of anti-colonialism. The Dutch fought ardently to prevent Indonesian independence (A) in the early days of the struggle, while the creation of the Commonwealth of Nations came more as a response to anti-colonialism than a cause for it (B). The French (D) were very hesitant to give up their colonies, as seen in Indo-China, and the struggle between Hitler and the Allies (E) was simply seen by Asian and Africans as a case of Europeans killing Europeans for world domination.

79. **(A)** The Baltic peoples long maintained—and the Soviets under Gorbachev have conceded—that they were illegally annexed in 1939 by Stalin. The Soviets did not withdraw their troops (B), but they had given no such promise to do so at Yalta. The Baltic peoples, at least the Estonians and Latvians, were under Russian domination from the time of Peter the Great to 1919 (C), when they gained their independence in the wake of the Russian Revolution. They are ethnically different, although each of the Baltic states has a sizeable number of ethnic Russians living in them (D). They have no desire to be under German control (E).

80. **(C)** "Come the Revolution," Marx held out the vision of the rise of a classless "workers' paradise." While the idea of the unity of the workers of the world (A) was a facet of Marx's doctrines, it was seen as merely a step in the desired end of a workers' paradise. Marx opposed nationalism (B), which he thought weakened the true goals of the ultimate revolution. He did not speak of an elite leadership (D) (this was Lenin's idea) and he did not perceive of an alliance (E) between the working and middle classes, seeing them as actually enemies.

Sample Answer to Document-Based Question

The major states of Western Europe had, in the course of the 16th century, begun to assume a more modern form. As competition among the nations both intensified and increasingly became of a global nature, the need for both internal unity and strength against potential foreign foes increased. Yet, emerging from the medieval period, there remained in the states numerous domestic forces that hampered the development of truly centralized administrations, strong administrations which were essential if the state was to survive and thrive. Feudal aristocracies jealous of the privileged position, a peasant class whose concept of political loyalty frequently did not extend beyond the local village or, at best, their own province, and deep divisions along religious lines were but a few of these divisive elements.

Lacking anything but the vaguest perception of the modern idea of nationalism, it was the princes who became—and deliberately made of themselves—the focal point of the state, the symbol about which the people of the state were expected to rally and to whom they were to give their unswerving obedience. This was the age of the absolute monarch and the divine right monarch. Documents 1 through 4 present both visual and written portraits of, and justification for, such rulers. As is seen in the illustration from Hobbes's *Leviathan*, the monarch is conceived of as embodying in his person all of his subjects. James I Stuart of England, one of the most ardent exponents of "divine-right" rule, saw the monarchs' unchallengeable status as being derived from God: princes were indeed, in his eyes, no less than gods on earth. Whether he actually believed this or, fearing that a state lacking a supreme, unquestioned sovereign power would fall into a state of confusion as held by Bishop Bossuet, simply sought to wrap his rule in a cloak of divinity is difficult to determine. Certainly King Louis XIV of France, tutored by Bossuet, was convinced that an aura of the divine shrouded his reign. James's vision of his status did not, in fact, go unchallenged, for in England, unlike France, there existed a strong middle-class element and a parliamentarian tradition to stand in opposition, one so strong that it eventually brought his son Charles I to the execution block. It was as a consequence of the Puritan Revolution that Hobbes, horrified by what he perceived as anarchy, argued for the need to vest absolute power in the hands of one man or body of men: his argument was based not on any concept of the ruler possessing a mandate from God but, rather, the belief that the only alternative was the confusion Bossuet had prophesied.

Locke (Document 5), like Hobbes, admitted man, if completely unchecked by authority, could be a threat to the welfare of others. But while recognizing the need for authority, unlike Hobbes he did not believe that men, in forming a covenant with a sovereign power, surrendered completely all their rights and freedoms, rights which, in the course of the "Glorious Revolution" of 1688, an event in which Locke was intimately involved, the English embodied in their Bill of Rights. That revolution established the fact that England's monarch, far from being a divine or absolute ruler, was a constitutional monarch and that ultimate power rested in the hands of parliament and the representatives of the people—or in 1688 at least that small segment of the people who actually had a political voice.

While Louis XIV, the "Sun King," who had proclaimed "I am the State," had been extremely successful in surrounding himself with the trappings of majesty, by the time of his death in 1715 the "Age of Absolutism" had given way to the "Age of Reason." Reflecting the achievements of the men of the Scientific Revolution, emphasis was placed on reason as seen in Voltaire's (Document 6) call for a prince who "furthers the development of reason"—an "Enlightened Despot" who sought to rule according to "reason" and the "laws of nature." Such a monarch was Frederick II (Document 7) who, denying any divinity, claimed only to be the "first servant of the state." It was still absolutism, but in a new dress.

By the mid-18th century a new concept of the state was emerging in the more developed nations of Europe—that the state was not the prince, but the totality of the individuals who composed it. This is seen in Rousseau's *Social Contract*, where his "General Will" is conceived of as being, in essence, the consensus view as to what was in the best interests of the whole community: sovereignty is found in the people, not the prince or assembly.

The French Revolution and Napoleonic era served to reinforce this concept of the State being, in fact, the people. Indeed, it went further: the "State" or Nation came to possess an existence of its own—it was seen as a living organism that was more than the total of all its parts (i.e., its citizens). The conservative Burke (Document 9) saw the English "Nation" as a legacy of that land's long history, one the living had to nurture and pass on to future generations. This concept was greatly amplified in the course of the 19th century as various peoples of Europe struggled to free themselves of foreign masters or to extend their liberties against reactionary regimes. In the mind of Mazzini (Document 10), the Romantic Italian, his country became his "mother" and "father," a parent to whom he owed everything and for whom he was prepared to sacrifice everything. Increasingly the concept of the State as an entity having a life of its own came to be associated with a common language, a common heritage, a common race. Such a vision of the State was transmitted beyond Europe, as seen in the words of Liang Ch'i-ch'ao, subsequently a founder of the Communist Party of China.

The second half of the 19th century saw other ideological concepts which influenced the vision of the State and the citizens relations to it. Social Darwinism, placing emphasis on the idea of "survival of the fittest," gave rise to the idea of the State in constant competition—warfare declared or undeclared—with its rivals. For Treitschke (Document 13), a Prussian historian, the State is seemingly perceived of as an army, its citizens little more than soldiers in the ranks who must obey. This vision of the ever-aggessive state, combined with an emphasis upon the unity—and superiority—of a particular race (*Volk*), and yet another ideological spin-off of Social Darwinism, elitism, combined to produce a concept of the State which plagued the first half of the 20th century, the Fascist, or Totalitarian, regime. This concept was succinctly stated in Hitler's *Mein Kampf* (Document 16), where the deification of the State as a "living organism," the exaltation of the "leader" as the personification of that State, and the ultimate contempt for the individual citizen, stupid and cowardly, is clearly set forth. Absolutism had returned in a terrifying form.

There were, of course, other views of the nature of the state and of its relations to the individual. Both Constant (Document 11) and, even more so, Mill (Document 12) argued that the authority of the State is limited and that the individual always retains certain rights which cannot be alienated: the State exists for the protection of the citizen, but it cannot infringe upon his liberties as long as those do not threaten others.

Lenin (Document 15) represented a different concept of the State, one also having its roots in 19th century ideology, that of Marxism. In theory what was envisioned was a classless State or, indeed, *no state*, for a State existed only as a tool of class oppression and, in a classless society would not be necessary. What emerged from the Russian Revolution was, of course, quite different than the theory—a totalitarian State in which an elite, the Communist Party member and a cult leader, Stalin, dominated a subservient citizenry—totalitarianism in a different guise.

Sample Answers to Essay Questions

1. The conflict, sparked by a relatively absurd conflict between Russia and France over the protection of Christian holy sites in Jerusalem, had its real roots in the "Eastern Question." Great Britain and France, having commercial, military, and political interests in the eastern Mediterranean and Near East, were opposed to any Russian encroachment upon the Turkish Straits or Turkish territory in that region. When a war broke out between Russia and Turkey, both Great Britain and France, fearing Russian intentions, quickly came to the Turks' support. The conflict itself, characterized by military ineptitude on all sides—ineptitude personified by the gallant but senseless "charge of the Light Brigade"—and the humanitarian activities of Florence Nightingale, ended in the defeat of Russia.

For Russia, defeat brought more than defeat on the battlefield. It brought clearly to the fore the backwardness of the Russian economic, social, and political structure. In the aftermath of the war the new Czar, Alexander II, inaugurated a series of reforms, including the emancipation of the serfs, introduction of *zemstvos* or provincial parliaments, and the extension and liberalization of the educational system. While these reforms did not go far enough, particularly in regard to the emancipation of the serfs, and were subsequently further hamstrung by Alexander's successors and conservative elements in Russian society, they were reflective of the severe domestic problems confronting Russia, problems that grew in subsequent decades. On the international scene, defeat in the war had served to block Russia's territorial ambitions in the Near East and Balkans temporarily: as a consequence, these were directed towards the Far East, where in the 1860s they annexed the Maritime Provinces, regions claimed by Manchu China, and southward towards Afghanistan. This expansion in the Asian area gave rise to increasing tensions with Great Britain and, eventually, the emerging Japan.

The Austro-Hungarian Empire, while not directly involved in the war, pursued a policy that was to have marked repercussions for it and, indeed, for all of Europe. In 1849, in accordance with the principles of the "Concert of Europe," Russia had come to the military assistance of Austria when it was confronted with a Hungarian uprising. When the Crimean War erupted, Russia looked to Austria for assistance, if only of a diplomatic nature, only to find her pursuing a policy of "neutrality." When, a decade later, Austria found itself faced with the threat presented by Otto von Bismarck's efforts to unify Germany under the leadership of Prussia, Russia, angered at Austria's "ingratitude" offered no help to her former ally: the "Concert of Europe" had been broken. Bismarck, on the other hand, while pursuing a policy of "friendly neutrality," secretly assisted Russia, thus reinforcing cordial relations to be utilized when the moment arrived.

The circumstances surrounding the Crimean War presented Austria with still another danger. Piedmont-Sardinia's Prime Minister Cavour, while having no real interest in the conflict, brought his country into the war on the side of Great Britain and France. Envisioning the unification of Italy, he realized that this would mean a war with Austria, a war his country could not win without the support of a powerful ally. France, whose ruler was Napoleon III, a man already sympathetic to the idea of Italian unification, was the logical choice. Permitted to plead his cause at the peace conference held in Paris, he was able to win Napoleon's promise of military support in Piedmont's inevitable war with Austria. Austria, isolated, fell victim to the unification ambitions of both Bismarck and Cavour and, with the eventual unification of Germany and Italy, the map— and history—of Europe were dramatically changed.

Britain, while a victor in the war, came away with a bitter taste, convinced of the wisdom of returning to a policy of "splendid isolation," seeking to avoid involvement in the affairs of the Continent. Time was to suggest this policy was a serious error, coming as it did on the eve of the unification of Germany and Italy and the beginning of the formation of a series of alliances which were to contribute significantly to the outbreak of World War I.

The Crimean War, albeit a "silly war" fought on the periphery of the Continent, clearly had major consequences which extended far beyond the battlefield or the specific terms ending it, consequences which were to markedly alter the subsequent course of European history.

2.   Decades before Luther posted his Ninety-Five Theses, religious unrest had been smouldering throughout Europe, unrest occasionally erupting in revolt as seen in the movements of Wycliffe in England and John Hus in Bohemia. In these spiritual movements, nationalistic sentiments were also involved. This was particularly evident in England, where Wycliffe began to translate the Bible into English and called for the King of England, not the Pope, to be recognized head of the English church. Clearly Wycliffe's ideas, aside from doctrinal convictions,

reflected a nationalistic spirit arising from England's involvement in the Hundred Years' War and a conviction that the Avignon papacy was a mere tool of the French. Wycliffe's movement also revealed another protest, this of a social nature. The Lollards, his followers, came largely from the lower class. Hungering for land, unhappy with the failings of the church and jealous of its wealth, suffering from the impact of the Black Death and the war, their anger was directed as much against the feudal and manorial system, the great landowners, and a regime which imposed hated dues and taxes upon them and sought to keep them in a socially subservient position as it was against doctrinal concepts. The Peasants' Revolt of 1381, numbering among its leaders the Lollard priest John Bull, was an overt display of this social unrest.

These and other protests and calls for change emerged even more clearly following Luther's revolt. He early translated the Bible into German, a national language. In his *Address to the Christian Nobility of the German Nation*—a nation that in fact did not exist—he made a frankly patriotic appeal to his countrymen to reject the authority of the papacy and argued that, as the church could not reform itself, the secular authorities must do so. Depending heavily upon the German princes for support, he early established the close relationship that would long exist between the Lutheran Church and the state. Nor was this alliance of state and church limited to Lutheran regions. In England, Henry VIII's "Reformation," motivated on his part more by "reasons of state" than those of a religious nature, created a national religion, Anglicanism, adherence to which was demanded as a sign of loyalty to king and state. This trend to national religions was not limited to Protestant states, for French monarchs worked to create a "Gallican Church," Catholic but controlled by the throne rather than the papacy. The unity of Christendom was giving way to national religions. Neither the Germans nor the Czechs, however, were to benefit from this trend.

Luther emphasized the Bible as the ultimate source of truth. Many took his words to heart: the problems such pursuits of truth presented quickly became evident, for the Scriptures and the picture they painted of the primitive Christian community lent themselves to diverse and at times revolutionary social, economic, and political interpretations. As early as the 1520s, peasants of southwestern Germany, suffering under the pressure of customary rents and services imposed upon them by their lords in a decaying feudal and manorial system, argued that they could find no Scriptural justification for their burdens. Many revolted in 1524, seeking to throw off the hated obligations. While they found some support from religious leaders such as Zwingli, Luther was now in close alliance with the princes of Protestant Germany, and turned violently on them.

The "Anabaptists," a term of derision applied to sects holding a broad spectrum of beliefs but having in common the practice of adult baptism, were seen by more conservative Protestants and Catholics alike as a danger to the social order. Communal ownership of property, including wives, the imminent return of Christ, anarchism, and withdrawal from the affairs of the secular state were among the ideas certain sects adhered to. In 1525 in Münster, Thomas

Munzer, once an associate of Luther, established a communistic theocratic society, only to be crushed before the end of the year. More radical were the Melchorites who, under the leadership of John of Leiden, gained control over the ordinary workers and craft guilds in Münster and established their "heavenly Jerusalem." Burning all books except the Bible, abolishing private property, introducing polygamy, they lived in an atmosphere of abandon and chaos—although probably not as much as their critics maintained—awaiting the coming of the Messiah. The Protestants and Catholics allied to crush them brutally. The more moderate Anabaptists, viewing themselves as a Christian community which, while recognizing the authority of the state, sought to live as an entity apart from the state, were long cruelly persecuted by Lutherans, Calvinists, and Catholics. Interestingly, the Anabaptists were among the earliest to advocate yet another "revolutionary" idea—religious toleration.

The revolutionary calls for changes in the social, economic, and political spheres on the part of the religious groups did not end with the close of the 16th century, nor were they confined to the German area. Seventeenth century England saw such movements as the Levellers,who called for the vote for all adult males and the yearly parliamentary elections, Fifth Monarchy Men, and the communist Diggers.

3.   While the term "imperialism" dates only from the 1880s, the objectives it implied are as old as history, to be seen when the first state sought to politically, economically, or culturally dominate another. The appearance of the term, however, indicated that the earlier goals, and the motives behind them, had been formulated into a more cohesive concept.

The "Old Imperialism" saw Europeans explore many corners of the globe and, where possible, colonize extensively. As with the subsequent "New Imperialism," the forces which led the Europeans to do so were varied. Much emphasis has been placed by scholars since the time of Marx upon the economic factors that drove Europeans to expand their influence in the colonial regions after *circa* 1871. Yet economic factors were not lacking in the earlier period. Certainly the vision of "El Dorados" to match the vast treasures of the Aztecs and Incas long led men to explore uncharted lands. In addition to the dream of vast hoards of gold, silver, and precious stones that drove the earlier explorers, the spices, jewels, cottons, silk, and porcelains of India, China, and the East Indies, together with the slaves of Africa, provided an economic stimulus to the European merchants and the countries they represented. The nations of the age of the "New Imperialism" saw their colonies as sources of raw materials and as markets for their finished products: the same was no less true of the earlier period, particularly in relation to their holdings in the New World.

Yet another reason advanced for the imperialistic surge of Europe in the late 19th century has been the missionary zeal of many Europeans: yet the earlier "God" of the cry of "God, Gold, and Glory" symbolized the ardent, even fanatical drive on the part of explorers to spread their faith, whether by sword or teaching. Nor was the quest for "glory" on the part of men such as Cortez,

Pizarro and others wholly lacking from men such as Cecil Rhodes or Henry M. Stanley.

Any study seeking to compare the "Old Imperialism" with the "New" will disclose other factors broadly parallel. The European states of the late 19th century enjoyed, as a consequence of the Industrial Revolution and a strong scientific and technological orientation, marked advantages, particularly in the military area: the gunboat and machine gun came to be symbols of European imperialism. But four centuries earlier the Portuguese, Spanish, and those who followed them also enjoyed the advantage of superior ships and firepower. The acquisition of colonies for strategic purposes or to deter the expansion of rival European powers was also characteristic of imperialism in the two periods, as was the pursuit of economic policies of mercantilism or "Neo-Mercantilism."

If there are many broad parallels between the Old Imperialism and the New, are there any differences? Three stand out. In the 1500s the Spanish encountered great civilizations in the New World: these, however, were not able to resist European firepower, discipline, and disease. In North America the natives, at best, could offer only temporary resistance. The result was that the lands of the New World were largely open to European exploitation and colonization. The situation in Asia and Africa was markedly different, for such dynasties as the Moghuls of India, Mings and Manchus of China, and Togukawa of Japan were able to control the handful of Europeans who came to their ports, while the adverse health conditions of sub-Saharan Africa deterred penetration of the interior. Nor did pre-industrial Europe have any items for sale really desired by those lands. As a result, European merchants went as supplicants, content to purchase the items so desired in the West. After the mid-19th century this situation altered dramatically. On one hand the Asian dynasties were undergoing internal decay, a situation the Westerners quickly exploited. Too, the rise of native elements in these regions who saw advantages in cooperating with the Europeans provided another wedge the latter could exploit. In Africa, medical advances permitted the Europeans to penetrate and exploit the interior.

In the economic sphere, the Industrial Revolution and second Commercial Revolution had also altered the picture dramatically. There was now extensive surplus capital to be invested for high profits in overseas areas. As these investments mounted, it was only natural that there was a desire on the part of the investors that their governments "protect" their interests, even if this necessitated military intervention or outright annexation. As the industrial plants of Europe demanded more and more raw materials, governments sought spheres of influence where these could be guaranteed: such spheres for the sale of the finished products of the plants were also sought. The consequence of these forces was that by 1900 virtually every nation and people of Africa and Asia was either governed directly or under the strong influence of a Western power.

In the era of the Old Imperialism the inevitable clashes of interest between the European powers in the colonial regions had often resulted in war. In the later period, while tensions remained, diplomacy often resolved before war erupted.

4.   There developed in the millennium before 1500 a concept of the universe and of man's place in it providing an ordered, hierarchical structure, preordained by the Creator. In this universe every object, animate or inanimate, knew its place: to upset this balance was in the eyes of the Church, since it had been established by God, a sin. This "Medieval Synthesis," reaching its culmination in the 11th and 12th centuries, was an amalgam of the scientific ideas of Aristotle, Ptolemy, and Galen, the "authorities" of Antiquity, and the doctrines of the Church. At the heart of this synthesis was its conception of the cosmos. At the center of the universe was the earth, motionless, changing, and corruptible. It was surrounded by nine crystalline spheres with which the sun, moon, planets, and stars were associated. Moving in perfect circular orbits, this heavenly realm was one of perfection and incorruptibility. Beyond the ninth sphere was the empyrean, the region of the blessed spirits.

Even before the 16th century questions were being raised regarding the validity of the medieval synthesis. Professors at Oxford, Padua, and Paris began to apply mathematical reasoning to problems of physics and astronomy, raising questions regarding the theories of Aristotle and Ptolemy, while the study of anatomy by Renaissance artists served to undermine the authority of Galen; humanists, in their studies of antiquity, discovered Greek philosophers who held theories in opposition to Aristotle and Ptolemy. The consequence of this doubting and questioning became clear in the 16th century with the publication of Vesalius' *On the Structure of the Human Body* and Copernicus' *On the Revolution of Heavenly Bodies*. Vesalius, while not rejecting wholly the authority of Galen, demonstrated the value of information gained through dissection. Copernicus' work, although advanced only as a theory, struck a sharper blow at a fundamental tenet of the Medieval Synthesis. Aware of ancient theories that the sun was the center of the universe and that the earth moved about it, he utilized mathematics to demonstrate that the universe constructed on these concepts presented a simpler, more logical explanation for the movements of the heavenly bodies than Ptolemy's complex system of epicycles. While Copernicus did not reject Ptolemy's ideas entirely, retaining the concept of the circular orbits of heavenly bodies and a finite sphere of fixed stars, he had sharply challenged authority.

In the decades that followed, Francis Bacon emphasized the need for inductive reasoning and empirical research while René Descartes reenforced the essential role of mathematical analysis and theory in scientific investigation. Others, using these new tools, steadily increased man's pool of knowledge: Gilbert in magnetism, Harvey in the circulation of blood,desedd Torricelli with vacuums, while others were expanding man's mathematical tools—Descartes with analytical geometry, Newton and Leibniz with calculus. Contributing to the advance of science was the beginning of an alliance of the artisan with the skills to construct superior equipment and the scientist who used them, an alliance that proved fruitful.

The 17th century, the "Century of Genius," saw a seemingly unbroken chain of discoveries which totally altered man's conception of the universe, the forces behind it, and man's place in it. Kepler, substituting elliptical orbits for Ptolemy's perfect circles, corrected Copernicus' error and validated the heliocentric theory. Galileo, using the newly invented telescope, revealed the moon was not a perfect globe and that the sun was not changeless, that the earth moved, and hinted that the earth and heavens were subject to the same forces and laws. Newton, drawing on Kepler's astronomy, Galileo's physics, his own mathematical skills and inductive reasoning, removed the distinctions between celestial and earthly physics: the "Medieval Synthesis" had been destroyed, replaced by the "World Machine" of Newton.

Man, in a sense, had been displaced from the center of the universe by Copernicus, Kepler, and Galileo: his mind, if not his physical being, had been restored to that position by the accomplishments of Descartes, Newton, and other scientists. They had demonstrated that, through the application of the proper tools—inductive reasoning, empiricism, and mathematics—the secrets of the universe could be unveiled. In doing so, they had also challenged and severely weakened the "Authorities," those of antiquity and of the Church. But the achievements of these scientists had provided man with a new vision, that of an ordered universe governed by "natural" laws, and new "authorities"—science, the scientific method, and his own reason. Intellectuals of Western Europe, deeply impressed with the achievements of the scientists, were convinced that through the proper application of these tools not only could the mysteries of the physical world be solved, but those of society itself. The 18th century, the "Age of Reason," saw men, the *philosophes*, seek to find solutions to the social, economic, and political problems they perceived to exist. Imbued with a spirit of optimism, they believed it possible to discover, through reason, the natural laws which governed society and man's relations with man. They, like the scientists, were prepared to challenge authority, whether that of the monarch, the church, or the established traditions of the day. That their conception of what was wrong in society was frequently based upon personal or class convictions did not deter their conviction that reason would lead to the reconstruction of society in accord with the laws of nature.

5.   Any discussion of Hitler's rise to power must take into consideration numerous factors pre-dating his emergence as an historical figure or over which he had no control. These, rather than being shaped by Hitler, served to shape him.

Certainly the most significant of these was Germany's defeat in World War I. That conflict was a devastating experience for all participants, its cost in destroyed lives and property immense. The same was also true in terms of the psychological impact of the struggle, the spirits of the victors and vanquished alike being shattered. For the Germans this was particularly true, for their propaganda had convinced them they were actually winning the war. When defeat came, many could not believe that their military establishment, long of paramount importance in German society, had been beaten. Quickly the myth arose that the army had been "stabbed in the back" by Jews, socialists, and other "traitors," a myth which the military and others propagated and Hitler subsequently exploited. The Treaty of Versailles, imposing on Germany what most of its citizens believed a harsh, extremely unjust, and humiliating burden, served to enhance their bitterness. The fact that politicians of the Weimar Republic, the successor to the German Empire, had signed the hated treaty or, in the minds of the Germans, the "Diktat," brought down on that government the hatred of many, an enmity which contributed to its ultimate fall.

In the immediate aftermath of the war, Europe, and the defeated nations in particular, were in social turmoil. Bolshevism's vision of an impending "World Revolution" terrified the middle and upper classes. The activities of the Spartacists and Kurt Eisner in Germany, as well as those of Bela Kun in Hungary, made the threat seem very real. While these movements failed, the specter of a "Red Revolution" remained strong in the minds of many. It was a fear contributing to Mussolini's rise to power in Italy a decade before Hitler became chancellor.

Another factor which, while aiding Hitler attain power, was beyond his control, were the economic problems confronting Germany and, indeed, the entire world in the inter-war years. In 1923 Germany suffered, as a result of the Franco-Belgian occupation of the Ruhr, a depression of monumental proportions. The savings of the middle class were virtually destroyed and political upheaval threatened from both the Left and the Right. It is not strange that it was at this time that Hitler, now head of the Nazi Party, tried unsuccessfully to overthrow the Bavarian government, the first step in the envisioned takeover of all Germany.

Certainly the strongest evidence that Hitler's rise to power was not inevitable or wholly within his control is seen in the fact that after 1923, as economic stability was restored to Germany and she re-entered the "family of nations," his following diminished greatly, reduced to only the hard-core cadre.

The crucial event in his rise was unquestionably the "Great Depression" of 1929, a development which, again, he could not control but which he could exploit. As unemployment spread across Germany, the Communists again became active. The Social Democrats, who controlled the Weimar Republic, could not find solutions to the plight of the people. The Nazis, now seeking power legally, increased their strength in the both national Reichstag and state governments. In January 1933, although winning only a simple majority in the elections, Hitler was named chancellor in a coalition government. A year later virtually all political opposition had been eliminated.

The despair and anger over the World War I settlement, the fear of Bolshevism, the economic crises, were factors which, while assisting Hitler in his quest for power, he could not control. Even the fanatical ideology he espoused—the anti-Semitism, the Aryan supremacy, the ardent nationalism, the vision of "*Lebensraum*"—were derived from ideas long present in Germany and Austria.

To what extent was his ultimate triumph the result of his own "will to power"? His political genius lay in his ability to read the minds of the German people, their fears, animosities, and aspirations, and to hold out to them the vision of fulfillment of their dream of restoring Germany, a Germany cleansed of impure and undesirable elements, to the status of a world power. A charismatic speaker understanding his audience, he held out to all segments of society—

workers, farmers, students, middle and upper classes, the military, industrialists alike—the promises they wanted to hear. While many Germans had marked reservations regarding the Nazis, alarmed by their brutality and fanaticism, it seemed to them that, in light of the failure of the Social Democrats, their alternatives were limited to the Nazis or the Communists, the latter a choice unacceptable to a majority of the German people. Some believed they could control Hitler, others that the responsibility of office would temper his extremism: they quickly learned they were wrong.

6.   The Agricultural and Industrial Revolutions dramatically altered the economic structure of England and changed forever the physical face of the country as it shifted from a land dominated by small, peasant operated farms to one where large industrial cities and big, capitalist-oriented agricultural establishments dotted the countryside. Many other changes, even more significant if not so visible, also took place in the ideological, social, and political structure and outlook of English society.

The Agricultural Revolution and the Enclosure Movement had seen many peasants forced from the land. Some found employment as tenant farmers or agricultural laborers. Others, moving into the blossoming industrial cities, constituted the basis of the expanding industrial working class. The new urban, industrial centers of England tended to be in Wales, the Midlands, and the north, this as a result of the location of ore and coal deposits. This population expansion was enhanced by the fact that from the early 1600s England, like many regions of the world, experienced a steady increase in its birthrate and, perhaps more significant, a lowering mortality rate and increased longevity. Previously these regions had been underpopulated and, more significant, had little or no representation in Parliament. By contrast, the south and southeast of England, in earlier days the agricultural heartland of England, dominated Parliament. Even though the population was shifting away from the south, political power long remained in the hands of the landowners and commercial class of that region who, through their control of "rotten" and "pocket" boroughs, were in a position to manipulate large segments of the House of Commons in their own interests. The powerful House of Lords also represented the older, vested interests. In the decades before the French Revolution, tensions were mounting as the new industrial middle and upper class demanded they receive more equitable representation. While their demands were pushed into the background by that conflict, with its end they came to the fore once again, now assuming a more threatening nature, as seen in the "Peterloo Massacre" (1819) and the abortive Cato Street Conspiracy of 1820. Following a period of repressive efforts on the part of conservative elements in the government to repress the calls for reforms, after 1822 more liberal elements began to introduce reforms, including weakening the protective mercantile system, a reform desired by manufacturers, revising antiquated criminal laws, and repealing the Combination Acts which prohibited the formation of unions. These reforms were capped by the Third Reform Bill of 1832: this abolished more than fifty "rotten" and "pocket" boroughs, redistributing the seats in Parliament to areas previously without representation, and the extension of the vote to a larger segment of the middle class, including those in the industrial sphere. In the decades that followed, although political change came gradually, *it did come.* This was due, in part, to the competition between the two major parties for the vote, a factor that led to an increasing extension of the franchise to a larger segment of the male population (women would have to wait until the 1920s to obtain the vote). Another factor was the increasing political activism of the middle and lower classes. The working class, initially lacking political cohesion, began to become more articulate and, through the formation of political parties, gain a voice in the chambers of Parliament. By 1911, virtually every male in Great Britain had gained the right to vote, the secret ballot had been introduced, and the powers of the House of Lords, normally a reactionary body, had been dramatically curtailed. Parliament had assumed a very "modern appearance."

The changes which were taking place in the political structure of England were mirrored in and influenced by changes in the social structure of the country. Those who were in the fore of the industrialization of England came, in many cases, from a different social strata than the aristocratical, landowning and commercial elements which had dominated Parliament since the "Glorious Revolution" of 1688. Thus many were members of the "dissenting churches," such as the Quakers and Methodists, rather than the "established" or Anglican Church. Many traced their roots back to the artisan or, in the 19th century, even working, class. As such, they tended to be viewed as outsiders or *nouveau riche* by the dominant element in society. However, as their economic role in society became more and more important and, eventually, dominant, they gradually gained social as well as political acceptance. Social mobility being greater in Great Britain than it was in many nations of the Continent, marriage between the industrial capitalists and the old families became increasingly common. They were becoming, politically and socially, part of the Establishment.

If the gradually enhanced status of the middle and upper class of England's industrial society was taking place, the same was true of those who, at the outset of the Industrial Revolution, had constituted the lower strata, the working class enduring wretched working conditions in the factories, miserable pay, and generally intolerable living conditions. Gradually, albeit very gradually, working conditions improved through the enactment of various labor regulations. Their incomes began to rise, permitting many to enter the ranks of the middle class. Increasingly their voice in the political arena became louder.

Clearly by the advent of the 20th century the Agricultural and Industrial Revolutions had brought into being a "new" England, its face changed physically, socially, and politically.

THE ADVANCED
PLACEMENT EXAMINATION IN

European
History

ANSWER SHEETS

Section II

Use the following pages on which to write your essays. If you need more space than is provided here use your own standard ruled paper on which to complete additional pages.

REA's Test Preps

The Best in Test Preparation

- REA "Test Preps" are **far more** comprehensive than any other test preparation series
- Each book contains up to **eight** full-length practice tests based on the most recent exam
- **Every** type of question likely to be given on the exams is included
- Answers are accompanied by **full** and **detailed** explanations

REA has published over 60 Test Preparation volumes in several series. They include:

Advanced Placement Exams (APs)
Biology
Calculus AB & Calculus BC
Chemistry
Computer Science
English Language & Composition
English Literature & Composition
European History
Government & Politics
Physics
Psychology
Statistics
Spanish Language
United States History

College-Level Examination Program (CLEP)
Analyzing and Interpreting Literature
College Algebra
Freshman College Composition
General Examinations
General Examinations Review
History of the United States I
Human Growth and Development
Introductory Sociology
Principles of Marketing
Spanish

SAT II: Subject Tests
American History
Biology E/M
Chemistry
English Language Proficiency Test
French
German

SAT II: Subject Tests (cont'd)
Literature
Mathematics Level IC, IIC
Physics
Spanish
Writing

Graduate Record Exams (GREs)
Biology
Chemistry
Computer Science
Economics
Engineering
General
History
Literature in English
Mathematics
Physics
Psychology
Sociology

ACT - ACT Assessment

ASVAB - Armed Services Vocational Aptitude Battery

CBEST - California Basic Educational Skills Test

CDL - Commercial Driver License Exam

CLAST - College-Level Academic Skills Test

ELM - Entry Level Mathematics

ExCET - Exam for the Certification of Educators in Texas

FE (EIT) - Fundamentals of Engineering Exam

FE Review - Fundamentals of Engineering Review

GED - High School Equivalency Diploma Exam (U.S. & Canadian editions)

GMAT - Graduate Management Admission Test

LSAT - Law School Admission Test

MAT - Miller Analogies Test

MCAT - Medical College Admission Test

MSAT - Multiple Subjects Assessment for Teachers

NJ HSPT- New Jersey High School Proficiency Test

PPST - Pre-Professional Skills Test

PRAXIS II/NTE - Core Battery

PSAT - Preliminary Scholastic Assessment Test

SAT I - Reasoning Test

SAT I - Quick Study & Review

TASP - Texas Academic Skills Program

TOEFL - Test of English as a Foreign Language

TOEIC - Test of English for International Communication

RESEARCH & EDUCATION ASSOCIATION
61 Ethel Road W. • Piscataway, New Jersey 08854
Phone: (732) 819-8880   **website: www.rea.com**

Please send me more information about your Test Prep books

Name _____

Address _____

City _____ State _____ Zip _____

REA's Test Prep Books Are The Best!
(a sample of the <u>hundreds of letters</u> REA receives each year)

(more on next page)

REA's Test Prep Books Are The Best!

(a sample of the <u>hundreds of letters</u> REA receives each year)

(more on previous page)